Photoshop Elements 7
THE MISSING MANUAL

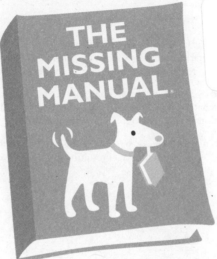

Barbara Brundage

POGUE PRESS™
O'REILLY®

Beijing • Cambridge • Farnham • Köln • Sebastopol • Taipei • Tokyo

Photoshop Elements 7: The Missing Manual

by Barbara Brundage

Published by O'Reilly Media, Inc., 1005 Gravenstein Highway North, Sebastopol, CA 95472.

O'Reilly books may be purchased for educational, business, or sales promotional use. Online editions are also available for most titles (*safari.oreilly.com*). For more information, contact our corporate/institutional sales department: (800) 998-9938 or *corporate@oreilly.com*.

Printing History:

September 2008:   First Edition.

ISBN: 978-0-596-52133-2

[V]

Table of Contents

Part Three: Retouching

Chapter 7: Basic Image Retouching 183

The Missing Credits

About the Author

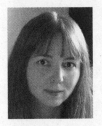 **Barbara Brundage** is the author of *Photoshop Elements 6: The Missing Manual*, an Adobe Community Expert, and a member of Adobe's prerelease groups for Elements 3, 4, 5, 6, and 7. She's been teaching people how to use Photoshop Elements since it first came out in 2001. Barbara first started using Elements to create graphics for use in her day job as a harpist, music publisher, and arranger. Along the way, she joined the large group of people finding a renewed interest in photography thanks to digital cameras. If she can learn to use Elements, you can, too! You can reach Barbara at *bbrundage@me.com*.

About the Creative Team

Peter Meyers (editor) is the managing editor for O'Reilly's Missing Manual series. He lives with his wife, daughter, and cats in New York City. Email: *meyers@oreilly.com*.

Nellie McKesson (production editor) is a graduate of St. John's College in Santa Fe, NM. She currently lives in Jamaica Plain, MA, and spends her spare time making t-shirts for her friends to wear (*mattsaundersbynellie.etsy.com*). Email: *nellie@oreilly.com*.

Sohaila Abdulali (copy editor) is a freelance writer and editor. She has published a novel, several children's books, and numerous short stories and articles. She recently finished an ethnography of an aboriginal Indian woman. She lives in New York City with her husband Tom and their small but larger-than-life daughter, Samara. She can be reached through her Web site at *www.sohailaink.com*.

Doug Nelson (technical reviewer) is the founder of RetouchPRO, a free resource for anyone interested in digital imaging. RetouchPRO offers tutorials, contests, challenges, user galleries, and an active community forum. Doug invites you to stop by and show your work, ask for help, help someone else, or just say hello. Web site: *www.retouchpro.com*.

Raymond Robillard (tech editor) is a software analyst for human interface applications. He enjoys playing video games and designing graphics on his computer. He's been teaching online for over five years (*eclecticacademy.com*) and has been, until recently, very active in user forums helping newcomers as well as more advanced users of Photoshop Elements and Macintosh computers.

Acknowledgements

Many thanks to Doug Nelson and Ray Robillard for reading this book and giving me the benefit of their advice and corrections. I'm also grateful for the help I received from everyone at Adobe, especially Bob Gager, Mark Dahm, and Rich Coencas.

Special thanks also to graphic artist Jodi Frye (*www.frontiernet.net/~jlfrye/Jodi_Frye*) for allowing me to reproduce one of her Elements drawings to show what can be done by those with more artistic ability than I have. My gratitude also to Florida's botanical gardens, especially McKee Botanical Garden (*www.mckeegarden.org*), Historic Bok Sanctuary (*www.boktower.org*), Heathcote Botanical Gardens (*www.heathcotebotanicalgardens.org*), and Harry P. Leu Gardens (*www.leugardens.org*), for creating oases of peace and beauty in our hectic world. Finally, I'd like to thank everyone in the gang over at the Adobe Photoshop Elements support forum for all their help and friendship.

The Missing Manual Series

Missing Manuals are witty, superbly written guides to computer products that don't come with printed manuals (which is just about all of them). Each book features a handcrafted index; cross-references to specific pages (not just chapters); and RepKover, a detached-spine binding that lets the book lie perfectly flat without the assistance of weights or cinder blocks.

Recent and upcoming titles include:

Access 2007: The Missing Manual by Matthew MacDonald

AppleScript: The Missing Manual by Adam Goldstein

CSS: The Missing Manual by David Sawyer McFarland

Creating Web Sites: The Missing Manual by Matthew MacDonald

Digital Photography: The Missing Manual by Chris Grover and Barbara Brundage

Dreamweaver 8: The Missing Manual by David Sawyer McFarland

Dreamweaver CS3: The Missing Manual by David Sawyer McFarland

Excel 2003: The Missing Manual by Matthew MacDonald

Excel 2007: The Missing Manual by Matthew MacDonald

Facebook: The Missing Manual by E.A. Vander Veer

FileMaker Pro 8: The Missing Manual by Geoff Coffey and Susan Prosser

FileMaker Pro 9: The Missing Manual by Geoff Coffey and Susan Prosser

Flash 8: The Missing Manual by E.A. Vander Veer

Flash CS3: The Missing Manual by E.A. Vander Veer and Chris Grover

FrontPage 2003: The Missing Manual by Jessica Mantaro

Google Apps: The Missing Manual by Nancy Conner

The Internet: The Missing Manual by David Pogue and J.D. Biersdorfer

iMovie 6 & iDVD: The Missing Manual by David Pogue

iMovie '08 & iDVD: The Missing Manual by David Pogue

iPhone: The Missing Manual, Second Edition by David Pogue

iPhoto '08: The Missing Manual by David Pogue

iPod: The Missing Manual, Sixth Edition by J.D. Biersdorfer

JavaScript: The Missing Manual by David Sawyer McFarland

Mac OS X Leopard: The Missing Manual, by David Pogue

Microsoft Project 2007: The Missing Manual by Bonnie Biafore

Office 2004 for Macintosh: The Missing Manual by Mark H. Walker and Franklin Tessler

Office 2007: The Missing Manual by Chris Grover, Matthew MacDonald, and E.A. Vander Veer

Office 2008 for Macintosh: The Missing Manual by Jim Elferdink

Photoshop Elements 6 for Mac: The Missing Manual by Barbara Brundage

PowerPoint 2007: The Missing Manual by E.A. Vander Veer

QuickBooks 2008: The Missing Manual by Bonnie Biafore

Quicken 2008: The Missing Manual by Bonnie Biafore

Switching to the Mac: The Missing Manual, Leopard Edition by David Pogue

Wikipedia: The Missing Manual by John Broughton

Windows XP Home Edition: The Missing Manual, Second Edition by David Pogue

Windows XP Pro: The Missing Manual, Second Edition by David Pogue, Craig Zacker, and Linda Zacker

Windows Vista: The Missing Manual by David Pogue

Windows Vista for Starters: The Missing Manual by David Pogue

Word 2007: The Missing Manual by Chris Grover

Your Brain: The Missing Manual by Matthew MacDonald

Introduction

Wow, have times changed. A few years ago a digital camera was still an expensive novelty, owned by a few people. Today, just about everyone has one. If you're like most people, you probably take and keep way more digital photos compared to the days of film when you had to pay to develop each picture. Not only that, but most folks have broadband Internet connections, which makes posting and sharing your work online that much easier.

Adobe has kept up right along with you. To begin with, Photoshop Elements was a terrific program for editing, improving, and printing photos. Then Adobe added the Organizer, which lets you easily keep track of thousands of photos, as well as whip up all sorts of easy-to-complete projects, like photo books and greeting cards. With Elements 7, Adobe gives you a free basic account at Photoshop.com, making it incredibly easy to share photos online, back them up automatically, and sync what you do online with your home computer. You even get your own personal Web page.

Why Photoshop Elements?

Adobe's Photoshop is the granddaddy of all image-editing programs. It's the Big Cheese, the industry standard against which everything else is measured. Every photo you've seen in a book or magazine in the past 15 years or so has almost certainly passed through Photoshop on its way to being printed. You just can't buy anything that gives you more control over your pictures than Photoshop does.

But Photoshop has some big drawbacks—it's darned hard to learn, it's horribly expensive, and many of the features in it are just plain overkill if you don't plan to work on pictures for a living.

For several years, Adobe tried to find a way to cram many of Photoshop's marvelous powers into a package that normal people could use. Finding the right formula was a slow process. First came PhotoDeluxe, a program that was lots of fun but came up short when you wanted to fine-tune *how* the program worked. Adobe tried again with Photoshop LE, which many people felt just gave you all the difficulty of full Photoshop but still too little of what you need to do top-notch work.

Finally—sort of like "The Three Bears"—Adobe got it just right with Photoshop Elements. It took off like crazy because it offers so much of Photoshop's power in a program that almost anyone can learn. With Elements, you, too, can work with the same wonderful tools that the pros use.

The earliest versions of Elements had something of a learning curve. It was a super program but not one where you could just sit down and expect to get perfect results right off the bat.

In each new version, Adobe has added lots of push-button-easy ways to correct and improve your photos. In Elements 7 the improvements focus on new ways for you to share your photos online more easily than ever.

What You Can Do with Elements 7

Elements not only lets you make your photos look great, but it also helps you organize your photos, and gives you some pretty neat projects in which to use them. The program also comes loaded with lots of new ways to share your photos. The list of what Elements can do is pretty impressive. You can use Elements to:

- Enhance your photos by editing, cropping, and color correcting them, including fixing exposure and color problems.

- Add all kinds of special effects to your photos, like turning a garden-variety photo into a drawing, painting, or even a tile mosaic.

- Combine photos into a panorama or a montage.

- Move someone from one photo to another, and even remove people (your ex?) from last year's holiday photos.

- Repair and restore old and damaged photos.

- Organize your photos and assign keywords to them so you can search by subject or name.

- Add type to your images, and turn them into things like greeting cards and flyers.

- Create slideshows to share with friends, regardless of whether they use Windows, a Mac, or even just a cellphone.

- Automatically resize photos so that they're ready for email. Elements even lets you send your photos inside specially designed emails.

- Create digital artwork from scratch, even without a photo to work from.

- Create and share incredible online albums and email-ready slideshows that will make your friends actually ask to see the pictures from your latest trip.

- Store your photos online, so that you can get to them from any computer. You can organize your photos online, and upload new photos directly to your personalized Photoshop.com Web site. You can also keep an online backup of your photos, and even sync albums so that when you add a new photo from another computer, it automatically gets sent to your home computer, too. Nice.

- Create and edit graphics for Web sites, including making animated GIFs (pictures that move animation-style).

- Create wonderful collages that you can print or share with your friends digitally. Scrapbookers—get ready to be wowed.

It's worth noting, though, that there are still a few things Elements *can't* do. While Elements handles text quite competently, at least as photo-editing programs go, it's still no substitute for QuarkXPress, InDesign, or any other desktop publishing program. And Elements can do an amazing job of fixing problems in your photos, but only if you give it something to work with. If your photo is totally overexposed, blurry, and the top of everyone's head is cut off, there may be a limit to what even Elements can do to help you out. (C'mon, be fair.) The fact is, though, you're more likely to be surprised by what Elements *can* fix than by what it can't.

What's New in Elements 7

Elements 7 brings some really cool online features as well as enhancements that let you even more easily edit and generally glamorize your photos:

- **Online Photo Sharing**. Sign up for a free Photoshop.com account (page 18), and you can easily share photos with friends and family (or the world at large), using beautiful, dramatic slideshow and gallery templates (page 467). You even get your own unique URL (Web address) at Photoshop.com.

  NOTE For now, you must be in the US to use Photoshop.com. If you're in another country, you can still create and share online albums, but you do so at Adobe's Photoshop Showcase (*www. photoshopshowcase.com*), a site first created for folks using Elements 6. Your serial number tells Elements to use the correct location. A few features are available only with Photoshop.com, so for now, these features are US-only.

- **Online Backups (US only)**. Create an album (a handpicked collection of photos) on your PC, and you can tell Elements to automatically back up your pictures to your Photoshop.com space (page 66). Once you set this up, you don't have to do anything—no scheduling or remembering to back up today's shots.

- **Access your photos from anywhere**. You don't have to be at your home computer to view your photos. Just log into your Photoshop.com account from any Web browser, and you can view, organize, and even tag (label) your photos (page 50). The online organizer works just like the one built into Elements.

- **Sync your photos (page 66) (US only).** Make changes to your photos online. and the next time you start Elements on your home computer, Elements can automatically make the same changes to your photos on your desktop. You can even upload pictures from another computer, and Elements can dispatch them back to your home computer—a great feature for travelers.

- **Get tutorials from right within Elements (US only).** The new Photoshop Inspiration Browser (page 30) links you to all sorts of tutorials, in video or PDF form, right from Elements. There's something for everyone from beginners to the most advanced Elements old-timers.

- **Use Photoshop Actions in Elements.** The new Actions Player (page 380) makes it super simple to add actions (little automated scripts that automatically run through multi-step projects) to Elements.

- **Smart Brush.** This new tool makes all sorts of corrections and enhancements as easy as drawing a line (page 189).

- **Download extra graphics, frames, backgrounds (US only).** The Content palette (page 427) displays thumbnails for additional items you can download right from within Elements.

- **New Touch-Up tools.** With just a quick click and drag you can whiten teeth, make the sky bluer, or convert part of your photo to black and white, right in the Elements Quick Fix window (page 113).

- **Scene Cleaner.** Eliminate unwanted elements (like other, unknown tourists) from your photos to create just the scene you want (page 313).

- **Improve Skin Texture.** The new Surface Blur filter (page 377) lets you soften areas without melting edges or losing detail. Great for use on portraits.

- **New Special Effects.** For example, Guided Edit (page 28) now includes new ways to create effects like a pencil sketch.

- **Adjustable Brightness.** If you used Elements 6, and didn't like the darker color scheme of the overall program, you'll be thrilled to know that Elements 7 has sliders that let you set the program's windows and menus to be as dark or as light as you choose (page 15).

If you've used Elements before and you're not sure which version you've got, a quick way to tell is to look for the version number on the CD. If the program is already installed, see page 14 for help figuring out which version you have.

Incidentally, all seven versions of Elements are totally separate programs, so you can run all of them on the same computer if you like, as long as your operating system is compatible. (Adobe doesn't recommend trying to have more than one version open at a time, though.) So if you prefer the older version of a particular tool, then you can still use it. If you've been using one of the earlier versions, then you'll still feel right at home in Elements 7. You'll just find that it's easier than ever to get stuff done with the program.

If You Have a Mac

This book covers Elements 7 for Windows. The current version of Elements for Mac is Photoshop Elements 6, and there's a Missing Manual just for it: *Photoshop Elements 6 for Mac: The Missing Manual*. As this book went to press, Adobe hadn't said when, or even if, they'd be releasing Elements 7 for Mac, but if and when they do, there'll be a separate Mac edition of this book.

If you have a Mac with an Intel processor and you don't want to wait for the Mac version of Elements 7, note that the Windows version works well in Apple's Bootcamp software or in the Parallels (*www.parallels.com*), or Fusion (*www.vmware.com*) virtualization programs. Of course, to use any of these programs, you have to install Windows on your Mac.

Elements vs. Photoshop

You could easily get confused about the differences between Elements and the full version of Adobe Photoshop. Because Elements is so much less expensive, and because many of its more advanced controls are tucked away, a lot of Photoshop aficionados tend to view Elements as some kind of toy version of their programs.

They couldn't be more wrong. Elements is Photoshop, but it's Photoshop adapted for use with a home printer, and for the Web. The most important difference between Elements and Photoshop is that Elements doesn't let you work or save in CMYK mode, which is the format used for commercial color printing. (CMYK stands for Cyan, Magenta, Yellow, and blacK. Your inkjet printer also uses those ink colors to print, but it expects you to give it an RGB file, which is what Elements creates. This is all explained in Chapter 7.)

Elements also lacks several tools that are basic staples in any commercial art department, like writing Actions or scripting (to help automate repetitive tasks), the extra color control you can get from Selective Color, and the Pen tool's special talent for creating vector paths. Also, for some special effects, like creating drop shadows or bevels, the tool you'd use—Layer styles—doesn't have as many settings in Elements as it does in Photoshop. The same holds true for a handful of other Elements tools.

And although Elements is all most people need to create graphics for the Web, it doesn't come with the advanced tools in Photoshop, which let you do things like automatically slice images into smaller pieces for faster Web display. If you use Elements, then you have to do those tasks manually or look for another program to help out.

The Key to Learning Elements

Elements may not be quite as powerful as Photoshop, but it's still a complex program, filled with more features than most people ever end up using. The good news is that the Quick Fix window (Chapter 4) lets you get started right away, even if you don't understand every last option that Quick Fix presents you with. And you also get the Guided Edit mode (page 28), which provides a step-by-step walk-through for some popular editing tasks, like sharpening your photo or cropping it to fit on standard photo paper.

As for the program's more complex features, the key to learning how to use Elements—or any other program, for that matter—is to focus only on what you need to know for the task you're currently trying to accomplish.

For example, if you're trying to use Quick Fix to adjust the color of your photo and crop it, don't worry that you don't get the concept of "layers" yet. You won't learn to do everything in Elements in a day or even a week. The rest will wait until you need it. So take your time and don't worry about what's not important to you right now. You'll find it much easier to master Elements if you go slowly, and concentrate on one thing at a time.

If you're totally new to the program, then you'll find only three or four big concepts in this book that you really have to understand if you want to get the most out of Elements. It may take a little time for some concepts to sink in—resolution and layers, for instance, aren't the most intuitive concepts in the world—but once they click, they'll seem so obvious that you'll wonder why things seemed confusing at first. That's perfectly normal, so persevere. You *can* do this, and there's nothing in this book that you can't understand with a little bit of careful reading.

The very best way to learn Elements is just to dive right in and play with it. Try all the different filters to see what they do. Add a filter on top of another filter. Click around on all the different tools and try them. You don't even need to have a photo to do this. See page 43 for how to make an image from scratch in Elements, and read on to learn about the many downloadable practice images you'll find at this book's companion Web site, *www.missingmanuals.com*. Get crazy—you can stack up as many filters, effects, and Layer styles as you want without crashing the program.

About This Book

Elements is such a cool program and so much fun to use, but figuring out how to make it do what you want is another matter. Elements 7 comes only with a quick reference guide, and it doesn't go into as much depth as you might want. The Elements Help files are very good, but of course you need to know what you're looking for to use them to your best advantage. (The Help files that ship with Elements are sometimes incomplete, but you can download a more polished version from Adobe's Elements support pages at *www.adobe.com/support/documentation/en/ photoshop_elements/*.)

You'll find a slew of Elements titles at your local bookstore, but most of them assume that you know quite a bit about the basics of photography and/or digital imaging. It's much easier to find good intermediate books about Elements than books designed to get you going with the program.

That's where the Missing Manual comes in. This book is intended to make learning Elements easier by avoiding technical jargon as much as possible, and explaining *why* and *when* you'll want to use (or avoid) certain features in the program. That approach is as useful to people who are advanced photographers as it is to those who are just getting started with their first digital cameras.

> **NOTE** This book periodically recommends *other* books, covering topics too specialized or tangential for a manual about Elements. Careful readers may notice that not every one of these titles is published by Missing Manual parent O'Reilly Media. While we're happy to mention other Missing Manuals and books in the O'Reilly family, if there's a great book out there that doesn't happen to be published by O'Reilly, we'll still let you know about it.

You'll also find instructions throughout the book that refer to files you can download from the Missing Manual Web site (*www.missingmanuals.com*) so you can practice the techniques you're reading about. And throughout the book, you'll find several different kinds of short articles. The ones labeled "Up to Speed" help newcomers to Elements do things or explain concepts with which veterans are probably already familiar. Those labeled "Power Users' Clinic" cover more advanced topics that won't be of much interest to casual photographers.

> **NOTE** Since Elements 7 works in both Windows Vista and Windows XP, you'll see screenshots from both operating systems in this book. Most things work exactly the same way in both programs; only the styles of some windows are different. In a few instances, the file paths for certain program files aren't exactly the same. If that's the case, then you'll be given the directions for both operating systems. Also, since the darkness/brightness of the program is adjustable (page 15), in the illustrations you'll see whichever setting best displays the given feature.

About the Outline

This book is divided into six parts, each focusing on a certain kind of task you may want to do in Elements.

- **Introduction to Elements.** The first part of this book helps you get started with Elements. Chapter 1 shows how to navigate Elements' slightly confusing layout and mishmash of programs within programs. You learn how to decide which window to start from, as well as how to set up Elements so it best suits your own personal working style, and how to set up your Photoshop.com account. You also learn about some important basic keyboard shortcuts, and where to look for help when you get stuck. Chapter 2 covers how to get photos into Elements, the basics of organizing them, and how to open files and create new images from scratch, as well as how to save and back up your images, either on your home computer or using Photoshop.com. Chapter 3 explains how to rotate and crop photos, and includes a primer on that most important digital imaging concept—resolution.

- **Elemental Elements.** Chapter 4 shows how to use the Quick Fix window to dramatically improve your photos. Chapter 5 and Chapter 6 cover two key concepts—making selections and layers—that you'll use throughout the book.

- **Retouching.** Having Elements is like having a darkroom on your computer. In Chapter 7, you'll learn how to make basic corrections, such as fixing exposure, adjusting color, sharpening an image, and removing dust and scratches. Chapter 8 covers topics unique to people who use digital cameras, like Raw conversion and batch processing your photos. In Chapter 9, you'll move on to some more sophisticated fixes, like changing the light, using the clone stamp for repairs, making a photo livelier by adjusting the color intensity, and light and shadows in an image. Chapter 10 shows you how to convert color photos to black and white, and how to tint and colorize black-and-white photos. Chapter 11 helps you to use Elements' Photomerge feature to create a panorama from several photos, and to make perspective corrections to your images.

- **Artistic Elements.** This part covers the fun stuff—painting on your photos and drawing shapes (Chapter 12), using filters and effects to create a more artistic look (Chapter 13), and adding type to images (Chapter 14).

- **Sharing your images.** Once you've created a great image in Elements, you'll want to share it, so this part is about how to create fun projects like photo books (Chapter 15); how to get the most out of your printer (Chapter 16); how to create images for the Web and email (Chapter 17); and how to make slideshows and share them in online albums (Chapter 18).

- **Additional Elements.** You can find literally hundreds of plug-ins and additional styles, brushes, and other nifty tools you can get to customize your copy of Elements and increase its abilities; the Internet and your local bookstore are chock-full of additional information. Chapter 19 offers a look at some of these, as well as information about using a graphics tablet in Elements, and some resources to turn to after you've finished this book.

For Newcomers to Elements

This book has a lot of information, and if you're new to Elements, then you don't need to digest it all at once, especially if you've never used any kind of photo-editing software before. So what do you need to read first? Here's a simple five-step way to use the book if you're brand-new to photo editing:

1. **Read all of Chapter 1.**

   That's important for understanding how to get around in Elements.

2. **If your photos aren't on your computer already, then read about the Photo Downloader.**

   The Downloader gets your photos from your camera's memory card into Elements. It's explained in Chapter 2.

3. **If you want to organize your photos, then read about the Organizer.**

   It doesn't matter where your photos are right now. If you want to use the Organizer to label and keep track of them, then read Chapter 2.

4. **When you're ready to edit your photos, read Chapters 3 and 4.**

   Chapter 3 explains how to adjust the view of your photos in the Editor. Chapter 4 shows you how to use the Elements Quick Fix window to easily edit and correct your photos. Guided Edit (page 28) can also be very helpful when you're just getting started. If you skipped Chapter 2 because you're not using the Organizer, go back there now, and read the parts about saving your photos, so you don't lose your work.

5. **When you're ready to print or share your photos, flip to the chapters on sharing your images.**

   Chapter 16 covers printing, both at home and from online services. Chapter 17 explains how to email photos, and Chapter 18 explains how to post your photos at Photoshop.com.

That's all you need to get started. You can come back and pick up the rest of the information in the book as you get more comfortable with Elements, and want to explore more of the wonderful things it can do for your photos.

The Very Basics

This book assumes that you know how to perform basic activities on your computer like clicking and double-clicking your mouse, and dragging objects onscreen. Here's a quick refresher: to *click* means to move the point of your mouse or trackpad cursor over an object on your screen, and then press the left mouse or trackpad button once. To right-click means to press the right mouse button once, which produces a menu of special features. To *double-click* means to press the left button twice, quickly, without moving the mouse between clicks. To *drag* means to click an object, and use the mouse to move it while holding down the left button so you don't let go of it. Most selection buttons onscreen are pretty obvious, but you may not be familiar with *radio buttons*: To choose an option, you click one of these little empty circles arranged like a list. If you're comfortable with basic concepts like these, then you're ready to get started with this book.

In Elements, you'll often want to use keyboard shortcuts to save time, and this book gives keyboard shortcuts when they exist (and Elements has a lot). So if you see "Press Ctrl+S to save your file," that means to hold down the Control key while pressing the S key.

About → These → Arrows

Throughout this book (and in any Missing Manual, for that matter) you see arrows that look like this: "Go to Editor → Filter → Artistic → Paint Daubs." This is a shorthand way of helping you find files, folders, and menu choices without having to read through excruciatingly long, bureaucratic-style instructions. So, for example, the sentence in the previous paragraph is a short way of saying: "Go to the Editor component of Elements. In the menu bar, click the Filter choice. In that menu, choose the Artistic section, and then go to Paint Daubs in the pop-out menu." Figure I-1 shows you an example in action.

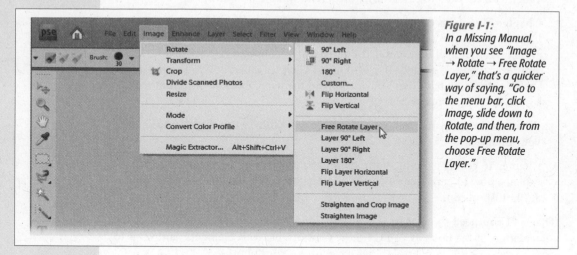

Figure I-1:
In a Missing Manual, when you see "Image → Rotate → Free Rotate Layer," that's a quicker way of saying, "Go to the menu bar, click Image, slide down to Rotate, and then, from the pop-up menu, choose Free Rotate Layer."

File paths are shown in the conventional Windows style, so if you see "Go to *C:\ Documents and Settings\<your user name>\My Documents\My Pictures*", that means you should go to your C drive, open the Documents and Settings folder, look for your user account folder, and then find the My Documents folder. In that folder, open the My Pictures folder that's inside it. When there are different file paths for Vista and Windows XP, then you'll find them both listed.

About MissingManuals.com

If you head on over to this book's Missing CD page (*www.missingmanuals.com*), you can find links to downloadable practice images mentioned throughout this book.

A word about these downloadable files: To make life easier for folks with dial-up Internet connections, the file sizes have been kept pretty small. So you probably won't want to print the results of what you create (since you'll end up with a print about the size of a match book). But that doesn't really matter because the files are really meant for onscreen use. You'll see notes throughout the book about which images are available to practice on for any given chapter.

At the Web site, you can also find articles, tips, and updates to the book. If you click the Errata link, then you'll see any corrections to the book's content, too. If you find something you think is wrong, feel free to report it by using this link. Each time the book is printed, we'll update it with any confirmed corrections. If you want to be certain that your own copy is up to the minute, this is where to check for any changes. And thanks for reporting any errors or suggesting corrections.

We'd love to hear your suggestions for new books in the Missing Manual line. There's a place for that on missingmanuals.com, too. And while you're online, you can also register this book at *www.oreilly.com* (you can jump directly to the registration page by going here: *http://tinyurl.com/yo82k3*). Registering means we can send you updates about this book, and you'll be eligible for special offers like discounts on future editions.

Safari® Books Online

 When you see a Safari® Books Online icon on the cover of your favorite technology book, that means the book is available online through the O'Reilly Network Safari Bookshelf.

Safari offers a solution that's better than e-books. It's a virtual library that lets you easily search thousands of top tech books, cut and paste code samples, download chapters, and find quick answers when you need the most accurate, current information. Try it for free at *http://safari.oreilly.com*.

CHAPTER 1

Finding Your Way Around Elements

Photoshop Elements lets you do practically anything you want to your digital images. You can colorize black-and-white photos, remove demonic red-eye stares, or distort the facial features of people who've been mean to you. The downside is that all those options can make it tough to find your way around Elements, especially when you're new to the program.

This chapter helps get you oriented in Elements. You'll learn about what to expect when you launch the program, how to use Elements to fix photos with just a couple of keystrokes, and how to sign up for and connect to all the goodies that await you on Photoshop.com. You'll also learn how to use Guided Edit mode to help get started editing your photos. Along the way, you'll find out about some of Elements' basic controls, and how to get hold of the program's Help files if you need them.

The Welcome Screen

When you launch Elements for the first time, you get a slew of options, all neatly laid out on the Welcome screen (Figure 1-1).

Interestingly, the Welcome screen isn't actually Elements. It's a launching pad that, depending on the button you click, starts up one of two different programs:

• **The Organizer**, which lets you store and organize your image files.

• **The Editor**, which lets you edit your images.

Which Version of Elements Do You Have?

This book covers Photoshop Elements 7. If you're not sure which version you've got, then the easiest way to find out is to look at the program's icon (the file you click to launch Elements). The icon for Elements 7 is quite distinctive—it's a blue square with the letters PSE (Elements' initials) on it. But if you're still not sure, click once on the Elements icon on your desktop, and you should see the full name of the program, including the version number, appear below the icon if it wasn't already visible. You can also check the Windows Start menu: Elements is listed along with its version number, or, if Elements is running, go to Help → About Photoshop Elements.

You can use this book if you have an earlier version of Elements because a lot of the basic editing procedures are the same. But Elements 7 is a little different, especially because of all the connections to online features, so you'd probably feel more comfortable with a reference book for the version you have. There are *Missing Manuals* for Elements 3, 4, 5, and 6, too, and you may prefer to track down the right book for your version of Elements.

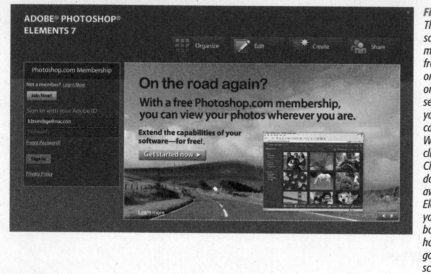

Figure 1-1:
The Elements Welcome screen gives you four main activities to choose from, as well as the area on the left for signing onto Photoshop.com and seeing information about your account there. You can't bypass the Welcome screen just by clicking the upper-right Close button. When you do, the screen goes away—but so does Elements. Fortunately, you've got options: The box on page 16 tells you how to permanently say goodbye to the Welcome screen.

You can quite easily go back and forth between the Editor and the Organizer—which you might call the two different faces of Elements—and you probably won't do much in one without eventually needing to get into the other. But in some ways, they still function as two separate programs. In any case, the Welcome screen offers you no fewer than four choices for getting into Elements:

- **Organize** takes you to the Organizer, where you can store and sort all your images.

- **Edit** takes you to the Editor, which is the digital darkroom/art studio where you edit photos, and create artwork from scratch.

- **Create** starts you up in the Organizer, and gives you a choice of making a photo book, calendar, collage, online gallery, or slideshow from your photos.

- **Share** also takes you to the Organizer, only this time you can choose to create an online gallery, email photos, order prints, or create a CD or DVD.

If you start in the Organizer, then once you've located a photo to edit, you have to wait a few seconds while the Editor loads. And when you have both the Editor and the Organizer running, just quitting the Editor doesn't close the Organizer. You have to close both programs independently. When both programs are running, you can switch back and forth by clicking the button at the upper right of the screen. The button reads "Organizer" when you're in the Editor and "Editor" when you're in the Organizer. (The Organizer button just takes a click, but the Editor button includes a pull-down menu where you choose the editing mode you want.) You can also just click the Editor or the Organizer icon in the Windows taskbar to switch from one to the other.

Adobe has built Elements around the assumption that most people work on their photos in the following way: First, you bring photos into the Organizer to sort and keep track of them. Then, you open photos in the Editor to work on them, and save them back to the Organizer when you've finished making changes. You can work differently, of course, like opening photos directly in the Editor and bypassing the Organizer altogether, but you may feel like you're always swimming against the current if you choose a different way of working. The next chapter has a few hints for disabling some Elements features if you really find they're getting in your way.

In addition, the Welcome screen in Elements 7 serves as your connecting point for creating or signing onto Photoshop.com. Page 18 has more about Photoshop.com, but for now you just need to know that a basic account is free if you're in the US (it's not available yet in other countries), and it gives you access to all the interesting new features in Elements 7 that require an Internet connection.

WORKAROUND WORKSHOP

Turning the Lights Back On

You may find the snazzy dark color scheme for Elements hard to see or just plain annoying. If so, you'll be pleased to know that in Elements 7, you can adjust the brightness to suit yourself. Both the Editor and the Organizer have sliders that let you determine how dark or light the program looks (although only up to a point). In either component, just go to Edit → Preferences → General → Appearance Options, and then put the User Interface Brightness slider where you like. This change takes effect immediately, so you don't need to restart Elements to see the difference. The Editor and Organizer adjustments are independent, so you can have each at a different brightness level, if you like.

Say Goodbye to the Welcome Screen

How do I get rid of the Welcome screen?

If you get to feeling like you've been welcomed enough, you probably want to turn off the Welcome screen so you don't have to click through it every time you start the program. Well, in Elements 7, you can't. Every time you start Elements, you start in the Welcome screen. If this is unwelcome news, don't fret: There's a workaround.

So how, you ask, am I supposed to directly launch the Editor or the Organizer? Simple—create a desktop shortcut. Go to C:\Program Files\Adobe\Photoshop Elements 7.0, and then find the actual application file (the one ending in *.exe*) for the Editor or the Organizer. Right-click it, and then choose Create Shortcut. This makes a direct shortcut to the component of your choice, right on the

desktop. In the future, double-click the shortcut to launch your preferred part of Elements. (You can make shortcuts for both the Editor and the Organizer, if you like.)

The tradeoff is that the Welcome screen is the most direct sign-on route to your Photoshop.com account. But you still have plenty of ways to get there. In either the Editor or the Organizer, in the menu bar, just click the little house icon. That summons the Welcome screen, where you can sign onto your account. If you do something while working with your photos that requires a connection to Photoshop.com, like clicking the Share button for an Album (page 53), then that also brings up the sign-in window, without the Welcome screen.

Organizing Your Photos

The Organizer is where your photos come into Elements and go out again (when it's time to print or email them). The Organizer stores and catalogs your photos, and you automatically come back to it for any activities that involve sharing your photos, like printing a photo package or making a slideshow. The Organizer's main window (Figure 1-2) is sometimes called the *Photo Browser*. It lets you view your photos, sort them into albums, and assign keyword labels to them.

The Organizer has lots of really cool features you'll learn about throughout this book when they're relevant to the task at hand. The next chapter shows you how to use the Organizer to import and organize your photos, and Appendix A covers all the Organizer's different menu options. What's more, in Elements 7, if you sign up for a Photoshop.com account (page 18), then you can access and organize your photos from any computer, not just at home.

Where the Heck Did Elements Go?

If you know that you've installed Elements but can't seem to figure out how to launch it, no problem.

Windows automatically creates a shortcut to Elements on your desktop once you've installed the program. You can

also go to the Start menu, and then click the Adobe Photoshop Elements 7.0 icon. If you don't see Elements in the Start menu, then click the arrow next to All Programs, and you should find it in the pop-up menu.

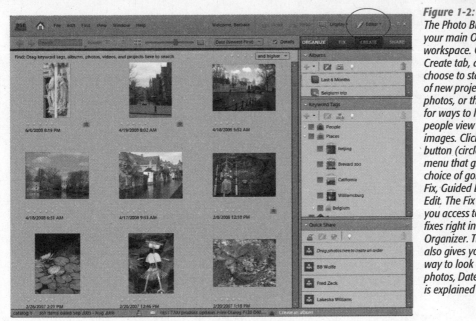

Figure 1-2:
The Photo Browser is your main Organizer workspace. Click the Create tab, and you can choose to start all kinds of new projects with your photos, or the Share tab for ways to let other people view your images. Click the Editor button (circled) for a menu that gives you a choice of going to Quick Fix, Guided Edit, or Full Edit. The Fix tab gives you access to some quick fixes right in the Organizer. The Organizer also gives you another way to look at your photos, Date View, which is explained in Chapter 2.

Photo Downloader

Actually, Elements has yet another component, which you may have seen already if you've plugged a camera into your computer after installing Elements: the Photo Downloader (Figure 1-3), which helps get photos straight into the Organizer directly from your camera's memory card.

If you've used Elements before, then you'll be pleased to know that one of the new features in Elements 7 is a politer version of the Downloader. In previous versions of Elements, the Downloader ran constantly as a separate program (whether Elements was running or not), racing to be first on the scene whenever it detected any newly-connected device that might have photos on it, and popping up its own window before the standard Windows dialog box could appear. For a few people, this was mighty convenient. But for the majority of folks who didn't want the Downloader every time they plugged some photo-bearing device into their computer, it was a big nuisance. If you have an iPod, for instance, then you know how aggravating this was.

So in Elements 7, the Downloader appears as only one of your options in the regular Windows dialog box that you see when you connect a device. If you want to use the Downloader, then just choose it from the list. No more interference with your iPod, and no extra dialog box to close every time you don't want to use the Downloader. It's a major improvement.

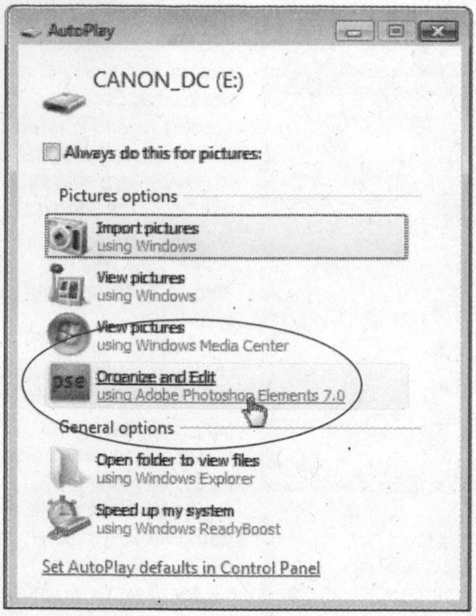

Figure 1-3:
Adobe's Photo Downloader is yet another program you get when you install Elements. Its role in life is to pull your photos from your camera (or other storage device) into the Organizer. To use the Downloader, just click "Organize and Edit using Adobe Photoshop Elements 7.0" (circled). After the Downloader does its thing, you end up in the Organizer.

You can read more about the Downloader in Chapter 2. If you plan to use the Organizer to catalog photos and assign keywords to them, then reading the section on the Downloader can help you avoid hair-pulling moments.

Photoshop.com

Adobe's new Photoshop.com service is the star feature in Elements 7. A basic account is free, and it's nicely integrated into Elements, making it very easy to use. The things you can do with a Photoshop.com account include:

- **Create your own Web site**. You can make beautiful online albums that display your photos in elaborate slideshows—all accessible via your own Photoshop.com URL (Web address). Great for dazzling friends and family. They can even download your photos or order prints, if you choose to let them. (See page 467.)

- **Automatically back up and sync your photos**. Frequent worriers and travelers, prepare to be amazed. You can set Elements to sync your PC-based photos to storage space on Photoshop.com, providing you with a backup, just in case. What's more, you can upload photos to your albums from *other* computers, and they automatically appear in the Organizer the next time you start Elements. See page 66 for more about how to use this nifty feature.

- **Access your photos from other computers**. When you're not at home, pop over to your Photoshop.com account to see and even organize your photos. That way, when you visit friends, you don't need to lug your own computer along— just log into your account from their computers.

- **Download lots of extra goodies.** In Elements 7, the Content palette (page 467) displays thumbnails for additional backgrounds, frames, graphics, and so on, that you can download right from Photoshop.com.

- **Get lots of great free advice.** Install the Photoshop Inspiration Browser (page 30), and you can choose from a whole range of helpful tutorials for all sorts of Elements tasks and projects.

The bad news is that for Elements 7, the Photoshop.com features are initially available only in the US. Adobe says it plans to expand this offering worldwide later on. (For now, you get some of the same features, like the ability to create online albums and galleries, at Adobe's Photoshop Showcase site. See page 3 for more about the regional differences.) To sign up for a free account:

1. **Tell Adobe you want an account.**

   Just click the Join button on the Welcome screen (page 13) or at the top of either the Organizer or the Editor's main window.

2. **In the window that opens, fill in your information to create your Adobe ID.**

   You need to give the usual address, phone, email, and so on, and also pick what you'd like for your unique Adobe Web address (Hint: something like *http://johnspictures.photoshop.com* is probably already taken, so you may need to try a few alternatives. When you click Create Account, you get a message if the Web address you chose is already in use.) Turn on the checkbox that says you agree to Adobe's terms and conditions. Finally, for security purposes you need to enter the text you see in a box on the sign-up screen.

3. **Create your account.**

   Click the Create Account button. Adobe tells you if it finds any errors in what you submitted, giving you a chance to go back and fix them.

4. **Confirm your account.**

   You'll get an email from Adobe. Just click the link in the email to confirm that you want to create an account, and you're all set. You need to click the link within 24 hours of creating your account, or you may have to start the whole process all over again.

Once you have an account, you can get to it from the left side of the Welcome screen, as shown in Figure 1-4. You can also click Sign In at the top of the Editor or Organizer. Once you're signed in, you see "Welcome < your name >" instead of Sign In, and you can click that to go to your account settings.

A free Photoshop.com account is a pretty amazing deal. It even gives you 5 GB of space on Adobe's servers for backing up and storing your photos. However, you can also upgrade to a paid account (called Plus), which gives you more of everything: more template designs for Online Albums, more downloads from the Content palette, more tutorials, and more storage space: 20 to 100 GB (depending on what

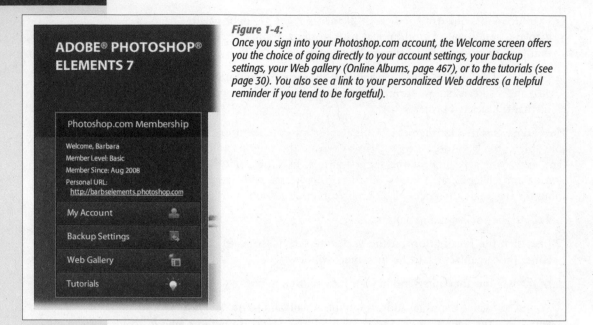

ADOBE® PHOTOSHOP® ELEMENTS 7

Photoshop.com Membership

Welcome, Barbara
Member Level: Basic
Member Since: Aug 2008
Personal URL:
   http://barbselements.photoshop.com

My Account

Backup Settings

Web Gallery

Tutorials

Figure 1-4:
Once you sign into your Photoshop.com account, the Welcome screen offers you the choice of going directly to your account settings, your backup settings, your Web gallery (Online Albums, page 467), or to the tutorials (see page 30). You also see a link to your personalized Web address (a helpful reminder if you tend to be forgetful).

level membership you choose). However, the Plus account costs $49.99 for 20 GB and more as your storage amount increases, so you might want to try the free account first to see whether you'll really use it enough to justify the price.

Once you sign into your account, you get logged in automatically every time you start Elements. If you don't want that to happen, just click your Account settings, and then, in the window that opens, choose Sign Out.

> **NOTE** Photoshop.com replaces the now-retired Photoshop Express. Both services actually do the same thing; Adobe is simply changing the name. If you forget your personalized Photoshop.com URL when you want to log in away from home, you can always just go to *www.photoshop.com*, and log in that way.

Editing Your Photos

In addition to the Organizer, the Editor is the other main component of Elements (Figure 1-5). This is the fun part of Elements, where you get to edit, adjust, transform, and generally glamorize your photos, and where you can create original artwork from scratch with the drawing tools and shapes.

You can operate the Editor in any of three different modes:

• **Quick Fix**. For many beginners, Quick Fix (Figure 1-6) ends up as your main workspace. Adobe has gathered together the basic tools you need to improve most photos. It's also one of the two places in Elements where you can choose to have a before-and-after view while you work. (Guided Edit, described below, is the other.) Chapter 4 gives you all the details on using Quick Fix.

- **Full Edit.** The Full Edit window gives you access to Elements' most sophisticated tools. You have far more ways to work on your photo in Full Edit than in Quick Fix, and if you're fussy, it's where you'll do most of your retouching work. Most of the Quick Fix commands are also available via menus in the Full Edit window.

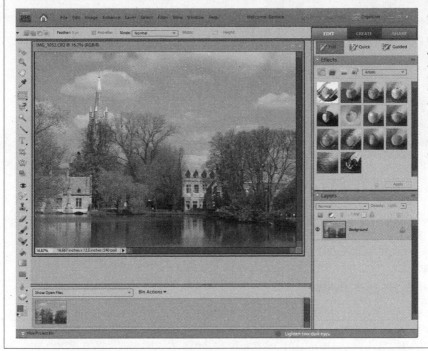

Figure 1-5:
The main Elements editing window, which Adobe calls Full Edit. In some previous versions of Elements it was known as the Standard Editor, something you might want to remember in case you ever try any tutorials written for Elements 3 or 4.

- **Guided Edit.** This window can be enormously helpful if you're a newcomer to Elements. Basically, it provides a step-by-step walkthrough for popular projects such as cropping your photos, and removing blemishes from them. Like Quick Fix, Guided Edit offers a before-and-after view of your photo as you work on it. Guided Edit is explained on page 28. In Elements 7, Guided Edit also features some advanced activities, like the new Actions Player (page 380).

The rest of this chapter covers some of the basic concepts and key tools in the Editor.

NOTE If you leave a photo open in the Editor, then when you switch back to the Organizer, you see a red band with a padlock across the photo's Organizer thumbnail as a reminder. To get rid of the lock and free up your image for Organizer projects, go back to the Editor and close the photo there.

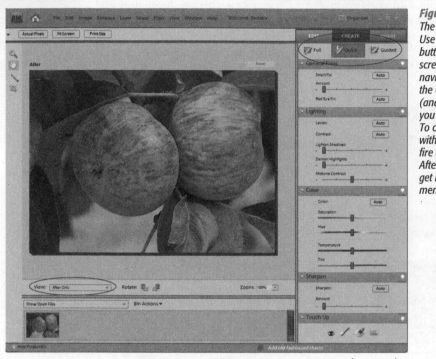

Figure 1-6:
The Quick Fix window. Use the navigation buttons at the top of the screen (circled) to navigate from Full Edit to the Quick Fix window (and to Guided Edit, if you like) and back again. To compare your fixes with the original photo fire up the "Before and After" view, which you get by clicking the View menu (circled).

Your Elements Tools

Elements gives you an amazing array of tools to use when working on your photo. You get almost two dozen primary tools to help select, paint on, and otherwise manipulate photos, and many of the tools have as many as six subtools hiding beneath them (see Figure 1-7). Bob Vila's workshop probably isn't any better stocked than Elements' virtual toolbox.

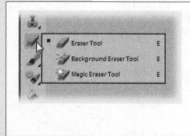

Figure 1-7:
Like any good toolbox, the Elements Toolbox has lots of hidden drawers tucked away in it. Many Elements tools are actually groups of tools, which are represented by tiny black triangles on the lower-right side of the tool icon. (You can't really see the triangle in the illustration because the pop-out menu obscures it, but if you look at the tools above the Eraser—the Clone Stamp and the Healing Brush—their triangles are visible.) Holding the mouse button down as you click the icon brings out the hidden subtools. The little black square next to the regular Eraser tool means it's the active tool right now.

TIP   When you want to explore every cranny of Elements, you need to open a photo (in the Editor, choose File → Open). Lots of the menus are grayed out if you have no file opened.

The long, skinny strip on the left side of the Full Edit window is the main Elements Toolbox, as you can see in Figure 1-7. It stays perfectly organized so that you can always find what you want without ever having to lift a finger to tidy it. And what's more, if you forget what a particular tool does, then hold your mouse over the tool's icon, and a label (called a tooltip) appears. To activate a tool, click it. Any tool that you select comes with its own collection of options, as shown in Figure 1-8.

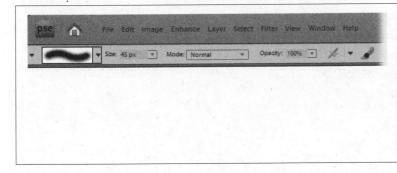

Figure 1-8:
When a tool is active, the Options bar changes to show its available settings. Elements tools are highly customizable, letting you do things like adjust a brush's size and shape. Here you see the options for the Brush tool. (The caterpillar-like thingy at the left is a sample of the stroke you'd get from the current brush settings.)

Incidentally, your screen size determines the number of columns in the Toolbox. In Elements 7, if you meet the minimum screen size requirements, then you start with a single column Toolbox, but if you reduce the height of the Elements window too much, then it becomes a double columned one. If you prefer a more compact Toolbox, see the box "Doubling Up."

POWER USERS' CLINIC

Doubling Up

If you have a single column Toolbox and you'd prefer the double-columned Toolbox (maybe you think it would be more efficient not to have your tools spread out so much, for example), good news—you can tear the Toolbox loose from its moorings and collapse it into a double column by grabbing its top edge, and pulling it off the Options bar. But keep in mind that a double-columned Toolbox is a bit quirky. When you put it too close to the left edge of the screen, it springs back to its original form.

Another advantage to having a floating Toolbox is that you can use the Tab key to hide it along with your other loose palettes. Press Tab again to bring them all back. (Like the anchored Toolbox, the bins and top bars of Elements don't go away when you press the Tab key.)

Other windows in Elements, like Quick Fix and the Raw Converter (see page 224), also have toolboxes, but none is as complete as the one in Full Edit.

NOTE   If you've used Elements 5 or earlier, you'll find an important difference in getting to subtools in Elements 7. Now you can choose a tool from a group only by using the tool's pop-out menu in the Toolbox. You can't switch from one tool in a subgroup to another in the Options bar anymore.

Don't worry about learning the names of every tool right now, but if you want to see them all, they're all on display in Figure 1-9. It's easier to remember what a tool is once you've used it. And don't be concerned about how many tools you have available. You probably have a bunch of Allen wrenches in your garage toolbox that you don't use more than a couple of times a year. Likewise, you'll find that you tend to use certain Elements tools more than others.

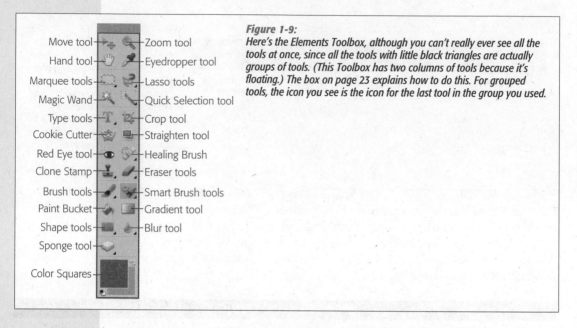

Move tool — Zoom tool
Hand tool — Eyedropper tool
Marquee tools — Lasso tools
Magic Wand — Quick Selection tool
Type tools — Crop tool
Cookie Cutter — Straighten tool
Red Eye tool — Healing Brush
Clone Stamp — Eraser tools
Brush tools — Smart Brush tools
Paint Bucket — Gradient tool
Shape tools — Blur tool
Sponge tool
Color Squares

Figure 1-9:
Here's the Elements Toolbox, although you can't really ever see all the tools at once, since all the tools with little black triangles are actually groups of tools. (This Toolbox has two columns of tools because it's floating.) The box on page 23 explains how to do this. For grouped tools, the icon you see is the icon for the last tool in the group you used.

TIP   You can activate any tool with a keyboard shortcut, thereby saving a *ton* of time, since you don't have to interrupt what you're doing to trek over to the Toolbox. To see a tool's shortcut key, hover your mouse over the icon. A label pops up indicating the shortcut key (it's the letter in parentheses).

FREQUENTLY ASKED QUESTION

The Always-On Toolbox

Do I always have to have a tool selected?

Yes. When looking at the Toolbox, you'll probably notice that one tool icon is highlighted, indicating that the tool is active. You can deactivate it by clicking a different tool. But what happens when you don't want *any* tool to be active? How do you fix things so that you don't have a tool selected?

You don't. In the Editor, one tool must always be selected, so you probably want to get in the habit of choosing a tool that won't do anything damaging to your image if you click it accidentally. For instance, the Pencil tool, which leaves a spot or line where you click, is probably not a good choice. The Marquee selection tool (page 123), the Zoom tool (page 87), and the Hand tool (page 88) are your safest choices.

Panels, Bins, and Palettes

Whether you're in the Editor or the Organizer, the right side of your screen is always pretty busy. Adobe calls this area the *Task panel*. Use it to select different modes, like whether to organize photos or share them by email (in the Organizer), or whether to edit a photo or use it in a project (in the Editor).

NOTE You can collapse the main part of the Task panel to get it out of your way by clicking its left edge, but the main tabs are always visible. Click the edge again to bring the panel back.

The Project bin

In the Editor, the long narrow photo tray hogging the bottom of your screen is called the *Project bin*. It shows you what photos you currently have open, as explained in Figure 1-10, but it does a lot more than that.

At the upper left of the Project bin are two pull-down menus:

- **Show Open Files.** This menu lets you determine what the Project bin is going to display: the photos currently open in the Editor, selected photos from the Organizer, or any of the albums (page 53) you've made. If you send a bunch of photos over from the Organizer at once, then you may think something went awry because no photo appears on your desktop or in the Project bin. If you switch the menu over to "Show Files from Organizer", then you see your photos waiting for you in the bin.

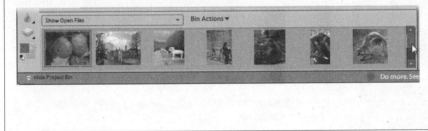

Figure 1-10:
The Project bin runs across the bottom of the Editor's screen. It holds a thumbnail of every photo you have open, as well as photos you sent over from the Organizer that are waiting to be opened.

- **Bin Actions.** This is where the Project bin gets really useful. You can choose to use the photos in the bin in a project (via the Create tab), share them by any of the means listed under the Task Panel's Share tab, print them out, or make an album right there in the bin without ever going to the Organizer.

TIP If you don't use the Organizer, then the Project bin is a particularly great feature, because it lets you create groups of photos you can call up all together. Just put them in an album (page 53), and then, from the Show Open Files menu, choose the name of the album when you want to see that group again.

You can drag your photos' thumbnails in the bin to rearrange them if you want to use the photos in a project.

The Project bin is a useful feature, but if you have a small monitor, sometimes you may prefer to have the space for your editing work. You can choose to make the bin collapse and hide until you move your mouse down to the bottom of the screen, causing it to jump back into view. Go to Editor → Edit → Preferences → General → "Project Bin auto-hide". This method works well only on a fast and powerful computer, though—if you don't have a lot of horsepower, the bin can take a while to reappear.

If you find auto-hide too slow but don't want to see the bin all the time, then go ahead and collapse and expand it manually. To close the bin, click the Hide Project Bin arrow at the lower left of your screen. Click the arrow again when you want the Project bin to reappear.

The Palette bin

When you're in Full Edit, the Task panel displays the Palette bin. These palettes let you do things like keep track of what you've done to your photo (Undo History palette) and apply special effects to your images (Effects palette and Content palette).

You might like the Palette bin, but many people don't. If you don't have a large monitor, you may find it wastes too much desktop acreage, and in Elements, you need all the working room you can get. Fortunately, you don't have to keep your palettes in the bin; you can close the bin and just keep your palettes floating around on your desktop, or you can minimize them.

Open and close the bin by clicking the Palette bin's left edge (anywhere along the thin vertical bar). You can also pull palettes out of the bin by dragging the name bar of any palette. Figure 1-11 shows how to make palettes even smaller once they're out of the bin. You can also combine freestanding palettes with each other, as shown in Figure 1-12.

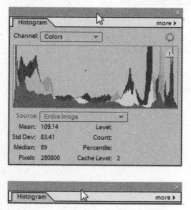

Figure 1-11:
You can free up even more space by collapsing your palettes, accordion-style, once they're out of the bin.

Top: To collapse a palette, double-click the palette's top bar.

Bottom: A shrunken palette.

At first, the Palette bin contains only two palettes: Layers and Effects. To see how many more palettes Elements actually gives you, check out the Editor's main Window menu (the one at the top of your screen). When you select a new palette, it appears floating on the desktop. If you want to put a palette into the bin, click the little double arrow at the upper right of the palette, choose "Place in Palette Bin when Closed", and then click the Close button. The palette jumps into the bin. To take a palette out of the bin, drag it out, go back to the menu, and then deselect "Place in Palette Bin when Closed". The next time you close the palette, it disappears, and you have to choose it from the Window menu to see it again.

TIP If you've been going crazy trying to get rid of one of the bin's original palettes (either the Layers or Effects palette), but every time you close it, it just hops back into the bin, in the upper-right corner of the palette, click the More button (the double arrows), and then turn off "Place in Palette bin when Closed". Next time you close the palette, it goes away and doesn't return til you choose it again from the Window menu.

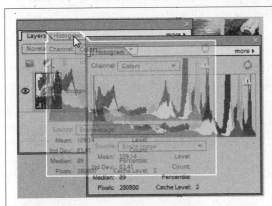

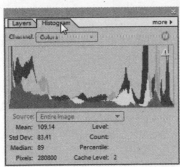

Figure 1-12:
You can combine two or more palettes once you've dragged them out of the bin.

Top: The Histogram palette is being pulled into, and combined with, the Layers palette. To combine palettes, drag one of them (by clicking on the palette's name bar) and drop it onto the other palette.

Bottom: To switch from one palette to another after they're grouped, just click the tab of the one you want to use. To remove a palette from a group, simply drag it off the palette window. If you want to return everything to how it looked when you first launched Elements, then go to Window → Reset Palette Locations.

NOTE Elements has one palette-related quirk. In the Window menu, visible palettes should have checks next to their names. (Palettes that are open in another tab but not currently visible have dashes next to their names.) But if you collapse a palette, even though the palette's name stays on your desktop, it remains unchecked in the Window menu. If you lose a collapsed palette (they occasionally get hidden behind the Options bar when you switch back and forth from Full Edit to Quick Fix or the Organizer), then just select the palette's name in the list again to bring it back to the front where you can reach it. If all else fails, choosing Reset Palette Locations in the Window menu puts everything back in its original position.

Getting Help

Wherever Adobe found a stray corner in Elements, they stuck some help into it. You can't move anywhere in this program without being offered some kind of guidance. Here are some of the ways you can summon assistance if you need it:

- **Help menu.** Choose Help → Photoshop Elements Help, or simply press F1. Elements launches your Web browser, and you see the Elements Help files displayed there. In the Help window, you can search or browse a topic list and glossary. ·

- **Tooltips.** When it's blue, the text that pops up under your mouse as you move around Elements is linked to the appropriate section in Elements Help. Click a tooltip for more information about whatever your mouse is hovering over.

- **Dialog box links.** Most dialog boxes have a few words of bright blue text somewhere in them. That text is actually a link to Elements Help. If you get confused about what the settings for a filter do, for instance, then, in the settings dialog box, click the blue text for a reminder.

Guided Edit

If you're a beginner, your biggest help in Elements may be Guided Edit, shown in Figure 1-13. It walks you through a variety of popular editing tasks, like cropping, sharpening, correcting colors, and removing blemishes. It also includes some features that are useful even if you're an old Elements hand, like the Actions Player (page 380) and the new Scene Cleaner (page 313).

Guided edit is really easy to use:

1. **Go to Guided Edit.**

   Click the Edit tab → Guided.

2. **Open a photo.**

   Press Ctrl+O, and then, from the window that appears, choose your photo. If you already have a photo open, it appears in the Guided Edit window automatically. If you have several photos in the Project bin, then you can switch images by double-clicking the thumbnail of the one you want to work on.

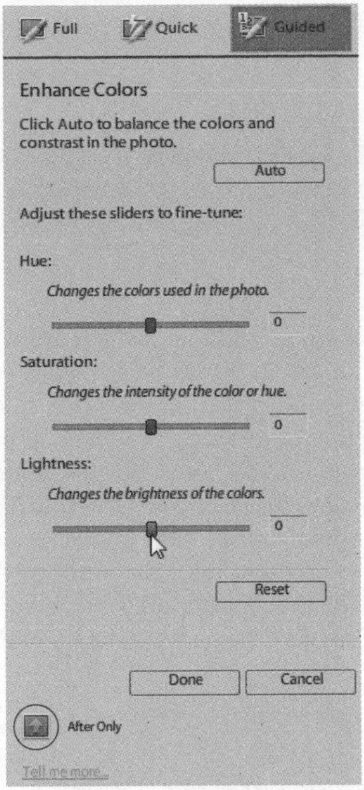

Figure 1-13:
Guided Edit gives you step-by-step help with basic photo editing. Just use the tools that appear in the task panel once you choose an activity. After you've selected a task, you can change the view of your photo to "Before and After". Keep clicking the little blue button (circled) at the bottom of the window to toggle views between "After Only", "Before & After—Horizontal", and "Before & After—Vertical".

Enhance Colors

Click Auto to balance the colors and constrast in the photo.

Auto

Adjust these sliders to fine-tune:

Hue:
Changes the colors used in the photo.
0

Saturation:
Changes the intensity of the color or hue.
0

Lightness:
Changes the brightness of the colors.
0

Reset

Done   Cancel

After Only

Tell me more...

3. **Choose what you want to do.**

Your options are grouped into major categories like Basic Photo Edits and Color Correction, with a variety of individual projects under each heading. Just click the task you want in the list on the right side of the window. The Task panel displays the relevant buttons and/or sliders for your task.

4. **Make your adjustments.**

Just move the sliders and click the buttons till you like what you see. If you want to start over, click Reset. If you change your mind about the whole project, click Cancel.

If several steps are involved, then Elements shows you just what you need to use for the current step, and then switches to a new set of choices for the next step as you go along.

5. **Click Done to finish.**

If there are more steps, then you may see another set of instructions. If you see the main list of topics again, you're all through. Don't forget to save your changes (page 58). To close your photo, press Ctrl+W, or leave it open and switch to another tab to share it or use it in a project.

If you need to adjust your view of your photo while you work on it, Guided Edit has a little toolbox with the Hand (page 87) and Zoom (page 88) tools to help you out.

> **NOTE** Guided Edit shows you quick and easy ways to change your image, but you don't always get the best possible results. It's a great tool for starting out, but don't make the mistake of thinking what you see here is the best you can possibly do for your images. Once you're more comfortable in Elements, Quick Fix (Chapter 4) is a good next step.

Photoshop Inspiration Browser

You've probably noticed the little text alerts that zip in and out at the bottom of both the Editor and the Organizer windows, as shown in Figure 1-14. If you click one, then you get a pop-up window that suggests a tutorial explaining how to do whatever the text suggested. Click the arrow where it says "Learn how", and, if you haven't already done so, Adobe offers to install the Photoshop Inspiration Browser. The Browser is a dedicated mini-program that lets you view tutorials. Viewing material in the Browser requires a Photoshop.com account (available only for US residents; see page 18), but if you have an account, it's well worth installing, because the Browser is a direct connection to a slew of tutorials for things you might want to do with Photoshop Elements or Premiere Elements (Adobe's movie editing program).

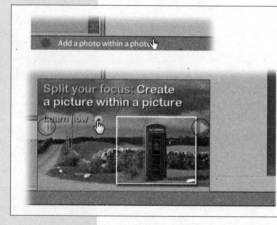

Figure 1-14:
Top: Click these little text banners for more information about the topic.

Bottom: In these pop-up windows you can either click "Learn how" to go directly to that particular tutorial, or click the faintly ghosted left and right arrows (circled; they get brighter when you mouse over them) in the window to read about other available tutorials.

To get started, just click through the screens to install the Inspiration Browser. If you don't already have it, then you have to install yet *another* Adobe program: Adobe AIR, which lets other programs show you content stored online without using a Web browser.

This process may seem like a lot of work, but it's well worth the effort, since you can find tutorials on everything from beginner topics like creating albums to advanced subjects like working with Displacement Maps (a sophisticated technique used for things like making your photo look like it's painted on a brick wall, letting the brick texture show through, or making a page of text look like a crumpled newspaper). The tutorials are all in either PDF or video format. You'll see tutorials from well-known Elements gurus here, but anyone can submit a tutorial for the Inspiration Browser. So if you figure out how to do a project you think might be useful to others, you can create a tutorial yourself and send it in for approval. (You need to create your tutorial as either a PDF or, for a video tutorial, in the Flash FLV format; submit by clicking the Submit button and entering the requested information in the window that appears.)

Search the tutorials using the box on the left, or, after clicking All Tutorials, filter them by category or product (so you don't have to see Premiere Elements topics if you have only Photoshop Elements, for example). You can also click on one of the column headings to see the available tutorials arranged by Title, Author, Difficulty, Date Posted, Category, Type (video or PDF), or the average star rating given it by the people who've tried it. Use the buttons at the upper right of the window to change the view from a list to a larger thumbnail view; information about each tutorial appears below the thumbnail.

The Inspiration Browser is a wonderful resource and may well give you most of the help you need with Elements beyond this book.

> **TIP**   If the author of a tutorial has a Web site, then the tutorial's page has a link to it. Exploring these links can bring you to a great many useful Elements-related learning resources, as well as useful add-on tools that extend Elements' capabilities (see Chapter 19).

Escape Routes

Photoshop Elements has a couple of really wonderful features to help you avoid making permanent mistakes: the Undo command and the Undo History palette. After you've gotten used to them, you'll probably wish it were possible to use these tools in all aspects of your life, not just Elements.

Undo

No matter where you are in Elements, you can almost always change your mind about what you just did. Press Ctrl+Z, and the last change you made goes away. Pressing Ctrl+Z works even if you've just saved your photo—but only while it's still open. (If you close your picture, your changes are permanent.) Keep pressing Ctrl+Z and you keep undoing your work, step by step.

If you want to *redo* what you just undid, just press Ctrl+Y. These keystroke commands are great for toggling changes on and off while you decide whether you really want to keep them. The Undo/Redo keystroke combinations work in the Organizer as well as the Editor.

> **TIP**   You do have a bit of control over the key combination you use for Undo/Redo, if you don't like the Ctrl+Z combination. Go to Edit → Preferences → General. Elements gives you two other choices, both of which involve pressing the Z key in combination with the Control, Alt, and Shift keys.

Undo History palette

In the Full Edit window, you get even more control over the actions you can undo, thanks to the Undo History palette (Figure 1-15); open it by choosing Window → Undo History.

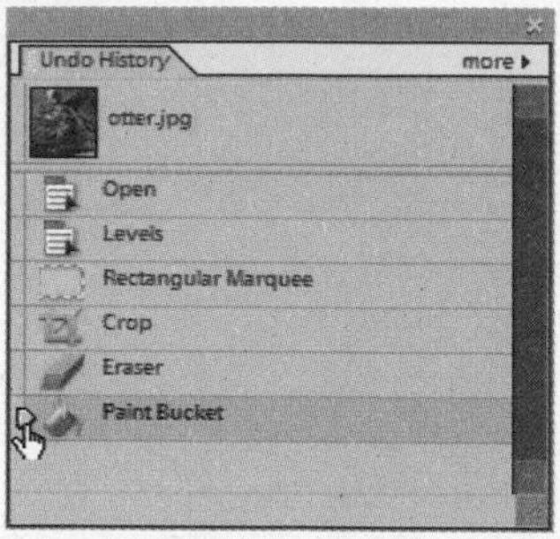

Figure 1-15:
For a little time travel, just slide the pointer up and watch your changes disappear one by one. You can go back only sequentially. Here, for instance, you can't go back to Crop without first undoing the Paint Bucket and the Eraser. Slide the pointer down to redo your work. You can also move to a different point in your work by just clicking the place in the list where you want to go, instead of using the slider.

This palette holds a list of the changes you've made since you opened your image. Just push the slider up and watch your changes disappear one by one as you go. Undo History even works if you've saved your file: As long as you haven't closed your file, the palette tracks every action you take. You can also slide the other way to redo changes that you've undone.

Be careful, though. You can back up only as many steps as you've set Elements to remember. Elements lets you keep track of as many as 1,000 steps. You can regulate this number in Preferences, as explained in Figure 1-16.

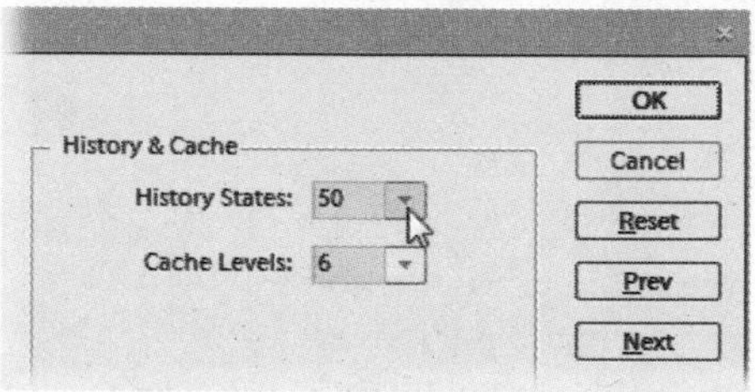

Figure 1-16:
You can set the number of steps the Undo History palette remembers in Edit → Preferences → Performance → History & Cache. Elements initially sets it to 50, but you can set it as high as 1,000. Beware, though—remembering even 100 steps may slow your system to a crawl if you don't have a superpowered processor, plenty of memory, and loads of disk space. If Elements runs slowly on your machine, then reducing the number of history states it remembers (try 20) may speed things up a bit.

The one rule of Elements

As you're probably beginning to see, Elements lets you work in lots of different ways. What's more, most people who use Elements approach projects in different ways. What works for your neighbor with her pictures may be quite different from how you would choose to work on the very same shots.

However, you'll hear one suggestion from almost every Elements veteran, and it's an important one: *Never ever work on your original. Always, always, always make a copy of your image and work on that.*

The good news is that if you store your photos in the Organizer, you don't need to worry about accidentally trashing your original. Elements automatically creates a copy when you edit a photo that's cataloged in the Organizer, so that you can always revert to your original.

> **NOTE** The Organizer's *version sets* provide another great safety net. They let you make as many different editions of your photo as you like without compromising your original. Page 59 has full details.

If you're determined not to use the Organizer, then follow these steps to make a copy of your image:

1. **Right-click the title bar of the Image window, and then choose Duplicate, or go to File → Duplicate.**

   The Image window is the smaller window within the Editor where your photo appears.

2. **Name the duplicate, and then click the close button (the X at the upper right of the image window) on the original.**

   Now the original is safely tucked out of harm's way.

3. **Save the duplicate using Ctrl+S.**

   Choose Photoshop (.psd) as the file format when you save it. (You may want to choose another format after you've read Chapter 3, and understand more about your different format options.)

Now you don't have to worry about making a mistake or changing your mind, because you can always start over if you want to.

> **NOTE** Elements doesn't have an autosave feature, so you should get into the habit of saving frequently as you work. Read more about saving on page 58.

Getting Started in a Hurry

If you're the impatient type, and you're starting to squirm because you want to be up and doing something to your photos, here's the quickest way to get started in Elements: Adjust the brightness and color balance all in one step.

1. **While you're in the Editor, open a photo.**

   Press Ctrl+O and navigate to the image you want, and then click Open.

2. **Press Alt+Ctrl+M.**

   You've just applied Elements' Auto Smart Fix tool (Figure 1-17).

Voilà! You should see quite a difference in your photo, unless the exposure, lighting, and contrast were almost perfect before. The Auto Smart Fix tool is one of the many easy-to-use features in Elements. (Of course, if you don't like what just happened to your photo, no problem—simply press Ctrl+Z to undo it.)

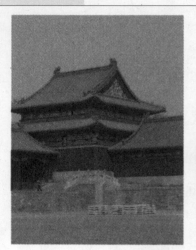
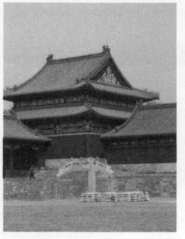
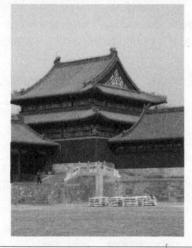

Figure 1-17:
Auto Smart Fix is the easiest, quickest way to improve the quality of your photos.

Top left: The original, unedited picture.

Top right: Auto Smart Fix makes quite a difference, but the colors are still slightly off.

Bottom: By using some of the other tools you'll learn about in this book (like Auto Contrast and Adjust Sharpness), you can make things look even better.

If you're the really impatient type, jump right to Chapter 4 to learn about using the Quick Fix commands. But it's worth taking the time to read the next two chapters so you understand which file formats to choose, and how to make some basic adjustments to your images, like rotating and cropping them.

Don't forget to give Guided Edit a try if you see what you want to do in the list of topics. Guided Edit can be a big help when you're first learning your way around.

CHAPTER 2

Importing, Managing, and Saving Your Photos

Now that you've had a look around Elements, it's time to start learning how to get photos *into* the program, and also how to keep track of where these photos are stored. As a digital photographer, you may no longer be facing shoeboxes stuffed with prints, but you've still got to face the menace of photos piling up on your hard drive. Fortunately, Elements gives you some great tools for organizing your collection and quickly finding individual pictures.

In this chapter, you'll learn how to import photos from cameras, memory card readers, and scanners. You'll also find out how to import individual frames from videos, open files already on your computer, and create a new file from scratch. At that point you're ready for a quick tour of the Organizer, where you can sort and find pictures once they're in Elements. Finally, you'll learn about photo preservation: saving and backing up your precious files.

Importing from Cameras

Elements gives you lots of different ways to get photos from camera to computer, but the simplest tool is Adobe's Photo Downloader. Even if you don't like the Downloader, read on. Later in this section, you'll learn about other ways to import your photos.

> **NOTE** Take a moment to carefully read the instructions from your camera manufacturer. Those directions should always take precedence over anything you read here that suggests doing something differently.

The Photo Downloader

When you plug your camera or memory card reader into your computer, you get a standard Windows dialog box (shown on page 18) asking what you want to do. To use the Photo Downloader to get your photos into Elements, just click "Organize and Edit using Adobe Photoshop Elements 7.0". The Downloader's job is pretty straightforward: to shepherd your photos as they make the trip to your PC and to make sure Elements knows where your new images are stored. Your job is to help it along by adjusting the following settings (on display in Figure 2-1).

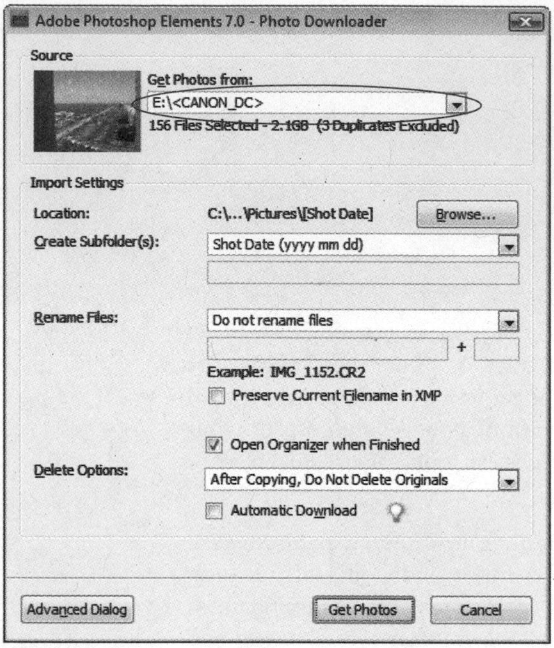

Figure 2-1:
When the Photo Downloader first launches, you see this dialog box, which lets you choose where your photos go and what names they're given (say goodbye to names like IMG_0327.JPG). To start, choose your camera or card reader from the list of devices (circled). If you want to browse through your photos to decide which ones to import, click Advanced Dialog, where you can pick and choose which photos to grab and fine-tune other settings.

• **Get Photos From.** Choose your camera or card reader from the list of available devices, as your first step to downloading. (You may also see a more generic "Camera or Card Reader" choice rather than the name of your camera. If that's all you see, pick that option.) Just below this menu, you'll see a list of how many photos the Downloader found, and also how many duplicates (of images already in the Organizer) it plans to skip.

• **Location.** Your photos usually get stored in a folder named for the date you imported them. (This folder is located inside the directory *C:\Users\<your user-name>\Pictures\<date>* [in XP, it's *C:\<your user name>\My Documents\My Pictures\Adobe\Digital Camera Photos*]. If you download more photos the same day, you get a second folder, with the same name with "-1" added to it.) If you want to change where your photos are headed, click the Browse button and choose another location. You can permanently change the standard location by going to Organizer → Edit → Preferences → "Camera or Card Reader". Set a new location, and from now on, the Downloader always puts your photos in the folder you chose.

- **Create Subfolder(s)**. If you want to have more organization, you can choose to put your files into a subfolder *inside* the folder you chose in Location, with a name you pick (instead of a date-stamped one). Or you can choose to have a subfolder named for the date of your import, or the date when the photo was shot (with the date displayed in your choice of several different formats).

> **TIP**   When you name the folder, you can apply that name as a tag (label) to all the photos in the folder with just one click (once you're in the Photo Browser window). Read more about tags—and how they can help you quickly find photos—later in this chapter.

- **Rename Files**. You can choose to give all the files a custom name, if you like. So if you type *obedience_school_graduation*, then you get photos named obedience_school_graduation001, obedience_school_graduation002, and so on, or you can choose to use a combination of a custom name and the shot date, if you prefer. You can also choose to use just the shot date or today's date, or the name of the subfolder. In each case, you'll get the three-digit number to distinguish the files. You can also choose to leave this setting at "Do not rename files", in which case you keep the camera's file names and numbers.

- **Preserve Current Filename in XMP**. Turn this on if you want the photos' current filenames to be used as the filename stored in the photo's metadata. (More about metadata on page 59.)

- **Open Organizer when Finished**. If you're going to put your files in the Organizer, usually you'd leave this turned on, but you can turn it off if you don't use the Organizer, or if you'd rather wait till later to get organized. (You won't see this option if the Organizer is already running when you import your photos.)

- **Delete Options**. You can choose to let the Downloader delete your files when done. Figure 2-2 explains more about this option.

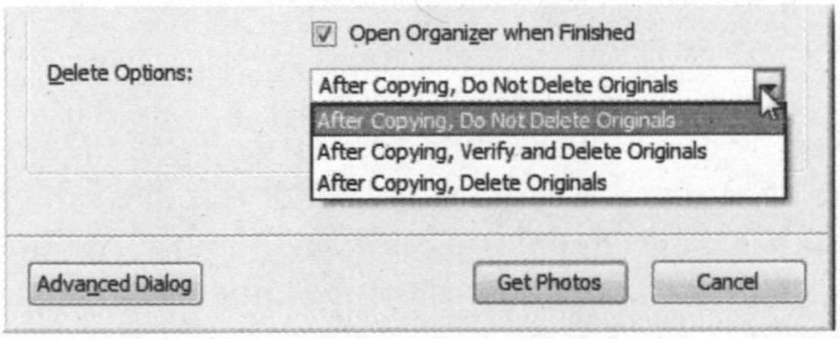

Figure 2-2:
The Photo Downloader offers to delete the files from your camera or memory card reader once they've been imported. This feature seems handy, but prudent people may want to think twice about whether to actually delete the files. The Downloader's pretty reliable, but it's always a good idea to wait until you've reviewed all your photos in Elements before deleting the originals. If you must use this option, at least choose "After Copying, Verify and Delete Originals", which forces Elements to check that it's copied your files correctly before vaporizing the originals.

- **Automatic Download**. If you like to live dangerously, you can turn on this checkbox and Elements will download any new photos it detects without showing you the dialog box. In almost all circumstances, it's best to leave Automatic Download off so that you have some control over what's going on. (This checkbox appears only after you've selected a device in the "Get Photos from" menu.) If you decide to take this risky route, you can set the parameters for downloading in Organizer → Edit → Preferences → "Camera or Card Reader".

The Downloader is smart enough to recognize any photos that it's already imported, and it doesn't reimport those. If you want to see your duplicates and for some reason download them again, or if you want to pick and choose which photos to import, then click the Advanced Dialog button at the bottom of the window to bring up the larger dialog box shown in Figure 2-3.

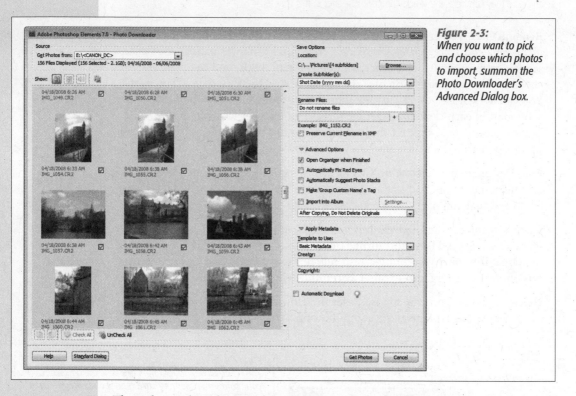

Figure 2-3:
When you want to pick and choose which photos to import, summon the Photo Downloader's Advanced Dialog box.

The Advanced Dialog window gives you all the options you see in the Downloader's standard window, plus a few more. The Advanced window is divided into two main parts. On the left side are the thumbnails of your photos. The little checkmarks next to each image indicate which photos will be imported; just turn off the checkboxes for the ones you don't want to bring into the Organizer. If you've already imported some of the images, the Organizer tells you so and doesn't import them again. You can also import video and sound files. The four buttons above the preview area (described here, from left to right) let you choose which files you see:

- **Show/Hide Images**. If you want to temporarily hide your photos (so you can look at just your video files, for instance), click this button or press Ctrl+M.

- **Video files**. This button is grayed out unless Elements finds any movie or video files on your memory card. If it does, you can hide them by clicking this button. You might do that if you're only interested in importing still photos right now. To see the video files again, click the button once more.

- **Audio files**. This button works just like the video button, but it becomes active when Elements finds audio files you may want to import.

- **Show Duplicates**. If Elements has already imported some of the photos on your memory card, but you want to see those files again, click this button and you can reimport them (or just see them for comparison's sake). In the preview area, the thumbnails of the files you've already imported will show an icon to indicate that they're duplicates. The icon appears on the upper-right corner of the photo thumbnails; it looks just like the Show Duplicates button.

    NOTE   Although much of this chapter talks about importing your pictures from a camera, most memory card readers work the same way. Use a card reader if you have one, since you'll spare your camera's batteries and subject your camera to less wear and tear.

The right side of the window is where you can adjust the settings for where your pictures are stored on your PC and how their folders are named. Most of these choices are the same ones you get in the Photo Downloader's standard dialog box, but you also get a few extras:

- **Automatically Fix Red Eyes**. When you leave this checkbox turned on, Elements searches through all your newly imported photos looking for pictures of people with red eyes (caused by camera flash) and then fixes them automatically. It sounds great, but it's not 100 percent reliable and tends to "fix" things like bright white teeth, as well. It's not destructive, because Elements makes a Version set (page 59) with your original, so you can ditch the new version if you don't like what Elements did. But the extra time it takes while Elements analyzes all your photos and the time you waste looking for mistakes mean you're better off leaving this option turned off and using another method to fix red eyes later. See page 104 for more about Elements' Red Eye tool. (You may find you also need to turn off Automatically Fix Red Eyes in Organizer → Edit → Preferences → "Camera or Card Reader" to keep this setting from turning itself back on again.)

- **Automatically Suggest Photo Stacks**. The Organizer lets you group related photos together into stacks (page 507). Turn this checkbox on to use the auto stack feature, where Elements automatically finds photos that should be grouped together. This feature works only for photos taken in your camera's burst (rapid advance) mode—in other words, photos of the same subject, taken very close together in time.

- **Make 'Group Custom Name' a Tag.** If you chose a custom name for your images, you can assign the name as a tag here. (Tags are explained on page 51.)

- **Import into Album.** Turn this on, and your current download automatically goes to the album you choose. Click the Settings button to select an existing album or create a new one. This feature is especially useful if you've chosen albums to automatically sync to Photoshop.com (page 18).

- **Apply Metadata.** If you want to write your name or copyright information right into the file's metadata (page 59) so that anyone who views your file will know it's yours, you can do that here.

Once you're done adjusting the Downloader's settings, click Get Photos. The Downloader slurps down the photos and launches the Organizer so you can review your pictures.

> **TIP**   You can tell the Organizer to "watch" folders that you often bring graphics (or even sound files or video) into. When you set a watched folder, Elements keeps an eye on it and lets you know when you have new photos there. Elements either imports the new files or tells you they're waiting for you, depending on which option you choose. Go to File → Watch Folders and click the Add button, and then browse to the folder you want Elements to watch.

Opening Stored Images

If you've got photos already stored on your computer, you have several options for opening them with Elements. If the file format is set to open in Elements, then double-click the file's icon to launch Elements and open the image. (If you want to change which files open automatically in Elements, see the box on page 41.) You've also got a few ways to open files from within Elements:

- **From the Organizer, for files not yet in the Organizer.** Go to File → "Get Photos and Videos" → "From Files and Folders", or press Ctrl+Shift+G, and then select your file. The other options in the Get Photos menu (like opening files stored on a cellphone) are covered on page 502.

- **From the Editor, for files already in the Organizer.** You can select an image that's stored in the Organizer and open it directly in the Editor. To do so, in the Organizer, click the file's thumbnail, and then press Ctrl+I, or go to the Editor button at the upper right of your screen → Full Edit. If you'd rather go to Quick Fix (page 99), choose Editor → Quick Fix instead. If you want to go to Guided Edit, click a photo's thumbnail, and then, in the upper right of your screen, click the Editor button → Guided Edit. Or you can click the Fix tab and choose any of the three Editor buttons there.

> **NOTE**   When your photo gets to the Editor, it should appear in the main editing space. If you don't see anything there, go down to the Project bin and choose "Show Files from Organizer". (If you send multiple images at once, they always appear in "Show Files from Organizer", not Show Open Files.)

- **From the Editor, for files anywhere on your computer.** Go to File → Open or press Ctrl+O and select your file. You can also drop a file right onto the Editor's desktop and it will open.

People who are new to Elements often get confused about the message shown in Figure 2-4. This appears whenever you go back to the Organizer with photos left open in the Editor.

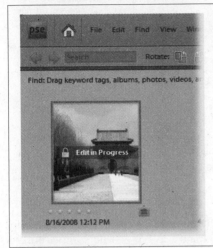

Figure 2-4:
This red locked band confuses many Elements newbies. It just means that you left your photo open in the Editor when you came back to the Organizer. To unlock it so that you have access to it in the Organizer again, just switch back to the Editor and close the photo there.

FREQUENTLY ASKED QUESTION

Picking the File Types That Elements Opens

How do I stop Elements from opening all my files?

Many people are dismayed to discover that once they install Elements, it opens every time they double-click any kind of graphics file—whether they want the file to open in Elements or not. Windows makes it pretty easy to change that behavior. First, find a file of the type you want to change. Then:

1. Right-click the icon of the closed file.

2. From the pop-up menu, in Vista choose Open With → Choose Default Program. In Windows XP, choose: Open With → Choose Program.

3. Select the program you want to use to open the file. Turn on "Always use the selected program to open this kind of file" to change the program for all files of this type.

Working with PDF Files

If you open a PDF file in Elements, you'll see the Import PDF dialog box (Figure 2-5), which gives you lots of options for how you want Elements to treat your file. You can choose to import whole pages or just the images on the pages, you can import multiple pages (if the PDF is more than one page), and you can choose the color mode (page 45) and the resolution, as well as whether or not you want anti-aliasing (page 135).

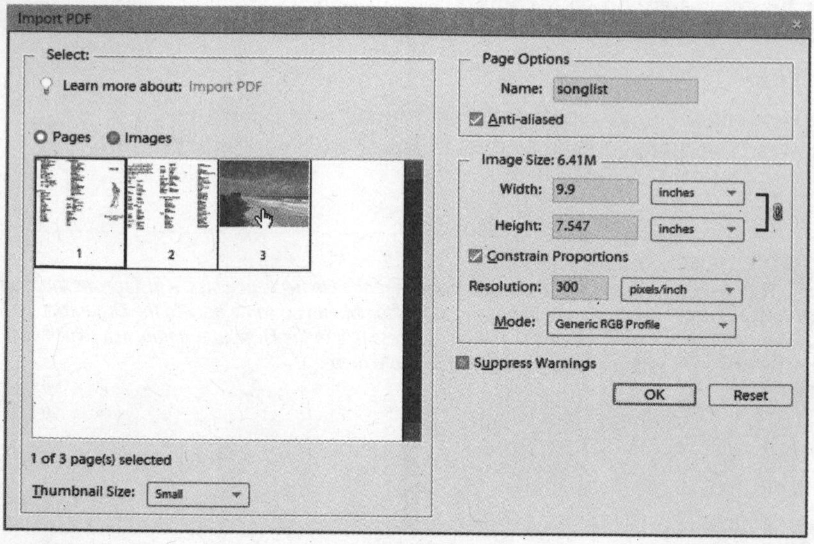

Figure 2-5:
You can open multipage PDF files in Elements. If you want to open just one page of the file, double-click the thumbnail of the page you want, and Elements opens it right up. To open multiple pages of the file, Shift-click to select the pages you want before you double-click to open them. You can catalog PDF files in the Organizer, too.

Scanning Photos

Elements comes bundled with many scanners because it's the perfect software for making scans look their best. You have two main ways of getting scanned images into Elements. Some scanners come with a *driver plug-in*, a small utility program that lets you scan directly into Elements. Look on your scanner's installation software for information about Elements compatibility or check the manufacturer's Web site for a Photoshop plug-in to download. (If you can scan into Photoshop, you should be able to scan into Elements.) You may also be able to scan into Elements if your scanner uses the *TWAIN interface*, which is an industry standard used by many scanner manufacturers.

If you don't have an Elements plug-in for your scanner and the Adobe TWAIN driver doesn't work for you, you'll need to use the scanning program that came with your scanner. Then, once you've saved your scanned image in a format that Elements understands, like TIFF (.tiff, .tif) or Photoshop (.psd), open the file in Elements like any other photo.

To control your scanner from within Elements, you can choose to scan from either the Editor or the Organizer. In the Editor, go to File → Import, and you'll find your scanner's name on the list that appears. In the Organizer, go to File → "Get Photos and Videos" → From Scanner, or press Ctrl+U. You should check out your available options for both locations because they're probably different. For instance, you may find that you have different file formats available to you in the Editor than you do in the Organizer.

TIP   If you do a lot of scanning, check out the Divide Scanned Photos command (page 71) for helpful tips on how to quickly scan in lots of photos at the same time. Also, you can save yourself a lot of drudgery in Elements if you make sure that both your scanner glass and the prints you're scanning are as dust-free as possible before you start.

Capturing Video Frames

Elements lets you capture a single frame from a video and use it the way you would any still photo. This feature works best if you choose a movie that's already on your computer (versus one that's streaming to your PC from the Web).

Elements can read many popular video file formats, including .avi, .wmv, and .mpeg. You do need to have a program on your computer (besides Elements) that's capable of viewing the video file.

NOTE   The video capture tool in Elements isn't really designed for use with long movies. You'll get the best results with clips that aren't more than a minute or two long.

To import a video frame, in the Editor, go to File → Import → Frame From Video, and then in the Video import dialog box:

1. **Find the video that contains the frame you want to copy.**

   Click the Browse button and navigate to the movie you want. After you choose the movie, the first frame should appear in the window in the Frame From Video dialog box.

2. **Navigate to the frame you want.**

   Either click the Play button or use the slider below the window to move through the movie until you see what you want.

3. **Copy the frame you want by clicking Grab Frame.**

   You can grab as many frames as you want. Each frame shows up in the Elements Editor as a separate file.

4. **When you have everything you need, click Done.**

   While grabbing video frames is a very fun thing to be able to do, it does have certain limitations. Most important, your video is going to appear at a fairly low resolution, so don't expect to get a great print from a video frame.

Creating a New File

You may want to create a new blank document when you're using Elements as a drawing program or when you're combining parts of other images together, for example.

To create a new file, go to the Editor, and choose File → New → Blank File (or press Ctrl+N) to bring up the New File dialog box. You have lots of choices to make each time you start a new file; they're all covered in the following sections.

> **TIP** You can't create a new blank file in the Organizer, but Elements gives you a quick shortcut from the Organizer to the Editor so you can open up a new, fresh file there. To open a new file, choose File → New → Blank File, and the Organizer creates a virgin file for you and automatically hops you and the new blank file over to the Editor. If you want to create a new file based on a photo that's in the Organizer, select the thumbnail, press Ctrl+C to copy it, and then choose File → New → "Image from Clipboard". Elements switches you to the Editor, where you'll see your copied photo awaiting you, all ready to work on.

Picking a File Size

The first thing you need to decide, logically enough, is how big you want your document to be. In Elements 7, there are two ways to do this:

- **Start with a Preset.** Preset, the first menu item in the New File window, lets you choose the general kind of document you want to create. If you want to create a file for printing, pick from the second group in the menu. The third group contains choices for onscreen viewing. Once you make a selection in this menu, the next menu—Size—changes to show you suitable sizes for your choice. Figure 2-6 shows you how it works.

> **NOTE** If you're into scrapbooking, you'll be pleased to see that Elements 7 offers some standard scrapbook page sizes as presets.

- **Enter the numbers yourself.** Just ignore the Preset and Size menus and type in what you want. You can choose inches, pixels, centimeters, millimeters, points, picas, or columns as your unit of measurement. Just pick the one you want in the Width and Height pull-down menus and then enter a number.

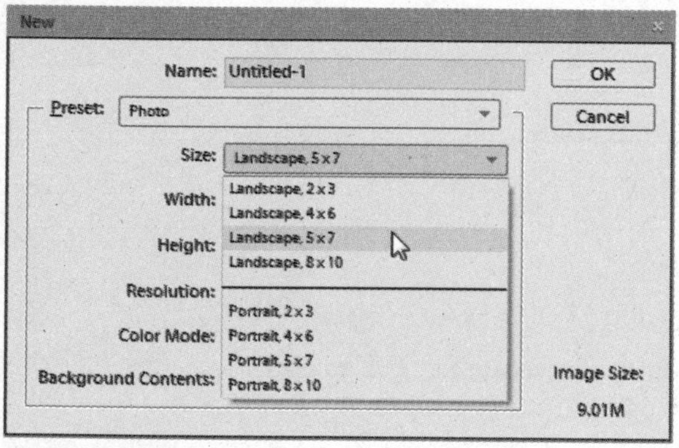

Figure 2-6:
Elements helps you pick an appropriate size when you use the Preset Menu. Choose a general category—here, Photo is the choice. The Size menu then changes to show you standard sizes for photo paper, each available in either landscape or portrait orientation. The size that Elements automatically selects if you don't choose anything from the menus (and you don't have anything copied to the clipboard) is 6"×4" at 300 pixels per inch, which works well if you're just playing around and trying things out.

Choosing Resolution

If you decide not to use one of the presets, you need to choose a resolution for your file. You'll learn a lot more about resolution in the next chapter (page 89), but a good rough guide is to choose 72 pixels per inch (ppi) for files that you'll look at only on a monitor, and 300 ppi for files you plan to print.

Choosing Color Mode

Elements gives you lots of color choices throughout the program, but Color Mode is probably your most important one because it determines which tools and filters you can use in your document. Your options are:

- **RGB Color.** Choosing RGB (red, green, and blue) means that you're creating a color document, as opposed to a black-and-white one. You'll probably choose RGB Color mode most of the time, even if you don't plan on having color in your image, because RGB gives you access to all of Elements' tools. Page 20 has lots more about picking colors. You can use RGB Color mode for black-and-white photos if you like, and many people do, since it gives you the most options for editing your photo.

- **Bitmap.** Every pixel in a bitmap mode image is either black or white. Use Bitmap mode for true black-and-white images—shades of gray need not apply here.

- **Grayscale.** Black-and-white photos are called *grayscale* because they're really made up of many shades of gray. In Elements, you can't do as much editing on a grayscale photo as you can in RGB (for example, you can't use some of the filters on a grayscale photo).

> **TIP** Sometimes you may need to change the color mode of an existing file to use all of Elements' tools and filters. For example, there are quite a few things you can do only if your file is in the RGB color mode. So if you need to use a filter (page 364) on a black-and-white photo and your choice is grayed out, go to Image → Mode and select RGB Color. Choosing RGB Color won't suddenly colorize your photo; it just changes the way Elements handles the file. You can always change back to the original color mode when you're done. If you use the "Convert to Black and White" feature in Elements (page 283), you still have an RGB mode photo afterward, not a grayscale mode.

If you find yourself in possession of a 16-bit file (page 238) you need to convert it to 8-bit color or you won't have access to many of the commands and filters in Elements. Make the change by choosing Image → Mode → 8 Bits/Channel. You're most likely to have 16-bit files if you import your images in Raw format (page 224); some scanners also offer you an option of creating 16-bit files. JPEG photos are always 8-bit.

Choosing Your File's Background Contents

The last choice you have to make when creating a new file is the *background contents* of the file. Choosing your file's background contents is where you tell Elements the color to use for the empty areas of the file, like, well, the background. You can be a traditionalist and choose white (almost always a good choice), or else choose a particular color or transparency. More about transparency in a minute.

If you want to choose a color other than white, use the Foreground/Background color squares to do so, as shown in Figure 2-7.

Figure 2-7:
To choose a new Background color, just click the Background color square (the purple one shown here) to bring up the Color Picker. Then choose the color you want. Your new color appears in the square, and the next time you do something that involves using a Background color, that's the shade you get. The whole process of picking colors is explained in much more detail on page 208.

Transparency is the most interesting option. To understand transparency and why it's such a wonderful invention, you need to know that every digital image, every single one, is either rectangular or square. A digital image *can't* be any other shape.

But digital images can *appear* to be a different shape—sunflowers, sailboats, or German Shepherds, for example. How? By placing your object on a transparent background so that it looks like it was cut out and only its shape appears, as shown in Figure 2-8. The actual photo is still a rectangle, but if you placed it into another image, you'd see only the shell and not the surrounding area, because the rest of the photo is transparent.

To keep the clear areas transparent when you close your image, you need to save the image in a file format that allows transparency. JPEGs, for instance, automatically fill transparent areas with solid white, so they're not a good choice. TIFFs, PDFs, and Photoshop files (.psd), on the other hand, let the transparent areas stay clear. Page 452 has more about which formats allow transparency.

Using the Organizer

The Organizer is where you keep track of your photos and start most of the projects that involve sharing your photos with others (posting them online, for example). You can see thumbnails of all your photos in the Organizer, assign keywords (called *tags*) to make it easier to find the pictures you want, and search for your photos in lots of different ways. In Elements 7, Photoshop.com (page 18) also hosts a version of the Organizer that works just the way it does on your desktop.

The Photo Browser is the main Organizer window. Date View (Display → Date View, or press Ctrl+Alt+D) offers a calendar-based system for looking at and searching for photos, as explained in Figure 2-9. But the Photo Browser is more versatile: It's your main Organizer workspace, which is what the rest of this section is about.

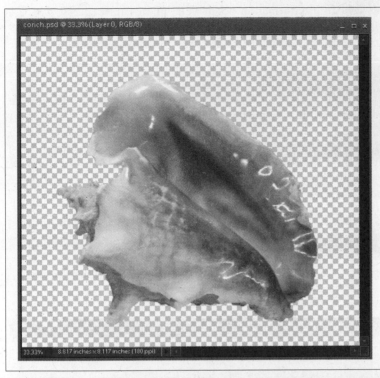

Figure 2-8:
The checkered background is Elements' way of indicating that an area is transparent. (It doesn't mean you've somehow selected a patterned background.) If you place this photo into another image, all you'll see is the seashell itself, not the checkerboard or the rectangular outline of the photo. If you don't like the size and color of the grid, you can adjust them in Edit → Preferences → Transparency.

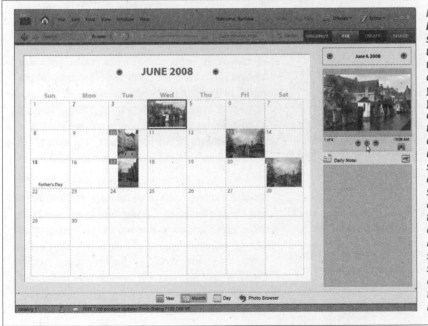

Figure 2-9:
Date View offers you the same menu options as the main Photo Browser window, but instead of a contact sheet–like view of your photos, you see your images laid out on a calendar. Click a date (in this example, June 4 is chosen), and in the upper-right corner of the screen, you can view or advance through a slideshow view of that day's pictures, by using the controls where the cursor is in the figure. Date View is fun, and sometimes handy for searching, but it doesn't offer many useful functions that aren't also in the Photo Browser.

The Organizer stores the information about your photos in a special database called a *catalog*. You don't have to do anything special—Elements creates your catalog (named *My Catalog*) automatically the first time you import photos. It's possible to have more than one catalog, but most people don't because you can't search more than one catalog at a time.

Your catalog can include photos stored anywhere on your computer, and even photos that you've moved to external hard drives and CDs or DVDs. There aren't any limits on where you can keep your originals. But once your photos appear in the Organizer, you must move them from within the Organizer as opposed to using another method (like Windows Explorer), if you want the Organizer to know where you put them. You aren't limited to photos, either—you can store videos and audio files in the Organizer as well.

> **TIP** The Organizer lets you choose to edit in programs other than Elements by going to Organizer → Edit → Preferences → Editing → Supplementary Editing Application. So if you want to supplement Elements with a program like Paint Shop Pro, it's easy to do. If you have Photoshop installed on your computer, it automatically appears as an editing option without you having to do anything.

WORKAROUND WORKSHOP

Avoiding the Organizer

Nobody's neutral about Adobe's decision to include the Organizer with Elements. People either love the Organizer or they hate it. If you're in the latter group, try to see if you can come to terms with the Organizer because it has some very useful features. You'll lose a lot if you give up the Organizer because it's the only place in Elements where you get a visual preview of your images before opening them.

However, if you find you just can't abide the Organizer, or if you prefer to use a different program, like Lightroom or Vista's Windows Photo Gallery, to organize your photos—or you just like to be disorganized—then you can avoid the Organizer altogether.

Create a desktop shortcut, as described on page 16, so that you always start up in the Editor.

Remember to keep "Include in Organizer" and version sets turned off in the Save dialog box whenever you're saving a picture. Once you turn off "Include in Organizer" in the Save As dialog box, it stays off until you turn it back on, or until you open a photo from the Organizer (after which it turns itself back on again). You may find you

need to turn it off once every editing session (maybe not, if you're lucky) but you don't have to keep remembering to turn it off every time you save.

You can also go to Control Panel (Classic View) → Administrative Tools → Services and find *Adobe Active File Monitor V7*. (In Vista, you'll also have a system dialog box or two asking for permission to continue.) This is a *service*, a small program that always runs in the background when your computer is on, even when Elements is closed. Highlight Active File Monitor, and then go to Action → Properties and set the Startup to Disabled.

There's a downside to disabling this service. The File Monitor also keeps track of the databases for the Content and Effects palettes, so if you disable it, any new layer styles, effects and so on that you add to Elements (See Chapter 19) won't appear in their palettes at all. The workaround is to turn Adobe Active File Monitor back on before the next time you start Elements after adding new material. Then you can disable it again till the next time you add something new.

The Photo Browser

Although the Photo Browser (Figure 2-10) may look a little intimidating the first time you see it, in fact it's really very logical. By using the different menu choices in the Photo Browser, you can choose to import photos, print them, share them, create projects, edit your photos, or customize your view in various ways. In the Photo Browser you see thumbnails for all your images in the main part of the window (sometimes called the *image well*).

On the right side of the Photo Browser is the *Task pane*, just as you see it in the Editor. It has the same Create and Share tabs, but also two tabs unique to the Organizer. The first is the Organize tab. That's where you *tag*, or label, your photos with keywords for easy searching. (Tagging is probably the first thing you'll want to do to your photos in the Organizer; you'll find directions on how to tag in the next section.)

At the bottom of the Organize pane is a shortcut staging area, called Quick Share, that makes it easy to order prints. (You can read about how to use Quick Share on page 437.) The other Organizer-only tab is the Fix tab. Here you can apply a number of auto fixes (like Auto Smart Fix or Auto Contrast) to your photo without ever going to the Editor, or you can send your photos to any of the three Edit modes from this pane.

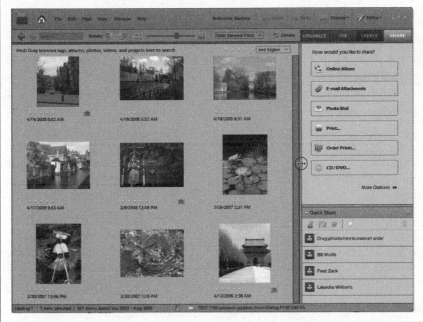

Figure 2-10:
The Photo Browser is your main Organizer workspace. Click the divider (circled) to hide or show the Task panel. Notice how the cursor morphs into a double-headed arrow when you're in the correct spot for clicking. If you want to change the way your photos are sorted in the Photo Browser, click the Display menu in the upper-right corner.

If you'd like to get a simultaneous look at your pictures and the folders on your PC where they're stored, go to Display → Folder Location. A new pane on the left side of the Photo Browser's window appears, showing the folder structure of your computer. If you click a thumbnail once you're in Folder Location view, the folder pane shows you the exact location of the current batch of photos. Click a folder's icon to see the photos it contains displayed in the image well.

> **TIP** If you've used early versions of the Organizer and you miss the Timeline, you can still have it in Elements 7. Just go to Window → Timeline or press Ctrl+L to bring back your old friend. For folks new to Elements, the Timeline is explained on page 56.

You can also move your photos directly within this Folder view pane by dragging them between folders. Moving your photos via the Folder view pane is better than moving them by, say, using Windows Explorer, because doing so lets Elements keep track of where your photos are (Figure 2-11).

> **TIP** Once you get your photos into the Organizer, you can use Display → "View Photos in Full Screen" or "Compare Photos Side by Side" to see a larger, slideshow-like view of your photos (either singly or in pairs, depending on the Display option you select) and choose the ones you want to print or edit (page 515). You can even choose music to accompany them. If you don't want something that elaborate, just double-click a thumbnail in the Photo Browser to see your photo enlarged to fit the available space in the Photo Browser. Double-click it again to go back to thumbnail view.

As if all these ways weren't enough, Elements gives you yet another way to view your images: arranged on a Yahoo map. When you first import your photos, Elements gives you the option of assigning them to a location on a map of your choice, and you can assign any tag to a map location, too. Page 487 explains more about using Yahoo maps in the Organizer, and also about sharing your maps with your friends.

Creating Categories and Tags

The Organizer's got a great system for quickly finding photos, but it works only if you use special keywords, called *tags*, which the Organizer uses to track down your pictures.

A tag can be a word, a date, or even a rating (as explained in the box below). When you import photos to the Organizer, the photos are automatically tagged with the date of import (and with any other tag choices you may have made in the Photo Downloader), but you may want to add more tags to make it easier to search for the subject of the photo later on. You can give a photo as many tags as you like.

Elements lets you group tags into *categories*. You get a certain number of preset categories, like People, Places, and Events, and you can create your own categories, too. You can also create as many subcategories within categories as you like. You may have a category of "Vacations," with "China trip" and "Cozumel" as subcategories, for instance. Your photos in those categories may have the tags "Jim and Helen," "silk factory," or "snorkeling."

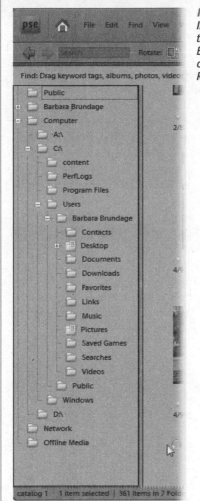

Figure 2-11:
If you want to move photos around on your PC after you've brought them into the Organizer, go to File → Move, or drag them within this pane of the Photo Browser. If you move photos around when you're not in the Organizer, Elements can't easily find them again. If Elements loses track of a photo, you can use the Reconnect command (File → Reconnect) to help Elements find it again.

Working with tags and categories

Elements gives you a few generic tags to help you get started, but you'll want to learn how to create your own tags, too. After all, by the time you've got 5,000 or so photos in the Organizer, searching for "Family" probably isn't going to help narrow things down.

When you're ready to create a new tag:

1. **Call up the Create Tag dialog box.**

   Press Ctrl+N, or go to Organize → Keyword Tags → New (the green plus sign) → New Keyword Tag. The Create Tag dialog box appears. (You can also choose to create a new Category or Sub-Category from the same menu.)

ORGANIZATION STATION

Special Tags

Elements starts you off with two special kinds of tags:

- **Favorites**. This tag lets you assign a one- to five-star rating to your photos. It's a good way to mark the ones you want to print or edit. Ratings are a great search tool because you can tell Elements to find, say, all your pictures that have ratings of four or more stars. (See page 57 for details on how to perform a search.) To assign ratings, just click the star under the photo thumbnail that corresponds to your rating. In other words, to assign a three-star rating, click the third star from the left. To search by ratings, click the star you want at the top of the Photo Browser (it works the same way as assigning tags—the second star from the left is the two-star rating) and then choose a qualifier from the pull-down menu at the right of the stars. You can search for all photos rated four stars or higher, for instance, or those rated two stars or lower, and so on. To change or remove a rating, right-click Thumbnail → Ratings, and choose what you want. You can also change a rating by clicking a different star under the thumbnail.

- **Hidden**. When you apply this tag to a photo, the photo disappears from the Photo Browser—once you select View → Hidden Files → Hide Hidden Files. The Hidden tag is useful for archiving those photos that didn't come out quite right but that you're not ready to trash. You can save these pictures (just in case) without having them cluttering up your screen while you're working with your good photos. To assign the Hidden tag, right-click the photo and choose Visibility → "Mark as Hidden". To bring it back into the open, go to View → Hidden Files → Show All Files, which makes all your hidden files visible. Then right-click it again and go to Visibility → "Mark as Visible" to keep it in view. To put the rest of your hidden files back out of sight, go to View → Hidden Files again. You can also see *only* your hidden files by going to View → Show Only Hidden Files.

2. **Name the new tag and assign it to a category.**

Enter the name you want to use in the text box where it says Name. Then, assign the tag to a category by picking from the Category pull-down menu. (You can change the category later if you want.) You can also edit the icon for your tag, as explained in Figure 2-12.

To assign the tag to a photo, just drag the tag's icon from the Organize bin onto the photo's thumbnail. It's as easy as that.

You can also delete tags, rearrange their order by dragging them, and even change the size of your tag icons by right-clicking a photo or tag and choosing what you want to do from the pop-up menu. You can also drag tags from one category to another in the Organize bin.

After you've assigned a tag to a photo, here's what to do if you decide you want to remove it:

- **From a single photo**. Right-click the photo's thumbnail, select Remove Tag, and then choose the tag you want to get rid of.

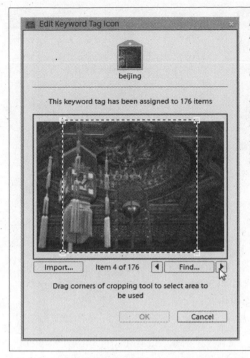

Figure 2-12:
Many people like to edit the icons Elements uses to represent different tags. Editing the icons makes it easy to search for a tag visually as well as by its name. To change the picture associated with a tag, click the tag in the Organize pane's Keyword Tags section. Then click the Edit Tag button (the pencil) → Edit Icon. In the Edit Keyword Tag Icon dialog box (shown here), the arrows on either side of the Find button let you advance through all the photos that use that tag. (The Find button shows you those photos all at once.) Or you can click the Import button to use a different image stored on your computer. Once you've chosen the picture you want, drag the dotted square to use only a certain part of your photo.

- **From a group of photos.** Select the photos, right-click one of them, select "Remove Tag from Selected Items", and then choose the tag you want to remove.

> **TIP** When an image first gets imported into the Organizer, the image well shows only the photos in the batch of photos you've just imported. You'll see an icon in the upper-right corner of the image well called Instant Tag (when in Folder view). Clicking it assigns the photo's folder name as a tag to all the photos in the group.

Albums and Smart Albums

You can group your photos into *albums*, which are great for gathering together pictures taken at a particular event. They can also be used to prepare groups of photos that you plan on using in one of the Create projects, like slideshows or Photo Collages (page 419). When you create an album, you're not actually making a copy of all the photos you're including; instead, you're simply creating a group of virtual "pointers" to each image. That means albums can hold as many pictures as you want without taking up much space and, even better, you can include the same pictures in different albums. Photos inside an album can appear in any order you choose, which is important, for instance, if you want to control the order of photos in a slideshow.

GEM IN THE ROUGH

Face Tagging

Elements includes an interesting way to sort through your photos so that you can easily tag them: Face Tagging. Go to Find → "Find Faces for Tagging", or click the "Find Faces for Tagging" button at the top of the Keyword Tags pane. (It's the outline of a person's head and shoulders with a tag next to it.) Elements then searches through your catalog for photos with people in them, and opens a new window showing the results. If you want to limit your search to a particular group of photos, select them before you start.

Face Tagging doesn't work quite the way you may have hoped: You can't tell Elements to find all the photos with Aunt Hildegarde. Elements just looks for what it thinks are human faces, and then shows you every photo it finds. If you have a camera with face recognition (which

works the same way), you may be less than thrilled with your Elements results; they may include a number of things, like leaves or parts of buildings, that look like faces to Elements—but not to you.

So what's the point if Elements can't tell one person from another? Face Tagging is designed on the theory that you're most likely to want to tag pictures of your family and friends. By using Face Tagging, you can easily spot all the untagged photos of your grandfather in a group of faces, for instance, and quickly tag them all at once. The Face Tagging dialog box gives you access to all your tags, and it also includes a handy Recent Tags section that rounds up the last few tags you've used so that you can quickly find them without having to navigate through the category structure.

Albums are particularly important in Elements 7 if you're using Photoshop.com, since you upload, sync, and back up your photos via albums rather than working with your whole catalog at once.

> **TIP** Albums are also good for gathering together groups of photos you want to export for use with another program.

There are several ways to create an album in Elements 7:

- **From the Organizer.** First Ctrl+click to select the photos you want to include. Then go to Organizer → Albums (at the top of the Organize pane), click the New Album button (the green plus sign), and choose New Album. Name your album and assign it to an album group (explained in a moment) if you wish, and then click Done. Your new album joins the list of albums. You can also choose to make an album from files anywhere on your computer, even if they're not in the Organizer—use the From File choice in the New Album button's popout menu.

- **From the Editor.** In the Editor, you can create an album in the Project bin's Bin Actions menu. No matter which method you use to make your album, it will appear in the lists of albums in both the Organizer and the Project bin's Show menu.

- **From the Create pane.** To create an online album (one that you upload to Photoshop.com), just click Online Album in the list of projects. Your album will appear in the Organizer's list of albums, too, when you're done.

Once you've created an album by either of the first two methods, you can upload it to your Photoshop.com account by clicking the Share button next to its name. (Albums you start from the Online Album button get uploaded automatically.) You get a lot of options for displaying your photos in a gallery and sharing them with friends. You can read more about working with online albums and sharing them in Chapter 18.

> **NOTE** You can also burn albums to a CD or DVD, or upload your slideshows and galleries to your own Web site. Page 467 explains how.

Once you've created an online album, you can edit it from any Web browser, including adding or deleting photos, reorganizing photos, tagging them, and so on. The online Organizer looks just like the regular desktop Organizer on your home computer and you use it the same way. You can synchronize your online album(s) so that changes you make online are reflected in the album(s) stored on your computer, and vice versa. Page 66 explains more about how to do this.

In the Organizer, to see the photos in your album, just click its name in the Albums palette. To return to all photos, click the binoculars next to the album name.

You can also create *album groups*, which are just what they sound like. If you have a lot of albums, you may want to group them into larger categories to make it easier to keep track of them. To make an album group, go to Organizer → Albums → New (the green plus sign) → New Album Group. Name your group and it appears in the Albums list. To add albums to the group, just drag their icons to the group's icon. To remove an album from a group, click the flippy triangle to the left of the album group name so you can see all the albums it contains. Then right-click the album you want to remove from the group and choose Edit <album name>. In the window that opens, go to Group → None (Top Level) and then click OK. You can also create groups within groups.

Smart Albums are another useful feature. They automatically collect all the photos that meet the criteria you specify, as shown in Figure 2-13. To create a new Smart Album, go to Organizer → Albums → New (the green plus sign) → New Smart Album.

Searching for Photos

Anyone who's been diligent enough to assign tags to all (or most) of their photos will be pleased to learn how easy Elements makes finding tagged photos. And as for the untagged masses? The good news is that Elements still gives you a few helpful ways to find your pictures. The next few sections take you through all your options.

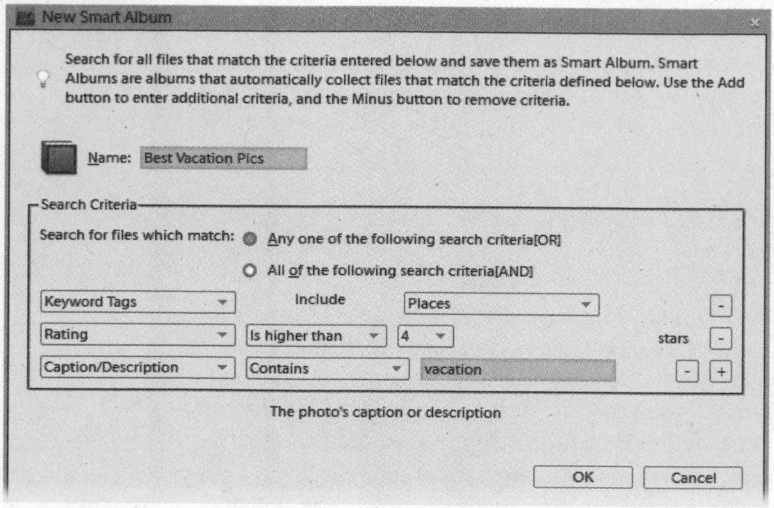

Figure 2-13:
When you create a new Smart Album, this dialog box appears. Choose the criteria for your album. Click the plus button to add another search parameter. Here, "Best Vacation Pics" is set up to include photos with tags in the Places category, ratings of more than four stars, and the word "vacation" in the caption or description. All the photos that meet all three criteria automatically join the album.

Browsing Through Photos

When you don't know exactly which photo you're looking for, Elements gives you a few ways to search through groups of pictures. These methods are also great if you don't want to look through your entire collection.

- **Text search**. In Elements 7, you can just type what you're looking for into the Search box at the upper left of the main Organizer window. Enter a filename, caption, date, tag, or anything that's in the file's metadata (see the box on page 59), and Elements will find it. You can adjust your terms by using *and*, *or*, or *not* with multiple terms. You can also restrict what you want to search for, so if you enter, for example, *Tag:Birthday* in the Search box, you'll get photos with the Birthday tag attached to them.

- **Folders**. You can navigate through the folders stored on your computer, just as you do when using a program like Windows Explorer. First, turn on Folder view if you haven't already done so (Display → Folder Location or press Ctrl+Alt+1).

   NOTE Generally, you only see folders that contain Organized photos. If you want to move photos to a folder the Organizer can't see, the workaround is to put a photo in the folder and then import it into Elements. After that, the Organizer will see the folder.

   Navigate by expanding the folders you want and working your way down to the ones that contain the photos you want. When you reach a folder that contains photos, the photos appear in the image well.

- **Timeline**. Go to Window → Timeline, and the Timeline appears above the Find bar at the top of the image well. Each bar in the Timeline represents a group of photos. Click a bar, and you see the photos in that batch.

- **Date View.** You see your photos, listed by date, on a calendar page. Just click the date of the group you want to see. To get to Date view, go to Display → Date View.

- **Map.** If you've chosen to put your photos on a Yahoo map, go to Display → Show Map, and then click the various pins stuck in the map to see your photos. (Page 487 has more on how to work with Yahoo maps.)

TIP The Find menu, covered on page 509, also lets you search for photos with similar colors. Choose Find → "By Visual Similarity with Selected Photo(s)". This option is great when you're looking for similarly toned graphics to use in a project.

Using Tags and Categories to Find Photos

Of course, when you're looking for a particular picture, you can use all the previously listed ways to find photos and just keep clicking through groups of photos until you find the one you want. But searching by tags and categories is the easiest way to find a particular photo.

- **Organize pane.** Click the empty square next to a tag or category, and Elements finds all the photos associated with those tags and categories. (A pair of binoculars appears inside the square to indicate it's being used to search for photos.) Click as many tags and categories as you want, and Elements searches for them all.

  You can exclude a tag from a search by right-clicking the tag's name and, in the menu, choosing to exclude it. So you could search for photos with the tags "sports" and "rock-climbing," but not "broken leg," for instance.

- **Find bar.** The Organizer's Find bar gives you another way to perform a tag search. Figure 2-14 shows how to use it.

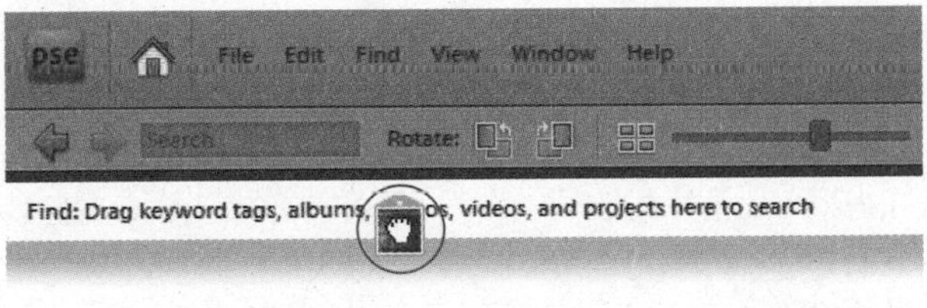

Figure 2-14:
To use the Find bar to search for pictures, just drag any tag, category, or photo onto the bar above the thumbnails (circled). When you get near the bar, it gets lighter so you can see it better (normally its boundaries really aren't visible). Your tag can hit the bar anywhere, not just where the lettering is.

Searching by Metadata

As explained in the box on page 59, your camera stores a great deal of information about your images in the form of *metadata*. In the Organizer, you can search your photos by their metadata, looking for, say, all the photos you took with a particular camera model at a certain aperture and exposure. Figure 2-15 explains how. You can save your results as a Smart Album (page 55), so that any future files with the same characteristics will be grouped together.

NOTE One of the new features in Elements 7 is that you can now search for more metadata categories in non-photo files, like your videos and audio files.

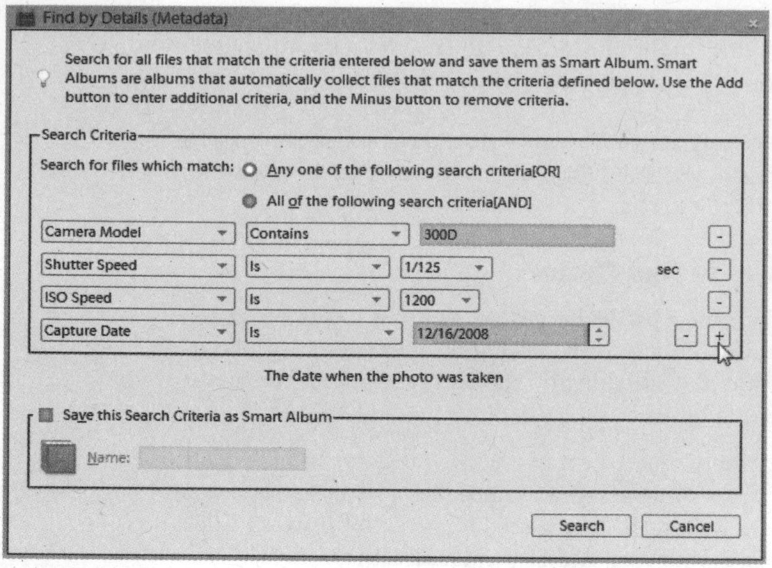

Figure 2-15:
To perform a search using your photos' metadata, go to Find → By Details (Metadata) to bring up this window. Choose the category of metadata from the drop-down menu on the left and enter your term or choose the exact setting in the box on the right. Click the plus button to add additional search terms, up to a total of 10. To remove a criterion, click the search term's minus button.

TIP If you want to share your tag information with people using the full Photoshop or Photoshop Elements for Mac, select the photos you want, then go to File → "Write Keyword Tag and Properties Info to Photo(s)". This transforms your tags into IPTC metadata keywords, which can then be read by those programs, as well as by the old File Browser in Elements 2 and 3, if you have friends still using those versions.

Saving Your Work

You've heard it before: save your files early and often. Saving your work is easy in Elements. (You don't need to do anything special to save information in the Organizer like tags or collections; you need to save only images you've created or changed, and you do that in the Editor.) When you're ready to save your file, press Ctrl+Shift+S to bring up the Save As dialog box, shown in Figure 2-16.

The top part of the Save As window is pretty much the same as it is for any program—you choose where you want to save your file, what you want to name it, and the file format you want. (More about file formats in a moment.) You also get some important choices that are unique to Elements:

- **Include in the Organizer.** This checkbox is always turned on the first time you use Elements. Leave it on and your photo gets saved in the Organizer. Turn it off if you don't want the new file to go to the Organizer. If you don't use the Organizer, turn it off (see page 48), and Elements should remember to leave it off, at least for this editing session, or until you save a photo that came from the Organizer.

Viewing Data about Your Images

The Organizer is just packed with information about your images. From captions you've written to statistics captured by your camera, the Properties window is chockfull of interesting tidbits. To launch the Properties window, select any photo in the Organizer and press Alt+Enter, or right-click any photo and choose Show Properties from the pop-up menu. You get four different kinds of information to choose from (you get to each by clicking the icon on the top of the Properties window):

- **General**. This is information that includes the file's name, location (on your PC), size, date you took the picture, caption (just put your cursor in the box and start typing to add one), and a link to any audio files associated with it (see page 480). You can also change the photo's file name here by highlighting the name and typing in a new one.

- **Metadata**. The information about the photo that's stored in the photo file itself is called *metadata*. Most notably, this is where you view your *EXIF*

(Exchangeable Image Format) data. EXIF data is information that your camera stores about your photos, including the camera you used, when you took the picture, the exposure, file size, ISO speed, aperture setting, and much more.

- **Tags**. If you've assigned any tags to your photo, they're listed here.

By paying attention to your EXIF data, you can learn lots about what works for making good shots...and what doesn't.

The Metadata screen includes many other kinds of information besides the EXIF data. Click the Complete button at the bottom of the window to see the full listing (clicking the Brief button shows you only highlights).

- **History**. Look here to find out when the file was created, imported, and edited, and also where you imported it from (your hard drive, for instance).

- **Save in Version Set with Original**. This option tells the Organizer to save your image (including any edits you've made) as a new version, separate from your original. Your photo gets the name of the original plus an ending to indicate it's an edited version.

  You can create as many versions as you want. Then you can go directly to any state of your image that you've saved as a version. It's a very handy feature. When you choose to start a version set, from now on, you'll get the Save As dialog box every time you save (instead of being able to just save your changes). Elements does that to give you the chance to create a new version each time.

- **Layers**. If your image has layers, turn on this checkbox to keep them. When you turn off this setting, Elements usually forces you to save as a copy. To avoid having to save as a copy, flatten your image (page 175) before saving it. Remember that once you close a flattened image, you can't get your layers back again—flattening is a permanent change.

- **As a Copy**. When you save an image as a copy, Elements makes the copy, names it "[OriginalFileName] copy", and puts the copy away. The original version remains open. If you want to work on the copy, you must open it. Sometimes Elements forces you to save as a copy—for instance, if you want to save a layered image and you turn off the layers option. (See Chapter 6 for more about layers.)

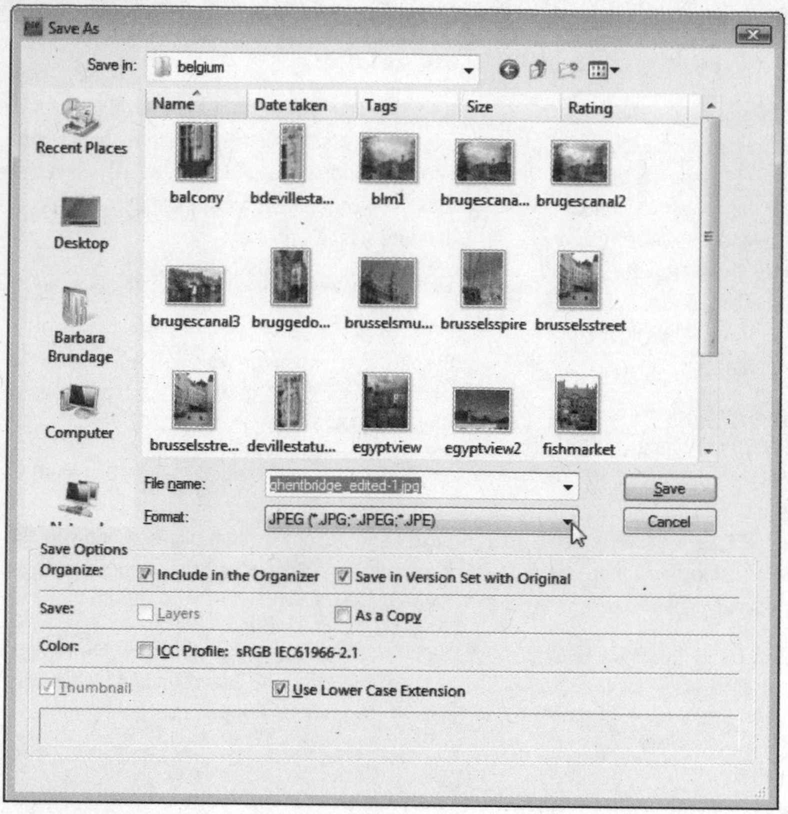

Figure 2-16:
The Elements Save As dialog box actually varies a little depending on what you're saving, but this example is pretty typical. When you click the Format pull-down menu (indicated by the cursor), you'll see a long list of file formats to choose from.

- **ICC Profile.** You can choose to embed a color profile in your image. Page 196 explains color profiles.

- **Use Lower Case Extension.** Using Lower Case Extension causes Elements to save your file as yourfile.jpg rather than yourfile.JPG, for example. Leave this setting on unless you have a reason to turn it off.

The File Formats Elements Understands

Elements gives you loads of file format options. Your best choice depends on how you plan to use your image.

- **Photoshop (.psd, .pdd).** It's a good idea to save your files as .psd files—the native file format for Elements or Photoshop—before you work on them. A .psd file can hold lots of information, and you don't lose any data by saving in this format. Also, it allows you to keep layers, which is very important, even if you haven't used them for much yet.

GEM IN THE ROUGH

Options for Saving Your Work

Elements gives you several options for saving a file. Before choosing one, you need to consider whether you want to create version sets (page 59) of your photos.

To tell Elements how to react to the Save command, go to Editor → Edit → Preferences → Saving Files. You see a pull-down menu labeled On First Save. By choosing how Elements behaves here, you can control (to some extent) when you're going to see a dialog box offering you options for saving your file, and when Elements will behave like any other program and just save your changes without needing any input from you.

For most people, it's fine to leave things as they are. (Elements uses the "Ask if Original" choice—explained below—unless you change it.) However, if you want more control over how Elements saves your photos (if you always want the option to create a new version set without having to remember to choose Save As, for instance), you can configure Elements to suit your working method.

Here's what the three options do:

- **Always Ask**. Choose Always Ask and, when you press Ctrl+S, Elements brings up the Save As dialog box the first time you save—if it's the first time you've opened the file in this session of Elements. Close the file and reopen it while Elements is still running, and you won't see the Save As dialog box the next time you save. But once you exit Elements and launch it again, you get the Save As dialog box the first time you press Ctrl+S. You might think of this choice as short for "Always ask the first time I save a file in an editing session and then don't bug me anymore."

- **Ask if Original**. If you're editing your original file (as opposed to a version) and don't have any version sets (page 59), you get the Save As dialog box the first time you save the file. On subsequent saves, or if you already have a version set, Elements just saves right over the existing version (unless you do a Save As to create a new version).

"Ask if Original" is meant to help you avoid inadvertently creating dozens of Organizer versions for each file as you edit it.

- **Save Over Current File**. When you select this option, Elements overwrites your existing file when you press Ctrl+S, without offering you the Save As dialog box at all. This is the way most other programs behave when saving—if you save an existing file in Word, for instance, you don't get a dialog box; Word just saves your changes, writing over the previous version of the file. If you choose this menu option and then, while you're working, decide you want to Save As instead of Save, press Ctrl+Shift+S (or just choose Save As from the Editor's File menu).

You'll have certain situations where Elements presents you with the Save As dialog box no matter *what* you choose here. For instance, say you add layers (explained in Chapter 6) to a JPEG file; you can't save a JPEG with layers, so Elements brings up the Save As dialog box to let you choose a different file format for saving your work.

The File Saving Options section of the Saving Files preferences window has two other menus (Image Previews → Always Save, and File Extensions → Use Lower Case), but you probably won't ever need to change the settings in those menus.

You can also use the Saving Files preferences window to control how well your image file works with other programs. With the Maximize PSD File Compatibility pull-down menu set to Always, a flattened image gets embedded into your file for the benefit of programs that don't understand Elements Layers. That makes for a substantially larger file, but with disk space so cheap these days, it's usually best to let Elements maximize compatibility. If you choose Ask, you'll encounter the dialog box in Figure 2-17 when you save a layered .psd file.

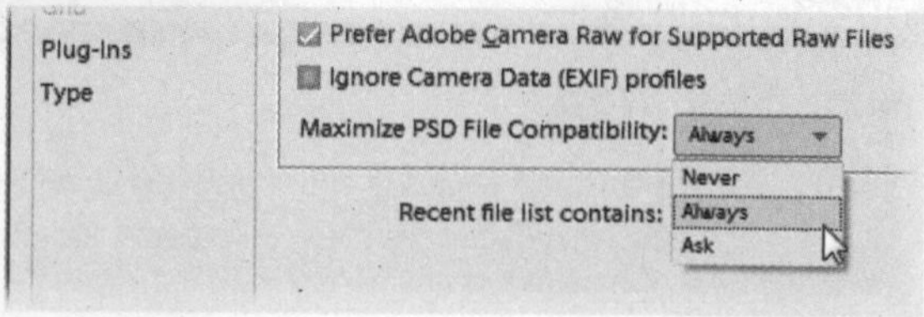

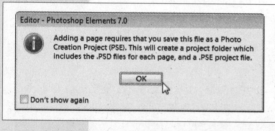

Figure 2-17:
Choose Always in the "Maximum compatibility" menu if you want people who don't have Elements to be able to open your image. The downside: larger files.

- **Photo Project (.pse).** This is a special format, only for multi-page Elements photo creations (see Figure 2-18 as well as page 427).

- **TIFF (.tif, .tiff).** This is another format that, like the Photoshop format, preserves virtually all of your photo's information and allows you to save layers. And like Photoshop files, TIFF files can be very large. TIFFs are used extensively in print production, and some cameras allow you to choose TIFF as a shooting option.

- **JPEG (.jpg, jpeg, .jpe).** Almost everyone who uses a computer has run into JPEGs at one time or another. Most digital cameras offer the JPEG format as an option. Generally, when you bring a JPEG into Elements, you want to use another format when you save it, to avoid data loss. Keep reading for more about why.

Figure 2-18:
If you add pages to a file (page 425), you see this warning message box. Elements is telling you it needs to save your multi-page project in a format that almost no other programs can open. To learn more about working with this format, and how to get your project out of Elements for online printing or use by other programs, see the box on page 427.

Editor - Photoshop Elements 7.0

Adding a page requires that you save this file as a Photo Creation Project (PSE). This will create a project folder which includes the .PSD files for each page, and a .PSE project file.

OK

☐ Don't show again

UP TO SPEED

File Formats

After you've spent hours creating a perfect image, you want other people to be able to see your picture, too. If everyone who wanted to view your images needed a copy of Elements, you probably wouldn't have a very large audience for your creations. So, Elements lets you save in lots of different *file formats*.

What does that mean? It's pretty simple, really. A file format is a way in which your computer saves information so that another program or another computer can read and use the file.

Because there are many different kinds of programs and several different computing platforms (Windows, Linux, and Mac, for example), the kind of file that's best for one use may be a really poor choice for doing something else. That's why many programs, like Elements, can save your work in a variety of different formats, depending on what you want to do with your image. There are many formats, like TIFF and JPEG, that many different programs can read. Then there are other formats, like the .pub files that Microsoft Publisher creates—which are easily read only by the program that created them.

- **JPEG 2000 (.jpf, .jpx, .jp2).** This newer variation of the JPEG format makes small files without losing any data, and it also supports transparency. There aren't many Web browsers that can display these files, though, so this format is not a good choice for the Web.

- **PDF (.pdf, .pdp).** Adobe invented PDF, or Portable Document Format, which lets you send files to people with Adobe Reader (formerly Acrobat Reader) so they can easily open and view the files. Elements uses PDF files to create presentations like slideshows.

- **CompuServe GIF (.gif).** (Everywhere except this menu, this format is known simply as GIF. CompuServe gets added here because they invented and own the code for the format.) This format is used primarily for Web graphics, especially files without a lot of subtle shadings of color. For more on when to choose GIFs, see Chapter 17. GIFs are also used for Web animations; see page 458 for help creating animated GIFs.

- **PICT (.pct).** PICT is an older Mac format that's still used by some applications. AppleWorks, for example, handles PICTs better than any other graphics format. Also, sometimes larger file formats like Mac-created TIFFs generate their thumbnail previews as PICT Resource files (the type of PICT used within the TIFF file).

- **BMP (.bmp).** This format is an old Windows standby. It's the file format used for many graphics tasks by the Windows operating system.

- **PNG.** Here's another Web graphic format, created to overcome some of the disadvantages of JPEGs and GIFs. It has its own disadvantages, though. See page 452 for more about these files.

- **Photoshop EPS (.eps).** EPS (Encapsulated PostScript) format is used to share documents among different programs. You generally get the best results when the documents go to a PostScript printer (some laser printers are PostScript printers; inkjets usually aren't).

- **Digital Negative (.dng).** Elements can't save files in this format (except in the Raw converter), but it can open DNG files. DNG is a format developed by Adobe to create a more universal way to store all the different camera Raw file formats. You can download a special DNG Converter from the downloads area of Adobe's support Web site (*www.adobe.com/downloads*); it lets you convert your camera's own Raw formatted photos into DNG files. DNG files aren't ready to use the way JPEG or TIFF files are—you still need to run your DNG files through the Raw Converter before you can use them in projects. See page 240 for more about DNG.

The not-so-common file formats

Besides the garden-variety formats in the previous list, Elements lets you save in some formats you may never have heard of. Here's a list, and then you can forget all about them, probably.

- **Filmstrip**. This format is for use with Premiere, Adobe's video-editing program. You won't even see this option if Premiere isn't installed on your computer.

- **PIXAR**. Yup, *that* Pixar. This is the special format for the movie studio's high-end workstations, although if you're working on one of those, it's extremely unlikely that you're reading this page.

- **Scitex CT**. This format is used for prepress work in the printing industry.

- **Photoshop Raw**. No, it's not the same as your camera Raw file, but rather an older Photoshop format that consists of uncompressed data.

- **Targa TGA**, or Targa. Developed for systems using the Truevision video board, this format has become a popular graphics format, especially for games.

- **PCX**. This format was very popular for graphics back in the days of DOS (remember PC Paintbrush?). Nowadays it's mostly used by some kinds of fax systems and a few document management programs.

About JPEGs

In the next chapter, you'll read about how throwing away pixels can lead to shoddy-looking pictures (page 96). Well, certain file formats were designed to make your file size as small as possible. They make the file smaller by throwing out information by the bucketful. These formats are known as *lossy* because they throw out, or lose, some of the file's data every time you save it, to make the file as small as possible.

Sometimes you want that to happen, like when you want a small-size (and hence, fast-loading) picture for a Web site. Therefore, many of the file formats that were developed for the Web, most notably JPEG, are designed to favor smallness over any other quality. They compress the file sizes by allowing some data to escape.

NOTE   Formats that preserve all your data intact are called *lossless*. (You may also run across the term *non-lossy*, which means the same thing.) The most popular file formats for people who are looking to preserve all their photos' data are PSD and TIFF.

If you save a file using the JPEG format, every time you hit the Save button and close the file your computer is squishing some of the data out of the photo. What kind of data? It's the information needed for displaying and printing the fine details. You don't want to keep saving your file as a JPEG over and over again. Every time you do, you lose a little more potential detail from your image. You can usually get away with saving as a JPEG once or twice, but if you keep it up, sooner or later you start to wonder what happened to your beautiful picture.

It's OK that your camera takes photos and saves them as JPEGs. Those are pretty enormous JPEGs, usually. Just importing a JPEG won't hurt your picture, and neither will opening it to look at it, as long as you don't make any changes. But once you get your files into Elements, save your pictures as Photoshop or TIFF files while you work on them. When you want another JPEG as the final result, change the format back to JPEG *after* you're done editing it.

TIP   Your camera may give you several different JPEG compression options to help you fit more pictures on your memory card. Always choose the *least* compression possible. Your photo file sizes are slightly larger, but the quality is much, much better. It's worth sacrificing the space.

Changing the File Format

It's very easy to change the format of a file in Elements. Just press Ctrl+Shift+S or go to File → Save As and, from the Format pull-down menu, select the format you want. Elements makes a copy of your file in the new format and asks you to name it.

Backing Up Your Files

With computers, you just never know what's going to happen, so "Be prepared" is a good motto. If your computer crashes, it won't be nearly so painful if all your photos are safely backed up someplace else. Thanks to Elements' new Photoshop.com service, you can make that happen automatically. In the event of a problem with your home computer, you can restore your photos—or at least the ones you've chosen to sync on Photoshop.com. The Photoshop.com-as-backup system has two main downsides: First, it only comes with 5 GB of space; if you want to back up more than that, you have to pony up for more storage, as explained on page 19. And you can only back up and sync albums, not your entire catalog.

NOTE   As of this writing, the Photoshop.com service is restricted to US residents.

If those limitations turn you off, you'll be glad to know that Elements also makes it very easy to save your files to any add-on storage device, like an external hard drive, or to a CD or DVD. All these options are covered in the pages ahead.

TIP Elements offers one frequently-requested feature for making backups: You can create *multi-session* discs. That means you can tell Elements to leave your CD or DVD open, so that you can come back later and use the disc again to add more files to it, instead of wasting an entire CD or DVD to burn a handful of pictures. To use this feature, go to Organizer → Edit → Preferences → Files, and then turn on "Enable multisession burning to CD/DVD".

Online Syncing and Backups

If you have a Photoshop.com account and you've created an online album (page 467), it's super simple to set things up so that any changes you make to either your online album or the album on your home computer appear in both places. In other words: Welcome to Perfect Backup Land. All you need to do is turn on the Backup/Synchronize checkbox when creating your album. After you do that the first time, Elements automatically provides the same syncing service for any additional albums you create. If you *don't* want that to happen, see Figure 2-19.

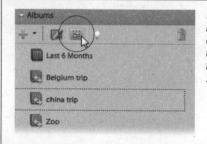

Figure 2-19:
If an album is set to sync with your Photoshop.com account, then you see two arrows on its icon, like the ones shown on the album names here. If you want to prevent Elements from syncing an album, or want to turn off syncing for future albums, just click the Sync icon (circled) to bring up the Backup/Synchronization preferences, where you can change what happens.

You can control how syncing and automatic backing up work from several places in Elements:

- **The Organizer's Album pane.** Click the Sync icon, shown in Figure 2-19.
- **The Welcome screen.** Just click Backup Settings.
- **Organizer preferences.** Go to Edit → Preferences → Backup/Synchronization.

Any of these options takes you to the Organizer's Backup/Synchronization preferences window. Here you have a lot of control over what Elements does. You can turn off syncing altogether, turn off syncing for new albums, turn syncing on and off for particular albums, and set a folder for where Elements puts new photos it finds in your Photoshop.com account. You can also see how much of your Photoshop.com space you've used, and buy more if you want. If you're worried about space, you can tell Elements to skip syncing files over a certain size, too.

NOTE   Photoshop.com includes a mini set of editing tools. If you use these tools to edit one of your online photos, then Elements creates a version set (page 59) on your home computer. That way your original file is preserved.

However, be careful! Despite this, Photoshop.com doesn't really understand version sets. If you send a version set to Photoshop.com, you're only backing up the top version (the one that's visible in the Organizer when the set is collapsed). And if you edit a photo on your home computer after backing up it up online (whether it's in a version set or not), your edited version replaces the stored original at Photoshop.com.

Once you have syncing turned on, Elements automatically makes backups of the albums you sync. A sync icon appears in the system tray at the bottom of your screen from now on. Right-click it, and you can also stop or start syncing there, and tell Elements to sync your photos only when your computer is idle, rather than as soon as you make a change.

If you have photos on Photoshop.com and something happens to your home computer, you can restore your online photos to your home machine, or to any other computer by just turning on the sync settings in the preferences, as explained earlier. Of course you need to have Elements installed to have the Organizer preferences checkbox to turn on. That's all you have to do: Turn on Backup/Synchronization for each album you want (or choose Select All for the whole kit and kaboodle), log into your account, and wait (it may take a while if you've got a lot of photos to restore).

If you're the sort of person who's not good about remembering to back up, Photoshop.com is a terrific, effortless way to get the job done. The downside is that it backs up only albums, not your whole catalog (page 48), so you'll probably want to make regular backups, too. These backups are also easy, if not quite as automatic.

NOTE   While online backups are swell, extra cautious people don't rely on them as a sole backup source. Make sure you have at least one other backup someplace else, because there's always a chance that things can happen to the computers that power online storage Web sites, too.

Organizer Backups

The Organizer offers a really helpful way to back up your photos. It's one of the best parts of Elements, and it's certainly very thorough, even going so far as to remind you to label the disc you create. You can back up your catalog, or just copy specific photos. Just follow these steps:

1. **Make sure your catalog is in tip-top shape.**

   Go to File → Catalog → Repair, just in case. It's also not a bad idea to go to File → Reconnect → All Missing Files, although the Organizer warns you if you have unconnected files when you start your backup.

2. **Call up the Backup dialog box, and let Elements make sure your catalog is in shape for backing up.**

   Go to File → "Backup Catalog to CD, DVD, or Hard Drive", or press Ctrl+B.

3. **Decide what kind of backup to make.**

   In the window that opens, you have to decide whether to back up your whole catalog or make an incremental backup. *Full Backup* backs up *everything* in your catalog. Pick that one the first time you make a backup, or if you're backing up everything to move to a new computer. *Incremental Backup* finds only the stuff that's new since the last time you made a backup, and that's all it copies—a major time and space saver. (You must make a full backup at least once before Elements will let you do an incremental backup.)

   Your backup will have the same name as your catalog. You can see the name in the dialog box, but you won't be allowed to change it. Click Next to continue.

   NOTE If you have multiple catalogs, you can back up only one catalog at a time.

4. **Choose a destination for your files.**

   Your choices include a CD, a DVD, or any hard drive connected to your computer (either built-in or external). Choose by selecting from the list in the Select Destination Drive dialog box.

   If you're backing up to a hard drive, click the Backup Path Browse button to select the location where you want Elements to create your backup. Navigate through the folder structure in the window that appears, and create a new folder if you'd like to keep your backups tidy (a good idea). Once you're done, the path appears in the Backup window.

   If you're making an incremental backup, you have to show Elements where to find your previous backup. Either insert the CD or DVD with the original full backup, or click the letter name of the drive where you made your previous backup and use the "Previous Backup file" Browse button to show Elements the existing backup file.

5. **If you're backing up to a CD or DVD, insert a disc in the drive when Elements asks you to. (If you're backing up to any other kind of media, including internal or external hard drives, skip ahead to step 6.)**

   Elements needs to calculate how many discs you need to create your backup. As Elements burns each disc, it asks if you want Elements to verify the disc to be sure it's OK. You do. Elements prompts you to feed it more discs if your backup doesn't all fit on one disc.

   You can also change the write speed for your disc, if you wish. Just choose one of the other options from the pull-down menu. (A slower speed takes longer but may be more reliable.) As Elements burns each disc, it asks if you want to verify the disc. Do this, so that Elements can check for any burn errors.

NOTE Always check your backup discs once you've burned them, even if you verified them during backup. Take a moment to put the disc in your computer and make sure that all your files are there. If there's an error, you want to know about it now, not six months from now.

6. **Create your backup.**

Click Done, and Elements generates your backup. If you decide you don't want to make a backup, click Cancel instead.

If you chose to burn CDs or DVDs, don't forget to label the discs when Elements finishes burning them, so you'll know what they are.

NOTE These directions cover how to back up your images and your catalog. Some people also like to back up their catalog database (the data file where the Organizer keeps track of where your photos are) by itself every once in a while. To back up just the catalog information, use Windows Explorer to search for files with the extension .psedb, and burn those files to a CD or copy them to an external hard drive.

When you want to restore your catalog, in the Organizer, just go to File → "Restore Catalog from CD, DVD, or Hard Drive" and follow the onscreen directions. The Organizer asks for the last disc from your backup, not the first one as you might expect. (You may want to back up and then restore your catalog if you have to reinstall Windows, for example.) Be aware that a backup made using these steps is for the use of Elements, not for you: If you open the discs, you'll see files with weird numerical names and you can't just rummage around to find a particular photo you accidentally deleted. You have to let Elements handle restoring the files.

Making Quick CDs/DVDs

So far, you've learned how to back up your photos so that you can restore them to the Organizer with all your cataloging information intact. But what if you just want to burn a few photos or a project to a disc and you don't care about the tags and such? Say you want to send your latest editing masterpieces to a friend, for instance. In Elements, it's a snap to do this.

1. **Select the photos and/or projects you want to burn.**

You can start from either the Editor or the Organizer, but in the Editor make sure you save your work first.

2. **Go to Share → CD/DVD.**

A window pops up where you must select the drive you want to use for burning. Just click its name in the window. If you want, you can also name your disc here. If you don't enter any text, the disc will be named with today's date.

3. **Insert a blank CD or DVD when Elements asks you to, and click OK.**

Elements has to see a disc to know how many photos will fit on it and to figure out how many discs you'll need, if all your photos won't fit on one disc. When the program is through figuring this out, you'll see the size and write time (how long it will take Elements to burn the disc) in the "Make a CD/DVD" window, in the Size area.

4. **Click OK to create your CD or DVD.**

When Elements is done, it asks if you want to verify the disc. This is always a good idea. When Elements is done verifying your disc, it ejects it and reminds you to write its name on it so you'll know what it is.

When you make copies of just a few photos (rather than the whole catalog), you're copying only the photos, not the catalog information about the photos. If you want to include your tags along with the photos, before you start, go to File → "Write Keyword Tag and Properties Info to Photos". This makes your tags part of the files' EXIF data (see the box on page 59), so that if you send the photos to someone using Photoshop or another program that can read metadata, the tags appear as keywords in the file info.

> **NOTE** One drawback to including your tag and property info is that you can't use Elements to remove tags from the metadata later. So, for instance, if you attach a "stupid boss" tag to a photo and then have second thoughts, you can remove that tag from your catalog, but it will still exist in the files themselves, unless you use another program to edit the metadata. Exifer (*www.exifer.friedemann.info*) is a popular program you can use to remove that "stupid boss" tag from the file's metadata before you email the photo to the editor of the company newsletter.

CHAPTER 3

Rotating and Resizing Your Photos

In the last chapter, you learned how to get your photos *into* Elements. Now it's time to look at how to trim off unwanted areas and straighten out crooked photos. You'll also learn how to change the overall size of your images and how to zoom in and out to get a better look at things while you're editing.

NOTE From here through Chapter 14, you need to be in the Elements Editor. If you're still in the Organizer, press Ctrl+I to go to the Full Edit window.

Straightening Scanned Photos

Anyone who's scanned old photos can testify about the hair-pulling frustration when your carefully placed pictures come out crooked onscreen. Whether you're feeding in precious memories one at a time or scanning batches of photos to save time, Elements can help straighten things out.

Straightening Two or More Photos at a Time

If you've got a pile of photos to scan, save yourself some time and lay as many of them as you can fit on your scanner. Thanks to Elements' wonderful Divide Scanned Photos command, you'll have individual images in no time.

Start by scanning in the photos (Figure 3-1). The only limit is how many can fit on your scanner at once. It doesn't matter whether you scan directly into Elements or use your scanner's own software. (See page 42 for more about scanning images into Elements.)

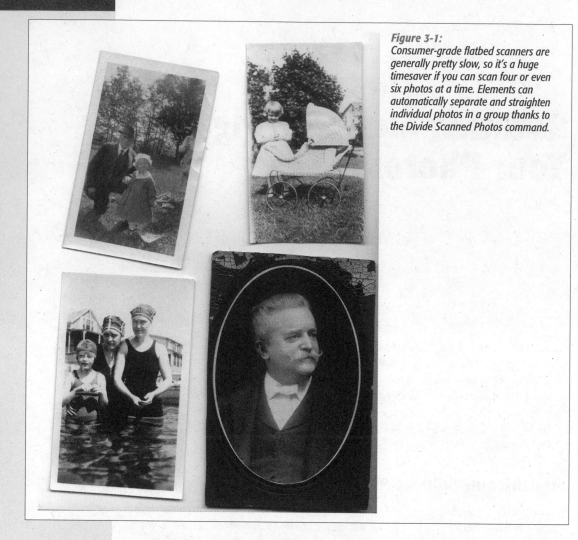

Figure 3-1:
Consumer-grade flatbed scanners are generally pretty slow, so it's a huge timesaver if you can scan four or even six photos at a time. Elements can automatically separate and straighten individual photos in a group thanks to the Divide Scanned Photos command.

TIP Sometimes it pays to be crooked. Divide Scanned Photos does its best work if your photos are fairly crooked, so don't waste time trying to be precise when placing your pictures on the scanner.

When you're done scanning, follow these steps:

1. **Open your scanned image file in the Editor.**

   It doesn't matter what file format you used when saving your scanned group of photos: TIFF, JPEG, PDF, whatever. Elements can read 'em all.

2. **Divide, straighten, and crop the individual photos.**

   Go to Image → Divide Scanned Photos. Sit back and enjoy the view as Elements carefully calculates, splits, straightens out, and trims each image. You'll see the individual photos appear and disappear as Elements works through the group.

3. **Name and save each separated image.**

When Elements is done, you'll have the original group scan as one image and a separate image file for each photo Elements has carved out. Once you're done, import the cut-apart photos into the Organizer. To do that, just make sure that "Include in Organizer" is turned on in the Save As dialog box (see page 58).

Elements usually does a crackerjack job splitting your photos, but once in a while it chokes, leaving you with an image file that contains more than one photo. Figure 3-2 shows you what to do when Elements doesn't succeed in splitting things up.

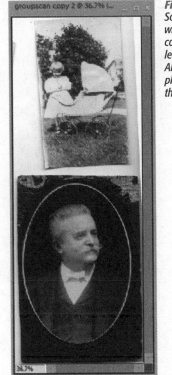

Figure 3-2:
Sometimes Elements just can't figure out how to split up your photos, and you wind up with something like these two not-quite-split-apart images. Rescan the photos that confused Elements, but this time, make sure they're more crooked on the scanner and leave more space between them. Elements should then be able to split them correctly. Also, check for positioning problems like you see here, where Elements can't split the photos because it can't draw a straight line to divide these two without chopping off the corners. Put a little more space between the photos and Elements can split them.

TIP Occasionally you may find that Elements can't accurately separate a group scan, no matter what you do. In that case, use the Marquee tool (page 123) to select each individual image, paste it into its own document (File → New → "Image from Clipboard"), and then save it.

Straightening Individual Photos

Elements can also straighten out and crop (trim) a single scanned image. Simply choose Image → Rotate → "Straighten and Crop Image", and Elements tidies things up for you. You can also choose just Straighten Image if you'd rather crop the edges yourself. Better still, you can use Divide Scanned Photos on a single image, as explained in the previous section. (Cropping is explained on page 79.)

Rotating Your Images

Owners of print photographs aren't the only ones who sometimes need a little help straightening their pictures. Digital photos sometimes need to be rotated, because some cameras don't include data in their image files that tells Elements (or any other image-editing program, for that matter) the correct orientation. Certain cameras, for example, send portrait-orientated photos out on their sides, and it's up to you to straighten things out.

Fortunately, Elements has rotation commands just about everywhere you go. If all you need to do is get Dad off his back and stand him upright, here's a list of where you can perform a quick 90-degree rotation on any open photo:

- **Quick Fix** (page 99). Click either of the Rotation buttons at the bottom of the preview area.

- **Full Edit.** Go to Image → Rotate → 90° Left (or Right).

- **Project bin.** Right-click a thumbnail and choose Rotate 90° Left (or Right).

- **RAW Converter** (page 224). Click the left or right arrow at the top of the Preview window.

- **Organizer** (page 46). You can rotate a photo almost any time in the Organizer by pressing Ctrl plus the left or right arrow key. You can also choose Edit → Rotate 90° Left (or Right). Finally, there's a pair of Rotate buttons to click at the top of the Photo Browser window. Whichever method you choose, you may see the dialog box shown in Figure 3-3.

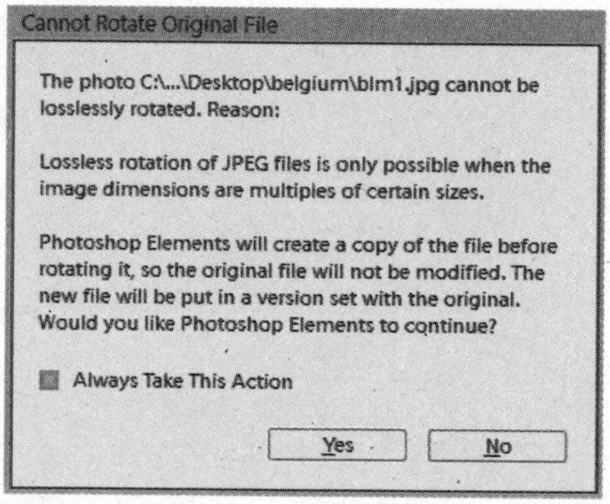

Figure 3-3:
The first time you try to rotate any JPEG-formatted (page 64) photo in the Organizer, Elements gives you this warning. What's that all about? As you learned in Chapter 2, every time you change and save a JPEG image, the picture's image quality degrades a bit. Rotating a JPEG qualifies as a change, so Elements is telling you that it's going to create and preserve a copy of your (unchanged) original. The copy automatically gets saved in a version set, so you always have both versions. (If you're wondering about what the dialog box means when it says that lossless rotation is possible at "multiples of certain sizes," that's pretty technical, but you can learn all about it at www.ammara.com/support/technologies/lossless-jpeg-rotation.html.)

Cannot Rotate Original File

The photo C:\...\Desktop\belgium\blm1.jpg cannot be losslessly rotated. Reason:

Lossless rotation of JPEG files is only possible when the image dimensions are multiples of certain sizes.

Photoshop Elements will create a copy of the file before rotating it, so the original file will not be modified. The new file will be put in a version set with the original. Would you like Photoshop Elements to continue?

☐ Always Take This Action

[Yes] [No]

Those commands all get you one-click, 90-degree changes. But Elements has all sorts of other rotational tricks up its sleeve, as explained in the next section.

Rotating and Flipping Options

Elements gives you several ways to change the orientation of your photo. To see what's available, in the Editor, go to Image → Rotate. You'll notice two groups of

Rotate commands in this menu. For now, it's the top group you want to focus on. (The second group does the same things, only those commands work on layers, which are explained in Chapter 6.)

In the first group of commands, you'll see:

- **90° Left or Right.** These commands produce the same rotation as the rotate buttons explained earlier. Use these commands for digital photos that come in on their sides.

- **180°.** This turns your photo upside down and backward.

- **Custom.** Selecting this command brings up a dialog box where, if you're mathematically inclined, you can type in the precise number of degrees to rotate your photo.

- **Flip Horizontal.** Flipping a photo horizontally means that if your subject was gazing soulfully off to the left, now she's gazing soulfully off to the right.

- **Flip Vertical.** This command turns your photo upside down without changing the left/right orientation (which is what Rotate 180° does).

NOTE   When you're flipping photos around, remember you're making a mirror image of everything in the photo. So someone's who's writing right-handed becomes a lefty, any text you can see in the photo is backward, and so on.

Figure 3-4 shows these commands in action.

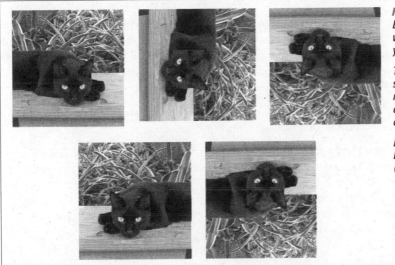

Figure 3-4:
Even the most uncooperative cat will turn somersaults for you if you use the rotate commands.

Top row: From left to right, you see the original, the photo rotated 90 degrees to the right, and the photo rotated 180 degrees.

Bottom row: The photo flipped horizontally (left) and vertically (right).

If you want to position your photo at an angle on a page (as you might in a scrapbook), use Free Rotate Layer, described on page 78.

Straightening the Contents of Your Image

What about all those photos you've taken where the main subject (a person or a building, say) isn't quite straight? You can flip those pictures around forever, but if your camera was off-kilter when you snapped the shot, your subjects will lean like a certain tower in Pisa. Elements has planned for this problem, too, by including a nifty Straighten tool that makes adjusting the horizon as easy as drawing a line.

> **NOTE** About 95 percent of the time, the Straighten tool will do the trick. But for the few cases where you can't get things looking perfect, you can still use the old school Elements method—the Free Rotate Layer command, described on page 78.

Straighten Tool

If you can never seem to hold a camera perfectly level, you'll love the Elements Straighten tool. It lives just below the Cookie Cutter tool in the Full Editor's toolbox. To straighten a crooked photo:

1. **Open the photo, and then activate the Straighten tool.**

   Its icon is two little photos, one crooked and one not. Or, on the keyboard, just press P.

2. **Make any changes to the Options bar settings for the Straighten tool before you use the tool.**

   Your choices are described in a moment.

3. **Tell Elements where the horizon is.**

   Drag to draw a line in your photo to show Elements where horizontal *should* be. Figure 3-5 shows how—by drawing a line that traces the boundary between the ocean and the sky. Your line appears at an angle when you draw it. That's fine, because Elements is going to level out your photo, making your line the true horizontal plane in the image.

4. **Elements responds by automatically straightening your photo. It also crops the photo if you chose that setting in the Options bar.**

   If you don't like what Elements did, press Ctrl+Z to undo it and draw another line. If you're happy, you're all done, except for saving your work (Ctrl+S).

> **TIP** If you have a photo of trees, sailing ships, skyscrapers, or any other subject where you'd rather straighten vertically than horizontally, just hold down Ctrl while you drag. The line you draw determines the vertical axis of your photo.

The Options bar gives you some choices about how to handle the edges of your newly straightened photo. Once your picture's straightened, the edges are going to be a bit ragged, so you can choose what you want Elements to do about that:

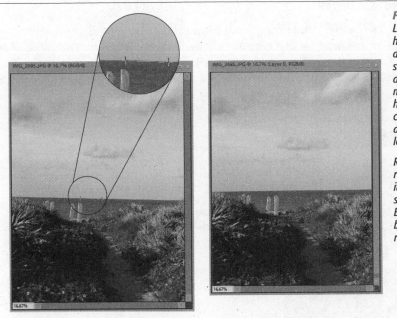

Figure 3-5:
Left: To correct the crooked horizon in this photo, just draw a line along the part that should be level. It's easiest to do this by choosing a clearly marked boundary like the horizon in this photo, but you can actually draw a line across anything you want to make level.

Right: Elements automatically rotates the photo to straighten its contents. In this case, you see the results of selecting Trim Background (in the Options bar), which crops off all the ragged edges for you.

- **Grow or Shrink Canvas to Fit.** Elements adds extra space around the edges of your photo to make sure that every bit of the original edges is still there. It's up to you to crop your photo afterward (see page 79).

- **Trim Background.** Elements chops off the ragged edges to give you a nice rectangular image. The downside to this option is that you lose some of the perimeter of your image—though just a bit, so usually it's not a big deal.

- **Original Size.** Elements makes sure the dimensions of your photo stay exactly the same—even if that means including some blank spaces along the perimeter.

If your photo has layers (see Chapter 6), you can use the Straighten tool to straighten only the active layer (page 153) by going to the Options bar and turning off Rotate All Layers. If you want Elements to straighten your whole photo, leave this checkbox turned on.

The Straighten tool is best for photos where you were holding the camera crooked. If you try it and it makes things look very odd in your photo, perhaps straightening isn't really what you need. Architectural photos, for instance, may look a bit crooked before you use this tool—but a lot worse afterward. If that house is *still* leaning, even though you're sure the ground line has been leveled correctly, then most likely your real problem is *perspective distortion* (a visual warping effect). To fix that, use Correct Camera Distortion (see page 316).

TIP You can also straighten photos right in the RAW Converter. There's a Straighten tool in its toolbox, right between the Crop tool and the Red Eye tool. You use it just like the Editor's Straighten tool. Page 229 tells you more.

Free Rotate Layer

You can also use the Rotate commands to straighten your photos, or to turn them at angles for use in scrapbook pages or album layouts you create. The rotate command that's best for this use is Free Rotate Layer, which lets you grab your photo and spin it to your heart's desire. And if you aren't sure where straight is, Elements gives you some help figuring it out, as shown in Figure 3-6.

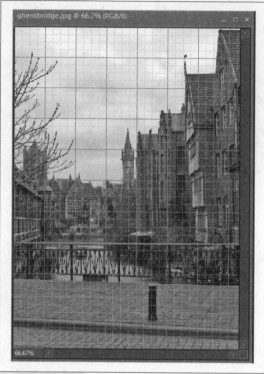

Figure 3-6:
If you need some help figuring out where straight is, in the Editor, go to View → Grid to toggle these handy guidelines on and off. You can adjust the grid spacing in Edit → Preferences → Grid. For a photo like this one, you could also change the color of the grid to make it show up better. To do that, click the color square in the grid preferences window and choose a color from the Color Picker (page 209).

All the rotate commands are also available for use on individual layers, incidentally. (Chapter 6 tells you all about layers, but you don't have to understand layers to use the Free Rotate Layer command.)

To use Free Rotate Layer:

1. **Go to Image → Rotate → Free Rotate Layer.**

   Elements asks if you want to "make this background a layer." Say yes. (Again, Chapter 6 tells you everything you need to know about layers.)

2. **Name the layer if you want to.**

   A dialog box appears, giving you a chance to name the layer (helpful if your image has lots of layers, but not necessary). Click OK.

3. Use the handle or the curved arrows to adjust your photo (Figure 3-7).

Your picture may look kind of jagged while you're rotating. Don't worry about that—Elements smoothes things out once you're done.

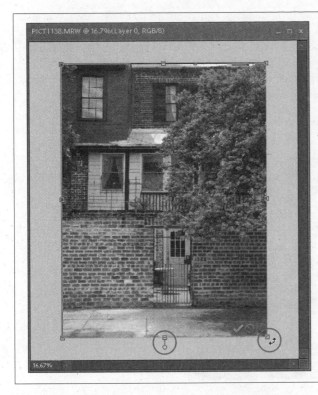

Figure 3-7:
You have two ways to straighten the contents of your photo—or even spin it around in a circle. Just grab either the handle at the bottom center of your photo or a corner (both circled). (When you move your cursor into the image window, it turns into a curved, two-headed arrow.) Then drag to adjust your photo the way you'd straighten a crooked picture on the wall. Click the green OK checkmark when you're happy with what you've done, or the red "no" symbol to cancel.

4. When you've got your image positioned where you want it, click the green OK checkmark or press Enter. (If you don't like what you did, press the red "no" symbol to cancel the rotation.)

Now you've got a nice straight picture, but the edges are probably pretty ragged since the original had slanted, unrotated sides. You can take care of that by cropping your photo, which is covered in the next section.

Cropping Pictures

Whether or not you straightened your digital photo, sooner or later you'll probably need to *crop* it—trim it to a certain size. Most people crop their photos for one of two reasons: If you want to print on standard size photo paper, you usually need to cut away part of your image to make it fit on the paper. Then there's the "I don't want *that* in my picture" reason. Fortunately, Elements makes it easy to crop away distracting background objects or people you'd rather not see.

A few cameras produce photos that are proportioned exactly right for printing to a standard size like 4"×6". But most cameras give you photos that aren't the same proportions as any of the standard paper sizes like 4"×6" or 8"×10". (The width-to-height ratio is also known as the *aspect ratio*.)

The extra area most cameras provide gives you room to crop wherever you like. You can also crop out different areas for different size prints (assuming you save your original photo). Figure 3-8 shows an example of a photo that had to be cropped to fit on a 4"×6" piece of paper. If you'd like to experiment with cropping or changing resolution (explained on page 90), download the image in the figure (*waterfall.jpg*) from the Missing CD page at *www.missingmanuals.com*.)

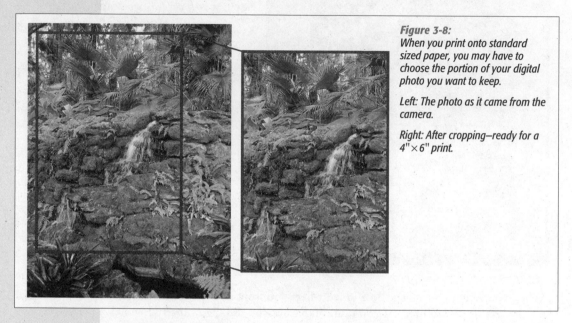

Figure 3-8:
When you print onto standard sized paper, you may have to choose the portion of your digital photo you want to keep.

Left: The photo as it came from the camera.

Right: After cropping—ready for a 4"×6" print.

If your photo isn't in the Organizer (which automatically saves your originals), it's best to perform your crops on a copy, since trimming is going to throw away the pixels outside the area you choose to keep. And you never know—you may want those pixels back someday.

Using the Crop Tool

You can use the Crop tool in either the Full Edit or Quick Fix window. The Crop tool includes a helpful list of preset sizes to make your work easier. In most cases the preset sizes are what you need, but if you do want to crop to a custom size, here's how:

1. **Activate the Crop tool.**

   Click the Crop icon in the Toolbox or press C.

2. **Drag anywhere in your image to select the area you want to keep.**

The area outside the boundaries of your selection is covered with a dark shield, indicating what you're discarding. To move the area you've chosen, just drag the bounding box (the outline) to wherever you want it.

You may find the Crop tool a little crotchety sometimes. See the box on page 82 for help making it behave.

3. **To resize your selection, drag one of the little handles on the sides and corners.**

They look like little squares, as shown in Figure 3-9. You can drag in any direction, so you can also change the proportions of your crop if you want to.

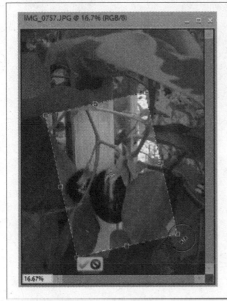

Figure 3-9:
If you want to change your selection from horizontal to vertical or vice versa, just move your cursor outside the cropped area and you'll see the rotation arrows (circled). Use them to rotate the crop frame the same way you would an entire photo. Changing your selection doesn't rotate your photo—just the boundaries of the crop. When you're done, press Enter or the green checkmark (for OK) to tell Elements you're satisfied. The red "no" symbol cancels your crop. (The OK and cancel symbols appear when you let go of the mouse.)

4. **If you change your mind, press Cancel (the "no" symbol) on the photo, or press the Escape key.**

That undoes the selection so you can start over.

5. **When you're sure you've got the crop you want, press Enter or OK (the checkmark) on the photo, or double-click inside the cropping mask, and you're done.**

Cropping Your Image to an Exact Size

You don't have to eyeball things when cropping a photo. You can enter any dimensions you want in the width and height boxes in the Options bar, or, from the Aspect Ratio menu, you can choose one of the Presets, which automatically enters a set of numbers for you. The Aspect Ratio menu offers you several standard photo sizes, like 4"×6" or 8"×10", to choose from. The Use Photo Ratio

---

TROUBLESHOOTING MOMENT

Crop Tool Idiosyncrasies

The Crop tool is crotchety sometimes. People have called it "bossy," and that's a good word for it. Here are some settings that may help you control it better.

- **Snap to Grid**. You may find that you just cannot position the crop selection exactly where you want it. Does the edge keep jumping slightly away from where you put it? Like most graphics programs, Elements uses a grid of invisible lines—called the *autogrid*—to help place things exactly. Sometimes a grid is a big help, but in situations like this, it's a nuisance. If you hold down Ctrl, you can temporarily disable the autogrid. You can also get rid of the autogrid or adjust the spacing on it. To turn it off, first make the grid visible by going to View → Grid.

Then select "Snap to" → Grid. You can adjust the grid settings—things like the spacing, color, and whether you see a solid or dotted line—in Edit → Preferences → Grid.

- **Clear the Crop Tool**. Occasionally you may find that the Crop tool won't release a setting you entered, even after you clear the Options bar boxes. For example, if the Crop tool won't let you drag where you want and keeps insisting on creating a particular sized crop, you need to reset the Crop tool. Simply click the triangle at the left of the Options bar, and then choose Reset Tool from the shortcut menu, as shown in Figure 3-10.

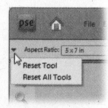

Figure 3-10:
If the Crop tool stops cooperating, there's an easy way to make it behave again. Click this tiny triangle in the Options bar, and then choose Reset Tool from the menu that appears. If you want to make sure that all your tools go back to their original settings, choose Reset All Tools.

---

choice in the Presets list lets you crop your image using the same width/height proportions (the *aspect ratio*) as in the original. Figure 3-11 shows you a timesaver: how to quickly switch the width and height numbers.

> **WARNING** If you enter a number in the Resolution box that's different from your image's current resolution, the Crop tool resamples your image to match the new resolution. (Resolution is explained in the section on resizing, starting on page 89.) See page 96 to understand what resampling is and why it isn't always a good thing.

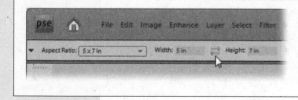

Figure 3-11:
If you want to change which number is the width setting and which is the height, just click these little arrows to swap them. So if you chose 5"×7" from the presets but want to switch to a landscape orientation, click the arrows (shown just above the cursor) to get 7"×5" instead.

Cropping with the Marquee Tool

The Crop tool is very handy, but it wants to make the decisions for you about several things you may want to control yourself. For instance, the Crop tool may decide to resample the image (see page 96) whether you want it to or not. The Crop tool gives you no warning that it's resampling. It just does it.

For better control, and also for making elliptical crop effects (great for oval vignettes), you may prefer to use the Marquee tool. It's no harder than using the Crop tool, but you get to make all the choices yourself.

There's one other big difference between using the Marquee tool and the Crop tool: With the Crop tool, all you can do to the area you selected is crop it. The Marquee tool, in contrast, lets you make many other changes to your selected area, like adjusting the color, which you may want to do before you crop.

To make a basic crop with the Marquee tool follow these steps:

1. **Activate the Marquee tool.**

   Click the little dotted square in the Toolbox or press M. Figure 3-12 shows you the shape choices you get within the Marquee tool. For cropping, choose the Rectangular Marquee tool.

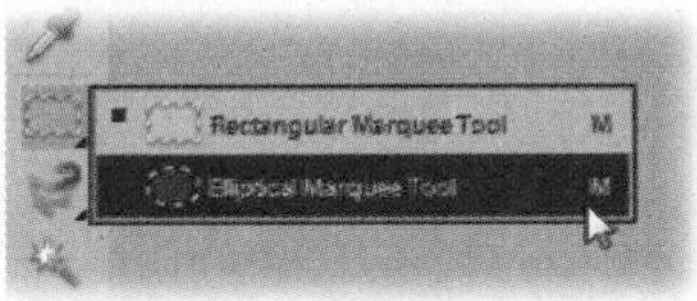

Figure 3-12:
Click the Marquee tool, and then choose the particular shape you want from this pop-out menu. The Toolbox icon shows you the shape that's currently selected.

2. **Drag the selection marquee across the part of your photo you want to keep.**

   When you let go, your selected area is surrounded by the dotted lines shown in Figure 3-13. These are sometimes called "marching ants." (Get it? The dashes look like ants marching around your picture.) The area inside the marching ants is the part of your photo you're keeping. (There's a lot more about making selections in Chapter 5.) If you make a mistake, press Ctrl+D to get rid of the selection and start over.

3. **Crop your photo.**

   Go to Image → Crop. The area outside your selection disappears, and your photo is cropped to the area you selected in step 2.

If you want to crop your photo to a particular aspect ratio, you can do that easily. Once the Marquee tool is active, but before you drag, go to the Options bar. In the Mode menu, choose Fixed Aspect Ratio. Then enter the proportions you want in the Width and Height boxes. Drag and crop as described earlier. Your photo will end up with exactly the proportions you entered in the Options bar.

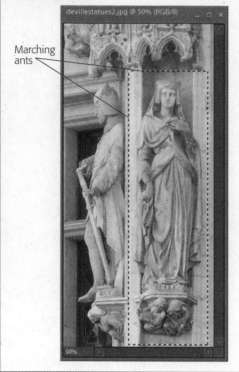

Marching
ants

Figure 3-13:
When you let go after making your Marquee selection, you see the "marching ants" around the edge of your selection. You can reposition the marquee by dragging it. To do so, just put your cursor anywhere inside the selection marquee and then drag it.

You can also crop to an exact size with the Marquee tool:

1. **Check the resolution of your photo.**

   Go to Image → Resize → Image Size (or press Alt+Ctrl+I) and make sure the ppi number is somewhere between 150 and 300 if you plan to print your cropped photo. You'll see that 300 is best, for reasons explained on page 93. If the ppi is OK, click OK and go to step 2.

   If the ppi is too low, change the number in the Resolution box to what you want. Make sure that the checkbox in the Resize dialog box that says Resample Image is turned off, and then click OK.

2. **Activate the Marquee tool.**

   Click the Marquee tool in the Toolbox (the little dotted square) or press M. Choose the Rectangular Marquee tool.

3. **Enter your settings in the Options bar.**

   First, go to the Mode menu and choose Fixed Size. Next, enter the dimensions you want in the Width and Height boxes.

4. **Drag anywhere in your image.**

   You get a selection the exact size you chose in the Options bar.

5. **Crop your Image.**

Go to Image → Crop.

The Cookie Cutter tool also gives you a way to create really interesting crops, as shown in Figure 3-14.

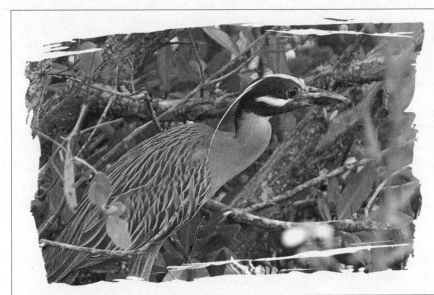

Figure 3-14:
With the Elements Cookie Cutter tool, you don't have to be square anymore. The Cookie Cutter tool lets you crop your images to various shapes, from the kind of abstract border you see here, to heart- or star-shaped outlines. More on how to use the Cookie Cutter tool in Chapter 12.

TIP   If you're doing your own printing, there's really no reason to tie yourself down to standard photo sizes like 4" × 6"—unless, of course, you need the image to fit a frame of that size. But most of the time, your images could just as well be square, or long and skinny, or whatever proportions you want. You can be especially inventive when sizing images for the Web. So don't feel that every photo you take has to be straitjacketed into a standard size.

Zooming and Repositioning Your View

Sometimes, rather than changing the size of your photo, all you want to do is change its appearance in Elements so you can get a better look at it. For example, you may want to zoom in on a particular area, or zoom out so you can see how edits you've made have affected your photo's overall composition.

This section is about how to adjust the view of your image inside Elements. Nothing you do with the tools and commands in this section changes anything about your actual photo. You're just changing the way you see it. Elements gives you lots of tools and keystroke combinations to help with these new views; soon you'll probably find yourself making these changes without even thinking about them.

Image Views

Before you start resizing your view of your photos, Elements gives you several different ways to position your image windows. When you first use Elements, if you have more than one photo open at a time, your photos overlap each other so that you can see as much as possible of the front photo, with only the edges of the photos behind it visible. This is a very efficient way to work, but if you don't like it, you're not stuck with it.

When you go to Window → Images, you get several choices for how you want your image to display:

- **Maximize Mode**. A single photo takes up the entire Elements desktop.

    TIP Switch to Cascade or Tile if you want to work on two or more photos simultaneously.

- **Tile**. Your image windows appear edge to edge so that they fill the available desktop space. With two photos open, each gets half the workspace; with four photos, each gets one quarter of it, and so on.

- **Cascade**. Your image windows appear in overlapping stacks. Most people find Cascade the most practical view when you want to compare or work with two images.

- **Match Zoom**. All your windows get the same magnification level as the active image window (the photo you're currently working on).

- **Match Location**. You see the same part of each image window, like the upper-right corner or the bottom-left. Elements matches the other windows to the active window.

You also get four handy commands for adjusting the view of your active image window. Go to the View menu, and you see:

- **New Window for**. Choose this command and you get a separate, duplicate window for your image. This view is a terrific help when you're working on very fine detail. You can zoom way in on one view while keeping the other window in a regular view so you don't lose your bearings for where you are in the photo. Don't worry about version control or keeping track of which window you're working in, since both windows just represent different glimpses of the same image.

- **Zoom In/Out**. These are shortcuts for zooming, explained on page 87.

    NOTE You can zoom in or out using the View menu, but it's much faster to learn the keyboard shortcuts so you don't have to keep trekking up to the menu. The short version: press Ctrl+= to zoom in and Ctrl+– (that's the Ctrl key plus the minus sign) to zoom out. The next section explains the Zoom tool in detail.

- **Fit on Screen.** This command makes your photo as large as it can be while still keeping the entire photo visible. You can also press Ctrl+0 for this view.

- **Actual Pixels.** For the most accurate look at the onscreen size of your photo, go with this option. If you're creating graphics for the Web, this view shows the size your image will be in your Web browser. Keystroke shortcut: Alt+Ctrl+0.

- **Print Size.** This view is really just a guess by Elements because it doesn't know exactly how big a pixel is on your monitor. But it's a rough approximation of the size your image would be if you printed it at the current resolution. (Resolution is explained in the section on resizing your photo, on page 89.)

To adjust the view of a particular image, Elements gives you three useful tools: The Zoom tool, the Hand tool, and the Navigator palette, all of which are explained in the following sections.

The Zoom Tool

Some of Elements' tools require you to get a very close look at your image to see what's going on. Sometimes you may need to see the actual pixels as you work, as shown in Figure 3-15. The Zoom tool makes it easy to zoom your view in and out.

The Zoom tool's Toolbox icon is the little magnifying glass. Click it or press Z to activate the tool. Once the tool is active, you see circle icons at the left of the Options bar. If you want to zoom in, click the one with the + sign on it. To use the Zoom tool, just click the spot in your photo where you want the zoom to focus. The point where you clicked becomes the center of your view, and the view size increases again each time you click.

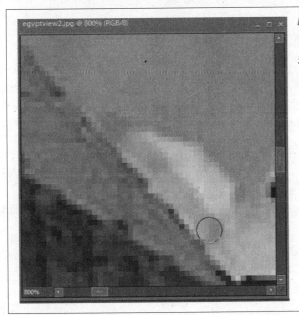

Figure 3-15:
There are times when you want to zoom way, way in. You may even need to go pixel by pixel in tricky spots, as shown here.

You can also select the Zoom Out tool in the Options bar, by clicking the circle with the minus (–) sign on it.

> **TIP** If you hold Alt as you click, the selected Zoom tool zooms in the opposite direction; for instance, the regular Zoom tool zooms out rather than in.

The Zoom tool has several Options bar settings:

- **Zoom percent.** Enter a number here and the view immediately jumps to that percentage. 3200 percent is the maximum, and 1 percent is the minimum.

- **Resize Windows to fit.** Turn this option on, and your image windows get larger and smaller along with the image size as you zoom. The image always fills the entire window with no gray space around it.

- **Ignore Palettes.** This setting lets windows resize so that they don't stop getting larger when they reach the edge of a palette. Instead, they continue resizing *underneath* the palette. At least that's how it's supposed to work. For the last few versions of Elements, palettes get ignored whether you turn this on or not.

- **Zoom All Windows.** If you have more than one image window, turn this option on, and the view changes in all the windows in sync when you zoom one window.

> **TIP** If you hold down the Shift key while zooming in, all your windows zoom together. You don't need to go to the Options bar to activate this feature.

The buttons for 1:1 (short for "Actual Pixels"), Fit Screen, and Print Size are the same as the menu commands described in the preceding section, "Image Views" (page 86).

> **TIP** You don't need to bother with the actual Zoom tool at all. Use your keyboard instead. Press Ctrl+= to zoom in and Ctrl+– (that's the Ctrl key plus the minus sign) to zoom out. Just hold down Ctrl and keep tapping the equal or minus sign until the view is what you want. You can also zoom to 100 percent by double-clicking the Zoom tool's icon.
>
> It doesn't matter which tool you're using at the time—you can always zoom in or out this way. Because you'll do a lot of zooming in Elements, this keyboard shortcut is one to remember.

The Hand Tool

With all that zooming, sometimes you can't see your entire image at once. Elements includes the Hand tool to help you adjust which part of your image appears onscreen. It's very easy to use. Just click the little hand in the Toolbox or press H to activate it.

When the Hand tool is active, your cursor turns to the little hand shown in Figure 3-16. Drag with the hand to move your photo around in the window. The hand tool is very helpful when you're zoomed in or working on a large image.

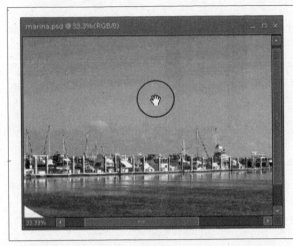

Figure 3-16:
The easiest way to activate the Hand tool is to press the Space bar on your keyboard. You can tell the Hand tool is active by this little white-gloved cursor. No matter what you're doing in Elements, pressing the Space bar calls up the Hand tool; it remains on until you release the Space bar. Then the tool you were previously using returns.

The Hand tool gives you the same "All Windows" option you get with the Zoom tool, but you don't have to use the Options bar to activate it. Just hold down Shift while using the Hand tool, and all your windows scroll in sync. The Hand tool also gives you the same three buttons (Actual Pixels, Fit Screen, and Print Size) that the Zoom tool does. Once again, they're the same as the menu commands described in "Image Views" on page 86.

Figure 3-17 shows the Hand tool's somewhat more sophisticated assistant, the Navigator palette, which is very useful for working in really big photos or when you want to have a slider handy for micro-managing the zoom level. Go to Window → Navigator to call it up.

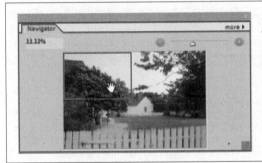

Figure 3-17:
Meet the Navigator. You can travel around your image by dragging the little red rectangle—it marks the area of your photo that you can see onscreen. You can also enter a percent number for the size you want your photo to display at, or move the slider or click the zoom in/out magnifying glasses on either side of the slider to change the view. The Navigator is perfect for keeping track of where you are in a large image.

Changing the Size of Your Image

The previous section explained how to resize the view of your image as it appears on your monitor. But sometimes you need to change the size of your actual image, and that's what this section is about.

Resizing your photo brings you up against a pretty tough concept in digital imaging: *resolution*, which measures, in pixels, the amount of detail your image can show. Where it gets confusing is that resolution for printing and for onscreen use (like email and the Web) are quite different.

For example, you need many more pixels to create a good-looking print than you do for a photo that's going to be viewed only onscreen. A photo that's going to print well almost always has too many pixels in it for onscreen display, and as a result, its file size is usually pretty hefty for emailing. So you often need two different copies of your photo for the two different uses. If you want to know more about the nitty gritty of resolution, a good place to start is *www.scantips.com*.

This section gives you a brief introduction to both screen and print resolution, especially in terms of what decisions you'll need to make when using the Resize Image dialog box. You'll also learn how to add more canvas (more blank space) around your photos. You'd add canvas to make room for captions below your image, for instance, or when you want to combine two photos.

To get started, open a photo you want to resize and go to Image → Resize → Image Size (Figure 3-18).

Resizing Images for Email and the Web

It's important to learn how to size your photos so that they show up clear and easy to view onscreen. Have you ever gotten an emailed photo that was so huge you could see only a tiny bit of it on your monitor at once? That happens when someone sends an image that isn't optimized for viewing on a monitor. It's very easy to avoid that problem—once you know how to correctly size your photos for onscreen viewing.

If you look at the Image Size dialog box, you see two main sections. The top one says Pixel Dimensions and below that is Document Size. You'll use the Pixel Dimensions settings when you know your image is only going to be viewed onscreen. (Document Size is for printing.)

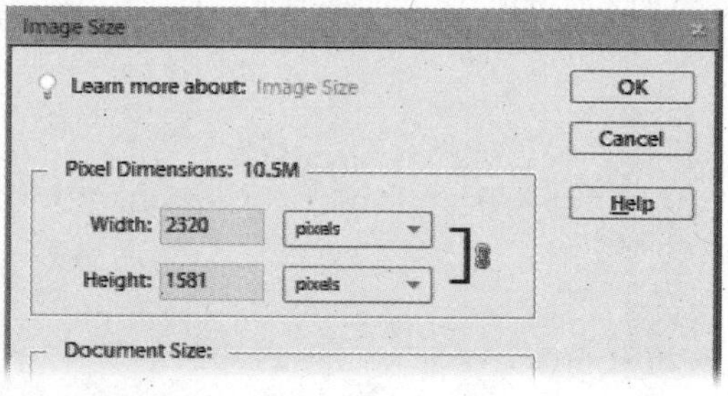

Figure 3-18:
The Image Size dialog box gives you two different ways to change the size of your photo. Use the Pixel Dimensions section (shown here) when preparing a photo for onscreen viewing. (The number immediately to the right of Pixel Dimensions—here, 10.5 M—indicates the current size of your file in megabytes [as in this example] or kilobytes.) Before you can make any changes here, you must turn on Resample Image in the bottom part of the dialog box (not visible here), since changing pixel dimensions always involves resampling (see page 96).

A monitor is concerned only with the size of a photo as measured in pixels, known as the *pixel dimensions*. On a monitor, a pixel is always the same size (unlike a printer, which can change the size of the pixels it prints out). Your monitor doesn't know anything about pixels per inch (ppi), and it can't change the way it displays a photo even if you change the photo's ppi settings, as shown in Figure 3-19. (It's true that graphics programs like Elements can change the size of your onscreen view by, say, zooming in, but most programs, like your Web browser, can't.)

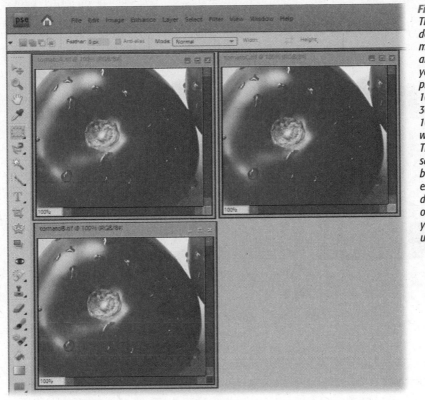

Figure 3-19:
This screenshot demonstrates that your monitor doesn't care about the ppi settings you enter. One of these photos was saved at 100 ppi, the second at 300 ppi, and the last at 1000 ppi. Can you tell which is which? Nope. They all look exactly the same on your monitor because they all have exactly the same pixel dimensions, which is the only resolution setting your monitor understands.

All you have to decide is how many pixels long and how many pixels wide you want your photo to be. You control those measurements in the Pixel Dimensions section of the Image Size dialog box.

What dimensions should you use? That depends a little on who's going to be seeing your photos, but as a general rule, small monitors today are usually 1024 (width) × 768 (height) pixels. Some monitors, like the largest Dell and Apple models, have many more pixels than that, of course. Still, if you want to be sure that people who see your photo won't have to scroll, a good rule of thumb is to choose no more than 650 pixels for the longer side of your photo, whether that's the width or the height. If you want people to be able to see more than one image at a time, you may want to make your photos even smaller. Also, some people still set their monitors to display only 800 pixels wide × 600 pixels high, so you may want to make even smaller images to send to them.

> **NOTE**   To get the most accurate look at how large your photo truly displays on a monitor, go to View → Actual Pixels.

Also, although a photo is always the same pixel dimensions, you really can't control the exact inch dimensions at which those pixels display on other people's monitors. A pixel is always the same size on any given monitor (as long as you don't change the monitor's screen resolution), but different monitors have different sized pixels these days. Figure 3-20 may help you grasp this concept.

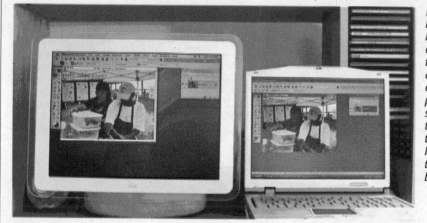

Figure 3-20:
Both these computers have a screen resolution of 1024 × 768 pixels, and the photo they're displaying takes up exactly the same percentage of each screen. But the picture on the left is larger because the monitor is physically larger—in other words, the individual pixels are bigger.

> **NOTE**   In the following sections, you'll be learning what to do when you want to *reduce* the size of an image. It's much easier to get good results making a photo smaller than larger. Elements does let you *increase* the size of your image, using a technique called upsampling (explained on page 96), but you often get mediocre results. The section on resampling (page 96) explains why.

To resize your photos, start by making very sure you're not resizing your original. You're going to be shedding pixels that you can't get back again, so resize your photos using a copy (File → Duplicate) if your photo's not already in the Organizer.

1. **Call up the Image Size dialog box.**

   Go to Image → Resize → Image Size.

2. **Turn on Resample Image at the bottom of the dialog box.**

   You won't be able to make any changes to the pixel dimensions in the top part of the window until you do this.

3. **In the Pixel Dimensions area, enter the dimension you want for the longer side
of your photo.**

   Usually you'd want 650 pixels or less. Be sure to choose pixels as the unit of
   measurement. You just need to enter the number for one side. Elements automatically figures the dimension for the other side as long as Constrain Proportions
   is turned on down near the bottom of the dialog box.

4. **Check the settings at the bottom of the dialog box.**

   Constrain Proportions should be turned on. (Scale Styles doesn't matter. Leave
   it off.) Resample Image should be turned on. (*Resampling* means changing the
   number of pixels in your image.) The Resample Image menu lists the different
   resampling methods. Adobe recommends choosing Bicubic Sharper when
   you're making an image smaller, but you may want to experiment with the
   other menu options if you don't like the results you get when using Bicubic
   Sharper.

5. **Click OK.**

   Elements resizes your photo, although you may not immediately see a difference
   onscreen. Go to View → Actual Pixels, before and after you resize, and you'll see
   the difference. Save your resized photo to make your changes permanent.

Sometimes Elements resizes an image automatically—for example, when you use
the Organizer's E-Mail command (see page 460). But the method described here
gives you more control than letting Elements make all the decisions for you.

> **TIP** If you're concerned about file size, use "Save for Web" (see page 452), which helps you create
> smaller files.

Resizing for Printing

If you want great prints, you need to think about your photo's resolution quite differently than you do for images that you're emailing. For printing, as a general
rule, the more pixels your photo has, the better. That's the reason camera manufacturers keep packing more megapixels into their new models—the more pixels
you have, the larger you can print your photo and still have it look terrific.

> **TIP** Even before you take your photos, you can do a lot toward making them print well if you
> always choose the largest size and the highest quality setting on your camera (typically Extra Fine,
> Superfine, or Fine).

When you print your photo, you need to think about two things: the size of your
photo in inches (or whatever your preferred unit of measurement is) and the resolution in pixels per inch (ppi). Those settings work together to control the quality
of your print.

Your printer is a virtuoso that plays your pixels like an accordion. It can squeeze the pixels together and make them smaller, or spread the pixels out and make them larger. Generally speaking, the denser the pixels (the higher the ppi), the higher the resolution of your photo, and the better it looks.

If you don't have enough pixels in your photo, the print will appear *pixelated*—very jagged and blurry looking. The goal is to have enough pixels in your photo so that they'll be packed fairly densely—ideally at about 300 ppi.

You usually don't get a visibly better result if you go over 300 ppi, though, just a larger file size. And depending on your tastes, you may be content with your results at a lower ppi. For instance, some Canon camera photos come into Elements at 180 ppi, and you may be happy with how they print. But 200 ppi is usually considered about the lowest density for an acceptable print. Figure 3-21 demonstrates why it's so important to have a high ppi setting.

To set the size of an image for printing:

1. **Call up the Image Size dialog box.**

   Go to Image → Resize → Image Size, or press Alt+Ctrl+I.

2. **Check the resolution of your image.**

   You want to look at the Document Size section of the dialog box (see Figure 3-22). Start by looking at the ppi setting. If it's too low, like 72 ppi, go to the bottom of the dialog box and turn off Resample Image. Then enter the ppi you want in the Document Size area. The dimensions should become smaller to reflect the greater density of the pixels. If they don't, click OK, and open the dialog box again.

3. **Check the physical size of your photo.**

   Look at the numbers in the Document Size area. Are they what you want? If so, you're all done. Click OK.

4. **If your size numbers aren't right, resize your photo.**

   If the proportions of your image aren't what you want, crop the photo using one of the methods described earlier, and then come back to the Image Size dialog box. Don't try to reshape an image using the Image Size dialog box.

   Once you've returned to the Image Size dialog box, go to the bottom of the window and turn on Resample Image. Choose Bicubic Smoother in the menu. (This menu choice is Adobe's recommendation, but you may find that you prefer one of the other resampling choices.)

   Now enter the size you want for the width or height. Make sure that Constrain Proportions is turned on. If it is, Elements will calculate the other dimension for you. (Scale Styles doesn't matter. Leave it off.)

5. **Click OK.**

   Your photo is resized and ready for printing.

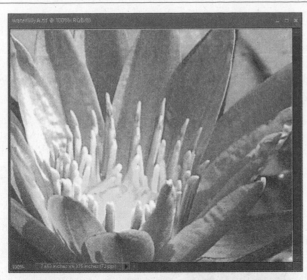

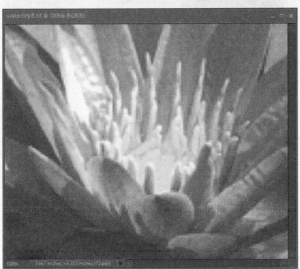

Figure 3-21:
Different resolution settings can dramatically alter the quality of a printout.

Top: A photo with a resolution of 300 ppi.

Bottom: The same photo with resolution set to 72 ppi. Too few pixels stretched too far causes this kind of blocky, blurry printing. When you can see the individual pixels, a photo is said to be pixelated.

Figure 3-22:
Crop your image to the shape you want (see page 79), then use this middle section of the Image Size dialog box to set its size for printing.

Resampling

Resampling is an image editing term for changing the number of pixels in an image. When you resample, your results are permanent, so you want to avoid resampling an original photo if you can help it. As a rule, it's easier to get good results when you *downsample*—that is, make your photo smaller—than when you *upsample*, which you do when you want to make your photo larger.

When you upsample, you're *adding* pixels to your image. Elements has to get them from somewhere, so it makes them up. Elements is pretty good at this, but these pixels are never as good as the pixels that were in your photo to begin with, as you can see from Figure 3-23. You can download the figure (russian_box.jpg) from the Missing CD page at *www.missingmanuals.com* if you'd like to try this out for yourself. Zoom in very closely so you can see the pixels.

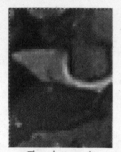 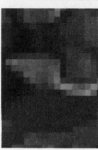 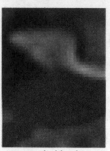

Figure 3-23:
Here's a close-up look at what you're doing to your photo when you resample it.

The photo as it came from the camera.

Downsampled to 72 ppi.

Upsampled back to the original resolution. See how soft the pixels look compared to the original?

When you enlarge an image to more than 100 percent of its original size, you'll definitely lose some of the original quality. So, for example, if you try to stretch a photo that's 3" wide at 180 ppi to an 8" × 10" print, don't be surprised if you don't like the results.

Elements offers you several resampling methods, and they do a very good job when you find the right one for your situation. You select them in the Resample Image menu in the Image Size dialog box. Adobe recommends choosing Bicubic Smoother when you're upsampling (enlarging) your images and Bicubic Sharper when you're downsampling (reducing) your photos, but you may prefer one of the others. It's worth experimenting with them all to see which you like.

Adding Canvas

Just like the works of Monet and Matisse, your photos appear in Elements on a digital "canvas." Sometimes you may want to add more canvas to make room for text or if you're combining photos into a collage.

To make your canvas larger, go to Image → Resize → Canvas Size. You can change the size of your canvas using a variety of measurements. If you don't know exactly how much more canvas you want, choose Percent. Then you can guesstimate that you want, say, 2 percent more canvas or 50 percent more. Figure 3-24 shows how to get your photo into the right place on the new canvas.

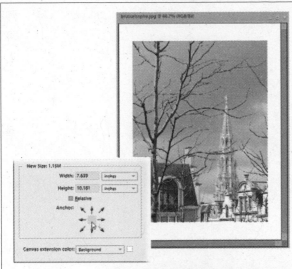

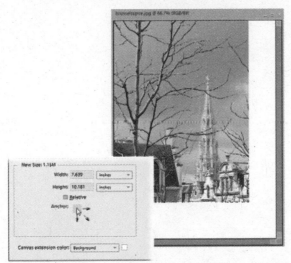

Figure 3-24:
The Canvas Size dialog box isn't as complicated as it looks. The strange little Anchor grid with arrows pointing everywhere lets you decide exactly where to add new canvas to your image. The Anchor box represents your photo's current position, and the arrows surrounding it show where Elements will add the new canvas. By clicking in any of the surrounding boxes, you tell Elements where to position your photo on the newly sized canvas. In the top pair of images, the new canvas has been added equally around all sides of the existing image. In the bottom pair, the new canvas has been added below and to the right of the existing image.

NOTE   Changing the size of your canvas doesn't change the size of your picture any more than pasting a postcard onto a full-size sheet of paper changes the size of the postcard. In both cases, all you get is more empty space around your picture.

The Quick Fix

With Elements' Quick Fix tools, you can dramatically improve the appearance of a photo with just a click or two. The Quick Fix window gathers easy-to-use tools that help adjust the brightness and color of your photos and make them look sharper. You don't even need to understand much about what you're doing. You just need to click a button or slide a pointer, and then decide whether you like how it looks.

If, on the other hand, you *do* know what you're doing, you may still find yourself using the Quick Fix window for things like shadows and highlights because Quick Fix gives you a before-and-after view as you work. Also, the Temperature and Tint sliders can come in very handy for advanced color tweaking, like finessing the overall color of your otherwise finished photo. You also get two tools—the Selection brush and the Magic Selection brush—to help make changes to only a certain area of your photo.

What's more, with Elements 7, you get some clever new fixes. You've always been able to correct red pupils in Elements, but do you want to whiten teeth or make the sky more blue? It's a snap to do any of these in the Quick Fix window. You can even make part of a picture black and white, right in the Quick Fix window.

In this chapter, you'll learn how (and in which order) to use the Quick Fix tools. If you have a newish digital camera, you may find that Quick Fix gives you everything you need to take your photos from pretty darn good to dazzling.

> **NOTE** If an entire chapter on Quick Fix is frustratingly slow, you can start off by trying out the ultra-fast Auto Smart Fix—a quick-fix tool for the truly impatient. Page 105 tells you everything you need to know. Also, Guided Edit may give you enough help to accomplish what you want to do; page 28 has the full story.

The Quick Fix Window

Getting to the Quick Fix window is easy. If you're in the Editor, just click the Edit tab → Quick button. If you're in the Organizer, click the Fix tab → Quick Fix, or right-click a photo and choose Quick Fix from the shortcut menu.

Incidentally, you can also make a lot of quick fixes right from the Organizer. Click the Fix tab for buttons that let you automatically fix red eye, apply Auto Smart Fix, Auto Color, Auto Levels, Auto Contrast, Auto Sharpen, or crop your photo without even launching the Editor. For more selective editing you'll still want the Editor, but if Auto's your thing, you'll be very happy staying in the Organizer. If you use the Organizer, you get the added benefit of having your fixes automatically made on a copy, which Elements saves in a version set (page 59) with your original. Read on for more about what these tools do. They work the same way regardless of where you are when you use them.

The Quick Fix window looks like a stripped-down version of the Full Edit window (see Figure 4-1).

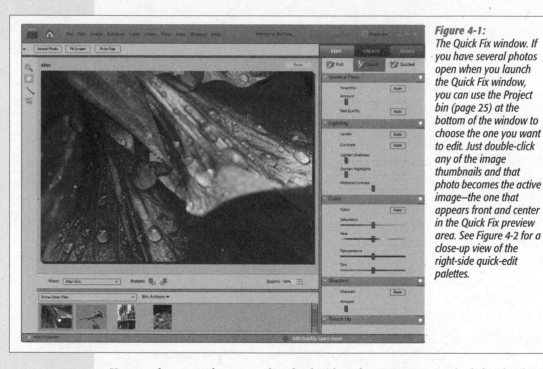

Figure 4-1:
The Quick Fix window. If you have several photos open when you launch the Quick Fix window, you can use the Project bin (page 25) at the bottom of the window to choose the one you want to edit. Just double-click any of the image thumbnails and that photo becomes the active image—the one that appears front and center in the Quick Fix preview area. See Figure 4-2 for a close-up view of the right-side quick-edit palettes.

Your tools are neatly arranged on both sides of your image: On the left side, there's a four-item Toolbox; on the right side, there's a collection of quick-edit palettes (Figure 4-2) stored inside the Control Panel. First, you'll take a quick look at the tools Quick Fix provides you with. Then, later in the chapter, you'll learn how to actually use them.

TIP If you need extra help, check out Guided Edit (page 28), which walks you step by step through a lot of basic editing projects.

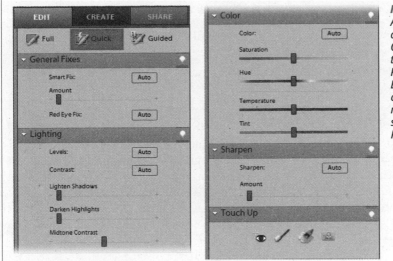

Figure 4-2:
A closeup look at all the ways you can enhance your photos with Quick Fix. The left figure shows the top section of the Control Panel; the right, the bottom half. Besides these handy tools, you can also use most of the Full Edit menu commands if you need something more than the Control Panel provides.

The Quick Fix Toolbox

The Toolbox holds an easy-to-navigate subset of the Full Edit window's larger tool collection. All the tools work the same way in both modes, and you can also use the same keystrokes to switch tools here. From top to bottom, here's what you get:

- **The Zoom tool** lets you telescope in and out on your image—perfect for getting a good close look at details or pulling back to see the whole photo. (See page 87 for more on how the Zoom tool works.) You can also zoom by using the Zoom pull-down menu in the lower-right corner of the image preview area.

- **The Hand tool** helps move your photo around in the image window—just like grabbing it and moving it with your own five fingers. You can read more about the Hand tool on page 88.

- **The Quick Selection tool** lets you apply Quick Fix commands to select portions of your image. The regular Elements Selection brush is also available in Quick Fix. To get to the Selection brush, in the Toolbox, just click the Quick Selection tool's icon and choose the Selection brush from the menu that appears. What's the difference between the two tools? The Selection brush lets you paint a selection exactly where you want it (or mask out part of your photo to keep it from getting changed), while the Quick Selection tool makes Elements figure out the boundaries of your selection based on your much less precise marks on the image. The Quick Selection tool is much more automatic than the regular Selection brush. You can read more about these brushes beginning on page 126.

To get the most out of both these tools, you need to understand the concept of selections. Chapter 5 tells you everything you need to know, including the details of using these brushes.

- **The Crop tool** lets you change the size and shape of your photo, by cutting off the areas you *don't* want (see page 79).

> **NOTE** If the contents of your photo need straightening (see page 76), you need to do that in Full Edit before bringing it into the Quick Fix window, since the Quick Fix Toolbox doesn't include the Straighten tool.

The Quick Fix Control Panel

When you switch to Quick Fix, the Task panel presents you with the Quick Fix Control Panel. The Control Panel is where you make the majority of your adjustments. Elements helpfully arranges everything into five palettes—General Fixes, Lighting, Color, Sharpen, and Touch Up—listed in the order you'll typically use them. In most cases, it makes sense to start at the top and work your way down until you get the results you want. (See page 116 for more suggestions on what order to work in.)

> **NOTE** There is one exception to this top-to-bottom order of operations: If you need to fix red eye problems (page 104). The Red Eye tool is in the Touch Up panel at the bottom of the window. You may want to jump down there first and use the Red Eye tool before you do your other editing.

The Control Panel always fills the right side of the Quick Fix screen. There's no way to hide it, and you can't drag the palettes out of the Control Panel as you can in Standard Edit mode. But you can expand and collapse them, as explained in Figure 4-3.

> **NOTE** If you go into Quick Fix mode *before* opening a photo, you won't see the pointers in the sliders, just empty tracks. Don't worry—they'll automatically appear as soon as you open a photo and give them something to work on.

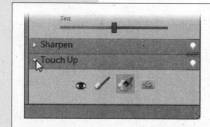

Figure 4-3:
Clicking any of these flippy triangles collapses or expands that section of the Control Panel. If you have a small screen the Touch Up section at the bottom is usually collapsed, so just click the triangle to expand it when you want those tools. There's no need to collapse another section before expanding it—the Sharpen section automatically collapses to make room for Touch Up when you open it.

Different Views: After vs. Before and After

When you open an image in Quick Fix, your picture first appears by itself in the main window with the word "After" above it. Elements keeps the Before view—your original photo—tucked away, out of sight. But you can pick from three other layouts, which you can choose at any time: Before Only, "Before and After—Horizontal", and "Before and After—Vertical". Both of the "Before and After" views are especially helpful when trying to figure out if you're improving your picture—or not—as shown in Figure 4-4. Switch between views by picking the one you want from the pop-up menu just below your image.

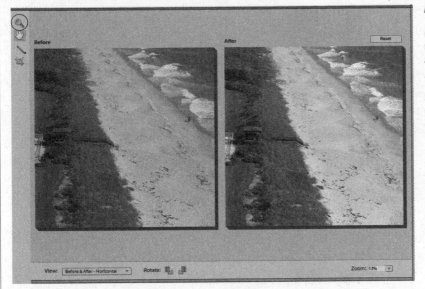

Figure 4-4:
The "Before and After" views in the Quick Fix window make it easy to see how you're changing your photo. Here you see "Before and After–Horizontal", which displays the views side by side. To see them one above the other, choose "Before and After–Vertical". If you want a more detailed view, use the Zoom tool (the magnifying glass icon–circled) to focus on just a portion of your picture.

NOTE   Quick Fix limits the amount of screen space available for your image. If you want a larger view while you work, click over to Full Edit.

Editing Your Photos

The tools in the Quick Fix window are pretty simple to use. You can try one or all of them—it's up to you. And whenever you're happy with how your photo looks, you can leave Quick Fix and go back to the Full Edit window or the Organizer.

If you want to rotate your photo, click either of the Rotate buttons, below the image preview area. (See page 74 for more about rotating photos.) These Rotate buttons only appear when you actually have a photo open in Quick Fix.

NOTE   If you click the Quick Fix Reset button, just above your image, you'll return your photo to the way it looked *before* you started working in Quick Fix. This button undoes *all* Quick Fix edits, so don't use it if you want to undo a single action only. For that, just use the regular undo command: Edit → Undo or Ctrl+Z.

Fixing Red Eye

Everyone who's ever taken a flash photo has run into the dreaded problem of *red eye*—those glowing, demonic pupils that make your little cherub look like someone out of an Anne Rice novel. Red eye is even more of a problem with digital cameras than with film, but luckily, Elements has a simple and terrific Red Eye tool for fixing it. All you need to do is click the red spots with the Red Eye Removal tool, and your problems are solved.

To use the Quick Fix Red Eye tool:

1. **Open a photo.**

   The Red Eye Removal tool in Elements 7 is in the Touch Up section at the very bottom of the Control Panel. This tool works the same whether you get to it from Touch Up in the Quick Fix or from the main Toolbox in Full Edit.

2. **Zoom in so you can see where you're clicking.**

   Use the Zoom tool to magnify the eyes. You can also switch to the Hand tool if you need to drag the photo so that the eyes are front and center.

3. **Activate the Red Eye tool.**

   You may need to expand the Touch Up section by clicking the triangle next to its name (see Figure 4-3); then click the Red Eye icon or press Y (this keystroke works in Full Edit, too).

4. **Click in the red part of the pupil (see Figure 4-5).**

   That's it. Just one click should fix it. If a single click doesn't fix the problem, you can also try dragging the Red Eye tool over the pupil. Sometimes one method works better than the other. You can also adjust two settings on the Red Eye tool: Darken Amount and Pupil Size, as explained later.

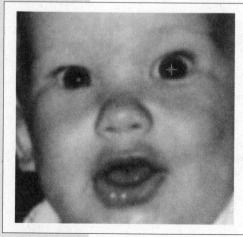

Figure 4-5:
Zoom in when using the Red Eye tool so you get a good look at the pupils. The eye on the left side of the picture has already been fixed. Don't worry if your photo looks so magnified that it loses definition—just make the red area large enough so you can hit it right in the center. Notice what a good job the Red Eye tool does of keeping the highlights (called catchlights) in the eye that's been treated.

5. **Click in the other eye.**

Repeat the process on the other eye, and you're done.

> **TIP**   You can also apply the Organizer's Auto Red Eye Fix in either the Quick Fix or Full Edit window. In either Quick Fix or Full Edit, just press Ctrl+R, or go to Enhance → Auto Red Eye Fix. In Full Edit you can also activate the Red Eye tool and click the Auto button in the Options bar. The only tradeoff to using the Auto Red Eye Fix in the Editor is you don't automatically get a version set (as you do when using the tool from within the Organizer). But you can create a version set when you save your changes, as explained on page 59.

POWER USERS' CLINIC

Another Red Eye Fix

The Red Eye tool does a great job most of the time, but it doesn't always work, and it doesn't work on animals' eyes. Elements gives you a couple of other ways to fix red eye that work in almost any situation. Here's one:

1. Zoom way, way in on the eye. You want to be able to see the individual pixels.

2. Use the Eyedropper tool (page 211) to sample the color from a good area of the eye, or from another photo. Confirm that you've got the color you want by checking the Foreground Color Picker (page 208).

3. Get out the Pencil tool (page 338) and set its size to 1 pixel.

4. Now click the bad or empty pixels of the eye to replace the color with the correct shade. Remember to leave a couple of white pixels for a catchlight (the pupil's glinting center highlight).

This solution works even if the eye is *blown out* (that is, all white with no color information left).

If you're a layers fan, you can also fix red eye by selecting the bad area, creating a Hue/Saturation adjustment layer (page 176), and desaturating the red area, but this method doesn't work so well if the eye is blown out.

If you need to adjust how the Red Eye tool works, the Options bar gives you two controls, although 99 percent of the time you can ignore them:

- **Darken Amount.** If the result is too light, increase the percentage in this box.

- **Pupil Size.** Increase or decrease the number here to tell Elements how much area to consider part of a pupil.

> **NOTE**   You can also fix red eye right in the Raw converter (page 224), if you're dealing with Raw format photos.

Smart Fix

The secret weapon in the Quick Fix window is the Smart Fix command, which automatically adjusts a picture's lighting, color, and contrast, all with one click. You don't have to figure anything out. Elements does it all for you.

You'll find the Smart Fix in the General Fixes palette, and it's about as easy to use as hitting the speed dial button on your phone: Click the Auto Smart Fix button, and if the stars are aligned, your picture will immediately look better. (Figure 4-6 gives you a glimpse of its capabilities. If you want to see for yourself how this fix works, download this photo—*finch.jpg*—from the Missing CD page at *www.missingmanuals.com.*)

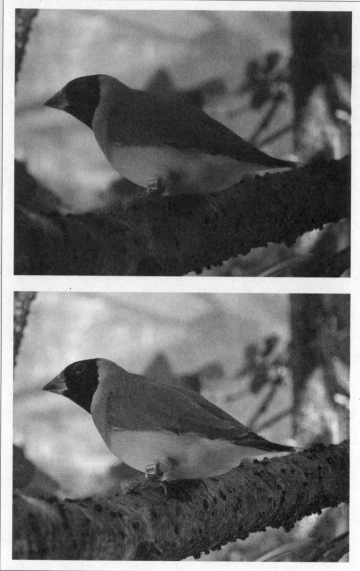

Figure 4-6:

Top: This photo is so dark you may think it's beyond help.

Bottom: The Auto Smart Fix button improved it significantly with just one click. (A click of the Auto Sharpening button, explained on page 112, was added to make it look really spiffy.)

TIP   You'll find Auto buttons scattered throughout Elements. The program uses them to make a best-guess attempt to implement whatever change the Auto button is next to (Smart Fix, Levels, Contrast, and so on). It never hurts to at least try clicking these Auto buttons; if you don't like what you see, you can always perform the magical undo: Edit → Undo or Ctrl+Z.

If you're happy with the Auto Smart Fix button's changes, you can move onto a new photo, or try sharpening your photo a little (see page 112) if the focus appears a little fuzzy. You don't need to do anything to accept the Smart Fix changes. But if you're not ecstatic with your results, take a good look at your picture. If you like what Auto Smart Fix has done, but the effect is too strong or too weak, press Ctrl+Z to undo it, and try playing with the Smart Fix Amount slider instead.

The Amount slider does the same thing Auto Smart Fix does, only you control the degree of change. Watch the image as you move the slider to the right. If your computer is slow, there's a certain amount of lag time, so go slowly to give it a chance to catch up. If you happen to overdo it, sometimes it's easier to press the Reset button above your image and start again. Use the checkmark and the cancel button (which appears next to the General Fixes label, as shown in Figure 4-7) to accept or reject your changes.

TIP   Usually you get better results with a lot of little nudges to the Smart Fix slider than with one big sweeping movement.

Incidentally, these are the same Smart Fix commands you see in two places in the Editor's Enhance Menu: Enhance → Auto Smart Fix (Alt+Ctrl+M), and Enhance → Adjust Smart Fix (Shift+ Ctrl+M).

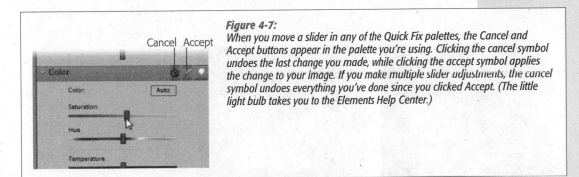

Cancel Accept

Figure 4-7:
When you move a slider in any of the Quick Fix palettes, the Cancel and Accept buttons appear in the palette you're using. Clicking the cancel symbol undoes the last change you made, while clicking the accept symbol applies the change to your Image. If you make multiple slider adjustments, the cancel symbol undoes everything you've done since you clicked Accept. (The little light bulb takes you to the Elements Help Center.)

Sometimes Smart Fix just isn't smart enough to do everything you want, and sometimes it does things you *don't* want. Smart Fix is better with photos that are underexposed than overexposed, for one thing. Fortunately, you still have several other editing choices, covered in the following sections. If you don't like the effect Smart Fix has had, undo it before going on to make other changes.

TIP Auto Smart Fix is one of the commands you can apply from within the Organizer, so there's no need to launch the Editor at all if you want just this tool. Simply click your photo and press Ctrl+Alt+M, or right-click your picture and choose Auto Smart Fix from the pop-up menu. You can also get to the Auto Smart Fix command via the Organizer's Fix pane or the Edit menu.

Adjusting Lighting and Contrast

The Lighting palette lets you make very sophisticated adjustments to the brightness and contrast of your photo. Sometimes problems that you thought stemmed from exposure or even focus may be fixed by these commands.

Levels

If you want to understand how Levels really works, you're in for a long technical ride. On the other hand, if you just want to know what it can do for your photos, the short answer is that it adjusts the brightness of your photo by redistributing the color information; Levels changes (and hopefully fixes!) both brightness and color at the same time.

If you've never used any photo-editing software before, this may sound rather mysterious, but photo-editing pros will tell you that Levels is one of the most powerful commands for fixing and polishing your pictures. To find out if its magic works for you, click the Auto Levels button. Figure 4-8 shows what a big difference it can make. Download this photo (*squirrel.jpg*) from the Missing CD page at *www.missingmanuals.com*, if you'd like to try this out yourself.

What Levels does is very complex. Chapter 7 contains loads more details about what's going on behind the scenes and how you can apply this command much more precisely.

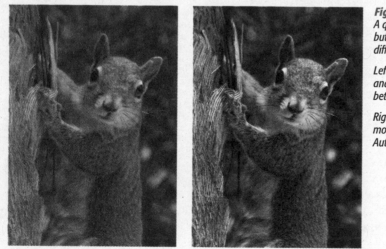

Figure 4-8:
A quick click of the Auto Levels button can make a very dramatic difference.

Left: The original photo isn't bad, and you may not realize how much better the colors could be.

Right: This image shows how much more effective your photo is once Auto Levels has balanced the colors.

FREQUENTLY ASKED QUESTION

Calibrating Your Monitor

Why do my photos look awful when I open them in Elements?

Do you find that when opening your photos in Elements they look really terrible, even though they look decent in other programs? Maybe your photos look all washed out, or reddish or greenish, or even black and white?

If that's the case, you need to calibrate your monitor, as explained on page 194. It's easy to do and it makes a big difference.

Elements is what's known as a *color-managed* program. You can read all about color management on page 192.

For now, you just need to understand that color-managed programs pay much more attention to the settings for your monitor than regular programs like word processors do.

Color-managed programs like Elements are a little more trouble to set up initially, but the advantage is that you can get truly wonderful results if you invest a little time and effort when you're getting started.

Contrast

The main alternative to Auto Levels in Quick Fix is Auto Contrast. Most people find that their images tend to benefit from one or the other of these options. Contrast adjusts the relative darkness and lightness of your image without changing the color, so if Levels made your colors go all goofy, try adjusting the contrast instead. You activate Contrast the same way you do the Levels tool: just click the Auto button next to its name.

> **NOTE** After you use Auto Contrast, look closely at the edges of the objects in your photo. If your camera's contrast was already high, you may see a halo or a sharp line around the photo's subject. If you do, the contrast is too high and you need to undo Auto Contrast (Ctrl+Z) and try another fix instead.

Shadows and Highlights

The Shadows and Highlights tools do an amazing job of bringing out details that are lost in the shadows or bright areas of your photo. Figure 4-9 shows what a difference these tools can make.

The Shadows and Highlights tools are a collection of three sliders, each of which controls a different aspect of your image:

- **Lighten Shadows.** Nudge the slider to the right and you'll see details emerge from murky black shadows.

- **Darken Highlights.** Use this slider to dim the brightness of overexposed areas.

- **Midtone Contrast.** After you've adjusted your photo's shadows and highlights, your photo may look very flat and not have enough contrast between the dark and light areas. This slider helps you bring a more realistic look back to your photo.

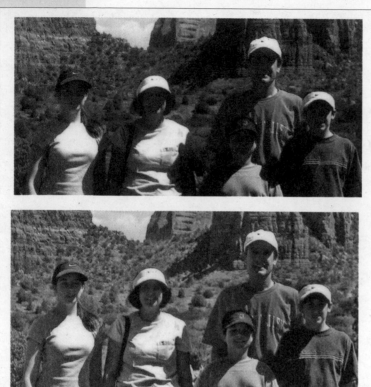

Figure 4-9:

Top: This photo shows a classic vacation picture problem: The day is bright, the scenery's beautiful, but everyone's faces are hidden in the dark shadows cast by their hats.

Bottom: The Shadows and Highlights tools brought back everyone's faces, but now they look a tad orange. Use the color sliders to make them look healthy again.

> **TIP** You may think you need only lighten shadows in a photo, but sometimes just a smidgen of Darken Highlights may help, too. Don't be afraid to experiment by using this slider even if you've got a relatively dark photo.

Go easy. Getting overenthusiastic with these sliders can give your photos a very washed-out, flat look.

Color

The Color palette lets you—surprise, surprise—play around with the colors in your image. In many cases, if you've been successful with Auto Levels or Auto Contrast, you won't need to do anything here.

Auto Color

Once again, there's another one-click fix available: Auto Color. Actually, in some ways Auto Color should be up in the Lighting section. Like Levels, it simultaneously adjusts color and brightness, but it looks at different information in your photos to decide what to do with them.

When you're first learning to use Quick Fix, you may want to try all three—Levels, Contrast, and Auto Color—to see which generally works best for your photos. Undo between each change and compare your results. Most people find they like one of the three most of the time.

Auto Color may be just the ticket for your photos, but you may also find that it shifts your colors in strange ways. Give it a click and see what you think. Does your photo look better or worse? If it's worse, just click Reset or Ctrl+Z to undo it, and go back to Auto Levels or Auto Contrast. If they all make your colors look a little wrong, or if you want to tweak the colors in your photo, move on to the Color sliders, explained in the next section.

Using the Color sliders

If you want to adjust the colors in your photo without changing the brightness, check out the Color sliders. For example, your digital camera may produce colors that don't quite match what you saw when you took the picture; or you may have scanned an old print that's faded or discolored; or you may just want to change the colors in a photo for the heck of it. If so, the sliders below the Auto Color button are for you.

You get four ways to adjust your colors here:

- **Saturation** controls the intensity of your photo's color. For example, you can turn a color photo to black and white by moving the slider all the way to the left. Move it too far to the right and everything glows with so much color that it looks radioactive.

- **Hue** changes the color from, say, red to blue or green. If you aren't looking for realism, you can have some fun with your photos by really pushing this slider to create funky color changes.

- **Temperature** lets you adjust color from cool (bluish) on the left to warm (orangeish) on the right. Use Temperature for things like toning down the warm glow you see in photos taken in tungsten lighting, or just for fine-tuning your color balance.

- **Tint** adjusts the green/magenta balance of your photo, as shown in Figure 4-10.

You probably won't use all these sliders on a single photo, but you can use as many of them as you like. Remember to click the Accept checkmark that appears in the Color palette if you want to accept your changes. Chapter 7 has much more information about how to use the full-blown Editor to really fine-tune your image's color.

> **TIP**   If you look at the color of the slider's track, it shows you what happens if you move in that direction. So there's less and less color as you go left in the Saturation track, and more and more to the right. Looking at the tracks can help you know where you want to move the slider.

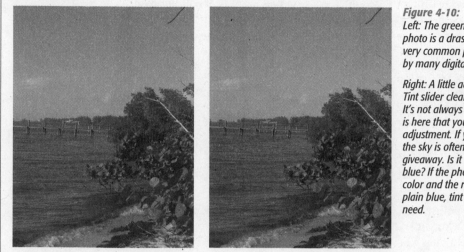

Figure 4-10:
Left: The greenish tint in this photo is a drastic example of a very common problem caused by many digital cameras.

Right: A little adjustment of the Tint slider clears it up in a jiffy. It's not always as obvious as it is here that you need a tint adjustment. If you aren't sure, the sky is often a dead giveaway. Is it robin's egg blue? If the photo's sky is that color and the real sky was just plain blue, tint is what you need.

Sharpening

Now that you've finished your other corrections, it's time to *sharpen* your photo. Sharpening gives the effect of better focus by improving the edge contrast in your photo. Most digital camera photos need some sharpening because the sharpening your camera applies is usually deliberately conservative. Once again, a Quick Fix Auto button is at your service. Give the Auto Sharpen button (located in the Sharpen palette) a try to get things started. Figure 4-11 shows what you can expect.

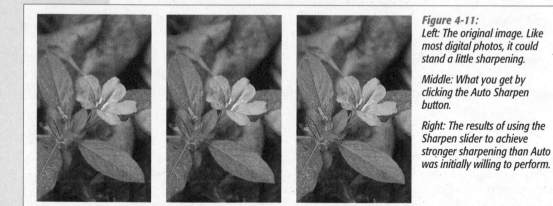

Figure 4-11:
Left: The original image. Like most digital photos, it could stand a little sharpening.

Middle: What you get by clicking the Auto Sharpen button.

Right: The results of using the Sharpen slider to achieve stronger sharpening than Auto was initially willing to perform.

The sad truth is that there really isn't any way to actually improve the focus of a photo once it's taken. Software sharpening just increases the contrast where the program perceives edges, so using it first can have strange effects on other editing tools and their ability to understand your photo.

If you don't like what Auto Sharpening does (you very well may not), you can undo it (press Ctrl+Z) and try the slider. If you thought the Auto button overdid things, go very gently with the slider. Changes vary from photo to photo, but usually Auto's results fall at around the 30 to 40 percent mark on the slider.

> **TIP** If you see funny halos around the outlines of objects in your photos, or strange flaky spots (making your photo look like it has eczema), those are artifacts from too much sharpening; reduce the Sharpening settings till they go away.

Always try to view Actual Pixels (View → Actual Pixels) whenever you sharpen because that gives you the clearest idea of what you're actually doing to your picture. If you don't like what the button does, undo it, and then try the slider. Zero sharpening is all the way to the left. Moving to the right increases the amount of sharpening applied to your photo.

As a general rule, you want to sharpen more for photos you plan to print than for images for Web use. You can read lots more about sharpening on page 214.

> **NOTE** If you've used photo-editing programs before, you may be interested to know that the Auto Sharpen button applies Adjust Sharpness (page 216) to your photo. The difference is that you don't have any control over the settings, as you would if you applied it from the Enhance menu. But the good news is that if you want it, or if you prefer to use Unsharp Mask (page 214), you can get this control—even from within Quick Fix. Just go to the Enhance Menu and choose the sharpener of your choice.

At this point, all that's left is cropping your photo, if you'd like to reduce its size. Page 79 tells you everything you need to know about cropping. However, you can also give your photo a bit more punch by using the new tools in the Touch Up panel, as explained in the next section.

Touch Ups

In Elements 7, you'll notice the new Touch Up panel at the very bottom of the Quick Fix Control Panel. (You can see it in Figure 4-12.) You've already learned how to use one of its main attractions—the Red Eye Removal tool—earlier in this chapter (page 104). There are also other three fixes available here:

- **Whiten Teeth**. As you probably guessed from the name, use this tool to make teeth look brighter. What's especially nice is that it doesn't create a fake, overly-white look.

- **Make Dull Skies Blue**. It's such a common problem with digital cameras—your exposure for the subject is perfect, but the sky is all washed out looking. Unfortunately, if your sky is really gray or blown out (white looking), this tool won't help much. It should probably have been called "Make Blue Skies Bluer." It is useful for creating more dramatic skies, though.

- **Black and White High Contrast.** You're probably wondering what the heck *that* means. It's Adobe's way of saying, "transform the area I choose from color to black and white." This tool's a great timesaver when you want to create a photo where only part of the picture is in color. (High Contrast refers to the style of black and white conversion this tool uses.)

All three tools work pretty much the same way—just draw a line over the area you want to change, and Elements makes a detailed selection of the area and applies the change for you:

1. **Open a photo and make your other corrections first.**

   If you're an old hand at using Elements, use the Touch Up tools before sharpening. But if you're a beginner and not comfortable with layers (see Chapter 6), sharpen first. (See the note on page 116 for more about why.)

2. **Click the icon for the tool you want to use.**

   See Figure 4-12 if you aren't sure which is which.

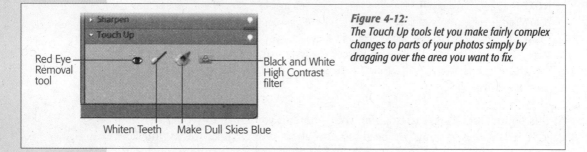

Figure 4-12:
The Touch Up tools let you make fairly complex changes to parts of your photos simply by dragging over the area you want to fix.

Red Eye Removal tool

Black and White High Contrast filter

Whiten Teeth   Make Dull Skies Blue

3. **Draw a line over the area you want to change.**

   When you click one of the Touch Up tools, your cursor turns to a circle with crosshairs in it. Just drag that over the area you want to change. Elements automatically expands the area to include the entire object it thinks you want. (It works just like the Quick Selection tool, only it also applies the changes to your image. You can learn more about using the Quick Selection tool on page 126.) You'll see the marching ants appear (page 122) around the area Elements is changing.

4. **If Elements included too much or too little, tweak the size of the selected area.**

   In the Options bar, you'll see three little brush icons. The left icon lets you start another new selection. Click the one on the right and drag over any area you want to remove, or click the middle one and drag to add to the area. You can also just drag to extend your selection, or Alt+drag if Elements covered too much area and you need to remove some of it, without going to the Options bar at all.

5. **Once you're happy with the area covered by the change, you're done.**

You can back up by pressing Ctrl+Z to undo your changes step by step. Just keep going to eliminate the change completely if you don't like it. (Clicking the Reset button doesn't undo the Touch Up changes, except for the Red Eye tool.)

The Touch Up tools can be very helpful, but they work based on the colors in your photo, so they may not always give you exactly the results you want, as you can see in Figure 4-13. If you want to use the Color sliders (page 111) to adjust things, you'll need to switch away from the Touch Up tools and use the Selection brush to reselect the area. That's because the sliders are not available when the Touch Up tools are active.

> **NOTE** The Touch Up tools (except for Red Eye) create a layered file. If you understand layers, you can also go back to Full Edit and make changes after the fact, like adjusting the opacity or blend mode of the layer (See Chapter 6 to learn about layers). You can always discard your Touch Up changes by discarding the layer they're on. And you can even edit the area affected by the changes by editing the layer mask, as explained on page 293, or you can use the Smart Brush tool (page 189) in Full Edit.

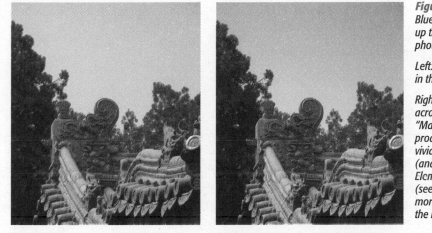

Figure 4-13:
Blue Skies can help punch up the sky color in your photos—sometimes.

Left: Smog makes the sky in this photo look very dull.

Right: One quick drag across the sky with the "Make Dull Skies Blue" tool produced a much more vivid sky, maybe too vivid (and maybe a tad green). Elements used a gradient (see page 385) to give a more realistic shading to the new sky color.

Also, if there isn't enough color to begin with, the Touch Up tools may not produce any visible result in your photo. If your subject has very white dentures, Whiten Teeth may not do anything, or Make Dull Skies Blue may prove to be a dud if your sky is just solid gray or completely overexposed. You may find, however, that after using a Touch Up tool, nothing happens when you try to make other changes to your photo. If you run into that problem, read the Note that follows.

NOTE As mentioned above, Elements leaves you with a layered file after the Touch Up tools (except for the Red Eye Removal tool). That isn't normally a problem, even if you don't know anything about layers, but once in a while you may find nothing happens when you try to make other changes to your photo.

If that happens, at the top of the page, click the Full button (under the Edit tab) to go back to Full Edit. Then find the Layers palette. It should be in the Palette bin unless you've removed it. (If you can't find it, go to Window → Layers to bring it back.) In the Layers palette, look for the word Background and click that. That part of the palette should be a lighter or darker gray (depending on your brightness slider settings) than the rest of the palette (the area that says Blue Skies, Pearly Whites, or whatever). If it isn't, click it again. Then you can go back to the Quick Fix and do whatever you want to your photo. However, the part you used the Touch Up tools on may behave differently from the rest of the photo. If that happens, and you haven't closed the photo since using the Touch Up tools, use Undo History (page 32) to back up to before the Touch Up.

Quick Fix Suggested Workflow

There are no hard-and-fast rules for what order you need to work in when using the Quick Fix tools. As mentioned earlier, Elements lays out the tools in the Control Panel, from top to bottom, in the order that usually makes sense. But you can pick and choose which tools you want, depending on what you think your photo needs. But if you're the type of person who likes a set plan for fixing photos, here's one order in which to apply the commands:

1. **Rotate your photo (if needed).**

   Use the buttons below the image preview.

2. **Fix red eye (if needed).**

   See page 104.

3. **Crop.**

   If you know you want to crop your photo, now's the time. That way, you get rid of any problem areas before they affect other adjustments. For example, say your photo has a lot of overexposed sky that you want to crop out. If you leave it in, that area may skew the effects of the Lighting and Color tools on your image. So if you already know where you want to crop, do it before making other adjustments for more accurate results.

4. **Try Auto Smart Fix and/or the Smart Fix slider. Undo if necessary.**

   Pretty soon you'll get a good idea of how likely it is that this fix will do a good job on your photos. Some people love it; others think it makes their pictures too grainy.

5. **If Smart Fix wasn't smart enough, work your way down through the other Lighting and Color commands until you like the way your photo looks.**

   Read the sections earlier in this chapter to understand what each command does to your photo.

6. **Sharpen.**

Try to perform sharpening as your last adjustment because other commands can give you funky results on photos that have already been sharpened. However, if you're a beginner and not comfortable with layers, you can sharpen *before* using Whiten Teeth, Make Dull Skies Blue, or "Black and White High Contrast" in the Touch Up panel. (See page 116 for more about why you'd wait to use these.)

NOTE When you're in Quick Fix mode, you can switch back to Full Edit at any point if you want tools not available in Quick Fix. Also, note that there's no Close button in Quick Fix. To close a photo there, use the File menu or Ctrl+W.

Adjusting Skin Tones

If you're like most amateur photographers, your most important photos are pictures of people: your family, your friends, or even just fascinating strangers. Elements gives you yet another tool for making fast fixes—one that's designed especially for correcting photos that have people in them. This is the "Adjust Color for Skin Tone" command, available in both the Quick Fix and Full Edit windows.

The name "Adjust Color for Skin Tone" may be a bit confusing. What this command actually does is adjust your *entire* image based on the skin tone of someone in the photo. The idea behind "Adjust Color for Skin Tone" is that you may well be much more interested in the way the people in your photos look than in how the background looks. This command gives the highest priority to creating good skin color. It's an automatic fix, but there's a dialog box where you can tweak the results once you've previewed Elements' suggested adjustments. To use the "Adjust Color for Skin Tone" command:

1. **Call up the "Adjust Color for Skin Tone" dialog box.**

In either Quick Fix or Full Edit, go to Enhance → Adjust Color → "Adjust Color for Skin Tone". The dialog box shown in Figure 4-14 appears. You may need to move it out of the way of your photo so you can see what's happening.

2. **Show Elements an area of skin to sample for calculating the color adjustments.**

Once the dialog box appears, your cursor turns to an eyedropper. Just find a portion of your photo where your subject's skin has relatively good color, and click it.

3. **Tweak the results.**

Elements is often a bit overenthusiastic in its adjustments. Use the sliders in the dialog box to get a more pleasing, realistic color. The Ambient Light slider works just like the Temperature slider in the Quick Fix control panel (page 111). Blush increases the rosiness of the skin as you move the slider to the right and decreases it to the left. Tan increases or decreases the browns and oranges in the

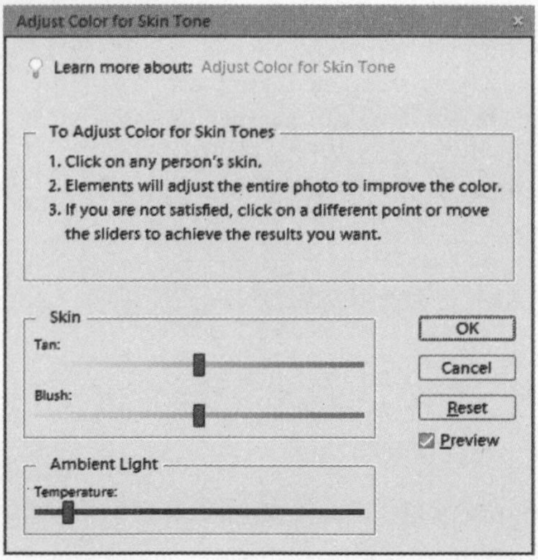

Figure 4-14:
When this dialog box appears, your cursor turns into a little eyedropper when you move it over your photo. Just click the best-looking area of skin you can find. You won't see any sliders in the tracks until you click. After Elements adjusts the photo based on your click, the sliders appear and you can use them to fine-tune the results. Clicking different spots gives different results, so you may want to experiment by clicking different places.

skin tones. You may get swell results with your first click, or you may have to use all the sliders to get a truly realistic result. It all depends on the photo.

You can preview the changes right in your photo as you work. If you mess up and want to start again, click Reset. If you decide you'd rather be using another tool instead, click Cancel.

NOTE The "Adjust Color for Skin Tone" sliders are like the Quick Fix sliders in that you can get an idea of which way to move them by looking at the colors in the slider tracks in the dialog box.

4. **When you like what you see, click OK.**

Elements applies your changes. If you want to undo them, press Ctrl+Z.

"Adjust Color for Skin Tone" seems to work best on fair skin, and not so well on darker skin tones. And it's most suited for making fairly subtle adjustments, so you may have to reduce the amount of change from what Elements first did.

Also, notice that not only the skin tones are changing. Elements is adjusting *all* the colors in the photo in sync with the skin tones (Figure 4-15). Sometimes you may find you've acquired quite a color cast by the time you've got the skin just right (see page 205). If this bothers you, try a different tool. On the other hand, you can create some very nice late afternoon light effects with this command.

While "Adjust Color for Skin Tone" is really meant as a kind of alternative fast fix, you may find it's most useful for making small final adjustments to photos you've already edited using other tools.

TIP If you understand layers (explained in Chapter 6), you may want to make a duplicate layer and apply this command to your duplicate. Then you can adjust the intensity of the result by adjusting the layer's opacity (see page 162).

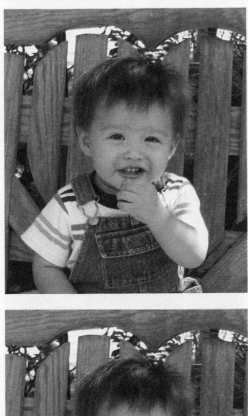

Figure 4-15:
Top: This photo shows a slight greenish cast, giving the little boy a somewhat unappealing skin tone.

Bottom: "Adjust Color for Skin Tone" is able to warm up his skin tones, and it even removes the greenish tinge to the wood of the bench he's sitting on.

CHAPTER 5

Making Selections

One of Elements' most impressive talents is its ability to let you *select* part of your image and make changes only to that area. Selecting something tells Elements, "Hey, *this* is what I want to work on. Just let me work on this part of my picture and don't touch the rest of it." You can select your entire image or any part of it.

By using selections, you can fine-tune your images in very sophisticated ways. You could change the color of just one rose in a whole bouquet, for instance, or change your nephew's festive purple hair color back to something his grandparents would appreciate. Graphics pros will tell you that good selections make the difference between shoddy amateurish work and a slick professional job.

Elements offers you a whole bunch of different selection tools to work with. You can draw a rectangular or a circular selection with the Marquee tools, for instance, or paint a selection on your photo with the Selection brush, or just draw a line with the Quick Selection tool and let Elements figure out the exact boundaries of your selection. When you're looking to pluck a particular object (a beautiful flower, say) from a photo, the Magic Extractor works wonders.

For most jobs, there's no right or wrong tool; with experience you may find you tend to prefer working with certain tools more than others. Often you'll use more than one tool to create a perfect selection. Once you've read this chapter you'll understand all the different selection tools and how to use each one. And in Elements 7, by using the new Smart Brush, you can even make a selection and apply your change at the same time. You can learn more about how to do that on page 189.

> **TIP** It's much easier to select an object that's been photographed against a plain, contrasting background. So, if you know you're going to want to select a bicycle, for example, shoot it in front of a blank wall rather than, say, a hedge.

Selecting Everything

Sometimes the only thing you want to do is select your entire photo. For instance, if you want to copy and paste your whole photo, you need to select all of it. Elements gives you some useful commands to help you make basic selections in a snap:

- **Select All** (Select → All or Ctrl+A) tells Elements to select your entire image. You'll see the "marching ants" (Figure 5-1) around the outer edge of your entire picture.

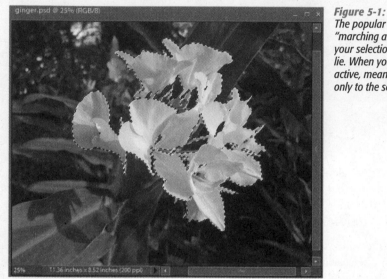

Figure 5-1:
The popular name for these dotted lines is "marching ants" because they march around your selections to show you where the edges lie. When you see the ants, your selection is active, meaning what you do next happens only to the selected area.

If you want to copy your image into another picture or program, performing a Select All is the fastest way to go. If your photo contains layers, which you'll learn about in Chapter 6, you may not be able to get everything you want with the Select All shortcut. In that case, use File → Copy Merged, or press Shift+Ctrl+C.

NOTE   If you're planning on pasting an image into another program, like Microsoft Word or PowerPoint, make sure you've got Export Clipboard turned on in Edit → Preferences → General.

- **Deselect Everything** (Select → Deselect, Escape, or Ctrl+D) removes any current selection. Remember the keystroke combination because it's one you'll probably use over and over again in Elements.

- **Reselect** (Select → Reselect or Shift+Ctrl+D) tells Elements to reactivate the selection you just canceled. Use Reselect if you realize you still need a selection you just got rid of. Or you can just press Ctrl+Z to back up a step.

- **Hide/View a Selection** (Ctrl+H) keeps your selection active while hiding its outline. Sometimes the marching ants make it hard to see what you're doing, or they can be distracting. To see the ants again, press Ctrl+H a second time.

TIP   Sometimes it's easy to forget you have a selection. When a tool acts goofy or won't do anything, start your troubleshooting by pressing Ctrl+H to be sure you don't have a hidden selection you forgot about.

If you want to quickly select an irregular area, try the Quick Selection tool, explained on page 126.

Selecting Rectangular and Elliptical Areas

Selecting your whole picture is all well and good, but many times your reason for making a selection is precisely because you *don't* want to make changes to the whole image. How do you select just part of the picture?

Well, the easiest way is to use the Marquee tools. You already met the Rectangular Marquee tool back in Chapter 3, in the section on cropping (page 79). If you want to select a block of your image or a circle or an oval from it, the Marquee tools are the way to go. As the winners of "Most Frequently Used Selection Tools," they get top spot in the Selection area of the Editor's Toolbox. You can modify how they work, like telling them to create a square instead of a rectangle, as explained in Figure 5-2.

To use the Marquee tools to make a selection:

1. **Press M or click the Marquee tool's icon in the Toolbox to activate it.**

   The Marquee tool is the little dotted square right below the Eyedropper icon in a single row toolbox, or below the Hand tool if you have two rows. (It may appear as a little dotted oval, if you used the Elliptical Marquee tool last.)

2. **Choose the Shape you want to draw: rectangle or ellipse.**

   In the Toolbox pop-out menu for the Marquee tools, choose the rectangle or the ellipse to set the shape.

3. **Choose a feather value if you want one.**

   Feathering makes the edges of your selection softer or fuzzier for better blending (when you're trying, say, to superimpose your face on Brad Pitt's body). See the box on page 135 for a look at how feathering (and anti-aliasing) work.

4. **Drag within your image to make your selection.**

   Wherever you initially place your mouse becomes one of the corners of your rectangular selection or a point just beyond the outer edge of your ellipse (you can draw perfectly circular or square selections, as shown in Figure 5-2). The selection outline expands as you drag your mouse.

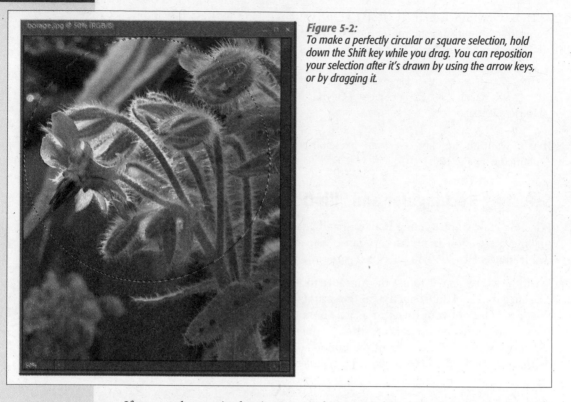

Figure 5-2:
To make a perfectly circular or square selection, hold down the Shift key while you drag. You can reposition your selection after it's drawn by using the arrow keys, or by dragging it.

If you make a mistake, just press the Escape key. You can also press either Ctrl+D to get rid of all current selections, or Ctrl+Z to remove the most recent selection.

The mode choices in the Options bar give you three ways to control the size of your selection: Normal lets you manually control the size of your selection; Fixed Aspect Ratio lets you enter proportions in the Width and Height boxes; and Fixed Size lets you enter specific dimensions in these boxes. The Anti-alias checkbox is explained in the box on page 135. Once you've made your selection, you can move the selected area around in the photo by dragging it (see page 84), or you can use the arrow keys to nudge your selection in the direction you want to move it. Changing the size of a Marquee selection once you've made it is pretty tricky, and it's far easier to just start over again, but you can add to or subtract from any selection you make in Elements. Page 126 tells you how.

Selecting Irregularly Sized Areas

It would be nice if you could always get away with making simple rectangular or elliptical selections, but is life really ever that neat? You aren't always going to want to select a geometric-shaped chunk of your image. If you want to change the color of one fish in your aquarium picture, selecting a rectangle or square isn't going to cut it.

UP TO SPEED

Paste vs. Paste Into Selection

Newcomers to Elements are often confused by the fact that there are two Paste commands in Elements: Paste and Paste Into Selection. Knowing what each one does will help you avoid problems.

- **Paste.** 99 percent of the time, Paste is the one you want. This command simply places your copied object wherever you paste it. Once you've pasted your object, you can move whatever you've pasted by moving the selected area.

- **Paste Into Selection**. This is a special command for pasting a selection into *another* selection. Your pasted object appears only *within* the bounds of the selection you're pasting into.

When you use Paste Into Selection, what you paste can still be moved around, but it won't be visible anywhere outside the edges of the selection you're pasting into. Paste Into Selection is very handy if you want to do something like putting a beautiful mountain view outside your window. Select the window, copy the mountain (Ctrl+C), and then use Paste Into Selection to add the view. You can maneuver the mountain photo around till it's properly centered. And if you move it outside the boundary of your window selection, it just disappears. Once you deselect, your material is permanently in place; you can't move it again.

If you understand layers (see Chapter 6), Paste creates a new layer, while Paste Into Selection puts what you paste on the existing layer.

Thankfully, Elements gives you other tools that make it easy for you to make very precise selections—no matter their size or shape. In this section, you'll learn how to use the rest of the selection tools. But first you need to understand the basic controls that they (almost) all share.

Controlling the Selection Tools

If you're the kind of person who never makes a mistake and you also never change your mind, you can skip this section. If, on the other hand, you're human, you need to know about the mysterious little squares you see in the Options bar when the selection tools are active (Figure 5-3).

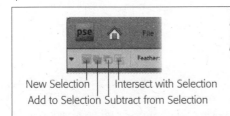

Figure 5-3:
These cryptic squares can save you hours of time once you understand how to use them to tell the selection tools how to behave.

New Selection | Intersect with Selection
Add to Selection Subtract from Selection

These selection squares don't look like much, but they tell the selection tools how to do their job: whether to start a new selection with each click, to add to what you've already got, or to remove things from your selection. They're available for all the selection tools except the Selection brush and the Quick Selection tool, which have their own sets of options. From left to right, here's what they do:

- **New Selection** is the standard selection mode that you'll probably use most of the time. When you click this button and start a new selection, your previous selection disappears.

- **Add to Selection** tells Elements to add what you select *in addition to* what you've already selected. Unless you have an incredibly steady mouse hand, this option is a godsend because it's not easy to get a perfect selection on the first try. (Holding down the Shift key while you use any selection tool is another way to add to a selection.)

- **Subtract from Selection** removes what you select next from any existing selection. (By holding down Alt while selecting the area you want to remove, you can accomplish the same thing.)

- **Intersect with Selection** is a bit confusing. It lets you take a selected area, make a new selection, and wind up with only the area where the selections overlap, as shown in Figure 5-4. (The keyboard equivalent is Alt+Shift.) Most people don't need this one much, but it can be useful for things like creating special shapes. If you need a selection shaped like a quarter of a pie, for instance, do a circle selection, then switch to "Intersect with Selection" and drag a rectangular selection from the circle's center point. You'll wind up with an arc-shaped area where they intersect.

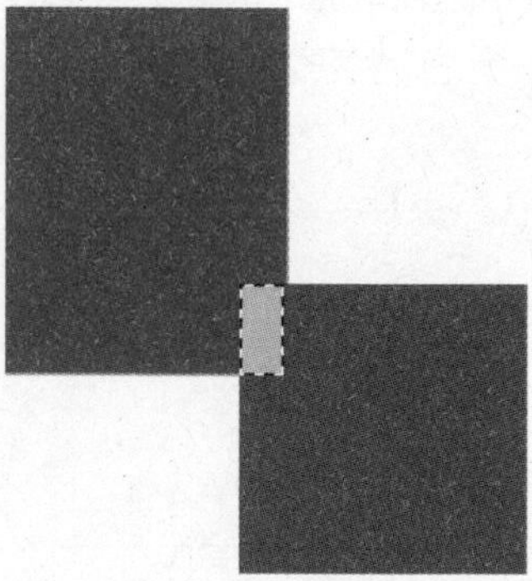

Figure 5-4:
"Intersect with Selection" lets you take two separate selections and select only the area where they intersect. If you have an existing selection, when you select again your new selection includes only the overlapping area. Here, the top blue rectangle is the first selection, and the bottom purple square is the second. The light area shows the final selection after you let go of the mouse button.

Selecting with a Brush

Elements also gives you two very special brushes to help make selections. The Selection brush has been around since Elements 2, so if you've used Elements before, you probably know how useful it is. These days it often takes a back seat to the amazing Quick Selection tool, which makes even the trickiest selections as easy as doodling. The Quick Selection tool automatically finds the bounds of the objects you drag it over, while the Selection brush only selects the area immediately under the brush cursor.

The Quick Selection tool and the Selection brush are grouped together in the Toolbox, and they appear in both Full Edit and Quick Fix because they're so useful. You may well find that with these two tools you rarely need the other selection tools.

It couldn't be easier to use the Quick Selection tool:

1. **Activate the Quick Selection tool.**

   Click it in the Toolbox or press A, and then choose it from the Toolbox pop-out menu. It shares a Toolbox slot with the regular Selection brush. Their icons are very similar, so look carefully—the Quick Selection tool looks more like a wand than a brush and it points up, while the regular Selection brush points down.

2. **Drag within your photo.**

   As you move the mouse, Elements calculates where it thinks the selection edges should be, and the selection outline jumps out to surround that area. It's an amazingly good guesser. There's no need to try to cover the entire area or to go around the edges of your object—Elements does that for you.

   There are a few Options bar controls, which are explained below, but you mostly won't need to think about them, at least not till you make your selection. Then you'll probably want to try Refine Edge (explained in the next section).

3. **Adjust the selection.**

   Odds are that you won't get a totally perfect selection that includes everything you wanted on the first click. To increase the selection area, drag in the direction where you want to add to the selection. A small move usually does it, and the selection jumps outward to include the area that Elements thinks you want, as shown in Figure 5-5.

   To remove an area from the selection, hold Alt and drag, or click in the area you don't want.

   Once you're happy with your selection, that's all, unless you want to tweak the edges using Refine Edge (see the next section)—and you probably do.

The Quick Selection tool does have a few Options bar choices, but you really don't need most of them:

- **New Selection, Add to Selection, Subtract from Selection.** These three brush icons work just like the equivalent selection squares in selection tools (page 125), but you don't need to use them. The Quick Select tool automatically adds to your selection if you drag toward an unselected area. Shift+drag to select multiple areas that are not contiguous. Alt+drag to remove areas from your selection.

- **Brush.** You can make all kinds of adjustments to your brush by clicking this pull-down menu, including choosing from many of the Brush Dynamics palette options (see page 331), although you'll rarely need any of these except maybe the brush size, once in a while.

- **All Layers.** Turn this on, and the Quick Selection tool selects from all visible layers in your image, rather than just the active layer.

- **Auto-Enhance.** This tells Elements to automatically smooth out the edges of the selection. It's a more automated way to make the same sort of edge adjustments that you make manually with Refine Edge.

- **Refine Edge.** This option lets you tweak the edges of your selection so that you'll get more realistic results when changing the selected area or copying and pasting it. Refine Edge is grayed out until you actually make a selection. It's explained in detail in the next section.

> **NOTE** Depending on what you plan to do with your selection, you may want to check out the new Smart Brush tool in Full Edit. It works just like Quick Selection, but it goes further than simply completing your selection for you; it also automatically applies the color correction or special effect you choose from its pull-down menu. See page 189 for more about working with the Smart Brushes.

Refine Edge

This is another tremendously helpful Elements feature. It allows you to create smooth, feathered, plausible edges on any selection—a must when you want to realistically blend edited sections into the rest of an image. It appears in the Options bar for some of the tools that allow you to make irregular selections (like Quick Selection), or you can use it on any active selection by going to Select → Refine Edge. To use it, first make a selection, and then:

1. **Call up Refine Edge.**

   If it's not currently available from the Options bar (it's not there when you use the Marquee tool, for example), go to Select → Refine Edge to bring it up.

2. **Adjust the edges of your selection.**

   Use the sliders, explained in the list that follows, to tweak and polish the edges of your selection. Use the view buttons to see your selection in either of two different ways, and zoom to 100 percent or more so you can see exactly how you're changing the image.

3. **When you like what you've done, click OK.**

   If you decide not to refine your edges, then click Cancel. To start over, Alt+click the Cancel button to turn it into a Reset button. If you play with the sliders and then decide you want to put them back where you started, click Default.

You get three sliders in Refine Edge; you may need to use only one, or any combination of them to improve your selection. Your choices are:

- **Smooth.** This removes the jagged edges around your selection. Set a value in pixels or use the slider (move it to the right for more smoothing, to the left for less). Be careful: You can go as high as 100 pixels, which is almost certain to be much more smoothing than you need.

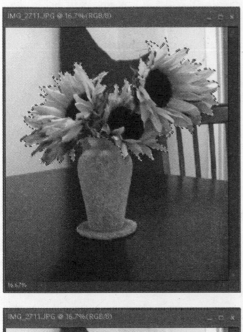

Figure 5-5:
Top: It would be a nuisance to select these sunflowers because of the many pointy-edged petals. A click and a couple of short drags, though, with the Quick Selection tool produced this selection. Notice how well the tool found the edges of the petals.

Bottom: It took only a tiny downward movement of the mouse to tell Elements to select the vase as well. The whole selection took less than 5 seconds to complete.

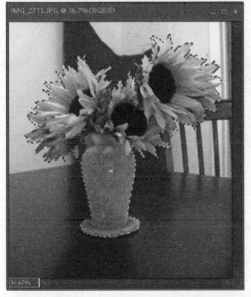

- **Feather.** Feathering is explained on page 135.

- **Contract/Expand.** You can use this to adjust the size of your selection. Move the slider to the left to contract the selection, or to the right to expand it outward.

It's easy to refine *too* much, so go in small increments and keep checking your selection. Adobe makes it easy to monitor things by giving you a choice of views.

The buttons above the Description area of the dialog box give you two different ways to see your selection:

- **Standard** shows the regular marching ants around your selection.

- **Custom Overlay** shows the red mask overlay you'd get when using the Selection brush in Mask mode (see page 130). The red area is not part of your selection. Using this view is a good way to check for holes and jagged edges.

> **TIP** Double-click the Custom overlay button and you can change the color and opacity of the overlay. You can hide the selection altogether by pressing X. Press X again to bring back the mask or the marching ants, and press F to toggle between Standard and Overlay views.

You also get icons for the Zoom (page 88) and Hand (page 89) tools, so you can adjust the view to see more or different details.

The Quick Selection tool doesn't work every time for every selection, but it's a wonderful tool that's worth grabbing first for any irregular selection. You can use the Selection brush or one of the other selection tools to clean up afterward, if needed.

The Selection Brush

The Selection brush is one of the greatest tools in Elements. Making complex selections and cleaning up selections are really, really easy with the Selection brush. You can use it on its own or as a complement to the Quick Selection tool, described in the previous section. The Quick Selection tool is awesome, but sometimes it just can't stop your selection exactly where you want. The Selection brush gives you total control because it only selects the area you cover with your brush stroke.

With the Selection brush, you simply paint over what you want to select by dragging over that area. You can let go, and each time you drag again, Elements automatically adds to your selection. There's no need to change modes in the Options bar or hold down the Shift key the way you do with the other selection tools.

Not only that, but the Selection brush also has a Mask mode, in which Elements highlights what *isn't* part of your selection. Mask mode is great for finding tiny spots you may have missed and for checking the accuracy of your selection outline. In Mask mode, anything you paint over gets *masked* out; in other words, it's protected from being selected.

Masking is a little confusing at first, but you'll soon see what a useful tool it is. Figure 5-6 shows the same selection made with and without Mask mode.

The Selection brush is pretty simple to use:

1. **Click the Selection brush in the Toolbox or press A.**

   The Selection brush is located in the Toolbox along with the Quick Selection tool. The Selection brush is the brush that looks like it's painting—the brush points down.

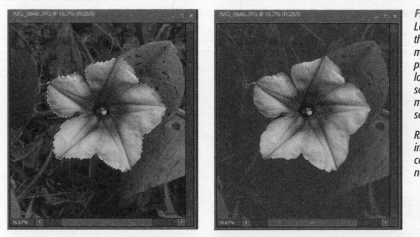

Figure 5-6:
Left: A selection made with the brush in Selection mode—dragged across the purple and white flower. It looks like a completed selection that you can make using any of the selection tools.

Right: The same selection in Mask mode. The red covers everything that's not part of your selection.

2. **In the Options bar, choose either Selection mode or Mask mode and the brush size you want.**

   Your Options bar choices are explained in the list below.

3. **Drag over the area you want.**

   If you're in Selection mode, the area you drag over becomes part of your selection. If you're in Mask mode, the area you drag over is excluded from becoming part of your selection.

The Selection brush gives you several choices in the Options bar:

- **Brush.** You can use many different brushes depending on whether you want a hard- or soft-edged selection. If you want a different brush, just choose it from the menu here. (For more about brushes, see page 327.)

- **Size.** To change the brush size, type a size in the box, or click the arrow and then use the slider. Or just press the close bracket key (]) to increase the size (keep tapping it until you get the size you want). The open bracket key ([) decreases the size of your brush. You can also just put your cursor on the word Size and scrub to the left or right to make the brush smaller or larger. (Don't know how to scrub? For more on this nifty Elements feature, see page 330.)

   TIP   The bracket key shortcut works with any brush, not just the Selection brush.

- **Mode.** This option is where you tell Elements whether you're creating a selection (Selection) or excluding an area from being part of a selection (Mask).

- **Hardness.** This option controls the sharpness of the edge of your brush, which affects your selection. See Figure 5-7.

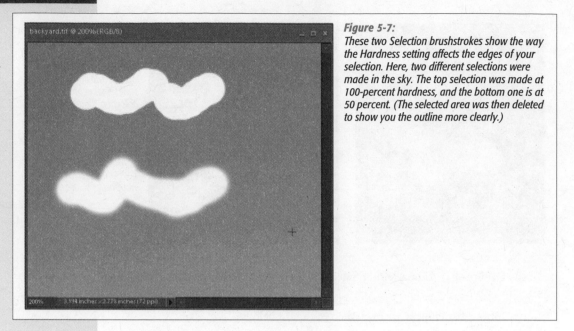

Figure 5-7:
These two Selection brushstrokes show the way the Hardness setting affects the edges of your selection. Here, two different selections were made in the sky. The top selection was made at 100-percent hardness, and the bottom one is at 50 percent. (The selected area was then deleted to show you the outline more clearly.)

Switching between Selection and Mask mode is a good way to see how well you've done when you finish making your selection. In Mask mode, the parts of your image that are *not* part of your selection have a red film over them, so that you can clearly see the selected area.

> **TIP**   You don't have to live with the red mask color. To change the mask's color, click the Overlay Color box in the Options bar while the Selection brush is active and in Mask mode. Use the Color Picker (page 209) to choose a color you prefer. You can also use the Overlay Opacity setting to adjust how well your image shows through the mask.

You can temporarily make the Selection brush do the opposite of what it's been doing by holding down Alt while you drag. This can save a lot of time in a tricky selection, since you don't have to keep jumping up to the Options bar to change what's happening, and you can keep the view (either your selection or the mask) the same. For example, if you're in Selection mode and you've selected too large an area, Alt+drag over the excess to remove it. If you're masking out an area, Alt+drag to add an area to the selection. This may sound confusing, but some things are easier to learn just by doing them.

> **TIP**   The Selection brush is great for fine-tuning selections made with the other selection tools. Quickly switching to the Selection brush in Mask mode is a great way to check for spots you may have missed—the red makes it really easy to spot them.

The Magic Wand

The Magic Wand is a slightly temperamental—and occasionally highly effective—tool for selecting an irregularly shaped, but similarly colored, area of an image. If you have a big area of a particular color, the Magic Wand can find its edges in one click. It's not actually all that magical: All it does is search for pixels with similar color values. But if it works for you, you may decide it should keep the "magic" in its name because it's a great timesaver when it cooperates, as Figure 5-8 shows.

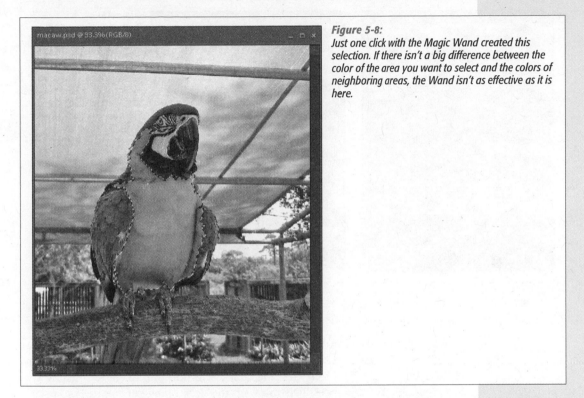

Figure 5-8:
Just one click with the Magic Wand created this selection. If there isn't a big difference between the color of the area you want to select and the colors of neighboring areas, the Wand isn't as effective as it is here.

Using the Magic Wand is pretty straightforward. You just click anywhere in the area you want to select. Depending on your *tolerance* setting (explained in the following bullet list), you may nail the selection at once, or it may take several clicks to get everything. If you need to click more than once, remember to hold down Shift so that each click adds to your selection.

The Magic Wand does its best job when you offer it a good solid block of color that's clearly defined and doesn't have a lot of different shades in it. But it's frustrating when you try to select colors that have any shading or tonal gradations. You have to click and click and click. Elements gives you two special Options bar settings that you can adjust to help the Wand do a better job:

• **Tolerance** adjusts the number of different shades that the tool selects at once. A higher tolerance includes more shades (resulting in a larger selection area), while a lower tolerance gets you fewer shades (and a more precise selection area). If you set the tolerance too high, you'll probably select a lot more of your picture than you want.

- **Contiguous** makes the Magic Wand select only color areas that actually touch each other. It's on by default, but sometimes you can save a lot of time by turning it off; Figure 5-9 explains all.

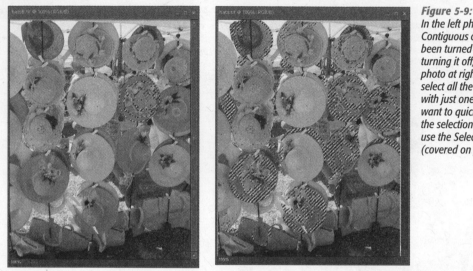

Figure 5-9:
In the left photo, the Contiguous checkbox has been turned on. By turning it off, as in the photo at right, you can select all the orange hats with just one click. If you want to quickly clean up the selection afterward, use the Selection brush (covered on page 130).

You also get access to the new Refine Edge command for fixing up the edges of your selection, as explained on page 128.

The big disadvantage to the Magic Wand is that it tends to leave you with unselected contrasting areas around the edge of your selection that are a bit of a pain to clean up. You may want to try out the Quick Selection tool (page 126) before trying the Magic Wand, especially if you want to select a range of colors. If you put a Magic Wand selection on its own layer (see Chapter 6 to understand how layers work), you can use Refine Edge (page 128) or the Defringe command (page 143) to help clean up the edges.

The Lasso Tools

The Magic Wand is pretty good, but it works well only when your image has clearly defined areas of color. A lot of the time, you'll want to select something from a cluttered background that the Magic Wand just can't cope with. Sometimes you may think the easiest way would be if you could just draw around the object you want to select.

Enter the Lasso tool. There are actually three Lasso tools: the Lasso tool, the Polygonal Lasso tool, and the Magnetic Lasso tool. Each tool lets you select an object by tracing around it.

Feathering and Anti-Aliasing

If you're old enough to remember what supermarket tabloid covers looked like before there was Photoshop, you probably had a good laugh at the obviously faked photos. Anyone could see where the art department had physically glued a piece cut from one photo onto another picture.

Nowadays, of course, the pictures of Brad and Angelina's vampire baby from Mars are *much* more believable looking. That's because with Photoshop (and Elements) you can add *anti-aliasing* and *feathering* whenever you're making selections.

Anti-aliasing is a way of smoothing the edges of a digital image so that it's not jagged-looking. When you make selections, the Lasso tools and the Magic Wand let you decide whether to use anti-aliasing. It's best to leave anti-aliasing on unless you have a reason to want a really hard-looking edge on your selection.

Feathering blurs the edges of a selection. When you make a selection that you plan to move to a different photo, a tiny feather can do a lot to make it look like it's always been part of the new photo. Some selection tools, like the Marquee tools, let you set a feather value before using them. Generally a 1- or 2-pixel feather gives your selection a more natural-looking edge without visible blurring.

If you apply a feather value that's too high for the size of your selection, you see a warning that reads "No pixels are more than 50% selected". Reduce the feather number to placate it.

A larger feather gives a soft edge to your photos, as you can see in Figure 5-10.

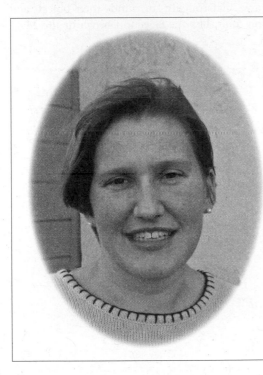

Figure 5-10:
Old-fashioned vignettes like this one are a classic example of where you'd want a fairly large feather. In this figure, the feather is 15 pixels wide. The higher the feather value, the softer the edge effect is.

You activate the Lasso tools by clicking their icon in the Toolbox (it's just below the Marquee tool) or by pressing L, and then selecting the particular variation you want in the Toolbox pop-out menu. You then drag around the outline of your object to make your selection. The following sections cover each Lasso tool. All the Lasso tools let you apply feathering and anti-aliasing as you make your selection (see the box on page 135), and the basic Lasso and the Polygonal Lasso give you access to Refine Edge (page 128) right in their Options bar settings.

The basic Lasso tool

The theory behind the basic Lasso tool is very simple. Click the tool, and your cursor changes to the lasso shape shown in Figure 5-11. Just click in your photo, and then drag around the outline of what you want to select. When the end of your selection gets back around to join up with the beginning, you've got a selection.

In practice, it's not always so easy to make an accurate selection with the Lasso, especially if you're using a mouse. A graphics tablet is a big advantage when using this tool, since tablets let you draw with a pen-shaped pointer. (There's more about graphics tablets on page 493.) But even if you don't happen to have a graphics tablet lying around, you can make all the tools work just fine with your mouse once you get used to their quirks.

It helps to zoom the view way in and go very slowly when using the Lasso. (See page 86 for more information on changing your view.) Many people use the regular Lasso tool to quickly select an area that roughly surrounds their object, and then go back with the other selection tools, like the Selection brush or the Magnetic Lasso, to clean things up.

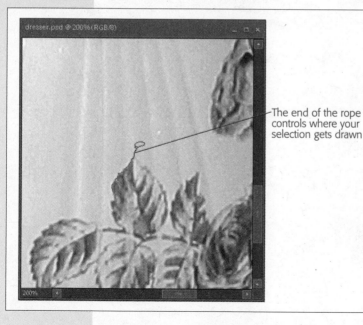

The end of the rope controls where your selection gets drawn

Figure 5-11:
The end of the rope, and not the lasso loop, is the selection-drawing point of the basic Lasso tool. If the cursor's shape bothers you, change it to crosshairs by pressing the Caps Lock key anytime as you select.

TIP   If you want to save time when you need to draw a straight line for part of your border, hold down Alt and click the points where you want your straight line to start and end. So if you're selecting an arched Palladian window, for instance, once you get around the curve at the top of the window and reach the straight side, press Alt and click at the bottom of the side to get the straight part of the side all in one go.

Once you've created a selection, you can use the new Refine Edge command from the Options bar to adjust and feather the edges (see page 135). Press Escape or Ctrl+D to get rid of your selection if you decide you don't want it anymore.

The Magnetic Lasso

The Magnetic Lasso is a very handy tool, especially if you were the kind of kid who never could color inside the lines or cut paper chains out neatly. The Magnetic Lasso snaps to the outline of any clearly defined object you're trying to select, so you don't have to follow the edge exactly.

As you might guess, the Magnetic Lasso does its best work on objects with clearly defined edges. You won't get much out of it if your subject is a furry animal, for instance. The Magnetic Lasso also likes a good strong contrast between the object and the background. (You can change the cursor shape with the Caps Lock key, just as with the basic Lasso.)

Click to start a selection. Then move your cursor around the perimeter of what you want to select; click again back where you began to finish your selection. You can also Ctrl+click at any point, and the Magnetic Lasso will immediately close up whatever area you've surrounded. You can also adjust how many points the Magnetic Lasso puts down and how sensitive it is to the edge you're tracing, as shown in Figure 5-12.

In addition to Feathering and Anti-aliasing (explained in the box on page 135), the Magnetic Lasso comes with four additional settings in the Options bar:

- **Width** tells the Magnetic Lasso how far away to look when it's trying to find the edge. The value is always in pixels, and you can set it as high as 256.

- **Edge Contrast** controls how sharp a difference the Magnetic Lasso should look for between the outline and the background. A higher number looks for sharper contrasts, and a lower number looks for softer ones.

- **Frequency** controls how fast Elements puts down the fastening points you see in Figure 5-12.

- **Use Tablet Pressure to Change Pen Width**—the little button with a pen at the right of the Options bar—only works if you have a graphics tablet. When you turn this setting on, how hard you press controls how Elements searches for the edge of objects you're trying to select. When you bear down harder, it's more precise. When you press more lightly, you can be a bit sloppier and Elements will still find the edge.

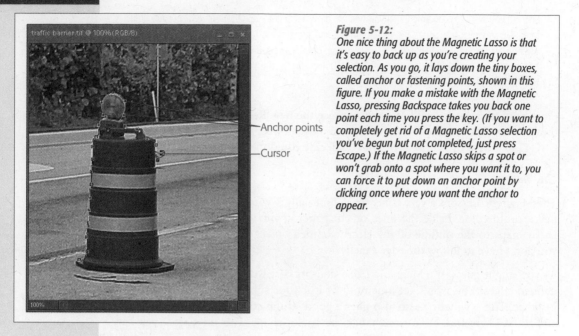

traffic barrier.tif @ 100%(RGB/8)

—Anchor points

—Cursor

100%

Figure 5-12:
*One nice thing about the Magnetic Lasso is that
it's easy to back up as you're creating your
selection. As you go, it lays down the tiny boxes,
called anchor or fastening points, shown in this
figure. If you make a mistake with the Magnetic
Lasso, pressing Backspace takes you back one
point each time you press the key. (If you want to
completely get rid of a Magnetic Lasso selection
you've begun but not completed, just press
Escape.) If the Magnetic Lasso skips a spot or
won't grab onto a spot where you want it to, you
can force it to put down an anchor point by
clicking once where you want the anchor to
appear.*

Many people live full and satisfying lives paying no attention whatsoever to these settings, so don't feel like you have to fuss with them all the time. You can usually ignore them unless the Magnetic Lasso misbehaves.

> **TIP** You get better results with the Magnetic Lasso if you go more slowly than if you speed around the object. Like most people, the Magnetic Lasso does better work if you give it time to be sure where it's going.

The Polygonal Lasso

At first, this may seem like a totally stupid tool. It works something like the Magnetic Lasso in that it puts down anchor points, but it creates only perfectly straight segments. So you may think, "Well that's great if I want to select a Stop sign, but otherwise, what's the point?"

Actually, if you're one of those people who just plain *can't* draw, and you even have a hard time following the edge of an object that's already on the screen, this is the tool for you. The trick is to use very short distances between clicks. Figure 5-13 shows the Polygonal Lasso in action.

The big advantage of using the Polygonal Lasso over the Magnetic Lasso is that it's much easier to keep it from getting into a snarl. Your only options for this tool are Feathering and Anti-aliasing (which are explained in the box on page 135) and Refine Edge (page 128).

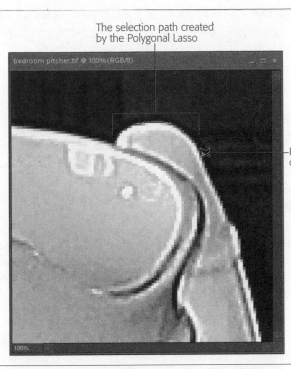

The selection path created
by the Polygonal Lasso

bedroom pitcher.tif @ 100% (RGB/8)

Polygonal Lasso
cursor

100%

Figure 5-13:
If you have limited dexterity, the Polygonal Lasso tool and a lot of clicks eventually get you a nice accurate selection. You need to zoom way, way in to use this tool to select an object that doesn't have totally straight sides. Here, the Polygonal Lasso easily made it around the curve of the handle by clicking to make extremely short segments.

Removing Objects from an Image's Background

Ever feel the urge to pluck an object out of your photo's background? For example, maybe you want to take an amazing shot you got of the moon and stick it in another photo. The traditional procedure is to make your selection, invert it (page 144), and then delete the rest of the image. But Elements streamlines this process with yet another "magic" tool—the Magic Extractor. It works much like the Quick Selection tool in that you just give Elements a few hints and let the program do the rest. When the Magic Extractor's done, your selection is isolated in all its lonely glory, surrounded by transparency and ready for use on its own. Like the Quick Selection tool, this tool does a surprisingly good job—most of the time. To conduct your own experiments, download the practice photo (*coralbean.jpg*) from the Missing CD page at *www.missingmanuals.com*.

> **TIP** You may find it faster to use the Quick Selection tool (page 126), followed by inverting and deleting the background area as explained on page 144. If that doesn't work, then it's time to try the Magic Extractor.

The Magic Extractor has an elaborate dialog box with tools not found elsewhere in Elements. To see it, go to Image → Magic Extractor (see Figure 5-14). You see a full-screen dialog box, including a Toolbox on the left side, instructions across the top, a preview of your image, and a set of controls at right. It looks complicated, but it's really just a bunch of easy-to-use options for tweaking what you've got before Elements extracts your object. Here's how to use this timesaving tool:

1. **Go to Image → Magic Extractor, or press Alt+Shift+Ctrl+V.**

   Your image appears in the preview area of the Magic Extractor window (Figure 5-14).

   NOTE   The Magic Extractor sometimes has problems with very large files. If you need to extract an object from a hefty image, you may get better results if you crop away any large, unnecessary areas first. See page 79 for more about cropping.

2. **If necessary, change the marker colors.**

   On the right side of the window, you see two color squares. Usually, you'll see red for the Foreground brush (the one you use to mark what to keep) and blue for the Background brush (the one that tells Elements what to discard from your image). To make the brush tools easier to see, you can click the squares for the Color Picker (page 209), and choose new colors.

3. **Use the Foreground brush to tell Elements what you want to extract.**

   Make some marks on the object you want to include. You can draw lines, as shown in Figure 5-14, but making dots on your object may work just as well. With a little practice, you'll soon get the hang of knowing what kind of marks you need for each object.

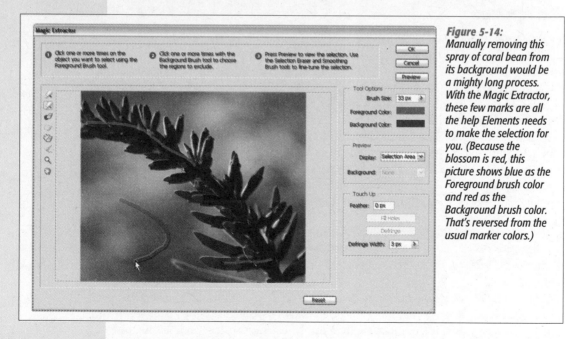

Figure 5-14:
Manually removing this spray of coral bean from its background would be a mighty long process. With the Magic Extractor, these few marks are all the help Elements needs to make the selection for you. (Because the blossom is red, this picture shows blue as the Foreground brush color and red as the Background brush color. That's reversed from the usual marker colors.)

4. **Click the Background brush and tell Elements what to exclude.**

Similarly, make some marks in the areas you *don't* want Elements to include in your selection.

5. **Click the Preview button.**

The Preview area shows what Elements thinks you want to do. If what you see isn't even close, press Reset and start over.

6. **If necessary, use the various tools to help Elements adjust the boundaries of your selection.**

For example, if Elements left off an area you want, usually just one click with the Foreground brush is enough to tell Elements what you want to add. If there are spots missing within the selection, click the Fill Holes button. If you need to get a better view of your work, use the Zoom and Hand tools (both of which are explained in more detail starting on page 87).

7. **Fine-tune the edges of your selection, if you wish.**

Add a feather (page 135), defringe (page 143), or smooth the edges of the selection with the Smoothing brush.

8. **When you like what you see, click OK.**

If you want to give up and try another method, click the Cancel button instead. Figure 5-15 shows what the Magic Extractor can do.

NOTE Once you understand layers (Chapter 6), you'll know that the Magic Extractor works only on the active layer of your photo. If you want to extract an object without wrecking the rest of your photo, make a duplicate layer (page 159) and work on that new layer.

The Magic Extractor gives you lots of ways to make sure Elements makes a perfect selection. The Toolbox contains a whole set of special tools just for the Extractor, as you can see in Figure 5-16. Each has its own keyboard shortcut to make it easy to switch tools while you work (given in parentheses after the tool's name in the list below). From top to bottom, you get:

- **Foreground brush** *(Keyboard shortcut: B)*. Use this brush to mark what you want to include in your extracted object. You can change the brush color by choosing a different foreground color in the square on the window's right side.

- **Background brush** *(P)*. This brush tells Elements what you want to cut away from your selection. Like the Foreground brush, this brush has a color square on the window's right side where you can choose a different marker color.

- **Point Eraser tool** *(E)*. If you mark something by mistake with the Foreground or Background brush, use this tool to erase the marks.

- **Add to Selection tool** *(A)*. For adding to the selection you already have.

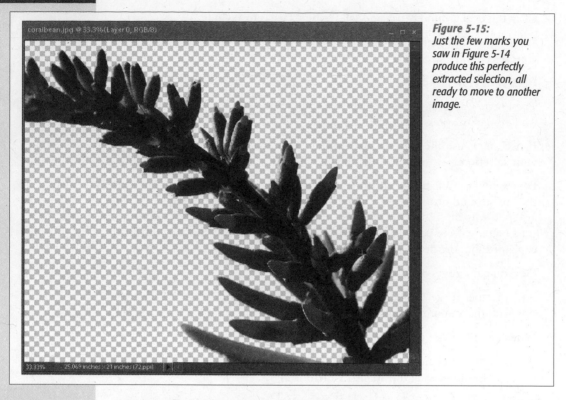

coralbean.jpg @ 33.3%(Layer 0, RGB/8)

33.33%   25.069 inches x 21 inches (72 ppi)

Figure 5-15:
*Just the few marks you
saw in Figure 5-14
produce this perfectly
extracted selection, all
ready to move to another
image.*

- **Remove from Selection tool** *(D)*. Whatever you paint over gets removed from your selection.

- **Smoothing brush** *(J)*. Once you've previewed your selection, you can use this brush to even out any ragged edges. Try the Touch Up commands from the right side of the window first because you may not need this brush.

- **Zoom tool** *(Z)* **and Hand tool** *(H)*. These are the same trusty standbys you use to adjust your view elsewhere in Elements. See page 87 for more about using the Zoom tool and page 88 for the Hand tool.

> **TIP**   Some of the fine-tuning tools, like the Smoothing brush, work much better if you zoom in pretty close before using them.

So you can see exactly what you're doing, Elements gives you several ways to adjust the tools and also your view of the image. These are found on the right side of the window:

- **Tool Options.** You can use the color squares to choose different colors for the Foreground and Background brushes by clicking these squares and using the Color Picker (page 209). You can also adjust the brush size, but that's hardly ever necessary, unless the brush is too big for the area you want to select. ·

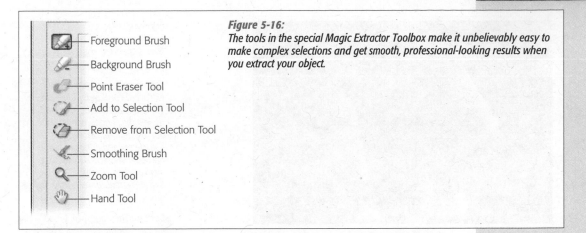

Foreground Brush
Background Brush
Point Eraser Tool
Add to Selection Tool
Remove from Selection Tool
Smoothing Brush
Zoom Tool
Hand Tool

Figure 5-16:
The tools in the special Magic Extractor Toolbox make it unbelievably easy to make complex selections and get smooth, professional-looking results when you extract your object.

- **Preview.** Choose whether to see just the selected area or your entire image. You can also choose what kind of background you want to see your selection against to get a clearer view. For example, you can choose None (the standard transparency grid), or a black, gray, or white matte, which puts a temporary solid background to make it easier to check the edges of your selection. Mask is just like working with the Selection brush in Mask mode (page 130). You can paint more of a mask or remove the mask to reveal a larger selection. (Remember that what's masked *isn't* selected.)

Once you've previewed your selection, you also get some very helpful options for making sure your selection is absolutely perfect. Most of these options are on the right side of the dialog box, under Touch Up.

- **Feather.** Enter the amount, in pixels, to feather the edge of your selection. (The box on page 135 explains feathering.)

- **Fill Holes.** If Elements left some gaps in your selection, you may be able to fill them by clicking this button. This tool works only for holes that are completely surrounded by selected material, though. If the edges of your selection have bites out of them, use the Smoothing brush instead, or give the area an extra click with the Foreground brush.

- **Defringe.** If your selection has a rim of contrasting pixels around it, this command can usually eliminate them. Figure 5-17 shows what a difference defringing can make. You can choose a different number of pixels for Elements to consider when defringing, but the standard setting is usually fine. Actually, recent versions of Elements are pretty good about making clean selections, so you probably won't need this button very often.

TIP If the edges of your selection are ragged but not contrasting, or if defringing alone doesn't clean things up enough, try the Smoothing brush (page 142). Just run it along the edge of your selection to polish it until it's smooth.

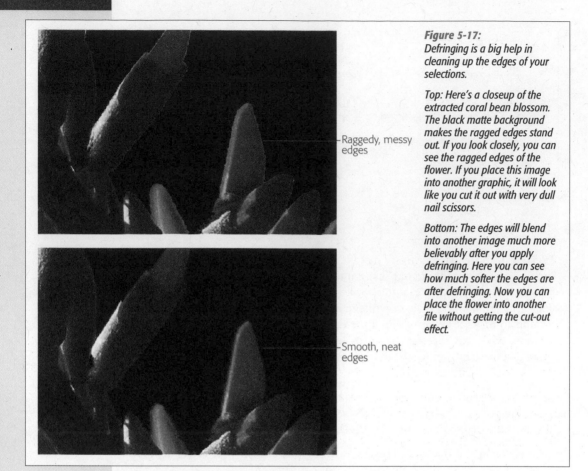

Figure 5-17:
Defringing is a big help in cleaning up the edges of your selections.

Top: Here's a closeup of the extracted coral bean blossom. The black matte background makes the ragged edges stand out. If you look closely, you can see the ragged edges of the flower. If you place this image into another graphic, it will look like you cut it out with very dull nail scissors.

Bottom: The edges will blend into another image much more believably after you apply defringing. Here you can see how much softer the edges are after defringing. Now you can place the flower into another file without getting the cut-out effect.

Raggedy, messy edges

Smooth, neat edges

Extracting objects used to be a very time-consuming process, often involving expensive third-party plug-ins to make the job easier. But now the Magic Extractor is all you need in most situations.

Changing and Moving Selections

Now that you know all about making selections, it's time to learn some of the finer points about using and manipulating them. Elements gives you several handy options for changing the areas you've selected and for actually moving images around once they're selected. You can even save a tough selection so you don't have to do *that* again.

Inverting a Selection

One thing you often want to do with a selection is *invert* it. That means telling Elements, "Hey, you know the area I've selected? Well, I want you to select everything *except* that area."

Why would you want to do that? Well, sometimes it's easier to select what you *don't* want. For example, suppose you have an object with a complicated outline, like the building shown in Figure 5-18. Say you want to use just the building in a scrapbook of your trip to Europe. It's going to be difficult to select. But the sky is just one big block of color. It's a lot faster to select the sky with the Magic Wand than to try to get an accurate selection of the building itself.

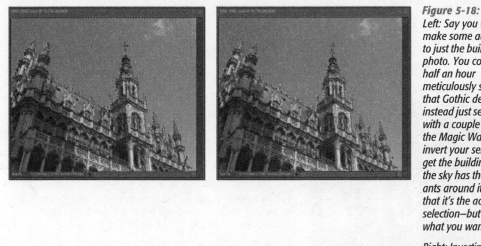

Figure 5-18:
Left: Say you want to make some adjustments to just the building in this photo. You could spend half an hour meticulously selecting all that Gothic detail, or instead just select the sky with a couple of clicks of the Magic Wand and invert your selection to get the building. Here, the sky has the marching ants around it to show that it's the active selection—but that's not what you want.

Right: Inverting the selection (Select → Inverse) gives you the ants around the buildings without the trouble of tracing over all the elaborate lacy details of the roofline.

To invert a selection:

1. **Make a selection.**

   Usually, you first select what you *don't* want if you're planning to invert your selection. You can select with any tool that suits your fancy.

2. **Go to Select → Inverse, or press Shift+Ctrl+I.**

   Now the part of your image that you *didn't* select is selected.

Making a Selection Larger or Smaller

What if you want to tweak the size of your selection? Sometimes you may want to move the outline of a selection outward a few pixels to expand it. Figuring out how to do so confuses people because Elements offers two similar-sounding ways to do it: Grow and Expand. They sound like they should do the same thing, but there's a slight but important difference between them.

- **Grow** (Select → Grow) moves your selection outward to include more similar contiguous colors, no matter what shape your original selection was. Grow doesn't care about shape; it just finds more matching contiguous pixels.

- **Expand** (Select → Modify → Expand) preserves the shape of your selection and just increases the size of it by the number of pixels you specify.

- **Similar** (Select → Similar) does the same thing as Grow but looks at all pixels, not just the adjacent ones.

- **Contract** (Select → Modify → Contract) shrinks the size of a selection.

So what's the big difference between Expand and Grow? Look at Figure 5-19 to see how differently they behave.

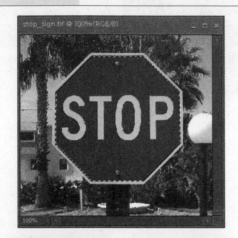

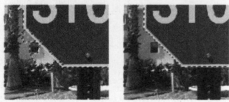

Figure 5-19:

Top: In the original selection, everything in the Stop sign has been selected except the small white border on the outside of the sign.

Bottom left: If you use Grow to enlarge the selection, you also get parts of the building that are similar in tone. As a result, your selection isn't shaped like a Stop sign anymore.

Bottom right: But if you use Expand instead, the selection still has the exact shape of the sign, only now the edges of the selection move outward to include the sign's white border area.

Moving Selected Areas

Often you make selections because you want to move objects around—like putting that dreamboat who wouldn't give you the time of day next to you in your senior year class photo. You can move a selection in several ways.

Here's the simplest, tool-free way to move something from one image to another:

1. **Select it.**

   Make sure you've selected everything you want. It's really annoying when you paste a selection from one image to another and find you missed a spot.

2. **Press Ctrl+C to copy it.**

   Or you could use Ctrl+X if you want to cut it out of your original. Just remember that Elements leaves a hole if you do it that way.

3. **If you want to dump the selection into its very own document, choose File → New → "Image from Clipboard".**

   Doing so creates a new document with just your selection in it. If you want to place the selection into an existing photo, follow the instructions in the next step.

4. **If you want to add the selection to another photo, then just use Ctrl+V to paste it into another image in Elements.**

   Once your selection is where you want it, you can use the Move tool (page 148) to position it, rotate it, or scale it to fit the rest of the photo. You can even paste your selection into a document in *another* program. Just be sure you've turned on Export Clipboard in Edit → Preferences → General.

   TIP   If you copy and paste a selection, and you see it's got partially transparent areas in it, back up and go over your selection again with the Selection brush using a hard brush. Then copy and paste again.

POWER USERS' CLINIC

Smoothing and Bordering

You'll probably use Refine Edge most of the time, but Adobe still includes some alternative ways to tweak the edges of your selections.

- **Smoothing** (Select → Modify → Smooth) is a sometimes-dependable way to clean up ragged spots in a color-based selection (like you'd make with the Magic Wand, for instance). You enter a pixel value, and Elements evens out your selection based on the number you entered, by searching for similarly colored pixels.

  For example, if you enter 5 pixels, Elements looks at a 5-pixel radius around each pixel in your selection. In areas where most of the pixels are already selected, it adds in the others. Where most pixels aren't selected, it deselects the ones that are selected to get rid of the jagged edges and holes in the selection.

This is handy, but smoothing is sometimes hard to control, and it doesn't affect only the edge of your selection. Usually it's easier to clean up your selection by hand with the Selection brush than to use Smoothing.

- **Bordering** (Select → Modify → Border) adds an anti-aliased, transparent border to your selection. You might say it selects the selection's outline. You could use it when your selection's edges are too hard and you want to soften them, although these days you'd probably be better off using Refine Edge (page 128). Choose a border size and click OK. Only the border is selected, so you can also apply a slight Gaussian blur (see page 374) to soften that part of the photo more if you like.

The Move tool

You can also move things around *within* your photo by using the Move tool, which lets you cut or copy selected areas. Figure 5-20 shows how to use the Move tool to conceal distracting details in photos.

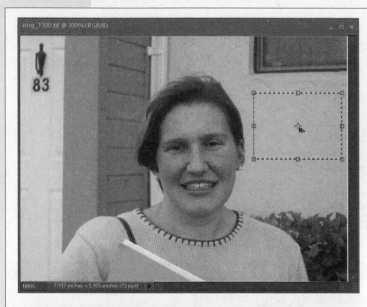

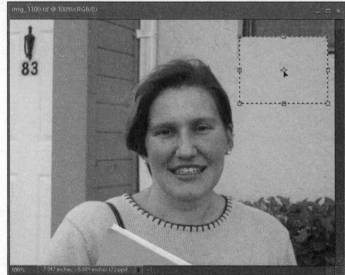

Figure 5-20:
Top: Here's the original version of the photo used for the feathered vignette on page 135. Let's say you wanted to get rid of the window in the upper-right corner of the top photo. By copying and moving a piece of the wall, you can cover up the window and create a simpler background to put the focus on the woman rather than the building. You select the area prior to moving it.

Bottom: Hold down the Alt key while using the Move tool to copy a selected area. The piece of wall slides into its new position as a window hider. (If you use the Move tool without holding down the Alt key, Elements cuts away the selection, leaving a hole in your photo.)

The Move tool lives at the very top of the Full Edit Toolbox. To use it:

1. **Make a selection.**

   Make sure your selection doesn't have anything in it that you don't want to copy.

2. **Switch to the Move tool.**

   Click the Move tool or press V. Your selection stays active but is now surrounded by a rectangle with box-shaped handles on the corners.

3. **Move the selection and press Enter when you're satisfied with its position.**

   As long as your selection is active, you can work on your photo in other ways and then come back and reactivate the Move tool. If you're worried about losing a complex selection, save it as described in the next section. If you're not happy with what you've done, just press Ctrl+Z (as many times as needed) to back up, and you can start over again.

You can move a selection in several different ways:

- **Move it.** If you just move a selection by dragging it, you leave a hole in the background where the selection was. The Move tool *truly* moves your selection. So unless you have something under it that you want to show through, that's probably not what you want to do.

- **Copy it and move the copy.** If you press the Alt key as you're moving, you'll copy your selection, so your original remains where it was. But now you'll have a duplicate to move around and play with.

- **Resize it.** You can drag the Move tool's handles to resize or distort your copy, which is great when you need to change the size of your selection. The Move tool lets you do the same things you can do with Free Transform (see page 322).

- **Rotate it.** The Move tool lets you rotate your selection the same way you can rotate a picture using Free Rotate (see page 78). Just grab a corner and turn it.

TIP   You can save a trip to the Toolbox and move selections without activating the Move tool. To move a selection without copying it, just place your cursor in the selection, hold down Ctrl, and move the selection. To move a copy of a selection, follow the same procedure but hold down the Alt key as well. You can drag the copy without damaging the original. To move multiple copies, just let go, then press Ctrl+Alt again and drag once more.

The Move tool is also a great way to manage and move objects that you've put on their own layers (Chapter 6). Page 168 explains how to use the Move tool to arrange layered objects.

Saving Selections

You can tell Elements to remember the outline of your selection so that you can reuse it again later on. This is a wonderful timesaver for particularly intricate selections and easy to do, too.

NOTE Elements' saved selections are the equivalent of Photoshop's *alpha channels*. Keep that in mind if you decide to try tutorials written for the full-featured Photoshop. Incidentally, alpha channels saved in files in Photoshop show up in Elements as saved selections, and vice versa.

To save a selection:

1. **Make your selection.**

2. **Choose Select → Save Selection, name your selection, and save it.**

   When you want to use the selection again, go to Select → Load Selection, and there it is, waiting for you.

   TIP When you save a feathered (page 135) selection, use the Refine Edge command (page 128) if you change your mind later on about how much feather you want. You can also save a hard-edged selection, load it, and then go to Select → Feather to add a feather if you need one. That way you can change the amount each time you use the selection, as long as you remember not to save the change to the selection.

Making changes to a saved selection

It's probably just as easy to start your selection over if you need to tweak a saved selection, but it is possible to make changes if you want. This can save you some time if your original selection was really tricky to create.

Say you've got a full-length photo of somebody, and you've created and saved a selection of the person's face (called, naturally enough, "Face"). Now, imagine that after applying a filter to the selection, you decide it would look silly to change only the face and not the person's hands, too.

So you want to add the hands to your saved selection. There are a couple of ways to do this.

The simplest is just to load up "Face," activate your selection tool of choice, put the tool in "Add to Selection" mode, select the hands, and then save the selection again with the same name.

But how about if you've already selected the hands and you want to add *that* new selected area to the existing facial selection? Here's what you'd do:

1. **Go to Select → Save Selection.**

   Choose your saved "Face" selection. All the radio buttons in the dialog box become active.

2. **Choose "Add to Selection".**

   What you just selected is added to the original selection and saved, so now your "Face" selection also includes the hands.

CHAPTER 6

Layers: The Heart of Elements

If you've been working mostly in the Quick Fix window so far, you've probably noticed that once you close your file, the changes you've made are permanent. You can undo actions while the file's still open, but once you close it, you're stuck with what you've done.

In Elements, you can keep your changes (most kinds, anyway) and still revert to the original image if you use *layers*, a nifty system of transparent sheets that keeps each element of your image on a separate sliver that you can edit. Layers are one of the greatest image editing inventions ever. By putting each change you make on its own layer, you can constantly rearrange the composition of your image, and add or subtract changes whenever you want.

If you use layers, then you can save your file and quit Elements, come back days or weeks later, and still undo what you did or change things around some more. There's no statute of limitations for the changes you make when using layers.

Some people resist learning about layers because they fear layers are too complicated. But they're actually very easy to use once you understand how they work. And once you get started with layers, you'll realize that using Elements without them is like driving a Ferrari in first gear. This chapter gives you the information you need to get comfortable working with layers.

Understanding Layers

Imagine you've got a bare-bones drawing of a room you're thinking about redecorating. To get an idea of your different decorating options, imagine that you've also got a bunch of transparent plastic sheets, each containing an image that changes the room's look: a couch, a few different colors for the carpet, a standing lamp, and so on. Your decorating work is now pretty easy, since you can add and remove, and mix and match the transparencies with ease.

Layers in Elements work pretty much the same way. With layers, you can add and remove objects, and also make changes to the way your image looks. And you can modify or discard any changes later on.

Figure 6-1 shows an Elements file that includes layers. Each object in that flyer is on a different layer, so you can easily remove or rearrange things. (If you want to follow along with a layers-heavy file, you can download a version of this file from the Missing CD page at *www.missingmanuals.com*. Look for *harvestfestwin.psd*.)

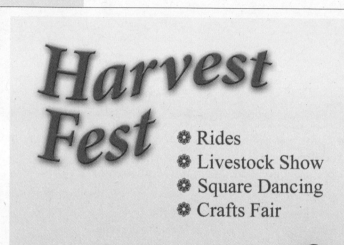

It's that time of year again! Everybody's favorite weekend for appple bobbing, corn husking, pumpkin pie eating, and general merriment is almost here. Get your crops in and come join us the last weekend in October for our annual town festival and fair. The fun starts at 8 am Saturday.

For more information and livestock show entry forms, please call 555-9876.

Saturday, October 30
County Fairgrounds
8 am till Midnight

Figure 6-1:
Every object in this flyer—the background, the scarecrow, the pumpkins, each block of text—is on its own layer, which makes changing things a snap. Want to change the background, get rid of the pumpkins, or change the phone number? With layers, you can easily do any of these things.

NOTE   It's important to understand that photos from your camera start out with just one layer. That means if you've got a photo like the one pictured in Figure 6-2, top, the individual objects— the two people, the ground they're standing on, and so on—all exist on the same layer. At least they do until you select and place a particular object on its own layer. That said, Elements does occasionally generate layers for you. For example, Elements automatically creates layers when you do certain things, like move an object from one photo to another, or use the new Smart Brush tool (page 189), which thoughtfully puts the changes it makes on their own layer.

You can also use layers for many adjustments to your photos, giving yourself the chance to tweak or eliminate those changes later on. For instance, say you used Quick Fix's Hue slider but then decided the next day you didn't like what you did—you're stuck (unless you can dig out a copy of your original). But if you'd used a Hue/Saturation Adjustment *layer* (page 176) to make the change, you could just throw out that layer and keep all your other changes intact. You can also use layers to combine parts of different photos, as shown in Figure 6-2.

Once you understand how to use layers, you'll feel much more comfortable making radical changes to an image because mistakes are much easier to fix. Not only that, but by using layers, you can easily make lots of very sophisticated changes that are otherwise very difficult and time-consuming. But the main reason to use layers is for creative freedom. Layers let you easily create lots of special effects that would be very difficult otherwise.

The Layers Palette

The Layers palette is your control center for any kind of layer-related action you want to perform, like adding, deleting, or duplicating layers. Figure 6-3 shows you the Layers palette for an image that already has lots of layers. Each layer displays its name and a little thumbnail icon previewing the layer's contents. You can adjust the size of the icon or turn it off altogether if you prefer, as shown in Figure 6-4.

TIP   It helps to keep the Layers palette readily available whenever you work with layers, not only for the information it gives you, but because you can generally manipulate layers more easily from the palette than directly in your image. There are many changes, like renaming a layer, that you can make only in the palette.

The Layers palette usually contains one layer that's *active*, meaning that any action you take, like painting, is going to happen on that layer (and that layer only). The active layer is darker so you can see which one it is.

NOTE   If you use the layer selection options described on page 167, then you can wind up with multiple active layers or none, but for general working purposes, usually you want to have only one active layer.

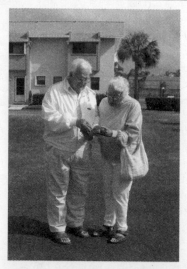

Figure 6-2:
Layers make it easy to combine elements from different photos. You may not be able to afford to send your grandparents on a real trip to Europe, but once you understand layers, you can give them a virtual vacation. When you copy part of one photo into another image, as was done here, Elements automatically places the pasted-in material on its own layer. You don't have to do anything special to create the layer—it just happens. There's more about combining elements from different photos on page 179.

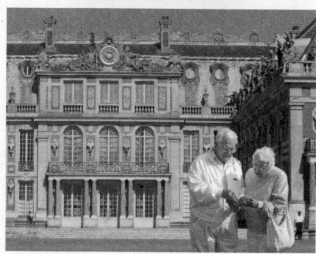

When you look at an image that contains layers, you're looking down on the stack of layers from the top, just the way you would with overlays on a drawing. The layers appear in the same order in the Layers palette—the top layer of your image is the top layer in the stack in the Layers palette. (Layer order is important because whatever is on top can obscure what's beneath it.)

Elements lets you perform lots of different maneuvers right in the Layers palette. You can make a layer's contents invisible and then visible again, change the order in which layers are stacked, link layers together, change the opacity of layers, add and delete layers—the list goes on and on. The rest of this chapter covers all these options and more.

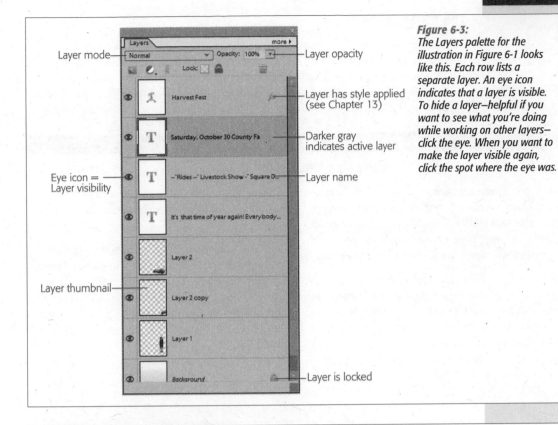

Layer mode

Layer opacity

Layer has style applied
(see Chapter 13)

Darker gray
indicates active layer

Eye icon =
Layer visibility

Layer name

Layer thumbnail

Layer is locked

Figure 6-3:
*The Layers palette for the
illustration in Figure 6-1 looks
like this. Each row lists a
separate layer. An eye icon
indicates that a layer is visible.
To hide a layer—helpful if you
want to see what you're doing
while working on other layers—
click the eye. When you want to
make the layer visible again,
click the spot where the eye was.*

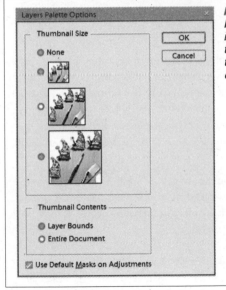

Figure 6-4:
*If you want to change the size of the thumbnail icons in the Layers palette,
in the palette's upper-right corner, click the arrows (or the More button, if
the palette is out of the bin) to open the pop-out menu. At the bottom of
the menu, choose Palette Options, and the dialog box shown here
appears. In this case, the medium size icon is selected.*

The Background

The bottom layer of any image is a special kind of layer called the *Background*. If you bring any image or photo into Elements, then the first time you open it, you see its one existing layer is called Background. (That's assuming that nobody else has already edited the file in Elements and changed things.) The name Background is only logical because whatever else you do will be on top of this layer.

A TIDY WORKSPACE

Managing the Layers Palette

The Layers palette sometimes ends up in a fairly inconvenient location at the bottom of the Palette bin. The flippy triangle to the left of its name lets you open (or close) the palette, but sometimes on small monitors, the palette contents are hidden below the bottom edge of the bin.

The Layers palette is important, so you probably want to get it out where you can see it all the time, at least while you're working with layered files. To do so, just grab the top bar of the palette near the name, and then pull it out of the bin onto your desktop. (For tips on keeping track of the Layers palette once it's out of the bin, see page 26.)

You can collapse the Layers palette once it's on the desktop, but Elements gurus usually like to keep it easily accessible.

If you have a big monitor and room to keep the Palette bin open while you work, then it's fine to leave the Layers palette in the bin if you prefer. You can drag the Layers palette up or down in the bin to put it in the most convenient position. The idea is to get that palette where you can see it all the time, and easily get to it with your mouse.

NOTE Elements has two exceptions to the first-layer-is-always-the-Background rule. First, if you create a new image by copying something from another picture, then you just have a layer called "Layer 0." Second, Background layers can't be transparent, so if you choose the Transparency option (page 167) when creating a file from scratch, then you have a Layer 0 instead of a Background layer.

As for content, the Background can be totally plain or busy, busy, busy. A Background layer doesn't mean that it literally contains the background of your photograph—your entire photo can be a Background layer. It's entirely up to you to decide what's on your Background layer, and what you place on other, newly added layers. With photographs, people often keep the photo's image on the Background layer, and then perform adjustments and embellishments (like adding type) on other layers.

You can do a lot to Background layers, but there are a few things you *can't* do: If you want to change a Background layer's blending mode (see page 164), opacity (page 167), or position in the layer stack, then you need to convert that Background into a regular layer.

TIP The Background and Magic Erasers automatically turn a Background layer into a regular layer when you click a background with them. If you have a single object on a solid background and you want transparency around the object, then one click with the Magic Eraser turns your background into a layer, eliminates a solid-colored background, and replaces it with transparency. (There's more on the Eraser tools on page 348.)

You can change a Background layer to a regular layer by double-clicking the Background layer in the Layers palette. Or, if you try to make certain kinds of changes to the background (like using the Transform commands [page 322]), then Elements prompts you to change the Background layer to a regular layer.

You can also transform a regular layer into a Background layer if you want. One reason to do this transformation is to send a layer zipping down to the bottom of the stack in a many-layered file. To do so:

1. **In the Layers palette, click the layer you want to convert to a Background layer.**

2. **Select Layer → New → "Background from Layer".**

   It may take a few seconds for Elements to finish calculating and to respond after you tell it what to do. The layer you've changed moves down to the bottom of the layer stack in the Layers palette, and automatically gets renamed "Background."

   NOTE   You can't have more than one Background layer in an image. So what do you do if you want to change a regular layer to a Background layer and you've already got a Background layer? Well, you need to change the existing background into a regular layer first. Otherwise, the command is unavailable. (If you add a background from the Content palette, it automatically replaces the contents of your current background layer.)

COMPATIBILITY

Which File Types Can Use Layers?

You can add layers to any file you can open in Elements, but not every file format lets you *save* those layers for future use.

For instance, if your camera shoots JPEGs, you can open the JPEG in Elements, and create lots of layers. But when you try to save the file, Elements presents you with the Save As dialog box instead of just saving your file. If you turn off the dialog box's option to save layers, a warning tells you that you have to save as a copy. That's because you can't have layers in a JPEG file, and Elements is reminding you that you need to save in another format to keep those layers.

You usually want to choose either Photoshop (.psd) or TIFF as your format when saving an image with layers, because they both let you keep your layers for future use. PDF files can also have layers. (On the other hand, if you don't need the layers, then just save your JPEG as a copy, close the original file, and say No when asked if you want to save changes.)

If someone using the full-featured Photoshop sends you an image that has layers, then you see them in the Layers palette when you open the file in Elements. Likewise, Photoshop can see layers you create in Elements.

If you open a Photoshop file with a layer that says "indicates a set" when you mouse over it, you have what Photoshop calls a Layer Group or *layer set* (a way to group *layers* into what are essentially folders in the layers palette), depending on the version of Photoshop that created the file. Elements doesn't understand those sets, so ask the sender to expand the layer sets and send you the file again. Alternatively, you can use Layer → Simplify to convert the set to an uneditable single layer.

Creating Layers

As you learned earlier in the chapter, your image doesn't automatically have multiple layers. Lots of newcomers to Elements expect the program to be smart enough to put each object in a photo onto its own layer. It's a lovely dream, but even Elements isn't that brainy. To experience the joy of layers, you first need to add at least one layer to your image, which is what you'll learn how to do in the next few sections.

> **TIP** It may help you to follow along through the next few sections if you get out a photo of your own or create a new file to use for practice. Or, you can download either the *harvestfestwin.psd* or *leaves.jpg* file from the Missing CD page at *www.missingmanuals.com*. (See page 43 for details on how to create a new file; if you do so, choose a white background.)

Adding a Layer

Elements gives you several different ways to add new layers. You can use any of the following methods:

- Choose Layer → New → Layer.
- Press Shift+Ctrl+N.
- In the Layers palette, click the "Create a new layer" icon (the little square shown in Figure 6-5).

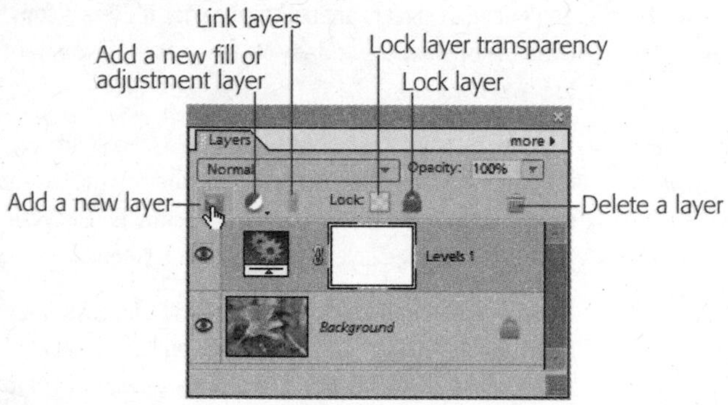

Figure 6-5:
More controls on the Layers palette. On the left side of the Layers palette, click the little "Create a new layer" icon when you want to quickly add a new layer.

When you create a new layer using any of these commands, the layer starts out empty. You don't see a change in your image until you use the layer for something (for example, painting on it). If you look at the Layers palette, then you see that any new layer you add appears just above the layer that was active when you created the new layer.

> **NOTE** The only practical limit to the number of layers your image can have is your computer's processing power. But if you find yourself regularly creating projects with upward of 100 layers, you may want to upgrade to Photoshop, which has tools that make it easier to manage large numbers of layers.

Some actions create new layers automatically. For instance, if you copy and paste an object from another photo (see page 179 for instructions) or add artwork from the Content palette, then the object automatically arrives on its own layer. And that's very handy for arranging the new item just where you want it, without disturbing the rest of your composition.

Deleting Layers

You can easily delete layers, if you decide you don't want a particular layer anymore. Figure 6-6 shows the simplest way.

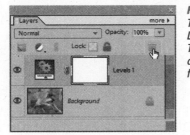

Figure 6-6:
To make a layer go away, either drag the layer to the Trash can icon on the Layers palette or, after selecting the layer, just click the "Delete layer" icon (the Trash can [where the cursor is here]). Elements responds by asking if you want to delete the active layer. Say yes, and it's history. Once you delete a layer, it's gone forever.

Elements also gives you a few other ways to delete a layer. You can:

• Select Layer → Delete Layer.

• Right-click the layer in the Layers palette, and then, from the pop-up menu, choose Delete Layer.

• On the Layers palette, click the More button (the arrows), and then, from the pop-up menu, choose Delete Layer.

Duplicating a Layer

Duplicating a layer can be very useful. Many Elements commands, like filters or color modification tools, don't work on a brand-new *empty* layer. This limitation poses a dilemma because if you apply those changes to the layer containing your main image, then you alter it in ways you can't undo later. The workaround is to create a *duplicate layer* and make your changes on that new layer. Then you can ditch the duplicate later if you change your mind, and your original layer is safely tucked away unchanged.

If all this seems annoyingly theoretical, try going to Enhance → Adjust Color → Adjust Hue/Saturation, for example, when you're working on a new blank layer, and see what happens. You see the stern dialog box shown in Figure 6-7 if you try to work on a blank layer.

> **NOTE**   Very rarely, you may still encounter the dreaded "no pixels are selected" warning. Several things can cause this, but the most common are too large a feather value on a selection (see the box on page 135) or trying to work in the empty part of a layer that contains objects surrounded by transparency.

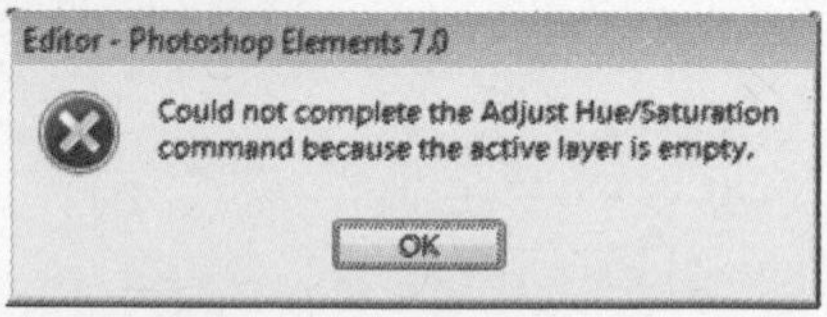

Figure 6-7:
Elements is usually pretty helpful when you try to do something that just isn't going to work, like applying a Hue/Saturation adjustment to an empty layer. The solution here is just to switch the Layers palette focus to a layer that has something in it.

Editor - Photoshop Elements 7.0

Could not complete the Adjust Hue/Saturation command because the active layer is empty.

OK

Elements gives you a few ways to duplicate an existing layer and its content. Select the layer you want to duplicate to make it the active layer, and then do one of the following:

- Press Ctrl+J.

- Choose Layer → Duplicate Layer.

- In the Layers palette, drag the layer you want to copy to the "Create a new layer" icon.

- In the Layers palette, right-click the Layer, and then, from the pop-up menu, choose Duplicate Layer.

- Click the More button (the double arrows to the right of the Layers palette's name), and then choose Duplicate Layer.

Creating a new layer using any of these methods copies the entire contents of the active layer into the new layer. You can then mess with the duplicate as much as you want without damaging the original layer.

GEM IN THE ROUGH

Naming Layers

You might have noticed that Elements isn't terribly creative when it comes to naming your layers. You get Layer 1, Layer 2, and so on. Fortunately, you don't have to live with those titles. You can quite easily rename your layers in Elements.

Maybe renaming layers sounds like a job for people with too much time on their hands, but if you get started on a project that winds up with many layers, you may find that you can pick out the layers you want more quickly if you give them descriptive names.

Incidentally, you can't rename a Background layer. You have to change it to a regular layer first. Also, Elements

helps you out with Text layers (see page 399) by naming them using the first few words of the text they contain. To rename a layer:

1. Double-click its name in the Layers palette.

   The name becomes an active text box.

2. Type in the new name.

   You don't even need to highlight the text—Elements does that for you automatically.

As with any other change, you have to save your image afterward if you want to keep the name.

Copying and Cutting from Layers

You can also make a new layer that consists of only a *piece* of an existing layer. (Helpful for things like applying a Layer style to one object from the layer, for instance.) But first you need to decide whether you want to *copy* your selection or *cut* it out and place it on the new layer.

What's the difference? It's pretty much the same as copying versus cutting in your word processing program. When you make a "New Layer via Copy", the area you select appears in the new layer while remaining in place in the old layer, too. On the othe hand, "New Layer via Cut" removes the selection from the old layer, and then places it on a new layer, leaving a corresponding hole in the old layer. Figure 6-8 shows the difference.

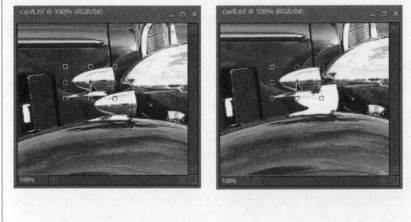

Figure 6-8:
The difference between "New Layer via Copy" and "New Layer via Cut" becomes obvious when you move the newly created layer and reveal what's beneath it.

Left: With "New Layer via Copy", the original light is still in place in the underlying layer.

Right: When you use "New Layer via Cut", the excised light leaves a hole behind.

Once you've selected what you want to move or copy, your new layer is only a couple of keystrokes away.

- **New Layer via Copy**. You can most easily copy your selection to a new layer by pressing Ctrl+J. (You can also go to Layer → New → "Layer via Copy".) Whichever you use, if you don't select anything beforehand, your whole layer gets copied. That makes it a good shortcut for creating a duplicate layer.

- **New Layer via Cut**. To cut your selection out of your old layer and put it on a layer by itself, press Shift+Ctrl+J (or go to Layer → New → "Layer via Cut"). Just remember that you leave a hole in your original layer when you do this.

If for some reason you want to cut and move the entire contents of a layer, you can press Ctrl+A first, although usually it's easier just to move your layer instead. Just drag it up or down the stack in the Layers palette to put it where you want it.

TIP   If you want to use a layer as the basis for a new document, Elements gives you a quick way to do so. Instead of copying and pasting, you can create a new document by going to Layer → Duplicate Layer. You get a dialog box containing a pull-down menu that gives you the option of placing the duplicate layer into your existing image, into any image currently open in the Editor, or into a new document of its own. (This maneuver works only from the menu. Ctrl+J doesn't bring up the dialog box.)

Managing Layers

The Layers palette lets you manipulate your layers in all kinds of ways, but first you need to understand a few more of the palette's cryptic little icons. Some of the things you can do with layers may seem tiresomely obscure when you first read about them, but once you're actually using layers, you'll quickly see why many of these options exist. The next few sections explain how to manipulate layers in several different ways: how to hide them, how to group them together, how to change the way you see them, and how to combine layers.

Making Layers Invisible

You can turn the visibility of layers off and on at will. This feature is tremendously useful, if you think about it. If the image you're working on has a busy background, for example, you often find it hard to see what you're doing when working on a particular layer. Making the Background layer invisible can really help you focus on the layer you're interested in. To turn off visibility, in the Layers palette, click the eye icon to hide the layer. Click the eye once more to make the layer visible again.

TIP   If you have a bunch of hidden layers and decide you don't want them anymore, go to Layers Palette → More (the double arrows) → Delete Hidden Layers to get rid of them all at once.

Adjusting Transparency

Your choices for layer visibility aren't limited to on and off. You can create immensely cool effects in Elements by adjusting the *opacity* of layers. In other words, you can make a layer partially transparent so that what's underneath it shows through.

To adjust the opacity of a layer, click the layer in the Layers palette, and then either:

• Double-click in the Opacity box, and then type in the percentage of opacity you want.

• If you'd rather make the adjustment visually (as opposed to entering numbers), then click the triangle to the right of the Opacity percentage and adjust the pop-out slider, or just put your cursor on the word Opacity and "scrub" (drag) left for less opacity and right for more. (Figure 6-9 explains the advantage of scrubbing.) You can download *leaves.jpg* from the Missing CD page at *www.missingmanuals.com*, if you'd like to experiment with creating Fill and Adjustment layers (page 176) and changing their modes and opacity.

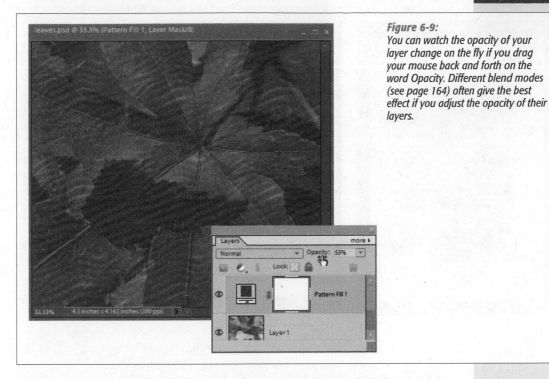

When you create a new layer using either the keyboard shortcut (Shift+Ctrl+N) or the menu (Layer → New → Layer), you can set the opacity right away in the New Layer dialog box. If you create a new layer by clicking the New Layer icon in the Layers palette, then you need to Alt+click the New Layer icon—the New Layer dialog box appears and you can change the opacity.

> **NOTE** You can't change the opacity of a Background layer. You have to convert it to a regular layer first; page 157 explains how.

Locking Layers

You can protect your image from yourself by *locking* any of the layers. Locking keeps you from changing a layer's contents. You can also lock just the transparent parts of a layer—helpful when you want to modify an object that sits atop a transparent layer, like the seashell shown in Figure 6-10. When you do that, the transparent parts of your layer stay transparent no matter what you do to the rest of it. (You're actually locking the pixels' current transparency level, so if you have pixels that are only partly transparent, then they stay at their current transparency level, too.)

To lock the transparent parts of a layer, select the layer, and then, in the Layers palette, click the little "Lock transparent pixels" checkerboard. It works like a button, and it's grayed out if you have no transparency in your photo. When you lock the transparency, a light gray padlock appears in the layers palette on the right side of the layer. To unlock, just click the checkerboard again.

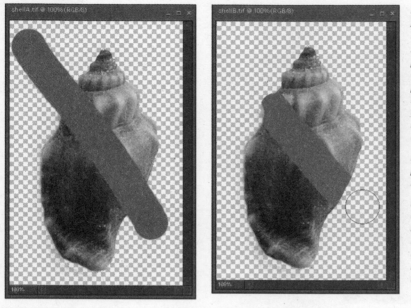

Figure 6-10:
After you've isolated an object on its own layer, sometimes you want to paint only on the object—and not on the transparent portion of the layer. Elements lets you lock the transparent part of a layer, making it easy to paint only the object itself.

Left: On a regular layer, paint goes wherever the brush does.

Right: With the layer's transparency locked, the stroke stops at the edge of the seashell, even though the brush (the circle) is now on the layer's transparent portion.

To lock the contents of a whole layer so that no changes can be made to it, click the "Lock all" icon (the dark gray padlock in the Layers palette next to the checkerboard). A dark gray padlock appears in the layers palette at the right of your layer, and the "Lock all" icon shows a dark gray outline around it. Now if you try to paint on that layer or use any other tools, your cursor turns into the shape of the universal "no" symbol (circle with a diagonal line through it) as a reminder that you can't edit that layer. You'll also see a lock icon next to the layer name in the Layers palette. To unlock the layer, just click the "Lock all" icon once more.

> **NOTE** Locking only preserves the layer from edits. It doesn't keep the layer from being merged into another layer or flattened, and it doesn't keep your image from being cropped.

Blend Mode

In the Layers palette, you also see another little menu that says "Normal" or, in the New Layer dialog box, "Mode: Normal". This setting is for your *blend mode*. When used with layers, blend modes control how the objects in a layer combine, or *blend*, with the objects in the layer beneath it. By using different blend modes, you can make your image lighter or darker, or even make it look like a poster, with just a few bold colors in it. Blend modes can also control how some tools—those that have Blend Mode settings—change your image. Changing a tool's blend mode can sometimes dramatically change the results you get.

Blend modes are an awful lot of fun once you understand how to use them. You can use them to fix under- or overexposed photos, or to create all kinds of special visual effects. You can also use some of the tools, like the Brush tool, in different blend modes to achieve different effects. The most common blend mode is Normal, in which everything you do behaves just the way you would expect: An object shows its regular colors, and paint acts just like, well, paint.

Page 343 has lots more about how to' use blend modes. For now, take a look at Figure 6-11, which shows how you can totally change the way a layer looks just by changing the layer's blend mode.

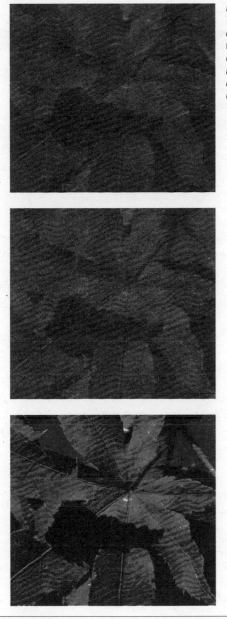

Figure 6-11:
This photo of some leaves has a Pattern Fill layer over it, showing three different modes. In normal mode at 100-percent opacity, the pattern would completely hide the leaves, but by changing the blend mode and opacity of the pattern layer, you can create very different looks. (There's more about Pattern layers on page 343.) From top to bottom, the modes are Normal, Dissolve, and Hard Mix. Notice how Dissolve gives a grainy effect and Hard Mix produces a vivid, posterized effect.

NOTE   The blend modes are grouped together in the menu according to the way they affect your image.

Not every blend mode makes a visible change in every circumstance. Some of them may seem to do nothing—that's to be expected. It just means that you don't have a condition in your current image that's responding to that particular mode change. See page 219 for one example of a situation where a mode change makes an enormous difference.

POWER USERS' CLINIC

Fading in Elements

One great thing you get in the full-featured Photoshop that Elements lacks is the ability to *fade* special effects and filters. Fading gives you great control over how much these tools change an image. (Often, filters generate harsh-looking results, and Photoshop's Fade command helps adjust a filter's effect until it's what you intended.)

In Elements, you can approximate the Fade tool: First, apply filters, effects, or layer styles to a duplicate layer. Then, reduce the layer's opacity till it blends in with what's below (and change the blend mode if necessary) to get exactly the result you want.

Rearranging Layers

One of the truly amazing things you can do with Elements is move your layers around. You can change the order in which layers are stacked so that different objects appear in front of or behind each other. For example, you can position one object behind another if they're both on their own layers. In the Layers palette, just grab the layer, and then drag it to where you want it.

NOTE   Remember, you're always looking down onto the layer stack when you look at your image, so moving something up in the list moves it toward the front of the picture.

Figure 6-12 shows the early stages of the flyer for a Fall Harvest Festival (originally shown in Figure 6-1). The pumpkins are already in place, and the scarecrow was dragged in from another image. The scarecrow comes in at the top of the stack, in front of the pumpkins. You can put the scarecrow behind the pumpkins by simply dragging the scarecrow layer below the pumpkin layer in the Layers palette.

NOTE   A Background layer is the only kind of layer you *can't* move. If you want to bring a Background layer to another spot in the layer stack, first convert the Background layer to a regular layer (page 157), and then you can move it.

You can also move layers by going to Layer → Arrange, and then choosing the command of your choice:

• **Bring to Front** (Shift+Ctrl+]) sends the selected layer to the top of the stack so the layer's contents appear in the foreground of your image.

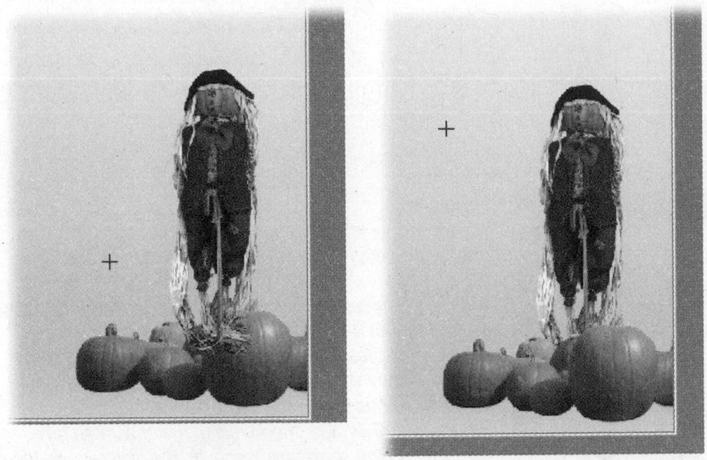

Figure 6-12:
Left: When you bring a new element into an image, it comes in on top of the active layer. In this case that move happened to make the scarecrow the front object.

Right: Move the new layer down in the stack, and the new object appears behind the existing content of the layers you move below, just as the scarecrow moves behind the pumpkins here.

- **Bring Forward** (Ctrl+]) moves the layer up one level in the Layers palette, so it appears one step closer to the front of your image.

- **Send Backward** (Ctrl+[) moves the layer down one level so it's sent back one step in the image.

- **Send to Back** (Shift+Ctrl+[) puts the layer directly above the Background layer so it appears as far back as you can move anything.

- **Reverse** (no keystroke shortcut) switches two layers' locations in the stack; you must select two layers in the palette (by Ctrl+clicking, for example) before this command becomes available.

> **TIP** These commands (except Reverse) are now also available from the Move tool's Options bar or by right-clicking in your photo when the Move tool is active. As a matter of fact, the Move tool can be a great way to rearrange layers in your image, as the next section explains.

Arranging layers with the Move tool

Using the Move tool, you can locate and arrange layers right in your image window, without trekking all the way over to the Layers palette. (If you need a refresher on Move tool basics, check out page 148.)

To arrange layers with the Move tool:

1. **Activate the Move tool.**

   Click its icon in the Toolbox or press V.

2. **Select the layer(s) you want to move.**

   As soon as you activate the Move tool, you see the bounding box (the dotted lines) around the active layer in the Layers palette. As you move your cursor over the image, you see a blue outline around the layer the cursor is over—no matter how far down the layer stack the object is (see Figure 6-13). When you click to select the layer you want to move, a dotted line bounding box appears around that layer. Shift+click to select multiple layers, and the bounding box expands to include all that you've selected.

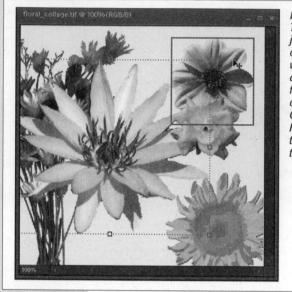

Figure 6-13:
The Move tool lets you select objects from any layer, not just the active one. When you move the cursor over any object, you see the blue outline around its layer. Here, the water lily is the active layer (you can see the bounding box around it), but the Move tool is ready to select the pink flower, even though it's not on the active layer. If all these outlines annoy you, then you can turn them off in the Options bar (via the Show Bounding Box or "Show Highlight on Rollover" checkboxes). If you want to force the Move tool to concentrate only on the active layer, then turn off Auto Select Layer.

3. **Move the Layer.**

For example, choose Layer → Arrange, or click the Options bar's Arrange Menu, or right-click inside the bounding box in the image. You see the same choices ("Bring to Front", Bring Forward, and so on) described in the previous section, except for Reverse, which is available only from the Layer menu. You can also use keystroke shortcuts (again, except for Reverse).

NOTE If you selected multiple layers, you may find that some of the commands are grayed out (that is, you can't select them). If that's a problem, just click elsewhere in the image to deselect the layers, and then send them one at a time instead of as a group.

Aligning and Distributing Layers

You can easily align objects in any image, thanks to the Move tool. The Move tool's *aligning* feature arranges the objects on each layer so that they line up straight along their top, bottom, left, or right edges, or through their centers. So, for example, if you align the top edges of your objects, then Elements makes sure that the top of each object is exactly in line with the others.

You'll also find it a breeze to evenly distribute the *space* between multiple objects. The Move tool's *distributing* feature spaces out the distance between objects, also letting you choose edges or centers as a guide. If you distribute the top edges, for example, Elements makes sure there's an even amount of space from the top edge of one object to another.

> **TIP** Distributing objects in this way is especially handy when you're creating projects like those described in Chapter 15.

Aligning and distributing layers with the Move tool works much like rearranging layers:

1. **Activate the Move tool.**

   Click its icon in the Toolbox or press V.

2. **Select the objects you want to align.**

   This maneuver works only if each object is on its own layer. If you have multiple objects on one layer, then move them to their own layers, one at a time, by selecting each object, and then pressing Ctrl+Shift+J.

   Shift+click inside the blue outline to select each layer you want to work with, or Shift+click in Layers palette to select the layers you want.

3. **Choose how you want to align or distribute the objects by selecting from the Options bar menus.**

   The Align and Distribute menus both give you the same choices: Top Edges, Vertical Centers, Bottom Edges, Left Edges, Horizontal Centers, and Right Edges. You can most easily find the choice you want by looking at the little thumbnails next to each label—they show you exactly how your objects will line up.

> **TIP** You can apply as many different align and distribute commands as you like, as long as the layers you're working with are still inside the bounding box. Figure 6-14 also gives you an example of how these commands work.

Grouping and Linking Layers

What if you want to move several layers at once? For instance, in the Harvest Festival image back on page 155, two layers have pumpkins on them. It's kind of a pain to drag each one individually if you need to move them in front of the scarecrow. Fortunately, you don't have to; Elements gives you a way to keep your layers united.

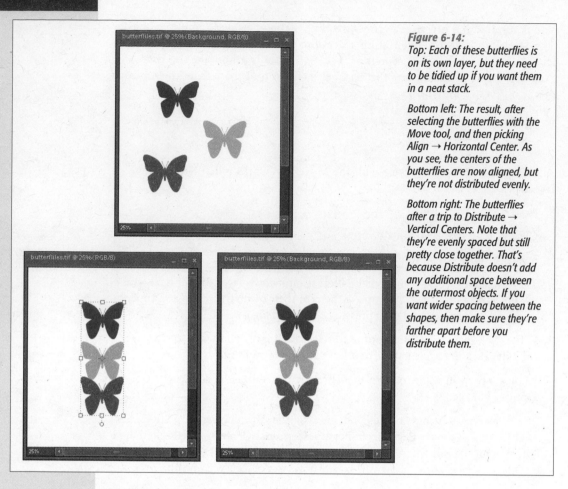

Figure 6-14:
Top: Each of these butterflies is on its own layer, but they need to be tidied up if you want them in a neat stack.

Bottom left: The result, after selecting the butterflies with the Move tool, and then picking Align → Horizontal Center. As you see, the centers of the butterflies are now aligned, but they're not distributed evenly.

Bottom right: The butterflies after a trip to Distribute → Vertical Centers. Note that they're evenly spaced but still pretty close together. That's because Distribute doesn't add any additional space between the outermost objects. If you want wider spacing between the shapes, then make sure they're farther apart before you distribute them.

Linking layers

You can *link* layers together, and then they'll travel as a unit, as shown in Figure 6-15.

If you want to remove a link between layers, then select the linked layers by clicking one, and then clicking the same chain icon to turn it off again. You can always merge the layers (covered in the next section) into one layer if you want. Sometimes, though, you'll want to keep layers separate, while still being able to move the layers as a group. You perform this trick by linking. You can also use the layer selection choices, described in the box "Selecting Layers", and skip the linking. As long as your layers all stay selected, they travel as a group. Linking's advantage is that your layers stay associated until you unlink them. There's no need to worry about accidentally clicking somewhere else in the palette and losing your selection group.

Selecting Layers

You can quickly target multiple layers when you want to manage them, like linking, moving, or deleting your layers. For your quick-selection pleasure, Elements gives you a whole group of layer selection commands, which you'll find in the Select menu. Here's what they do:

- **All Layers**. Choose this command, and every layer except the Background layer gets selected. Even if you've turned off visibility (page 162) on a particular layer, that layer still gets selected.

- **Deselect Layers**. When you're done working with your layers as a group, you can choose this option, and you won't have any layers selected until you click one.

- **Similar Layers**. This command is the most useful. Choose this option, and every layer of the same type gets selected, no matter where it is in the stack. So, for example, if you have a Text layer as your active layer when you choose Similar Layers, then all your Text layers get selected. If, on the other hand, you had an Adjustment layer active, then all your Adjustment layers get selected. You may use this command to quickly select a stack of Adjustment layers you want to drag to another image, for instance, using the technique described on page 252.

You can also Shift+click to select multiple layers that are next to each other in the palette, or Ctrl+click to select layers that are separated. That way, you can avoid the menu altogether. Once you're done, you can either use the Deselect Layers command from the menu, or just click another layer to make it the active layer.

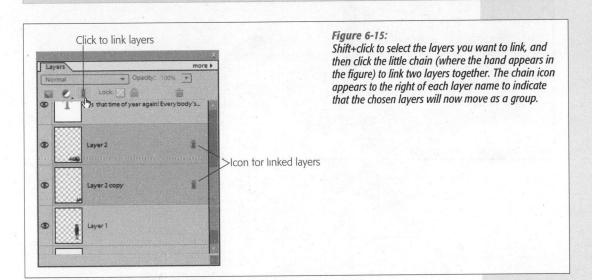

Click to link layers

Icon for linked layers

Figure 6-15:
Shift+click to select the layers you want to link, and then click the little chain (where the hand appears in the figure) to link two layers together. The chain icon appears to the right of each layer name to indicate that the chosen layers will now move as a group.

NOTE   The chain icon at the top of the Layers palette behaves like the "Lock Transparent Pixels" button does. You click the chain icon to link your layers, but it doesn't look any different once you've got some layers linked together (contrast that with the way the "Lock All" transparency button looks pushed in when active). The Linked layer chain next to the layer name is the only hint you get that a layer is linked.

Grouping layers

An even more powerful way to combine separate layers is to *group* them. With grouping, you can let one layer influence the other layers it's grouped with. Grouping layers isn't anything like linking them. You can probably understand grouping most easily by looking at the example shown in Figure 6-16, which shows how you can crop an image on one layer using the shape of an object on another layer. (This kind of grouping is also called a *clipping mask* in Photoshop, and sometimes in Elements as well.)

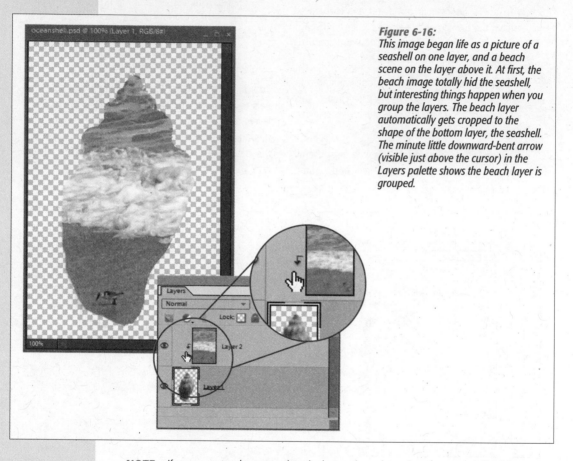

Figure 6-16:
This image began life as a picture of a seashell on one layer, and a beach scene on the layer above it. At first, the beach image totally hid the seashell, but interesting things happen when you group the layers. The beach layer automatically gets cropped to the shape of the bottom layer, the seashell. The minute little downward-bent arrow (visible just above the cursor) in the Layers palette shows the beach layer is grouped.

NOTE If you group two layers together, the bottom layer determines the opacity of both layers.

Once the layers are grouped, you can still slide the top layer around with the Move tool to reposition it so that you see exactly the part of it that you want. So in Figure 6-16, the beach layer was maneuvered around till the sandpiper showed in the bottom of the shell shape.

To group two layers together, make the top layer (of the two you want to group) the active layer. Then choose Layer → "Group with Previous". You can also group layers using the keyboard. First, make sure the top layer is the active layer, and then press Ctrl+G.

You can also group right in the Layers palette. Hold down Alt, and then, in the Layers palette, move your cursor over the dividing line between the layers. Click when you see two linked circles appear by your cursor. Now your layers are grouped.

If you get tired of the layer grouping or you want to delete or change one of the layers, then select Layer → Ungroup or press Shift+Ctrl+G to remove the grouping.

> **TIP** You have an even easier way to group layers: The New Layer dialog box has a checkbox for "Group with Previous Layer". Turn it on, and your new layer is pre-grouped with the layer below it.

Merging and Flattening Layers

By now, you've probably got at least an inkling of how useful layers are. But there's a downside to having layers in your image: They take up a lot of storage space, especially if you have lots of duplicate layers. In other words, layers make files bigger. Fortunately, you aren't committed to keeping layers in your file forever. You can reduce your file size quite a bit—and sometimes also make things easier to manage—by merging layers or flattening your image.

Merging layers

Sometimes you may have two or more separate layers that really could be treated as one layer, like the pumpkins shown in Figure 6-17. You aren't limited to linking those layers together; once you've got everything arranged to your satisfaction, you can merge them together into one layer. Also, if you want to copy and paste your image, many times the standard copy and paste commands (page 125) copies only the top layer. So it helps to get everything into one layer, at least temporarily.

You'll probably merge layers quite often when you're working with multilayered files (for example, when you've got multiple objects that you want to edit simultaneously).

To merge layers, you have a few different options, depending on what's active in your image at the time. You can get to any of the following commands from the Layers menu, or from the Layers palette's More button, or use keystroke shortcuts.

- **Merge Down.** This shortcut combines the active layer and the layer immediately beneath it. If the layer just below the active layer is hidden, then you don't see this option in the list of choices. Keyboard shortcut: Ctrl+E.

- **Merge Visible.** This shortcut combines all the visible layers into one layer. If you want to combine layers that are far apart, then just temporarily turn off visibility (by clicking the eye icon) for the ones in between and for any other layers that you don't want to merge (Shift+Ctrl+E).

- **Merge Linked.** Click any of your linked layers and you see this command, which joins the linked layers into one layer (Ctrl+E, just like Merge Down).

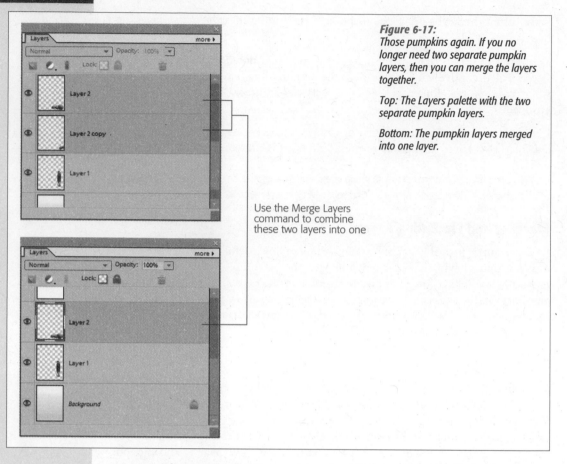

Figure 6-17:
Those pumpkins again. If you no longer need two separate pumpkin layers, then you can merge the layers together.

Top: The Layers palette with the two separate pumpkin layers.

Bottom: The pumpkin layers merged into one layer.

Use the Merge Layers command to combine these two layers into one

- **Merge Clipping Mask.** You need to select the bottom layer of a layer group to see this command. Choose it, and the grouped layers join into one layer (Ctrl+E).

POWER USERS' CLINIC

Stamp Visible

Sometimes you want to perform an action on all the visible layers of your image without permanently merging them together. You can easily do this—and quickly, too, even if you have dozens of layers in your file—by using what Adobe calls the Stamp Visible command. The Stamp Visible command combines the contents of all your layers into a new layer at the top of the stack.

Stamp Visible lets you work away on the new combined layer while still preserving your existing layers untouched, in case you want them back later on.

Just press Ctrl+Shift+Alt+E or hold down Alt while selecting the Merge Visible command from the Layers menu (or from Layers palette's More menu). Elements creates a new top layer for you, and fills it with the combined contents of all your other layers.

If you want to keep a layer or two from being included in this new layer, then just turn off the visibility of those layers you don't wish to include before using the Stamp Visible command.

It's important to understand that once you merge layers and save and close your file, you can't just un-merge them again. While your file is still open, of course, you can use any of the undo commands (page 31). But once you've gotten past the undo limit you've set in Preferences (page 32), you're stuck with your merged layers.

> **TIP** The box on page 174 shows you another way to combine all your layers, while still keeping a separate copy of the individual layers.

Sometimes if your layer contains type or shapes drawn with the Shape tool, you can't merge the layer right away. Elements asks you to *simplify* the layer first. Simplifying a layer means that you've converted its contents to a *raster object*. In other words, now it's just a bunch of pixels, subject to the same resizing limitations as any photo. So, for example, if you have a type layer, then you can apply filters to the type or paint on it, but you can no longer edit the words. (See page 355 for more about simplifying and working with shapes, and see Chapter 14 for working with type.)

Flattening an image

While layers are simply swell when you're working on an image, they're a headache when you want to share your image, especially if you're sending it to a photo-printing service (their machines usually don't understand layered files). And even if you're printing at home, the large size of a layered file can make it take forever to print. Also, if you plan to use your image in other programs, very few non-Adobe programs are totally comfortable with layered files, so you may get some odd results if you feed them a layered file.

In these cases, you may want to squash everything in your picture into a single layer. You can do this easily in Elements by flattening your image. Do so by going to Layer → Flatten Image, or on the Layers palette, choose the More button (the double arrows) → Flatten Image. Or, to keep your original intact, save as a copy, and then turn off Layers in the Save As dialog box.

> **TIP** Saving your image as a JPEG file automatically gets rid of layers, too.

There's no keystroke shortcut for flattening, because it's something you don't want to do by accident. Like merging, flattening is a permanent change. Many cautious Elements veterans always do a Save As, instead of a plain Save, before flattening. That way you have a flattened copy and still have your working copy with the layers intact, just in case. Organizer version sets (page 59) can help you here, too, because they let you save different states of your image. So, you could have a version with layers and a flattened version, too.

> **NOTE** Flattening creates a background layer out of the existing layers in your image, which means that you lose transparency, just as with a regular background layer. If you want to create a single layer with transparency, then use Merge Visible instead of Flatten Image.

Adjustment and Fill Layers

Adjustment layers and *Fill layers* are special types of layers. Adjustment layers let you manipulate the lighting, color, or exposure of the layers beneath them. If you're mainly interested in Elements to spruce up your photos, then you'll probably use Adjustment layers more than any other kind of layer. Adjustment layers are great because they let you undo or change your edits later on if you want to.

You can also use Adjustment layers to take the changes you've made on one photo and reapply those changes to another photo (see the Note on page 252). And after you've created an Adjustment layer, you can limit future edits so they change only the area of your photo affected by the Adjustment layer.

You'll find out much more about all the things you can do with Adjustment layers in the next few chapters. For now, you just need to learn how to create and manipulate them.

Fill layers are just what they sound like: layers filled with a color, a pattern, or a gradient (a rainbow-like range of colors). There's more about gradients on page 385.

> **TIP**   Digital photographers should check out the Photo Filter Adjustment layers, which let you digitally make the sort of adjustments that you used to do by attaching a colored piece of glass to the front of your camera's lens. You can read more about what you can do with photo filters on page 242.

GEM IN THE ROUGH

Adjustment Layers for Batch Processing

Page 245 shows you how to perform *batch* commands: simultaneously applying adjustments to groups of photos, using the Process Multiple Files tool. The drawback with Process Multiple Files is that you have access only to some of the auto commands there—your editing options are very limited. So what do you do if you're a fussy photographer who's got 17 shots that are all pretty much the same, and you'd like to apply the same fixes to all of them? Do you have to edit each one from scratch?

Not in Elements. You can open the photos you want to fix, and then drag an Adjustment layer from the first photo onto each of the other photos (page 179 shows you how to drag layers between images). The new photo gets the same adjustments at the same settings. It's not as fast as true batch processing, but it saves a lot of time compared with editing each photo from scratch.

Adding Fill and Adjustment Layers

Creating an Adjustment or Fill layer is easy. In the Layers palette, just click the black-and-white circle, as shown in Figure 6-18. The button displays a menu of all the Adjustment and Fill layer choices in one list (the first three choices are Fill layers; the rest are Adjustment layers).

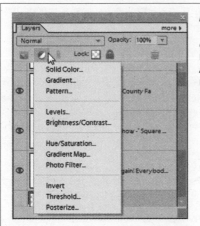

Figure 6-18:
To create a new Adjustment or Fill layer, click the black-and-white circle to get a drop-down menu that lets you choose the type of Adjustment or Fill layer you want. If you'd rather work from the menu bar, then go to Layer → New Adjustment Layer (or Layer → New Fill Layer), and choose the layer type you want.

Whichever type of layer you choose, you get a dialog box that lets you tweak the layer's settings (Invert, which doesn't give you any choices, is the exception). After you make your choices, click OK, and the new layer appears.

Elements gives you three Fill layer choices: Solid Color, Gradient (a rainbow-like range of colors), and Pattern. See more about patterns on page 264, and gradients on page 385.

Here are the kinds of Adjustment layers you can select from:

- **Levels.** This is a much more sophisticated way to apply Levels than using the Auto Levels button in Quick Fix or the Auto Level command from the Enhance menu. Page 198 has more information about using Levels. For most people, Levels is the most important Adjustment layer.

- **Brightness/Contrast.** This does pretty much the same things as the Quick Fix adjustment (covered on page 109).

- **Hue/Saturation.** Again, it's very much like the Quick Fix command (page 111), only with slightly different controls.

- **Gradient Map.** This is very tricky to understand, and is explained in detail on page 396. It maps each tone in your image to a new tone based on the gradient you select. That means you can apply a gradient so that the colors aren't just distributed in a straight line across your image.

- **Photo Filter.** Use Photo Filter to adjust the color balance of your photos by adding warming, cooling, or special effects filters, just like you might attach to the lens of a film camera. See page 242.

- **Invert.** This reverses the colors of your image to their opposite values, for an effect similar to a film negative. See page 281.

- **Threshold.** Use this to make everything in your photo pure black and pure white. See page 282.

- **Posterize.** Reduces the numbers of colors in your image to give a poster-like effect. See page 281.

You can change the settings for a Fill or Adjustment layer by highlighting the layer in the Layers palette, and then going to Layer → Layer Content Options, or, in the Layers palette, double-clicking the left icon for the layer. The layer's dialog box reappears, and you can adjust its settings. Deleting Fill and Adjustment layers is a tad different from deleting a regular layer, as explained in Figure 6-19.

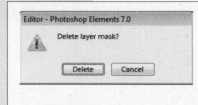

Figure 6-19:
When you click the Layers palette Delete icon, Elements asks if you want to "Delete layer mask?" Click Delete. Then you have to click the Trash can icon again to fully delete the layer. If you want to get rid of the layer in one step, then you've got a few choices: Use the Layer menu, right-click the layer in the Layers palette, or use the More button (the arrows) to delete it. In each case, you should see a Delete Layer choice. The next section has more about layer masks.

Layer Masks

Adjustment and Fill layers use something called a *layer mask*, which dictates which parts of the layer are affected when you make your changes (see Figure 6-20). By changing the area covered by the layer mask, you can control which part of your image the layer adjustments affect.

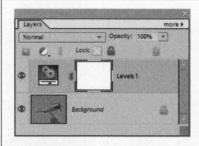

Figure 6-20:
Adjustment and Fill layers, like the top-most "Levels 1" layer shown here, always have two icons in the Layers palette. The left-side icon indicates that the layer's making an adjustment (Levels, in this case). You can double-click that icon to bring up the dialog box to make changes to your settings. (Note to Elements veterans: In Elements 7, Fill Layers still have a unique icon for each type of layer, but now all Adjustment layers show the little gear icon you see here. Individual icons for the different types of adjustment layers don't exist anymore.) The right icon is for the Layer Mask; you can use it to control the area that's covered by the adjustment.

Full Photoshop uses layer masks for many other purposes, but in Elements, Adjustment and Fill layers are the only place you encounter a layer mask. The great thing about layer masks is that you can edit them by painting on them, as explained on page 293. In other words, you can go back later and change the part of your image that the Adjustment layer affects.

Incidentally, the term *layer mask* may be a bit confusing if you're thinking about masking with the Selection brush. With the Selection brush, masking prevents something from being changed. A layer mask really works the same way, but by definition, it starts out empty; in other words, you can use the mask to prevent your adjustment from affecting parts of the layer, but not until you mask out parts of your image by painting on the layer mask. So to begin with, your entire layer is affected by your change. You can learn how to edit layer masks on page 293.

Moving Objects Between Images

If you use layers, then you can easily combine parts of different photos. Just put what you want from photo A into its own layer, and then drag it onto photo B. The trick is that you have to drag the layer *from the Layers palette*. If you try to drop one photo directly onto another photo's window, then you'll just wind up with a lot of windows stacked on top of each other (unless you activate the Move tool, described on page 148). Figure 6-21 shows you the correct way to move a layer between photos.

NOTE In some earlier versions of Elements, you could also drag a photo directly from the Photo bin into another image. That maneuver doesn't work in Elements 7.

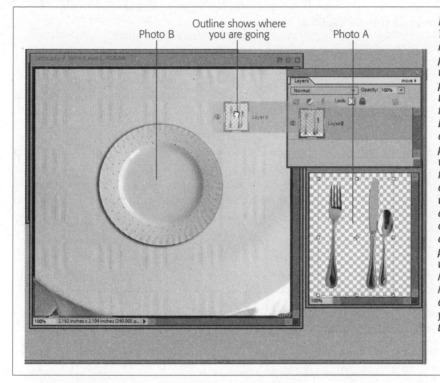

Photo B

Outline shows where you are going

Photo A

Figure 6-21:
This figure shows how to move objects from one photo to another, working from the Layers palette. Here, the goal is to get the silverware from photo A (whose Layers palette is visible) onto the tablecloth in photo B (whose image is visible). You always drag from the Layers palette onto a photo window when combining parts of different images into a composite. (If you try to drag from a photo to a photo, then it doesn't work unless you click the Move tool first.) Use the Move tool to adjust your object's placement once you've dropped it into the image.

But what if, rather than moving an entire layer, you just want to move a particular object—say, a person—to another layer? Just follow these steps:

1. **Open both photos in Full Edit.**

   If you're in Maximize mode, go to Window → Images, and then choose Tile or Cascade so you can see both photos at once.

2. **Prepare both photos for combining.**

Go to Image → Resize → Image Size, and then make sure both photos have the same pixels per inch (ppi) setting before you start (see page 89 if you need a refresher on resizing and resolution). Why? If one photo is hugely bigger than the other, then the moved object could easily blanket the entire target image. You don't absolutely have to perform this size balancing, but it'll make your life a lot easier, since it helps avoid having your pasted object be enormous or tiny after you move it. See below for more advice about resolution when moving objects and layers.

3. **Select what you want to move.**

Use the selection tools of your choice (see Chapter 5 if you need help making selections). Add a one or two pixel feather to your selection (see page 135) to avoid a hard, cut-out looking edge.

4. **Move the object.**

There are several ways to get material from one image to another:

- **Copy and Paste.** Start by pressing Ctrl+C to copy the object from the first photo. Next, click the second photo to make it the active photo, and then press Ctrl+V to paste what you copied.

- **Use the Move Tool.** Activate the Move Tool (page 148), and then drag from one photo to the other. As you're moving, you may see a hole in the original where the selection was, but as long as you don't let go till you get over the second photo, this fixes itself after you let go. (If seeing this bothers you, just Alt+drag to move a copy of the selection.)

- **Drag the layer.** If the object you want to move is already on its own layer, surrounded by transparency, then you can just drag the layer from the layers palette of the first photo into the main image window of the photo where you want to put it.

It doesn't matter which method you use—whatever you move appears on its own layer in the combined image.

5. **If necessary, use the Move tool to position or scale the object after you've moved it, as shown in Figure 6-22.**

See page 148 for more about using the Move tool; scaling objects is covered on page 384.

6. **Save your work when you're done.**

If you may want to make further adjustments to the moved object, then save your file as a TIFF or Photoshop (.psd) file to keep the layers. Remember that if you save your file as a JPEG, then you lose the layers, and you can't easily change or move the new object anymore.

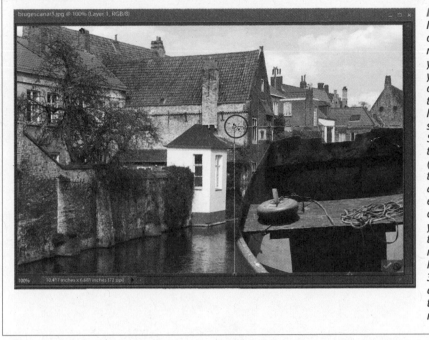

Figure 6-22:
If you forget to balance out the relative size and resolution of the photos you're combining, then you wind up with a giant object in your photo—like the boat in this picture's lower-right corner. The solution is simple: Just Shift+drag a corner of the oversized item (circled). You may need to drag the new object around a bit in order to expose the size-adjusting corner. Don't forget that you can use all the Move tool features on your new object. Here, a little Free Transform (page 322) could adjust the angle of the boat relative to the water for optimal realistic positioning.

Here are a few points to keep in mind when copying from one image to another:

- **Watch out for conflicting resolution settings** (see page 90). The bottom image (that is, the one receiving the moved layer or object) controls the resolution. So if you bring in a layer that's set to 300 pixels per inch (ppi), and place it on an image that's set to 72 ppi, then the object you're moving is now set to 72 ppi; its overall size will increase proportionately as the pixels get spread out more.

> **NOTE** Remember that you can't work with multiple images when you have the Elements screen view set to Maximize mode. Instead, go to Window → Images, and then choose Tile or Cascade. Cascade gives you the most flexibility for positioning your photos.

- **Lighting matters.** Objects that are lit differently stand out if you try to combine them. If possible, plan ahead and choose similar lighting for photos you're thinking about combining.

- **Center your moved layer.** If you're dragging the layer and want your layer to center itself in the new image, then Shift+drag the layer.

- **Feather with care.** A little feathering (page 135) goes a long way toward creating a realistic result.

> **NOTE** If you'd like more practice using layers and moving objects between photos, visit the Missing CD page at *www.missingmanuals.com*, and download the Table Tutorial. It walks you through most of the basic layer functions.

CHAPTER 7

Basic Image Retouching

You may be perfectly happy using Elements only in Quick Fix mode. And that's fine, as long as you understand that you've hardly scratched the surface of what the program can do for you. Sooner or later, though, you're probably going to run across a photo where your best Quick Fix efforts just aren't good enough. Or you may just be curious to see what else Elements has under its hood. That's when you finally get to put all your image-selecting and layering skills to good use.

Elements gives you loads of ways to fix your photos beyond the limited options in Quick Fix. This chapter guides you through fixing basic exposure problems, shows you new ways of sharpening your photos, and most important, helps you understand how to improve the colors in your photos. You'll also learn how to use the amazing new Smart Brush tool that lets you apply many common fixes by just brushing over the area you want to correct.

If you want to get the most out of Elements, you need to understand a little about how your camera, computer, and printer think about color. Along with resolution, color is the most important concept in Elements. After all, almost all the adjustments that image-editing programs make consist of changing the color of pixels. So quite a bit of this chapter is about understanding how Elements—and by extension, you—can manipulate your image's color.

TIP Most of Elements' advanced-fixes dialog boxes have a "preview" checkbox, which lets you watch what's happening as you adjust the settings. It's a good idea to keep these checkboxes turned on so you can decide if you're improving things. And for a handy "before" and "after" comparison, toggle the checkbox on and off.

Fixing Exposure Problems

Incorrectly exposed photos are *the* number one problem all photographers face. No matter how carefully you set up your shot and how many different settings you try on your camera, it always seems like the picture you really, really want to keep is the one that's over- or underexposed.

The Quick Fix commands (page 99) can really help your photo, but if you've tried to bring back a picture that's badly over- or underexposed, you've probably run into the limitations of what Quick Fix can do. Similarly, the Shadows/Highlights command (page 109) can do a lot, but it's not intended to fix a photo whose exposure is totally botched—just ones where the contrast between light and dark areas needs a bit of help. And if you push Smart Fix to its limits, your results may be a little strange. In those situations, you need to move on to some of Elements' more powerful tools to help improve your exposure.

> **TIP** In this section, you'll learn about the more traditional ways of correcting exposure in Elements, as well as how to use the new Smart Brush tool for corrections. But also be sure to check out the Elements Camera Raw Converter (page 224), which can help with your JPEG and TIFF photos, too. Your results with non-Raw photos may vary, but the Raw Converter just might turn out to be your best choice.

UP TO SPEED

Understanding Exposure

What exactly *is* exposure, anyway? You almost certainly know a poorly exposed photo when you see it: It's either too light or too dark. But what exactly has gone wrong?

Exposure refers to the amount of light your film (or the sensor in your digital camera) received when you released the shutter.

A well-exposed photo shows the largest amount of detail in *all* parts of your image—light and dark. In a properly exposed photo, shadows aren't just pits of blackness, and bright areas show more than washed-out splotches of white.

Deciding Which Exposure Fix to Use

When you open a poorly exposed photo in Elements, the first thing to do is figure out what's wrong with it, just like a doctor diagnosing a patient. If the exposure's not perfect, what exactly is wrong? Here's a list of common symptoms to help figure out where to go next:

- **Everything is too dark.** If your photo is really dark, try adding a Screen layer, as explained on page 185. If it's just a bit too dark, try using Levels (page 198).

- **Everything is too light.** If the whole photo looks washed out, try adding a Multiply layer (explained on page 185). If it's just a bit too light, try Levels (page 198).

- **The photo is mostly OK, but your subject is too dark or the light parts of the photo are too light.** Try the Shadows/Highlights adjustment (page 187) or the new Smart Brush tool (page 189).

Of course, if you're lucky (or a really skilled photographer), you may not see any of these problems, in which case, skip to page 198 if you want to do something to make your colors pop.

> **NOTE** You may have noticed that you didn't see Brightness/Contrast mentioned anywhere in the previous list. A lot of people tend to jump for the Brightness/Contrast controls when facing a poorly exposed photo. That's logical—after all, these dials usually help improve the picture on your TV. But in Elements, about 99 percent of the time, you've got a whole slew of powerful tools—like Levels and the Shadows/Highlights command—that can do much more than Brightness/Contrast can. However, in recent versions of Elements, Brightness/Contrast is much improved from earlier versions, so feel free to give it a try when you only need to make very subtle changes.

Fixing Major Exposure Problems

If your photo is completely over- or underexposed, you need to add special layers to correct the problems. You follow the same steps to fix either problem. The only difference is the layer blend mode (page 164) you choose: *Multiply layers* darken your image's exposure while *Screen layers* lighten it. Figure 7-1 shows Multiply layers in action (and also gives you an idea of the limitations of this technique if your exposure is really far gone). You can download the file *window.jpg* from the Missing CD page at *www.missingmanuals.com* if you'd like to try the different exposure fixes for yourself.

Be careful, though. If your entire photo isn't out of whack, using Multiply or Screen layers can ruin the exposure of the parts that were OK to start with, because they'll increase or decrease the exposure on the entire photo. Your properly exposed areas may blow out (see page 187) and lose the details if you apply a Screen layer, for example. So, if your exposure problem is spotty (as opposed to problems that affect the entire image), try the new Smart Brush (page 198) or Shadows/Highlights (page 187) first. If your whole photo needs an exposure correction, here's how to use layers to fix it:

1. **Create a duplicate layer.**

   Open your photo and press Ctrl+J or go to Layer → Duplicate Layer. Check to be sure the duplicate layer is the active layer.

2. **In the Layers palette, change the mode for the new layer in the pop-up menu.**

   Choose Multiply if your photo is overexposed, or Screen if it's underexposed. Make sure you change the mode of the duplicate layer, not the original layer.

3. **Adjust the opacity of the layer if needed.**

   If the effect of the new layer is too strong, in the Layers palette, move the Opacity slider to the left to reduce the new layer's opacity.

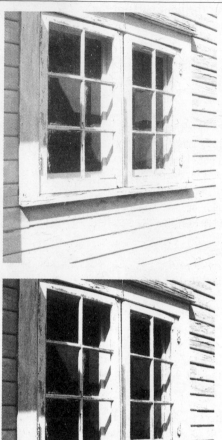

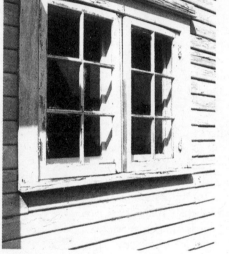

Figure 7-1:
For those who think photographically, each Multiply layer you add is roughly equivalent to stopping your camera down one f-stop, at least as far as the dark areas are concerned.

Top: This photo is totally overexposed, and it looks like there's no detail there at all. Multiply layers darken things enough to bring back a lot of the washed-out areas. This technique can bring out the detail quite a bit.

Bottom: As you can see in the corrected photo, even Elements can't do much in areas where there's no detail at all.

4. **Repeat as necessary.**

   You may need to use as many as five or six layers if your photo is in really bad shape. If you need extra layers, you'll probably want them at 100 percent opacity, so you can just keep pressing Ctrl+J, which will duplicate the current top layer.

You're more likely to need several layers to fix overexposure than you are for underexposure. And, of course, there are limits to what even Elements can do for a blindingly overexposed image. Overexposure is usually tougher to fix than underexposure, especially if the area is blown out, as explained in the box on page 187.

IN THE FIELD

Avoiding Blowouts

An area of a photo is *blown out* when it's so overexposed that it appears as just plain white—in other words, your camera didn't record any data at all for that area. (Elements isn't all that great with total black, either, but that doesn't happen quite so often. Most underexposed photos have some tonal gradations in them, even if you can't see them very well.)

A blowout is as disastrous in photography as it is when you're driving. Even Elements can't fix blowouts because there's no data for it to work from. So, you're stuck with the fixes discussed in this chapter, which are never as good as a good original.

When you're taking pictures, remember that it's generally easier to correct underexposure than overexposure. Keep that in mind when choosing your camera settings. If you live where there's extremely bright sunlight most of the time, you may want to make a habit of backing your exposure compensation down a hair. Depending on your camera, your subject, and the average ambient glare, you should try starting at −.3 and adjusting from there.

You can also try *bracketing* your shots—taking multiple shots of exactly the same subject with different exposure settings. Then you can combine the two exposures for maximum effect (the box on page 243 explains how to combine images).

The Shadows/Highlights Command

The Shadows/Highlights command is one of the best features in Elements. It's an incredibly powerful tool for adjusting only the dark or light areas of your photo without messing up the rest of it. Figure 7-2 shows what a great help it can be.

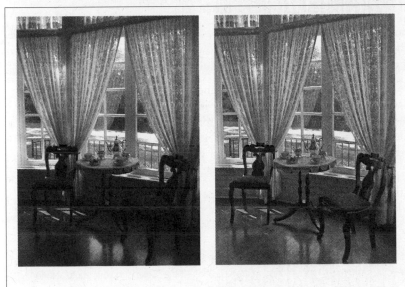

Figure 7-2:
The Shadows/Highlights command can bring back details from photos where you were sure there was no information at all—but sometimes at a cost.

Left: This photo suffers from the worst of both worlds—a severely underexposed interior along with the overly bright exterior visible through the windows.

Right: The Shadows/Highlights tool brings out the hidden detail and reduces the background glare, but it can't bring back the blown out sidewalks visible through the windows.

The Shadows/Highlights command in the Full Editor works pretty much the same way it does in Quick Fix (page 109). The single flaw in this great tool is that you can't apply it as an Adjustment layer (page 176), so you may want to apply Shadows/Highlights to a duplicate layer. Then, later on, you can discard the changes if you want to take another whack at adjusting the photo. In any case, it's not difficult at all to make amazing changes to your photos with Shadows/Highlights. Here's how:

1. **Open your photo and duplicate the layer (Ctrl+J) if you want to.**

   Duplicating your layer makes it easier to undo Shadows/Highlights later if you change your mind.

2. **Go to Enhance → Adjust Lighting → Shadows/Highlights.**

   Your photo immediately becomes about 30 shades lighter. Don't panic. As soon as you select the command, the Lighten Shadows setting automatically jumps to 25 percent, which is way too much for most photos. Just shove the slider back to 0 to undo this change before you start making your corrections.

3. **Move the sliders around until you like what you see.**

   The sliders do exactly what they say: Lighten Shadows makes the dark areas of your photo lighter, and Darken Highlights makes the light areas darker. Pushing the slider to the right increases the effect for either one.

4. **Click OK when you're happy.**

The Shadows/Highlights tool is a cinch to use because you just make decisions based on what you're seeing. Keep these tips in mind:

- You may want to add a smidgen of the opposite tool to balance things out a little. In other words, if you're lightening shadows, you may get better results by giving the Darken Highlights slider a teeny nudge, too.

- Midtone Contrast is there because your photo may look kind of flat after you're done with Shadows/Highlights, especially if you've made big adjustments. Move the Midtone Contrast slider to the right to increase the contrast in your photo. It usually adds a bit of a darkening effect, so you may need to go back to one of the other sliders to tweak your photo after you use it.

- You can overdo the Shadows/Highlights tool. When you see halos around the objects in your photo, you've pushed the settings too far.

TIP   If the Shadows/Highlights tool looks like it washed out your photo's colors—making everyone look like they've been through the laundry too many times—adjust the color intensity with one of the Saturation commands, either in Quick Fix or in the Full Editor (as described on page 271). Watch people's skin tones when increasing the saturation—if the subjects in your photo start looking like sunless-tanning lotion disaster victims, you've gone too far. Also check out the Vibrance slider in the Raw Converter (page 236), or you can try adjusting colors with Elements' Color Curves feature (page 267).

Correcting Part of an Image

Shadows/Highlights is great if you want to adjust *all* the light or dark areas of a photo, but what if you want to tweak the exposure only in certain areas? Or what if you like the photo's background just fine, but you want to tweak the subject a little? Of course, you can always make a selection in your photo (see Chapter 5 for more about selecting), or copy the selected area to a new layer, and then make your adjustments to that layer. But in Elements 7, Adobe has provided a super simple way to apply a correction to just the area you want, using the new Smart Brush tools.

Correcting color with a brush

The Smart Brush is actually two different tools (the Smart Brush and the Detail Smart Brush) that work just like the Quick Selection tool and the regular Selection brush, respectively—only instead of merely selecting a region of your photo, they also edit it as you brush. So you may be able to do very tightly targeted adjustments to different areas of your photo, just by drawing a line over it. The Smart Brushes don't always work, but they're truly amazing when they do.

In this section you'll learn how to use the Smart Brush to correct exposure, but you have a whole menu of different things you can choose to do with the Smart Brush: Change the color of someone's jacket, apply different special effects, add lipstick to a woman's lips, convert the area you select to black and white—the list goes on and on. As a matter of fact, if you've been using the Quick Fix, you may well have met the Smart Brush already, although it doesn't go by that name there: The new Touch Up tools (page 113) in the Quick Fix all use the Smart Brush to apply their effects.

Here's how to put this nifty pair of tools to work:

1. **Open a photo in Full Edit, and then activate the Smart Brush.**

   Click its icon in the Toolbox (it's the brush with the gears next to it) or press F. Use the flyout menu to be sure you have the regular Smart Brush. It shares its Toolbox slot with the Detail Smart Brush, which works like the Selection Brush. That is, it changes only the area directly under the brush, instead of automatically expanding your selection to include the entire object you brush over. For now, see if the regular Smart Brush is smart enough to select the area you want.

2. **Choose the correction you want to apply.**

   Go to the Options Bar, and then, choose from the pull-down menu. (Both Smart Brushes have the same options bar settings, discussed below. The important one is explained in Figure 7-3.) Adobe calls these choices Smart Paint.

3. **Drag over the area you want to change.**

   This step is just like using the Quick Selection tool—no need to make a careful selection, since Elements calculates the area it thinks you want to include and create the selection for you. A simple line should do it.

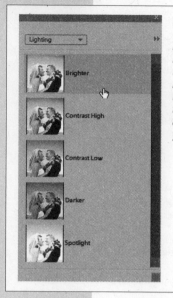

Figure 7-3:
Your Smart Paint options (the things you can do with the Smart Brush) are grouped into the categories listed in the pull-down menu. Each thumbnail picture shows an individual option applied to the same photo. For exposure issues, start by looking at the choices in the Lighting section. You can choose to make the area darker, brighter, make the contrast low or high, or even put a spotlight effect on it. Just scroll through the list to find the effect you want, click it, and then click somewhere outside your photo to minimize the menu list again. You can also tear the list loose from the Options bar and place it where you want, if you'd like to keep it available and out of the way of your photo.

4. **Tweak the selection, if necessary.**

   If Elements didn't quite select everything you want, then you can add to the selection by brushing again. If you still need to modify the selection, then use the selection editing tools, explained in Figure 7-4. If you're really unhappy with the Smart Brush's selection talents, then head back to the Toolbox, and try the Detail Smart Brush.

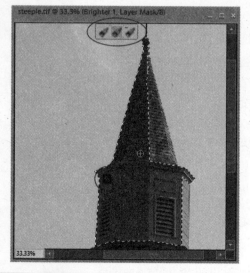

Figure 7-4:
Once you've used the Smart Brush, a pin (circled) appears in your photo, indicating that the selected region is now under the power of the Smart Brush. Click it, and you see a trio of icons (circled) which let you edit your selected area. From left to right the icons mean New Selection, "Add to Selection", and "Remove from Selection". If you're pressed for time, there's an even quicker route to modifying your selection: Just drag again to add to the area affected by the Smart Brush (or to use the same adjustment on another part of your photo) or Alt-drag to remove changes from an area. You see the pin any time the Smart Brush is activated again, even after you've closed and saved your photo.

You can invert a selection (page 144) by turning on the Inverse box in the Options bar. Then what you select with the brush is *excluded* from your selection; everything else is included in the selection. You can turn on the checkbox before or after using the Smart Brush, as long as it's still the active tool. If you come back to the Smart Brush after using another tool, then you need to click the pin shown in Figure 7-4 before you can invert the selection, thus inverting the area covered by the effect.

5. **Once you like the selection, you can also adjust the effect, if you want.**

   The Smart Brush gives you several ways to change what it's done:

   - **Change what happens to the selected area.** While the selection is active, in the Options bar, just go to the Smart Paint setting, and then choose a different Smart Paint adjustment. It automatically updates your previous choice.

   - **Add a different kind of Smart Paint.** At the far left of the Options bar, click the tiny triangle and choose Reset Tool. Then the Smart Brush puts down an *additional* adjustment when you use it, instead of just changing what you've already done. You can also use this to double up an effect—to add Lipstick twice, for instance, if you thought the first pass was too faint. Each Smart Brush adjustment gets its own pin, so if you have two Smart Brush adjustments in your photo, then you have two pins in it, too. Each pin is a different color.

   - **Change the settings for Smart Paint you've already applied.** Rather than adding another Smart Paint layer to increase the effect, you can just adjust the settings for the changes you've already made. Right-click the pin in your image, and then choose Change Adjustment Settings to bring up a dialog box where you can adjust the effect you're brushing on. The Smart Brush uses Adjustment layers for the changes it makes. The available settings that are the same as they would be if you created a regular Adjustment layer—if you're using the Brighter option, as shown in Figure 7-4, for example, then you get the settings for a Brightness/Contrast Adjustment layer.

6. **When you're happy with what you have, you're all done.**

   You can always go back to your Smart Paint changes again. Just activate the Smart Brush (click it in the Toolbox or press F) and the pin(s) appear again, to let you easily change what you've done. You can eliminate Smart Brush changes by right-clicking the adjusted area, and then choosing Delete Adjustment (the Smart Brush needs to be active), or by going to the Layers palette and discarding their layers (you can do this anytime, whether the Smart Brush is active or not). You can also edit the Layer mask of a Smart Brush adjustment the way you'd edit any other Layer mask, as described on page 293. But usually it's easier just to click the pin, and then adjust your selection.

The Smart Brush is especially handy for projects like creating images that are partly in color and partly black and white, or even for silly special effects like making one object from your photo look like it's been isolated on a 60's-style psychedelic background.

The Smart Brush has several Options bar settings, but you usually don't need to use them:

- **New Selection.** Click the left brush icon, and you can add the same effect elsewhere in your photo. Actually, though, just clicking someplace else with the brush does the same thing.

- **Add to Selection.** You can click this option to put the Smart Brush in add-to-selection mode, but again, the brush does that automatically without using the icon.

- **Remove from Selection.** Did the Smart Brush take in more area than you wanted? Click this icon before brushing away what you don't want, or just Alt-drag.

- **Brush characteristics.** You can change the size, hardness, spacing, angle, or roundness of the brush here.

- **Inverse.** If you want to apply your chosen correction to the area you *didn't* select with the Smart Brush, then just turn on this checkbox to invert the selection.

- **Refine Edge.** Use this if you want to make the edges of your effect sleeker. See page 128.

- **Smart Paint.** Click the thumbnail for a pop-out menu of all the possible Smart Brush adjustments, grouped into categories. (Incidentally, if you hover your mouse over the thumbnail, then the tooltips text just says "Choose a Preset", but Adobe calls these settings Smart Paint in the Help files and elsewhere.)

If you like the idea of the Smart Brush, but never seem to find exactly the adjustments you want, or if you always find that you want to change the settings you apply, then you can even create your own Smart Paint options, as described in the box on page 193.

> **NOTE** If you make a mistake creating your preset, and don't catch it till after starting the Editor again, correct it, go to *C:\ProgramData\Adobe\Photoshop Elements\7.0\Locale\en_US* (this is different if you aren't in the US), and then delete MediaDatabase.db3 to refresh the list of presets, if you're using Vista. In XP, it's in *C:\Documents and Settings\All Users\Application Data\Adobe\ Photoshop Elements\7.0\ Locale\en_US* (or your location).

Controlling the Colors You See

You want your photos to look as good as possible and to have beautiful, breathtaking color, right? That's probably why you bought Elements. But now that you've got the program, you're having a little trouble getting things to look the way you want. Does this sound familiar?

- Your photos look great onscreen but your prints are washed out, too dark, or the colors are all a little wrong.

- Your photos look just fine in other programs like Word or Windows Explorer, but they look just awful in Elements.

Making Smart Paint

While the Smart Brush offers a lot of different Smart Paint choices (the various settings for correcting and enhancing your photos), you may find it slightly frustrating that Elements doesn't have a setting for the particular corrections you use most frequently. No problem—you can create your own Smart Paint settings. As long as you can use Adjustment layers (page 176) to achieve the effect you want, you can configure your own Smart Paint choices, and they appear in the menus right along with the ones from Adobe.

To get started, if you're using Vista go to *C:\Program-Data\Adobe\Photoshop Elements\7.0\Photo Creations\ adjustment layers*. (In XP, it's *C:\Documents and Settings\All Users\Application Data\Adobe\Photoshop Elements\7.0\ Photo Creations\Adjustment Layers*.) These files are hidden, so you need to turn on viewing hidden files to see them. You see three files for each Smart Paint preset:

- **A PSD file**. This file contains the actual settings for the preset.

- **A thumbnail file**. These files are necessary if you want to have a little preview in the menu.

- **An XML file**. This file tells Elements where in the menus to display the preset, whether to show it in "Black and White" or in Lighting, for instance. The XML files all have the word "metadata" in their names, so you can easily find them.

Essentially, you need to edit *copies* of these files to make new ones for each choice you want to add. Here's how:

1. **Open one of the .psd files in the Editor**. To start with, pick the one that's the closest to what you want to do. Notice how the file is put together. You see it's a 160-pixel square .psd file with an adjustment layer on it. Save the file under a new name so you don't inadvertently mess up the original.

2. **Change the settings**. Double click the Adjustment layer's left icon to bring up the adjustment settings. Move the settings where you want them, and then save the file.

3. **Create a new thumbnail**. You can just save the original thumbnail with your new name. (Thumbnails are 74-pixel square JPEGs, in case you feel creative and want to make a new one from scratch.)

4. **Create a new XML file**. For most people, this is the trickiest part. Open the XML file and save it as XML with the name of the new Smart Paint choice you just created. (If you don't have anything else to use, you can use Notepad. In the "Save as" dialog box, choose All Files in the "Save as type" menu.) Then look at the contents of the file. Most of it won't make much sense to non-geeks, but what you're looking for is a line that looks like this:

```
<name value="$$$/content/adjustmentlayers/
ContrastHigh=Contrast High" />
```

In this example, you'd be adapting the Contrast High preset, so you just find the two instances of the name (note that there's no space in the first one), and then change them to the name of your new preset. If you're ambitious, you can also edit the text for tooltips (the text that appears when you hover your mouse over the thumbnail) and the category. You can use an existing category or create a new one. When you're finished making your changes, save the file. The file should be named *my effect.metadata*—just replace "my effect" with the name you gave your new preset.

Make sure all three files are in the Adjustment Layers folder. The next time you start Elements, you should see your new Smart Paint right there along with the ones that came with Elements.

What's going on? The answer has to do with the fact that Elements is a *color-managed* program. That means that Elements uses your monitor information for guidance when deciding how to display images. Color management is the science of making sure that the color in your images is always exactly the same, no matter who opens your file or what kind of hardware they're viewing it on or printing it from. If you think of all the different monitor and printer models out there, you get an idea of what a big job this is.

Graphics pros spend their whole lives grappling with color management, and you can find plenty of books about the finer points of color management. On the most sophisticated level, color management is complicated enough to make you curl up into the fetal position and swear never to create another picture.

Lucky for you, Elements makes color management a whole lot easier. Most of the time, you have only two things to deal with: your monitor calibration and your color space. The following pages cover both.

> **NOTE**   There are a couple of other color-related settings for printing, too, but you can deal with those when you get ready to print. Chapter 16 explains them.

Calibrating Your Monitor

Most of programs pay no attention to your monitor's color settings, but a color-managed application like Elements relies on the *profile*—the information your computer stores about your monitor's settings—when it decides how to print or display a photo onscreen. If that profile isn't accurate, neither is the color in Elements.

So, you may need to *calibrate* your monitor, which is a way of adjusting its settings. A properly calibrated monitor makes all the difference in the world in getting great-looking results. If your photos look bad only in Elements, or if your pictures in print don't look anything like they look onscreen, you can start fixing the problem by calibrating your monitor.

Getting started with calibrating

Calibrating a monitor sounds intimidating, but it's actually not that difficult—some people think it's even kind of fun. You get an extra added benefit in that your monitor may look about a thousand times better than you thought it could. Calibrating may even make it easier to read text in Word, for instance, because the contrast is better. Your options for calibrating your monitor, from best to only okay, are:

- **Use a colorimeter**. This method may sound disturbingly scientific, but it's actually the easiest. A *colorimeter* is just a hardware device with special software that does your calibration for you. The device is much more accurate than calibrating by eye. For a long time, only a pro could afford one, but these days if you shop around you can find the Pantone Huey or the Spyder2Express for about $70 or less. More pro-oriented calibrators like the Eye One Display 2 or the Monaco Optix Spyder are about $200 or less. If you're serious about controlling your colors in Elements, hardware is by far your best option for calibrating.

NOTE   Your calibration software probably asks you to set the brightness and contrast before you begin, even though most newer LCD monitors don't have adjustable dials for these anymore. If you're happy with your monitor's current brightness and contrast, you can safely ignore this step. And unless you have a reason to choose differently, for an LCD monitor you usually want to set your white point to 6500 (Kelvin) and your gamma to 2.2.

- **Software on your computer.** There's a good chance that the drivers (utility software) for your graphics card include some kind of calibration tool. Figure 7-5 shows a typical example. Right-click anywhere on the desktop and choose Display Settings → Color Management (in Windows XP: Display → Properties → Settings → Advanced) to see what you have.

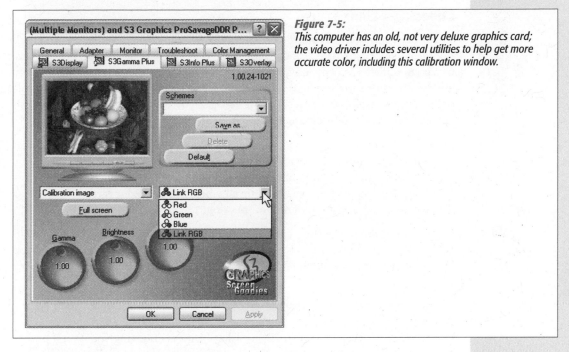

Figure 7-5:
This computer has an old, not very deluxe graphics card; the video driver includes several utilities to help get more accurate color, including this calibration window.

- **Adobe Gamma.** If you have an older version of Elements (Elements 5 or earlier) you may have this program, which used to come with Elements. It's pretty ancient, was never meant to work with anything but the old CRT monitors (the big fat ones like old-fashioned televisions), and will not work in Vista at all. If you happen to have Adobe Gamma, it may be better than nothing, but it's probably less useful than any other utility you might have for adjusting your display.

If your photos still look a little odd even after you've calibrated your monitor, you may need to turn on the Ignore EXIF setting in the Editor's preferences; see Figure 7-6.

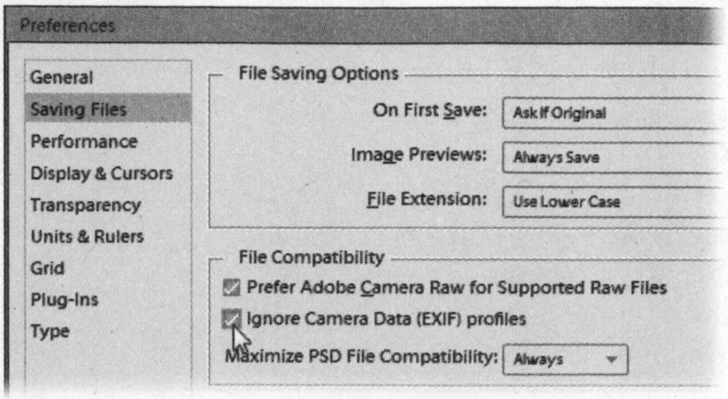

Figure 7-6:
If you still see a funny color cast (usually red or yellow) on all your digital camera photos, go to Edit → Preferences → Saving Files and turn on "Ignore Camera Data (EXIF) profiles". Some cameras embed nonstandard color information in their files, and Elements' Ignore EXIF utility just tells Elements to pay no attention to it, allowing your photos to display and print properly.

Choosing a Color Space

The other thing you may need to do to get good color from Elements is to check the *color space* Elements is using. Color space refers to which standard (out of several possibilities) Elements uses to define your colors. Color space can seem pretty abstruse the first time you hear about it, but it's simply a way of defining what colors mean. For example, when someone says "green," what do you envision: a lush emerald color, a deep forest green, a bright lime, or something else?

Choosing a color space is a way to make sure that everything that handles a digital file—Elements, your monitor, your printer—sees the same colors the same way. Over the years, the graphics industry has agreed on standards so that everyone has the same understanding of what you mean when you say red or green—as long as you specify which set of standards you're using.

Elements only gives you two color spaces to pick from: *sRGB* (also called *sRGB IEC61966-2.1* if you want to impress your geek friends) and *Adobe RGB*. When you choose a color space, you tell Elements which set of standards you want it to apply to your photos.

If you're happy with the color you see on your monitor in Elements and you like the prints you're getting, you don't need to make any changes. If, on the other hand, you aren't perfectly satisfied with what Elements is giving you, you'll probably want to modify your color space, which you can do in the Color Settings dialog box. Go to Edit → Color Settings or press Shift+Ctrl+K. Here are your choices:

• **No Color Management**. Elements ignores any information that your file already contains, like color space information from your camera, and doesn't attempt to add any color info to the file data. (When you do a Save As, there's a checkbox that offers you the option of embedding your monitor profile. Don't turn on this checkbox, since your monitor profile is best left for the monitor's own use, and putting the profile into your file can make trouble if you ever send the file someplace else for printing.)

- **Always Optimize Colors for Computer Screens.** Choose this option and you're looking at your photo in the sRGB color space, which is what most Web browsers use; this is a good choice for when you're preparing graphics for the Web. Many online printing services also prefer sRGB files. (If you've used an early version of Elements, this is the same as the old Limited Color Management option.)

- **Always Optimize for Printing.** This option uses the Adobe RGB color space, which is a wider color space than sRGB. In other words, it allows more gradations of color than sRGB. Sometimes this is your best choice for printing—but not always. So despite the note you'll see in the Color Settings dialog box about "commonly used for printing," don't be afraid to try one of the other two settings instead. Many home inkjet printers actually cope better with sRGB or no color management than with Adobe RGB. (For old Elements hands, this setting used to be called Full Color Management.)

- **Allow Me to Choose.** This option assumes that you're using the sRGB space, but lets you assign either an Adobe RGB tag, an sRGB tag, or no tag at all. If you've selected "Allow Me to Choose", each time you open a file that isn't sRGB, you see the dialog box shown in Figure 7-7. You can use this dialog box to assign a different profile to a photo. Just save it once without a profile (turn off the ICC [International Color Consortium] Profile checkbox in the Save As dialog box), and then reopen it and choose the profile you want from the dialog box. Or there's an easier way to convert a color profile if you need to make a change. See the box on page 198 to learn how.

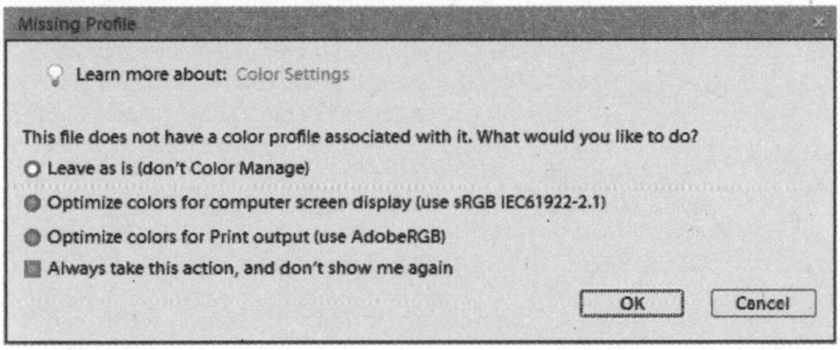

Figure 7-7:
If you select the "Allow Me to Choose" option for color management, you see the Missing Profile dialog box each time you open a previously untagged image. Here's where you can decide whether or not to tag your file and how to tag it. (See page 50 for more about tags.)

NOTE Elements automatically opens files tagged with a color space other than the one you're working in without letting you know what it's just done. (Except when you open a file in a color mode that Elements can't handle at all, like CMYK. In that case, Elements offers to convert it to a mode you can use.) So, if you have an Adobe RGB file and you're working in "Always Optimize Colors for Computer Screens", Elements doesn't warn you about the profile mismatch the way early versions of the program did—it just opens the file.

So what's your best option? Once again, if everything is looking good, leave it alone. Otherwise, for general use, you're probably best off starting with No Color Management. Then try the others if that doesn't work well for you.

Converting Profiles in Elements

If you're a color-management maven, Elements gives you a feature you'll really appreciate—the ability to convert an image's ICC profile from one color space to another. If you've been working in, say, sRGB, and now you want your photo to have the Adobe RGB profile, you can convert it by going to Image → Convert Color Profile and choosing Apply Adobe RGB Profile in the pop-out menu.

You can choose to remove a profile, or convert to sRGB or Adobe RGB; your current color profile choice is grayed out.

This is a true conversion. Your photo's colors don't shift the way they might if you just tag a photo with a different profile. Why would you want to perform such a conversion? Well, for example, if you use Adobe RGB when editing your photos, but you're sending your pictures to an online printing service that wants sRGB instead, then you may want to think about converting.

If you choose one of the other three options, when you save your file, Elements attempts to embed the file with a *tag*, or information about the file's color space— either Adobe RGB or sRGB. (Incidentally, this tag isn't related to the Organizer tags that you read about in Chapter 2.) If you don't want a color tag—also known as an *ICC Profile*—in your file, just turn off the checkbox before you save your file. Figure 7-8 shows where to find the profile information in the Save As dialog box, and how to turn the whole process off.

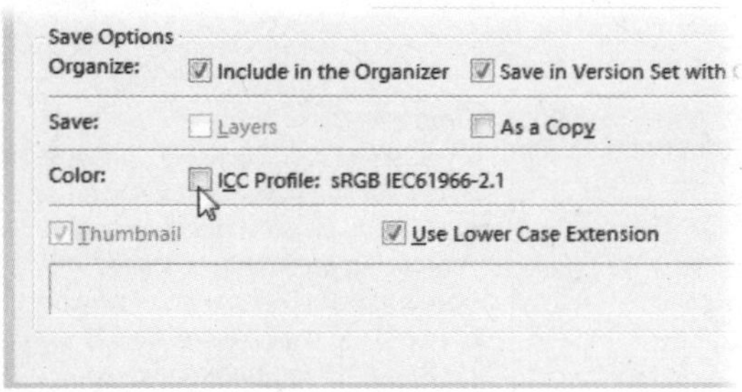

Figure 7-8:
When you save a file, Elements offers to embed the color tag in the file. You can safely turn off the ICC Profile checkbox and leave the file untagged. (Assigning a profile is helpful because then any program that sees your file knows what color standards you're working with. But if you're new to Elements, you'll usually have an easier time if you don't start embedding profiles in files without a good reason.)

Using Levels

People who've used Elements for a while will tell you that the Levels command is one of the program's most essential tools. You can fix an amazing array of problems simply by adjusting the level of each *color channel*. (On your monitor, each color you see is composed of red, green, and blue. In Elements, you can make very precise adjustments to your images by adjusting these color channels separately.)

Just as its name suggests, Levels adjusts the amount, or level, of each color within an image. There are several different adjustments you can make using Levels, from general brightening of your colors to fixing a color cast (more about color casts later in this chapter). Many digital photo enthusiasts treat almost every picture they take to a dose of Levels, because there's no better way to polish up the color in your photo.

The way Levels works is fairly complex. Start by thinking of the possible range of brightness in any photo on a scale from 0 (black) to 255 (white). Some photos may have pixels in them that fall at both those extremes, but most photos don't. And even the ones that do may not have the full range of brightness in each individual color channel. Most of the time, there's going to be some empty space at one or both ends of the scale.

When you use Levels, you tell Elements to consider the range of colors available in *your* photo as the *total* tonal range it has to work with. Elements redistributes your colors accordingly. Basically, you just get rid of the empty space at the ends of the scale of possibilities. This can dramatically readjust the color distribution in your photo, as you can see in Figure 7-9.

It's much, much easier to use Levels than to understand it, as you know if you've already tried Auto Levels in Quick Fix (page 108). That command is great for, well, quick fixes. But if you really need to massage your image, Levels has a lot more under the hood than you can see there. The next section shows you how to get at these settings.

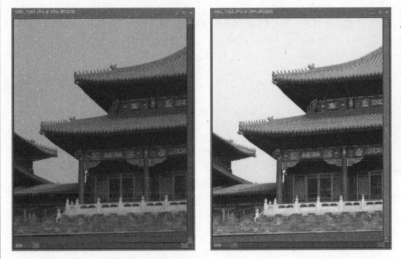

Figure 7-9:
A simple Levels adjustment can make a huge difference in the way your photo looks.

Left: The gray-green cast to this photo makes everything look dull.

Right: Levels not only got rid of the color cast, but the photo also gives the impression of having better contrast and sharpness.

Understanding the Histogram

Before you can get started adjusting Levels, you first need to understand the heart, soul, and brain of the Levels dialog box: the Histogram (shown in Figure 7-10).

The Histogram is the black bumpy mound in the window. It's really nothing more than a bar graph indicating the distribution of the colors in your photo. (It's a bar graph, but there's no space between the bars, which is what causes the mountainous look.)

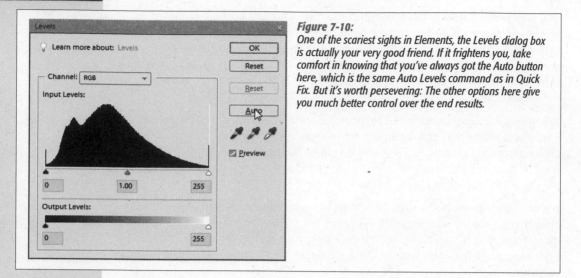

Figure 7-10:
One of the scariest sights in Elements, the Levels dialog box is actually your very good friend. If it frightens you, take comfort in knowing that you've always got the Auto button here, which is the same Auto Levels command as in Quick Fix. But it's worth persevering: The other options here give you much better control over the end results.

From left to right, the Histogram shows the brightness range from dark to light (the 0 to 255 mentioned earlier in this section). The height of the "mountain" at any given point shows how many pixels in your photo are that particular brightness. You can tell a lot about your photo by where the mound of color is before you adjust it, as demonstrated in Figure 7-11.

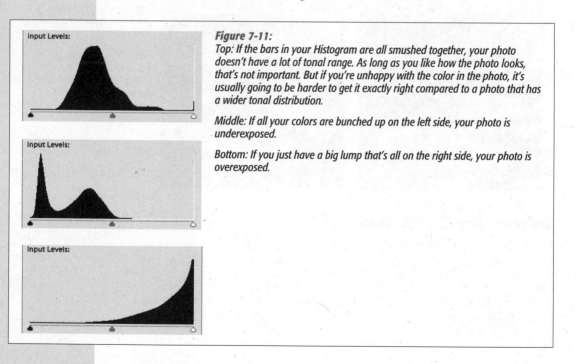

Figure 7-11:
Top: If the bars in your Histogram are all smushed together, your photo doesn't have a lot of tonal range. As long as you like how the photo looks, that's not important. But if you're unhappy with the color in the photo, it's usually going to be harder to get it exactly right compared to a photo that has a wider tonal distribution.

Middle: If all your colors are bunched up on the left side, your photo is underexposed.

Bottom: If you just have a big lump that's all on the right side, your photo is overexposed.

If you look above the Histogram, you can see that there's a little menu that says RGB. If you pull that down, you can also see a separate Histogram for each individual color. You can adjust all three channels at once in the RGB setting, or change each channel separately for maximum control of your colors.

The Histogram contains so much information about your photo that Adobe also makes it available in the Full Editor in its own palette (Figure 7-12); this way, you can always see it and use it to monitor how you're changing the colors in an image. Once you get fluent in reading Histogramese, you'll probably want to keep this palette around.

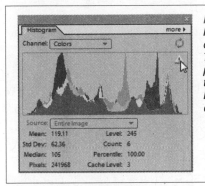

Figure 7-12:
If you keep the Histogram on your desktop, you can always see what effect your changes are having on the color distribution in your photo. To get this nifty Technicolor view, go to Window → Histogram and then choose Colors from the pull-down menu on the palette. To update a Histogram, click the upper-right triangle as shown here. If you're really into statistical information, there's a bunch of it available at the bottom of this palette, but if you're not a pro, you can safely ignore these numbers.

The Histogram is just a graph, and you don't do anything to it directly. What you do when you use Levels is use the Histogram as a guide so that you can tell Elements what to consider as the black and white points—that is, the darkest and lightest points, in your photo. (Remember, you're thinking in terms of brightness values, not shades of color, for these settings.)

Once you've set the end points, you can adjust the *midtones*—the tones in between that would appear gray in a black-and-white photo. If that seems complicated, it's not—at least, not when you're actually doing it. Once you've made a Levels adjustment, the next time you open the Levels dialog box, you'll see that your Histogram now runs the entire length of the scale because you've told Elements to redistribute your colors so that they cover the full dark-to-light range.

The next two sections show you—finally!—how to actually adjust your image's Levels.

TIP Once you learn how to interpret the Histograms in Elements, you can try your hand with your camera's histogram (if it has one). It's really hard to judge how well your picture turned out when all you have to go by is your camera's tiny LCD screen, so the histogram can be a big help. By looking at your camera's histogram, you can tell how well exposed your shot was.

Adjusting Levels: The Eyedropper Method

One way to adjust Levels is to set the black, white, and/or gray points by using the eyedroppers on the right side of the Levels dialog box. It's quite simple—just follow these steps:

1. **Bring up the Levels dialog box by selecting Layer → New Adjustment Layer → Levels.**

   If for some reason you don't want a separate layer for your Levels adjustment, go to Enhance → Adjust Lighting → Levels or press Ctrl+L instead. But making the Levels changes on an Adjustment layer gives you more flexibility for making changes in the future.

2. **Move the Levels dialog box out of the way so that you get a good view of your photo.**

   The dialog box loves to plunk itself down smack in the middle of the most important part of your image. Just grab it by the top bar and drag it to where it's not covering up a crucial part of your photo.

3. **In the Levels dialog box, click the black eyedropper.**

   From left to right, the eyedroppers are black, gray, and white.

4. **Move your cursor back over your photo and click an area of your photo that should be black.**

   Should be, not *is*. That's a mistake lots of people make the first time they use the Levels eyedroppers. They click a spot that appears the same color as the eyedropper rather than one that *ought to be* that color.

5. **Repeat with the other eyedroppers for their respective colors.**

   In other words, now find a white point and a gray point. That's the way it's supposed to work, but it's not always possible to use all of the eyedroppers in any one photo. Experiment to see what gives you the best-looking results.

   NOTE   You don't always need to set a gray point. If you try to set it and think your photo looked better without it, just skip that step.

6. **When you're happy with what you see, click OK.**

See, it's not so hard. If you mess up, just click the Reset button, and you can start over again.

Adjusting Levels: The Slider Controls

The eyedropper method works fine if your photo has spots that should be black, white, or gray, but a lot of the time, your picture may not have any of these colors.

Fortunately, the Levels sliders give you yet another way to apply Levels, and it's by far the most popular method, giving you maximum control over your colors.

Levels Before Curves

I never know where to start adjusting the colors in my photos. Some photo mavens talk to me about using Levels, others about Curves. Which should I use?

Elements includes a much requested feature from Photoshop–*Color Curves*. Despite the name, the Curves tool isn't some kind of arc drawing tool. Instead, it's yet another sophisticated method of adjusting the color in your photos. Curves works something like Levels, but with many more available points of correction.

In Elements, you get a simplified version of the Photoshop Curves dialog box, with a few preset settings.

Because the Elements version doesn't have quite as many points of adjustment, you get much of the advanced color control of Curves without all the complexity.

Generally speaking, a quick Levels adjustment is usually all you need to achieve good, realistic color. If you still aren't satisfied with the contrast in your image, or you want to create funky artistic effects, check out Color Curves (explained in detail on page 267).

If you look directly under the Histogram, you'll see three little triangles, called *Input sliders*. The left triangle is the slider for setting the black point in your photo, the right slider sets the white point, and the middle slider adjusts your midtones (gray). You just drag them to make changes to the color levels in your photo, as shown in Figure 7-13.

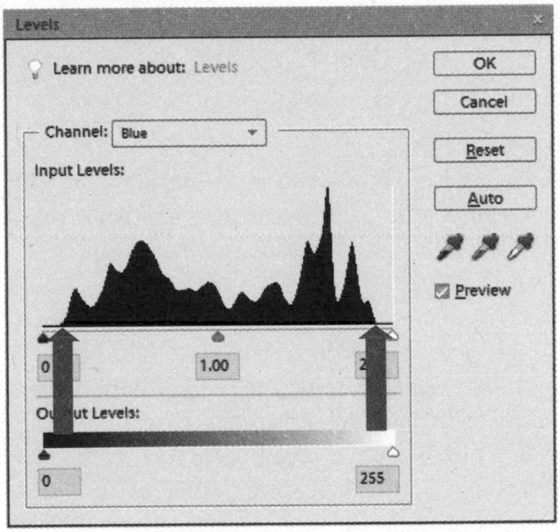

Figure 7-13:
Here's how to use the Levels sliders. You want to move the left and right sliders from the ends of the track until they're under the outer edges of the color data in the graph. If there's empty space on the end, just move the slider until it's under the first mound of data. The red arrows in this figure show where you'd position the left and right sliders for this photo.

When you move the left Input slider, you tell Levels, "Take all the pixels from this point down and consider them black." With the right slider, you're saying, "Make this pixel and all higher values white." The middle slider, the midtones slider, adjusts the brightness values that are considered medium gray. All three adjustments improve the contrast of your image.

NOTE If there are small amounts of data, like a flat line at the ends or if all your data is bunched in the middle of the graph, watch the preview in your photo to decide how far toward the mountain you should bring the sliders. Moving it all the way in may be too drastic. Your own taste should always be the deciding factor when you're adjusting a photo.

The easiest way to use the Levels sliders is to:

1. **Bring up the Levels dialog box.**

   Use one of the methods described in step 1 of the Eyedropper method (page 202).

2. **Move the Levels dialog box so you've got a clear view of your photo and then grab the black Input slider.**

   That's the one on the left side of the Histogram box.

3. **Slide it to the right, if necessary.**

   Move it over until it's under the farthest left part of the Histogram that has a mound of color in it. If you glance back at Figure 7-13, you'd move the left slider to where the left red arrow is. (Incidentally, although you're adjusting the colors in your image, the Levels Histogram stays black and white no matter what you do—you don't get any color in the dialog box itself.)

   You may not need to move the slider at all if there's already a good bit of data at the end of the Histogram. It's not mandatory to adjust each slider every time.

4. **Grab the white slider (the one on the right side) and move it left, if necessary.**

   Bring it under the farthest right area of the Histogram that has a mound of data in it.

5. **Now adjust the gray slider.**

   This is called the *midtones* slider, and it adjusts the midtones of your photo. Move it back and forth while watching your photo until you like what you see. Midtones makes the most impact on the overall result, so take some time to play with this slider.

6. **Click OK.**

You can adjust your entire image or just each color channel individually. The most accurate way is to first choose each color channel separately from the Channel drop-down menu in the Levels dialog box. Adjust the end points for each channel by itself, and then go back to RGB and tweak just the gamma slider.

TIP If you know the numerical value of the pixels you want to designate for any of these settings—you geek!—you can type that information into the Input Levels boxes. You can set the gamma value from .10 to 9.99. It's set at 1.00 automatically.

The last control you may want to use in the Levels dialog box is the Output Levels slider. Output Levels work roughly the same way as your brightness and contrast controls on your TV. Moving these sliders makes the darkest pixels darker and the lightest pixels lighter. Among pros, this is known as adjusting the tonal range of a photo.

Adjusting Levels will improve almost every photo you take, but if your photo has a bad *color cast*—if it's too orange or too blue—you may need something else. The next section shows you how to get rid of unwanted color.

Removing Unwanted Color

It's not uncommon for an otherwise good photo to have a *color cast*—that is, to have all the tonal values shifted so that the photo is too blue, like Figure 7-14, or too orange.

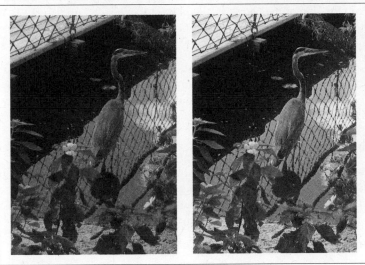

Figure 7-14:
Left: You may wind up with a photo like this one of a heron every once in a while if you forget to change the white balance—your camera's special setting for the type of lighting conditions you're shooting in (common settings are daylight, fluorescent, and so on). This is an outdoor photo taken with the camera set for tungsten indoor lighting.

Right: Elements fixes that wicked color cast in a jiffy. The photo still needs other adjustments, but the color is back in the ballpark.

Elements gives you several ways to correct color cast problems:

- **Auto Color Correction** doesn't give you any control over the changes, but it often does a good job. To use it, go to Enhance → Auto Color Correction or press Ctrl+Shift+B.

- **The Raw Converter** may be the easiest way to fix problems, though it works only on Raw, JPEG, and TIFF files. Just run your photo through the Raw converter (page 224) and adjust your white balance there.

- **Levels** gives you the finest control of all the methods in this list. You can often eliminate a color cast by adjusting the individual color channels till the extra color is gone (as explained in the previous section). The drawbacks are that Levels can be very fiddly for this sort of work, sometimes this method doesn't work at all if the problem is severe, and one of the other ways may be much faster at getting you the results you want.

- **Remove Color Cast** is the special command for correcting a color cast with one-click ease. The next section explains how to use this tool.

- **The Color Variations** dialog box is helpful in figuring out which colors you need more or less of, but it has some limitations. It's covered on page 207.

- **The Photo Filter command** gives you much more control than the Color Cast tool, and you can apply Photo Filters as Adjustment layers, too. Photo Filters are covered on page 242.

- **The Average Blur Filter**, used along with a blend mode, lets you fix a color cast. As you'll read on page 376, it's something like creating a custom photo filter.

- **Adjust Color for Skin Tone** lets Elements adjust your photos based on the skin colors in the image. In practice, this adjustment may be more likely to introduce a color cast than to correct one, but if your photo has a slight bluish cast that's visible in the skin of the people in the photo (as explained on page 117), it may do the trick. This option works best for slight, annoying casts that are too subtle for the other methods in this list.

All these tools are useful for fixing a color cast, depending on exactly what your problem is. Usually you'd start with Levels and then move on to the Color Cast tool or the Photo Filter. (To practice any of the fixes you're about to learn, download the photo *heron.jpg* from the Missing CD page at *www.missingmanuals.com*.)

Using the Color Cast Tool

The Color Cast tool is another eyedropper sampling tool that adjusts the colors in your photo based on the pixels you click. In this case, you show Elements where a neutral color should be. As you saw with the heron in Figure 7-14, the Color Cast command can make a big difference with just one click. To use it:

1. **Go to Enhance → Adjust Color → Remove Color Cast.**

   Your cursor should change to an eyedropper when you move it over your photo. If it doesn't change, go to the dialog box and click the Eyedropper icon.

2. **Click an area that should be gray, white, or black.**

   You only have to click once in your photo for this tool to work. As with the Levels eyedropper tool, click an area that *should be* gray, white, or black (as opposed to looking for an area that's currently one of these colors). If several of these colors appear, you can try different spots in your photo, clicking Reset in between each sample, until you find the spot that gives you the most natural-looking color.

3. **Click OK.**

The Color Cast tool works pretty well if your image has areas that should be black, white, or gray, even if they're very tiny. The tricky thing is when you have an image that doesn't have a good area to sample—when there isn't any black, white, or gray anywhere in the picture. If that's the case, consider using the Photo Filter (page 242).

TIP   If you generally like what Auto Levels does for your photos, but you feel like it leaves behind a slight color cast, a click with the Color Cast tool may be just the right finishing touch.

Using Color Variations

The Color Variations window (Figure 7-15) is very appealing to many Elements beginners, because it gives you a visual clue about what to do to fix the color in your photo. You just click the little preview thumbnail that shows the color balance you like best, and Elements applies the necessary change to make your photo look like the thumbnail.

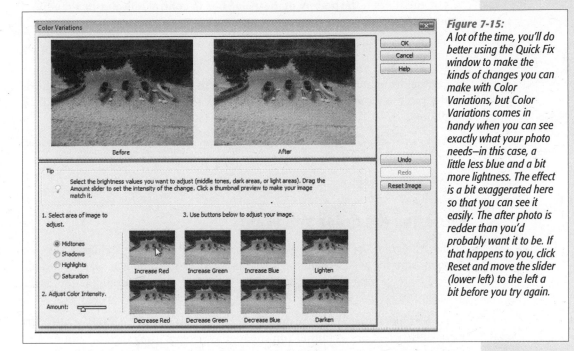

Figure 7-15:
A lot of the time, you'll do better using the Quick Fix window to make the kinds of changes you can make with Color Variations, but Color Variations comes in handy when you can see exactly what your photo needs–in this case, a little less blue and a bit more lightness. The effect is a bit exaggerated here so that you can see it easily. The after photo is redder than you'd probably want it to be. If that happens to you, click Reset and move the slider (lower left) to the left a bit before you try again.

However, Color Variations has some pretty severe limitations, most notably the microscopic size of the thumbnails. It's very hard to see what you're doing, and even newcomers can usually get better results in Quick Fix (page 111).

Still, Color Variations is useful for those times when you know something is not quite right in your color but you can't figure out exactly what to do about it. And because it's adjustable, Color Variations is good for when you do know what you want but you want to make only the tiniest sliver of a difference to your photo's color. To use the Color Variations tool:

1. **Open your photo.**

   You may want to make a duplicate layer (page 159) for the adjustments, so that you'll have the option to discard your changes if you're not happy with them. If you don't work on a duplicate, keep in mind that the changes you make here aren't undoable after you've closed the photo.

2. **Go to Enhance → Adjust Color → Color Variations.**

   You see the dialog box pictured in Figure 7-15.

3. **On the lower-left corner of the dialog box (where it says "Select area of image to adjust"), click a radio button to choose whether you want to adjust midtones, shadows, highlights, or saturation.**

   Color Variations begins by selecting midtones, which is usually what you want. But experiment with the other settings to see what they do. The Saturation button works just like Saturation in Quick Fix (page 111).

4. **Use the slider at the bottom of the dialog box to control how drastic the adjustment should be.**

   The farther you push the slider to the right, the more dramatic the change. Usually, just a smidgen is enough to make a noticeable change.

5. **Just below where it says "Use buttons below to adjust your image", click one of the color buttons to make your photo look more like one of the thumbnail photos.**

   You can always Undo or Redo using the buttons on the right side of the window, or use Reset Image to put your photo back to where it was when you started.

6. **When you're happy with the result, click OK.**

Choosing the Color You Want

So far, the color corrections you've been reading about in this chapter have all done most of the color assigning for you. But a lot of the time, you want to be able to *tell* Elements what colors to work with—like when you're selecting the color for a background or Fill layer (page 176), or when you want to paint on an image.

Although you can use any of the millions of colors your screen can display, Elements loads only two colors at a time. You choose these colors using the Foreground and Background color squares at the bottom of the Toolbox (see Figure 7-16).

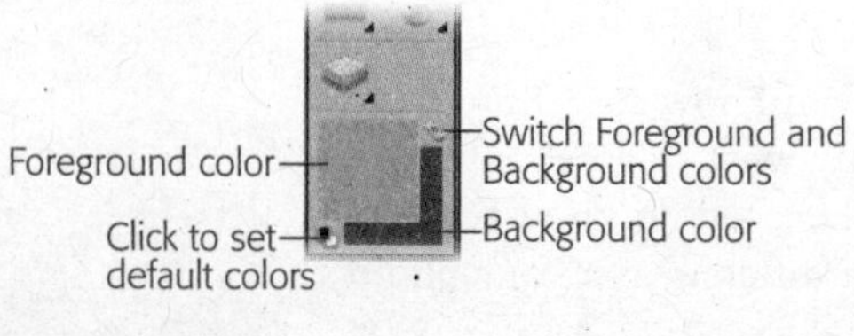

Foreground color—
Click to set—
default colors
—Switch Foreground and
Background colors
—Background color

Figure 7-16:
The top square (aqua) displays the Foreground color; the bottom displays the Background color. To quickly reset the standard black and white colors, either click the two tiny squares at the bottom left or press D. Click the curved double-headed arrows or press X to swap the Foreground and Background colors.

Foreground and Background mean just what they sound like—use the Background color to fill in backgrounds, and use the Foreground color with Elements tools, like the Brush or the Paint Bucket. You can use as many colors as you want, of course. The color-picking tools at the bottom of the Toolbox let you control the color you're using in a number of different ways:

- **Reset default colors.** Click the tiny black and white squares to return to the standard settings of black for the Foreground color and white for the Background color.

- **Switch Foreground and Background colors.** Click the little curved arrows above and to the right of the squares, and your Background color becomes the Foreground color, and vice versa. This is very helpful when you've inadvertently made your color selection in the wrong box. (For example, if you've set the Foreground color to yellow, but you actually meant to make the Background color yellow, just click these arrows, and you're all set.)

- **Change either the Foreground or Background color to whatever color you want.** You can choose any color you like for either color square. Click either square to call up the Color Picker (explained later) to make your new choice. There's no limit on the colors you can select to use in Elements. Well, technically there is, but it's in the millions, so you should find enough choices for anything you want to do.

You actually have a few different ways to select your Foreground and Background colors. The next few sections show you how to use the Color Picker, the Eyedropper tool (to pick a color from an existing image), or the Color Swatches palette.

When working with some of the Elements tools, like the Type tool, you can choose a color in the tool's Options bar settings. Adobe knows that, given a choice, most people prefer to work with either Color Swatches or the Color Picker, so they've come up with a clever way to accommodate both camps, as shown in Figure 7-17.

Click here for the Click here for the
Color Picker   Color Swatches

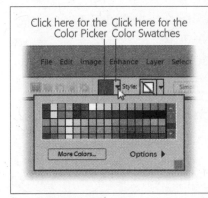

Figure 7-17:
Whether you prefer using Color Swatches or the Color Picker, you can choose your favorite (for most tools) in the Options bar. Click the color sample in the box to bring up the Color Picker, or, if you're a Swatcher, click the arrow to the right of the box to reveal the Color Swatches palette.

The Color Picker

Figure 7-18 shows you the Color Picker. It has an intimidating number of options, but, most of the time, you don't need them all. Picking a color is as easy as clicking wherever you see the color you want.

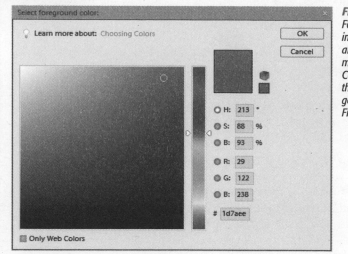

Select foreground color:

Learn more about: Choosing Colors

OK

Cancel

H: 213 °
S: 88 %
B: 93 %

R: 29
G: 122
B: 238

1d7aee

Only Web Colors

Figure 7-18:
For the majority of beginners, the most important parts of the Elements Color Picker are the vertical rectangular slider in the middle (called, appropriately enough, the Color Slider), and the big square box, called the Color Field. Use the Slider to get the general color you want, and then click in the Field for the exact shade.

The Color Picker is actually pretty simple to use:

1. **Click the Foreground or Background color square in the Toolbox.**

   The Color Picker launches. Some other tools—like the Paint Bucket (page 339) and the mask color option for the Selection brush (page 130)—also use the Color Picker. It works the same way no matter how you get to it.

2. **Choose the color range you want to select from.**

   Use the vertical Color Slider in the middle of the Color Picker. Slide through the spectrum until you see the color you want in the Color Field.

3. **Click the exact spot in the Color Field where you see the particular shade you want.**

   You can keep clicking around to watch the color in the top box in the window change to reflect the color you've chosen. The bottom box continues to show your original color for comparison.

4. **Click OK.**

   The color you selected is now your option in the Foreground or Background square in the Toolbox.

That's the basic way to use the Color Picker. See the box on page 213 for ways to enter a numeric value for your color if you know it, or to change the shades the Color Picker is offering you.

TIP   You're not limited to Elements' Color Picker. You can also opt to use the Windows Color Picker instead, if you prefer. (If you're used to working with the Windows Picker, you might want to use what you're most comfortable with, for example.) To change the Color Picker, in the Elements Editor, go to Edit → Preferences → General. The Windows Color Picker opens up looking pretty feeble—just a few colored squares and some plain white ones, but if you click "Define Custom Colors", it expands, giving you access to most of the features in the Adobe picker. (The plain white squares are like little pigeonholes where you can save your color choices.)

The Eyedropper Tool

If you've ever repainted your house, you've probably had the frustrating experience of spotting the *exact* color you want somewhere—if only there were a way to capture that color. That's one problem you'll never run into in Elements, thanks to the handy Eyedropper tool that lets you sample any color you see on your monitor and then automatically make it the Foreground color in Elements. If you can get a color into your computer, Elements can grab it.

Sampling a color (that is, snagging it for your own use) couldn't be simpler than it is with the Eyedropper. Just move your cursor over the color you want and click. It even works on colors that aren't already in Elements, as explained in Figure 7-19. Sampling is perfect for projects like scrapbook pages, where you might want to use, say, the color from an event program cover as a theme color for the project. Just scan the program and sample the color with the Eyedropper.

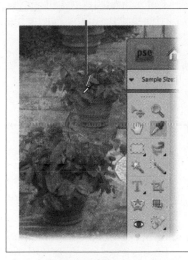

Figure 7-19:
To use the Eyedropper tool to sample colors outside of Elements, start by clicking anywhere inside your Elements file. Then, while still holding your mouse button down, move your cursor over to the non-Elements object (a Web page, for instance), until the eyedropper is over the area you want to sample. Then you can let go, and you'll see the new color in the Elements color squares. If you let go before you get to the non-Elements object, it won't work. Here, the Eyedropper (where the arrow is pointing) is sampling the green color from a photo in Vista's Windows Photo Gallery. If you don't have a big monitor, it can take a bit of maneuvering to get the program windows positioned so that you can perform this procedure.

By now, you may be thinking that Elements has more eyedroppers than your medicine cabinet. But this time, the Eyedropper in question is the Official Elements Eyedropper tool that has its own place in the Toolbox. It's one of the easiest tools to use:

1. **Click the Eyedropper in the Toolbox or just press I.**

   Your cursor changes into a tiny eyedropper.

2. **Move the Eyedropper over the color you want to sample.**

   If you want to watch the color change in the Foreground color box as you move the Eyedropper around, hold the mouse button down as you go.

3. **Click when you see the color you want.**

   Your color choice is loaded up, ready to use, as your Foreground color in the Color Squares. To make it a Background color instead, Alt+click the color in your source.

If you want to keep your color sample around so that you can use it another time without having to get the Eyedropper out again, you can save your color samples in the Swatches palette. Then you can quickly choose those exact colors again any time you want. See the next section for directions on how to do this.

> **TIP** Since there may be some slight pixel-to-pixel variation in a color, you can set the Eyedropper to sample a little block of pixels and average them. In the Eyedropper Options bar settings, you can choose between the exact pixel you click (point sample), a 3-pixel square average or a 5-pixel square average. Oddly enough, this Eyedropper setting also applies to the Magic Wand. Change it here and you change it for the Wand, too.

The Color Swatches Palette

The Color Swatches palette holds several little preloaded libraries of sample colors for you to use in picking a color. Go to Window → Color Swatches to call up the Color Swatches palette. You can park the Color Swatches palette in the Palette bin just like any other palette, if you like, or leave it floating on your desktop. When you're ready to choose a color, just click the swatch you want, and it appears in the Foreground color square or the color box of the tool you're using.

The Color Swatches palette is very handy when you want to keep certain color choices at your fingertips. For instance, you can put your logo colors into it, and then you always have those colors available for any graphics or ads you create in Elements.

Elements starts you off with several different libraries (groups) of Color Swatches. Click the pull-down menu on the Swatches palette to see them all. A swatch you create appears at the bottom of the current library, and you can save it there, or you can create your own swatch libraries if you'd rather do that.

Using the Color Swatches to select your Foreground or Background color is as easy as using the Eyedropper tool. Figure 7-20 shows you how.

To use the Color Swatches palette:

- **To pick a foreground color:** Click the color you want. It appears as the Foreground color choice.

- **To pick a background color:** Ctrl+click a color, and Elements makes it the Background color.

Paint by Number

The Elements Color Picker also includes some very sophisticated controls that most folks can live a long and happy life without ever understanding. For the curious or more advanced, here's what the rest of the Color Picker does.

- **HSB buttons**. These numbers control the hue, saturation, and brightness of your color. The settings control pretty much the same values as the Hue/Saturation adjustment. (See page 271 for more about hue and saturation.)

- **RGB buttons**. The RGB buttons let you specify the amount of red, green, and blue you want in the color you're picking. Each button can have a numerical value anywhere from 0 to 255. A lower number means less of the color, a higher number means more. For example, 128, 128, 128 is neutral gray. By changing the numbers, you can change the blend of the color.

- **Hex number**. Below the radio buttons is a box that lets you enter a special six-character hexadecimal code that you use when you're creating Web graphics. These codes tell Web browsers which colors to display. You can also click a color in the window to see the hex number for that shade.

- **Only Web Colors checkbox**. Turning on this box ensures that the colors you see in the main color box are drawn only from the 216 colors that antique Web browsers can display. For example, if you're creating a Web site and you're really worried about color compatibility with Netscape 4.0, this box is for you. If you see a tiny cube just to the right of the color sample box, the color you're using isn't deemed Web safe.

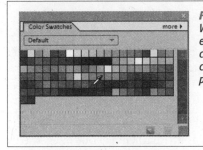

Figure 7-20:
When you move your cursor over the Color Swatches palette, it changes to an eyedropper. Click to select a color. If you're using a preloaded palette you'll see color name labels as you move over each square. If you use the swatches a lot, choose "Place in Palette Bin when closed" from the More menu so the Swatches palette is always there.

You can also change the way the Color Swatches palette displays swatch information, as shown in Figure 7-21.

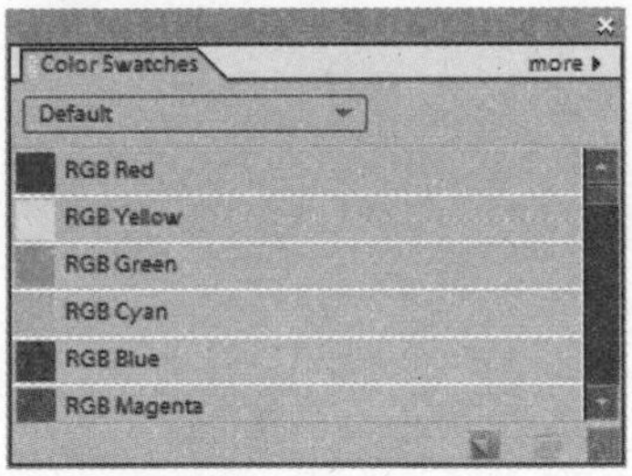

Figure 7-21:
On the Color Swatches palette, click the More button → Small List, and depending on the collection you're using, you can see the names or hex numbers for each color (in addition to a small thumbnail of the color). Some of the tools, like the Type tools, have Options buttons for their swatches viewer instead of the palette's More button.

Saving colors in the Swatches palette

Any colors you've picked using the Color Picker or Eyedropper tool, you can save as swatches. If you don't save them, you lose them as soon as you select a different library or close the palette.

To add a swatch, you can do one of two things:

- **Click the New Swatch icon at the bottom of the Color Swatch palette.** It's the same square that stands for "new" in the Layers palette.

- **Click the More button on the palette, and choose New Swatch.**

In either case, you get a chance to name and save the new swatch. The name shows up as a pop-up label when you hover your mouse over the swatch in the palette. (Don't change the save location if you want Elements to continue to recognize it as a swatch.) Your swatch gets saved at the bottom of the current swatch library. To delete a swatch that you've saved, drag it to the Trash icon in the Color Swatches palette, or Alt+Click the swatch.

You can also create your own libraries, if you want to keep your own swatches separate from the ones Elements gives you. Go to the More button on the palette and pick Save Color Swatches. Then give your new library a name and save it.

> **NOTE** When you save a new swatch library, it doesn't show up in the list of libraries until the next time you start Elements.

Sharpening Your Images

Digital cameras are wonderful, but often it's hard to tell how well you've focused until you download the photos to your computer. And because of the way a camera's digital sensors process information, most digital image data usually needs to be *sharpened*. Sharpening is an image-editing trick that makes your pictures look more clearly focused.

Elements includes some almost miraculous tools for sharpening your images. (It's pretty darned good at blurring them, too, if you want; see page 374.)

> **NOTE** If you've used early versions of Elements, you may be searching in vain on the Filter menu for the Sharpen filters. It's true—your old friends Sharpen and Sharpen More are gone. In their place, Adjust Sharpness appears at the bottom of the Enhance menu, along with Unsharp Mask. (Both of these features are explained in the following sections.) If you miss the one-click ease of Sharpen and Sharpen More, just head over to the Quick Fix and use its Auto button to get the same effect.

Unsharp Mask

Although it sounds like the last thing you'd ever want to do to a photo, Unsharp Mask reigned as the Supreme Sharpener for many generations of image correction, despite the fact that it has the most counterintuitive name in all of Elements.

To be fair, it's not Adobe's fault. *Unsharp Mask* is an old darkroom term, and it actually does make sense if you know how our film ancestors used to improve a picture's focus. (Its name refers to a complicated darkroom technique that involved making a blurred copy of the photo at one point in the process.)

For several versions of Elements, Unsharp Mask ranked right up there with Levels as a contender for most useful tool in Elements, and some people still think it's the best way to sharpen a photo. Figure 7-22 shows how much a little Unsharp Mask can do for your photos.

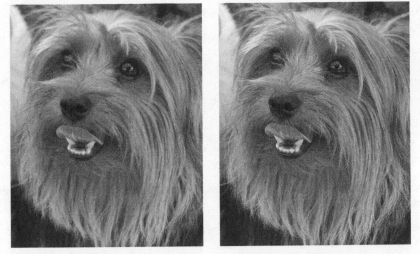

Figure 7-22:
Left: The photo as it came from the camera.

Right: The photo was treated with a dose of Unsharp Mask. Notice how much clearer the individual hairs in the dog's coat are and how much better defined the eyes and mouth are.

To use Unsharp Mask, first finish all your other corrections and changes. Unsharp Mask (or any sharpening tool) can undermine other adjustments you make later on, so always sharpen as the very last step. A good rule to remember when sharpening is "last and once." Repeatedly applying sharpening can degrade your image's quality.

> **NOTE**   An exception to the rule about sharpening only once occurs when you're converting Raw images (page 236). You can usually sharpen both in the Raw converter and then again as a last step without causing problems.

If you're sharpening an image with layers, be sure the active layer has something in it. Applying sharpening to a Levels Adjustment layer, for example, won't do anything. Also, perform any format conversions (page 65) before applying sharpening. Finally, you may want a duplicate layer for the sharpening if you want the ability to undo your changes later on. Press Ctrl+J to create the duplicate layer.

NOTE It's helpful to understand just exactly what Elements does when it "sharpens" your photo. It doesn't magically correct the focus. As a matter of fact, it doesn't really sharpen anything. What it does is deepen the contrast where colors meet, giving the impression of a crisper focus. So while Elements can dramatically improve a shot that's just faintly out of focus or a little soft, even Elements can't fix that old double exposure or a shot where the subject is just a blur of motion.

When you're ready to apply Unsharp Mask:

1. **Go to Enhance → Unsharp Mask.**

   You can use Unsharp Mask in either Full Edit or the Quick Fix.

2. **Adjust the settings in the Unsharp Mask dialog box until you like what you see.**

   Move the sliders until you're happy with the sharpness of your photo. Your adjustment options are explained in the following list. In the Preview window, you can zoom in and out and grab the photo to adjust which part you see. It's also a good idea to drag the dialog box off to the side so that you can watch your actual image for a more global view of the changes you're making.

3. **When you're satisfied, click OK.**

The sliders for Unsharp Mask work very much like the sliders in several of the other tools:

- **Amount** tells Elements how much to sharpen, in percent terms. A higher number means more sharpening.

- **Radius** lets Elements know how far from an edge it should look when increasing the contrast.

- **Threshold** is how different a pixel needs to be from the surrounding pixels before Elements should consider it an edge and sharpen it. If the threshold is left at zero—which is the standard setting—Elements sharpens all the pixels in an image.

There are many, many different schools of thought about which values to plug into each box. Whatever works for you is fine. The one thing you want to watch out for is oversharpening. Figure 7-23 tells you how to know if you've gone too far.

You'll probably need to do a bit of experimenting to find out which settings work best for you. Photos you want to print usually need to be sharpened to an extent that makes them look oversharpened when viewed on your monitor. Therefore, you may want to create separate versions of your photo (one for onscreen viewing and one for printing). Version sets (page 59) in the Organizer are great for keeping track of multiple copies like this.

Adjust Sharpness

Unsharp Mask has been around since long before digital imaging. A lot of people (including the folks at Adobe) have been thinking that, in the computer age,

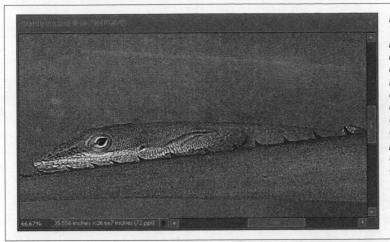

Figure 7-23:
The perils of oversharpening. This lizard may have a suspicious attitude, but he didn't have a skin condition. The flaky look comes from overapplying sharpening, and the white flecks are called artifacts. If you look very closely, oversharpening causes a halo effect around the lizard. The presence of halos is often your best clue that you've oversharpened an image.

there's got to be a better way to sharpen, and now there is. The latest tool in the war on poor focus is Adjust Sharpness.

The Unsharp Mask tool you learned about in the previous section helps boost a photo's sharpness by a process something like reducing Gaussian blur (page 374). Problem is, Gaussian blurring is rarely the cause of your picture's poor focus, so there's only so much Unsharp Mask can fix. In real life, blurry photos usually come from one of two causes:

- **Lens blur.** Your camera's prime focal point is not directly over your subject. Or perhaps your lens is not quite as sharp as you'd like it to be.

- **Motion blur.** You moved the camera—or your subject moved—while you pressed the shutter.

Adjust Sharpness is as easy to use as Unsharp Mask, and it gives you settings to correct all three kinds of blur—Gaussian, lens, and motion. When you first open the Adjust Sharpness dialog box, its settings are almost identical to Unsharp Mask. It's the extra things Adjust Sharpness can do that make it a more versatile tool. Here's how to use it:

1. **Make sure the layer you want to sharpen is the active layer in your photo.**

   See Chapter 6 if you need a refresher on layers.

2. **Go to Enhance → Adjust Sharpness.**

   You can reach this menu item from either Full Edit or Quick Fix.

3. **Make your adjustments in the Adjust Sharpness dialog box.**

   As shown in Figure 7-24, the dialog box gives you a nice big preview. It's usually best to stick to 50 or 100 percent zoom (use the plus and minus buttons below the preview) for the most accurate view. The settings are explained in detail in the list below.

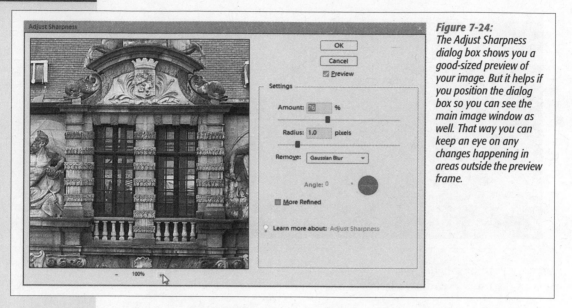

Figure 7-24:
The Adjust Sharpness dialog box shows you a good-sized preview of your image. But it helps if you position the dialog box so you can see the main image window as well. That way you can keep an eye on any changes happening in areas outside the preview frame.

4. **When you like the way your photo is sharpened, click OK.**

The first two settings in the Adjust Sharpness dialog box, Amount and Radius, work exactly the same way they do in Unsharp Mask. Adjust Sharpness also has a couple of additional settings of its own:

- **Remove.** Here's where you choose what kind of fuzziness to fix: Gaussian, lens, or motion blur, as explained on page 217. If you aren't sure which you want, try all three and see which best suits your photo.

- **Angle.** In a motion blur, you can improve your results by telling Elements the angle of the motion. For example, if your grip on the camera slipped, the direction of motion would be downward. Move the line in the little circle or type a number in degrees to approximate the angle. (It's awfully tricky to get the angle exactly right, so you may find it easier to sharpen without messing with this setting.)

- **More Refined.** Turn this checkbox on, and Elements takes a tad longer to apply sharpening since it sharpens more details. Generally you'll want to leave this setting off for photos with lots of little details, like leaves or fur (and people's faces, unless you like to look at pores). But you might want it on for bold desert landscapes, for example, or other subjects without lots of fiddly small parts. Noise, artifacts, and dust become much more prominent when you turn on More Refined, since they get sharpened along with the details of your photo. Experiment, and watch the main image window as well as the preview, to see how it's affecting your photo.

TIP Although Amount and Radius mean the same things as they do in Unsharp Mask, don't assume that you can just plug your favorite Unsharp Mask settings into Adjust Sharpness and get the same results. Experiment, and don't be surprised if you prefer very different numbers in these settings for the new tool.

Many people who've used Smart Sharpening in the full-featured Photoshop swear they'll never go back to plain Unsharp Mask. Try out Adjust Sharpness—the Elements version of Smart Sharpening—and see if you agree. To give you an idea of the difference between the two methods, Figure 7-25 shows the dog from Figure 7-22 again, only this time with Adjust Sharpness instead of Unsharp Mask.

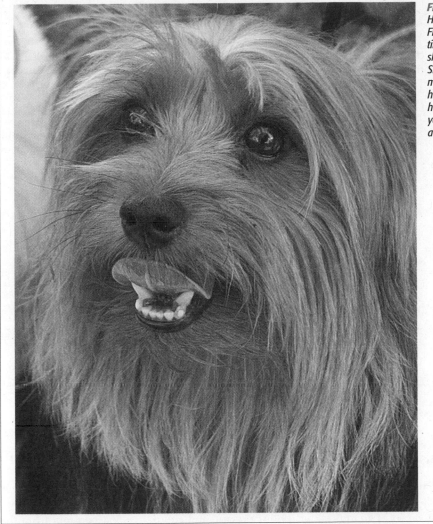

Figure 7-25:
Here's the terrier from Figure 7-22 only this time he's been sharpened using Adjust Sharpness. Notice how much more each hair in his coat stands out, and how much more detail you can see in his nose and mouth.

The High-Pass Filter

Unsharp Mask is definitely the traditional favorite, and Adjust Sharpness is the latest thing in sharpening, but there's an alternative method that many people prefer because you do it on a dedicated layer and can back the effect off later by adjusting the layer's opacity, if you like. Moreover, you can use this method to punch up the colors in your photo as you sharpen. It's called *High-Pass* sharpening. All sharpening methods have their virtues, and you may find that you choose your technique according to the content of your photo. Try the following procedure out for yourself by downloading the photo *waterlillies.jpg* from the Missing CD page at *www.missingmanuals.com*.

1. **Open your photo and make sure the layer you want to sharpen is the active layer.**

2. **Duplicate your layer by pressing Ctrl+J.**

   If you have a multi-layered image and you want to sharpen all the layers, first flatten your image or use the Stamp Visible command (see the box on page 174), so everything is all in one layer.

3. **Go to Filter → Other → High-Pass.**

   Your photo now looks like the victim of a mudslide, buried in featureless gray. That's what you want for right now.

4. **Move the slider until you can barely see the outline of your subject.**

   Usually that means picking a setting somewhere roughly between 1.5 and 3.5. If you can see colors, your setting is too high. If you can't quite eliminate every trace of color without totally losing the outline, a tiny bit of color is OK. Keep in mind that the edges you see through the gray are the ones that you'll be sharpening the most. Use that as your guide to how much detail to include.

5. **Click OK.**

6. **In the Layers palette, set the blend mode for the new layer to Overlay.**

   Ta-da! Your subject is back again in glowing, sharper color, as shown in Figure 7-26.

   TIP There's yet another way to create "pop" in your photos. Check out the Clarity setting in the Raw converter (page 236), which sharpens and enhances contrast at the same time. (If you know what "local contrast enhancement" means, this setting does something similar.) You can use it on Raw, JPEG, and TIFF files. It's especially useful for clearing haze from your shots.

The Sharpen Tool

Elements also gives you a dedicated Sharpen tool. It's a special brush that sharpens instead of adding color to the areas you drag it over; Figure 7-27 shows it in action. To get to it, go to the Blur tool or press R, and choose the Sharpen tool from the pop-out menu.

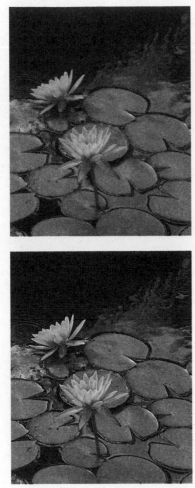

Figure 7-26:
Top: The original photo.

Bottom: High-Pass sharpening using Vivid Light makes the colors more vivid, but the ripples are much harder-edged than they were in the original. For high-pass sharpening, you can use any of the blend modes in the group with Overlay, except Hard Mix and Pin Light. Vivid Light can make your colors pop, but watch out for sharpening artifacts, since they'll be more vivid, too. Overlay gives a softer effect.

The Sharpen tool has some of the same Options bar settings as the Brush tool (see page 329 for more about brush settings). It also has a couple of settings of its very own:

- **Mode** lets you increase the visibility of an object's edge by choosing from several different blend modes, but usually Normal gives the most predictable results.

- **Strength** adjusts how much the brush sharpens what it passes over. A higher number means more sharpening.

- **All Layers** causes the Sharpen tool to work on all the visible layers in your image. Leave it off if you want to sharpen only the active layer.

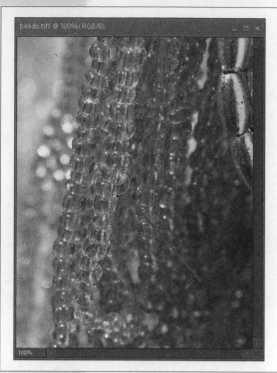

Figure 7-27:
The Sharpen tool isn't meant to sharpen an entire photo, but it's great for detail sharpening. Here, it's being used to bring out the detail in the front strand of beads. (The red arrow helps you find the cursor.) Approach this tool with caution; it's very easy to overdo things with it. One pass too many or a too-high setting, and you start seeing artifacts right away.

CHAPTER 8

Elements for Digital Photographers

If you're a fairly serious digital photographer, you'll be delighted to know that Adobe hasn't just loaded Elements with easy-to-use features, aimed at beginners. Elements is also brimming with a collection of pretty advanced tools pulled straight from the full-featured Photoshop.

Number one on the list is the Adobe Camera Raw Converter, which takes Raw files—a format some cameras use to give you maximum editing control—and lets you convert and edit them in Elements. In this chapter, you'll learn lots more about Raw, and why you may or may not want to use it in your own photography. Don't go away if your camera shoots only JPEGs, though. You can use the Raw Converter to edit JPEG and TIFF images as well as Raw files, which can come in really handy, as you'll see shortly.

> **NOTE**   Whereas JPEG and TIFF are acronyms for geeky photographic terms, the word Raw—which you may occasionally see formatted as RAW—actually refers to the pristine, unprocessed quality of these files.

You'll also get to know the Photo Filter command, which helps adjust image colors by replicating the old-school effect of placing filters over a camera's lens. And last but not least, Elements includes some truly useful batch-processing tools, including features to help rename files, perform format conversions, and even apply basic retouching to multiple photos.

The Raw Converter

Probably the most useful thing Adobe has done for photography buffs is include the Adobe Camera Raw Converter in Elements. For many people, this feature alone is well worth the price of the program, since you just can't beat the convenience of being able to perform conversions in the same program you use for editing.

If you don't know what Raw is, it's just a file format (a group of formats, really, since every camera maker has its own proprietary Raw format). But it's a very special one. Your digital camera actually contains a little computer that does a certain amount of processing to your photos right inside the camera itself. If you shoot in JPEG format, for instance, your camera has already made some decisions about things like sharpness, color saturation, and contrast before it saves the JPEG files to your memory card.

If your camera lets you shoot Raw files, on the other hand, then you get the unprocessed data straight from the camera. Shooting in Raw lets you make your own decisions about how your photo should look, to a much greater degree than with any other format. It's something like getting a negative from your digital camera—what you do to it in your digital darkroom is up to you.

That's Raw's big advantage—total control. The downside is that every camera manufacturer has its own proprietary Raw format, and the format varies even among models from the same manufacturer. No regular graphics program can edit these files, and very few programs can view them. Instead, you need special software to convert your Raw files to a format you can work with. In the past, that usually meant you needed software from the manufacturer before you could move your photo into an editing program like Elements.

Enter Adobe Camera Raw, which lets you convert your files right in Elements. Not only that, but the Adobe Camera Raw plug-in that comes with Elements lets you make very sophisticated corrections to your photos—before you even open them. Many times, you can do everything you need right in the Converter, so that you're done as soon as you open your converted file. (You can, of course, still use any of Elements' regular tools once you've opened a Raw file.) Using Adobe Camera Raw saves you a ton of time, and it's compatible with most cameras' Raw files.

> **NOTE** Adobe regularly updates the Raw Converter to include new versions produced by different cameras, so if your camera's Raw files don't open, check for a newer version of the plug-in. You can download the latest version by going to *www.adobe.com/downloads*, and scrolling down to the section for Photoshop Elements for Windows. (Elements and Photoshop use the same plug-in, but you don't see all the features in Elements.) You'll also find a standalone version of the DNG (digital negative) Converter there, which you can use without launching Elements; see page 240.

Using the Raw Converter

For all the options it gives you, the Raw Converter is very easy to use. Adobe has designed it so that it *automatically* calculates and applies what it thinks are the correct settings for exposure, shadows, brightness, and contrast. You can accept the

Converter's decisions or override them and do everything yourself—it's your call. While you may find all the various settings, tools, and tabs in the Converter a little overwhelming at first, it's really laid out quite logically. Here's a quick overview of how to use it:

- **Open your file in the Raw Converter**. You can call up the Raw Converter from either the Organizer or Full Edit, just by opening a Raw file.

- **Adjust your view and do any rotating, straightening, or (if you wish) cropping**. The Raw Converter has its own tools for all these tasks, so you don't need to go into the Editor for any of them.

- **Adjust the image settings**. This is the best part of shooting Raw format images: You can tweak settings for things like lighting and color. The Converter also lets you apply final touchups: noise reduction, sharpening, and so on.

- **Leave the Converter, go to the Editor**. The Raw Converter is a powerhouse for improving your photo's fundamental appearance, but to perform all the other adjustments Elements lets you make—applying filters, adding effects, and so on— you need to move your image to the Editor, which is also where you save the file in the standard graphics format of your choice (like TIFF, PSD, or JPEG).

If you'd like some practice with the Converter, you can find a sample image (Raw_practice.mrw) on the Missing CD page (*www.missingmanuals.com*), but be warned: It's a big file (7.2 MB).

To start converting your file, in the Organizer, highlight the file(s), and then click Editor → Full Edit (or press Ctrl+I) to bring up the Converter window. (If you send multiple files from the Organizer and the Converter doesn't open automatically, then you can find your files in the Project bin by choosing Show Files From Organizer. Select them all, and then double-click one thumbnail to display them in the Converter.) If you're starting from the Editor, just go to File → Open. You can work with multiple files in the Raw Converter, as Figure 8-1 explains.

> **NOTE** You may not be able to open your Raw files by double-clicking them outside Elements (from the Windows desktop, for instance). You'll probably get a message to the effect that your computer has no idea what program to use to open that file. You can make sure that your computer always uses Elements to open Raw files by following the steps described on page 41. (Windows may also offer to take you to a Web site where you can download the files necessary to let Windows Picture and Fax Viewer display your Raw photos.)

One important point about Raw files: Elements never overwrites your original file. As a matter of fact, Elements can't in any way modify the original Raw file. So your original is always there if you want to try converting it again later on using different settings. It's something like having a negative from which you can always get more prints. This also applies to any image you edit in the Raw Converter, not just Raw files. You can crop a JPEG file here, for instance, and your original JPEG is not cropped—only the copy you open from the Converter. There's more on working with non-Raw files in the Converter on page 239.

To Shoot in the Raw or Not

Should I shoot my pictures in Raw format?

It depends. Using Raw format has pros and cons. You may be surprised to learn that some professional photographers choose not to use Raw. For example, not many journalists use it, and it's not common with sports photographers, either. Here's a quick look at the advantages and disadvantages, to help you decide if you want to get involved with Raw.

On the plus side, you get:

- **More control**. With Raw you have a lot of extra chances to tweak your photos, and you get to call the shots, instead of the processing choices made by your camera.

- **More fixes**. If you're not a perfect photographer, Raw is more forgiving—you can fix a lot of mistakes in Raw, although even Raw can't make a bad photo into a great photo.

- **No need to fuss with your white balance all the time while shooting**. However, you'll get better input if your camera's white balance settings are correct.

- **Nondestructive editing**. The changes you make in the Raw Converter don't change your original image one jot. It's always there for a fresh start, if need be.

But Raw also has some significant drawbacks. For one thing, you can't just open a file and start using the photo the way you do with a JPEG file. You always have to convert it first, whether you use the Elements Converter or one supplied by the manufacturer. Other disadvantages include:

- **Larger file size**. Raw files are smaller than TIFFs, but they're usually much bigger than the highest quality JPEGs. Consequently, you need bigger (or more) memory cards if you regularly shoot Raw.

- **Slower Speed**. It generally takes your camera longer to save Raw files than JPEGs—a significant consideration for action shots. Newer cameras have a buffer that holds several shots and lets you keep shooting while the camera is working, but you may hit the wall pretty quickly if you're using burst (rapid-advance) mode, especially with a pocket-sized point-and-shoot camera that uses Raw. Then you just have to wait. (Most digital single-lens reflex cameras are pretty fast with Raw these days, but they're generally even faster with JPEG.)

- **Worse in-camera preview**. For many cameras, you have some pretty significant limitations for digitally zooming the view in the viewfinder when using Raw, and Windows may not be able to show previews of your Raw files, either, without a special browser.

You may want to try a few shots of the same subject in both Raw and JPEG to see whether you notice a difference in your final results. Generally speaking, Raw offers the most leeway if you want to make significant edits, but you need to understand what you're doing. JPEG is easier if you're a beginner.

It's really your call. Some excellent photographers wouldn't think of shooting in anything but Raw, and other excellent photographers think it's too time consuming.

NOTE   The Organizer can store your Raw files with no problems, but the Photo Downloader tends to be very slow about importing them, and has been known to choke when working with Raw files. You may well find you prefer to get your Raw photos into Elements using one of the other methods discussed on page 40. If you shoot Raw + JPEG (the camera takes one photo and saves it as both a Raw file and a JPEG file), then you definitely don't want to use the Downloader, since it finds this scenario completely confusing.

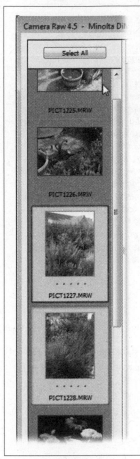

Figure 8-1:
When you open a bunch of files at once in the Raw Converter, you get a handy filmstrip view down the left side of the window. You can select a single image from the group by clicking it, and then your changes apply only to that file. Shift+click or Ctrl+click to select multiple files (or use the Select All button at the top of the list), and your selected files get changed along with the one in the main preview area. When you finish and click Open, all the files appear in the Project bin. If you want to save a group of them in another format, then use Process Multiple Files (page 245).

Adjusting the view

When the Raw Converter opens, you see something like Figure 8-2. Before you decide whether to accept the auto settings that Elements offers or to do your own tweaking, you need to get a good close look at your image. The Converter makes it easy to do this by giving you a large preview of your image, and a handful of tools to help adjust what you see.

- **Hand and Zoom tools.** These tools are in the Toolbox above the upper-left corner of the Converter window. You use them here exactly the same way you would anywhere else in Elements. You'll find more about the Hand tool on page 87; the Zoom tool is described on page 88. The keyboard shortcuts for adjusting the view (page 86) and scrolling (page 88) also work in the Raw Converter.

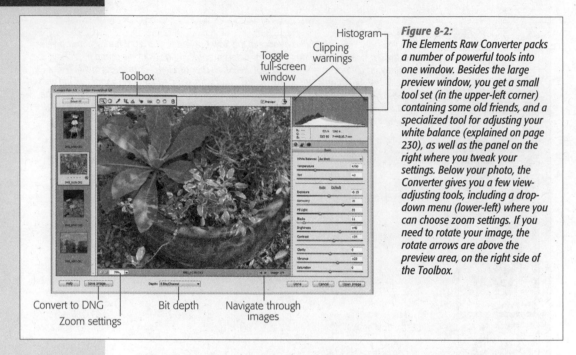

Figure 8-2:
The Elements Raw Converter packs a number of powerful tools into one window. Besides the large preview window, you get a small tool set (in the upper-left corner) containing some old friends, and a specialized tool for adjusting your white balance (explained on page 230), as well as the panel on the right where you tweak your settings. Below your photo, the Converter gives you a few view-adjusting tools, including a drop-down menu (lower-left) where you can choose zoom settings. If you need to rotate your image, the rotate arrows are above the preview area, on the right side of the Toolbox.

Histogram

Clipping warnings

Toggle full-screen window

Toolbox

Convert to DNG

Zoom settings

Bit depth

Navigate through images

- **View percentage.** You get a pop-up menu with preset sizes below the lower-left corner of the preview window. Just choose the size you want, or click the + or – buttons to zoom in or out.

  NOTE Some adjustments and some of the special views, like the mask views for sharpening, aren't available unless you zoom to 100 percent or more.

- **Full Screen.** If you click the icon that looks like a page with a left-facing arrow on it, just to the right of the preview checkbox above the image area, then you can put the Raw Converter window into full-screen view. Click it again to toggle back to the normal view.

- **Histogram.** If you look at the upper-right corner of the Converter, then you see a histogram at the top of the window. The Histogram helps you keep track of how your changes affect the colors in your photo. (Flip back to page 199 for more on the fine art of reading histograms.)

  TIP Another handy feature in the Raw Converter is the panel just below the Histogram, where you can see important shooting information about your photo, like the aperture and ISO speed (ISO is a digital camera's version of film speed). If you hover your cursor over a pixel in the image, the RGB values for that pixel appear here, as well.

Once you've gotten a good close look at your photo, you need to decide: Did Elements do a good enough job of choosing the settings for you? If so, you're done. Just click Open Image, and Elements opens your photo in the Editor, ready for any artistic changes or cropping. If you prefer to make adjustments to your photo in the Converter, read on. (If you're happy with Elements' conversion, but you want to sharpen your picture, then skip ahead to page 236.)

> **NOTE** Everyone gets confused by the Save Image button. That button is actually the DNG Converter (see page 240), and all you can do when you click it is create a DNG file. To save your edited Raw file, click Done if you just want to save the changes without actually opening the file, or click Open. and then save in the format of your choice in the Editor.

Rotating, straightening, and cropping

Before tweaking your settings, you can make these basic adjustments to your photo right in the Converter:

- **Rotate it.** Click one of the Rotation Arrows above the image preview if you need to rotate your photo.

- **Straighten it.** The Raw Converter contains its own Straighten tool, which you use just like the one in the Editor's toolbox (page 76), although it has a different icon and cursor. It's just to the right of the Crop tool in the Raw Converter's toolbox. However, you don't see your photo actually straighten out in the Converter. Elements just shows you the outline of where the edges of your straightened photo will be. Opening the photo in the Editor applies the straightening.

- **Crop it.** The Raw Converter gives you the same Crop tool you find in the Editor (page 80). You can crop to a particular aspect ratio (page 80) here, if you want. Just right-click your photo when the Crop tool is active for a list of presets to choose from. If you want to crop to a particular size, choose Custom from the menu, and then, in the dialog box that appears, enter the numbers. (You also need to select inches or pixels.) Your crop information gets saved along with the Raw file, so the next time you open the file in the Converter, you see the cropped version.

As with straightening, Elements just draws a mask over the area in the Converter; you can still see the outline of the entire photo. To adjust your crop, in the Raw Converter's toolbox, just click the Crop tool again. Then drag one of the handles that appear around the cropped area. To revert to the uncropped original later, right-click the Raw Converter's Crop tool, and then choose Clear Crop.

> **NOTE** You can also fix red eye in the Raw Converter. The Red Eye tool is in the Toolbox just to the right of the Straighten tool, and it works the same way it does everywhere else in Elements (page 104).

Adjusting White Balance

The long strip down the right side of the Raw Converter gives you many ways to tweak and correct the color, exposure, sharpness, brightness, and noise level of your photo. The strip is divided into three tabs. Start with the one labeled Basic, which contains the basic settings for the major adjustments.

First you want to check your white balance, which is at the top of the settings in the Basic tab. Adjusting white balance is often the most important change when it comes to making your photos look their best.

The White Balance control adjusts all the colors in your photo by creating a neutral white tone. If that sounds a little strange, stop and think about it for a minute. The color you think of as *white* actually changes depending on the lighting conditions. At noon there's no warmth (no orange/yellow) to the light because the sun is high in the sky. Later in the day when the sun's rays are lower, whites are warmer. Indoors, tungsten lighting is much warmer than fluorescent lighting, which makes whites rather bluish or greenish. Your eyes and brain easily compensate for these changes, but sometimes your camera may not do so, or may overcompensate, giving your photos a color cast. The White Balance setting in the Raw Converter lets you create more accurate color by neutralizing the white tones.

Most digital cameras have their own collections of white balance settings. Typical choices include Auto, Daylight, Cloudy, Tungsten, Fluorescent, and Custom. When you shoot JPEGs, picking the correct setting here really matters, because it's tough to readjust white balance, even in a program like Elements. (Unless, of course, you tweak your JPEG with the Raw Converter, and even then the results may not be what you want.) With Raw photos, you can afford to be a little sloppier about setting your camera's white balance, because you can easily fix things in the Raw Converter.

Getting the white balance right can make a very big difference in how your photo looks, as you can see in Figure 8-3.

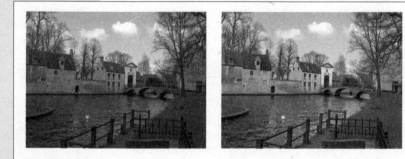

Figure 8-3:
Left: The lighting in this shot has a bluish cast that makes the scene look chilly.

Right: A single click on the swan with the White Balance tool makes the whole photo appear warmer. (It could stand a little additional tweaking, but already the better white balance makes the photo more vivid, and improves the contrast.)

The Raw Converter gives you several ways to adjust the white balance in your image:

- **Pull-down menu.** The menu just below the Histogram starts out by displaying As Shot, which means Elements is showing you your camera's settings. You can use the menu to change this setting, choosing from Auto, Daylight, Cloudy, and other options. It's worth giving Auto a try because it picks the correct settings a surprisingly high percentage of the time.

- **Temperature.** Use this slider to make your photo warmer (more orange) or cooler (more blue). Moving the slider to the left cools your photo; moving it to the right warms it. You can also type a temperature in the box in degrees Kelvin (the official measurement for color temperature), if you're experienced in doing this by the numbers. Use the Temperature slider and the Tint slider (described next) in conjunction for a perfect white balance.

- **Tint.** The tint control adjusts the green/magenta balance of your photo, pretty much the way it does in Quick Fix (see page 111). Move it to the left to increase the green in your photo, and to the right for more magenta.

- **White Balance tool.** The Raw window has its own special Eyedropper tool. Click any white or light gray spot in your photo with it, and Elements calculates the white balance based on those pixels. This is the most accurate of the methods listed here, but you may have a hard time finding neutral pixels on which to use it.

If you're a good photographer, then much of the time a good white balance and a little sharpening may be all your photo needs before it's ready to go out into the world.

Adjusting Tone

The next group of six settings—from Exposure down through Contrast—help you improve your image's exposure and lighting (also known as "tone"). If you like Elements to make decisions for you, click Auto, and Elements starts you off by selecting what it thinks are the best slider positions for each of the six settings. If you don't click anything, then Elements starts you off with the Default settings. Here's the difference between Auto and Default:

- **Auto.** Elements automatically adjusts your photo, using the same software-powered guesswork that powers the other Auto buttons throughout the program, as explained in Figure 8-4.

- **Default.** The Raw Converter contains a database of basic tone settings for each camera model. If you choose Default, then you see the baseline settings for your camera. It's up to you to make further adjustments to your photo, if you wish. You can set your own camera *defaults* (where the sliders are when your photo opens), too, as explained on page 235. If you don't like what you got with Auto, then just click Default to send your photo back to where it was when you opened it.

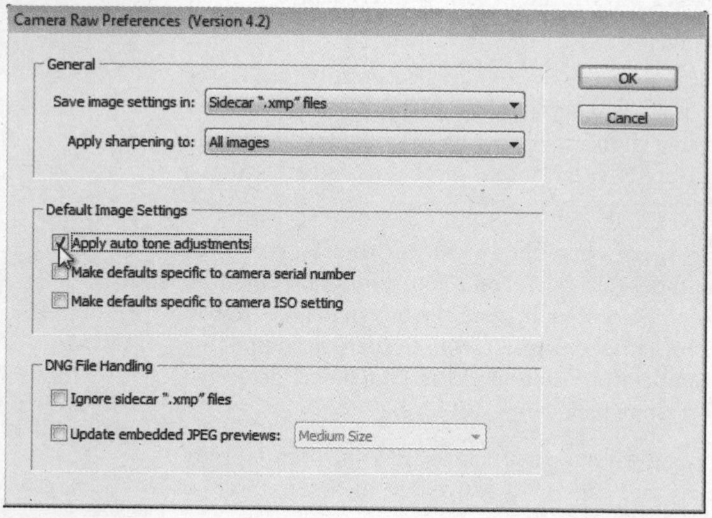

Figure 8-4:
If you want the Raw Converter to always open your photos with the auto settings applied, then open the Raw Converter's preferences dialog box (in the Raw Converter's Toolbox, next to the Red Eye tool, it's the icon with the three lines on it). Turn on this checkbox for "Apply auto tone adjustments", and from now on, the Raw Converter is in Auto mode, at least for the Tone settings.

After you've clicked Auto or Default, you can override any setting by moving the slider yourself. If you go to the trouble of shooting Raw, then you may well prefer to do so, as Figure 8-5 demonstrates.

Here's a blow-by-blow of each of the six settings:

- **Exposure.** A properly exposed photo shows the largest possible range of detail. Shadows contain enough light to reveal detail, and highlights aren't so bright that all you see is white. Move the slider to the left to decrease exposure and to the right to increase it. (Note to photo veterans: The values on the scale are equivalent to f-stops.) Too high a choice here will *clip* some of your highlights. (That is, they'll be so bright you won't see any detail in them.) See Figure 8-6.

- **Recovery.** This clever slider brings down overexposed highlights, recovering the details that were lost without underexposing the rest of the photo. Be very careful when using it—a little goes a long way.

- **Fill Light.** If your subject appears backlit, move this slider to the right to lighten up the shadowed areas, just the way a photographer's fill light does. The Elements Fill Light is clever enough to bring up the shadowed areas without clipping the highlights in your photos.

- **Blacks.** This slider increases the shadow values and determines which pixels become black in your photo. Increasing the Blacks value may give an effect of increased contrast in your photo. Move the slider to the right to increase shadows or to the left to decrease them. A very little change here goes a long way. Move too far to the right, and you clip your shadows. (In other words, they become plain black, with no details, and your colors may become very funky.)

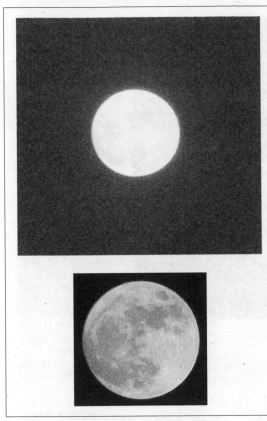

Figure 8-5:

Top: The Raw Converter's suggested Auto settings for this image of the moon. (If you've been wondering what noise is, this is an outstanding example of that annoying problem.)

Bottom: With a little bit of manual adjustment, the photo reveals that the camera actually captured plenty of detail.

- **Brightness.** This is somewhat similar to Exposure in that moving the slider to the right lightens your image and moving it to the left darkens it. But the Brightness slider doesn't clip your photo the way the Exposure setting may. Use this slider to set the overall brightness of your image after you've used the Exposure, Recovery, and Blacks sliders to set the outer range of your photo.

- **Contrast.** The Contrast control adjusts the midtones in your image. Move this slider to the right for greater contrast in those tones, and to the left for less. People usually use this slider last.

Most of the time, you'll want to use several of these sliders to get a perfectly exposed photo. Once you get things adjusted the way you want, you can go on to the lower group of settings and adjust the clarity and saturation of your photo. But if you want, you can also save custom settings for use with other photos, or undo all the changes you've made, as explained in the next section. If you don't have anything to save or undo, just skip ahead to "Adjusting Vibrance and Saturation."

Saving your settings

Most of the time, you'll probably want to use only the adjustments you're making on the particular photo or photos you're editing right now. But Elements also gives

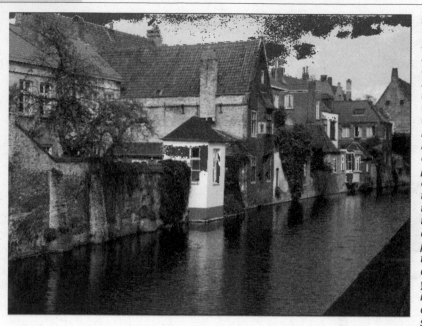

Figure 8-6:
To help you get the Tone settings right, Elements includes two triangles above the ends of the Histogram. Use these to turn on special "clipping warnings" that reveal where your highlights (in red) or your shadows (in blue) lose detail at your current settings. If the photo contains no clipped areas, then the triangle for that end of the Histogram is dark. If the triangle is white or colored, then you have a problem; click the triangle to turn the mask on to see the clipping. As you change your settings in the controls, the clipping mask changes to show the current state of your corrections. In this photo, Elements is warning you that the red and blue speckled areas will be clipped when you open the photo unless you adjust your settings.

you a bunch of ways to save time by saving your settings for future use. Just below the Histogram, on the far right side of the window, you see a small tab with a tiny square with some lines on it: the button for a pull-down menu. Whatever you choose in this menu determines how Elements converts your photo. Here's a look at what the choices mean:

- **Image Settings.** This is the "undo all my changes" option. In other words, if you've made some changes to your photo in the Converter, and you want to revert to the settings Elements originally presented you with, then choose this option.

- **Camera Raw Defaults.** The Raw Converter contains a profile of normal Raw settings for your camera model that it uses as its baseline for the adjustments it makes. That's what you get when you pick Camera Raw Defaults. In Elements 7, you can add your own camera profiles, too (see page 241).

- **Previous Conversion.** If you've already processed a photo and want to apply the same settings to the photo you're currently working on, then choosing this setting applies the settings from the last Raw image you opened (but only if it's from the same camera).

- **Custom Settings.** Once you start changing settings, you see this instead of one of the other choices.

Since individual cameras—even if they're the exact same model—may vary a bit (as a result of the manufacturing process), the Camera Raw Defaults settings may not be the best ones for *your* camera. You can override the default settings and create a new set of default settings for any camera.

- **To change your camera's settings:** If you know that you always want a different setting for one of the sliders—like maybe your Shadows setting should be at 13 instead of the factory setting of 9—move any or all of the sliders to where you want them, and then choose Save New Camera Raw Defaults. From now on, Elements opens your photos with these settings as your starting point.

- **To revert to the original Elements settings for your camera:** If you want to go back to the way things were originally, then click the Settings button, and choose Reset Camera Raw Defaults.

    NOTE   You can apply the same changes to multiple photos at once. See page 227 for more on how to do this.

The Raw Converter's preferences have a couple of special settings that may interest you. To bring up the Raw Converter's Preferences dialog box, in the Raw Converter's toolbox, click its icon (the three lines). These preferences can be very useful, especially if you have more than one camera.

- **Make defaults specific to a camera serial number.** Turn this on if you have more than one of a particular camera model; for instance, if you carry two bodies of the same model with different lenses when you shoot, or if both you and your spouse have the same camera model. This setting lets you have a different default for each camera body.

- **Make defaults specific to camera ISO setting.** Since you may shoot very differently at different ISO settings (ISO is equivalent to film speed), you can use this to create a default that applies only to photos shot at ISO 100, or at ISO 1600, and so on.

    NOTE   If you regularly share photos with people using other programs, you'll be pleased to know that the Elements Camera Raw preferences let you choose whether your settings get saved in the Camera Raw database or in a sidecar XMP file that goes along with the image. If you choose the XMP file, then your settings become portable along with your photo—that is, if you send the file to someone else, the settings travel along with the photo, as long as you send the XMP file, too.

You don't have to create default settings to save the changes you make to a particular photo. If you just want to save the settings for the photo or group of photos you're working on right now, without having to open them all in the Editor and save them in another format, make your changes, and then click Done to update the settings for the image file(s).

NOTE   In Elements 7, you can also add a whole new camera profile for the Raw Converter to use as a basis for adjusting your photos. Page 241 explains how.

Adjusting Vibrance and Saturation

The final group of settings on the Raw Converter's leftmost tab controls the vividness of your colors; you may or may not want to use them. Most Raw files have lower saturation to start with than you'd see in the same photo shot as a JPEG. Therefore people often want to boost their saturation a bit. Move the sliders to the right for more intense color, and to the left for more muted color. If you know you'll always want to change the intensity of the color, then you can change the standard setting by moving the slider until you have the intensity you want, and creating a new camera default setting, as described on page 235.

- **Saturation.** The Saturation slider controls how vivid your colors are by applying the same amount of change to the intensity of all the colors in your photo.

- **Vibrance.** While Saturation adjusts all the colors in your photo equally, the Vibrance slider is much smarter. It increases the intensity of the duller colors, while holding back on those colors that are already so vivid they may oversaturate. If you want to adjust saturation to make your photo pop, then try this slider first; it's one of the handiest features in the Raw Converter.

- **Clarity.** This slider appears first, and it's a bit different from the other two. Clarity isn't strictly a color tool, although it is an absolutely amazing feature. If you're an experienced Elements sharpener, you may have heard of the technique called Local Contrast Enhancement, where you use the Unsharp Mask (page 214) with a low amount setting and a high radius to eliminate haze and bring out details. That's sort of what Clarity does: Through an incredibly sophisticated technique, it creates an edge mask in your photo that it uses to increase detail. It can do wonderful things for many, maybe even most of your photos, to improve contrast and add punch. Give it a try, but be sure to look at your photo at 100 percent magnification (or more) so you can see how you're changing things. For some cameras you may find that the details in the converted photos look rather blocky when viewed at near 100 percent size. If that happens, reconvert the file with a lower Clarity setting.

Adjusting Sharpness and Reducing Noise

Once you've got your exposure and white balance right, you may be almost done with your photo. But in most cases, you still want to click over to the Raw Converter's Detail tab to do a little sharpening.

Two other important adjustments are available here as well: *Luminance* and *Color* (both described in a moment), used for reducing noise in your photos. None of the adjustments on this tab have Auto settings, although you can change the standard settings by moving their sliders where you want them, and then creating a new camera default, as described earlier.

Sharpening increases the edge contrast in your photo, which makes it appear more crisply focused. The sharpening tools in the Raw Converter are a bit different from those in the Editor. But some of the sliders should look familiar if you've sharpened before, since they're similar to the settings for Unsharp Mask (page 214) or Adjust Sharpness (page 216).

- **Amount** controls how much you want Elements to sharpen. The scale here goes from zero (no sharpening) to 150 (way too much sharpening).

- **Radius** governs how wide an area Elements should consider as an edge to sharpen. Its scale goes from .5 pixels to 3 pixels.

- **Detail** controls how the sharpening is applied to your image. At 100—the far end of the scale—the effect is most similar to Unsharp Mask (in other words, you can overdo it if you aren't careful). At zero, you shouldn't see any sharpening halos at all.

- **Masking** is a very cool feature that reduces the area where sharpening takes place so that only edges get sharpened. If you find that you're sharpening more details than you like, then use this slider to create an Edge Mask that restricts Elements from sharpening areas inside the edges. The farther you move the slider to the right, the more area is protected from sharpening. Masking is doing some amazing behind-the-scenes calculations, so don't be surprised if there's a little lag in the preview when you use this slider.

  Masking and Detail work together to create very accurate sharpening, which is why the sliders go so high—you won't like the effect from just one of them set all the way up, but by experimenting with the effect of using both sliders, you can create excellent sharpening for your photo.

You also get an extremely helpful view of your image if you hold the Alt key as you move the sliders, as explained in Figure 8-7 (but only if the view is set to at least 100%).

If you're not planning on making any further edits to your photo when you leave the Raw Converter, then go ahead and sharpen it here.

On the other hand, some people prefer to wait to sharpen until they finish all their other adjustments in Full Edit mode, so they skip these sliders. But in fact you can usually sharpen here, and then sharpen again later on, outside the Converter, without causing yourself any trouble.

The final two settings on this tab (under Noise Reduction) work together to reduce the *noise* (graininess) of your photo. Noise is a big problem in digital photos, especially with 5-plus megapixel cameras that don't have the large sensors found in single-lens reflex cameras. The Raw Converter gives you two adjustments here that may help:

- **Luminance.** This setting reduces grayscale noise, which causes an overall grainy appearance to your photo—something like what you'd see in old newspaper photos. The slider is always at zero to start with, since you don't want to use

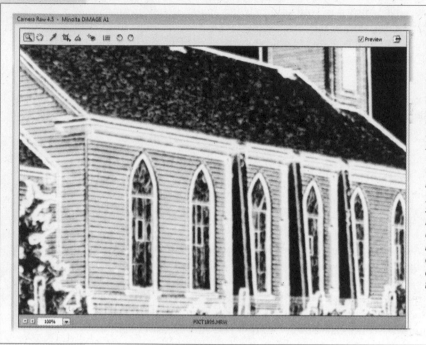

Figure 8-7:
If you've tried High-Pass sharpening (page 219), then you won't have any trouble understanding this helpful new view of your image. Set the view to 100 percent or higher, and then Alt+drag any of the sharpening sliders to see this black-and-white view of your image. Omitting the color makes it easy to focus on what you're doing to the edge sharpness in your photo. If you pay close attention, then you get a highly accurate view of exactly what you're doing as you manipulate the sliders.

more than you can help. That's because moving to the right reduces noise, but it also softens the detail in your photo.

- **Color.** If you look at what should be evenly colored areas of your photo, and you see obvious clumps of different-colored pixels, this setting can help smooth things out. Drag the slider to the right to reduce the amount of color noise.

In most cases, it may take a fair amount of fiddling with these sliders to come up with the best compromise between sharpness and smoothness. It helps if you zoom the view up to 100 percent or more when using the sliders.

Choosing bit depth: 8 or 16 bits?

Once you've got your photo looking good, you have one more important choice to make: Do you want to open it as an 8-bit or a 16-bit file? *Bit depth* refers to the number of pieces of color data, or *bits*, that each pixel in your image can hold. A single pixel of an 8-bit image can have 24 bits of information in it, 8 for each of the three color channels (red, green, and blue). A 16-bit image holds far more color information than an 8-bit photo. How much more? An 8-bit image can hold up to 16 million colors, while a 16-bit image can hold up to 281 *trillion* colors.

NOTE You can adjust 16-bit images with microscopic precision, but in the real world, your home printer provides only 8-bit color anyway. If you want to do all your editing (or at least 90 percent of it) in 16-bit color, then consider upgrading to Photoshop.

Non-Raw Files in the Raw Converter

If your camera shoots JPEG files and you've always been curious about what this Raw business is all about, you can find out for yourself—sort of. You can open JPEG or TIFF files with the Raw Converter, and then process them there. (If you want to try another kind of file, save it as a TIFF, and then open it with the Raw Converter. This way, you can take advantage of the special tools in the Converter, like Vibrance or Clarity, for any photo.)

To open non-Raw formats in the Editor, just use File → Open As, and then choose Camera Raw (*not* Photoshop Raw) as the format. Your file opens up in the Converter, and you can work on it just like a real Raw file. Actually, it's more accurate to say, "almost like a real Raw file." The thing about using other formats in the Converter is this: When your camera processed that JPEG file that it wrote to your memory card, it tossed out the information it didn't need for the JPEG, so Elements doesn't really have the same amount of information to work with that it has for a true Raw file. The Converter even lets you create a DNG—digital negative—file (page 240) from a JPEG if you wish, but it can't put back the information that wasn't included in the JPEG, so this is of limited usefulness for most people.

This means that your results can be very iffy. You may find that the Raw Converter does a bang-up job on your photo, or you may find that you liked it better before you started messing with it. There are so many variables involved that it's really hard to predict the results you'll get. But it's definitely worth giving it a try to see what you think.

If you find you like using the Raw Converter for JPEGs, then you might want to experiment with reducing the saturation, contrast, and sharpening in the camera if you have settings that let you do so. You're more likely to get good results from the Raw Converter if your image is fairly neutral to start with.

Most digital cameras produce Raw files with 10 or 12 bits per channel, although a few can shoot 16-bit files. You'd think it makes perfect sense to save your digital files at the largest possible bit depth. But the fact is you'll find quite a few restrictions on how much you can do to a 16-bit file in Elements. You can open it, make some corrections, and save it, but that's about all. You can't work with layers or apply the more artistic filters on a 16-bit file, but you can use many of the Auto commands in Elements 7. If you want to work with layers on a 16-bit file, then you need to upgrade to Photoshop.

> **NOTE**   Your scanner may say it handles 24-bit color, but this is actually the same as what Elements calls 8-bit. Elements goes by the number of bits per color channel, whereas some scanner manufacturers try to impress you by giving you the total for all three channels ($8 \times 3 = 24$). When you see very high bit numbers—assuming you aren't a commercial printer—you can usually get the Elements equivalent number by dividing by three.

Once you've decided between 8- and 16-bit color, just make your selection in the Depth drop-down menu (in the lower-left corner of the Raw Converter window). The Raw bit-depth setting is "sticky," so if you change it, all your images open in that color depth until you change it again. If you ever forget what bit depth you've chosen, your image's title bar tells you, as shown in Figure 8-8.

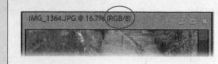

Figure 8-8:
You can always tell an image's bit depth by looking in the title bar of any image window. This image is 8-bit.

TIP If you do decide to create a 16-bit image and later become frustrated by your lack of editing choices, then you can convert your image to 8-bit by choosing Image → Mode → 8 Bits/Channel. You can't convert an 8-bit image to 16 bits.

If you want to take advantage of any 16-bit files you might have, you may want to use either Save As or the Organizer's version set option (see page 59) for the copy you plan to convert to 8-bit. That way you still have the 16-bit file for future reference. Incidentally, your Save options are different for the two bit depths. JPEG, for instance, is available only for 8-bit files. If you wonder why you only have choices like JPEG 2000 when you save a file, then you've got yourself a 16-bit file. (Regular JPEGs are always 8-bit files.)

A popular choice when you're thinking about your order of operations (*workflow*, in photo-industry speak) is to first convert your Raw file as a 16-bit image to take advantage of the increased color information while making any basic corrections, and then convert to 8-bit for the fancy stuff like the artistic filters or layer creation.

Finishing Up

Now that you've got your photo all tweaked and sleeked and groomed to look exactly the way you want, it's time to get it out of the Raw Converter. In order to do that, you need to click Open, which sends your photo to Full Edit, where you can save it in the format of your choice (TIFF or JPEG, for instance). Everyone gets confused by the Raw Converter's Save button—that's actually a link to the DNG converter, discussed in "Converting to DNG" below. If you just want to save your changes without actually opening the file, then you don't need to do anything: The next time you open your Raw file, the Raw Converter will remember where you left off.

Converting to DNG

There's been a lot of buzz lately about Adobe's DNG (digital negative) format, and if you shoot Raw, you should know what's going on. As you read at the beginning of this chapter, every manufacturer uses a different format for Raw files. Even the formats for different cameras from the same manufacturer differ. It's a recipe for an industry-wide headache.

Adobe's solution is the DNG format, which the company envisions as a more standardized alternative to Raw files. Here's how it works. If you convert your Raw file to a DNG file, then it still behaves like a Raw file—you can still tweak your settings in the Converter when you open it, and you still have to save it in a standard image format like TIFF or JPEG to use it in a project. But the idea behind DNG is that if

Working with Profiles

The Raw Converter has another trick up its sleeve. It's one you can safely ignore if you're a beginner, but for Raw experts it's a very big deal indeed. In Elements 7, the Raw Converter has a third tab: Camera Calibration. If you click it, all you see is a pull-down menu that seems to imply you're using an older version of Adobe Camera Raw. What's the point of this cryptic tab?

You can now create and edit your own camera profiles, and install them in Elements for the Converter to use. If you've ever thought, "Darn, I wish my Raw files opened looking as good as the JPEGs I shoot with my camera," or if you've stuck with another Raw converter (like the ones from Nikon or Canon because you just can't get the same results with Adobe's Converter), then this tab's for you.

You can't actually create or edit profiles in Elements, but Adobe has developed a standalone profile editor, along with profiles for many, many cameras. They're undertaking to eventually have profiles for every camera that shoots Raw, but they began with Nikon and Canon (since they're the most popular brands).

Editing camera profiles is beyond the scope of this book, but you can download the DNG Profile Editor and the initial set of camera profiles at *http://labs.adobe.com/wiki/index.php/DNG_Profiles*. There's an excellent tutorial at *http://www.luminous-landscape.com/reviews/accessories/dng-profiles.shtml*.

If you create and install profiles, then they appear in the pull-down menu on the Camera Calibration tab, and you can select the one you want to use as the basis for all your setting changes in the Raw Converter. If you haven't done this, and you're wondering why your list shows older Adobe Camera Raw versions like 4.2, that's because the list shows the version numbers for when the built-in Adobe Camera Raw profiles were last updated. So if you've been thinking, "You know, I think I liked the way my Raw files looked better a couple of versions ago," no problem. You can choose the older profile version for your camera from the list, and use that instead of the newest one.

you keep your Raw files in this format, then you don't have to worry about whether or not Elements version 35 can open them. Adobe clearly hopes that all camera manufacturers will adopt this standard, putting an end to the mishmash of different formats that make Raw files such a nuisance to deal with. If all cameras used DNG, then every time you bought a new camera you wouldn't have to worry whether your programs could view the camera's images.

You can create DNG files from your Raw files right in the Converter. At the bottom of the window, just click the Save Image button, and you see the DNG Converter, shown in Figure 8-9. Choose a destination, and then select how you want to name the DNG file. You get the same naming options as in Process Multiple Files (page 245), but since you convert only one file at a time here, you may as well keep the photo's current name, and just add the .DNG extension.

Of course, the jury is still out on whether DNG is going to become an industry standard, although it does seem to be gaining popularity. People have had other good ideas over the years, like the JPEG 2000 format (see page 63), that never really took off. Whether or not to create DNG files from your Raw files is up to you, but for now, it's probably prudent to hang onto the original files as well, if you decide in favor of DNG.

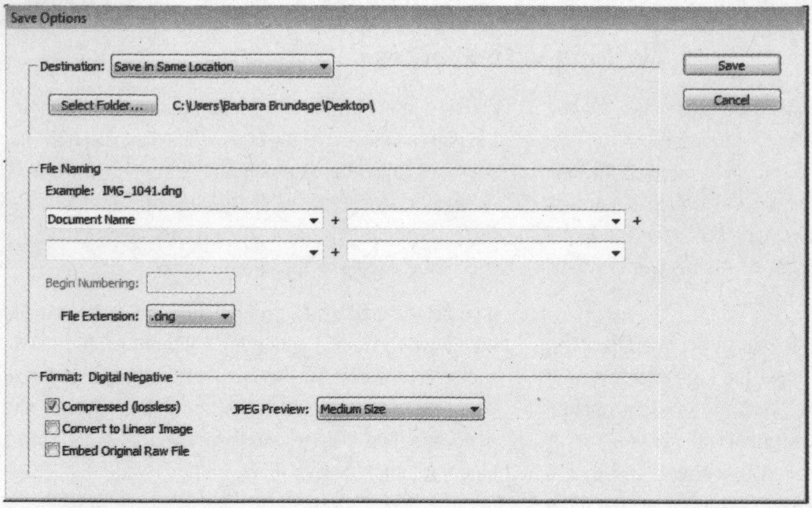

Figure 8-9:
The DNG Converter. The bottom section of the Converter window lets you choose whether or not to compress the file, how to handle the image preview, and whether or not to embed your original Raw file in the new one. Generally, you're best off leaving the settings in this section the way you see them in the illustration.

TIP If you want to convert a group of your Raw files to DNG in one batch, the easiest way is to go to Adobe's Web site (*www.adobe.com/downloads*) and search for "DNG"; download the stand-alone DNG Converter, which you can leave on your desktop. Then just drop a folder of Raw images onto its icon, and the DNG Converter lets you process the whole folder at once. The stand-alone Converter is part of the Raw Converter update (page 224). If your Raw Converter is up to date already, just remove the DNG Converter and discard the rest of the download. You can also batch-save images in the Raw Converter itself, by highlighting them in the list on the left side of the window, and then clicking Save Images.

Photo Filter

The Photo Filter command gives you a host of nifty photo filters. These filters are the digital equivalent of those lens-mounted filters used in traditional film photography. You can use them to correct problems with your image's white balance, as well as for a bunch of other fixes from the seriously photographic to the downright silly. For example, you can correct bad skin tone or dig out an old photo of your fifth-grade nemesis and make him green, literally. Figure 8-11 shows the Photo Filter in action.

Elements comes with 20 Photo Filters, but for most people, the top six are the important ones: three warming filters and three cooling filters. You use these filters to get rid of the color casts that come from a poor white balance (see page 230).

The filters are an improvement over the Color Cast eyedropper (page 206) because you can control the strength with which you apply them (using the Density slider, explained later). And you can also apply them as Adjustment layers (page 176), so you can tweak them later on.

POWER USERS' CLINIC

(Faking) HDR/Digital Blending

One of the big new buzz terms in photography is *high dynamic range*, or HDR for short. This technique has been around awhile, but before it was more often called *digital blending*. With most digital cameras, you're likely to hit the clipping point (page 234) in an image much sooner than you want to. If you up the exposure so that the shadows are nice and detailed, then about half the time you've blown the highlights. On the other hand, if you adjust your exposure settings down to favor the highlights, then your shadows are murkier than an Enron annual report.

HDR/digital blending is a technique photographers use to get around these limitations. To use HDR, you *bracket* your shots. That is, you take two or more identical shots of your subject at different settings—one exposed for shadows and one for highlights—and then combine them, choosing the best bits of each one. True HDR is a pretty complex process, but you can simulate it, to some extent, in Elements.

That technique is great for landscapes. But if you're shooting hummingbirds, roller-skating chimps, or toddlers, you know it's just about impossible to get two identical shots of a moving subject. And if you're like many amateur photographers, you may not realize you didn't capture what you wanted until you're home and see the shot on your computer.

If you shoot in Raw mode, you can use the Converter to help fake HDR, sort of. It's not as good as planning ahead, but you can often salvage another stop or two of detail. Just follow these steps:

1. Run your photo through the Converter twice, exposing once for the highlights and once for the shadows.

2. Drag one image onto the other—the way you would if you were creating a new layer (page 179).

3. Put the image with the largest area that you want to use on top, so you have less to change.

4. Use the Eraser tool (page 348) to rub out the bad spots on the top photo, revealing those areas in the bottom layer.

Figure 8-10 shows this process in action.

When you're done, you can merge the layers (page 173) if you want.

If you'd like to try your hand at the real thing, you'll find an excellent tutorial on Luminous Landscape (*http://luminous-landscape.com/tutorials/digital-blending.shtml*). Every digital photographer should bookmark this site. You're sure to find a ton of valuable information there, including lots of fine tutorials.

You can also purchase special plug-ins that automatically create HDR for you. *www.hdrlabs.com* and *www.hdrsoft.com* are good sources for popular plug-ins. (Always be sure to check with the developer for compatibility with Elements 7 before you spend money on a plug-in.)

To apply a Photo Filter:

1. **Open the Photo Filter dialog box.**

   Go to Layer → New Adjustment Layer → Photo Filter, or go to Filter → Adjustments → Photo Filter. The Photo Filter dialog box appears.

2. **Choose a filter from the pull-down list or click the Color radio button.**

   You get two choices. The pull-down list gives you a choice of filters in preset colors. If you want to choose your own custom color, then click the Color button instead.

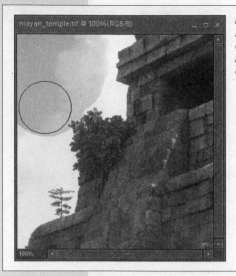

Figure 8-10:
Digital blending (see the box on page 243) in action. Here, the blown-out sky in the top image is being erased to reveal the blue sky in the bottom layer. This maneuver is similar to the technique you use for creating spot or accent color, explained on page 288.

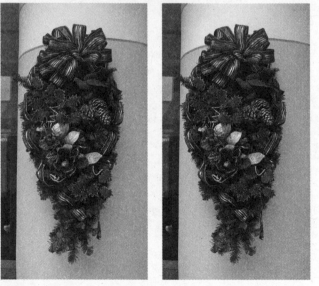

Figure 8-11:
You can use the Photo Filter to correct the color casts you get from artificial lighting.

Left: This photo had a strong bluish tinge from nearby fluorescent lighting.

Right: A Warming Filter (85) took care of it. Use Cooling Filter (80) or Cooling Filter (82) to counteract the orange cast from tungsten lighting. (The numbers stand for the numbers of glass filters you'd use on a film camera.)

3. **If you chose the Color button, then in the dialog box, click the color square to bring up the Color Picker (page 209), and choose the shade you want.**

   You can also sample a color from your image. The cursor turns to an eyedropper when you move it from the dialog box into your photo. Just click the color you want for your filter, and that color appears in the dialog box's color square.

4. **Move the Density slider to adjust the color.**

Moving the Density slider to the right increases the filter's effect; moving it to the left decreases it. If you leave Preserve Luminosity turned on, then the filter doesn't darken your image. Turn off Preserve Luminosity, and your photo gets darker when you apply the filter.

5. **Click OK.**

Processing Multiple Files

If you're addicted to batch processing your photos, then you'll love the Elements equivalent: Process Multiple Files. In addition to renaming your files and changing their formats, you can do a lot of other very useful things with this tool, like adding copyright information or captions to multiple files, or even using some of the Quick Fix auto commands.

To call up the batch-processing window, in Full Edit, go to File → Process Multiple Files. You see yet another headache-inducing, giant Elements dialog box. Fear not—this one is actually pretty easy to understand. If you look closely, then you see that the dialog box is divided into sections, each with a different specialty (see Figure 8-12).

> **TIP** Process *Multiple* Files is the name of the command, but you can run it on just one photo if you want, although you'll usually find it easier just to do a regular Save As (see Chapter 2 for more about saving files). Just open your photo, go to File → Process Multiple Files, and then choose Opened Files as your source. You can even opt to save the new version to the desktop without overwriting your original.

The following sections cover each main section of the Process Multiple Files dialog box. You have to use the first section (which tells Elements which files you want to process), but you'll probably want to make use of only one or two of the other sections at any one time. (Of course, you can use them all, as shown in Figure 8-12.)

> **TIP** If you're working in the Organizer, then you can do some batch processing without going to the Editor. Select the files you want, and then go to File → Export As New File(s) (or press Ctrl+E). You get a dialog box that lets you change the format, choose a new size from a list of presets, set a destination for the new images, and choose a new "common base name" if you want. If you choose this option, then your files get the new name plus a sequential number. (By the way, this export feature is a great way to create a folder of JPEGs to send to an online photo service.)

Choosing Your Files

In the first section of the dialog box, in the upper-left corner, identify the files you want to convert, and then tell Elements where to put them once it's processed them. You have several options here, which you pick from the Process Files From pull-down menu: your currently open files, the contents of a folder, or "Import".

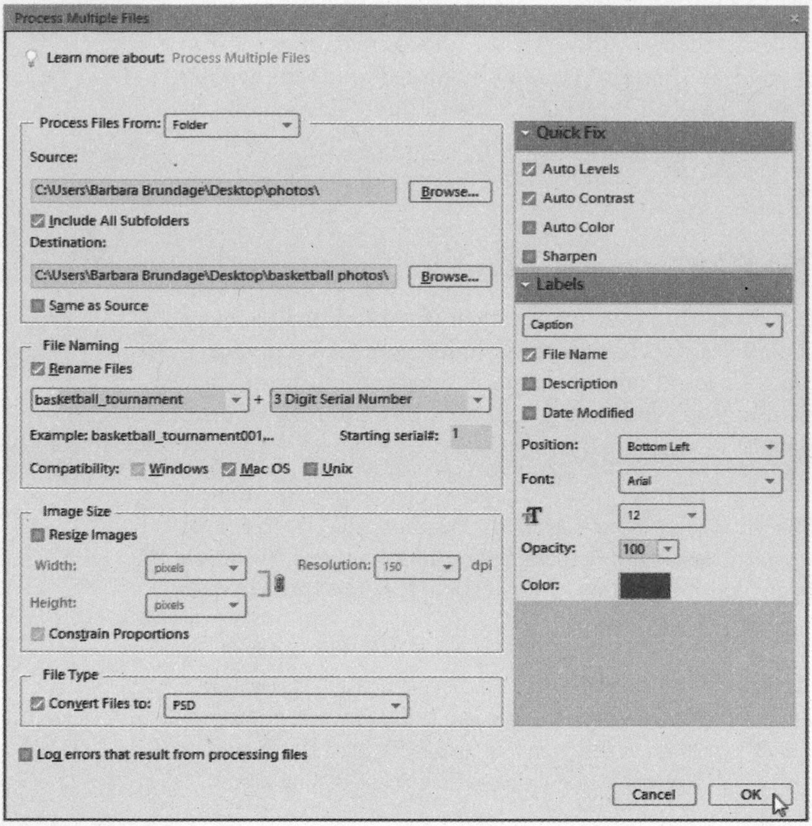

Figure 8-12:
You could also call Process Multiple Files "Computer: Earn Your Keep", because you can make so many changes at once. This dialog box is set up to apply the following changes: Rename every file (from PICT8983 to basketball_tournament001), change the images to the .psd format, apply Auto Levels and Auto Contrast, and add the file name as a caption. You make all that happen by clicking the OK button.

That last one brings up the same options you get when selecting File → Import. Use this option to convert files as you bring them into Elements—from a camera or scanner, for example.

If you want to include files scattered around in different locations on your hard drive, then speed things up by opening the files first or gathering them into one folder. If you have a couple of folders' worth of photos to convert, save time by putting all those folders into one folder, and using the "Include All Subfolders" option explained later. Then all the files get converted at once.

Here's a step-by-step tour of the process:

1. **Choose the files you want to convert.**

   Use the Process Files From pull-down menu to select which kind of files you want: opened files, a folder, or files imported from your camera or scanner.

2. **If you chose Folder, then tell Elements which folder you want.**

   Click the Browse button and, in the dialog box that appears, choose the folder you want. Files for processing must be in a folder if they aren't already open.

If you have folders within a folder and you want to operate on all those files, then turn on the Include All Subfolders checkbox. Otherwise, Elements changes only the files at the top level of the folder.

3. **Pick a destination.**

This step is when you decide where the files will end up once they've been processed. Most of the time, you'll want a new folder for this, so click Browse, and then, in the window that opens, click New Folder. Or you can choose an existing folder in the Browse window. A word of warning if you go this route: Be careful about choosing "Same as Source", as Figure 8-13 explains.

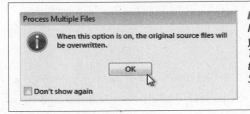

Figure 8-13:
If you turn on the "Same as Source" checkbox, then Elements warns you that it's going to replace your originals with the new versions. That's a timesaver, but it's dangerous, too. If something goes wrong, then your originals are toast. Bottom line: Don't choose the "Same as Source" checkbox unless you have backup copies someplace else.

Renaming Your Files

Being able to rename a group of files in one fell swoop is a very cool feature, but it has a few limitations. If you think it means you can give each photo a unique name like "Keisha and Gram at the Park", followed by "Fred's New Newt", and so on, you're going to be disappointed. Instead, what Elements offers is a quick way of applying a similar name to a group of files. That means you can easily transform a folder filled with files named *DSCF001.jpg*, *DSCF0002.jpg*, and so on, into the slightly friendlier *Keisha and Gram001.jpg*, *Keisha and Gram002.jpg*.

To rename your files, turn on the dialog box's Rename Files option. You see two active text boxes with pull-down menus next to them (a + sign separates the menus). You can enter any text you like, and it replaces every file name in the group. Or you can choose any of the options in the menus. (Both menus are the same.)

The menus offer you a choice of the document name (in three different capitalization styles), serial numbers, serial letters, dates, extensions, or nothing at all (which gives you just the trailing numbers without any kind of prefix). Figure 8-14 shows the many choices you get.

NOTE   If you want to add serial numbers, you can designate the starting number in the "Starting serial#" box. Your first choice is always 1, which actually shows up as 001 because your computer needs the leading zeros to recognize the file order. The tenth figure in your batch would be numbered 010, the hundredth would be 100, and so on.

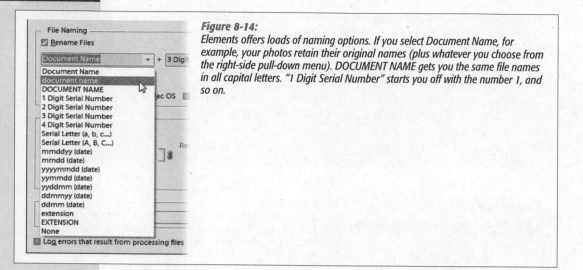

Figure 8-14:
Elements offers loads of naming options. If you select Document Name, for example, your photos retain their original names (plus whatever you choose from the right-side pull-down menu). DOCUMENT NAME gets you the same file names in all capital letters. "1 Digit Serial Number" starts you off with the number 1, and so on.

So if you type *tongue_piercing_day* in the text box and choose the three-digit serial number, then Elements names your photos *tongue_piercing_day001.jpg, tongue_piercing_day002.jpg*, and so on.

> **NOTE**   If you turn on "Same as Source", then the Rename Files option is grayed out. If you want to put your renamed files in the same folder with the originals, then leave "Same as Source" turned off, but select the same folder as the destination in the top part of the dialog box. Then Elements places your renamed files in the folder with the originals.

You also get to designate which operating systems' naming conventions Elements should respect when assigning the new names, as explained in Figure 8-15. If you send files to people or servers using other operating systems, then you know how important this is. If you don't, then play it safe and turn on all three checkboxes. You never know when you may need to send a photo to your nephew who uses Linux.

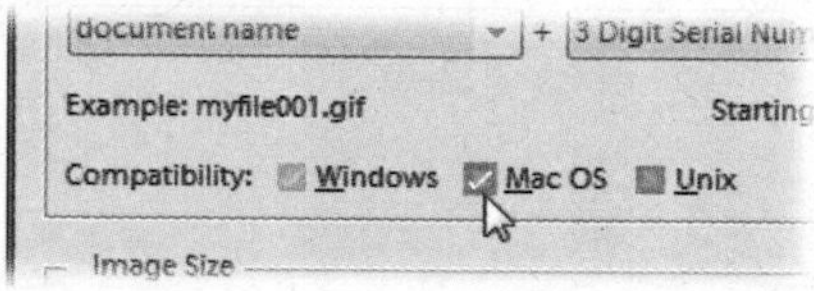

Figure 8-15:
The Compatibility checkboxes tell Elements to watch out for any characters that would violate the naming conventions of the operating systems you check. This is handy if, say, your Web site is hosted on a Unix server and you want to be sure your file names don't create a problem for it. You can choose to be compatible with either or neither of the other operating systems, but the Windows checkbox is always turned on.

Changing Image Size and File Type

The Image Size and File Type sections let you resize your photos and change your images' file formats. The Image Size settings work best when you're trying to reduce file sizes (for example, with a folder of images that you've converted for Web use but found are still too big).

NOTE   Before you make any big changes to a group of files, it's important for you to understand the concept of how changes in an image's resolution and file size affect its appearance. See page 89 for a refresher.

To apply image size changes, turn on the Resize Images checkbox, and then adjust the Width, Height, and Resolution settings, all of which work the same way as those described on page 93.

In the File Type section, you can convert files from one format to another. This is probably the most popular batching activity. If your camera creates JPEGs and you want TIFFs for editing work, then you can change an entire folder at once. From the pull-down menu, just select the file type you want to create.

The final setting in the left half of the window is the checkbox for logging errors in processing your files. It's a good idea to turn this checkbox on, as explained in Figure 8-16.

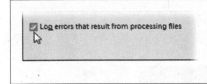

Figure 8-16:
If you turn on "Log errors that result from processing files", then Elements lets you know if it runs into any problems while converting your files. You'll find a little text log file in the folder with your completed images, whether there were problems or not. (If nothing went awry, it's blank.)

Applying Quick Fix Commands

In the upper-right corner of Process Multiple Files, you'll find some of the same Quick Fix commands you have in the regular Quick Fix window. If you consistently get good results with the Auto commands there, then you can run them on a whole folder at once here.

You can run Auto Levels, Auto Contrast, Auto Color, Auto Sharpen, or any combination of those commands that you like on all the files in your folder. (Unfortunately, you can't batch-run the Auto Smart Fix command from this window.) If you don't see the list, then click the flippy triangle next to Quick Fix to expand it. If you need a refresher on what each one does, then see Chapter 4, beginning on page 108.

If you want to batch run the Auto Smart Fix, or if your only reason for bringing up Process Multiple Files is to use any of the editing options, then you can save time by running these commands right from the Organizer, as explained on page 49.

TIP   Don't forget that you can also batch process corrections in the Raw Converter (see page 227). Then open the files, and use Process Multiple Files to save all the changed files at once.

Attaching Labels

The tools in the Labels section let you add captions and copyright notices, which Elements calls *watermarks*, to your images (see Figure 8-17). Watermarks and captions get imprinted right onto the photo itself. The procedure is the same for both; only the content differs. A watermark contains any text you choose, while a caption is limited to your choices from a group of checkboxes.

First, you need to choose between a watermark and a caption (choose from the pull-down menu right below the Label tab). You can't do both at once, so if you want both, add one, run Process Multiple Files, and then add the other, and run Process Multiple Files again on the resulting images. You can download *wagon-wheels.jpg* from the Missing CD page at *www.missingmanuals.com* if you want to practice adding your own watermarks and captions.

Watermarks

If you want to create a watermark, you first need to enter some text in the Custom Text box. Next, choose the position and appearance of your text as explained in a moment.

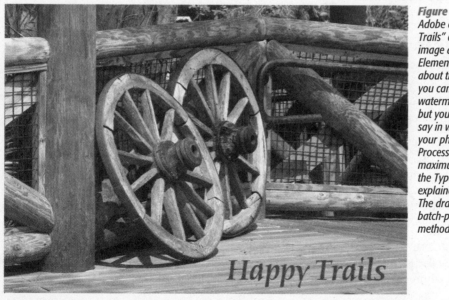

Figure 8-17:
Adobe calls the "Happy Trails" custom text in this image a watermark. Elements is very flexible about the fonts and sizes you can choose for a watermark or caption, but you don't get much say in where it goes on your photo if you use Process Multiple Files. For maximum flexibility, use the Type tool, as explained on page 252. The drawback: You can't batch-process using that method.

Text you enter here gets applied to every photo in the batch, so this is a great way to add copyright or contact info that you want on every photo. If you want different text on each photo, check out the Description option for captions, as shown in Figure 8-18.

TIP   If you want to include the copyright symbol (©), hold Alt while typing 0169 (on the number pad, not the top row of the keyboard). Or you can use the Character Map (Start → All Programs → Accessories → System Tools → Character Map).

Adding captions

For a caption, you can choose any of the following, separately or in combination:

- **File Name.** You can choose to show the file's name as the caption. If you decide to run the rename option at the same time, then you get the new name you're assigning.

- **Description.** Turn this checkbox on to use any text you have entered in the Description section of the File Info dialog box (File → File Info) as your caption. This option is your most flexible one for entering text, and the only way to batch different caption text for each photo. Just enter the text for each photo in File → File Info → Description.

- **Date Modified.** This is the date your file was last changed. In practice, that usually means today's date, because you're modifying your file by running Process Multiple Files on it.

Once you've decided what you want your caption to say, you need to make some choices about its position and size. These choices are the same whether you're adding a watermark or a caption, and if you switch from one to the other before actually running Process Multiple Files, then your previous choices appear.

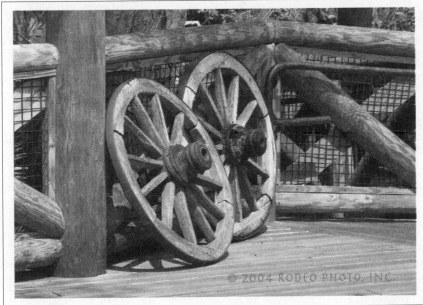

Figure 8-18:
You just can't beat Process Multiple Files for adding quick copyright information to your photo, although some other methods give a more sophisticated look, as described in the Tip at the end of this chapter (page 252).

CHAPTER 8: ELEMENTS FOR DIGITAL PHOTOGRAPHERS

- **Position.** This tells Elements where to put your caption. Your options are Bottom Left, Bottom Right, or Centered. Centered doesn't mean bottom center, incidentally. It puts the text smack in the middle of your image.

- **Font.** From the pull-down menu, choose any font on your system. Chapter 14 has much more information about fonts.

- **Size.** This setting determines the size of your type. Click the menu next to the two little Ts to choose from several preset sizes, up to 72 point.

- **Opacity.** Use this to adjust how solidly your text prints. Choose 100 percent for maximum readability or click the downward arrow and move the slider to the left for a watermark type that lets you see the image underneath it.

- **Color.** Use this setting to choose your text color. Click the box to bring up the Color Picker (page 209) and make your choice.

> **TIP** If you want to use a logo as a watermark, the Process Multiple Files tool can't help you. But there is a way to apply a logo to a bunch of images. Here's what you do: First, create your logo on a new layer in one of the images. Adjust the opacity with the slider in the Layers palette until you like the results. Save the file. Now you can drag that layer from the Layers palette onto the image window for each photo where you need it. (If you Shift+drag the layer, then it goes to exactly the same spot on each image, assuming they're all the same size.) You can also do this with Adjustment layers (page 176) to give yourself a sort of batch-processing capability for applying the same adjustments to multiple files.

CHAPTER 9

Retouching: Fine-Tuning Your Images

Basic edits like exposure fixes and sharpening are fine if all you want to make are simple adjustments. But Elements also gives you the tools to make sophisticated changes that aren't hard to apply, and that can make the difference between a hohum photo and a fabulous one. This chapter introduces you to some advanced editing maneuvers that will greatly help either rescue damaged photos or give good ones that little extra zing.

The first part of the chapter shows how to get rid of blemishes—not only those that affect skin, but also dust, scratches, stains, and other photographic imperfections. You'll also learn some powerful color-improving techniques, including the Color Curves tool, which offers a great way to improve your image's contrast and color.

Fixing Blemishes

It's an imperfect world, but in your photos, it doesn't have to be. Elements gives you some amazing tools for fixing your subject's flaws: Erase crow's feet and blemishes, eliminate power lines in an otherwise perfect view, or even hide objects you wish weren't in your photo. Not only that, but these same tools are great for fixing problems like tears, folds, and stains—the great foes of photoscanning veterans. With a little effort, you can bring back photos that seem beyond help. Figure 9-1 shows an example of the kind of restoration you can accomplish with a little persistence and Elements.

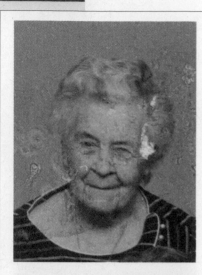

Figure 9-1:
You can do some amazing repair work with Elements if you have the patience.

Top: Here's a section of a water-damaged family portrait. The grandmother's face is almost obliterated.

Bottom: The same image after being repaired with Elements. It took a lot of cloning and healing to get even this close, but if you keep at it, you can do the kind of work that would have required professional help before Elements. If you're interested in restoring old photos, check out Katrin Eismann's books on the subject (Photoshop Restoration and Retouching [New Riders, 2006] is a good one to start with). They cover full-featured Photoshop, but you can adapt most of the techniques for Elements. You might also want to investigate The Photoshop Elements 5 Restoration and Retouching Book (Peachpit, 2007) by Matt Kloskowski. (Although it's for Elements 5, the techniques are still usable in Elements 7.)

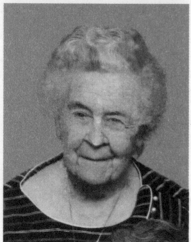

Elements gives you three main tools for this kind of work:

- **The Spot Healing brush** is the easiest way to repair your photo. Just drag over the area you want to fix. Elements searches the surrounding area and blends that information into the troubled spot, making it indistinguishable from the background. This brush usually works best on small areas, for the reasons explained later.

- **The Healing brush** works much like the Spot Healing brush, only you tell the Healing brush the part of your photo to use as a source for the material you want to blend in. This makes the Healing brush better suited to large areas, because you don't have to worry about inadvertently dragging in unwanted details.

- **The Clone Stamp** offers another way to make repairs. It works like the Healing brush in that you sample a good area and apply it to the area you want to fix. But instead of blending the repair in, the Clone Stamp actually covers the bad area with the replacement. The Clone Stamp is best for situations when you want to completely hide the underlying area, as opposed to letting any of what's already there blend into your repair (which is how things work with the Healing brushes). The Clone Stamp is also your best option when you want to create a realistic copy of detail that's elsewhere in your photo. You can clone over some leaves to fill in a bare branch, or replace a knothole in a fence board with good wood, for instance.

All three tools work similarly: You just drag each tool over the area you want to change. It's as simple as using a paintbrush. In fact, each of these tools requires you to choose a brush, just like the ones you'll learn about in Chapter 12. But brush selection is pretty straightforward; in this chapter you'll learn everything you need to make basic brush choices.

> **TIP** If you want to smooth out blotchy or blemished skin, check out the new Surface Blur filter, explained on page 377. It's good to try if you want to do minor touchups that affect large areas. In contrast, the tools described in this section give you more control for fixing individual imperfections.

The Spot Healing Brush: Fixing Small Areas

The Spot Healing brush excels at fixing minor blemishes: pimples, lipstick smudges, stray lint, and so on. Simply paint over the area you want to repair, and the Spot Healing brush automatically searches the surrounding areas and blends that into the spot you're brushing. Figure 9-2 shows what a great job the Spot Healing brush can do. (Download the file *radish.jpg* from the Missing CD page at *www.missingmanuals.com*, if you'd like to do some experimenting with this tool.)

The Spot Healing brush's ability to borrow information from surrounding areas is great, but it's also a drawback. The larger the area you drag the brush over, the wider Elements searches for replacement material. So, if there's contrasting material too close to the area you're trying to fix, it can unintentionally get pulled into the repair. For instance, if you're trying to fix a spot on an eyelid, you may wind up with some of the color from the eye itself mixed in with your repair.

You get best results from this brush when you choose a brush size that just barely covers the spot you're trying to fix. If you need to drag to fix an oblong area, use a brush the minimum width that covers the flaw. The Spot Healing brush also works much better when there's a large surrounding area that looks the way you want your repaired spot to look.

The Spot Healing brush has only three settings in the Options bar:

- **Brush.** Use the pull-down menu to choose a different brush style if you prefer (see Chapter 12 for lots more about brushes), but generally, you're best off sticking to the standard brush that Elements starts out with and just changing the size, if necessary.

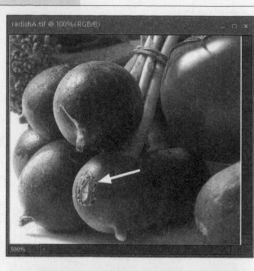

Figure 9-2:
The trick to using the Spot Healing brush is to work in very tiny areas. If you choose too large a brush or drag over too large an area, you're more likely to pick up undesired shades and details from the surrounding area.

Top: The radish in the bottom row has a large gouge in it.

Bottom: By dragging with a brush barely the width of the scar, you can make a truly invisible fix.

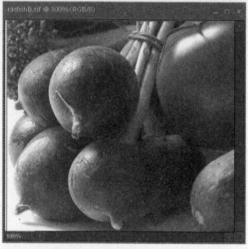

- **Size.** Use this slider to set the brush size.

- **Type.** Use these radio buttons to adjust how the brush works. Proximity Match tells the Spot Healing brush to search the surrounding area for replacement pixels, and Create Texture tells it to blend only from the area you drag it over. Generally speaking, if Proximity Match doesn't work well, you'll get better results by switching to the regular Healing brush than by choosing Create Texture.

    TIP Adobe suggests that you may like the results you get from Create Texture better if you drag over the spot more than once.

- **All Layers.** Turn this on if you want the brush to look for replacement material in all your photo's visible layers. (Another reason to turn this on: If you prefer to work on a new blank layer so that you can blend it in better later by adjusting the healed area's opacity.)

You won't believe how easy it is to fix problem areas with the Spot Healing brush. All you do is:

1. **Activate the Spot Healing brush.**

   Click the Healing brush icon (the Band-Aid) in the Toolbox, and then choose the Spot Healing brush—the one with the dotted selection lines extending from it—from the pop-out menu. (Keyboard shortcut: J.)

2. **Choose a brush size just barely bigger than the flaw.**

   You can choose your brush size from the Options bar Size slider or by pressing] (the close bracket key) for a larger brush or [(the open bracket key) for a smaller brush.

3. **Click the bad spot.**

   If the brush doesn't quite cover the flaw, drag over the area.

4. **When you release the mouse button, Elements repairs the blemish.**

   You won't see any change to your image while you drag—only after you let go.

Sometimes you get great results with the Spot Healing brush on a larger area if it's surrounded by a field of good material that's similar in tone to the spot you're trying to fix. Most of the time, though, you're better off with the regular Healing brush for large areas, as well as for flaws whose replacement material isn't right next to the bad spot.

The Healing Brush: Fixing Larger Areas

The Healing brush lets you fix much bigger areas than you can usually manage with the Spot Healing brush. The main difference between the two tools is that with the regular Healing brush, you choose the area that's going to be blended into the repair. The blending makes your repair look very natural. Figure 9-3 shows what great results you can get with this tool.

The repair material doesn't have to be nearby; in fact, you can sample from a totally different photo if you like. To sample material from another photo, just arrange both photos on the desktop so you can easily move the cursor from one to the other.

The basic procedure for using the Healing brush is similar to that for the Spot Healing brush: Drag over the flaw you want to fix. The difference is that with the Healing brush, you first Alt+click where you want Elements to look for replacement pixels.

Dust and Scratches

Scratched, dusty prints can create giant headaches when you scan them. Cleaning your scanner's glass helps, but lots of photos come with plenty of dust marks already in the print, or in the file itself if the lens or sensor of your digital camera was dusty.

A similar problem is caused by *artifacts*, blobbish areas of color caused by JPEG compression. If you take a close look at the sky in a JPEG photo, for instance, you may see that instead of a smooth swath of blue, you see lots of little distinct clumps of each shade of blue.

The Healing brushes are usually your best first line of defense for fixing these problems, but if the specks are widespread, Elements offers a couple other options.

The first is the JPEG artifacts option in the Reduce Noise filter (page 371). If you're lucky, that will take care of things.

If it doesn't, other possible solutions include the Despeckle filter (Filter → Noise → Despeckle). And if that doesn't get everything, undo it and try the "Dust and Scratches filter (Filter → Noise → "Dust and Scratches), or the Median filter (Filter → Noise → Median). The Radius setting for these last two filters tells Elements how far to search for dissimilar pixels for its calculations. Keep that number as low as possible. The downside to the filters in this group is that they smooth things out in a way that can make your image look blurred, so generally you'd probably prefer to make a selection first to confine their effects to the areas that need repair. Generally, Despeckle is the filter that's least destructive to your image's focus.

In Elements 7 you might also want to try creating a duplicate layer (Layer → Duplicate) and running the Surface Blur filter (page 377) and then, in the Layers palette, reducing the opacity of the filtered layer.

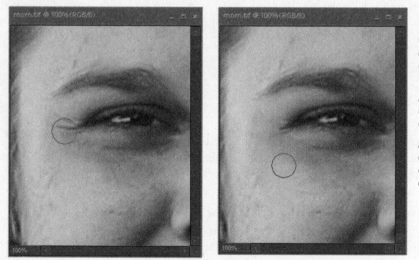

Figure 9-3:
The Healing brush is especially remarkable because it also blends the textures of the areas where you use it.

Left: This photo shows the crow's-feet at the corner of the woman's eye.

Right: The Healing brush eliminates them without creating a phony, airbrushed effect.

The Healing brush offers you quite a few choices in the Options bar:

- **Brush.** Click the brush thumbnail to bring up the Brush Dynamics palette, explained on page 331. This lets you customize the size, shape, and hardness of your brush. But generally, the standard brush works well, so you don't have to change things other than the size if you don't want to.

- **Mode**. You can choose some blend modes (page 343) here, but most of the time, you want one of the top two options: Normal and Replace. Normal is usually your best choice. Sometimes, though, your replacement pixels may make the area you work on show a visibly different texture than the surrounding area. In that case, choose Replace, which preserves the grain of your photo.

- **Source**. You can choose to sample an area to use as a replacement, or you can blend in a pattern. Using the Healing brush with patterns is explained on page 265.

- **Pattern thumbnails**. If you choose to use a pattern, this box becomes active. Click it to select the pattern you want to use.

- **Aligned**. If you turn on the Aligned checkbox, Elements keeps sampling new material in your source as you use the tool. The sampling follows the direction of your brush. Even if you let go of the mouse button, Elements continues to sample new material as long as you continue brushing. If you leave Aligned turned off, all the material comes from the area where you first defined your source point.

  Generally, for both the Healing brush and the Clone Stamp, it's easier to leave Aligned turned off. You can still change your source point by Alt+clicking another spot, but you often get better results if *you* make the decision about when to move on to another location rather than letting Elements decide.

- **All Layers**. If you turn on this option, Elements samples from all the visible layers (page 162) in the area where you set your source point. You'd also use it if you want to heal on a new blank layer. Turn it off and Elements samples only the active layer.

- **Overlay Options**. Click this icon (the little gray overlapping squares) for a pop-out menu that lets you turn on and adjust a visible overlay for your photo. It allows you to see a floating ghostly overlay of the source area where you're sampling in relation to your original, so you can see exactly how things line up to help you do very accurate healing. You can also adjust the opacity of the overlay or invert it (make the light areas dark and the dark areas light so that you can see details better, if necessary) for a better view. Autohide causes it to disappear at the moment you click so it's not in your way as you work.

  If you're a beginner, you'll probably want to leave this off, but advanced healers may find it very useful. It's also available for the Clone Stamp, and the settings you choose for one tool will appear when you switch to the other tool.

It's almost as simple to use the Healing brush as it is to use the Spot Healing brush.

1. **Activate the Healing brush.**

   Click the Healing brush icon (the Band-Aid) in the Toolbox and choose it from the pop-out menu. (Keyboard shortcut: J.)

2. **Find a good spot you want to sample to use in the repair and then Alt+click it.**

   When you click the good spot, your cursor temporarily turns into a circle with crosshairs in it to indicate that this is the point where Elements will retrieve your repair material from. (If you want to use a source point in a different photo, both the source photo and the one you're repairing must be in the same color mode. See page 45 for more about color modes.)

3. **Drag over the area you want to repair.**

   You can see where Elements is sampling the repair material from: A cross marks the sampling point.

4. **When you release the mouse, Elements blends the sampled area into the problem area.**

   Often you don't know how effective you were until Elements is through working its magic, because it may take a few seconds for the program to finish its calculations and blend in the repair. If you don't like what Elements did, press Ctrl+Z to undo and try again.

You can choose to heal on a separate layer. The advantage of doing this is that if you find the end result is a little too much—your granny suddenly looks like a Stepford wife—you can back things off a bit by reducing the opacity (page 162) of the healed layer to let the original show through. This is a good plan when using the Clone Stamp, too. Just press Ctrl+Shift+N to create a new layer and then turn on All Layers in the Options bar.

The Clone Stamp

The Clone Stamp is like the Healing brush in that you add material from a source point that you select. The main difference between the two is that the Clone Stamp doesn't *blend in* when the new material is applied. Instead, the Clone Stamp works by covering up the underlying area completely. This makes the Clone Stamp your tool of choice when you don't want to leave any visible trace of what you're repairing. Figure 9-4 shows an example of when cloning is a better choice than healing.

The choices you make in the Options bar for the Clone Stamp are very important in getting the best results possible.

- **Brush.** Use the pull-down menu to select a different brush style if you want (see Chapter 12 for more about brushes), but the standard brush style usually works pretty well. If the soft edges of your cloned areas bother you, you may be tempted to switch to a harder brush. But that usually makes your photo look like you strewed confetti on it, because hard edges don't blend well with what's already in your photo.

- **Size.** Choose a brush that's just big enough to get your sample without picking up a lot of other details that you don't want in your repair. While it may be tempting to clone huge chunks at once to get it done faster, most of the time you'll do better using the smallest brush that gets the sample you want.

- **Mode.** You can choose any blend mode (page 343) for cloning, but Normal is usually your best bet. Other modes can create interesting special effects.

- **Opacity.** Elements automatically uses 100-percent opacity for cloning, but you can reduce opacity to let some details from your original show through.

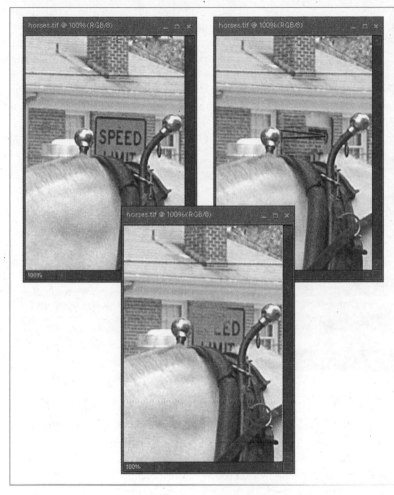

Figure 9-4:
Here's an example of when you'd choose cloning over healing.

Top left: This photo has a very distracting Speed Limit sign just above the horse's collar.

Top right: In this photo, the Healing brush does a lousy job covering up the sign.

Bottom: The Clone Stamp works much better. Only the upper-left corner has been fixed, but you can see how much better the Clone Stamp covers up the sign.

TIP You gain more control by placing your clone on another layer (see page 158) than by adjusting the Clone Stamp's opacity.

- **Aligned.** This setting works exactly the way it does for the Healing brush (described earlier in this chapter). Turn it on and Elements keeps sampling at a uniform distance from your cursor as you clone. Turn it off and you keep putting down the same source material. Figure 9-5 shows an example of when you'd turn on Aligned.

- **All Layers.** When you turn on All Layers, Elements takes its samples from all the visible layers in the area where you set your source point. When it's off Elements samples only the active layer.

- **Overlay Options.** Click this (the two overlapping rectangles) and choose Show Overlay to turn on a pale overlay that shows the clone source area floating over the original, so you can see precisely how your possible source material aligns with the original. This is a little confusing at first, but once you get the hang of it, it's very helpful when cloning precise patterns. If you've ever used the Clone Stamp before and had the experience of inadvertently cloning from the wrong spot, or dragging in detail you didn't mean to grab, you'll love this option. The options for adjusting the overlay are the same as for the Healing brush (page 259), which shares this feature. Settings you choose here will appear when you use the Healing brush and vice versa.

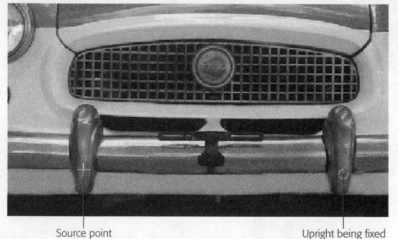

Figure 9-5:
The right-hand upright on this car's bumper was badly damaged. To restore it, the Clone Stamp's Aligned option was used to pull detail from the left bumper, replacing the missing pieces. Dragging with the Clone Stamp in Aligned mode replaces the entire bumper smoothly, rather than in hard-to-align brush-sized samples.

Source point

Upright being fixed

The Clone Stamp shares its space in the Toolbox with the Pattern Stamp, which is explained later. (You can tell which is which because the Pattern Stamp icon has a little blue checkerboard to its left.) Using the Clone Stamp is very much like using the Healing brush. Only the result is different.

1. **Activate the Clone Stamp.**

   Press S or click its icon (the rubber stamp) in the Toolbox, and then choose it from the pop-out menu.

2. **Find the spot in your photo that you want to repair.**

   You may need to zoom way, way in to get a good enough look at what you're doing. See page 87 for how to adjust the view.

3. **Find a good spot to sample as a replacement for the bad area.**

You want an area that has the same tone as the area you're fixing. The Clone Stamp doesn't do any blending the way the Healing brush does, so tone differences are pretty obvious.

WORKAROUND WORKSHOP

Repairing Tears and Stains

With Elements, you can do a great deal to bring damaged old photos back to life. The Healing brush and the Clone Stamp are major players when it comes to restoring pictures. It's fiddly work and takes some persistence, but you can achieve wonders if you have the patience.

That said, if you're lucky enough to have good-size useable replacement sections elsewhere in your photo, you can use the Move tool to copy the good bits into the problem area. First, select the part you want to copy. Then press M to activate the Move tool and Alt+drag the good piece where you want it. (There's more about the Move tool on page 148.)

You can use the Rotate commands to flip your selection if you need a mirror image. For example, if the left leg of a chair is fine but the right one is missing, try selecting and Alt+dragging the left leg with the Move tool. When it's where you want it, go to Image → Rotate → Flip Selection Horizontal to turn the copied left leg into a new right leg.

If you don't need to rotate an object, sometimes you may be able to just increase the Clone Stamp brush size and clone your object where you need a duplicate. Cloning objects works well only when your background is the same for both areas.

---

4. **Alt+click the spot you want to clone from.**

When you click, the cursor turns to a circle with crosshairs in it, indicating the source point for the repair. Once you're actually working with the Clone Stamp, you see a cross marking the sampling point.

5. **Click the spot you want to cover.**

Elements puts whatever you just selected down on top of your image, concealing the original. You can drag with the Clone Stamp, but it acts like it's in Aligned mode (described earlier) when you do, so often it's preferable to use multiple clicks instead for areas that are larger than your sample. (The only difference between real Aligned mode and what you get from dragging is that with dragging, when you let go of the mouse, your source point snaps back to where you started. If you turn on Aligned, your source point stays where you stopped.)

6. **Continue until you've covered the area.**

With the Clone Stamp, unlike the Healing brush, what you see as you click is what you get. Elements doesn't do any further blending or smoothing.

The Clone Stamp is a very powerful tool, but it's crotchety, too. See the box on page 264 for some suggestions on how to make it behave.

You can clone on a separate layer, just as you can use the Healing tool on a dedicated layer. This lets you adjust the opacity of your repair afterwards. Press Shift+Ctrl+N to create a new layer and then turn on Sample All Layers in the Options bar. It's almost always a good idea to clone on a separate layer when you can do so, since cloning is so much more opaque than healing. If you use a separate layer, you can adjust the opacity of the cloned area afterwards for a more subtle blend, if necessary.

TROUBLESHOOTING MOMENT

Keeping the Clone Stamp Under Control

The clone tool is a great resource, but it definitely has a mind of its own sometimes.

If you suddenly see spots of a different shade appearing as you clone, take a look in the Options bar at the Aligned box. It has a tendency to insist on staying turned on, and even if you turn it off, it can turn itself back on when you aren't paying attention.

Once in a great while, the Clone Stamp just won't reset itself when you try to select a new sampling point.

Try clicking the tiny down arrow on the extreme left side of the Options bar and choosing the Reset Tool option, as shown in Figure 9-6. If that doesn't do it, exit Elements and restart the Editor and delete Elements' preferences file. Here's how: hold down Ctrl+Alt+Shift immediately after launching the Editor. You get a dialog box asking if you want to delete the Elements settings. Say yes. This returns all your Elements settings to where they were the first time you launched the program. (Resetting the preferences cures about 80 percent of the problems you may run into in Elements.)

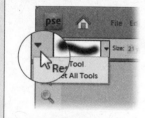

Figure 9-6:
You can reset the Clone Stamp (or, for that matter, any Elements tool) by clicking this tiny arrow at the left end of the Options bar, then choosing Reset Tool. If you want to reset the whole Toolbox, choose Reset All Tools. This clears up a lot of the little problems you may have when trying to make a tool behave correctly.

Applying Patterns

Besides giving you the ability to add solid colors to your images, Elements lets you add patterns too. You get quite a few patterns with Elements when you buy it, and you can also download more patterns from online sources (see page 495) or create your own. You can use patterns to add interesting designs to your image, or to give a more realistic texture to certain repairs.

You can use either the Healing brush or the Pattern Stamp to apply patterns. The Healing brush has a pattern option in the Options bar. The Pattern Stamp shares the toolbox slot with the Clone Stamp, and it works very much like the Clone Stamp, but it puts down a preselected pattern instead of a sampled area.

TIP   Elements actually gives you lots of ways to use patterns, including creating a Fill layer that's entirely covered with the pattern of your choice. Fill layers are covered on page 176.

The tool you choose to apply your pattern makes a big difference, as you can see from Figure 9-7. The next two sections explain how to use both tools.

The Healing Brush

The Healing brush in Pattern mode is great for things like improving the texture of someone's skin by applying just the skin texture from another photo.

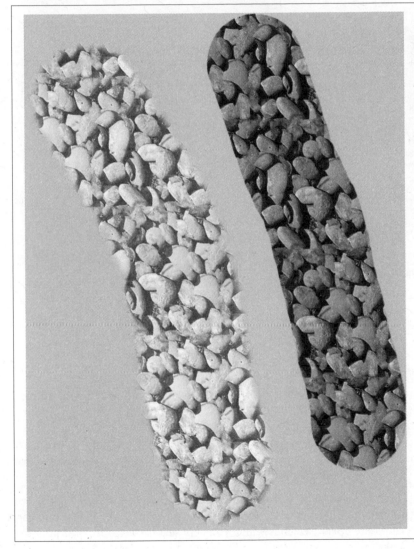

Figure 9-7:
The same pattern applied with the Healing brush (left) and the Pattern Stamp (right). The Healing brush blends the pattern into the underlying color (and texture, when there is any), while the Pattern Stamp just plunks down the pattern as it appears in the pop-out palette. (To get a softer edge on the Healing Brush pattern, set the Brush Hardness lower in the Brush Dynamics pop-out palette [page 331].)

Using patterns with the Healing brush is just as easy and works the same way as using the brush in normal healing mode: Just drag across the area you want to fix. The only difference is that you don't have to choose a sampling point, since the pattern is your source point. When you drag, the pattern you selected blends into your photo.

Click the Pattern button in the Options bar and then choose a pattern from the palette. There are more pattern libraries available if you click the right-facing arrow on the Pattern palette, or you can create and save your own patterns. Figure 9-8 explains how to create custom patterns for use with either the Healing brush or the Pattern Stamp.

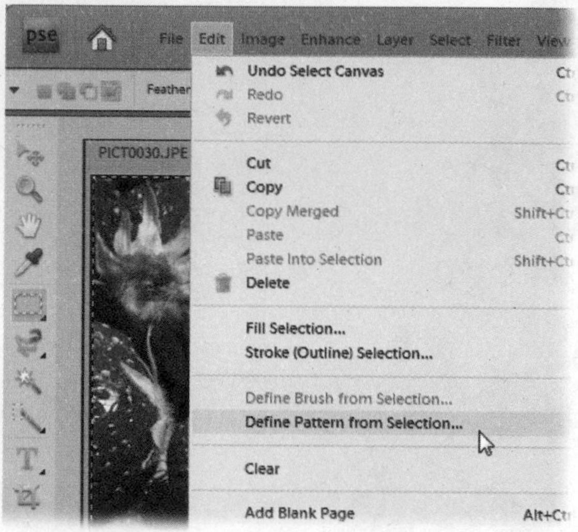

Figure 9-8:
You can create your own patterns very easily. On any image, make a rectangular unfeathered selection, and then choose Edit → "Define Pattern from Selection". Your pattern appears at the bottom of the current pattern palette, and a dialog box pops up and asks you to type a name. To use the whole image, don't make a selection, and go to Edit → Define Pattern. To rename or delete a pattern later, right-click it in the Pattern palette and make your choice. You can also download hundreds of different patterns from various online sources (see page 495).

TIP   You can create some very interesting effects by changing the blend mode (page 343) when using patterns.

The Pattern Stamp

The Pattern Stamp is just like the Clone Stamp, only instead of copying sampled areas, it puts down a predefined pattern that you select from the Pattern palette. The Pattern Stamp is useful when you want to apply a pattern to your image without mixing it in with what's already there. For instance, if you want to see what your patio would look like if it were a garden instead, you could use the Pattern stamp to paint a lawn and a flower border on a photo of your patio.

To get started, click the Clone stamp in the Toolbox, and then choose the Pattern Stamp from the pop-out menu. Click the pattern thumbnail in the Options bar. The Pattern palette opens, which is where you choose a pattern. Other options for this brush, like the size, hardness, and so on, are the same as for the Clone Stamp.

The main difference is the Impressionist option demonstrated in Figure 9-9, which is mostly useful for creating special effects.

Once you've selected a pattern, just drag in your photo where you want the pattern to appear.

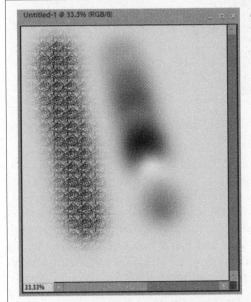

Figure 9-9:
If you turn on Impressionist in the Options bar, your pattern is blurred, giving an effect vaguely like an Impressionist painting. Here, you can see a pattern put down with the regular Pattern Stamp (left) and the Impressionist stamp (right).

Color Curves: Enhancing Tone and Contrast

If you hang around photo-editing veterans, you'll hear plenty of talk about how useful the Curves tool is. Contrary to what you might expect, Curves isn't a drawing tool. Instead, it works much like Levels (page 198), but with many more points of correction. Adobe calls the Elements version *Color Curves* to remind you what it's for. Unlike Levels, in which you set your entire photo's white point, black point, and gamma settings, Curves lets you target specific tonal regions. For instance, Curves lets you make only your shadows lighter or only your highlights darker. Maybe that's why some pros say, "Curves is Levels on steroids." (For advice on when to use Levels and when to use Color Curves, see the box on page 203.)

Elements' Color Curves tool is a fairly restricted version of its counterpart (just called Curves) in the full version of Photoshop. In the more powerful Curves tool, you can work on each color channel separately, as you do in the Levels dialog box. You can also drag any point on the Curves graph (like the one you see Figure 9-10) to manipulate it directly. For example, you can drag to adjust just the middle range of your greens. Elements doesn't give you that kind of flexibility.

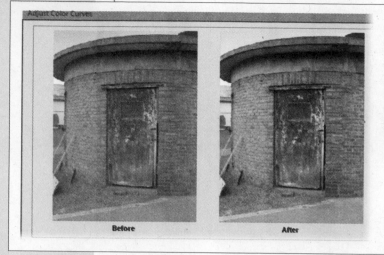

Figure 9-10:
Elements gives you a good look at what you're doing to your photo with these large before-and-after previews. Start by clicking around in the list of presets on the lower-left side of the window (not shown here), and then use the sliders in the middle of the lower section to fine-tune the effect if you need to.

Since Curves, in its original-strength version, is a pretty complicated tool, Adobe makes it easier to use in Elements. To start with, you get a group of preset adjustments to choose from (see Figure 9-10). These presets offer shortcuts to the types of basic enhancements you'll use most often. Just click the one that looks good to you. If you like what it does, you're done. But if you aren't quite satisfied with a preset, you have a simple way to make adjustments in the Adjust Color Curves dialog box's advanced options, to the right of the presets.

Here's how to improve a photo's appearance with Color Curves:

1. **Open your photo and make a duplicate layer.**

   Press Ctrl+J or go to Layer → Duplicate Layer. Elements doesn't let you use Color Curves as an Adjustment layer (unlike Photoshop), so you're safer applying it to a duplicate layer in case you want to change something later.

   TIP   If you want to restrict your adjustment to a particular area of your photo, select it first so that Color Curves changes only the selected area. For instance, if you're happy with everything in your shot of your son's Little League game except the catcher in the foreground, select him, and you can do a Color Curves adjustment that affects him alone—not the rest of the photo. See Chapter 5 if you need a refresher on selections.

2. **Go to Enhance → Adjust Color → Adjust Color Curves.**

   The Color Curves dialog box opens. You see your original image in the preview on the left.

3. **Choose a Color Curves preset.**

Scroll through the list in the lower left of the window and click the preset that seems closest to what you want your photo to look like. Feel free to experiment by clicking different presets. (As long as you're just clicking in the list, you don't need to click Reset between each one, since Elements starts from your original each time you click.)

The dialog box gives you a decently-sized look at how you're changing your image, but for important photos, you can also preview the effect right in your image. To do that, drag the dialog box out of the way and check your actual photo to get a closer look at how you're changing things before you make your final choice.

4. **Apply the changes, or tweak them some more.**

If you're satisfied, click OK. If not, go to the next step. (And if you don't want to apply any Color Curves adjustments at all, click Cancel.)

5. **Make any further adjustments.**

If you think your photo still doesn't look quite right, use the sliders shown in Figure 9-11 to make any additional changes. (The sliders are described in the list on page 270.) Click Reset if you want to undo any of the changes you make with the sliders.

TIP   Easy does it here. Notice how subtle the preset curves are. A tiny nudge of these sliders makes a big difference, so be gentle with the sliders.

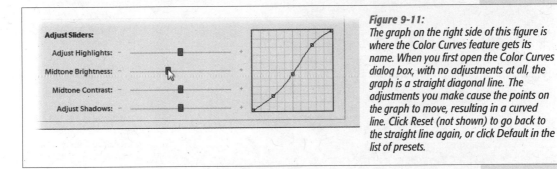

Figure 9-11:
The graph on the right side of this figure is where the Color Curves feature gets its name. When you first open the Color Curves dialog box, with no adjustments at all, the graph is a straight diagonal line. The adjustments you make cause the points on the graph to move, resulting in a curved line. Click Reset (not shown) to go back to the straight line again, or click Default in the list of presets.

6. **When you're happy with your photo's new look, click OK.**

Don't forget to save your changes. If you used the duplicate layer, you can always change your mind about them later on and start over on a fresh layer.

NOTE   If you've used Curves add-ons in an old version of Elements (like those from Richard Lynch or Grant Dixon, for example), or if you've used the Photoshop Curves Adjustment Layers, the Color Curves tool may take some getting used to. (You power user, you!) You may prefer the more fully-featured free add-on Curves tool for Elements at *http://free.pages.at/easyfilter/curves.html*.

Once you've got some Color Curves experience under your belt, you probably won't be satisfied with the results you get from the presets. So don't hesitate to use the sliders to adjust different tonal regions in your photo:

- **Adjust Highlights.** Move the slider to the left to darken your photo's highlights; move it to the right to lighten them.

- **Midtone Brightness.** If you'd like the middle range of colors to be darker, move this slider to the left. Move it to the right to make the midtones brighter.

- **Midtone Contrast.** This slider works just like the one in the Shadows/Highlights feature (see page 187). Move it to the right to increase your photo's contrast, and to the left to reduce it.

- **Adjust Shadows.** If you want to lighten shadows, move the slider to the right. To darken shadow areas, move it to the left.

As you move the sliders, you can see the point you're adjusting move on the graph and watch the curve change shape. Although it's fun to see what's going on in the graph, you should pay more attention to what's happening in your photo.

Color Curves is such a potent tool, it can change your photo in ways you don't intend. Rather than using Color Curves to make huge adjustments, try another tool first. Then come back and use Color Curves for the final, subtle tweaks. On the other hand, you can also use Color Curves to create some wild special effects, if that's what you're after. See Figure 9-12 for an example.

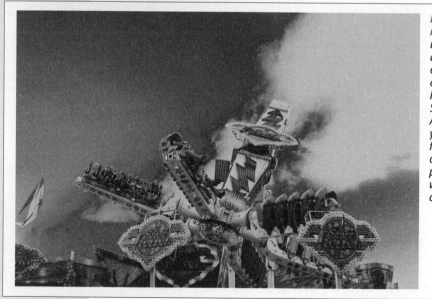

Figure 9-12:
Many people prefer to use Color Curves for artwork and special effects rather than adjusting photos. Jimi Hendrix fans may like the Solarize preset, which Adobe includes to give you a starting point for funky pictures like this one. (Others say this preset should serve as a warning about going overboard with this tool.)

NOTE You can also apply the Solarize adjustment to part of your photo by using the Smart Brush tool (page 189). But you can't edit the settings afterwards, so you may prefer to apply Solarize using Color Curves on a duplicate layer (page 159).

Making Your Colors More Vibrant

Do you drool over the luscious photos in travel magazines, the ones that make it look like the world's full of vivid destinations that make regular life seem pretty drab in comparison? What *is* it about those photos that makes things look so dramatic?

Often the answer is the *saturation*, or intensity, of the colors. Supersaturated color makes for darned appealing landscape and object photos, regardless of how the real thing may rate on the vividness scale.

There are various ways to adjust the saturation of your photos. Some cameras offer you settings to help control it, but Elements lets you go even further. For example, by increasing or decreasing a photo's saturation, you can shift the perceived focal point, change the mood of the picture, or just make your photo more eye-catching in general.

By increasing your subject's saturation and decreasing it in the rest of the photo you can focus your viewer's attention, even in a crowded photo. Figure 9-13 shows a somewhat exaggerated use of this technique; you can download the photo (*strawberries.jpg*) from the Missing CD page at *www.missingmanuals.com* to try it out for yourself.

It's quite easy to change saturation. You might want to start out with the Raw Converter's Vibrance slider if your photo is in either the Raw, TIFF, or JPEG format (see page 236). If that doesn't work well for you, try using either of the more traditional methods: the Hue/Saturation dialog box or the Sponge tool, which are explained in the following sections. For big areas, or when you want a lot of control, use Hue/Saturation. If you just want to quickly paint a different saturation level (either more or less saturation) on a small spot in your photo, the Sponge tool is faster.

NOTE Many consumer-grade digital cameras are set to crank the saturation of your JPEG photos into the stratosphere. That's great if you love all the color. If you prefer not to live in a Technicolor universe, you may wish to desaturate your photos in Elements to remove some of the excess color.

Using the Hue/Saturation Dialog Box

Hue/Saturation is one of the most popular commands in Elements. If you aren't satisfied with the results of a simple Levels adjustment, you may want to work on the hue or saturation as the next step toward getting really eye-catching color.

Hue simply means the color of your image—whether it's blue or brown or purple or green. Most people use the saturation adjustments more than the hue controls, but both hue and saturation are controlled from the same dialog box. You can adjust both or just one.

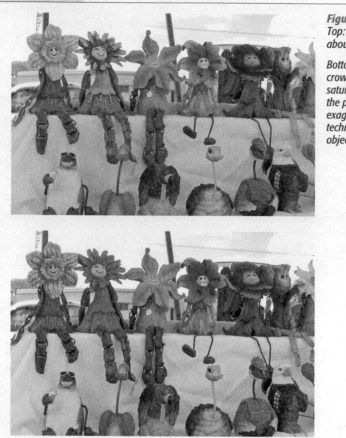

Figure 9-13:
Top: In this photo, all the shelfsitter figures are about equal in brightness.

Bottom: To make one figure stand out from the crowd, the figure was selected and the saturation was increased. Meanwhile, the rest of the photo was desaturated. The effect is exaggerated here, but a subtler use of this technique can work wonders for spotlighting objects in your photos.

In Elements, you can use the Hue slider to actually change the color of objects in your photos, but you probably want to adjust saturation far more often than you want to shift the hue of a photo.

When you use Hue/Saturation, it's a good idea to first make the most of your other corrections—like Levels or exposure corrections (see page 184). When you're ready to use the Hue/Saturation command, just follow these steps:

1. **If you want to adjust only part of your photo, select the area you want.**

   Use whatever selection tools you prefer. (See Chapter 5 for more about making selections.)

2. **Call up the Hue/Saturation Adjustment dialog box.**

   Go to Enhance → Adjust Color → Adjust Hue/Saturation, or go to Layer → New Adjustment Layer → Hue/Saturation. As always, if you don't want to make changes that you can't easily reverse, use an Adjustment layer instead of working directly on your photo.

3. **Move the sliders until you see what you want.**

If you want to adjust only saturation, just ignore the Hue slider. Move the Saturation slider to the right to increase the amount of saturation (more color) or to the left to decrease it. If necessary, move the Lightness slider to the left to make the color darker, or move it to the right to make the color lighter. Incidentally, you don't have to change all the colors in your photo equally. See Figure 9-14 for how to focus on individual color channels.

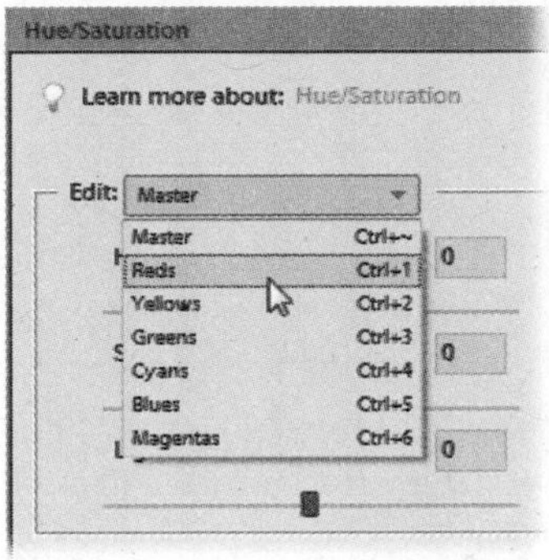

Figure 9-14:
The Hue/Saturation dialog box has a pull-down menu like the Levels dialog box, so you can adjust individual color channels. If only the reds are excessive (a common problem with digital cameras), you can choose to lower the saturation only for the reds without changing the other channels.

TIP   Generally speaking, if you want to change a pastel to a more intense color, you'll need to reduce the lightness (move the slider to the left) in addition to increasing the saturation—if you don't want your color to look radioactive.

Adjusting Saturation with the Sponge Tool

The Sponge tool gives you another way to adjust saturation. Although the tool is very handy for working on small areas, all that dragging gets old pretty fast when you're working on a large chunk of your image. For those situations, use the Hue/Saturation dialog box instead.

Even though it's called a sponge, the Sponge tool works like any other brush tool in Elements. Choosing the size and hardness are just the same as choosing them for any other brush (see page 328). The Sponge has a couple of unique settings of its own as well:

• **Mode.** Choose here whether to saturate (add color) or desaturate (remove color).

• **Flow.** Flow governs how intense the effect is. A higher number means more intensity.

To use the Sponge tool, drag over the area you want to change. Figure 9-15 shows an example of the kind of work the Sponge does.

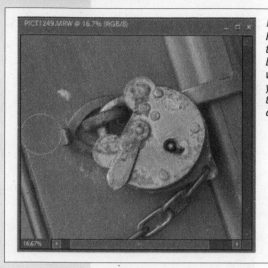

Figure 9-15:
Here, the Sponge tool has been applied to the upper-left side of the wood behind the lock, increasing the color saturation and bringing out the reddish paint colors. Approach the Sponge tool with some caution. It doesn't take much to cause degradation in your image, especially if you've made lots of other adjustments to it. If you start to see noise (graininess), undo your sponging and try it again at a reduced setting.

You may want to press Ctrl+J to create a duplicate layer before using the Sponge. Then you can always throw out the duplicate layer later on if you don't like the changes.

1. **Activate the Sponge tool.**

   Press O or click the icon in the Toolbox, and then choose the Sponge from the pop-out menu. Choose the brush size and the settings you want in the Options bar.

2. **Drag in the area you want to change.**

   If you aren't seeing enough of a difference, increase the Flow setting a little. If it's too strong, reduce the number for the Flow.

   TIP If you have a hard time coloring (or decoloring) inside the lines, select the area you want before starting with the sponge. Then the brush won't do anything outside the selection, allowing you to be as sloppy as you like.

Changing the Color of an Object

In Chapter 4, you saw one way to change the color of an object—select it and use the Hue and Saturation sliders in Quick Fix. Elements also gives you some other ways to do this: You can use an Adjustment layer, the Replace Color command, or the Color Replacement tool. And now, in Elements 7, the Smart Brush tools (page 189) have a whole menu full of color changes, too.

The method you choose depends to some extent on your photo and to some extent on your own preference. Using an Adjustment layer gives you the most flexibility if you want to make other changes later on. Replace Color is the fastest way to change one color that's widely scattered throughout your whole image, and the Color Replacement tool lets you quickly brush a replacement color over the color you want to change. Whichever method you choose, Figure 9-16 shows the kind of complex color change you can make in a jiffy using any one of these methods.

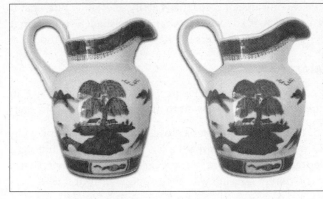

Figure 9-16:
What if you have a blue and white jug, but what you really want is a brown and white one? Just call up the Replace Color tool. Elements actually gives you several ways to make a complicated color substitution like this one, all of which are covered in this section.

NOTE The Smart Brush lets you target the area you want to change and make a quick color adjustment, but the color presets are pretty limited (and pretty ugly). Also, the Smart Brush doesn't just apply a single color, but uses color gradients (page 385). If you can find the effect you like in the Smart Brush, go for it. But it's much harder to adjust the color with this tool by changing the settings, since you must pick a different gradient or edit the gradient the Smart Brush used (page 391 tells you how). On the whole, the methods described in the following pages are much simpler to control.

Using an Adjustment Layer

You can use a Hue/Saturation Adjustment layer to make the same kind of changes to the color that you saw on page 272. The advantage of the Adjustment layer is that later on, you can change the settings or the area affected by the layer (as opposed to changing your whole image). The procedure is exactly the same as that described in the section "Using the Hue/Saturation Dialog Box", only this time, you start by selecting the object you want to change.

1. **Select the object whose color you want to change.**

   Use any of the Selection tools (see Chapter 5). If you don't make a selection before creating the Adjustment layer, you'll change your entire photo.

2. **Create a new Hue/Saturation Adjustment layer.**

   Go to Layer → New Adjustment Layer → Hue/Saturation. The new layer affects only the area you selected.

3. Use the sliders in the dialog box to adjust the color until you see what you want, and then click OK.

Use the Hue slider to start and pick the color you want. When you've gotten close to the desired color, use the Saturation slider to adjust the new color's vividness and the Lightness slider to adjust the darkness.

This method is fine if you have one area of color that's easily selectable. But what if you have a bunch of different areas or you want to change one shade everywhere it appears in your photo? For that, Elements offers the Replace Color command.

Replacing Specific Colors

Take a look at the blue and white pitcher in Figure 9-16 again. Do you have to tediously select each blue area one by one if you want to make a brown and white jug?

You can do it that way, of course, but far easier is to use the Replace Color command. It's one of those Elements dialog boxes that look a bit intimidating, but it's a snap to use once you understand how it works. Replace Color changes every instance of the color that you select, no matter how many times it appears in your image.

You don't need to start by making a selection when you use Replace Color. As usual, if you want to keep your options for future changes open, make a duplicate layer (Ctrl+J). When you start, be sure your active layer isn't an Adjustment layer, or Replace Color won't work.

1. **Open the Replace Color dialog box.**

Go to Enhance → Adjust Color → Replace Color. The Replace Color dialog box in Figure 9-17 appears.

TIP   If you want to protect a particular area of your chosen color from being changed, paint a mask on it by using the Selection brush in Mask mode (page 130) before you start.

2. **Move your cursor over your photo.**

The cursor changes to an eyedropper. Take a moment to confirm that the left eyedropper in the Replace Color dialog box is the active one (the one without a plus or minus sign).

3. **Click an area of the color you want to replace.**

All the areas matching that particular shade are selected, but you won't see the marching ants in your image the way you do with the Selection tools. If you click more than once, you just change your selection instead of adding to it, just the way you would with any of the regular Selection tools. To add to your selection (that is, to select additional shades), Shift+click in your photo.

Another way to add more shades is to select the middle eyedropper (the one with the + sign next to it) and click in your photo again. To remove a color, select the right eyedropper (with the minus sign) and click. Alternatively,

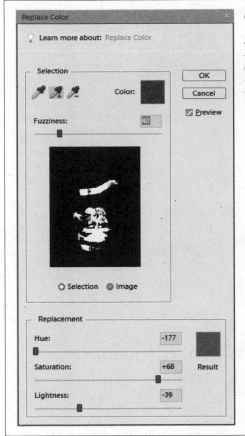

Figure 9-17:
The funny area that looks like a negative in the Replace Color window shows you where the sliders will affect the color. Use the Hue/ Saturation sliders to adjust the replacement color (shown in the bottom color square) the way you would with a regular Hue/ Saturation adjustment. Fuzziness works like a Tolerance Setting for the Magic Wand, as explained in Figure 9-18.

Alt+click with the first eyedropper, and the shade you click is removed from the selection. If you want to start your selection all over again, Alt+click the Cancel button to turn it to a Reset button.

4. **When you've selected everything you want to change, move the sliders to replace the color.**

The Hue, Saturation, and Lightness sliders work exactly the way they do in Hue/Saturation (explained earlier in this chapter). Move them and watch the color box in the Replace Color window to see what color you're concocting. You can also click the color box to bring up the Color Picker (page 209) and choose a color there. If you need to tweak the area of color you're changing, the Fuzziness slider adjusts the range of colors that Color Replacement affects, as shown in Figure 9-18.

Look at your photo after you've chosen your replacement color. If the preview doesn't show the color in all the areas you want, just click the missing spots with the middle eyedropper to fix them.

5. **Click OK.**

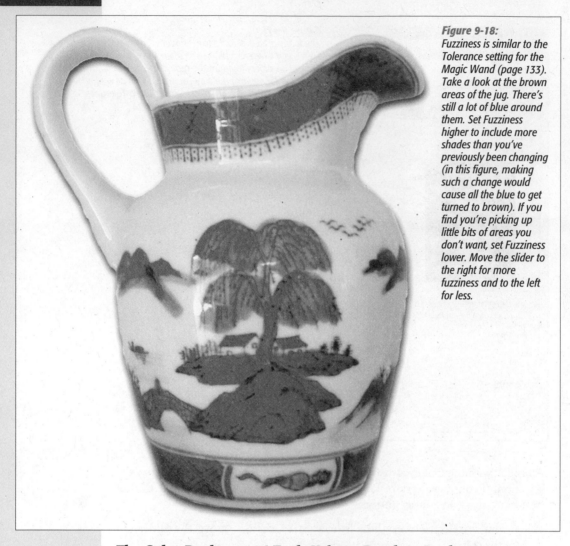

Figure 9-18:
Fuzziness is similar to the Tolerance setting for the Magic Wand (page 133). Take a look at the brown areas of the jug. There's still a lot of blue around them. Set Fuzziness higher to include more shades than you've previously been changing (in this figure, making such a change would cause all the blue to get turned to brown). If you find you're picking up little bits of areas you don't want, set Fuzziness lower. Move the slider to the right for more fuzziness and to the left for less.

The Color Replacement Tool—Using a Brush to Replace Colors

Besides the Smart Brush, Elements gives you yet another way to brush on a color change—the Color Replacement tool. It lets you brush a replacement color onto the area you want to change, without changing any other colors in your photo except the one you target. Your color choices with the Color Replacement tool are pretty much any color you want, so it's more versatile than the Smart Brush for changing colors. Figure 9-19 shows how great this tool is for changing hard-to-isolate areas like feathers.

The Color Replacement tool shares a slot with the Brush tool in the Toolbox. To select it, press B or click the Brush tool, and then choose the Color Replacement tool from the pop-out list.

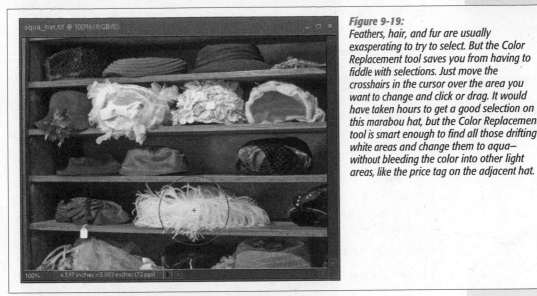

Figure 9-19:
Feathers, hair, and fur are usually exasperating to try to select. But the Color Replacement tool saves you from having to fiddle with selections. Just move the crosshairs in the cursor over the area you want to change and click or drag. It would have taken hours to get a good selection on this marabou hat, but the Color Replacement tool is smart enough to find all those drifting white areas and change them to aqua—without bleeding the color into other light areas, like the price tag on the adjacent hat.

The Options bar settings make a big difference in the way the Color Replacement tool works:

- **Brush Options.** These settings (size, hardness, angle, and so on) work the same way they do for any brush. See Chapter 12 for more information about brushes.

- **Mode.** This is the blend mode (page 343) the tool uses. Generally you want Color or Hue, although you can get some funky special effects with Saturation.

- **Sampling.** These choices appear as icons in the Options bar. Click one to tell the tool how to look for colors in your image. From left to right, they stand for Continuous, Once, and Background Swatch. If you choose Continuous, the brush changes every color that falls under the crosshairs as you move through your photo. Choosing Once means that no matter how far you travel while holding the mouse button, Elements replaces only the color that was under the crosshairs when you first clicked. Background Swatch means that Elements replaces only the color currently featured in the Toolbox's Background color swatch.

- **Limits.** This setting tells the Color Replacement tool which areas of your photo to look at in its search for color. Contiguous means only areas that touch each other get changed. Discontiguous means the tool changes all the places it finds a color—whether they're touching one another or not.

- **Tolerance.** This is just like the Tolerance setting for the Magic Wand: The higher the number, the more shades of color are affected by the tool. Getting this setting right is the key to getting good results with the Color Replacement tool.

- **Anti-alias.** This setting smoothes the edges of the replacement color. It's best to leave it turned on.

Using the Color Replacement tool is very straightforward:

1. **Pick the color you're going to use as a replacement.**

   Elements uses the current Foreground color as the replacement color. To choose a new Foreground color, click the Foreground color square in the Toolbox and choose a new color from the Color Picker (page 209) when it appears.

2. **Activate the Color Replacement tool and pick a brush size.**

   Click the Brush tool in the Toolbox and then choose the Color Replacement tool from the pop-out menu. (Keyboard shortcut: B.) See Chapter 12 for help using brushes. Generally for this tool, you want a fairly large brush, as shown in Figure 9-19.

3. **Click or drag in your photo to change the color.**

   Elements targets the color that is under the crosshairs in the center of the brush.

The Color Replacement tool is great for changing large areas of color to an equivalent tone, but if you want to replace dark red with pale yellow you probably won't like the results. It's not great for colors where the lightness is very different.

> **TIP** You may want to use the Color Replacement tool on a duplicate layer (Ctrl+J) so that you can adjust the layer opacity to control the effect.

Special Effects

Elements gives you some other useful ways of drastically changing the look of your image. You can apply these effects as Adjustment layers (Layer → New Adjustment Layer) or by going to Filter → Adjustments (there's much more about filters in Chapter 13). Either way gives you the same options for their settings. You can see them in action in Figure 9-20.

In most cases, you use these adjustments as steps along the way in a more complex treatment of your photo, but they're effective by themselves, too. Here's what each does:

- **Equalize** makes the darkest pixel black and the lightest white, and redistributes the brightness values for all the colors in a photo to give them all equal weight. When you have an active selection, you see a dialog box that lets you choose between simply equalizing your whole photo and equalizing it based on a selection. It doesn't always work, but sometimes Equalize is great for bringing up the brightness level of a dim photo. This choice is not available as an adjustment layer, only as a filter.

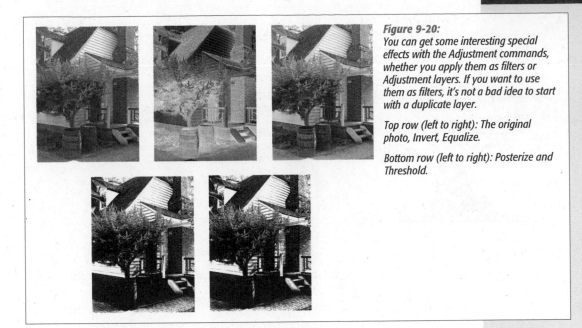

Figure 9-20:
You can get some interesting special effects with the Adjustment commands, whether you apply them as filters or Adjustment layers. If you want to use them as filters, it's not a bad idea to start with a duplicate layer.

Top row (left to right): The original photo, Invert, Equalize.

Bottom row (left to right): Posterize and Threshold.

- **Gradient Map** is pretty complicated. According to Adobe, it "maps the gray-scale range of an image to the colors of a specified gradient fill." If you want to know what the heck *that* means, turn to page 396. Basically, a gradient map lets you apply a gradient based on the light and dark areas of your photo. The gradient colors replace the existing colors in your photo. There's a lot more to it than that, though.

- **Invert** makes your photo look like a negative. It's so useful in doing artistic effects that Elements also lets you invert in the Editor at any time just by pressing Ctrl+I. (If you want to invert part of an image, check out the new Smart Brush tools [page 189]. There are some interesting variations on inversion in its Special Effects menu choices.)

NOTE If you think choosing the Invert option sounds like a great way to get your negatives scanned in with a basic flatbed scanner and turned to positive images, sorry, but that won't work. Color negatives have an orange mask on them that Elements can't easily undo. You're best off with a dedicated film scanner that's designed to cope with negatives, or at least with a scanner that has software designed to deal with the mask.

- **Posterize** reduces the total number of colors in your photo, giving a less detailed, more poster-like effect. The lower the number you enter in the dialog box, the fewer colors you'll get (thus, the more extreme the result). If you want blocky, poster-like edges in your photo, try Filter → Artistic → Poster Edges instead of or in addition to this.

• **Threshold** turns every pixel in your photo to pure white or pure black. You won't find any shades of gray here. Figure 9-21 explains how to adjust the settings for the Threshold command.

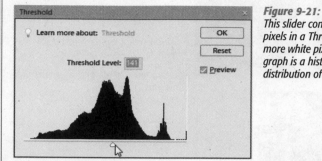

Figure 9-21:
This slider controls the dividing point between black and white pixels in a Threshold adjustment. Slide to the left if you want more white pixels, and to the right for more dark ones. The graph is a histogram (page 199) showing the light to dark distribution of the pixels in your image.

• **Photo Filter** makes color corrections, like removing color casts from your photos. You can read about it in detail on page 242.

CHAPTER 10

Removing and Adding Color

If you love classic black-and-white photography, or if you yearn to be the next Ansel Adams, then you'll be over the moon with the high-quality black-and-white conversion in Elements. If you can't imagine why anyone would willingly abandon color, consider that in a world crammed full of eye-popping colors, black and white really stands out. Also, you may be planning to have something printed where you can't use color illustrations. And, of course, for artistic photography there's still nothing like black and white, where tone and contrast make or break the photo, without any pretty colors to distract you from the picture's underlying structure.

In this chapter, you'll learn how to make a color photo black and white, and how to create images that are partly in color and partly in black and white. You'll also learn how to colorize a black-and-white image, and, along the way, how to use and edit *layer masks*, an important technique for advanced Elements work.

Method One: Making Color Photos Black and White

A good black-and-white image is so much more than just a color photo without color. Generally, just removing the color from a photo produces a pretty flat-looking, uninteresting image. A good black-and-white photo usually needs more contrast. You can create very different effects and totally different moods in your photo, depending on what you decide to emphasize in the black-and-white version.

Black-and-white conversion has traditionally been regarded as a pretty complicated process. When you do a Google search, you can find literally dozens of different recipes for making conversions. Fortunately for you, Elements makes it really easy to perform these conversions, and even to do sophisticated tweaking of the different color channels.

Just follow these steps:

1. **Open the photo you want to convert.**

   If the photo has multiple layers, then flatten it (Layer → Flatten Image), or make sure the layer you want to convert is the active layer (click it in the Layers palette). If you want to convert only a part of your photo, then select the area you want to make black and white. As always, it's best to do this on a copy, not your original photo.

2. **Go to Enhance → "Convert to Black and White", or press Alt+Ctrl+B.**

   The "Convert to Black and White" dialog box appears. It includes a helpful before and after preview of your image, and the controls shown in Figure 10-1.

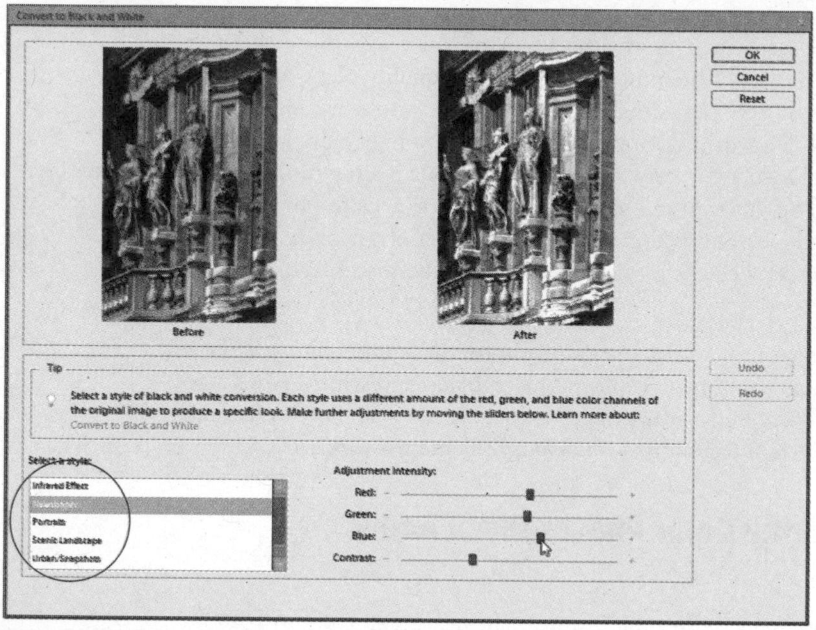

Figure 10-1:
The "Convert to Black and White" dialog box makes it very easy to create effective transformations, even if you don't have any idea what you're doing. First, choose a conversion style from the list on the left (circled), and then use the sliders to tweak your conversion, if necessary.

3. **Choose a conversion style.**

   Elements gives you various preset styles for the conversion. Click a style in the list to apply it to your photo. Try different styles to see which suits your photo best.

4. **Tweak the conversion, if necessary.**

Use the Adjustment Intensity sliders below the preview area (Red, Green, and so on) to increase or decrease the prominence of each color channel. Watch the preview to see how you're changing your photo. Go gently—it doesn't take much to make quite a difference in your image.

Once you move a slider, Undo and Redo buttons appear. Use them to step backwards and forwards through your changes. If you want to start from scratch, then click Reset.

5. **When you're satisfied with how your photo looks, click OK.**

Be sure to examine your actual image carefully. Don't rely on just the smallish preview window. Move the "Convert to Black and White" dialog box around your screen so that you can see all the regions of your photo before you accept the conversion. If you decide against creating a black-and-white image, then click Cancel.

TIP Very often, you may prefer to emphasize certain details in your photo without making additional changes to the overall tonality. To do that, use the Dodge and Burn tools (page 340), once you've completed your conversion.

While the different conversion styles have descriptive names, like Portraits and Scenic Landscape, don't put too much stock in the names themselves. Instead, test out the various styles to see which best matches your photo. For instance, you may vastly prefer the way Uncle Julio looks when you choose the Newspaper style instead of the Portraits style. Basically, the names are just a less intimidating way of describing preset collections of settings to the color channels in your photo.

But wait a minute: changes to the color channels? That's right. Back in Chapter 7, you read about how your photo consists of three separate color channels: red, blue, and green. What you may not realize is that, in your original camera file, each of these channels is recorded merely as variations in light and dark tones; in other words, a black-and-white image. Your image file tells the computer or printer to render a particular channel as all red, blue, or green, and the blending of the three monotone channels makes all the colors you see.

Now when you convert your photo back to black and white, each of these channels contains varying amounts of details from your photo, depending on the color of your original subject. So, the green channel might have more detail from your subject's eyelashes, while the red channel may have more detail from the bark on the tree she's standing under. (Remember, the color channels themselves don't necessarily correspond to the color of the objects you see in your final photo. Or, put another way: Your camera needs to use a mixture of red, blue, and green to create what looks like bark to us humans.) Noise (graininess) often happens much more in one channel than the others, as well.

The Adjustment Intensity sliders in the dialog box (More Red, More Green, and so on) let you increase or decrease the presence of each color channel. So you can adjust how prominent various details in your photo are by changing the importance of that color channel in the complete photo. These adjustments can greatly change the appearance of the final conversion. The Contrast slider adjusts the contrast for the combined channels.

That's the theory behind those color channel sliders, but fortunately you don't have to understand it to use them effectively. Just be sure you can get a good view of your photo (zoom and, if necessary, move the dialog box around), and slide till you're happy with what you see. If you plan to print your converted photo, read the box on page 287 for some tips on how to get a good black-and-white print from a color inkjet printer.

> **NOTE** Elements gives you an easier way to convert your photo to black and white, but it's an all-or-nothing scenario—you don't get any options for adjusting the tones in your image. The Effects palette includes a very nice black-and-white tint effect. Go to Effects → Photo Effects → Monotone Color, and then double-click the black-and-white apple to apply the effect. Also, some frames in the Frames section of the Content palette (page 427)—like some of the Color Tint frames—automatically convert your photo to black and white when you place it in the frame. See page 419 for details on how to use these frames.

Method Two: Removing Color from a Photo

Since one size never fits all, Elements gives you a few other, fundamentally different ways to remove the color from your image. Most times, you should follow the instructions in the preceding section to convert your photo to black and white. But if you want to drain the color from a particular part of your photo, or if you're looking to do something artistic, like changing a color photo into a drawing or a painting, then you'll probably want to try one of these three methods:

- **Convert Mode.** You may remember from page 45 that you need to choose a color mode for your photo: RGB, Bitmap, or Grayscale. You can remove the color from your photo by changing its mode to Grayscale. Choose Image → Mode → Grayscale. This method is quick, but it's also a bit destructive, since you can't apply it to a layer: Your entire photo is either grayscale or not.

- **Remove Color.** You can also keep your photo as an RGB file and drain the color from it, by going to Enhance → Adjust Color → Remove Color (or pressing Shift+Ctrl+U). This command removes the color only from the active layer, so if your photo has more than one layer, then you need to flatten it first (Layer → Flatten Image), or the other layers keep their color.

    Remove Color is really just another way to completely desaturate your photo—just as you might when using the Hue/Saturation command (described in the next option). Remove Color is faster but you don't get the control that the Hue/Saturation command gives you. Figure 10-2 shows the difference between applying the Remove Color command versus converting your entire image to grayscale.

- **Hue/Saturation.** You can also call up the Hue/Saturation dialog box (page 271), and move the Saturation slider all the way to the left, or type *–100* into the Saturation box. The advantage of this method is that if you don't care for the shade of gray you get, then you can desaturate each color channel separately by using the pull-down menu in the dialog box. With this method, you can tweak your settings a bit to eliminate any color cast you may get from your printer.

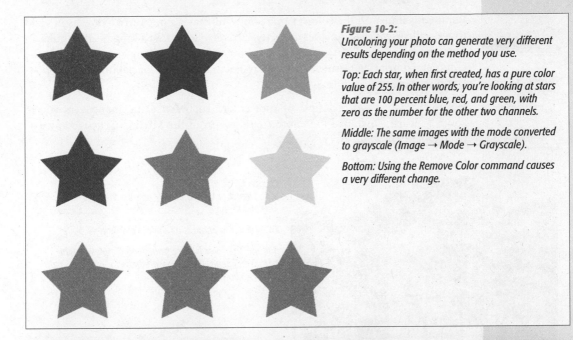

Figure 10-2:
Uncoloring your photo can generate very different results depending on the method you use.

Top: Each star, when first created, has a pure color value of 255. In other words, you're looking at stars that are 100 percent blue, red, and green, with zero as the number for the other two channels.

Middle: The same images with the mode converted to grayscale (Image → Mode → Grayscale).

Bottom: Using the Remove Color command causes a very different change.

OUTSIDE ELEMENTS

Digital Black and White

If you love black-and-white photography, there's good news for you in the digital world. The quality of digital black-and-white printing is improving by leaps and bounds, and now you can get decent black-and-white photos from even some of the lowest-priced printers.

For all the wonders of digitizing, though, there's still nothing that can exactly duplicate the effect of a traditional silver print—although digital printing has made great strides in the past couple of years.

If you want to print black-and-white photos, you may still want to look into buying a photo printer that lets you substitute several shades of gray for your color cartridges. The special inks available are constantly improving, and you can get much better prints now than you could even a year or two ago. You can now purchase special grayscale ink cartridge sets for even very inexpensive inkjet printers, and more printer drivers have settings for grayscale printing. (Printer driver controls appear when you launch the Elements Print dialog box, as explained on page 440.)

TIP   If you're planning to print the results of your conversion, the paper you use can make a *big* difference in the gray tones you get. If you don't like the results from your usual paper, try a different weight or brand. You'll need to experiment because the inks for different printer models react differently with different brands of paper.

Creating Spot Color

Removing almost all the color from a photo but leaving one or two objects in vivid tones, called *spot color*, is a very effective artistic device that's long been popular in the print industry. (The term can also have a different meaning among those in the commercial printing business, where it refers to the use of special ink for a particular color in a multicolor image.)

Figure 10-3 shows an example of spot color. To practice the maneuvers you're about to learn, download the photo (*barn.jpg*) from the Missing CD page at *www. missingmanuals.com*.

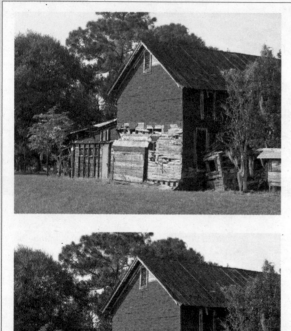

Figure 10-3:
With Elements, you can easily remove the color from only part of an image.

Top: Here, the photo is a regular color image.

Bottom: The color is gone from everything except the barn. You'll learn three easy methods for removing color in this section.

This section walks you through four of the easiest methods to create spot color. (The fifth way, explained earlier in this chapter [page 283], is to select the area you want to make black and white, and then use "Convert to Black and White".) You can paint out color, erase your way back to color, change only a selected area to black and white, or use an Adjustment layer. With the last method, you'll also learn how to edit the layer mask of an Adjustment layer so that you can change the area that the adjustment affects.

The end result looks the same no matter which method you choose. Just select the one you find easiest for the particular photo you want to change.

> **TIP** If you have a newish digital camera, check your special effects settings for a spot or accent color setting. Many cameras can now create a black-and-white image with only one shade left in color.

Brushing Away Color

Creating black-and-white areas in a color photo has never been as easy as it is in Elements 7. You can use the new Smart Brush to convert an area to black and white while making your selection (see Figure 10-4). In other words, you paint the object you wish to make black and white, and Elements selects and converts it—all while preserving the color in the rest of your photo. If you want to keep most of your image in color while converting only small portions of it to black and white, this method is definitely the one to try first.

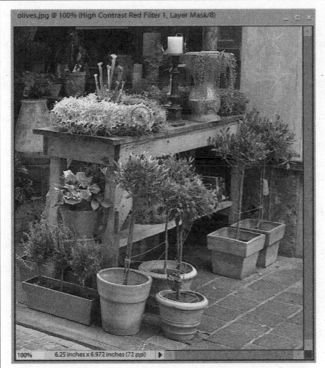

Figure 10-4:
With the Smart Brush, converting part of your photo to black and white is as simple as making a selection. It would be a nuisance to accurately select all the curly edges of the grass wreath on the table, but the brush does a fairly good job of automatically finding the wreath's edges as you drag your cursor over it. The end result? A wreath that's soon to be black and white, all without changing the color of the rest of the photo.

To paint away color with the Smart Brush:

1. **Open a photo in Full Edit mode, and then activate the Smart Brush.**

   Press F, or click its icon in the Toolbox, and then choose the brush from the pop-out menu. The Smart Brush puts its changes on their own layer, so you don't need to create a duplicate layer before using it.

2. **Choose the style of black and white conversion you want.**

   At the right end of the Smart Brush options, you'll see a small thumbnail. This is actually the pop-out menu for the Smart Brush presets (which Adobe calls Smart Paint). Go to the "Black and White" section, and then choose the thumbnail that looks most like what you want. (If you don't like it once it's applied, you can always change it later.) Elements has a number of different conversion styles, and the names don't mean much, really. It's best to go by the thumbnail preview when choosing a conversion style.

3. **Drag over the object in your photo that you want to make black and white.**

   The Smart Brush should select the object and convert it, all in one go. If you have a hard time getting a good selection, then go back to Elements' main Toolbox, and use the Detail Smart Brush (page 189) instead. (That one works like the regular Selection brush, changing only the area directly under the cursor, so you'll have more work to do, but you'll get a more accurate selection.)

That's all there is to it. If you don't like the conversion style you've chosen, or want to change the area the brush affects, then just click the pin that appears when the Smart Brush is active; then make your changes. See page 191 for more about how to fine-tune Smart Brush edits. You can also adjust the affected area by editing the Smart Brush's layer mask, as explained on page 293.

The Smart Brush is great when you want a photo that's mostly in color with only a small area of black and white showing. If you want a photo that's mostly black and white with only a small area of color, brush over the area you want to keep in color and then, in the Options bar, turn on the Invert checkbox, which reverses the area changed by the effect. The part of your image you made black and white gets recolored, while the rest of the photo (where you didn't brush) turns black and white. You can also use one of the methods listed in the following sections.

Erasing Colors from a Duplicate Layer

You can also easily remove colors from parts of your image with the Eraser tool. (See page 348 for more about the different Erasers.) Using this method, you place a color-free layer over your colored original, and then erase bits of the top layer to let the color below show through.

1. **Make a duplicate layer.**

   Press Ctrl+J or go to Layer → Duplicate Layer. This layer is going to be black and white.

2. **Remove the color from the new top layer.**

   Go to Enhance → "Convert to Black and White", or to Enhance → Adjust Color → Remove Color. (Be sure the top layer is the active one before you do this.) You should now see only a black-and-white image.

3. **Erase the areas on the top layer where you want to see color.**

   Use the Eraser tool (page 348) to remove parts of the top layer so the colored layer underneath shows through. Usually you'll get the best results with a fairly soft brush.

If you want an image that's mostly colored with only a few black-and-white areas, then reverse the technique—remove the color from the bottom layer, and leave the top layer in color. Then erase as described above.

When finished, you can flatten the layers if you want. But by keeping them separate, you preserve the option to go back and erase more of the top layer later on. And you'll still have the option of trashing the layer you erased and making a new duplicate of the bottom layer, if you want to start over.

Removing Color from Selections

If you don't want to have multiple layers, you can also use the Enhance menu's "Convert to Black and White" option or the Remove Color command on a selection. Just make sure you save your image as a version (page 59) or perform this method on a copy, if your photo isn't in the Organizer. You don't want to risk wrecking your original photo. While the Smart Brush is the handiest tool for uncoloring small areas, as explained above, the method described here is best if you don't like any of the Smart Paint presets or if you're absolutely dead set against having a new layer.

The procedure for changing a selected area to black and white is very simple:

1. **Mask out the area where you want to keep the color in your image.**

   Use the Selection brush in Mask mode (see page 130) to paint a mask over the area where you want to *keep* the color, to protect it from being changed in step 2. In other words, you're going to make everything black and white *except* where you paint with the Selection brush.

   If you want to keep the color in most of your photo and remove the color from only one or two objects, then paint over them with the brush in Selection mode instead of Mask mode, or use the Quick Selection tool.

2. **Remove the color from the selected area.**

   Go to Enhance → "Convert to Black and White", or to Enhance → Adjust Color → Remove Color, or press Shift+Ctrl+U. The color disappears from the areas not protected by the mask, but the area under the mask is untouched. (You can also do this step by going to Enhance → Adjust Color → Adjust Hue/Saturation, and then moving the Saturation slider all the way to the left.)

You should see a photo with color only in the areas that you didn't select. This method is the least flexible of all the ones described in this chapter. Once you close your image, the change is permanent and not undoable, which is why you don't want to use this method on your original photo.

SPECIAL EFFECTS

Hints for Coloring Old Photographs

It's easier to put each element of a face that you're going to color—lips, eyes, cheek color, skin—on a separate layer. That way, you can change just one color later without a lot of hassle. You can always merge the layers (Layer → Merge Visible, or Merge Down) later, once you know for sure that you're done. Here are some other tips when you're aiming for that 19th century look:

- If you want the effect of a photo that was hand-colored a century ago, paint at less than 100-percent opacity. The tinting on old photos is very transparent.

- If you select the area before you paint, then you don't have to worry about getting color outside of where you want it, because your paint is confined to your selection.

- Skin colors are very hard to create in the color picker. Try sampling skin tones from another photo instead. If it's a family photo, after all, the odds are good that the current generation's basic skin tones are reasonably close to Great-Granddad's.

Using an Adjustment Layer and the Saturation Slider

If you'd like to keep the option of easily changing your mind about which areas keep the color, and you don't like any of the Smart Brush presets, it's best to remove the color with a Hue/Saturation Adjustment layer. This choice is the most flexible (though it doesn't offer you the tone adjustments you can make when using the Enhance menu's "Convert to Black and White" option). Using an Adjustment layer lets you both add and subtract areas of color later if you like.

1. **Select the area where you want to remove the color.**

   Use any Selection tool you like (see Chapter 5 for more about Selection tools). If you think it would be easier to select the area where you want to keep the color, do that. Then press Shift+Ctrl+I to invert your selection—now the area that's going to lose the color is selected instead.

2. **Create a Hue/Saturation Adjustment layer.**

   Go to Layer → New Adjustment Layer → Hue/Saturation, or click the New Adjustment Layer icon on the Layers palette, and then choose a Hue/Saturation layer.

3. **In the Hue/Saturation dialog box that appears, remove the color.**

   Move the Saturation slider all the way to the left to remove the color.

Why is this method better? Well, for one thing, you can always discard the Adjustment layer if you change your mind. But that's not all. You can actually edit the Adjustment layer's layer mask (see page 178 for more about layer masks) so that you can change which parts of your photo are in color, even days or weeks later.

Don't want that tree as well as the vine on the house? Or maybe you wish you'd left all the window frames in color? You can easily fix everything by editing the layer mask. The next section tells you how.

Editing a layer mask

Elements lets you make changes to the layer mask of an Adjustment layer any time you want—as long as the layer hasn't been merged into another layer and the image hasn't been flattened. You may want to edit your layer mask if you think your original selection needs some cleaning up, or you want to make changes to the area the Adjustment layer affects. You can use this same technique to change the area affected by a Smart Brush adjustment, too, although usually it's simpler just to click the pin in the image and activate the layer mask that way (see page 191 for more details on how all *that* works).

> **NOTE** Remember that masking something means it *won't* be affected by a change. So the area that shows up in black or red on your layer mask is the area that isn't going to be changed by your adjustment. If you don't see any black or red when looking at a layer mask, then the Adjustment layer is going to change your whole photo.

You can work on the mask directly, or make the layer mask visible and work on the mask itself. Here's the simplest way to make changes to the area covered by a layer mask:

1. **Make sure the Adjustment layer is the active layer.**

   If it isn't, then click it in the Layers palette.

2. **Set your foreground/background colors to black and white.**

   Just press D. If you want to paint with white, press X to swap the colors so that white (the background) becomes the foreground color.

3. **Paint directly on your image.**

   Use the Brush tool to paint on the image. Paint with black to keep an area from being affected by your adjustment. Paint with white to increase the area affected by the adjustment. In other words, black masks an area, while white increases your selected area.

   You can also use the Selection tools (the same way you would on any other selection) to change the mask's area. Just keep in mind that what's selected gets changed by the adjustment, while what's masked doesn't change. See Chapter 5 if you need help making selections. If you watch the layer mask icon in the layers palette, then you'll see that it also changes to show where you've painted.

To make a layer mask visible, click it in the Layers palette. Elements gives you a choice of two different ways to see the masked area, as shown in Figure 10-5. You merely Alt+click the right thumbnail for the Adjustment layer in the Layers palette, and then you'll see the black layer mask (instead of your photo) in the image window. Add the Shift key when you click to see a red overlay on the photo instead of the black-and-white view. Press the same keys again to get back to a regular view of your image.

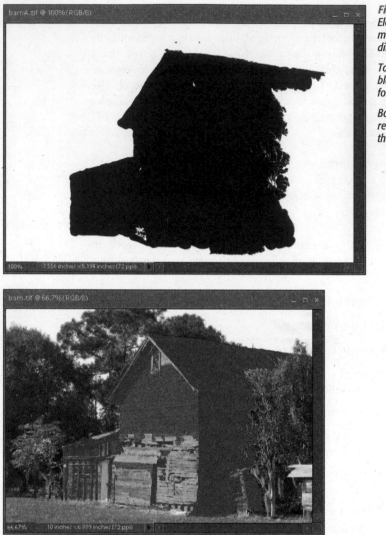

Figure 10-5:
Elements lets you edit your layer mask and also gives you two different ways to see it.

Top: To see the masked area in black, Alt+click the right thumbnail for the layer in the Layers palette.

Bottom: To see the masked area in red, Alt+Shift+click the layer's thumbnail.

The black mask view shows only the mask itself, not your photo beneath it. This is a good choice when checking to see how clean the edges of your selection are. If you're adding or subtracting areas of your photo, then choose the red overlay view so you can see the objects in your photo as you paint over them. You can use the method described above to paint in either view.

That's all there is to it, but that's not all you can do to edit a layer mask. You can use shades of gray to adjust the transparency of the mask. When you paint on your mask with gray, you can change the opacity of the changes made by the Adjustment layer. You can let a little color show through the mask, for instance, without letting the full vividness of the color come through. Figure 10-6 shows an example of how you'd use this technique. The lighter the shade of gray you choose, the more color shows through.

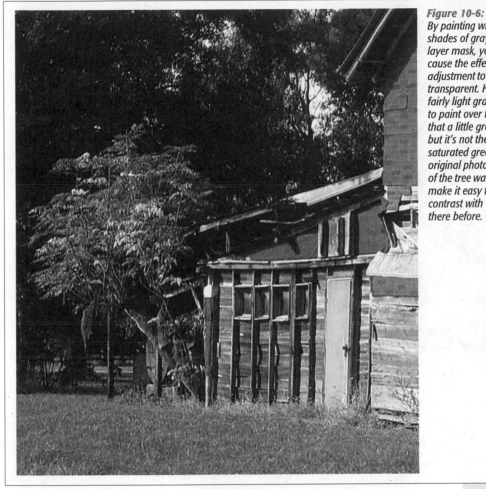

Figure 10-6:
By painting with different shades of gray on the layer mask, you can cause the effect of the adjustment to be partially transparent. Here, a fairly light gray was used to paint over the tree so that a little green shows, but it's not the bright, saturated green of the original photo. Only part of the tree was painted to make it easy to see the contrast with what was there before.

Colorizing a Black-and-White Photo

So far, you've read about ways to make all or part of a color photo black and white. But what about when you've got a black-and-white photo and you want to add color to it? Elements makes things easy (or if not easy, then at least possible). For instance, you can give an old photo the sort of hand-tinted effect you sometimes see in antique prints, as shown in Figure 10-7.

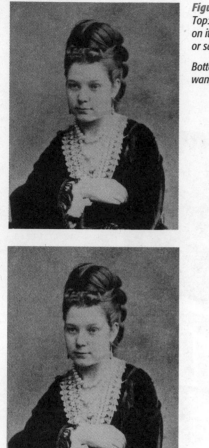

Figure 10-7:
Top: If you decide to color an old black-and-white or sepia photo, put each color on its own layer. That way you can adjust the transparency or change the hue or saturation of one color without changing the other colors, too.

Bottom: A very low opacity is enough for really old photos like this one if you want to give the effect of a print that was hand-colored.

You can easily color things with Elements. Before you start tinting a photo, first make any needed repairs. See page 263 for repair strategies. For fixes to the exposure, see page 184.

1. **Make sure your photo is in RGB mode.**

   Go to Image → Mode → RGB Color. Your photo must be in RGB mode or you can't color it.

2. **Create a new layer in Color blend mode.**

   Go to Layer → New → Layer and select Color as the layer mode. By choosing Color as your layer mode, you can paint on the layer and the image details still show through.

3. **Paint on the layer.**

Use the Brush tool (page 328) and choose a color in the Toolbox's Foreground color square (page 208). Keep changing the foreground color as much as you need to. If the coverage is too heavy, then in the Options bar, reduce the opacity of the brush.

You can also paint directly on the original layer. (Try switching the brush blend mode to Color for this.) But with that method, you'll find it far more difficult to fix things if you make a mistake when you're well into your project. Using the original layer also doesn't give you much of an out if you decide later on that the lip color you painted first doesn't look so great with the skin color you just chose.

The method just described is handy for when you want to use many different colors on a photo, but if you want to add only a single color to part of the photo, in Elements 7 the easiest way is to use the Smart Brush:

1. **Be sure your photo is in RGB mode.**

Go to Image → Mode → RGB Color. Your photo must be in RGB mode or the Smart Brush only paints in shades of gray rather than the color you select.

2. **Activate the Smart Brush, and then choose a color to paint with.**

Press F or click the Smart Brush in the Toolbox, and then go to the Smart Paint setting in the Options bar (the thumbnail to the right of Refine Edge) and choose Color. From the menu thumbnails, select the color you want.

3. **Drag over what you want to color.**

The Smart Brush automatically creates your selection, and colors it. If you don't get a good selection with the regular Smart Brush, switch to the Detail Smart Brush.

4. **Tweak the effect.**

The color choices tend to be pretty heavy, so you may prefer to go to the Layers palette and reduce the opacity of the Smart Brush layer (see page 162 for more about layer opacity).

The Smart Brush works well if you happen to like one of the available color choices. If you don't like any of the colors it offers, then use the new layer method described earlier in this section, which is much more flexible, since you can choose any color you want.

Tinting an Entire Photo

You can give an entire photo a single color tint all over, even if the original is a grayscale photo. Tinting is a great way to create a variety of different moods.

You have two basic ways to tint photos. Actually, there are a lot more than two, but two should get you started. The first method (Layer style) described here is faster, but the second (Colorize) lets you tweak your settings more. Figure 10-8 shows the result of using the Layer style method on a color photo. (For a more subtle effect, you can also use Photo Filters, described on page 242.) Photo Effects also has some terrific monotone tint effects, as explained on page 379.

For either method, if you want to keep the original color (or lack thereof) in part of your photo, then use the Selection brush in Mask mode (page 130) to mask out the area you don't want to change.

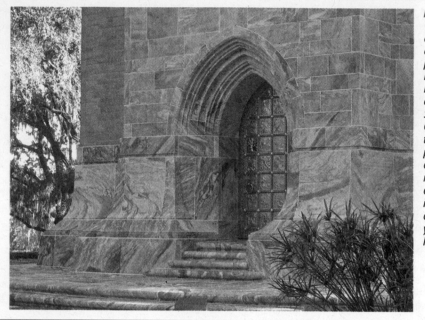

Figure 10-8:
You can most easily create a monochrome color scheme for your photo with the Photographic Effects Layer styles, which are explained in Chapter 13. Shown here is the Gray-Green Tone style applied to the original color photo. It removes any existing color and recolors your image in one click. The downside is that you can't edit the color once you're done if you decide you'd rather have, say, orange.

TIP Some of the frame effects in the Content palette automatically add a tint to your photo when you apply them. The Effects palette also has some handy monochrome tint effects in its Photo Effects section.

Using a Layer style

Although many people never dig down far enough to find them, Adobe gives you some Photographic Effects Layer styles that make tinting a photo as easy as double-clicking. You'll learn more about Layer styles on page 382, but this section tells you all you need to know to use the Photographic styles. It's a very simple procedure:

1. **Create a duplicate layer.**

   Go to Layer → Duplicate Layer or press Ctrl+J. (If you don't create a duplicate layer and your original has only a Background layer, then you'll get asked to convert it to a layer when you apply the style. Say yes.)

2. **If necessary, change the mode to RGB.**

   Go to Image → Mode → RGB Color. With this method, it doesn't matter if your original is in color or not. The Layer style gets rid of the original color, and tints the photo all at the same time.

3. **Choose a Layer style.**

   Go to the Effects palette → Layer Styles → Photographic Effects. Double-click the style of your choice, drag it to the photo, or click it once in the palette, and then click Apply. You can click around and try different styles to see which you prefer. Undo (Ctrl+Z) after each style that you try.

4. **When you see what you like, click OK.**

   The drawback to this method is that you can't easily go back and edit the color you get from the Layer style. When you call up the Style Settings (see page 385), you don't see any active checkboxes, because these styles don't use those settings. Instead, you'd need to use a Hue/Saturation adjustment (see page 271) or Color Variations (page 207) to go back later and change the Layer style's tint color.

Additional tint effects from the Content palette

The Content palette includes some frames that automatically apply a tint to your photo, as shown in Figure 10-9. These range from simple all-over colors like Sepia, to fading gradients. (See page 385 for more about gradients.)

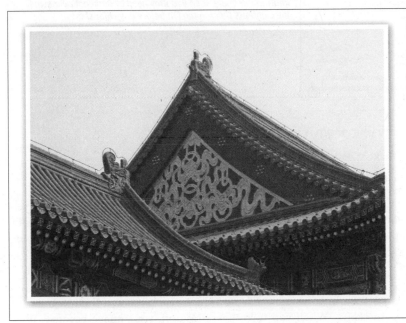

Figure 10-9:
Using the Content palette, you can apply elaborate effects, like this fading gradient, drop shadow, and frame, with just a double-click. The effect used here is the Color Tint Blue Fadeout 20px.

You can read more about using the Frames from the Content palette on page 419. To tint your photo, choose Type → Frames, and then scroll down towards the bottom of the list of thumbnails.

The Photo Effects section of the Effects palette also has some very effective color tints. Read about how to apply Effects on page 379.

Using Colorize

You can use the Colorize checkbox in the Hue/Saturation dialog box to add a color tint to a grayscale photo or to change the color of a photo that already has color in it. With this method, you can choose any color you like, as opposed to the limited color choices of the Layer styles in the previous section. You can also adjust the intensity of the color with the Saturation slider once you've selected the shade you want.

Figure 10-10 explains how the Colorize setting changes the way the Hue/Saturation command works.

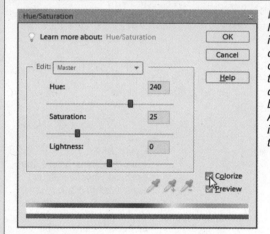

Figure 10-10:
If you want to color something that has no color information in it, like a white shirt or a grayscale image, in the Hue/Saturation dialog box, turn on Colorize (where the cursor is here) to add color to the image. If you don't turn on the Colorize checkbox, then you can adjust the hue, saturation, and lightness of white all day long—all you'll do is go from white to gray to black because there's no color info there for Elements to work with. Also, if something is pure white (that is, contains no color information at all), then you may need to darken it by moving the Lightness slider to the left before any color shows.

1. **Make sure your photo is in RGB mode.**

   Go to Image → Mode → RGB Color.

2. **Remove the color from your photo, if necessary.**

   Press Shift+Ctrl+U to remove the color. Do this if the photo has become yellowed or discolored (because of age, for example). If your whites are really dingy, then you might want to make a Levels adjustment (page 198) to brighten them back up before removing the color.

3. **Colorize your photo on a new layer.**

   Go to Layer → New Adjustment Layer → Hue/Saturation, and then turn on the Colorize checkbox. When you turn this setting on, your image becomes filled with the foreground color. If you don't like it, that's fine. You're going to change it right now.

4. **Adjust the color until it looks the way you want it to.**

Move the sliders for Hue, Saturation, and Lightness until you find the look you want, and then click OK. Figure 10-11 shows the results.

TIP Want to turn a full-color photo to a monotone image in a hurry? Just turn on the Colorize checkbox—no need to remove the color first. Colorize automatically reduces your photo to just one color. The advantage to using the Colorize method (versus the layer style) is that you can use the sliders to create any color you want.

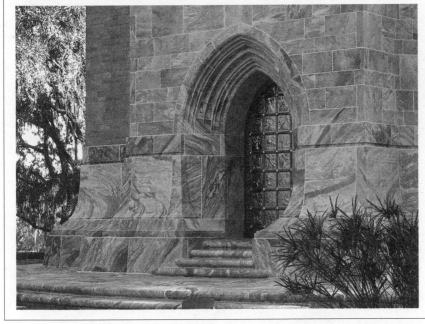

Figure 10-11:
Here's the photo from Figure 10-8. It was tinted with a purple tone by turning on the Colorize checkbox in the Hue/ Saturation dialog box. The door was masked out so that it stays in full color.

If you selected and masked an area, then that part should still show the original color.

You can change your mind about the colorizing by double-clicking the left icon on the layer in the Layers palette. That brings up the controls for the Hue/Saturation adjustment again so you can change your settings. And you can also edit the layer mask, as described on page 293, if you want to change the area that's affected by the Adjustment layer.

When you're done, if you merge layers (or press Ctrl+Alt+Shift+E to produce a new merged layer above the existing layers), then you can use Levels (page 198), Color Variations (page 207), and the other color-editing tools to tweak the tint effect.

CHAPTER 11

Photomerge: Creating Panoramas, Group Shots, and More

Everyone's had the experience of trying to photograph an awesome view—a city skyline or a mountain range, say—only to find the whole scene won't fit into one picture because it's just too wide. Elements, once again, comes to the rescue. With Elements' Photomerge command, you can stitch together a group of photos you've taken while panning across the horizon. You end up with a panorama that's much larger than any single photo your camera can take. Panoramas can become addictive once you've tried them, and they're a great way to get those wide, wide shots that are beyond the capability of your camera lens.

Elements includes the same great Photomerge feature that's part of Photoshop CS3, which makes it incredibly easy to create super panoramas.

Not only that, but Adobe gives you a couple of fun twists on Photomerge that are unique to Elements: Faces and Group Shot, which let you easily move features from one face to another, and replace folks in a group photo. And Elements 7 brings yet another new kind of merge: Scene Cleaner, for all those times when your almost perfect vacation shot is spoiled by strangers managing to get into your perfect scenic composition.

If you're into photographing buildings (especially tall ones), then you know that you often need some kind of perspective correction: The building appears to be leaning backward or sideways as a result of distortion caused by your camera's lens. This chapter shows you how to use the Correct Camera Distortion filter to straighten things back up. You'll also learn how to use the Transform commands to adjust or warp your images.

Creating Panoramas

It's incredibly simple to make fabulous panoramas in Elements. (If you're upgrading from Elements 5 or earlier, then you know that lots of other programs made better, easier panoramas than Elements used to. Not anymore: The Elements Photomerge does an amazing job, totally automatically.) To make a panorama in Elements now, about 99 percent of the time, you just tell Elements which photos you want to use, and Elements automatically stitches together a perfect panorama. Figure 11-1 shows what a great job it does.

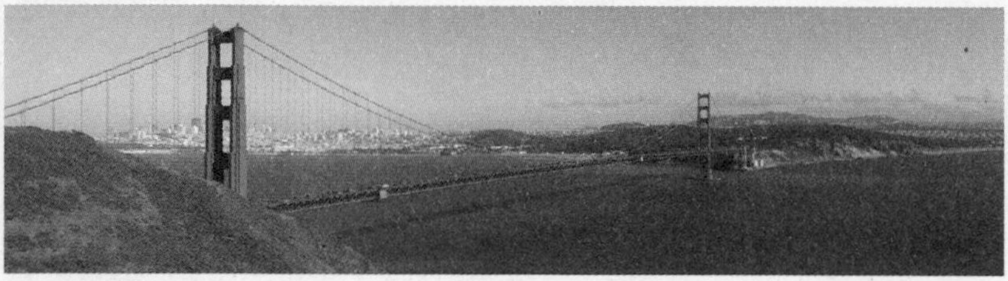

Figure 11-1:
For subjects like the Golden Gate Bridge, you can never capture the entire scene in one shot. Here's a five-photo panorama made with Photomerge. The individual photos had huge variations in exposure and were taken without a tripod. Elements takes the images—straight from the camera with no adjusting—and blends them seamlessly.

Elements can merge as many photos as you want to include in a panorama. The only real size limitation comes when printing out your compositions. If you create a five-photo horizontal panorama but your paper is letter size, then your printout is only a couple of inches high, even if you rotate the panorama to print lengthwise. However, you can buy a printer with an attachment that lets you print on rolls of paper, so that there's no limit to the longest dimension of your panorama. These printers are very popular with panorama addicts. You can also use an online printing service, like the Kodak EasyShare Gallery, to get larger prints than you can make at home. See page 437 for more about how to order online prints via the Organizer.

You'll get the best results creating a panorama if you plan ahead when shooting your photos. The pictures should be side by side, of course, and they should overlap each other by at least 30 percent. Also, you'll minimize the biggest panorama problem—matching the color in your photos—if you make sure they all have identical exposures. While Elements can do a lot to blend exposures that don't match well, for the best panorama, adjust your photos before you begin, as explained in Figure 11-2. (The box on page 309 has more tips for taking merge-ready shots.)

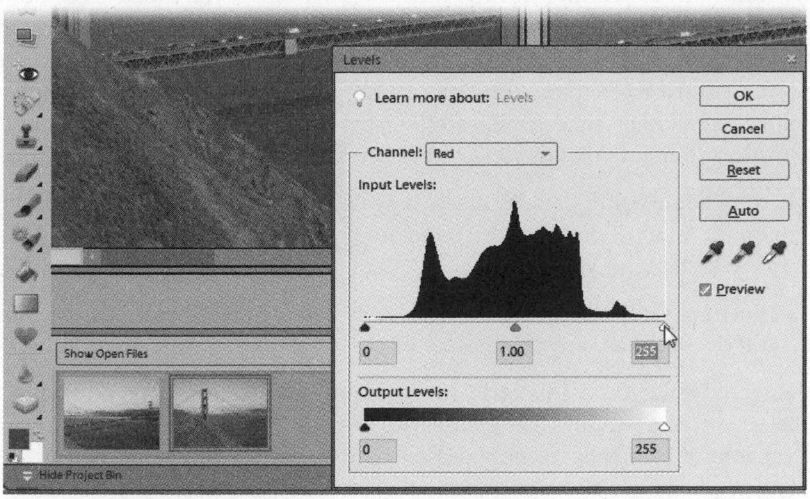

Figure 11-2:
While Elements did a very credible job with the bridge panorama in Figure 11-1, if you look closely you can see the photos on the left were much lighter than those on the right. For even better results, use Elements to correct your photos so that the colors are as close as possible before beginning your panorama. It helps to keep them side by side so that you can compare them as you work.

When you're ready to create a panorama, just follow these steps:

1. **Start your merge.**

   In the Editor, go to File → New → Photomerge Panorama. The Photomerge dialog box appears.

2. **Choose your photos.**

   If the photos you want to include are already open, then just click Add Open Files. Otherwise, in the pull-down menu, choose Files or Folder; then click the Browse button to navigate to the ones you want. As you click them in the window that appears, Elements adds them to the list in the Photomerge window.

   Add more files by clicking Browse again. To remove a file, click it in the list, and then click Remove.

   NOTE   You can merge directly from Raw files, although of course you don't have any controls for adjusting the file conversions. Photomerge works only with 8-bit files, so if you have 16-bit files, it asks if you want to convert them when it begins merging. For faster Raw merges, set the Raw converter to 8 bits (page 238) before you start.

3. **From the Layout list on the left side of the window, choose a merge style.**

   Ninety-nine percent of the time you want to choose Auto, the first Layout option. That's usually all you need to do. When you click OK, your completed panorama is darned near perfect. You also get some other merge style choices for use in special situations:

   • **Perspective.** Elements adjusts the other images to match the middle image using such methods as skewing and other Transform commands to create a realistic view.

- **Cylindrical.** Sometimes when you adjust perspective, you create a panorama shaped like a giant bow tie. Cylindrical mapping corrects this distortion. (It's called "cylindrical" because it gives an effect like looking at the label on a bottle—the middle part seems the largest, and the image gets smaller as it fades into the distance, similar to the label wrapping around the sides of the bottle.) You may want this style for very wide panoramas.

   If you choose Auto, then Elements may use either Perspective or Cylindrical mapping when it creates your panorama, depending on what it thinks will do the best job for your photos.

- **Reposition Only.** Elements overlaps your photos and blends the exposure, but it doesn't make any changes to the perspective of the images.

- **Interactive Layout.** This style lets you position your images manually. It takes you to a window that's similar to the old Photomerge window in early versions of Elements; the next section gives a detailed explanation.

4. **Click OK to create your panorama.**

   Elements whirls into action, combining, adjusting, looking for the most invisible places to put the seams, and whips up a completed panorama for you. That's all there is to it.

   > **NOTE** Elements has a lot of complex calculations to make when creating a panorama, especially if you have lots of images or big exposure differences between the photos, so it may take awhile. Don't assume that Elements is stuck; give it time to think about what it's doing. It may need a few minutes to finish everything.

You'll probably want to crop your panorama (page 79), but otherwise, you're all done. You can use any of the editing tools on the final panorama once Photomerge is through, if you like. You can do anything to your panorama that you can do to any other photo.

> **NOTE** Elements has a quirk that may cause the program to give you an out-of-memory error message when saving a panorama. If you run into this, then just flatten your panorama (Layer → Flatten Image) and you should be able to save it.

Manual Positioning with Interactive Layout

If you find that you absolutely must do some manual positioning of your photos, choose Interactive Layout from the Layout list. When you click OK, Elements does its best to combine your photos, and presents them to you in the window shown in Figure 11-3.

Here you can help Elements blend your photos better. Your panorama in its current state appears in the large preview area, surrounded by special tools to help you get a better merge. On the left of the window, you see a special toolbox. The Lightbox,

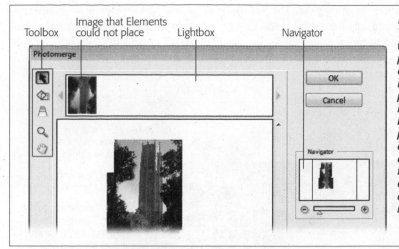

Toolbox   Image that Elements   Lightbox   Navigator
           could not place

Figure 11-3:
You don't often need to intervene when Elements makes a panorama, but if you want to control the process yourself, Interactive Layout lets you position your photos manually. Note how obvious the differences in exposure are in the merged photos in the graphic. Elements applies Advanced Blending only after you click OK to create your final panorama. Then the obvious exposure banding you see here disappears so you get a smooth merge.

which contains the photos that Elements couldn't figure out how to place, is across the top, and you see special controls down the right side. You can use any combination of these features to improve your panorama.

You can manually drag files from the Lightbox into the merged photos, and also reposition photos already in your panorama. Just grab them with the Select Image tool (explained below), and then drag them to the correct location in the merge.

If you try to nudge the position of a photo and it keeps jumping away from where you've placed it, turn off "Snap to Image" on the right side of the Photomerge window. Then you should be able to put your photo exactly where you want it. However, Elements isn't doing the figuring for you anymore, so use the Zoom tool to get a good look at the alignment afterward. You may need to micro-adjust the photo's exact position.

There's a little toolbox at the top left of the Photomerge window. Some tools are familiar, and others are special tools just for panoramas:

- **Select Image.** Use this tool to move individual photos into or out of your merged photos or to reposition them. When the Select Image tool is active, you can drag photos into or out of the Lightbox. Press A or click the tool to activate it.

- **Rotate Image.** Elements usually rotates images automatically when merging them, but if it doesn't or if it guesses wrong, press R to activate this tool, and then click the photo you want to rotate. You see handles on the image, just the way you would with the regular Rotate commands (page 78). Just grab a corner, and then turn the photo until it fits in properly. Usually, you don't need to drastically change a photo's orientation, but this tool helps make the small changes often needed to line things up better.

- **Set Vanishing Point.** To understand what this tool does, think of standing on a long, straight, country road and looking off into the distance. The point at which the two parallel lines of the road seem to converge and meet the horizon is called the *vanishing point*. The Vanishing Point tool in Elements tells Photomerge where you want that point to be in your finished panorama. Knowing the vanishing point helps Elements figure out the correct perspective. Press V to activate the *Vanishing Point* tool. Figure 11-4 shows an example of how it can change your results.

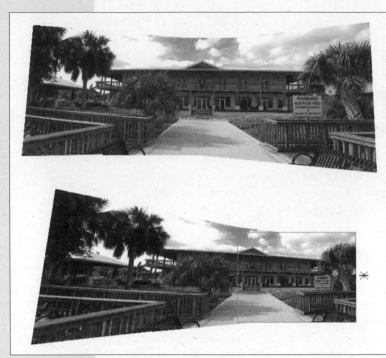

Figure 11-4:
You can radically alter the perspective of your panorama by selecting a vanishing point.

Top: The result of clicking in the merge's center photo.

Bottom: The result of clicking on the right-hand image. Note that the tool selects only a particular image in the merge group, not the actual point within the photo. You can click any photo to put your vanishing point there, but if you subsequently try to tweak it by clicking a higher or lower point within the same photo, then nothing happens. To change the Vanishing point you've set, just click a different photo.

- **Zoom tool.** This is the same Zoom tool (page 87) you meet everywhere else in Elements. Click the magnifying glass in the Toolbox or press Z to activate it.

- **Move View tool.** Use the Move View tool exactly the way you'd use the Hand tool (page 88) when you need to scoot your *entire* merged image around to see a different part of it. Click the hand icon in the Toolbox or press H to activate it. When moving an individual photo within your panorama, use the Select Image tool instead of the Hand tool.

To control your onscreen view of your panorama, on the right side of the Photomerge window, Elements gives you the Navigator, which works just like the regular Navigator described on page 89. Move the slider to resize the view of your panorama.

Drag to the right to zoom in on one area, or to the left to shrink the view so that you can see the whole thing at once. If you want to target a particular spot in your merge, then drag the red rectangle to control the area that's onscreen.

Shooting Tips for Good Merges

The most important part of creating an impressive and plausible panorama starts before you even launch Elements. You can save yourself a lot of grief by planning ahead when shooting photos for a panorama.

Most of the time, you know *before* you shoot that you'll want to try to merge your photos. You don't often say, "Wow, I can't believe I've got seven photos of the Sponge-Bob SquarePants balloon at the Thanksgiving Day parade that just happen to be exactly in line and have a 30-percent overlap between each one! Guess I'll try a merge."

If you know you want to create a panorama, when you're taking pictures, set your camera to be as much in manual mode as possible. The biggest headache in panorama making is trying to get the exposure, color, brightness, and so on to blend seamlessly. Elements is darned good about blending the outlines of the physical objects in your photos. Lock your camera settings so that the exposure of each image is as identical as possible.

Even on small digital cameras that don't have much in the way of manual controls, you may have some kind of panorama setting, like Canon's Stitch Assist mode, that does the same thing.

(To be honest, your camera may make merges itself that work at least as well as what Elements can do, because the camera's doing the image-blending internally. Check out whether your model has a panorama feature.)

The more your photos overlap, the better. Elements does what it can with what you give it, but it's really happy if you can arrange a 30 percent overlap between images.

Use a tripod if you have one, and *pan heads* (tripod heads that let you swivel your camera in an absolutely straight line) were made for panoramas. Actually, as long as your shots aren't wildly out of line, Elements can usually cope. But you may have to do quite a bit of cropping to get even edges on the finished result if you don't use a tripod.

Whether you use a tripod or not, keep the camera—rather than the horizon—level to avoid distortion. In other words, focus your attention more on leveling the body of the camera than what you see through the viewfinder. Use the same focal length for each image, and try not to use the zoom, unless it's manual, so that you can keep it exactly the same for every image.

Below the Navigator box you see two radio buttons—Reposition Only and Perspective—that adjust the viewing angle of your panorama. You can choose one or the other, but not both:

- **Reposition Only**. This button merely overlaps the edges of your photos, with no changes to the perspective. If you don't like the way the angles in your panorama look, then try clicking Perspective instead. (Advanced Blending is always on, so Elements always blends the exposure for a smooth transition. You can't turn it off.)

- **Perspective**. If you click this button, Elements tries to apply perspective to your panorama to make it look more realistic. Sometimes Elements does a bang-up job, but usually you get better results if you help it out by setting a vanishing point, as explained earlier. If you still get a totally weird result, go ahead and just create the merge anyway. Then correct the perspective yourself afterward using one of the Transform commands, covered in the next section.

Once you get your photos arranged to your satisfaction, just click OK, and Elements creates your final panorama.

> **NOTE** Elements always creates layered panoramas. If you're sending your panorama out for printing, flatten it (Layer → Flatten Image) before doing so, since most commercial printers don't accept layered files. Also, if you enlarge the view of your layered panorama and zoom in on the seams, then you may see what look like hairline cracks. Merging or flattening the layers gets rid of these cracks.

Merging Different Faces

Merging isn't just for making panoramas anymore. One of the Elements-only tools that Adobe gives you is Faces, a fun (okay, let's be honest—silly) feature that lets you merge parts of one person's face with another person's face. You can use it to create caricature-like photos, or for things like pasting your new sweetie's face over your old sweetie's face in last year's holiday photo. Figure 11-5 shows an example of what Faces can do. (Elements' other special tools, Group shot and the new Scene Cleaner, are explained later in this chapter.)

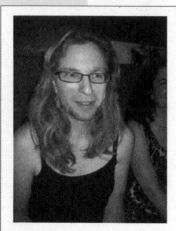

Figure 11-5:
Faces is really just for fun. You can create composite images like this one, and then use the Editor's other tools to make your photo even sillier, if you like.

Although you'd be hard put to think of a serious use for Faces, it can be fun to play with, and it's quite simple to use:

1. **Choose the photos to combine.**

   You need to have at least two photos available in the Project bin before you start.

2. **Call up the Faces feature.**

   You can get to it either from File → New → Photomerge Faces, or from Guided Edit → Photomerge → Faces.

A dialog box asks you to choose the photos you want to include. In the Project bin, Ctrl+click to select the photos you want to use, or choose Open All from the dialog box. Elements then opens the Faces window, which has a preview area on the left and an instruction pane on the right.

3. **Choose a Final photo.**

This photo is the main photo into which you're going to paste parts of the face from one or more photos. Just drag a photo from the bin into the Final Image area (on the right-hand preview).

4. **Choose your Source photo.**

This is the photo from which you're going to copy part of the face to move to the Background Image. Double-click it in the Project bin, and it appears in the left-hand preview area. You can copy from many different photos, but you can work only with one Source photo at a time. (When you're done working with one photo, just double-click the next one you want. This way you can use the ears from one photo, the nose from another, and so on.)

5. **Align your photos.**

This step is very important, because otherwise Elements can't adjust for any differences in size or angle between the two shots. Click the Alignment tool button in the Faces pane, and the three little targets shown in Figure 11-6 appear in each image.

Position the markers over the eyes and mouth in each photo, and then click Align Photos. (If you need help seeing what you're doing, there's a little Toolbox on the left with your old friends the Zoom [page 87] and Hand [page 88] tools, so you can reposition the photo for the best view.)

Elements adjusts the photos so they're the same size and sit at the same angle to make a good blend.

6. **Tell Elements what features to move from the Source image to the Final Image.**

Click the Pencil tool in the Faces pane and, in the Source photo, draw over the area you want to move. In a few seconds you should see the selected area appear in the Final photo. It takes only a quick line—don't try to accurately color over all the material you want to move. In the Options bar, you can adjust the size of the Pencil tool if it's hard to see what you're doing, or if it's grabbing too much of the surrounding area.

If Elements moves too much material from the Source photo, then use the Faces Eraser tool to remove part of your line. Watch the preview in the Final image to see how you're changing the selection. If you want to start over, then click Reset.

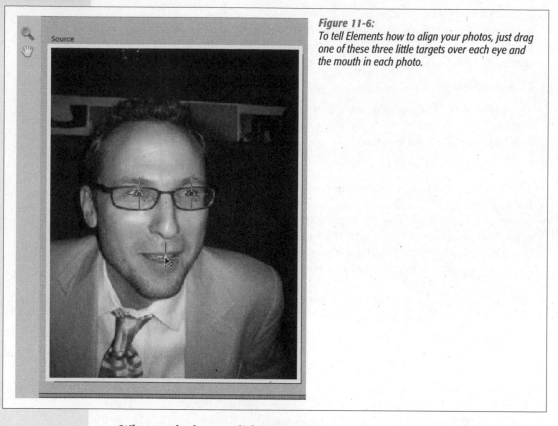

Figure 11-6:
To tell Elements how to align your photos, just drag one of these three little targets over each eye and the mouth in each photo.

7. **When you're happy, click Done.**

Elements creates your merge as a layered file. Now you can edit it using any of the Editor's tools, if you wish. You may want to clean up the edges a bit or to manually clone (page 260) a little more material than Elements moved. And you can make your image even sillier with the Transform commands (page 321), the Liquify filter (page 411), and so on.

You can adjust two settings in the Faces pane:

- **Show Strokes.** If you want to see what you're selecting, then leave this on.

- **Show Regions.** Turn this on, and you see a translucent overlay over the Background image, which makes it easier to tell which regions you're copying over from your Source photo. It's something like the overlay option for the Healing brush (page 257) and the Clone Stamp (page 260).

It would be nice if you could use this feature to merge things besides faces, but it doesn't do a very good job at all. Even for faces, if you're doing something important, like repairing an old photo with parts from another picture of the same person, then you may prefer to do your own selections, and manually move and adjust things (see page 179). However, the alignment tools in Faces can simplify the process enough that it's worth giving it a try to see if it can do what you need.

Arranging a Group Shot

Have you ever tried taking photos of a whole group of people? Almost every time, you get a photo where everything is perfect, except for that one person with his eyes shut. In another shot, that person is fine, but other people are yawning or looking away from the camera. You probably thought, "Dang, I wish I could move Ed from that photo to this one. Then I'd have a perfect shot."

Adobe hears your wishes, and Group Shot is the result. It's specifically designed for moving one person in a group from one photo to another, similar photo.

You launch Group Shot by going to File → New → Photomerge Group Shot, or Guided Edit → Photomerge → Group Shot.

The steps for using Group Shot are the same as for Faces, except that you don't normally need to align the photos, since Group Shot is intended for those situations where you were saying, "Just one more, everybody—and hold it!" as opposed to moving people from photos taken at different times with different angles and lighting.

But if you do need to align your photos, you can do that in the advanced options. Just place the markers the same way you do in Faces (see page 311). Another advanced option is Pixel Blending, which adjusts the moved material to make it closer in tone to the rest of the Final image.

> **NOTE**   It would be great if you could use Group Shot for things like creating a photo showing many generations of your family by combining images from photos taken over many years. However, Group Shot moves someone from the Source photo and pastes that person into the same spot in the Final photo, and then creates a composite layer in the completed merge. That means the relocated person is merged into the entire Background image, and isn't left as an extracted object, which makes it impossible to put that person in a completely different location. You need to do that the old-fashioned way, by moving each individual onto a separate layer (see page 179) and then repositioning everybody where you want them.

Tidying Up with Scene Cleaner

Elements 7 brings a useful new spin to photo merging. With Scene Cleaner, you can eliminate unwanted people or elements in your photos. Think of all those travel magazine photos that show famous sights in their lonely glory, without any tourists hanging around to clutter up the scene. If you've ever waited patiently for what seems like hours, trying to get a shot of a famous landmark, only to give up as busload after busload of tourists keep arriving, you'll appreciate Scene Cleaner.

Or you've probably had this experience when showing your vacation photos: "Here's a shot of Jodi and Taylor at the rim of the Grand Canyon…Oh, those other people—no, no idea who they are. Just got in front of the camera somehow." Scene Cleaner was made to fix photos like those.

Scene Cleaner is quite easy to use, but you'll get best results if you can plan ahead when taking your photos. In order to get a people-less landscape, then you need to shoot multiple photos from nearly the same angle. All the areas you want to feature should be uninhabited in at least one photo. So, for instance, if you can get one shot of the Statue of Liberty where all the tourists are in the left side of her crown and one where they're on the right side, you're all set. Then, to use Scene Cleaner to create a more perfect world:

1. **In the Editor, open the photos you want to combine.**

   In addition to being taken from nearly the same vantage point, they should have similar exposures. If a cloud is passing, for instance, so that one photo is bright and one is shadowy, then you'll have to do some fancy touchups afterwards to blend the tones together. It's usually easier to do this beforehand. Chapter 7 has the full story on exposure correction.

2. **Call up Scene Cleaner.**

   In Full Edit, go to File → New → Photomerge Scene Cleaner, or go to Guided Edit → Photomerge → Scene Cleaner. In either case, you wind up in Guided Edit to create your merged image. Elements automatically aligns your photos, so there may be a slight delay before you see the Scene Cleaner window.

3. **Choose a Final Image.**

   This is the base image into which you want to put parts of your other photo(s). Drag the photo you choose from the Project bin into the Final preview area (the right-hand slot).

4. **Choose a Source Image.**

   Look through your photos to find a photo that has an empty area with the people or objects you want to remove from the Final photo. Click that photo in the Project bin, and it appears in the Source Image preview area (the left-hand slot). (As with Faces, you can use many Source images, but you work with only one at a time—move on to the next Source photo when you're done.)

5. **Align your photos manually, if necessary.**

   Usually you don't need to do this, but if Elements didn't do a good job of automatically aligning your photos, click the flippy triangle next to Advanced Options, and then click the Alignment tool. You see the three markers described in the section on Faces (page 311). This time, instead of eyes and mouth, place them over three similar locations in each photo, and then click Align Photos.

6. **Tell Elements what you want to move.**

   If the Pencil tool isn't active, then click it in the right-hand pane of the window. Then, in the Source image, draw over the area you want to move to the Final photo. Just draw a quick line—Elements figures out the exact area to move.

(You can also go to the Final preview, and draw over the area you want to cover—Elements can figure it out either way.)

7. **Adjust the areas if needed.**

Use the Pencil tool again to add more areas, and the Eraser tool to remove bits if you moved too much. You can use the Eraser in either preview, Source or Final. If you have more than two photos to work with, in the Project bin, click another photo to move it to the Source slot, and then select the area you want. If you need to see the edges of the areas that Elements is moving, then turn on Show Regions, as explained in Figure 11-7.

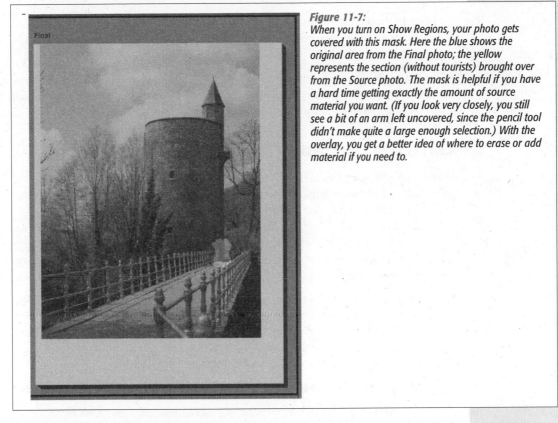

Figure 11-7:
When you turn on Show Regions, your photo gets covered with this mask. Here the blue shows the original area from the Final photo; the yellow represents the section (without tourists) brought over from the Source photo. The mask is helpful if you have a hard time getting exactly the amount of source material you want. (If you look very closely, you still see a bit of an arm left uncovered, since the pencil tool didn't make quite a large enough selection.) With the overlay, you get a better idea of where to erase or add material if you need to.

If the exposures don't blend well, go the Advanced Options and turn on Pixel Blending for a smoother merge.

8. **When you're happy, click Done.**

Don't forget to save your work. If you want to start over, then click Reset. If you decide to give up on the merge, then click Cancel.

Most of the time, you need only the Pencil tool and the Eraser, but Adobe does give you some additional options to help you out when necessary:

- **Show Strokes**. Leave this turned on, or you can't see where you're drawing with the tools.

- **Show Regions**. Scene Cleaner actually brings over chunks of the Source image. If you turn this option on, then you can see a blue and yellow overlay showing the exact size of the material you're moving. See Figure 11-7.

- **Alignment Tool**. This advanced option lets you manually set the comparison points. Use these points if you don't like Elements automatic choices. Step 5 explains how to use the Alignment tool.

- **Pixel Blending**. Just as in Faces, you turn on Pixel Blending when there's a discrepancy in color or exposure between your photos, so that they combine more seamlessly.

It's not always easy to get enough clear areas to blend, even with multiple photos, but when you have the right kind of source photos, you can create the impression that you and your pals had a private tour of your favorite places all to yourself.

Correcting Lens Distortion

If you ever photograph buildings, then you know that it can be tough getting good shots with a fixed-lens digital camera. When you get too close to the building, your lens starts to cause distortion, as shown in Figure 11-8. Special perspective-correcting lenses are available, but they're expensive (and if you have a pocket camera, they aren't even an option). Fortunately, you can use Elements' Correct Camera Distortion filter to fix photos after you've taken them. It's another very popular Photoshop tool that Adobe transferred over to Elements, minus a couple of advanced options.

Correct Camera Distortion is a terrifically helpful filter, and not just for buildings. You can also use it to correct the slight balloon effect you sometimes see in close-ups of people's faces (especially in shots taken with a wide-angle setting). You can even deploy the filter for creative purposes. For example, you can create the effect of a fish eye lens by pushing the filter's settings to their extremes.

Here are some telltale signs that it's time to summon Correct Camera Distortion:

- You've used the Straighten tool (page 76), but things still don't look right.

- Your horizon is straight, but your photo has no true right angles. In other words, the objects in your photo lean in misleading ways. For instance, buildings lean in from the edges of the frame, or back away from you.

- Every time you straighten to a new reference line, something else gets out of whack. For example, say you keep choosing different lines in your photo that ought to be level, but no matter which one you choose, something else in the photo goes out of plumb.

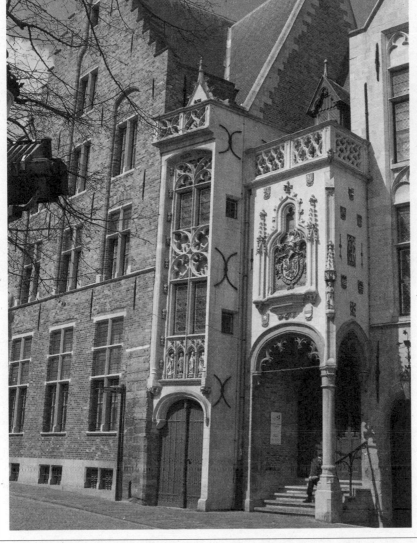

Figure 11-8:
Here's a classic example of a candidate for Elements' Correct Camera Distortion filter. This type of distortion is quite common when you're using a point and shoot camera in a very narrow space that doesn't let you get far enough away from your subject. You can fix such problems in a jiffy with the help of this filter.

- If you have a problem with vignetting—a dark, shadowy effect in your photo's corners—you can also fix that with Correct Camera Distortion. You can also *create* vignetting for special effects.

Adobe's made this filter extremely easy to use. Just follow these steps:

1. **Open a photo, and then go to Filter → Correct Camera Distortion.**

   The large dialog box shown in Figure 11-9 appears.

NOTE Even though Correct Camera Distortion is in the Filter menu, you can't reapply it using the Ctrl+F shortcut, the way you can with most other filters. You always have to select it from the Filter menu.

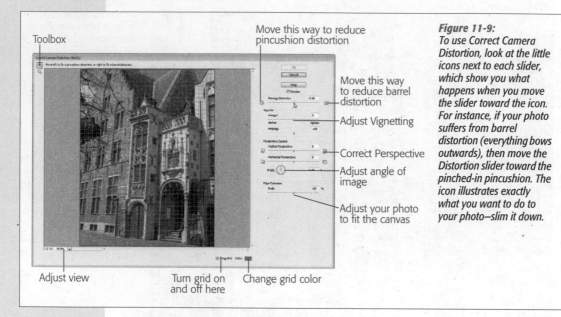

Toolbox

Move this way to reduce pincushion distortion

Move this way to reduce barrel distortion

Adjust Vignetting

Correct Perspective

Adjust angle of image

Adjust your photo to fit the canvas

Adjust view

Turn grid on and off here

Change grid color

Figure 11-9:
To use Correct Camera Distortion, look at the little icons next to each slider, which show you what happens when you move the slider toward the icon. For instance, if your photo suffers from barrel distortion (everything bows outwards), then move the Distortion slider toward the pinched-in pincushion. The icon illustrates exactly what you want to do to your photo—slim it down.

2. **If necessary, use the Hand tool (page 88) to adjust your photo in the window. You want a clear view of a reference line—something you know you want to correct, like the edge of a building.**

If the distortion is very bad, this mission may be impossible, but try to find at least one line as closely aligned to the grid as you can, so you have a reference for changing the photo. You can also use the usual view adjustment controls (including zoom in and out buttons) in the dialog box's lower-left corner. The Hand tool adjusts both your photo and the grid. That means you can't use it to position your photo *relative* to the grid. Also, the Hand tool doesn't do anything unless you set the view to more than 100%.

The Show Grid checkbox lets you turn the grid on and off, but since you're going to be aligning your image, you'll almost always want to keep it on. To change the color of the grid, next to the Show Grid checkbox, click the Color box.

3. **Make your adjustments.**

The filter lets you fix three different kinds of problems: barrel/pincushion distortion, vignetting, and perspective problems. These errors are the ones you're most likely to run into, and correcting them is as easy as dragging sliders around. The small icons on each side of some of the sliders show you how your photo will change if you move in that direction. You may need to make only one adjustment, or you may need many (the bulleted list that follows helps you decide which controls to use).

Watch the grid carefully to see how things are lining up. When you get everything straightened to your satisfaction, you're done. If you want to start over, Alt+click the Cancel button to change it to a Reset button, and return your photo to the state it was in when you brought it into this filter.

4. **Scale your photo, if you wish.**

As you make your adjustments, you'll probably notice some empty space appearing on either side of your canvas (the background area of your file). This phenomenon often happens when Elements pinches and stretches your photo to correct the distortion. To make things right, you've got two options. You can click OK now and crop the photo yourself (using any of the options you learned about back on page 79). Or, you can stay here and use the Edge Extension slider to enlarge your photo so that it fills up the visible window. If you use this method, then Elements crops some of the photo anyway.

Edge Extension is handy, but gives you little control over how the photo is cropped. After all the effort you made using this filter, you may as well do your own cropping to get the best possible results.

5. **Click OK to apply your changes.**

If you don't like the way things are turning out, then you can reset your photo by Alt+clicking the Cancel button. If you just want a quick look at where you started from (without undoing your work), then toggle the Preview checkbox on and off.

The Correct Camera Distortion filter gives you a few different ways to adjust your image. Your choices are divided into sections, according to the different kinds of distortion they fix:

- **Remove Distortion.** Use this slider to fix *barrel distortion* (objects in your photo balloon out, like the sides of a barrel, as shown in Figure 11-10), and its opposite, *pincushion distortion* (your photo has a pinched look, with the edges of objects pushing in toward the center). Move the slider to the right to fix barrel distortion, and to the left to fix pincushion distortion.

    TIP   Barrel distortion is usually worst when you use wide-angle lens settings, while pincushion distortion generally appears when a telephoto lens is fully extended. Barreling's more common than the pincushion effect, especially when you use a small point-and-shoot camera at a wide-angle lens setting. You can often reduce barrel distortion in a small camera by simply avoiding your lens's widest setting. For instance, if you go from f2.8 to f5.6, you may see significantly less distortion.

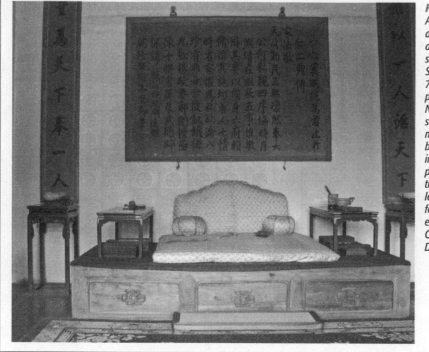

Figure 11-10:
A classic case of barrel distortion. This photo has already been straightened with the Straighten tool (page 76), but things are still pretty out of plumb here. Notice how the platform seems to sag in the middle, and the side banners on the wall lean in toward the top of the photo. Barrel distortion is the most common kind of lens distortion, but fortunately, you can easily fix it with the Correct Camera Distortion filter.

- **Vignette.** If you see dark corners in your photo (usually caused by shadows from the lens or lens hood), then you need to spend time with these sliders. Vignetting typically afflicts owners of digital single-lens reflex cameras, or people who use add-on lenses with fixed-lens cameras. Move the Amount slider to the right to lighten the corners, and to the left to darken them. The Midpoint slider controls how much of your photo is affected by the Amount slider. Move it to the left to increase the area (to bring it toward the center of the photo), or to the right to keep the vignette correction more toward the edges. Also consider turning off the Show Grid checkbox, so that you have an unobstructed view of how you're changing the lightness values in your photo. Turn it back on again if you have other adjustments to make afterward.

- **Perspective Control.** Use these sliders to correct objects like buildings that appear to be tilted or leaning backward. It's easiest to understand the sliders by looking at the icons at both ends; each icon shows you the effect you'll get by moving the slider in that direction. The Vertical Perspective slider spreads the top of your photo wider as you move the slider to the left, and makes the bottom wider as you move it to the right. (If buildings seem like they're leaning backward, move it to the left first.) The Horizontal Perspective slider is for when your subject doesn't seem to be straight on in relation to the lens (for example, if it appears rotated a few degrees to the right or left). Move the slider to the left to bring the left side of the photo toward you, and to the right to bring the right side closer.

- **Angle.** You can rotate your entire photo by moving the line in the circle to the angle you want, or by typing a number into the box. A very small change here has a huge effect. The circle tool is easy to work with, but if you prefer, you can type a precise angle, in degrees. Here's how it works: There are 360 degrees in a circle. Your photo's starting point is 0.00 degrees. To rotate your photo to the left (counterclockwise), start from 0.01, and then go up in small increments to increase the rotation. To go clockwise, start with 359.99, and then reduce the number. In other words, 350 is further to the right than 355.

> **TIP** Each of the adjustment settings is accompanied by a box where you can type a number instead of using the sliders. If you want to make the same adjustments to many photos, take note of the numbers you used to fix your first photo. Then just plug those numbers into the boxes for the other photos.

- **Edge Extension.** As explained earlier in the step on scaling your photo, when you're done fixing your photo, you're likely to end up with some blank areas along the edge of your photo's canvas. Move the Scale slider to the right to enlarge your photo, thereby getting rid of the blank areas. Moving the slider to the left shrinks your photo and increases the blank areas, but you'll rarely need to do that.

The Scale slider changes your actual photo, not just your view of it (as would be the case when using the Zoom tool). When you click OK, Elements resizes and crops your photo. If you want the objects in your photo to stay the same size they were, then don't use this slider. Instead, just click OK, and then crop using any of the methods discussed starting on page 79.

The most important thing to remember when using Correct Camera Distortion is that a little goes a long way. For most of the corrections, start small and work in small increments. These distortions can be very subtle, and you often need to make subtle adjustments to correct them.

> **TIP** The Correct Camera Distortion filter isn't just for corrections. You can use it to make your sour-tempered boss look truly prune-y, for example, by pincushioning him (just make sure you do it at home). Or, you can add vignettes to photos for special effects. You can also use the filter on shapes (simplify them first [page 355]), artwork, or anything else that strikes your fancy.

Transforming Images

You'll probably end up using the Correct Camera Distortion filter, as explained in the previous section, for most of your straightening and warp correction needs. But Elements also includes a series of Transform commands that you can use, as shown in Figure 11-11. For example, Transforming comes in handy when you want to make a change to just *one* side of a photo, or for final tweaking to a correction you made with Correct Camera Distortion. You can also apply these commands just for fun to create wacky photos or text effects.

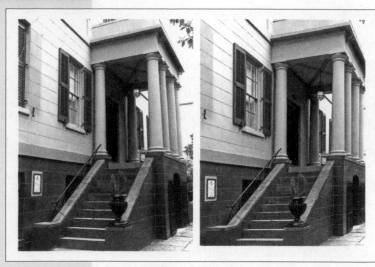

Figure 11-11:
Left: While you'd usually use Correct Camera Distortion (page 316) to straighten a slanting building like this, you can also use the Transform commands. You just have more limited choices with Transform.

Right: Here, it took only a dose of Skew and a bit of Distort to pull the building straight and make it tall again.

Skew, Distort, Perspective

Elements gives you four commands, including three specialized ones—skew, distort, and perspective—to help straighten up the objects in your photos. While they all move your photo in different directions, the way you use them is the same. The Transform commands have the same box-like handles that you see on the Move tool, for example. You choose the command you want, and then the handles appear around your photo. Just drag a handle in the direction you want your photo to move. Figure 11-12 shows how to use the Transform commands.

To see the list of Transform commands, go to Image → Transform. The first one, Free Transform, is the most powerful because it includes all the others. The next section has more about Free Transform.

> **NOTE** Transform works only on layers or active selections. If you have just a Background layer, then Elements offers to turn it to a regular layer so that you can use Transform.

The other Transform commands, which are more specialized, are:

• **Skew** slants an image. If you have a building that looks like it's leaning to the right, then you can use Skew to pull it to the left and straighten it back up again.

• **Distort** stretches your photo in the direction you want to pull it. Use it to make buildings (or people) taller and skinnier, or shorter and squatter.

• **Perspective** stretches your photo to make it look like parts are nearer or farther away. For example, if a building in your photo looks like it's leaning away from you, then you can use Perspective to pull the top back toward you.

Although Free Transform is the most capable command, it can also be trickier to use. You may find it easier to use one of the one-way commands from the previous list so you don't have to worry about inadvertently moving a photo in an unwanted direction.

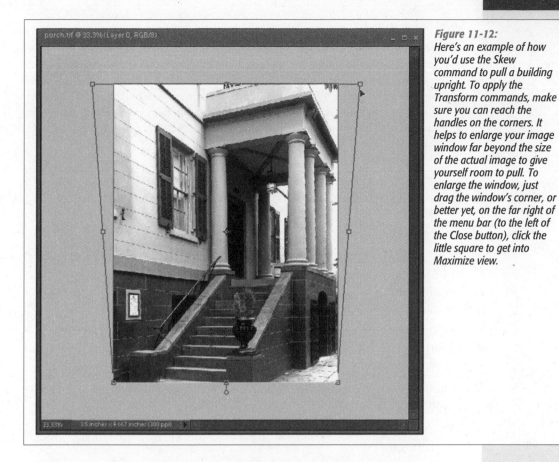

porch.tif @ 33.3%(Layer 0, RGB/8)

33.33%   3.5 inches x 4.667 inches (300 ppi)

Figure 11-12:
Here's an example of how you'd use the Skew command to pull a building upright. To apply the Transform commands, make sure you can reach the handles on the corners. It helps to enlarge your image window far beyond the size of the actual image to give yourself room to pull. To enlarge the window, just drag the window's corner, or better yet, on the far right of the menu bar (to the left of the Close button), click the little square to get into Maximize view.

TIP If you have an active selection in your image, then you can apply the Transform commands just to the selection, as long as you're not working on a background layer.

All the Transform commands, including Free Transform, offer the same settings in the Options bar, shown in Figure 11-13.

pse ⌂ File Edit Image Enhance Layer Select Filter View Window Help

W: 100.0%   H: 100.0%   ☑ Constrain Proportions   0.0

Reference point   Width and height   Rotate° Rotate   Skew
        Scale   Constrain aspect   Scale
                            ratio

Figure 11-13:
The Options bar for the Transform commands. The width and height boxes let you manually specify dimensions when resizing your image (click the Scale button to their left once you're done entering the numbers). To scale by dragging, click the Scale button towards the right side of the tool options, and then drag any of the scaling handles (not shown) that appear on the bounding box surrounding your image.

From left to right, the Options bar settings control:

- **Reference Point Location.** This strange little doodad (shown in Figure 11-14) lets you tell Elements where the fixed point should be when you transform something. It's a miniature cousin of the placement grid you see in the Canvas Size dialog box (page 97). The reference point starts out in the image's center, but you can tell Elements to move everything using the upper-left corner or the bottom-right corner as the reference point instead. To do that job, click the square you want to use as the reference.

Figure 11-14:
This nine-box icon in the Options bar is where you set the reference point for transformations, which tells Elements the central point for rotations. For example, if you want your photo to spin around the lower-left corner instead of the center, then click the lower-left square. For the Transform commands, this also tells Elements the point to work from.

- **Scale.** You can resize your image by dragging, or enter a percentage in the width or height box here. Turn on the Constrain Proportions checkbox to keep the original proportions of your image.

- **Rotate.** The box next to the little rotated squares (to the right of Constrain Proportions) in the Options bar lets you enter the number of degrees to rotate your image or selection.

- **Rotate.** Click this next pair of rotated squares, and you can grab a corner of your image to make a free rotation (see page 78).

  TIP   If you Shift+drag when turning your image, then you force it to turn in 15-degree increments.

- **Scale.** Click here if you want to resize your image by dragging—as opposed to entering numbers in the Scale boxes to the left of the Options bar.

- **Skew.** Click here, and you can pull a corner of your image to the left or right, the way you do with the Skew command. In most cases, you can transform your object without paying much attention to these settings. Truly, you can most easily transform your photo when you grab a handle and drag. Here's how you proceed:

1. **Position your image to give yourself room to work.**

   You need to position your photo so that you have room to drag the handles far beyond its edges. Figure 11-12 is a good example of an image window that's sufficiently expanded to make lots of transformations.

2. **Choose how you want to transform your image.**

   Go to Image → Transform, and then select the command you want. It's not always easy to tell which is best for a given photo, so you may want to try all three in turn. You can always change your mind and undo your changes by pressing Escape (Esc) before you accept a change, or undo using Ctrl+Z once the change has been made.

You can apply Transform commands only to layers, so if your image has only a Background layer, the first thing Elements does is ask you to convert that layer to a regular layer. Just say yes and go on. Once the Transform command is active, you see the handles around your image. (You can apply Transform commands to a selection on a Background layer without converting it to a regular layer, though.)

3. **Transform your image.**

Grab a handle, and then pull in the direction you want the image to move. You can switch to another handle to pull in a different direction, too. If you decide you made a mistake, then just press the Escape key (Esc) to return to your original photo.

4. **When you're happy with how your photo looks, accept the change.**

Click the Commit button (the checkmark) in your photo, or press Enter. Click the Cancel button (the "no" symbol) instead if you decide not to apply your transformation to your photo.

TIP Before clicking the Commit button, you can switch to another Transform command and add that transformation to your image, too.

Free Transform

Free Transform combines all the other Transform commands into one, and lets you warp your image in many different ways. If you aren't sure what you need to do, then Free Transform is a good choice.

Use Free Transform exactly the way you use the other Transform tools, following the steps listed earlier. The difference is that with Free Transform, you can pull in *any* direction, using keystroke combinations to tell Elements which kind of transformation you want to apply. Each particular transformation, listed as follows, does exactly the same thing it would if you selected that transformation from the Image → Transform menu:

- **Distort.** To make your photo taller or shorter, Ctrl+drag any handle. Your cursor turns into a gray arrowhead.

- **Skew.** To make your photo lean to the left or right, Ctrl+Shift+drag a handle in the middle of a side. You cursor is the gray arrowhead with a tiny double-arrow attached to it.

- **Perspective.** To correct the way an object appears to lean away from or toward you, press Ctrl+Alt+Shift and drag a corner. You see the same gray arrowhead that you see when you're distorting.

The Free Transform command is the most powerful of all the Transform commands, but when you're pulling in several different directions, it's tricky to keep your photo from becoming distorted. Consequently, some people prefer to use the simpler Transform commands, and apply multiple transformations instead.

CHAPTER 12

Drawing with Brushes, Shapes, and Other Tools

If you're not of the artistic persuasion, you may feel tempted to skip this chapter. After all, you probably just want to fix and enhance your photos. What do you care about brush technique? Surprisingly enough, you should care quite a lot. In Elements, brushes aren't just for painting a moustache and horns on a picture of someone you don't like, or for blackening your sister's teeth in that old school photo.

Many tools in Elements use brushes to apply their effects. So far, you've already run into the Selection brush, the Clone Stamp, and the Color Replacement brush, to name just a few. And even with the Brush tool, you can paint with lots of things besides color—like light or shadow, for example. In Elements, when you want to apply an effect in a precise manner, you're often going to use some sort of brush to do it.

If you're used to working with real brushes, their digital cousins can take some getting used to, but there are many serious artists now who paint primarily in Photoshop. With Elements, you now have access to most of the same tools as in the full Photoshop, if not quite all the settings available for each tool. Figure 12-1 shows an example of the detailed work you can do with Elements and some artistic ability.

This chapter explains how to use the Brush tool, some of the other brush-like tools (like the Erasers), and how to draw shapes even if you can't hold a pencil steady. You also get some practical applications for your new skills, like dodging and burning your photos to enhance them, and a super-easy way to create sophisticated artistic crops for your photos—a favorite feature for scrapbooking.

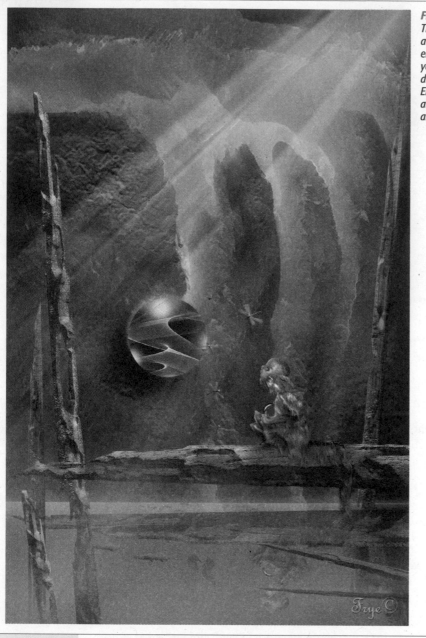

Figure 12-1:
This complex drawing by
artist Jodi Frye was done
entirely in Elements. If
you learn to wield all the
drawing power in
Elements, you can create
amazingly detailed
artwork.

Picking and Using a Basic Brush

If you look at the Toolbox, you'll see the Brush tool icon, which is below the Eraser
in a single-column Toolbox, or below the Clone Stamp if you have two columns of
tools. (Don't confuse it with the Selection brushes, which are up above the Crop or

Type tool, or the new Smart Brush [page 189], which is below the regular Brush tool or to the right of it, depending on whether you have one or two columns of tools.) Click the Brush tool's icon or press B to activate it.

The Brush is one of the tools that include a hidden pop-out drawer—you can choose between the Brush, the Impressionist brush, the Pencil tool, and the Color Replacement brush. You can read about the Impressionist brush and the Pencil tool later in this chapter, and about the Color Replacement brush on page 278. This section is about the regular Brush tool.

If you look at the Options bar (Figure 12-2), you can see that the Brush offers lots of ways to customize the tool.

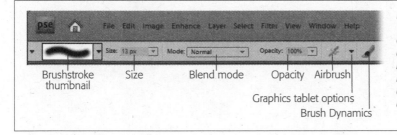

Figure 12-2:
The Brush tool's Options bar. By changing the settings shown here, as well as the hidden settings—revealed when you click the Brush Dynamics button—you can dramatically alter the behavior of any brush.

Here's a quick rundown (from left to right) of the available Brush options:

- **Brushstroke thumbnail.** The Options bar displays a thumbnail of the stroke you'd get with the current brush. Click the thumbnail to view the complete Brush palette. Elements gives you a bunch of basic brush collections, which you can view and select here. You can also download many more from various Web sites (see page 495).

  If you click the pull-down menu, you'll see that you get more than just hard or soft brushes of various sizes (see Figure 12-3). You also get special brushes for drop shadows, brushes that are sensitive to pen pressure if you're using a graphics tablet (you can also use them with a mouse, but you don't have as many options), and brushes that paint shapes and designs.

  NOTE One very cool feature of the brushes in Elements is that any changes you make to a brush are reflected in the little brushstroke thumbnail that appears in the Brush palette.

- **Size.** This slider lets you adjust the size of your brush—anywhere from 1 pixel up to sizes that may be too big to fit on your monitor. Or you can just type in a size. Figure 12-4 shows you an easy way to adjust brush size using your mouse. As you're working you can press the close bracket key (]) to quickly increase brush size, or the open bracket key ([) to decrease it.

- **Mode.** Choices in this pull-down menu determine your blend mode. The mode you choose determines how the brush color interacts with what's in your image.

  For example, Normal simply paints the current foreground color (more about all the Mode choices later).

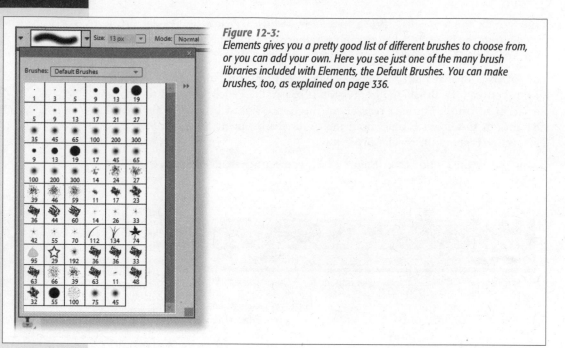

Figure 12-3:
Elements gives you a pretty good list of different brushes to choose from, or you can add your own. Here you see just one of the many brush libraries included with Elements, the Default Brushes. You can make brushes, too, as explained on page 336.

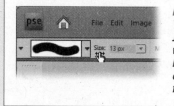

Figure 12-4:
You don't need to open pull-down menus like the one shown here that says "13 px". Just move your cursor onto the word "size", and your cursor changes into a hand-with-double-headed-arrow. Now you can "scrub" back and forth right on the Options bar to make the changes—left for smaller, right for larger. This trick also works anywhere you see a numerical pop-out slider (as in the Layers palette's Opacity menu, for example).

- **Opacity.** Here's the way to control how thoroughly your brushing covers what's beneath it. You can use the pull-down menu's slider or type in any percentage you like, from 1 to 100. The maximum—100 percent—gets you total coverage (at least in Normal mode). Or you can scrub, as shown in Figure 12-4.

- **Airbrush.** Clicking the little pen-like brush just to the right of the Opacity control lets you use the brush as an airbrush. Figure 12-5 shows you how this works.

- **Tablet Options.** Click the tiny arrow to the right of the airbrush. If you use a graphics tablet, you can use these settings to tell Elements which brush characteristics should respond to the pressure of your stroke. There's more about graphics tablets on page 493.

- **Brush Dynamics.** Clicking this icon gets you the Brush Dynamics palette, which gives you oodles of ways to customize your brush, all covered in the next section. If you're using your brush for artistic purposes, it pays to familiarize yourself with these settings, since this is where you can set a chiseled stroke or a fade, for example.

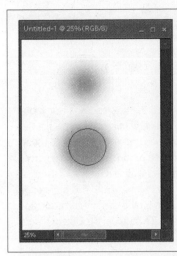

Figure 12-5:
As with real airbrushes, Elements' airbrush option causes Elements to continue to "spray" paint as long as you hold down the mouse button, regardless of whether the mouse is moving or not.

Top: Notice the effect of one click with the brush in Regular mode.

Bottom: Here's the effect of one click with the same brush in Airbrush mode. See how far the color has spread beyond the actual brush cursor (the circle) when using the airbrush? Not every brush offers the airbrush option.

TIP   If you ever want to return a brush to its original settings, click the Reset button (the tiny black arrow) on the far left side of the Options bar and then click Reset Tool from the pop-up menu.

To actually use the Brush, you enter your settings—make sure you've selected the color you want in the Foreground color square (page 208)—and then just drag across your image wherever you want to paint.

TIP   If you're used to painting with long, sweeping strokes, keep in mind that in Elements, that technique can be frustrating. That's because when you undo a mistake (by pressing Ctrl+Z), Elements undoes *everything* you've done while you've been holding down the mouse button.

In tricky spots, you can save yourself some aggravation by using shorter strokes so you don't have to lose that whole long curve you painstakingly worked on just because you wobbled a bit at the end. (The Eraser tool [page 348] is handy in these situations, too, for tidying up.)

One of the biggest differences between drawing with a mouse and drawing with a real brush is that, on a computer, it doesn't matter how hard you press the mouse. But if you've got a *graphics tablet*, an electronic pad that causes your pen movements to appear instantly onscreen, you can replicate real-world brushing, including pressure effects. Page 493 tells you all about using a tablet.

TIP   To draw or paint a straight line, hold down the Shift key while moving your mouse. If you click where you want the line to start, and press and hold Shift, and then click at the end point, Elements draws a straight line between those two points. It's important to click first and then press Shift, or you may draw lines where you don't want them.

Modifying Your Brush

When you click the Brush Dynamics button in the Options bar, you'll see a palette that lets you customize the brush in a number of ways. Its official name is the

TROUBLESHOOTING MOMENT

What Happened to My Cursor?

One thing that drives newcomers to Elements nuts is having the Brush cursor change from a circle to little crosshairs, seemingly spontaneously. This is one of those "It's not a bug; it's a feature" situations. Many tools in Elements offer you the option of what's called the *precise cursor*, shown in Figure 12-6. There are situations where you may prefer to see those little crosshairs so that you can tell *exactly* where you're working.

You toggle the precise cursor by pressing the Caps Lock key. So, if you hit that key by accident, you may find yourself in precise cursor mode with no idea of how you got there. Just press it again to turn it off.

There's one other way you may wind up with the precise cursor, and this time you have no choice in the matter. It happens when your image is so small in proportion to the cursor that Elements *must* display the crosshairs to show the brush in the right scale for your image. Zooming the view out usually gets your regular cursor back,

unless you're working with a 1-pixel brush, which always uses crosshairs.

There's another wrinkle to the mysterious cursor problem. Your cursor may look like a tiny icon instead of the brush circle. Once again, you can control this by adjusting an Elements preference setting. Go to Edit → Preferences → Display & Cursors → Painting Cursors → Normal Brush Tip to get back the normal brush. This preference window also lets you turn off the specialized cursors for tools like the Lasso tools. To do so, in the Other Cursors box, choose Precise.

You can also choose to always see the crosshairs within the regular cursor circle if you want. In the Preferences dialog box, at the bottom of the list of Brush Size options, turn on the checkbox for "Show Crosshair in Brush Tip", and you'll always have a mark for the exact center of your brush.

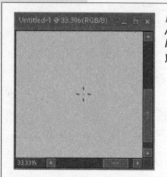

Figure 12-6:
Adobe calls these crosshairs the "precise cursor". Elements sometimes makes your tool look like this when you're zoomed way out on an image. To get the normal cursor back, you can zoom in some, and read the box above for further advice.

Brush Dynamics palette (it's also called Additional Brush Options). You'll also run into a version of this palette for some of the other brush-like tools, like the Healing brush. The Brush Dynamics palette lets you change the way your brush behaves in a number of sophisticated and fun ways. Mastering these settings goes a long way toward getting artistic results in Elements.

- **Fade** controls how fast the brush stroke fades out—just the way a real brush does when you run out of paint. Think of the numbers as sort of "how many steps" it would take to run out of paint. A lower number means it fades out very fast (very few steps) while a higher one means the fade happens later (more steps).

You can pick a number up to 9999, so with a little fiddling, you should be able to get just what you want. Zero is no fading at all—the stroke is the same at the end as it is at the beginning.

If the brush isn't fading fast enough, decrease the number. If it fades too fast, increase it. A smaller brush usually needs a higher number than a larger brush does. You may find that you need to set the brush spacing (see below) up into the 20s or higher to make fading show any visible effect.

• **Hue Jitter** controls how fast the brush switches between the background and foreground colors. Some brushes, especially the ones that you'd use to paint objects like leaves, automatically vary the color for a more interesting or realistic effect. The higher the number (percentage) here, the faster the color moves from foreground to background. A lower number means the brush takes a longer distance to get from one color to the other. Brushes that acknowledge hue jitter don't put down only the two colors, but a range of hues in between. Not all brushes respond to this setting, but for the ones that do, it's a pretty cool feature. Figure 12-7 shows how it works.

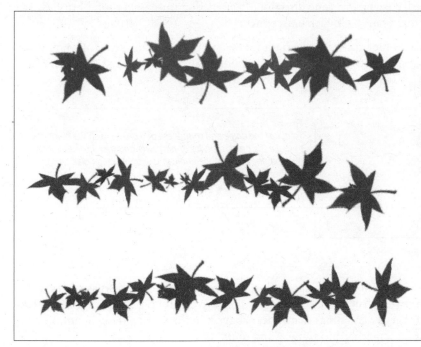

Figure 12-7:
Top: A brushstroke with no hue jitter.

Middle: The same brushstroke with a medium hue jitter value.

Bottom: The same brushstroke with a high hue jitter value. The foreground/ background colors here are red and blue. Notice how the brush automatically does a little shading, even without allowing for jitter. It takes a fairly high number to get all the way to blue in a stroke of this length.

• **Scatter** means just what it says—how far the marks get distributed in your brushstroke. (When you paint with an Elements brush, you're actually putting down many repetitions of the brush shape rather than an actual line.) If scatter is given a very low number (percentage), you get a dense, line-like stroke, whereas a higher value gives an effect more like random spots.

- **Spacing** controls how far apart the brush marks get laid down when you apply the brush. A lower number makes them close together, a higher number farther apart, as shown in Figure 12-8.

Figure 12-8:
The same brushstroke with the spacing set at 5 percent, 75 percent, and 150 percent (respectively, from top to bottom). You may have been wondering why some of the brush thumbnails look like long caterpillars, when the brush should paint an object, like a star or leaf. The reason? Cramped spacing: The thumbnail shows the spacing as Elements originally sets it. Widen the spacing to see separate objects instead of a clump.

- **Hardness** controls whether the brush edge is sharp or fuzzy. This setting isn't available with all brush types, but when it is, you can choose any value between zero and 100 percent. 100 percent is the most defined edge, zero the fuzziest.

- **Angle and Roundness.** If you've ever painted with a real brush, you should understand Angle and Roundness right away. They let you create a more chiseled edge to your brush and then rotate it so that it's not always painting with the edge facing the same direction. Painters don't use only round brushes, and you don't have to in Elements, either.

There are some brushes in the libraries that aren't round, like the calligraphy and chalk brushes. But you can adjust the roundness of any brush to make it more suitable for chiseled strokes, as shown in Figure 12-9.

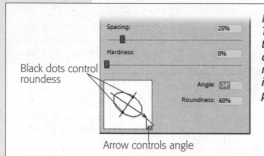

Black dots control roundess

Arrow controls angle

Figure 12-9:
To adjust the angle and roundness of a brush, push the black dots to make the brush rounder or narrower and then grab the arrow and spin the brush to the angle you want. You can also type a number directly into either the Angle or Roundness box. (The illustration shows the bottom portion of the Brush Dynamics palette.)

There's also a checkbox (called "Keep These Settings for All Brushes") you can turn on if you want to make all brushes behave exactly the same way. The checkbox only keeps the settings that appear above it in the palette, though, not the ones below it (spacing, hardness, angle, and roundness).

Saving Modified Brush Settings

If you modify a brush and like the result, you can save it as a custom brush. You can alter any of the existing brushes and save the result—a great feature if you're working on a project that's going to last awhile and don't want to have to keep modifying the settings again and again. (Don't worry: When you modify an existing brush, Elements preserves a copy of the original.) To create your own brush, just:

1. **Choose a brush to modify.**

   Select a brush in the Brush palette. You can customize any of the brushes.

2. **Make the changes you want.**

   Change the brush settings until you get what you're after. Watch the brush thumbnail in the Options bar as you go. It changes to reflect your new settings.

3. **Tell Elements you want to keep the new brush.**

   Click the arrow in the upper-right corner of the brush thumbnails palette and choose Save Brush. Elements asks you to name it. You don't absolutely have to, but naming brushes makes them easier to keep track of. (Your new name will appear as pop-up text when you hover over the brush icon, rather than in the actual thumbnail in the palette.)

4. **Click OK.**

   The brush shows up in the bottom of your current list of brushes. If you make lots of custom brushes you may want to create a special set for them. The Preset Manager (page 496) is helpful for this.

Deleting brushes is pretty straightforward. You can select the brush in the Brush palette and then choose Delete Brush from the pop-out menu. Or you can Alt+click the brush thumbnail. The cursor will change to a pair of scissors when you hold down the key. Clicking with the scissors deletes the brush.

You can also make a selection from an image and save it as a brush, if you like (the next section shows how). Just remember, though, that brushes by definition don't have color, so you save only the *shape* of the selection, not the full coloring of it. The color you get is whichever color you choose to apply. If you want to save a full color sample, try saving your selection as a pattern (page 266) or just use the clone stamp repeatedly instead.

The Specialty Brushes

So far you've been reading about brushes that behave pretty much as brushes do in the real world—they paint a stripe of something, whether color, light, or even transparency.

But in the digital world, a brush doesn't have to be just a brush. With some of the brushes included in Elements, you can paint stars, flowers, disembodied eyeballs, gravel, or even rubber ducks with just one swipe of the brush, as shown in Figure 12-10.

If you click the arrow next to the brush thumbnail in the Options bar, you'll see the list of brushes in the current category and a pull-down menu that lets you investigate the other brush sets available in Elements. The brushes used in Figure 12-10, for example, came from several different categories. Most brushes are sensitive to your pen pressure if you're using a graphics tablet (page 493).

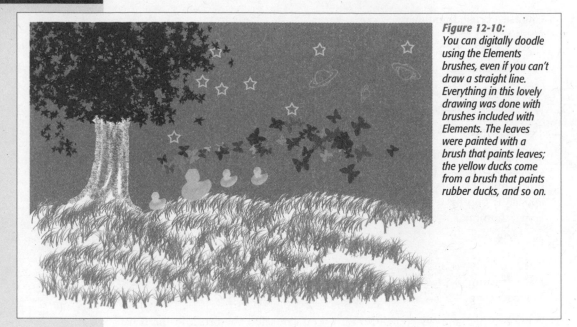

Figure 12-10:
You can digitally doodle using the Elements brushes, even if you can't draw a straight line. Everything in this lovely drawing was done with brushes included with Elements. The leaves were painted with a brush that paints leaves; the yellow ducks come from a brush that paints rubber ducks, and so on.

The Specialty brushes respond very readily to changes in the Advanced Brush Options settings (covered earlier in this chapter). Your choices there can make a huge difference in the effect you get—whether you're painting swaths of smooth grass, like a lawn, or scattered sprigs of dune grass, for instance. You get the exact same list of choices described in the previous section on the Advanced Brush Options palette: fade, hue jitter, scatter, and so on.

> **TIP** If you've tried some of the special effects brushes and found the results rather anemic, you can always go back once you've painted and punch up the color with a Multiply layer, just as you would do for an overexposed photo (see page 185).

Making a Custom Brush

You can turn any picture, or selection within a picture, into a brush that paints the shape you've selected. Figure 12-11 shows what a wreath looks—and behaves like—when it's been turned into a brush.

It's surprisingly easy to create a custom brush from any object you have a picture of.

1. **Open a photo or drawing that includes what you want to use as a brush.**

   You can choose an area as large as 2500 pixels square. (Remember, you can resize your selection once it's a brush, just the way you can resize any other brush, so don't worry if it's a big area. That said, of course, if you choose a tiny size for a super-detailed brush, you may lose some definition when you're actually using it.)

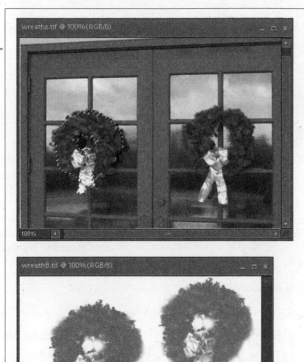

Figure 12-11:
Top: If you want to make a brush that draws holiday wreaths, just select a wreath in a photo and save it as a brush.

Bottom: You can paint better than you thought! Notice, too, that some of the ragged edges of the wreath were left out to improve the shape of the brush.

2. **Select the object or region you want.**

   Use any of the Selection tools. It's a good idea to inspect your selection with the Selection brush in Mask mode as a last step (page 130). That's because any stray areas you included by mistake get painted with each stroke—just as if you wanted them to be there.

3. **Create your brush.**

   Go to Edit → "Define Brush from Selection". You see a dialog box showing the shape and asking you to name the new brush. Check the thumbnail to be sure it's exactly what you had in mind. If not, click Cancel and try again. If you like it, click OK.

The new brush shows up at the bottom of your currently active list of brushes. If you want to get rid of it, highlight the thumbnail in the brush thumbnails, click the arrow on the right side of the palette, and go to Delete Brush, or Alt+click the brush thumbnail.

The Impressionist Brush

When you paint with the Impressionist brush, you blur and blend the edges of the objects in your photo, just like an Impressionist painting. At least that's what's *supposed* to happen. This brush is very tricky to control, but you can get some very interesting effects, especially if you paint with it on a duplicate layer and play with the Opacity control (page 162). Usually you want a very low opacity with this brush, or some of the curlier styles will make your image look like it's made from poodle hair.

The Impressionist brush has most of the same options as the regular Brush, but if you click the More Options button (the icon to the right of the Opacity setting), you'll see three new choices:

- **Style** determines what kind of brushstroke effect you want to create.

- **Area** tells Elements the size and number of brushstrokes.

- **Tolerance** is how similar in color pixels have to be before they're affected by the brush.

If you really want to create a hand-painted look, you may prefer the brushstroke filters (Filter → Brush Strokes). Page 364 explains how to use them. The Impressionist brush is really not the best tool for true Impressionist effects, although its blurring qualities can sometimes be useful because it covers large areas faster than the Blur tool. The Smudge tool (page 345) is another excellent, though time-consuming, way to create a painted effect.

The Pencil Tool

Basically just another brush, the Pencil tool shares the Brush tool's slot in the Toolbox. Choose the Pencil from the pop-out menu or press N to activate it.

The Pencil has many of the same setting options as the Brush—like size, mode, and opacity—but it offers only hard-edged brushes. In other words, you can't draw fuzzy lines with the pencil, not even the kind of lines you'd sketch with a soft pencil. The Pencil's lines are always very well defined. It's especially useful when you want to work on a pixel-by-pixel basis.

You use the Pencil tool the same way you use any other brush. The big difference is the Auto Erase option (the checkbox is located in the Options bar). Auto Erase makes the Pencil paint with the background color over areas that contain the foreground color. But if you start dragging in an area that doesn't contain the foreground color, it paints with the foreground color instead. This is really confusing until you try it, but then it's pretty easy to understand. Take a look at Figure 12-12 for some help in understanding what's going on, or better yet, create a blank file (page 43) and try it yourself.

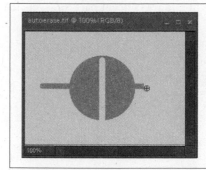

Figure 12-12:
The slightly confusing Auto Erase option was used to create two lines: a horizontal one consisting of the foreground color (blue) and a vertical one consisting of the background color (pink). The horizontal line was drawn by starting with the cursor in the background (thus, the pencil erased the pink, leaving a blue line across the circle). On the other hand, the pink line was drawn by starting inside the blue circle, causing the background color to be exposed.

The Paint Bucket

When you want to fill a large area with color in a hurry, the Paint Bucket's the tool for you. It's right next to the Brush in the Toolbox. If you click it (keyboard shortcut: K) and then click in your image, the entire available area (either your whole image or the current selection) gets flooded with color. It works something like the Magic Wand: Just as the Magic Wand selects the color you click, the Paint Bucket fills only the color you click.

TIP   Make any tool settings adjustments before clicking in your photo.

Most of the Options bar settings for the Paint Bucket are probably familiar:

- **Pattern**. Normally the Paint Bucket fills the area with the foreground color (page 208). Turn this on and it uses a pattern (page 264) instead. Choose from any of the existing patterns (listed in the Pattern drop-down menu on the Options bar). Or create your own, just as you would with the Pattern Stamp (see page 266).

- **Mode**. Use the Paint Bucket in any blend mode, as explained later in this chapter on page 343.

- **Opacity**. 100-percent opacity gives you total coverage; nothing shows through the paint you put down. Lower the percentage for a more transparent effect.

- **Tolerance**. This setting works the same way it does for the Magic Wand (page 133). The higher the number, the more shades the paint fills.

- **Anti-alias**. This setting smoothes the edges of the fill. Leave it turned on unless you have a specific reason not to.

- **Contiguous**. This is another old familiar option from the Magic Wand (page 134). If you leave Contiguous on, you change only areas of the chosen color that touch each other. Turn it off, and all areas of the color you click get changed, whether they're contiguous or not.

- **All Layers**. Fills any pixels that meet your criteria, no matter what layer they're on. (The Paint Bucket actually paints on the active layer, but it looks for pixels to change based on all the layers in your image.) To keep out just one layer, click the eye icon on the Layers palette to hide the layer you want to exclude. Don't forget that you can lock the transparent and translucent parts of layers in the Layers palette (see page 164).

You can undo a Paint Bucket fill with the usual Ctrl+Z.

> **TIP**   You can sometimes improve blown-out skies by using the Eyedropper to select an appropriate shade of blue from another photo and then filling the blown-out areas of your sky using the Paint Bucket at a very low opacity.

Dodging and Burning

Like Unsharp Mask, dodging and burning are old darkroom techniques to enhance photos and emphasize particular areas. Dodging *lightens* and brings out the hidden details in the range you specify (midtones, shadows, or highlights), and burning *darkens* and brings out details (you have the same range choices as for dodging). Both tools live with the Sponge tool in the Toolbox, so you may have run into them while using the Sponge.

You may think that, given the Shadows/Highlights command, you don't have any need for these tools. But they still serve a useful purpose because they let you make selective changes, rather than affecting the entire image or requiring tedious selections, the way Shadows/Highlights does. When you dodge or burn, you just paint your changes. Figure 12-13 gives an example of when you might need to work on a particular area. Of course, you can also make a selection and then use Shadows/Highlights just on that area, which is another technique that you may want to try as well as dodging and burning.

Skillful use of dodging and burning can greatly improve your photo, although it helps to have an artistic eye to spot what to emphasize and what to downplay. When using the black-and-white conversion feature (page 283), use the Dodge and Burn tools to emphasize certain areas of your photos. The real masters of black-and-white photography, like Ansel Adams, relied heavily on dodging and burning (in the darkroom, in those days) to create their greatest images.

Both the Dodge and Burn tools are really just variants of the Brush tool, except they don't apply color directly—they just affect the colors and tones already present in your photo. Adobe refers to these two as the "toning tools."

One caution about these tools, though—unless you use them on a duplicate layer, you can't undo the effect once you close your photo. So be careful how you use them. Actually, many people prefer to dodge and burn using the method described in the box on page 345, rather than with the actual Dodge and Burn tools, unless they're working on a black-and-white photo.

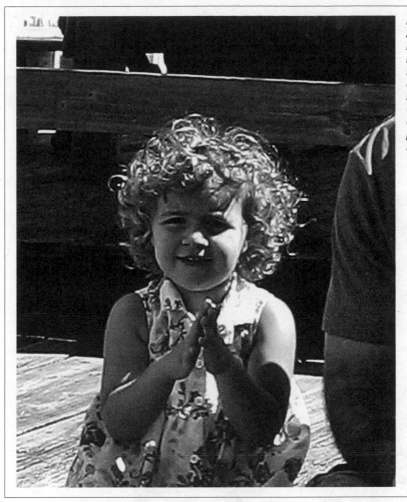

Figure 12-13:
Although the overall shadow/highlight balance of this photo is about right, the detail in the face of this little concert-goer is obscured by backlighting and by her father's shadow. Careful dodging and burning can really improve these problems, as you can see in Figure 12-14.

TIP In Elements 7, you may also want to try some of the Smart Brush (page 189) lighting settings for making selective adjustments to just part of your photo. A little experimenting will give you a sense for which tools you prefer to use in different situations.

Dodging

Use the Dodge tool to lighten areas of your image and to bring out details hidden in shadows. It's a good idea to create a separate layer (Layer → Duplicate Layer or Ctrl+J) when using this tool, to preserve your image if you go overboard. Be sure you're applying the Dodge tool to a layer that has something in it, or nothing happens.

1. **Activate the Dodge tool.**

Click the Sponge tool in the Toolbox or press O, and choose the Dodge tool (the lollipop-like paddle) from the pop-out menu You'll see the usual brush

---

options, but with two differences: a choice of whether the tool should work on highlights, midtones, or shadows, and a setting called Exposure, which determines the strength of the effect.

2. **Drag over the area you want to change.**

Choose a very low Exposure setting for the Dodge tool (and the Burn tool as well) and drag more than once to get a more realistic result (see Figure 12-14). After you're done, if you think the Dodge tool's effect is still too strong, you can always reduce the opacity of the layer in the Layers palette (as long as you're working on a duplicate layer).

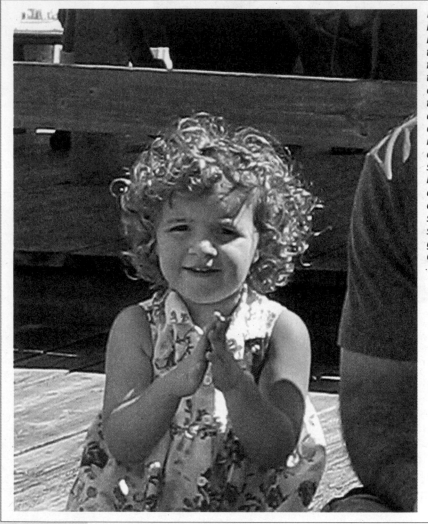

Figure 12-14:
Figure 12-13 after the Dodge and Burn tools did their work. The girl's features are much easier to see, but if you look closely, you can see that the colors in her face are a bit flat. See page 345 to compare a different method for selectively adjusting highlights and shadows. Both solutions have advantages and disadvantages. Things are deliberately a bit too strong in both figures to show you the perils of getting overzealous with either method.

Burning

The Burn tool does exactly the opposite of what the Dodge tool does: It darkens. Use the Burn tool to uncover more detail in your highlights. Of course, there have to be *some* details there for the tool to work. If your photo's highlights are blown out (see page 187), you won't get any results, no matter how much you apply the tool. The Burn tool is grouped with the Sponge and Dodge tools. Its icon is a hand striking a match, logically enough.

Apply the Burn tool the same way as the Dodge tool; most of the time, you'll probably want to use these tools in combination. They can help draw attention to specific parts of your photo, but they work best for subtle changes. Applying them too vigorously—especially on color photos—gives an obviously faked look to photos. Black-and-white pictures (or color images converted to black and white) can generally stand much stronger contrasts.

Blending and Smudging

In Elements, you can control how the color you add to an image blends with the colors that are already there. This section takes a look at blending in two different ways—using the Smudge tool to literally mix elements of your image together, and using *blend modes* to determine how the colors you paint change what's already in your image. Blend modes are almost limitless in the ways they can manipulate images.

Blend Modes

Blend modes control how the color you add when you paint reacts with the existing pixels in an image—whether you just add color (Normal mode), make the existing color darker (Multiply mode), or change the saturation (Saturation mode).

Image editing experts have found plenty of clever ways to use blend modes for some really sophisticated techniques. Thorough coverage of these maneuvers would turn this into a book the size of the Yellow Pages, but Figure 12-15 shows a few examples of how simply changing the brush blend mode can radically change your result.

There are so many ways to combine blend modes that even Elements pros can't always predict the results, so experimenting is the best way to learn about them.

Elements groups Blend modes according to the effects they have. The top group in the menu includes what you might call painting modes, followed by modes for darkening, lightening, adjusting light, special effects modes, and adjusting color.

It's also important to be aware that the modes work quite differently with layers than with tools. In other words, painting with a brush in Dissolve mode is going to produce an effect quite different than creating a layer in Dissolve mode and painting on it, as shown in Figure 12-16.

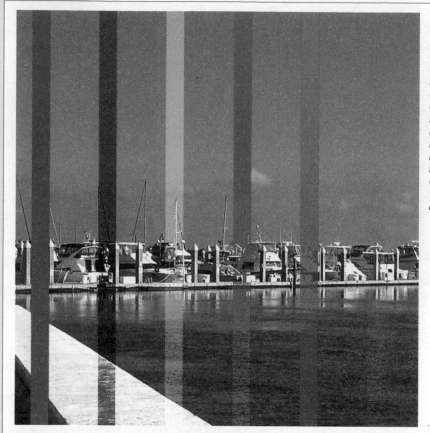

Figure 12-15:
This photo shows the effect of some of the different blend modes when used with the Brush tool. The same color was used for every one of the vertical stripes—you can see how different the result is from just changing the mode. From left to right, the modes are: Normal, Color Burn, Color Dodge, Vivid Light, Difference, and Saturation.

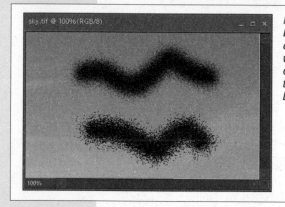

Figure 12-16:
Blend modes behave differently when used in layers than they do when using a tool in the same mode. Both these strokes were done using Dissolve mode in pure black at 100-percent opacity. The difference is that the top stroke is painted with the Brush tool in Dissolve mode while the bottom one is a brush stroke in normal mode on a Dissolve layer.

Modes are really cool and very useful once you get used to using them, but if you're just starting out in Elements, there's no need to worry about them right away.

TIP   If you'd like to learn more about how each mode works, there are a lot of useful tutorials on the Web. A good place to start is *www.photoshopgurus.com/tutorials/t010.html*. (Ignore the section "Additional blend mode information"—that's only for Photoshop.)

Blend Modes Instead of Dodge and Burn

You can do a lot in Elements without ever touching blend modes. But if you take a little time to familiarize yourself with them, you might find they become a regular part of your image editing toolkit. For instance, you may prefer the effect you get using a layer in Overlay mode to that of the Dodge and Burn tools.

To adjust a photo using an Overlay blend mode layer instead of the Dodge and Burn tools, first make basic adjustments like Levels or Shadows/Highlights. Then, when you're ready to fine-tune your photo by painting over the details you want to enhance, here's what you do:

1. **Create a new layer**.

   Go to Layer → New → Layer or press Shift+ Ctrl+N.

2. **Before dismissing the New Layer dialog box, choose the Overlay blend mode for your new layer**.

   Select Overlay in the Layer mode menu and turn on the box that says "Fill with Overlay-neutral color (50% gray)." You won't see anything happen yet.

3. **Set the foreground and background colors to their original settings**.

   Press D to set the colors in the Foreground/Background squares to black and white.

4. **Activate the Brush tool**.

   Choose a brush (set to Normal mode) and set the opacity very low, maybe 17 percent or even less. You'll need to experiment a bit to see how low a setting is low enough.

5. **Paint on the areas you want to adjust**.

   Paint with white to bring up the detail in dark areas and with black to darken overly light areas. (Remember that you can switch from one to the other by pressing X.) The detail on your photo comes up just like magic.

Figure 12-17 shows the results of using Overlay mode on the image from Figure 12-13 so that you can compare the different results. This method has the added advantage of being adjustable by changing the opacity of the Overlay layer. You can also carry this technique to extremes for very interesting results, when you want an artistic rather than a realistic result.

The Smudge Tool

The Smudge tool does just what its name says. You can use it to smear the colors in your image, just as if you had rubbed them with your finger. You can even "finger paint" with the Smudge tool, if you feel the call of your inner fifth grader. Adobe describes the effect of the Smudge tool as being "like a finger dragged through wet paint." It's sort of like a cousin to the Liquify filter (page 411), but without so many options.

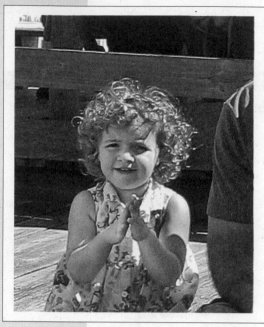

Figure 12-17:
*Here's the little girl from Figure 12-13 again, this time after
using Overlay blending, as described in the box on page 345.
Unlike the results from the actual Dodge and Burn tools, this
time the color isn't grayish—as dodging made it—but the
contrast where shadowed areas meet bright ones still needs
some work.*

If you're interested in turning your photos into paintings (Figure 12-18), the humble Smudge tool is your most valuable resource. For artistic smudging, you need a graphics tablet so you can vary the stroke pressure. You can use the Smudge tool without a tablet, but you won't get nearly as good an effect. If you'd like to learn more about this kind of smudging, some excellent tutorials can be found at the Retouching forum at Digital Photography Review (*www.dpreview.com*; search for *smudging*). The forums at *www.retouchpro.com* are also a favorite hangout for expert smudgers.

> **NOTE**   If you're serious about smudging, check out Scott Deardorff's online classes at *www.
> digitalartacademy.com*. (Most of the classes there are for a different program, Corel Painter, but
> his smudging classes cover Photoshop and Elements.) Scott is one of the most talented smudgers
> you can find.

A warning—if you have a slow computer, there's quite a bit of lag time between when you apply the Smudge tool and when the effect actually shows up. This delay makes the tool tricky to control, because you need to resist the temptation to keep going over the area until you see results.

You'll find the Smudge tool hidden under the Blur tool in the Toolbox. Click the Blur tool or press R and, from the pop-out menu, choose the Smudge tool (its icon is a finger that looks like it's painting).

The Smudge tool offers mostly the same settings as a regular brush, but it also includes the All Layers option (page 259), like you have for the Healing brush or the Clone Stamp. It also has two additional settings: Strength and Finger Painting.

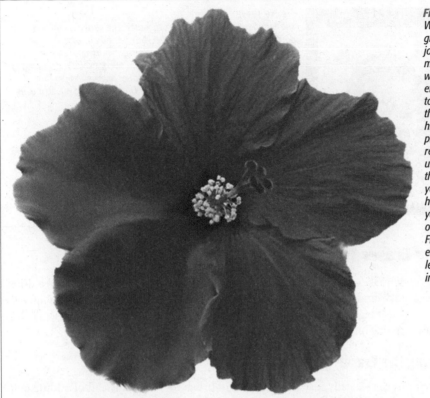

Figure 12-18:
With the help of a graphics tablet, you can join the ranks of the many skilled smudgers who create amazing effects using only this tool. The two petals on the left side of this hibiscus blossom show preliminary smudging results. The brushes you use determine whether the effect is smooth, as you see here, or more heavily stroked. When you want to blend in other colors, use the Finger Painting option. In effect, the Smudge tool lets you turn your photo into a painting.

- **Strength.** This setting means just what it says—it controls how hard the tool smudges the colors together. A higher number results in more blending.

- **Finger Painting.** Turning on this checkbox makes the Smudge tool smear the foreground color at the start of each stroke. When the box is turned off, the tool uses the color that's under the cursor at the start of each stroke. Figure 12-19 demonstrates the difference. This option is very useful for creating artistic smudges. If you want a bit of a contrasting color to help your strokes stand out more, choose a foreground color (page 208) and turn this checkbox on.

TIP Use the Eyedropper (page 211) to sample other areas of your image to add Finger Painting colors that harmonize well with the area you're smudging.

Once you've chosen your settings, smudge away.

NOTE When using the Smudge tool, you only see results where two colors come together. It blends together the pixel colors where edges meet. If you use Smudge in the middle of an area of solid color, nothing happens unless you've turned on Finger Painting.

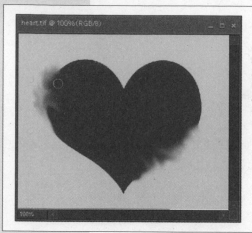

Figure 12-19:
The Smudge tool smears colors together. The stroke on the left was done with the Finger Painting checkbox turned on, which lets you introduce a bit of the foreground color (green, in this case) into the beginning of each stroke. This technique's very useful for shading or when you need to mix in just a touch of another color. The smudging on the right was done with Finger Painting off, so it uses only the colors that are already in your image.

The Eraser Tool

Everyone makes mistakes sometimes. Adobe has thoughtfully included three different mistake-fixers. If you click and hold the Eraser icon in the Toolbox, you'll see the Eraser, the Magic Eraser, and the Background Eraser. You'll probably use all three Erasers at one time or another. You can also activate the Eraser by pressing E.

Using the Eraser

The Eraser is basically just another kind of brush tool, only instead of adding color to your image, it removes color from the pixels. How it works varies a little, depending on where you use it.

If you use the Eraser on a regular layer, it replaces the color with transparency. On a Background layer, or one in which transparency is locked, it replaces whatever color is there with the background color (see Chapter 6 for more about how layers work).

The settings for the Eraser are pretty much the same as for any other brush—including brush style, size, and opacity—but with the Eraser a couple of them work differently:

- **Mode.** For the Eraser, Mode doesn't have anything to do with blend modes (page 343), but rather tells Elements the shape of the eraser you want to work with. Your choices are Brush, Pencil, and Block.

  You can see the difference in how the Eraser is going to work by watching the brush style preview in the Options bar as you change Modes. Picking the Brush or Pencil lets you use the Eraser as you would those tools—in other words, by choosing a brush, you can choose any brush you like. The Brush option lets you make soft-edged erasures, while Pencil mode makes only hard-edged erasures. Choosing Block changes the cursor to a square, so that you can use it just the way you would a regular artist's erasing block—sort of.

- **Opacity** determines how much of the color is removed—at 100 percent, it's all gone (or all replaced with the background).

To use the Eraser:

1. **Activate the Eraser.**

   Click the Eraser tool in the Toolbox (keyboard shortcut: E). The tool looks like an eraser, so it's easy to find.

2. **Choose your settings.**

   Choose the eraser's size, mode, and opacity. As noted earlier, the mode and opacity settings work differently here than they do for regular brushes.

3. **Drag anywhere in your image to remove what you don't want.**

   You may need to change the size of the Eraser a few times. It's usually easiest to use a small eraser (or the Background Eraser, which is explained later) to accurately clear around the edges of the object you want to keep, as shown in Figure 12-20. Then you can use a larger eraser brush size to get rid of the remaining chunks, once you don't have to worry about accidentally going into the area you want to keep.

   TIP   You can use a selection (see Chapter 5) to limit where the Eraser operates.

It's tedious to erase around a long outline or to remove entire backgrounds, so Elements has two other kinds of Erasers for those situations.

The Magic Eraser

Once you try it, you're likely to wonder why the heck Adobe gave this pedestrian tool such an intriguing name. What's so magic about the Magic Eraser?

Well, not much, really. It's called "magic" because it works very much like the Magic Wand tool (page 133). Use it to select pixels of a single color or range (depending on the tolerance settings). It even has the same little sparklies as the Magic Wand does in its icon to remind you of the relationship.

The problem, as Figure 12-21 shows you, is that the Magic Eraser isn't as clean in its work as the other erasers. Still, it can be a big help in eliminating large chunks of solid color. Moreover, if you're lucky, you may be able to clean the edges right up with Refine Edge (you'll need to make a selection to use it) or the Defringe command (Enhance → Adjust Color → Defringe Layer). To use Refine edge, you'll need to select the layer contents, or click in the empty background area with the Magic Wand (page 133) and then choose Select → Invert. There's more about Refine Edge on page 128 and about Defringing on page 143.

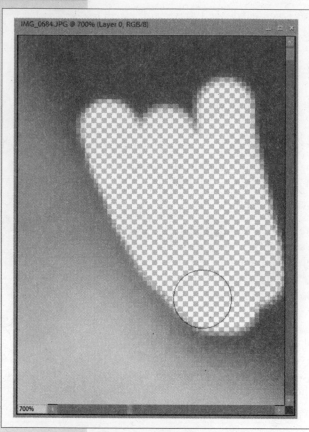

Figure 12-20:
Accurate erasing around an object usually means zooming way, way in so that you can control which pixels the Eraser is changing.

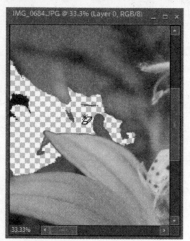

Figure 12-21:
This figure gives you a close-up look at the Magic Eraser at work on the background behind a bunch of flower petals. One click of the Magic Eraser got rid of a bunch of the background, and setting the Tolerance higher would've gotten even more. But if you look closely, you can see the disadvantage of the Magic Eraser: The edges of the flowers are fringed with dark ragged areas it didn't eliminate. The following fixes aren't always 100 percent successful but you may be able to clean up the edges with Enhance → Adjust Color → Defringe Layer (page 143), or the new Refine Edge command (page 128).

It's usually best to use the Magic Eraser in combination with at least one of the other erasers if you're looking to achieve really clean results. One sometimes useful side effect of the Magic Eraser is that if you click your photo with the Magic Eraser, it automatically transforms your Background layer into a regular layer, just the way the Background Eraser does. That means if you want to do something to the remaining object that requires a regular layer—applying a Layer Style, for instance—you save yourself a step.

The Background Eraser

Lots of people think this eraser deserves the name "Magic" much more than the Magic Eraser does. The Background Eraser is a tremendous help when you want to remove all the background around an object. For example, say you've got a photo of a football and want to quickly remove the ball from the background.

The Background Eraser erases all the pixels under the brush (but outside the edges of the object) and renders the area it's used on transparent, even if it's a Background layer. (If you click with it on a Background layer, your computer may hesitate initially because it's busy transforming your Background to a regular layer.)

Here's how to use it:

1. **Select the Background Eraser.**

   Press E or, in the Toolbox, click the Eraser icon. Then choose the Background Eraser from the pop-out menu. It's the eraser with a pair of scissors next to it.

2. **In the Options bar, choose a brush size.**

   The cursor turns to a circle with crosshairs in it. These crosshairs are important: They're the Background Eraser's "hot spot." Any color that you drag them over is turned to transparency. The circle size changes depending on how large a brush you've chosen, but the crosshairs stay the same size. As you can see in Figure 12-22, with a large brush, there may be a lot of space around the crosshairs. That makes it easy to remove big chunks of the background at once, since everything in the circle is going to get eliminated.

   If you start seeing *all* your brushes (not just the Background Eraser) as crosshairs, take a look at the box on page 332 to see how to get back to your regular cursor.

3. **Drag in your photo.**

   Move around the edge of the object you want to keep, being very careful not to let the crosshairs move into the object, or else you'll start erasing that, too. If you make a mistake, just use Ctrl+Z to undo your actions.

The Background Eraser has three Options bar settings to help refine how it works:

- **Brush.** If you want a different brush style, choose it from the pull-down menu.
- **Limits.** Do you want the Background Eraser to remove only contiguous color, or all patches of a certain color? This works exactly like the Contiguous setting for the Magic Wand (page 134).

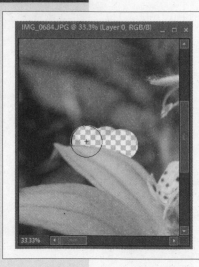

Figure 12-22:
The Background Eraser does a very careful job of separating the flowers from their background. Just be sure to keep the little crosshairs outside the color you want to keep. Here, because the crosshairs are outside the petals, only the background is getting removed. But if you moved the crosshairs into the flower, you'd be biting chunks out of it with the tool.

- **Tolerance.** This tells the Background Eraser how similar colors must be for it to remove them, again like the Magic Wand setting (page 133).

However, you may never need to change any of these settings to get the results you want.

If you want to remove the background from around an object, you may find it most effective to start with the Background Eraser around the edge of your object. Then, use the other Erasers to clean up afterward. The advantage of working this way is that you don't have to clean up junk left over from the Magic Eraser. It's also easier to maneuver the Background Eraser than the regular Eraser, especially if you don't have a graphics tablet.

Drawing with Shapes

Wow, so many brush options and Adobe still isn't done—there's yet another way to draw things in Elements. The program includes a Shape tool (actually a group of tools that share one slot in the Toolbox), which lets you draw geometrically perfect shapes, regardless of your artistic ability. And not just simple shapes like circles and rectangles. You can draw animals, plants, starbursts, picture frames—all sorts of things, as shown in Figure 12-23. This tool should appeal to anyone whose grade school masterpieces always seemed to get put up on the wall behind the piano somewhere.

Turning yourself into an artist by using Elements' Shape tool is easy. Just follow these steps:

1. **Open an image or create a new one.**

   You can add shapes to any file you can open in Elements.

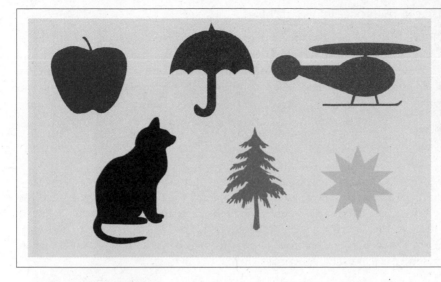

Figure 12-23:
Here are just a few of the shapes that you can draw with Elements, even if you flunked art class in elementary school. These objects look much more impressive once you gussy them up with Layer styles (page 382).

2. **Activate the Shape tool.**

   Click the Shape tool in the Toolbox, or press U. The Shape tool is sometimes a little confusing to newcomers to Elements, because the icon reflects the shape that's currently active—so you may see a rectangle, a polygon, or a line, for instance. (You see a blue heart shape—the Custom Shape tool's icon—before you've used this tool for the first time.)

3. **Select the kind of shape you want to draw.**

   Use the Toolbox menu to choose a rectangle, a rounded rectangle, an ellipse, a polygon, a line, or a custom shape. (If you choose the custom shape, you have many different shapes to choose from. Click the Shape pull-down menu in the Options bar to choose the one you want.) All the shapes, and their accompanying options, are described in the following sections.

4. **Adjust your settings in the Options bar.**

   Choose a color by clicking the color square in the Options bar or use the foreground color (page 208). If you click the Options bar color square, you see the Color Picker (page 209). If you click the arrow to the right of the square, you get the Color Swatches palette instead (page 212).

   If you have special requirements, like a rectangle that's exactly 1"×2", click the downward-facing arrow just to the right of the shape thumbnails for the Shape Options palette and enter the size of your shape.

   There's also an Options bar setting that lets you apply a layer style (see page 382) as you draw your shape. Just click the downward-facing arrow on the right side of the Style box and choose the style you want from the pop-out palette. To go back to drawing without a style, choose the rectangle with the diagonal red line through it.

5. **Drag in your image to draw the shape.**

Notice that *how* you drag the cursor affects the final appearance of the shape. For example, the way you drag determines the proportions of your figure. If you're drawing a fish, you can drag so that it's long and skinny or short and fat. Even with practice, it may take a couple of tries to get exactly the proportions you want.

> **NOTE** If you're trying to create exact copies of a particular shape, use the Shape Selection tool, described later, to create duplicates of the first shape.

The Shape tool automatically puts each shape on its own layer. If you don't want to do that, or need to control how shapes interact, use the squares in the middle of the Options bar. With one exception ("Exclude Overlapping Shape Areas"), they're the same as the ones for managing selections (page 125). Use them to add more than one shape to a layer, subtract a shape from a shape, keep only the area where shapes intersect, or exclude the areas where they intersect.

> **TIP** If you want to draw multiple shapes on one layer, click the "Add to Shape" rectangle in the Options bar. Then, everything you do is on the same layer. Shapes don't have to touch or overlap to use this option.

You can also turn any shape from a vector image (infinitely resizable) into a raster image (drawn pixel by pixel) by clicking the Simplify button in the Options bar. The box on page 355 tells you everything you need to know about the difference between vector and raster images.

You can also add custom shapes by choosing them in the Content palette. Just double-click the one you want, or click its palette thumbnail and then click Apply.

The following sections describe all of the main shape categories and their special settings.

Rectangle and Rounded Rectangle

The Rectangle and Rounded Rectangle tools work pretty much the same way and are very popular for creating Web page buttons. They both have Shape Options settings in the Options bar pull-down menu for:

- **Unconstrained.** Choose Unconstrained to draw a rectangle of whatever dimensions you want. How you drag determines the proportions of your shape.

- **Square.** To draw a square instead of a rectangle, click this radio button before you start, or just hold down the Shift key as you drag.

- **Fixed Size.** This setting makes Elements draw your shape the size you specify. Just enter the dimensions you want in inches, pixels, or centimeters.

- **Proportional.** Use this setting if you know the proportions you want your rectangle to have, but not the exact size. Just type in the proportions. So if you enter a width of 2 and a height of 1, no matter where you drag, the shape is always twice as long as it is high.

- **From Center.** This setting lets you draw your shape from its center instead of from a corner. It's useful when you know exactly where you want the shape but aren't sure exactly how big it needs to be.

- **Snap to Pixels.** This setting makes sure that the edge of your rectangle falls exactly on the edge of a pixel. You'll get crisper-looking edges with "Snap to Pixels" turned on. It's available only for the Rectangle and Rounded Rectangle tools.

UP TO SPEED

Rasterizing Vector Shapes

Back in Chapter 3, you read about how the majority of your images (definitely your photos) are just a bunch of pixels to Elements. These images are known as *raster* images. The shapes you draw with the Shape tools work a little differently. They're called *vector* images.

A vector image is made up of a set of directions, specifying what kind of geometric shapes should be drawn. The advantage of vector images is that you can size them way up or down without producing the kind of pixelation you see when you resize a raster image too much.

Your shape keeps its vector characteristics until you *simplify* the layer that it's on. Simplifying, also called *rasterizing*, just means that Elements turns your shape into regular pixels. Once you simplify, you have the same limitations on resizing as you do for a regular photo. For example, you can make your image smaller, but you can't make it larger than 100 percent without losing quality. Sooner or later, you may want to transform your vector image to a regular raster image so that you can do certain things to it, like adding filters or effects.

If you try to do something that requires simplifying a layer, Elements generally asks you to do so, via a pop-up dialog box. To rasterize your shape, just click OK, or click the Simplify button in the Options bar. Remember that once you've rasterized a shape, if you try to resize, you won't get the nice, clean unpixelated results that you got when it was a vector image. If you need to resize a shape, it's easiest to start over with a new shape—if that's feasible (which is yet another good reason to use layers).

Also, it may puzzle you that, where at one time you were able to change the color of an existing shape by clicking the color box, now all of a sudden the shape totally ignores what you do in the Options bar. That's because you simplified the shape layer. Simplifying always affects the entire layer—everything on it is simplified, or nothing is. Once your shape is simplified, you have to make a selection and change the color the way you would on any detail in a photo.

The Content palette brings yet another wrinkle to the raster/vector situation—Smart Shapes. The items in the Content palette (the frames, backgrounds, and other doodads) act as vector objects, except that they may seek out a particular place in the layer stack. (See page 425 for more on Smart Shapes.)

Most of the Shape tools have similar options. The Rounded Rectangle has one Options bar setting of its own, though: *Radius*, which is the amount (in pixels) that the corners are rounded off. A higher number means more rounding.

TIP Looking to add a simple, empty rectangle, square, circle, or ellipse? See the box on page 359.

Ellipse

The Ellipse tool has the same Shape Options as the Rectangle tool. The only difference is that you can opt for a circle instead of a square. The Shift key constrains the Ellipse to a circle.

Polygon

You can draw many kinds of regular polygons using this tool. Use the Options bar to set the number of sides. The shape options in the Options bar pull-down menu are a bit different for this tool:

- **Radius.** This setting sets the distance from the center to the outermost points.

- **Smooth Corners.** If you don't want sharp edges at the corners, choose Smooth Corners.

- **Star.** This setting inverts the angles to create a star-like shape, as shown in Figure 12-24.

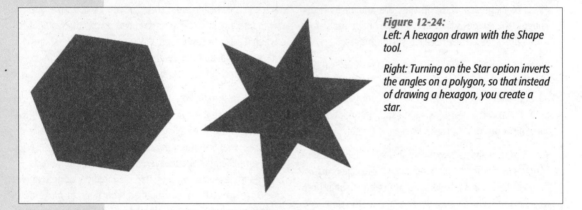

Figure 12-24:
Left: A hexagon drawn with the Shape tool.

Right: Turning on the Star option inverts the angles on a polygon, so that instead of drawing a hexagon, you create a star.

- **Indent Sides by.** If you're drawing a star, this sets how much (in a percentage) you want the sides to indent.

- **Smooth Indents.** Use Smooth Indents if you don't want sharp interior angles on your star.

Line Tool

Use this tool for drawing straight lines and arrows. Specify the weight (width) of the line in pixels in the Options bar. If you want an arrowhead on your line, the Shape options give you some settings for adding one to your line as you draw:

- **Start/End.** Do you want the arrowhead at the start or the end of the line you draw? Tell Elements your preference with this setting.

- **Width and Length.** This setting determines how wide and how long you want the arrowhead to be. The measurement unit is the percentage of the line width, so if you enter a number lower than 100, your arrowhead is narrower than the line it's attached to. You can pick values between 10 and 5,000 percent. If your length setting is too low, you get a shape that looks more like a T than an arrow.

- **Concavity.** Use this setting if you want the sides of the arrowhead indented. The number determines the amount of curvature on the widest part of the arrowhead. See Figure 12-25. Pick a setting between –50 percent and +50 percent.

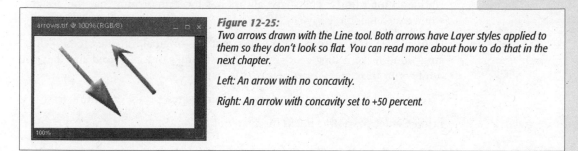

Figure 12-25:
Two arrows drawn with the Line tool. Both arrows have Layer styles applied to them so they don't look so flat. You can read more about how to do that in the next chapter.

Left: An arrow with no concavity.

Right: An arrow with concavity set to +50 percent.

TIP   If you prefer fancier arrows, you'll find some in the Custom Shape tool.

The Custom Shape Tool

The Custom Shape lets you draw a huge variety of different objects, as you can see in Figure 12-26. Its icon is the little blue heart in the Toolbox. Click it or press U and then choose the Custom Shape tool you want from the pull-down menu.

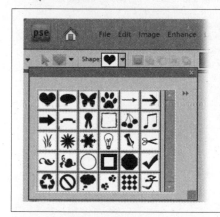

Figure 12-26:
Here's just a small part of the shape library you can choose from in the Shape Picker. To add more custom shapes to your repertoire, you can download and add them to C:\Program Files\Adobe\Photoshop Elements7.0\ Presets\Custom Shapes. Look for the file extension .csh when you want shapes that you can add to your library. Downloaded shapes that you add show up as drawing options when you click the More button (the double arrows) on the Shapes palette. See page 500 for more about adding shapes to Elements.

Once the Custom Shape tool is active, if you look in the Options bar, you see a little window labeled Shape with the arrow for a pull-down menu next to it. Click this arrow to bring up the Elements Shape Picker. Various shapes automatically come up, but if you click the More button (the double arrows) at the upper-right corner of the window, you get a menu giving you lots more choices. To scroll through all of them, just choose All Elements Shapes.

TIP There's a copyright symbol available in the custom shapes if you want something official looking.

The Custom shape also has a few optional settings:

- **Unconstrained.** Control the proportions of your shape by the way you drag.

- **Defined Proportions.** The shape always has the proportions that the designer who created the shape gave it.

- **Defined Size.** The shape is always the size it was originally created to be—dragging won't make it bigger or smaller. It just plinks out at a fixed size that you can't control, except by resizing after the fact.

- **Fixed Size.** Enter the dimensions you want in inches, pixels, or centimeters.

- **From Center.** Start drawing in the center of the object.

The Shape Selection Tool

The arrow in the Options bar just to the left of the any Shape tool's icon is the Shape Selection tool. This is a special kind of Move tool (page 148) that works only on shapes that haven't been simplified yet, as explained in Figure 12-27. (You can also activate the Shape Selection tool from the Toolbox pop-out menu.)

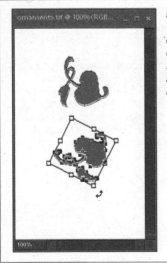

Figure 12-27:
The Shape Selection tool gives you the same kind of bounding box as the Move tool, and it works the same way, but only on shapes that haven't been simplified yet. You can also apply transformations like skewing and rotating (page 321) when the Shape Selection tool is active. Once you've simplified a shape layer, you need the regular Move tool to move it around. You can always use the Move tool, even on shapes that haven't been simplified, where you could use the Shape Selection tool instead.

It may seem unnecessary, but if you're working with shapes, it saves a lot of time not to have to keep switching tools when you want to move one shape.

Click the Shape Selection tool and then move your shape. Your shape doesn't have to be on the active layer. You can also use the Shape Selection tool to combine multiple shapes into one by clicking the Combine button. You also have the other options that you have when using any of the shape tools: add, subtract, intersect, and exclude.

The Shape Selection tool works just like the Move tool. You can drag to move, hold down Alt to copy (instead of moving) the original shape, drag the handles to resize the shape, and so on. Unfortunately, you can't align and distribute shapes with this tool the way you can with the Move tool. If you need to line things up, use the regular Move tool instead.

WORKAROUND WORKSHOP

Drawing Outlines and Borders

If you've played around at all with the Shape tool, you may have noticed that you can't draw shapes that are just outlines (that is, that aren't filled with color). No matter what you do, your shape is always a solid shape (except for the frame shapes).

Even if you haven't ever touched the Shape tool, you may be wondering how the heck to get a simple plain colored border around a photo.

The easiest way to create an outline is to make a selection using the Marquee tool or other selection tools and then select Edit → Stroke (Outline) Selection. The Stroke dialog box pops up and lets you enter the width of the line in pixels and choose a color.

You'll also see choices for Location, which tell Elements where you want the line—around the inside edge of the selection, centered on the edge of the selection, or around the outside. If you're bordering an entire photo, don't choose Outside, or the border won't show because it's off the edge of your image.

You can choose a blend mode (page 164) if you like and set the opacity. Using a mode can give you a more subtle edge than a normal stroke does. The Preserve Transparency setting just ensures that any transparent areas in your layer stay transparent. When you're finished adjusting the settings in the Stroke dialog box, click OK, turn off your Marquee, and you've got yourself an outlined shape.

Also check out some of the simpler frame designs in the Content palette (page 427). They let you apply a simple border with just a double-click.

The Cookie Cutter

At first glance, you may think the Cookie Cutter is a pretty silly tool. Actually, it's a very handy tool that you may use all the time, once you understand it. The Cookie Cutter creates the same shapes as the Custom Shape tool, but you use it on a photo to crop it to the shape you chose. Want a heart-shaped portrait of your sweetie? The Cookie Cutter is your tool. If you're a scrapbooker, with a couple of clicks you can get results that would have taken ages and a bunch of special scissors to create with paper.

If you're not into that sort of thing, don't go away, because hidden away in the shapes library are some of the most sophisticated artistic crop shapes you can find. You can use them to get the kinds of effects that people pay commercial artists big bucks to create—like creating abstract crops that give a jagged or worn edge to your photo (an effect that's great for contemporary effects).

You can also combine the result with a stroked edge, as explained in the preceding box ("Drawing Outlines and Borders"), and maybe even a Layer style (page 382). Even without any additional frills, your photo's shape will appear more interesting, as shown in Figure 12-28.

TIP   Elements gives you a couple of other ways to create cutouts and fancy edge effects, which you might want to check out. If you plan to print out your cropped photo, for use in a scrapbooking project, for example, check out the Picture Package (page 449). The frames there include some shape crops, and you can do everything right in the Organizer Print dialog box, if those shapes work for you. (Despite the name, you can make a Picture Package with only one print of one photo.)

The Frames section of the Content palette also includes a bunch of crops, ranging from simple shapes like stars to elaborate edges that make your photo look like a half-completed jigsaw puzzle.

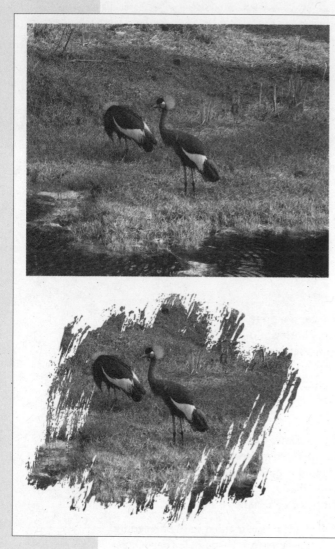

Figure 12-28:
A quick drag with the Cookie Cutter is all it took to create the bottom graphic from the top photo. If you want to create custom album or scrapbook pages, you can rotate or skew your crops before you commit them. See page 321 for how to rotate and skew your images.

Use the Cookie Cutter just like the Custom Shape tool, but you cut a shape from a photo, instead of drawing a shape:

1. **Activate the Cookie Cutter tool.**

   Click the Cookie Cutter in the Toolbox (the icon looks like a star), or press Q.

2. **Select the shape you want your photo to be.**

   Choose a shape from the Shapes palette by clicking the down arrow next to the shape display in the Options bar. You have access to all the Custom Shapes, but pay special attention to the Crop Shapes category. Click the More button (the arrows) on the Shape Picker to see all the shape categories it contains, or choose All Elements Shapes.

3. **Adjust your settings, if necessary.**

   You have the same Shape Options described earlier for the Custom Shapes (page 357), so you can set a fixed size or constrain proportions if you want. Click the Shape Options button to see your choices.

   You can choose to feather the edge of your shape, too. Just enter the amount in pixels. (See page 135 for more about feathering.) The other option, Crop, crops the edges of your photo so they're just large enough to contain the shape.

4. **Drag in your photo.**

   A mask appears over your photo and you see only the area that will still be there once you crop, surrounded by transparency.

5. **Adjust your crop if necessary.**

   You can reposition the shape mask or drag the corners to resize it. Although the cropped areas disappear, they'll reappear as you reposition the mask if you move it so that they're included again.

   Once you've created the shape, you'll see the Transform options (page 321) in the Options bar (which means that you can skew or distort it if you want) until you commit your shape, as explained in the next step. You can drag the mask around to reposition it if you'd like, or Shift+drag a corner to resize it without altering the proportions. It may take a little maneuvering to get exactly the parts of your photo that you want inside the crop.

6. **When you've gotten everything lined up the way you want, click the Commit button in the image window or just press Enter.**

   If you don't like the results, click the Cancel button in the window, or press Escape (Esc). Once you've made your crop, you can use Ctrl+Z if you want to undo it to try something else.

   TIP   The Cookie Cutter replaces the areas it removes with transparency. If the transparency checkerboard makes it too hard for you to get a clear look at what you've done, temporarily create a new white or colored Fill layer (page 176) beneath the cropped layer. You can delete it once you're sure you're happy with your crop.

CHAPTER 13

Filters, Effects, Layer Styles, and Gradients

There's a popular saying among artistic types who use software in their studios: *Tools don't equal talent*. And it's true: No mere program is going to turn a klutz into a Klimt. But Elements has a few special tools—*filters, effects*, and *Layer styles*—that can sure help you fool a lot of people. It's amazing what a difference you can make to the appearance of any image with only a couple of clicks.

Filters are a jaw-droppingly easy way to change the appearance of your image. You can use certain filters for enhancing and correcting your image, but Elements also gives you a bunch of other filters that are great for unleashing all your artistic impulses, as shown in Figure 13-1. You'll find the original photos (*courthouse.jpg* and *paulownia.jpg*) on the Missing CD page at *www.missingmanuals.com*, if you want to play around with these images yourself.

Most filters have settings you can adjust to control how the filter changes your photo. You get more than a hundred different filters with Elements, so there isn't room in this chapter to cover each filter individually, but you'll learn the basics of applying filters, and you'll get in-depth coverage of some of the filters you're most likely to use frequently.

Effects are like little macros or scripts, designed to make very elaborate changes to your image, like creating a three-dimensional frame around it or making it look like a pencil sketch or an oil pastel. They're super easy to apply—you just double-click a button—but you can't tweak their settings as easily as you can with filters, since effects are programmed to make very specific changes. (Adobe calls them Photo Effects, but you can apply them to any kind of image, not just a photo.)

If you've used Elements before, then you may know that the Effects are also known as *actions*. Full-featured Photoshop lets you record and save your own actions, and install actions created by others. Power users could always use these actions in a limited way in Elements, but it took a lot of doing. One of the great new features in Elements 7 is an actions player that lets you easily use Photoshop actions in Elements. You still can't *create* actions in Elements, but you can run them once someone creates them for you.

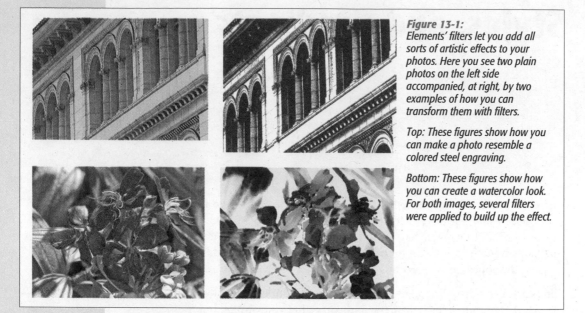

Figure 13-1:
Elements' filters let you add all sorts of artistic effects to your photos. Here you see two plain photos on the left side accompanied, at right, by two examples of how you can transform them with filters.

Top: These figures show how you can make a photo resemble a colored steel engraving.

Bottom: These figures show how you can create a watercolor look. For both images, several filters were applied to build up the effect.

Layer styles change the appearance of just one layer of your photo (see Chapter 6 for more about layers). They're very popular for creating impressive-looking text, but you also can apply them to objects and shapes. Most Layer styles include settings you can easily modify.

You can combine filters, effects, and Layer styles on the same image if you like. And you may spend hours trying different groupings, because it's addicting to watch the often-unpredictable results you get when mixing them up.

The last section of this chapter focuses on *gradients*. A gradient is a rainbow-like range of color that you can use to color in an object or a background. But that's not all gradients are good for. You can also use gradients and *Gradient Maps*—gradients that get distributed according to the brightness values in your photo—for very precise retouching effects.

Using Filters

Filters let you change the look of your photos in very complex ways. Using them is as easy as double-clicking a button. Elements gives you a huge number of filters, grouped in categories to help you choose the one that does what you need. This section offers a quick tour through the filter categories as well as some information about using a few of the most popular filters, like the Noise and Blur filters.

To make it easy to apply filters, Elements presents your filters in two different places: the Filter menu, where you choose them from the list that appears, and the Effects palette. (The menu is the only place where you can see every filter. Some filters, like the Adjustment filters, don't appear in the palette.) Elements also has a Filter Gallery, a great feature that makes it very easy to get a good idea of how your photo will look when you apply the artistic filters. The next part of this section explains how to use all three methods.

Applying Filters

In the Filter menu, you choose a filter by name from the list. In the Effects palette, thumbnail images give you a preview of what the filters do. The filters do exactly the same thing no matter which way you choose them.

The Filter Gallery gives you a good preview of what a filter looks like when applied to your image. Some filters automatically open the Filter Gallery when you choose them from the menu or the palette. Or you can call up the Gallery itself (without first choosing a filter) by going to Filter → Filter Gallery. You can't apply every filter from the Gallery—only some of the filters with adjustable settings.

> **TIP** In Elements, you can easily apply the same filter repeatedly. Press the Ctrl+F keyboard shortcut, and Elements automatically applies the last filter you used, with whatever settings you last used. The top listing in the Filter menu also shows the name of this same filter (selecting it works the same way as the keyboard shortcut: You get the same settings you just used). Press Ctrl+Alt+F to bring up the last filter you used, but with the dialog box open in case you want to change your settings.

Filter menu

The Filter menu groups filters into 14 main categories. Correct Camera Distortion (page 316) is all by itself at the top of the list. You'll also see a divider below the bottom category (called Other). When you first install Elements, the Digimarc filter is the only filter below this line, but other filters you download or purchase will appear here, too.

When you choose a filter from the list, one of three things happens:

- **Elements applies the filter automatically**. This happens if the filter's name in the list doesn't have an ellipsis (...) after it. Just look at the result in your photo, and then undo it (Ctrl+Z) if you don't like its effect. If you do like it, then you don't have to do anything else. If you don't, then you have no options for adjusting the settings on these filters.

- **You see a dialog box**. Elements filters that have adjustable settings have an ellipsis (...) after their names. Some of them (mostly corrective filters) open a dialog box where you can tweak the settings. Set everything as you want it, watching the small preview in the dialog box to see what you're doing. Then click OK.

- **You see the Filter Gallery.** Some of the more artistic, adjustable filters automatically call up the Filter Gallery so that you can get a nice large preview of what you're doing, and also rearrange the order of multiple filters before applying them. Applying filters from the Gallery is explained later.

Regardless of how you've applied the filter, once you're done, you can always undo it (Ctrl+Z) if you're not happy with the effect. If you like it, then there's no need to do anything else, except of course to eventually save your image.

> **TIP** Since you can't undo filters after you've closed your image, many people apply filters to a duplicate layer. Press Ctrl+J to create a duplicate layer.

Effects palette

If you're more comfortable with visual clues when choosing a filter, then you can also find most filters in the Effects palette (Figure 13-2), which is, logically enough, also where you apply effects.

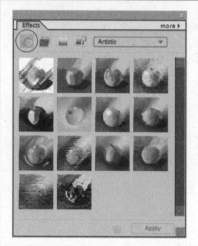

Figure 13-2:
The Effects palette gives you a preview of what every filter looks like when applied to the same picture of a green apple. Click the Filters button (circled), and then, from the pull-down menu, choose a category. If you know what you want a filter to do but don't know what name to look for, scrolling through these thumbnail images should help locate the one you want. To apply a filter from the palette, double-click the thumbnail, or click the thumbnail once and then click Apply. You can also drag the filter's thumbnail from the palette onto your image.

The Effects palette is one of the palettes in the Palette bin the first time you launch Elements. If it's not there waiting for you, go to Window → Effects, and then click the Filters button. Choose a Filter category from the pull-down menu or choose Show All. The categories are the same ones you see in the Filter menu, except that Adjustments is available only through the menu, and Sharpen appears in the palette but not the Filter menu.

To apply a filter from the palette, double-click its thumbnail, or drag the thumbnail onto your image. If the filter has adjustable settings, you see the same dialog box or Filter Gallery you'd see when applying the filter from the Filter menu, as described earlier.

One small drawback to applying filters from the palette is that you can't tell from the thumbnail whether a filter is one that applies automatically, with no adjustable settings. Elements doesn't give you any clue like an ellipsis (…) to tell you which group a filter falls into.

Filter Gallery

The Filter Gallery, shown in Figure 13-3, is one of Elements' more popular features. It gives you a large preview window, a look at all the little green apple thumbnails so you have a visual guide to what your filter will do, and, most important, it lets you apply filters like layers—you can stack them up and change the order in which they're applied to your image. Changing the order of filters can make some big differences in how they affect your image. For example, you get very different results if you apply Ink Outlines *after* the Sprayed Strokes filter compared to the other way around. The Gallery makes it easy to play around and see which order gives you the look you want. The layer-like behavior of the filters in the gallery is only for previewing, though—you don't end up with real layers.

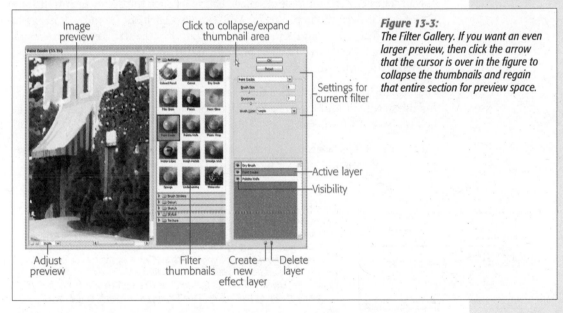

Figure 13-3:
The Filter Gallery. If you want an even larger preview, then click the arrow that the cursor is over in the figure to collapse the thumbnails and regain that entire section for preview space.

The Gallery is more for artistic filters than corrective filters. You can't apply the Adjustment or Noise filters from the Gallery, for instance. All the Gallery filters are in the artistic, brushstroke, distort, sketch, stylize, and texture categories. (See the next section for an overview of all the filter categories.)

The Filter Gallery is divided into three panes. On the left side is a preview of what your image will look like when you apply the filter. The center holds the thumbnails for the different filters, and the right side contains the settings for the currently chosen filter. Your filter layers are at the bottom of the settings pane. You can see what filters you've applied, add or subtract layers, and rearrange their order here.

NOTE Filter layers work something like regular layers (see Chapter 6) with one important difference: Your filter layers are what you might call "working layers." In other words, you have separate filter layers only until you click OK. Then all your chosen filters get applied to your image at once. You can't close your photo, come back later and still expect to see the filters as individual, changeable layers after you've actually applied the filters. And most important, your filters become part of the layer to which you apply them. You aren't creating a new permanent layer when you use the Filter Gallery.

If you've used the latest version of the full featured Photoshop, then be aware that Elements doesn't create editable smart filters the way Photoshop does—it handles filters the way earlier versions of Photoshop (Photoshop CS2 and below) did. This trait is good to keep in mind if you're trying to do something based on instructions written for Photoshop (instructions you've found online, say).

In addition to letting you adjust the settings for a given filter, the Filter Gallery lets you perform a few other tricks:

- **Adjust the preview magnification of your image.** In the Gallery's lower-left corner, click directly on the percentage listing or click the arrow next to it for a list of preset sizes to choose from. You can also click the + and – buttons to zoom the view in or out. Easier still, use the Ctrl+= (the Ctrl key plus the equal sign key) and Ctrl+– (the Ctrl key plus the minus key) shortcuts to zoom in and out from the keyboard.

- **Choose a new filter.** Just click a filter's thumbnail once, and you get the settings for the new filter and the preview image updates right away—usually. (See the box on page 371 for details.)

- **Add a new filter layer.** Each time you click the New Filter Layer icon (see Figure 13-4), you add another filter layer to the ones you already have.

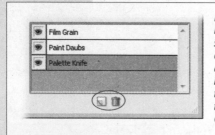

Figure 13-4:
If you've used layers before (see Chapter 6), then these little icons (circled) should look familiar. In the Filter Gallery, they make new filter layers instead of regular layers. Click the square icon (shown at the bottom of this figure) to add a new filter layer to your image. Click the Trash can icon to delete a filter layer. The eye icons next to your filter layers turn visibility on and off just as they do in the Layers palette. It's true that the filters preview in layers, but they don't show up as real layers in the Layers palette—only in the Filter Gallery.

- **Change the position of filter layers.** Just drag them up and down in the stack to change the order in which they'll get applied to your image.

- **Hide filter layers.** Click the eye next to a filter layer in the filter layer palette to turn off visibility, just like in the regular Layers palette (page 16).

- **Delete filter layers.** Highlight any filter layer by clicking it, and then click the trash icon to delete it.

• **Change the content of a layer.** You can change what kind of filter is in a particular layer. For instance, if you applied, say, the Smudge Stick, and you like all your other changes but wish you had used the Glass filter instead, then you don't have to delete the Smudge Stick layer. Instead, just highlight the Smudge layer, and then click the Glass filter button to change the layer's contents.

TIP   Ctrl+F reapplies all the filters that were in your last gallery set if you press it again after using the Filter Gallery. Ctrl+Alt+F brings up the dialog box for the last filter so you can change your settings before you apply it again.

Filter Categories

Elements divides filters into categories to help you more easily track down the one you want. Some of the categories, like Distort, contain filters that vary hugely in what they do to your photo. Other categories, like the Brush Stroke filters, contain filters that are all pretty obviously related to one another. Here's a quick breakdown of the categories:

• **Correct Camera Distortion.** This filter lets you correct perspective distortion (think: tall buildings) as well as vignetting (shadows) caused by your camera's lens. It's explained in detail on page 316.

• **Adjustments.** These filters apply some photographic, stylistic, and artistic changes to your photo. Most of the adjustments are explained on page 280; the Photo Filters are covered on page 242.

• **Artistic.** This is a huge group of filters that do everything from give your photo a cut-from-paper look (Cutout) to make it resemble a quick sketch (Rough Pastels). You generally get the best effects with these filters by using multiple filters or applying the same one multiple times.

• **Blur.** The blur filters let you soften focus and add artistic effects. They're explained later in this chapter.

• **Brush Strokes.** These filters apply brushstroke effects, and generate a hand-painted look.

• **Distort.** These filters warp images in a great variety of ways. The Liquify filter is the most powerful, and you'll find a tutorial for using it on page 411.

• **Noise.** Use these filters to add or remove grain. They're explained later in this chapter.

• **Pixelate.** The Pixelate filters break your image up in different ways, making it show the dot pattern of a magazine or newspaper's printed image (Halftone), or the fragmented look you see on television when a show is concealing someone's identity.

NOTE   The Color Halftone filter makes your photo look like a one-color *halftone*, an image whose dots simulate the shades of gray you see in a black-and-white photo. It's not the same as true halftone screening, which isn't available in Elements. If the print shop you're working with needs a halftone, you need to either use the full-featured Photoshop or ask the printer to do the conversion for you.

- **Render.** This group includes a pretty diverse bunch of filters that let you do things like create a lens flare effect (Lens Flare), transform a flat object so it looks three-dimensional (3D Transform), and make an effect that looks like fibers (Fibers) or clouds (Clouds). The Lighting Effects filter, a powerful but confusing filter that's like a whole program in itself, helps you change the way lighting appears in your image. For a full rundown on what this filter does, as well as how to use it, check out the Missing CD page at *www.missingmanuals.com*.

- **Sharpen.** Unsharp Mask (page 214) appears in the palette but not the Filter menu. (The sharpening commands are in the Enhance menu.)

- **Sketch.** These filters can make your photo look like it was drawn with charcoal, chalk, crayon, or some other material—and they can also make the photo look like it was embossed in wet plaster, photocopied, or stamped with a rubber stamp.

- **Stylize.** These filters create special effects by increasing the contrast in your photo, and displacing pixels. You can make your photo look radioactive, reduce it to outlines, or make it look like it's moving quickly.

- **Texture.** These filters change the surface of your photo to look like it was made from another material. Use them to create a crackled finish (the Craquelure filter), a stained glass look (Stained Glass), or a mosaic effect (Mosaic Tiles).

- **Video.** These filters are for creating and editing images for (and from) videos.

- **Other.** This is a group of fairly technical filters that you can highly customize. The High Pass filter is explained on page 219. You can use Offset to shift an image or a layer a little bit, or to position tiled image layers.

- **Digimarc.** Use this filter to check for Digimarc watermarks in photos. Digimarc is a company that lets subscribers enter their information in a database so that anyone who gets one of their photos can find out who holds the copyright.

You can find a number of filter plug-ins online, ranging from free to very expensive. Page 495 gives you some suggestions for places to start looking. Once you've installed new filters, you access them in the Filter menu, at the bottom of the list.

NOTE   Filters are platform specific, so you can't use plug-ins written for the Mac version of Elements if you're using Windows. Only Windows plug-ins work with the Windows version of Elements.

UNDER THE HOOD

Filter Performance Hints

If Elements could speak, it would say, "Easy for *you*," when it comes to filters and effects. Although you don't have to do much to apply them, Elements has a huge amount of work to do on its end. Elements 7 is pretty fast, but if your computer is slow or memory-challenged, it can take a long time to apply filters and even to update the preview. You can speed things up by applying filters to a selection for previewing. Filters that have their own dialog boxes (as opposed to the Filter Gallery) show a flashing line under the size percentage below the preview area to indicate the progress they're making. A few other filter-related tips are worth remembering:

- Filters don't do anything if they don't have pixels to work on, so be sure you're targeting a layer with something in it, and not an Adjustment layer.

- If you apply a filter to a selection, then you'll usually want to feather (page 135) or refine (page 128) the edges a fair amount to help the filter edges blend into the rest of your photo.

- Alt+click the Cancel button to turn it into a Reset button. Clicking Cancel makes the window go away, while Reset lets you start over without having to call up the filter again.

- If your filters are grayed out in the Filter menu, check to be sure you're not in 16-bit mode (page 238) or in grayscale, bitmapped, or index color (all these color modes are explained on page 45).

Useful Filter Solutions

This section shows how to use some of Elements' most popular and useful filters to correct your photos and create a few special effects. For instance, you'll learn how to modify graininess to create an aged effect or smooth out a repair job. And you'll also see how to blur photos to create a soft-focus effect, or to make subjects look like they're moving.

Removing noise: Getting rid of graininess

Noise, the appearance of undesired graininess in an image, is a big problem with many digital cameras, especially those with small sensors and high megapixel counts. It's rare to find a fixed-lens camera with more than 5 megapixels that doesn't have some trouble with noise, especially in underexposed areas. If you shoot using the Raw format, then you can correct a fair amount of noise right in the Raw Converter (page 237). But the Raw Converter may give unpredictable results if you use it on JPEGs. And even Raw files may need further noise reduction once you've edited your photo after converting it.

Elements includes the Reduce Noise filter, which is designed specifically to help get rid of noise in your photos. To get to it, go to Filter → Noise → Reduce Noise. You get a dialog box with a preview window on the left and settings adjustments on the right. To use the filter, first use the controls below the preview to set the view to at least 100 percent, or preferably even higher. You need to see the pixels in your photo so you can see how the filter is changing them as you adjust the settings.

You get three settings, each of which you control by using a slider:

- **Strength.** This setting controls the overall impact of the filter. It reduces the same kind of noise as the Luminance Smoothing setting in the Raw converter (page 237). The stronger you set it, the greater the risk of softening your photo.

- **Preserve Details.** Using noise reduction can soften the appearance of your photo. This setting tells Elements how much care to take to preserve the details of your image.

- **Reduce Color Noise.** This control adjusts uneven distribution of color in your image. You can set the slider pretty high without a negative impact on your photo.

You also have a checkbox for minimizing JPEG artifacts—the uneven areas of color caused by JPEG compression (see page 64). A mottled pattern in what should be a clear blue sky is one classic example of JPEG artifacting that you may have experienced. Turn on the checkbox to help smooth things out.

For each setting, move the slider to the right if you want more and to the left if you want less; watch the effect in the preview window to see how you like the changes. You may notice a little lag time before the preview updates. When you see what you want, click OK to apply the filter.

The Elements Reduce Noise filter does an OK job on areas with a small amount of noise, like the sky in many JPEG photos, but it's not one of the strongest tools in Elements. If your camera has major noise problems, you may find you still need third-party noise reduction software. Some of the most popular programs are Noise Ninja (*www.picturecode.com*), Neat Image (*www.neatimage.com*), and Noiseware (*www.imagenomic.com*). All have demo versions you can download to try out the programs. If you search on Google for "noise reduction software," you'll get a variety of other options as well, including several free programs.

Adding noise: Smoothing out repair jobs

Elements also gives you a filter for *creating* noise. Why do that when most of the time you try so hard to get rid of noise? One reason is when you're trying to age the appearance of your photo. If you wanted to make a photo look like it came from an old newspaper, for instance, you'd add some noise.

The other most common use for noise is to help make repaired spots blend in with the rest of an image. If you've altered part of a photo in Elements, especially by painting on it, odds are the repaired area is going to look perfectly smooth. That's great if the rest of the photo is noise free. But if the rest of the photo is a little grainy, that smooth patch is going to stand out like a sore thumb. Add a bit of noise to make it blend in better with the rest of the photo, as shown in Figure 13-5. Also, if you see color banding when you print, adding a little noise to the photo may help fix that in your next print.

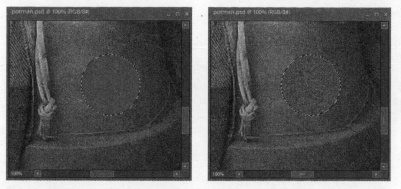

Figure 13-5:
Left: If you use the Average Blur filter in a repair on this noisy photo, the blended area stands out, making the repaired area obvious.

Right: By adding some noise, the changes become much less noticeable.

To add noise to a photo, start by selecting the area where you want to add the noise. Using a duplicate layer (Ctrl+J) for the noise is a safe step, since you can always undo changes if you've got them on a layer.

1. **Call up the Add Noise filter.**

   Go to Filter → Noise → Add Noise to bring up the dialog box with the settings for the filter.

2. **Adjust the settings to your liking.**

   The settings are explained in the following list. In the dialog box, use the preview window to check how the changes are affecting your photo.

3. **When you're satisfied, click OK.**

You have three options in the Add Noise dialog box:

- **Amount.** This option controls how heavy the noise is going to be. Just drag the slider to the right for more noise or to the left for less. You can also type in a number. A higher percentage means more noise.

- **Uniform or Gaussian.** These buttons let you control how the noise gets distributed through your image. Uniform is just what it says—the same all over. Gaussian distributes the noise to produce a more speckled effect.

  If you're adding noise to duplicate existing noise in a grainy photo, then you probably want a Gaussian distribution. For an old newspaper photo look, try Uniform. In either case, experiment until you get what you want.

- **Monochromatic.** This setting limits you to grayscale noise. Take a look at the middle image in Figure 13-6, and notice how many more colors you can see inside the noise, compared to the solid red of the original. The noise was applied with the Monochromatic setting turned off.

Noise can also help when you want to apply special effects to blocks of solid color, as shown in Figure 13-7. If you try to apply the Angled Strokes filter to a solid color, then you don't see the strokes. Adding noise gives the filter something to work on.

Figure 13-6:
Filters can really spruce up solid objects.

Top: An unfiltered solid red heart, drawn with the Shape tool (page 352).

Middle: Here's the same heart after adding some Uniform noise to it.

Bottom: Adding the Angled Strokes filter gives the heart a hand-painted look. If you don't add noise before applying the filter, then you won't see any texture change from the top graphic when applying the filter.

Gaussian Blur: Drawing attention to a foreground object

Probably the most frequently used of the Blur filters, the Gaussian Blur filter lets you control how much an image is blurred. Besides using it to blur large areas of a photo, like the background in Figure 13-7, bottom, you can apply the Gaussian Blur filter at a very low setting to soften lines—very useful when trying to achieve a sketched effect. If you'd like to try out the different blurs, download the hawk photo (*hawk.jpg*) from the Missing CD page at *www.missingmanuals.com*.

When using the Gaussian Blur, you have to set the *radius*, which controls how much the filter blurs things. A higher radius produces more blurring; use the filter's preview window to see what you're doing.

Radial Blur: Producing a sense of motion

As you can see in Figure 13-8, the Radial Blur really produces a sense of motion. It has two available styles: Zoom, which is designed to give the effect of a camera zooming in, and Spin, which produces a circular effect around your designated center point.

The Radial Blur dialog box may look a bit complicated, but it's really not. Unfortunately, you don't get a preview with this filter, because it drains so much processor power. That's why you have a choice between Draft, Good, and Best Quality. Use Draft for a quick look at roughly what you'll get. Then, most of the time, choose Good for the final version. Good and Best aren't very different except on large images, so don't feel that you must choose Best for the final version all the time.

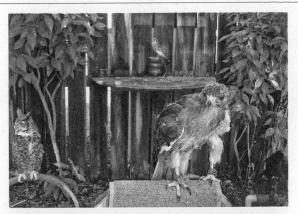

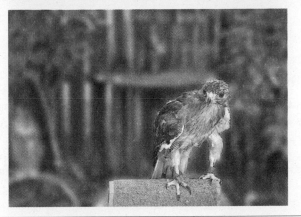

Figure 13-7:
Top: This photo could use some help from the Blur filters. The hawk is hard to distinguish from the rest of the photo; blurring helps center the focus on the hawk.

Bottom: With a Gaussian Blur filter applied to the background, the hawk becomes the photo's clear focal point.

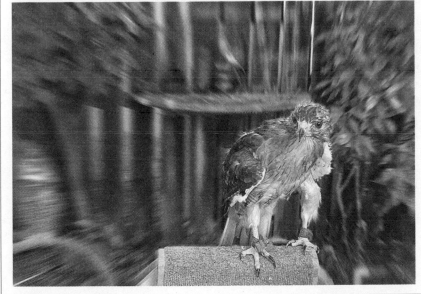

Figure 13-8:
A Radial Blur applied in Zoom mode. As you can see, this filter can produce an almost vertiginous sense of motion. If you don't want to give people motion sickness, go easy on the Amount setting.

Once you've chosen your method (Zoom or Spin), set the amount, which controls the intensity of the blur that's applied. Next, click inside the Blur Center box to identify the point where you want the blur to center, as shown in Figure 13-9. Finally, click OK when you're finished.

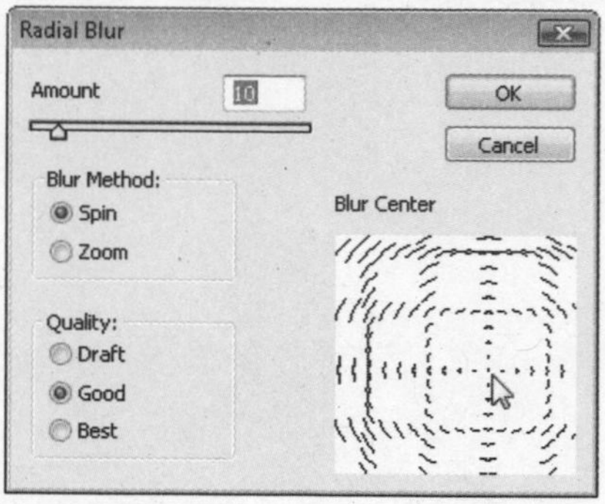

Figure 13-9:
The Blur Center box lets you identify the center point of the Radial Blur's effect (whether you've chosen Zoom or Spin mode). Drag the ripple drawing inside the box in any direction; here, the center point has been moved just to the right and down from its original position in the center of the box.

Color correcting with the Average Blur filter

If you've already given the Average Blur filter a whirl, then you may be wondering what on earth Adobe was thinking when they created it. Use it on your entire photo, and your image disappears under a hideous soup, something like what you'd get by pureeing together all the colors in your photo. Oddly enough, this effect makes the filter a great tool for getting rid of color casts (page 205). You can use the Average Blur to create a sort of custom Photo Filter (page 242) toned specially for the image you use it on. The secret is in using blend modes (page 164). Here's how:

1. **Open your image and make a duplicate layer.**

   Just press Ctrl+J, or go to Layer → Duplicate Layer.

2. **Apply the Average Blur filter.**

   Make sure your duplicate layer is the active layer (click it in the Layers palette if it isn't), and then go to Filter → Blur → Average. Your photo disappears under a layer of (probably) very unpleasing solid color, but you'll fix that next.

3. **Change the blur layer's blend mode.**

   In the Layers palette, from the Mode pull-down menu, choose Color. Already things are starting to look better.

4. **Invert the blur layer.**

   Press Ctrl+I to invert the colors.

5. **Reduce the opacity of the blur layer, and do other tweaking, if necessary.**

Use the Layers palette's opacity slider. Start with 50 percent. By now, the color should look right—no more color cast. Tweak if necessary, and then save your work.

You may want to add a Hue/Saturation layer (page 275) if you find that no matter how you adjust the opacity slider, the photo looks a little flat.

The Average Blur filter is a particularly good way to color-correct underwater photos, where it's very hard to get a realistic white balance using your camera's built-in settings.

Improving skin texture with the Surface Blur filter

Elements 7 brings yet another way to blur your photos—the Surface Blur filter. At this point you may be thinking that you have enough ways to eliminate details in your photos, but the Surface Blur filter is actually very handy, especially if you take pictures of people. The Surface Blur filter is smart enough to avoid blurring details and areas of high contrast, which makes it very handy for fixing skin. If you want to eliminate pores, for instance, or reduce the visibility of freckles, this is your tool, as shown in Figure 13-10, and it's pretty simple to use, too:

1. **Open your image, and then make a duplicate layer.**

Just press Ctrl+J, or go to Layer → Duplicate Layer.

> **TIP** For best results, you may want to start by selecting the area you want to blur (see Chapter 5 for help with selections). Then make your duplicate layer from the selection, in order to maintain maximum detail in the areas you aren't trying to fix. For example, select only the skin areas of your subject's face, leaving out the mouth and eye areas, so they won't be affected at all by the blur.

2. **Apply the Surface Blur filter.**

Make sure your duplicate layer is the active layer (click it in the Layers palette if it isn't already), and then go to Filter → Blur → Surface Blur. Move the dialog box out of the way, if necessary, so that you can watch what you're doing in the main image window as well as in the small preview area of the dialog box.

3. **Tweak the filter settings till you like the effect.**

The sliders are explained below. Be cautious—it doesn't take much to make your photo start to look like a painting. Click OK when you've got the flaws concealed as much as possible without losing important details like eyelashes.

4. **If you want, change the blend mode and/or the opacity for the duplicate layer.**

Use the Layers palette sliders to do this step. If you want to eliminate skin blemishes, try Lighten blend mode, for example.

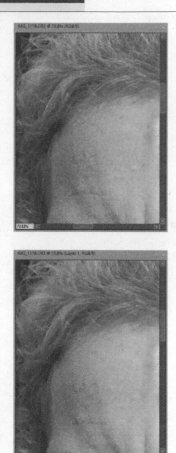

Figure 13-10:
The new Surface Blur filter is a very handy tool for creating better looking skin, minimizing lines and flaws, or reducing the visibility of pores.

Top: The original photo.

Bottom: A dose of Surface blur evens out fine lines in the skin and preserves individual hairs that have good definition. But if you look closely, the areas of hair with less definition got blurred along with the skin. In cases like that, use a selection to limit where the blur gets applied.

The Surface Blur filter isn't at all hard to understand, but you usually have to do a fair amount of fiddling with the sliders to get the best balance for the blur effect. Here's what the sliders do:

- **Radius.** As with other filters, this one controls how far Elements should blur your image. Move the slider to the left for a smaller blur, and to the right for a wider blur.

- **Threshold.** This slider controls the level at which Elements begins to blur. A low setting here means you see less blurring, a higher setting means more blurring.

> **TIP** When you have to do a lot of experimenting, sometimes it's easier just to highlight the number in the box for each setting, and use the up and down arrow keys to adjust the effect.

Adding Effects

Like filters, effects give you loads of ways to modify your photo's appearance—from adding green slime textures to surrounding your image with classy picture frames. Although you apply effects with a simple double-click of your mouse, these clicks actually trigger a sequence of changes that Elements diligently applies. Some effects involve many complex steps, although Elements works so quickly you might not even notice all the changes taking place.

> **NOTE** You usually can't customize or change an effect's settings. Effects are typically an all-or-nothing deal. For example, if you use one of the Frame effects, then you either take the frame size as Elements applies it to your image, or you don't. No need to ask if you can adjust the scale of the frame relative to your photo—you can't. (This quality is why most of the frames are now Smart Objects [page 425] that you apply from the Content palette, rather than effects—you have more control over Smart Objects.)

You'll find effects in a few different spots throughout Elements:

- The **Effects palette** is home to most photo effects—things like photo tinting (Figure 13-11)—and a few frames. Coverage starts after this bullet list.

- The **Content palette** houses some effects. They're intended primarily for text, but sometimes you can use them for other purposes. They create cool results on shapes, too, for instance. Page 427 has the full scoop.

- **Guided Edit.** Elements 7 has a few new effects that Adobe included as part of its let-us-show-you-how section; you'll find them at the very bottom of the list of tasks, and Guided Edit walks you through applying them. Page 28 tells you more about using Guided Edit.

To apply an effect from the Effects palette, choose Window → Effects, and then click the Photo Effects button. Just as with filters, use the pull-down menu on the Effects palette to see all your choices, or pick from only one category. The thumbnail images give you a preview of how the effect changes your image.

To apply an effect, in the Effects palette, double-click its thumbnail, or click the thumbnail once, and then click Apply. You can also just drag the thumbnail onto your photo. That's all there is to it. If you don't like the result, press Ctrl+Z to undo it, but you can't tweak much in the effects.

Here are a few other effects-related tips to help maximize these nifty but-quirky features:

- A few effects flatten (page 175) or simplify (page 355) your image. Therefore, it's usually best to make a copy of your image, or wait until you're done making all your other edits, before applying an effect.

- Many effects create additional layers; check the Layers palette once you're done applying them. You may want to flatten your image to reduce the file size before printing or storing it. (See Chapter 6 if you need a refresher on using layers.)

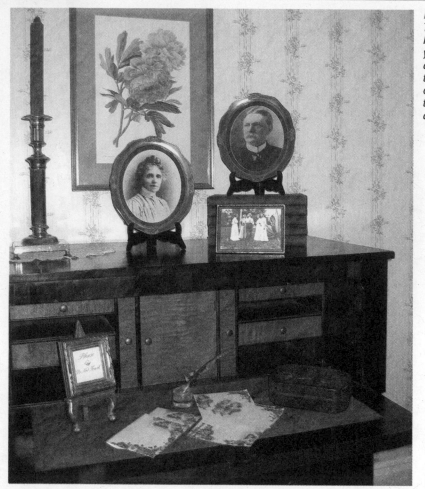

Figure 13-11:
The Effects palette's Photo Effects section lets you age a photo by applying an antique look to it, as shown in this color photo which has the Vintage Photo effect applied to it.

Using Actions in Elements

If you hang around people who use Photoshop, then you'll hear a lot of talk about *actions* and how useful they are. An action is a little script, like a macro in a program like Word, that automates the steps for doing something, thus saving you a ton of time. For example, you might create an action that applies your favorite filter and crops a photo to a certain size, or one that creates a complicated artistic effect, like a colorful watercolor look that would take many steps to do manually. Wouldn't it be great to be able to use actions in Elements?

Well, in a way Elements has always been able to use actions—under the hood, effects are really actions. And you could always add some Photoshop actions to Elements, although it's been pretty complicated to do so. Not any more, though— one of Elements 7's greatest new features is the Action Player, which lets you run many Photoshop actions right in Elements.

It's extremely easy to use actions in Elements 7. Adobe gives you a few useful ones to get you started, and you can add your own, too, as explained later in this section. To run an action:

1. **Open a photo in the Editor, and then go to the Action Player.**

   Click the Edit tab → Guided → Automated Actions → Action Player.

2. **From the first pull-down menu, choose the Action set you want.**

   Action sets are groups of related actions. (Earlier versions of Elements didn't understand action sets at all, so this is a big deal in Elements 7.) The action sets that come with Elements let you choose between actions to add captions (and canvas to display the captions), trim weight from your subjects, resize and crop your photos, or apply special effects to them.

3. **From the second pull-down menu, choose the specific action you want to use.**

   You can choose how much thinner to make someone with the Lose Weight actions, for example, or what color canvas (white, gray, or black) to add for a caption.

4. **Run the action.**

   Just click Play Action. If you don't like the results, click Reset or press Ctrl+Z to undo the action, and then try another action instead. (You can't step backwards in the Elements Action Player.)

   NOTE   The actions that come with Elements all happen pretty much instantly, but if you add actions from other sources, then you may see pop-up dialog boxes to adjust settings for some steps. Just make any changes, click OK, and the action resumes and completes itself automatically.

5. **When you like the result, click Done.**

   If you decide you don't want to use an action after all, click Cancel instead.

One of the Elements 7 Action Player's great qualities is that you can easily add more actions to it. You can't create new actions in Elements—you need Photoshop to record actions—but you'll find literally thousands of free actions available on the Internet that you can download and add to Elements. Page 495 gives you some places to look for them.

Once you download an action, if you're using Vista, just pop it into *C:\ ProgramData\Adobe\Photoshop Elements\7.0\Locale\en_US* (this is different if you aren't in the US)*\Workflow Panels\Actions*. For Windows XP, it's *C:\Documents and Settings\All Users\Application Data\Adobe\Photoshop Elements\7.0\Locale\en_ US* (this is different if you aren't in the US)*\Workflow Panels\Actions*. (You need to turn on hidden folder viewing for either operating system, since these are hidden files.) The next time you start Elements, you'll see your action in the drop-down menu shown in Figure 13-12.

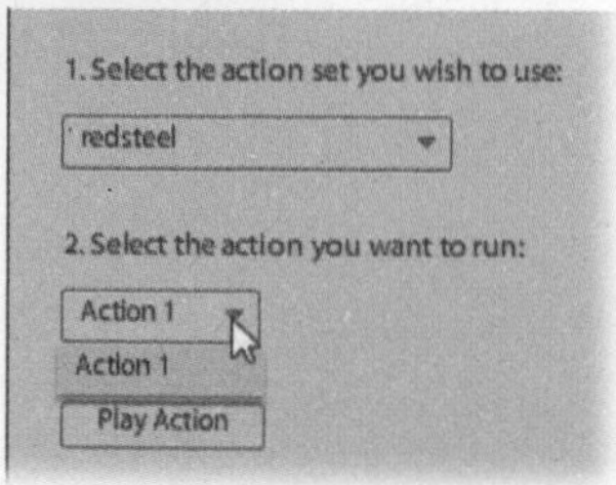

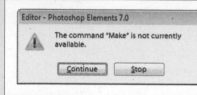

Figure 13-12:
If you add a single action that isn't part of an action set, then you still have to make a choice in both the Action Set menu and the Action menu. Just choose its name in the Action Set menu, and then, in the Action menu, choose Action 1. Redsteel is an action that contains the steps used to create the window image in Figure 13-1. You can download it from the Missing CD page at www.missingmanuals.com if you want to try installing actions. It works best on photos with lots of detail. On images with large blocks of color, the effect is more like pop art than a colored steel engraving.

It's important to understand a few differences between actions in Photoshop and in Elements. Photoshop can run an action on a whole folder full of images at once. Not so in Elements, where you're restricted to one photo at a time. Also, Elements can't quite carry out actions that invoke Photoshop-only commands. For example, if you run an action that includes the creation of a history snapshot, then you see the dialog box shown in Figure 13-13.

Figure 13-13:
When you run an action in Elements, you may see all kinds of dialog boxes asking for your input as the action works through the steps. However, if you see this dialog box, then you're trying to run an action that includes a step that Elements just can't do. You don't have to stop the action, but be aware that you won't get the same results as you would in Photoshop.

If you like to play it safe, you can find a number of actions written specifically for Elements. Page 495 tells you where to look for them.

> **NOTE** While the Actions player is great, there's one disadvantage to having it in Guided Edit: You don't have access to the Layers palette, which is annoying for those actions which require you to choose a layer to use in mid-action. The good news is that you can still install actions in the Effects palette, using exactly the same steps that you would have used in Elements 6. This lets you use actions in Full Edit, where you can get over to the Layers palette any time an action requires it. You can still use the various add-on tools to Elements that are actually actions, like the various free tool sets available online. You'll find much more about downloading and installing these in Chapter 19.

Adding Layer Styles

Like filters and effects, Layer styles let you transform objects by giving them new characteristics, like Drop Shadows, for instance. Layer styles are especially useful for modifying individual objects, like text and buttons, because you can edit the text and change the button's shape even *after* you've applied the Layer style.

Layer styles, as their name suggests, work on the contents of one layer—rather than on your whole image. That's important. A Layer style affects the *entire* contents of a layer. If you want to apply a Layer style to just one object in your picture, select the object, and then put it on a layer of its own (Ctrl+J or Layer → New → "Layer via Copy", or Ctrl+Shft+J or New → "Layer via Cut"). Figure 13-14 shows what you can do with Layer styles.

You apply Layer styles from the Effects palette (Window → Effects). Click the Layer Styles button, and then—from the pull-down menu—choose a Layer style category, or choose Show All. Finally, select the layer you want to modify (by highlighting it in the Layers palette), and then click the Layer style you want to use. The box on page 385 shows you how to modify any style's settings.

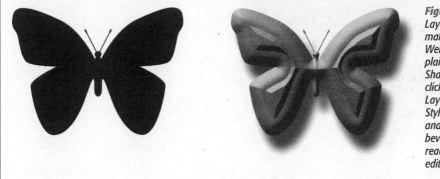

Figure 13-14:
Layer styles are great for making fancy buttons for Web sites. Changing this plain black Custom Shape was as simple as clicking the Sunset Sky Layer style (in Complex Styles), adding a bevel, and then making the bevel bigger. (Keep reading to learn how to edit Layer styles.)

NOTE   Some tools, like the Type tool (see page 399), have an Options bar setting that lets you choose a Layer style.

Here's a quick rundown of the choices available in each Layer style category:

- **Bevels** give objects a 3-D look by making them appear raised from the page or embossed into it. Figure 13-15 shows an example of how combining a bevel and a drop shadow can add a lot of dimension to even a simple shape.

- **Complex** includes a variety of elaborate Layer styles that make an object look like it's made from metal, cactus, or several other materials. These styles are particularly useful for applying to type.

- **Drop Shadows** adds shadow effects that make your object look like it's floating above the page.

  NOTE   Adding a drop shadow to an entire photo requires adding canvas (see page 96) to give the shadow someplace to fall.

- **Glass Buttons** are supposed to make objects look like glass buttons, but many people think they look more like plastic. They're useful for creating Web page buttons.

- **Image Effects** give you a wealth of ways to transform your photo, including fading it and making it look like the pieces of a puzzle or a tile mosaic.

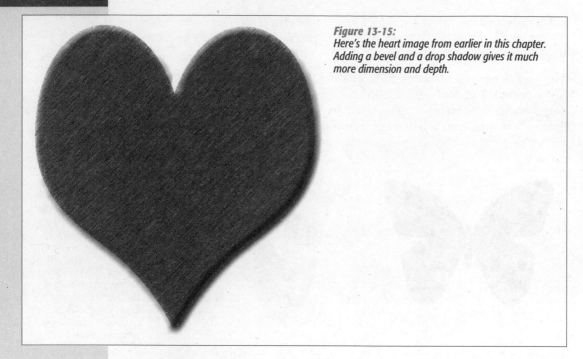

Figure 13-15:
Here's the heart image from earlier in this chapter. Adding a bevel and a drop shadow gives it much more dimension and depth.

- **Inner Glows** add light around the inside edge of your object.

- **Inner Shadows** give your image a hollow or recessed effect by casting a shadow within the object, rather than outside it the way drop shadows do.

- **Outer Glows** create the same kind of light effects that Inner Glows do, only they go around the outer edge of your image.

- **Patterns** apply an overall pattern to your image. Want to make something look like it's made from metal or dried mud, or want to fill in a dull background with a really vivid pattern? You'll find lots of choices here.

- **Photographic Effects** include several favorite traditional photographic techniques. You can add a variety of monochrome effects, like good old-fashioned sepia.

- **Strokes** let you put a black or colored border around the edge of a layer, or an object on its own layer. They're great for making outlined text, too.

- **Visibility** changes the opacity and visibility of your layer. Use them to create a ghosted effect—or when you're applying multiple Layer styles, and you want to use the outlined shape of an object without having the object itself visible.

- **Wow Chrome, Neon, and Plastic Styles** make an object look like it's made from shiny chrome, outlined in neon, or made from plastic.

NOTE   You can apply Layer styles only to regular layers, so if you try to apply one to a Background layer, then Elements asks you to convert it to a regular layer before the style can take effect.

If someone sends you a file made using Layer styles that you don't have, then you can snag them for your own use by highlighting the layer with the styles on it, and then going to Layer → Layer Style → Copy Layer Style. Then, in an image where you want to use the styles, click the layer that you want to modify, and then choose Layer → Layer Style → Paste Layer Style. This command applies all the styles used in the original image to the layer you targeted.

Editing Layer Styles

You can create highly customized Layer styles in Elements (see Figure 13-16). Start by applying a Layer style, and then you can edit it as much as you like. Just double-click the Layer Styles icon in the Layers Palette (the little italic "fx") or select Layer → Layer Style → Style Settings.

Once the Style Settings dialog box appears, you can edit your style in many different ways:

- **Drop Shadow**. You can change the shadow's direction, distance, opacity, or even its color. Once the Style Settings dialog box is open, you can drag the shadow around, right in your image window, until it's positioned where you want it.

- **Glow**. You can set the color, size, and opacity for both inner and outer glows, and turn each one on or off individually.

- **Bevel**. Change the size or direction of the bevel.

- **Stroke**. A stroke is a border around the edge of the style (like a line). You can change the color, size, and opacity of the stroke.

You can customize styles in so many ways that you can practically make your own style from any existing one. There's only one hitch: You can't change the standard settings for each style, so any changes you make affect the style only as you're currently applying it.

To remove a Layer style, in the Layers palette, right-click the layer, and then choose Clear Layer Style, or go to Layer → Layer Style → Clear Layer Style. These commands are all-or-nothing: If your layer has multiple styles, they all go away at once. To remove one style at a time, use the Undo History palette (page 32).

TIP   If you want to see what your image looks like without the styles you've applied to it, then go to Layer → Layer Style → Hide All Effects.

You can download hundreds of additional Layer styles from the Web (see page 495 for tips on where to look and how to install them). It's easy to get addicted to collecting Layer styles because they're so much fun to use.

Applying Gradients

You may have noticed that a few of the Layer styles and Photo Effects fade out a color at the edges. In fact, Elements lets you fade and blend colors in almost any

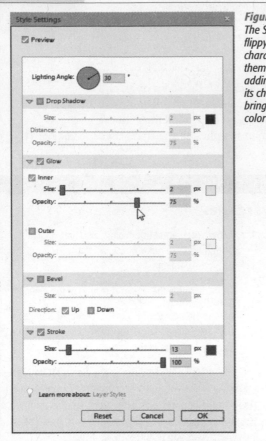

Figure 13-16:
The Style Settings dialog box gives you a lot of choices. Use the flippy triangles on the left to see the settings for a particular style characteristic or to collapse the ones you don't care about to get them out of your way. To apply a new characteristic to a style (like adding a glow to a style that doesn't already have one), just turn on its checkbox. Click the color squares to the right of the sliders to bring up the Color Picker (see page 209,) and then choose a new color for that setting.

way you can imagine by using *gradients*. Use gradients to create anything from a multicolor rainbow extravaganza to a single color that fades away into transparency. Figure 13-17 shows you a few examples of what you can do with gradients. The only limit is your imagination.

You can apply gradients directly to your image using the Gradient tool, or you can create *Gradient Fill layers*, which are entire layers filled with—you guessed it—gradients. You can even edit gradients and create new ones using the Gradient Editor. Finally, there's a special kind of gradient called a *Gradient Map* that lets you replace the colors in your image with the colors from a gradient. This section covers the basics of using all these tools and methods.

The Gradient Tool

If you want to apply a gradient to a particular object in your image, then the Gradient tool is the fastest way to do so. This tool may seem complicated when you first see it, but it's actually pretty easy to use. Start by activating the Gradient tool in the Toolbox (the yellow and blue rectangle) or by pressing G. Figure 13-18 shows the Gradient tool's Options bar.

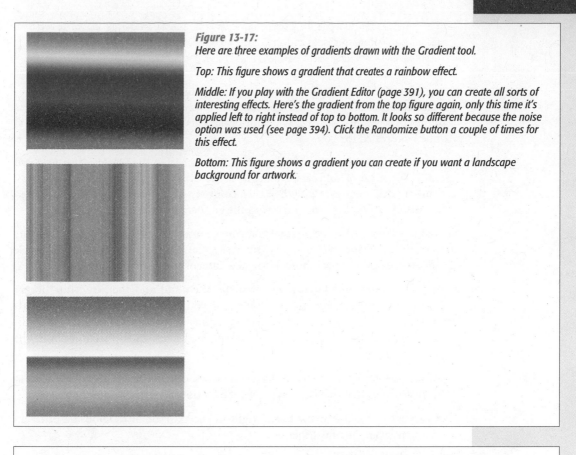

Figure 13-17:
Here are three examples of gradients drawn with the Gradient tool.

Top: This figure shows a gradient that creates a rainbow effect.

Middle: If you play with the Gradient Editor (page 391), you can create all sorts of interesting effects. Here's the gradient from the top figure again, only this time it's applied left to right instead of top to bottom. It looks so different because the noise option was used (see page 394). Click the Randomize button a couple of times for this effect.

Bottom: This figure shows a gradient you can create if you want a landscape background for artwork.

Figure 13-18:
The Gradient tool's Options bar gives you lots of choices for customizing how you apply your gradient.

Make changes to the gradient · Choose the blend mode · Make the gradient flow in the other direction · Turn on if you want to make transparency visible

Choose your gradient here · Pattern for applying the gradient · Choose the opacity level · Turn on smooth color blending

Using the Gradient tool is as easy as dragging. Click where you want the gradient to begin, and then drag to the point where you want it to stop (you'll see a line connecting your beginning and ending points). When you release the mouse, the gradient covers the entire available space.

For example, say you're using a yellow-to-white gradient. If you click to end the gradient one-third of the way into your photo, the yellow stops transitioning at that point, but the remaining two-thirds of your photo is covered with white. Drag the gradient within a selection if you want to confine the area it covers (see Chapter 5 if you need a refresher on making selections).

TIP   The Gradient tool puts the gradient on the same layer as the image you apply it to, which means that it's hard to change anything about your gradient after it's applied. If you think you might want to alter your gradient, use the Gradient Fill layer, described later.

Some of the gradients available in Elements use your chosen foreground and background colors as the two colors that generate the gradient. But Elements also offers a number of preset gradients, which are gradients in different color schemes that Adobe has created for you.

Click the arrow to the right of the gradient thumbnail in the Options bar, and you see a little palette of different gradients, some of which use your selected colors, and others that are preset with their own color schemes. The gradients are grouped into categories; you can work only with the gradients in one category at a time.

In the upper-right corner of the gradient thumbnails pop-out menu, click the arrows to see all the available gradient categories. Choose one, and the available gradients change to reflect those in the new category.

You can also download gradients from the Web and add them to your library using the Preset Manager (see page 496), or you can create your own gradients from scratch. (See page 495 for some suggestions of where to look for new gradients.) Creating and editing gradients is explained later, in the section about the Gradient Editor.

You can customize your gradient in several ways, even without using the Gradient Editor. When the Gradient tool is active, the Options bar offers several choices:

- **Gradient**. Click the arrow to the right of the thumbnail to choose a different gradient from the one displayed.

- **Edit**. Click this button to bring up the Gradient Editor (explained starting on page 391).

- **Gradient types**. Use this setting to determine the way the colors flow in your gradient. Click a thumbnail to choose how to apply the gradient. From left to right, your choices are: Linear (in a straight line), Radial (a sunburst effect), Angle (a counterclockwise sweep around the starting point), Reflected (from the center out to each edge in a mirror image), and Diamond. Figure 13-19 shows what each one looks like.

- **Mode**. You can apply a gradient in any blend mode (see page 164).

- **Opacity**. If you want your image to be visible through the gradient, then reduce the opacity here.

- **Reverse**. This setting changes the direction in which the colors are applied so that instead of yellow to blue from left to right, you get blue to yellow, for instance.

- **Dither**. Turning on this checkbox uses fewer colors but simulates the full color range using a noise pattern. It can help to prevent banding of your colors, making smoother transitions between them.

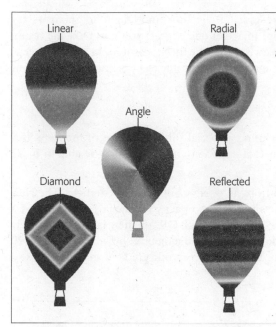

Linear
Radial
Angle
Diamond
Reflected

Figure 13-19:
The same gradient pattern applied using the different gradient types: Linear, Radial, Angle, Diamond, and Reflected.

- **Transparency.** If you want to shade to transparency anywhere in your gradient, then turn Transparency on. Otherwise, the gradient can't show transparent regions.

Using the Gradient tool

To apply a gradient with the Gradient tool, first make a selection if you don't want to see the gradient in your whole image. Then:

1. **Choose the colors you want to use for your gradient.**

   Click the Foreground/Background color squares (page 208) to choose colors. (Some gradient choices ignore these colors and use their own preset colors instead.)

2. **Activate the Gradient tool.**

   Click it in the Toolbox or press G.

3. **Select a gradient.**

   Go to the Options bar, click the Gradient thumbnail, and then choose the gradient style you want. Then make any other necessary changes to the Options bar settings, like reversing the gradient.

4. **Apply your gradient.**

   Drag in your image from the starting point to the ending point, marking where the gradient should run. If you're using a linear gradient, then you can make the gradient run vertically by dragging up or down. Or you can make it go left to right by dragging sideways. For Radial, Reflection, and Diamond gradients, try dragging from the center of your image to one edge. If you don't like the result, press Ctrl+Z to undo it. Once you like the way the gradient looks in your image, you don't need to do anything special to accept it, except of course to save your image before you close it.

Gradient Fill Layer

You can also apply your gradient using a special fill layer. Most of the time, this choice is better than the Gradient tool, especially if you want to be able to make changes to your gradient later on.

To create a Gradient Fill layer, go to Layer → New Fill Layer → Gradient. The New Layer dialog box appears, which lets you set the opacity for the layer, and choose a blend mode (page 164), if you like. Once you click OK, the new layer immediately fills with the currently selected gradient, and the dialog box shown in Figure 13-20 pops up. You can change many of the settings for your gradient here or choose a different gradient.

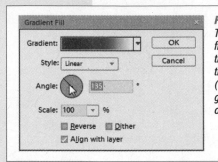

Figure 13-20:
The Gradient Fill dialog box gives you access to most of the same settings you find in the Options bar for the Gradient tool. The major difference is that in the fill layer, you set the direction of your gradient by typing in a number for the angle or by changing the direction of the line in the circle as shown here (the cursor is right on the line that you drag to change the angle). You don't get a chance to set the direction by dragging directly in your image, as you do with the Gradient tool.

The settings in the Gradient Fill dialog box are pretty much the same as those in the Options bar for the Gradient tool:

- **Gradient.** To choose a different gradient, click the arrow next to the thumbnail for the Gradient palette. To choose from a different gradient category, click the arrow on the palette, and then choose the category you want.

- **Style.** You get the same choices you do for the tool (for example, Linear, Diamond, and so on). In this case, you see only the name of the style. Choose a different style and it previews in the layer itself.

- **Angle.** This setting controls the direction the colors will run. Enter a number in degrees or spin the line in the circle by moving it with your mouse to change the direction of the flow.

- **Scale.** This setting determines how large your gradient is relative to the layer. 100 percent means they're the same size. If you choose 150 percent, then the gradient exceeds the size of your layer, which means you see only a portion of the gradient in the layer. For example, if you had a black-to-white gradient, you'd see only shades of gray in your image. If you turn off "Align with layer", you can adjust the location of the gradient relative to your image. Just drag the gradient in your image.

- **Reverse**. Turn Reverse on to make colors flow in the opposite direction.

- **Dither**. Use this setting to avoid banding, and create smooth color transitions.

- **Align with Layer**. This setting keeps the gradient in line with the layer. Turn it off, and you can pull the gradient around in your image to place it exactly where you want it.

When you've gotten the gradient looking the way you like, click OK to create your layer. You can edit it later in the Layers palette by double-clicking the left icon for the layer.

Editing a Gradient

The Elements Gradient Editor lets you create gradients that include any color combination you like. You can even make gradients in which the color fades to transparency, or you can modify existing gradients. For instance, you can easily make a two-color gradient where the fade is very one-sided, if you want a large plain area where you can put text (the plain area helps keep the text readable).

The Gradient Editor isn't the easiest tool in the world to use. This section will give you the basics you need to get started. Then, as happens so often with Elements features, a little bit of playing around with the Gradient Editor will help you understand how it works.

The Gradient tool must be active to launch the Gradient Editor. In the Options bar, click the Edit button to see the Gradient Editor (see Figure 13-21).

The Gradient Editor opens showing the currently selected gradient. You can choose a different gradient by picking from the thumbnails at the top of the Gradient Editor window, or by clicking the More button to the right, and then choosing a new category from the list. You'll learn how to save your gradients later in this chapter.

Using the Gradient Editor

To get started using the Gradient Editor, first choose your gradient's type and smoothness settings:

- **Gradient Type**. Your choices are Solid or Noise. Solid gradients are the most common; they let you create transitions between solid blocks of color. Noise gradients, which are covered later in this section, produce bands of color, as you might see in a spectrometer.

- **Smoothness**. This setting controls how even the transition appears between colors.

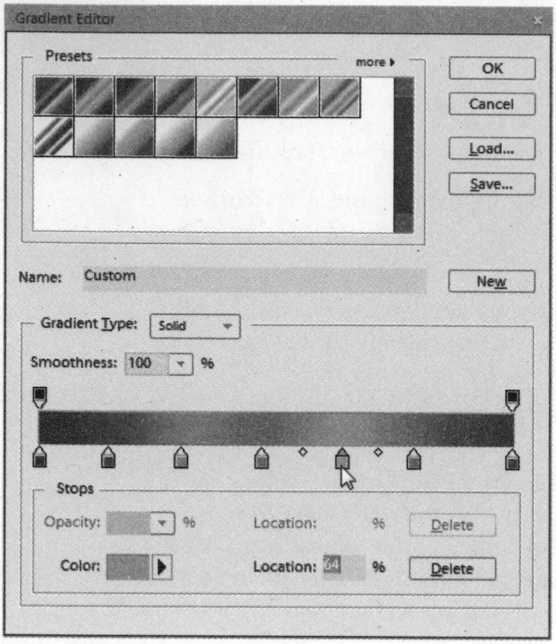

Figure 13-21:
The powerful and complex Gradient Editor. Here, the aqua-colored Stop (where the cursor is) has been clicked to make it active. The colored triangle on the Stop is Elements' way of telling you it's the active Stop. The two tiny diamonds on either side of the active Stop control the location of the midpoint of the transition between the selected color and its neighbors.

Most of the work you do in the Gradient Editor takes place in the *Gradient bar*, the long colored bar where your chosen gradient is displayed. The little boxes (also called *stops*) and diamonds surrounding the Gradient bar let you control the color and transparency of your gradient.

For now, you care only about the stops *beneath* the Gradient bar. Each is a Color Stop; it represents where a particular color falls in the gradient. You always need at least two Color Stops in a gradient.

If you click a stop, then the pointed end becomes colored, letting you know that it's the active stop. Anything you do at this point is going to affect the area governed by that stop. You can slide the stops around to change where the colors transition in your gradients. The Color Stops let you customize your gradient in lots of different ways. Using them, you can:

- **Change where the color transitions.** Click a Color Stop, and you see a tiny diamond appear under the bar. The diamond is the midpoint of the color change. Diamonds always appear between two Color Stops. You can drag the diamond in either direction to skew the color range between two Color Stops so that it more heavily represents one color over another. (You know you've successfully grabbed the diamond when it shows color.) Wherever you place the diamond tells Elements the point at which the color change should be half completed.

- **Change one of the colors in the gradient.** Click any Color Stop, and then click the color square (at the bottom of the Gradient Editor, in the Stops section) to bring up the Color Picker (page 209). Choose a new color, and the gradient automatically alters to reflect your change. You can also pick a new color by moving your cursor over the Gradient bar. The cursor turns to an eyedropper that lets you sample a color from the bar or from anywhere in your image.

- **Add a color to the gradient.** Click a Color Stop, and then click again (not in the bar, but anywhere just beneath it) to indicate where you want the new color to appear. You see a new Color Stop where you clicked. Next, click the color-picking window to choose the color you want to add. The new color appears in the gradient at the new stop. Repeat as many times as you want, adding a new color each time.

- **Remove a color from a gradient.** If a gradient is *almost* what you want but you don't like one of the colors, you don't have to live with it. You can remove a color by clicking its stop to make it the active color. Then click the Delete button to remove that color, or just drag its stop downward off the bar. The Delete button is grayed out if no Color Stop is active.

Transparency in gradients

You can also use the Gradient Editor to adjust the transparency in a gradient. Elements gives you nearly unlimited control over the transparency in your gradients, and the opacity of any color at any point in the gradient. Adjusting opacity in the Gradient Editor works very much like using the Color Stops to edit the colors. Instead of Color Stops, you use Opacity Stops.

> **TIP** Transparency is particularly nice in images for Web use, but remember that you need to save in a format that preserves transparency, like GIF, or you lose the transparency. If you save your file as a JPEG, the transparent areas become opaque white. See page 451 for more about file formats for the Web.

The Opacity Stops are the little boxes *above* the Gradient bar. You can move an Opacity Stop to wherever you want, and then adjust the transparency by using the settings in the Gradient Editor's Stops section. Click the Gradient bar wherever you want to add more Opacity Stops (click above the Gradient bar, rather than in it). The more Opacity Stops your Gradient bar has, the more points you have at which you can adjust your gradient's opacity.

Here's how to add an Opacity Stop, and then adjust its opacity setting:

1. **Click one of the existing Opacity Stops.**

   If the little square on the stop is black, it means the stop is completely opaque. A white square is totally transparent. The new stop has the same opacity as the stop you click, but you can adjust the new stop once you've created it.

---

2. **Add a stop.**

   Click anywhere along the Gradient bar where you want to add a stop. If you want your gradient to be precisely positioned, then you can enter numbers (indicating percentage) in the Location box below the gradient bar. For example, 50 percent positions a stop at the midpoint of the Gradient bar.

3. **Adjust the new stop's opacity.**

   Go to the Opacity box below the Gradient bar, either enter a percentage or click the arrow to the right of the number, and then move the slider to change the opacity setting. If you want to get rid of a stop, click its tab, and then press Delete, or drag it upward away from the bar.

By adding stops, you can make your gradient fade in and out, as shown in the background of Figure 13-22, which shows a simple vertical blue to transparent linear gradient that's been edited so that it fades in and out a few times.

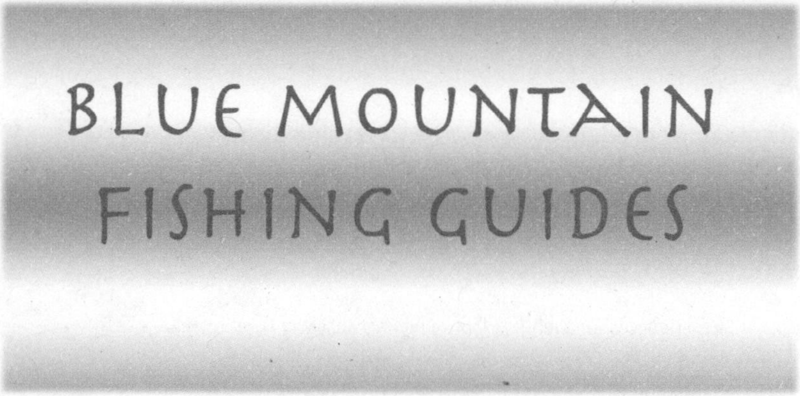

Figure 13-22:
You can make a gradient fade in and out like this background by adding more Opacity stops and reducing the opacity level of each stop.

Creating noise gradients

Elements also lets you create what Adobe calls *noise gradients*. A noise gradient isn't speckled (as you might expect if you're thinking of camera noise). Instead, noise gradients randomly distribute their colors within the range you specify, giving a banded or spectrometer-like effect to the gradient. The effect is interesting, but noise gradients can be a bit unpredictable. The noisier a gradient is, the more stripes of the colors you see, and the greater the number of random colors.

You can create a noise gradient by clicking the More button (the arrow at the upper right) on the Options bar gradient pop-out menu, and then, in the pop-out list of categories, selecting Noise Samples. Or you can click the Edit button to bring up the Gradient Editor, and then choose Noise as your Gradient Type.

Noise gradients have some special settings of their own in the Gradient Editor:

• **Roughness** controls how often the gradient transitions (see Figure 13-23).

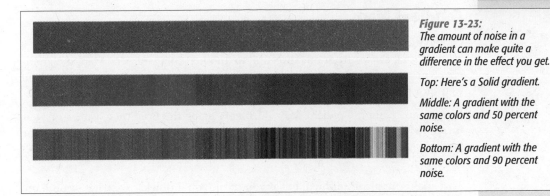

Figure 13-23:
The amount of noise in a gradient can make quite a difference in the effect you get.

Top: Here's a Solid gradient.

Middle: A gradient with the same colors and 50 percent noise.

Bottom: A gradient with the same colors and 90 percent noise.

- **Color Model** determines which color mode you work in—RGB or HSB. RGB gives you red, green, and blue color sliders, while HSB lets you set hue, saturation, and brightness (see page 213 for more information about these settings).

- **Restrict Colors** keeps your colors from getting too saturated.

- **Add Transparency** puts random amounts of transparency into your gradient.

- **Randomize.** Click this button to add random colors (and transparency if you turned on that checkbox). Keep clicking the Randomize button until you see an effect you like.

Saving Gradients

After all that work, you probably want to save your gradient so you can use it again. To save a gradient, you have two options:

- **In the Editor, click the New button.** In the Name box, enter a name for your new gradient. Your gradient gets added to the current category. Elements creates a new preset gradient for you that's now available in the Gradient thumbnails, in the currently visible set of gradients.

   TIP If you forget and click the New button before naming your gradient, or if you just want to change its name, in the Gradient Editor, right-click the thumbnail, and then choose Rename Gradient.

- **Click Save.** The Save dialog box appears, and Elements asks you to name the gradient. You'll save the new gradients in a special Gradients folder, which Elements automatically takes you to in the Save dialog box. When you want to use the gradient again, click Load, and then select it from the list of gradients that appears.

   NOTE You can also save and load gradients from the Options bar Gradient pop-out menu's More menu.

Gradient Maps

Gradient Maps let you use gradients in nonlinear ways. In other words, instead of a rainbow that shades from one direction to another, in a Gradient Map, the gradient colors are substituted for the existing colors in your image. You can use Gradient Maps for funky special effects or for serious photo corrections.

When you create a Gradient Map, Elements maps the brightness values of your image to a gradient (light to dark), and then replace the existing colors with the gradient you choose, using the lightness values as a guide for which color goes where.

That may sound complicated, but if you try it, you'll quickly see what's going on. Take a look at Figure 13-24, for instance. Applying a Gradient Map dramatically livens up this really dull photo, but that's not all Gradient Maps are good for. Gradients and Gradient Maps can also be valuable tools for straight retouching. See the box on page 398 for how to use gradients to fix the color in your photo.

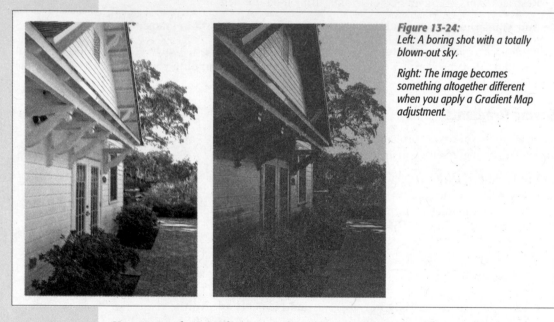

Figure 13-24:
Left: A boring shot with a totally blown-out sky.

Right: The image becomes something altogether different when you apply a Gradient Map adjustment.

You can apply a Gradient Map directly to your image by going to Filter → Adjustments → Gradient Map. (You can also apply a Gradient Map with the Smart Brush [page 189]. In the Smart Paint setting, choose Special Effects → Rainbow Map.) But most times, for maximum control you'll want to use a Gradient Map Adjustment layer, because it's easier to edit after you've created the layer. Here's how:

1. **Create a Gradient Map Adjustment layer.**

   Go to Layer → New Adjustment Layer → Gradient Map. You see the dialog box shown in Figure 13-25.

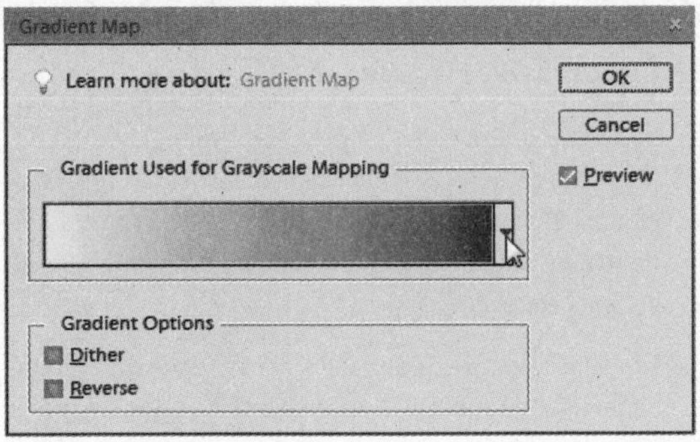

Figure 13-25:
The Gradient Map Adjustment layer dialog box. Clicking the tiny arrow at the right of the thumbnail (where the cursor is in the figure) gives you a drop-down menu showing the available gradient patterns. Click in the pattern preview area to bring up the Gradient Editor (page 391) if you want to make changes to the gradient you've chosen.

2. **Choose a gradient.**

   In the dialog box, you see a gradient. The gradient color is based on your current Foreground/Background colors (see page 208). That's the map of the lightness/darkness values that Elements has made for your image. If you want your image to show color, then you need to choose a color gradient. At the right of the Gradient bar, click the arrow, and then choose a color gradient.

   The Dither setting adds a little random noise to make smoother transitions. The Reverse setting switches the direction the gradient is applied to the map. For example, if you chose a red-to-green gradient, then reversing it would put green where it would have previously put red, and vice versa. It's worth giving this setting a try—you can get some very interesting effects.

3. **Click OK when you're satisfied with the result.**

   Elements automatically replaces the colors in your image with the equivalent values from the gradient you chose.

Remember, too, that you don't have to use your gradient in Normal mode. You can use any blend mode (page 164). You can spend hours playing around with the different effects you can get with the Gradient Map. Other filters and adjustments can produce unexpected results when used with it.

> **TIP**   Try Equalizing your image (Filter → Adjustments → Equalize) after applying a Gradient Map adjustment. The colors can shift quite dramatically. Equalize is a good thing to try if you find that your Gradient Map makes your image look dull or dingy. However, you may need to merge the layers (page 173) to get this command to work, since you can't equalize an Adjustment layer. (See page 280 for more about the Equalize command.)

Using Gradients for Color Correction

If your only interest in Elements is enhancing and correcting your photos, then you may think that all this gradient business is big waste of time. But keep in mind that gradients and Gradient Maps aren't just for introducing lurid colors into your photos. They're powerful tools to help you correct your photographs.

For instance, say you've got a photo where one side is much darker than the other. You may want to apply an Adjustment layer so it affects only the dark side of the image. You can do this trick by bringing up the layer mask of the Adjustment layer (see page 293), and then applying your gradient directly to the mask.

You can also use Gradient Map Adjustment layers in different blend modes to help balance out the colors in your photos, although you may need to use the Gradient Editor to play with the distribution of light and dark values to get the best effect.

Gradient maps are also useful for colorizing skin in black-and-white photos. Set up a gradient based on three or more skin tones, and you can get a more realistic distribution of color tones than you could get by painting.

CHAPTER 14

Type in Elements

If you want to add text to your images, Elements makes it easy. You can quickly create all kinds of fancy text to use on greeting cards, as newsletter headlines, or as graphics for Web pages.

Elements gives you lots of ways to jazz up your text: you can apply Layer styles, Effects, and gradients, or you can warp your type into psychedelic shapes. And the Type Mask tools let you fill individual letters with the contents of a photo. Best of all, most type tools let you change your text with just a few button clicks (see Figure 14-1). By the time you finish this chapter, you'll have learned about all the ways that Elements can add pizzazz to your text.

Adding Type to an Image

It's a cinch to add text to an image in Elements. Just select the Type tool, choose your font from the Options bar, and type away. The Type tool has a Toolbox icon that's easy to recognize: a capital T. Elements actually gives you four different type tools, all of which are hidden behind the Toolbox icon's pop-out menu: the Horizontal Type tool, the Vertical Type tool, the Horizontal Type Mask, and the Vertical Type Mask.

You'll learn about the Type Mask tools later in this chapter (see page 414). To get started, you'll focus on the regular Horizontal and Vertical Type tools. As their names imply, the Horizontal Type tool lets you enter type that runs left to right, while the Vertical Type tool is for creating type that runs down the page.

When you use the Type tools, Elements automatically puts your text on its own layer, which makes it easy to throw out that text and start over again later.

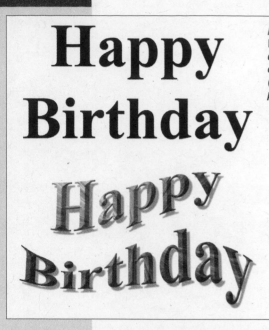

Figure 14-1:
With Elements, you can take basic type and turn it into the kind of snazzy headlines you see on greeting cards and magazine covers. It took only a couple of clicks—a couple of Layer styles (Angled Spectrum and a bevel) and some warping—to turn the plain black type (top) into an extravaganza (bottom).

TROUBLESHOOTING MOMENT

Why Does the Type Tool Turn My Photo Red?

If your image gets covered with an ugly orange-red film every time you click it with the Type tool, you've got one of the Type Masks turned on. (Type Masks, covered later in this chapter, are useful when you want to create text that's cut from an image.)

To switch over to the regular Type tools, click the Type tool icon in the Elements Toolbox. Use the pop-out menu to select either of the regular Type tools (horizontal or vertical).

Type Options

Whether you select the Horizontal or Vertical Type tool, the first thing you're going to want to do is take a look at the many settings available in the Options bar (Figure 14-2). These choices let you control pretty much every aspect of your type, including font selection, font color, and alignment.

Your choices from left to right are:

- **Font Family.** Choose your font, listed here by name. Elements uses the fonts installed on your computer.

  TIP The font menu displays the word "Sample" in the actual fonts to make it easier for you to find the one you want. To see all your fonts, in the Options bar, click the down arrow to the right of the font name box for a pop-out menu. You can also adjust the size of the preview samples by going to Edit → Preferences → Type.

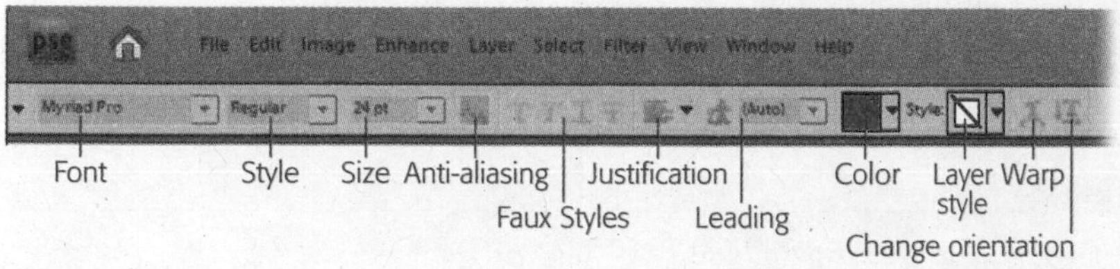

Figure 14-2:
The Type Options bar lets you control lots of different settings, most of which are pretty standard, like the font you want to use and the size of the letters. The choices toward the right end—like Warp and Layer style—are where the fun begins.

- **Font Style.** Here's where you select the styles available for your font, like Bold or Italic.

- **Size.** This is where you choose how big your type should be. Text is traditionally measured in *points*. You can choose from the list of preset sizes in the pull-down menu or just type in the size you want. You aren't limited to the sizes shown in the menu—you can type in any number you want. See the box on page 406 for help understanding the relationship between points and actual size in Elements.

  If points make you nervous, you can change the type measurement unit to millimeters, pixels, or points in Edit → Preferences → "Units and Rulers".

- **Anti-aliasing.** This setting smoothes the edges of your type. Turn it on or off by clicking the little square with the two As on it. Anti-aliasing is explained later, but usually you want it turned on.

- **Faux Styles.** Faux as in "fake." If your chosen font doesn't have a Bold, Italic, Underline, or Strikethrough version, you can tell Elements to simulate it here by clicking the appropriate icon. (This option isn't available for some fonts.)

- **Justification.** This pull-down menu tells Elements how to align your text, just like in a word processor. If you enter multiple lines of type, here's where you tell Elements whether you want it lined up left, right, or centered (for horizontal type). If you select the Vertical Type tool, you can align top, bottom, or middle.

NOTE If you choose the Vertical Type tool, your columns of type run from right to left (each time you start a new column) instead of left to right. If you want vertical type columns to run left to right, you need to put each column on its own layer and position them manually. You can use the Move tool's Distribute option to space them evenly (page 169).

- **Leading** (rhymes with "bedding"). This setting controls the amount of spacing between the lines of type, measured in points. For horizontal type, leading is the difference between the baselines (the bottom of the letters) on each line. For vertical type, leading is the distance from the center of one column to the center of the column next to it. Figure 14-3 demonstrates what a difference leading can make in the appearance of your text. The first setting you'll always see is Auto, which is Elements' guess about what looks best. You can change leading by choosing a number from the list or entering the amount you want (in points, unless you changed the measurement unit in the preferences).

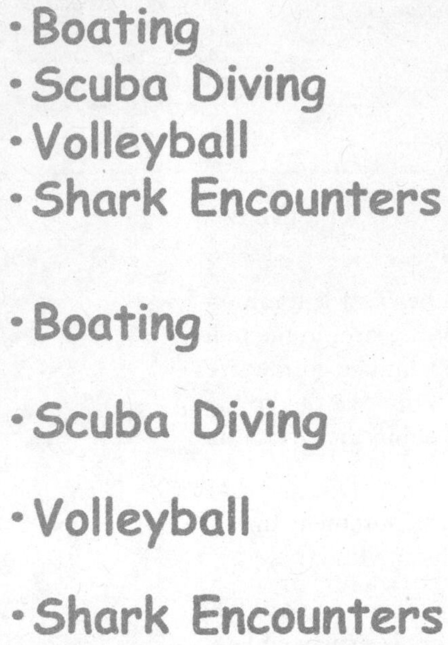

- Boating
- Scuba Diving
- Volleyball
- Shark Encounters

Figure 14-3:
Leading is the space between lines of type.

Top: A list of four items with Auto leading.

Bottom: The same list with the leading number set much higher. (If you change the leading of vertical type, you change the space between the vertical columns of type, rather than the space between letters in an individual column. See the box on page 408 for how to tighten up the space between letters that are stacked vertically.)

- Boating

- Scuba Diving

- Volleyball

- Shark Encounters

- **Color.** Click this square to set the color of your text. Or click the arrow to the right of the color square to bring up Color Swatches (page 212). When you've made your selection, the Foreground color square (page 208) changes to show the new color.

    NOTE When the Type tool cursor is active in your image, you can't use the keyboard commands to reset Elements' standard colors (black and white) or to switch them. You'll need to click the relevant buttons in the Toolbox instead. (See page 208 for how to use the Toolbox's color picking squares.)

- **Layer style.** You can add funky visual effects to your type with Layer styles (page 382). First, enter some text and then, on the Options bar, click the Commit button (the green checkmark). Next, click the Layer style box and choose a style from the pop-out palette. If you want to remove a style that you've just applied, choose Remove Style from the More button's menu (the double arrows on the upper-right corner of the Layers palette), or go to Layer → Layer Style → Clear Layer Style.

The next two choices are grayed out until you create some text for them to work on:

- **Warp.** The little T over a curved line hides a multitude of options for distorting your type in lots of interesting ways. There's more about this option on page 407. (The Warp Text command is also available from Layer → Type → Warp Text.)

- **Orientation.** This button changes your text from horizontal to vertical, or vice versa. You can also change type orientation by going to Layer → Type → Horizontal or Vertical.

These two choices don't show up at all until you've typed something:

- **Cancel.** When you add type to your image, the text automatically gets placed on its own layer. Click the Cancel button to delete this newly created text layer. This button works only if you click it before you click the Commit checkmark. To delete text after you've committed it, drag its layer to the Trash in the Layers palette.

- **Commit.** Click this green checkmark after you type on your image to tell Elements that yes, you want the text to remain as it appears. Committing your type gives you access to the other tools again.

If you see either of these buttons, you haven't committed your type, and many menu selections and other tools won't be available until you do. When you see the Cancel and Commit buttons in the Options bar, you're in what Elements calls "Edit mode", where you can make changes to your type, but most of the rest of Elements isn't available to you. Just click Commit or Cancel to get the rest of the program options back.

Creating Text

Now that you're familiar with the choices you've got in the Options bar, you're ready to start adding text to your image. You can add type to an existing image, or start by creating a new file (if you want to create type to use as a graphic by itself). To use either the Horizontal or Vertical Type tools, just follow these steps:

1. **Activate the Type tool.**

   Click the tool in the Toolbox or press T, and then select the Horizontal Type tool or the Vertical Type tool from the pop-out menu.

2. **Modify any settings you want to change on the Options bar.**

   See the list in the previous section for a rundown of your choices. You can make changes after you enter your type, too, so your choices aren't set in stone yet. Elements lets you edit your type until you simplify the layer. (See page 355 for more about what simplifying a layer means.)

3. **Enter your text.**

   Click in your image where you'd like your text to go and then begin typing. The Type tools automatically create a new layer for your text. If you're using the

Horizontal Type tool, the horizontal line you see is the baseline your letters sit on. If you're typing vertically, the vertical part of the cursor is the centerline of your character.

Type the way you would in a word processor, using the Enter key to create a new line. If you want Elements to *wrap* your type (adjust it to fit a given space), drag a text box with the Type tool before you start typing. Otherwise, you need to make your returns manually. If you create a text box, you can resize it to adjust the type flow by dragging the handles after you finish typing. This won't work anymore after you simplify the layer.

As noted earlier, if you want to use the Vertical Type tool, you can't make the columns of type run left to right. If you need multiple vertical columns of English language text, enter one column and then click the Commit button. Then start over again for the next column, so that each column is on its own layer.

4. **Move your text if you don't like where it's positioned.**

Sometimes the text isn't placed exactly where you want it. You can move text with the Text tool before committing it—just grab the little black square at the beginning of the baseline and drag. If you have trouble moving your text, try the Move tool, but note that switching to the Move tool automatically commits your text (see step 5). If you need to move vertical type columns, wait until you've committed the type to rearrange the columns.

5. **If you like what you see, click the checkmark in the Options bar to commit the type.**

When you commit your type, you tell Elements that you accept what you've created. The Type tool cursor is no longer active in your photo once you commit. If, on the other hand, you don't like what you typed, click the Cancel button in the Options bar, and the whole type layer goes away.

Once you've entered type, you can modify it using most of Elements editing tools—add Layer styles (page 382), move it with the Move tool (page 148), rotate it, make color adjustments, and so on.

> **NOTE** If you try to paste text into Elements by copying it from your word processor, the results are unpredictable. Sometimes things work fine, but you may find the text comes in as one endlessly long line of words. If that happens, it's often easier to type your text in Elements from scratch than to try to reformat the text.

Editing Type

In Elements, you can change your text after you've entered it, just like in a word processor. Elements lets you change not only words, but the font and its size, too, even if you've applied lots of Layer styles (see Figure 14-4). You modify text by highlighting it and making the correction or changing your settings in the Options bar.

TIP   As mentioned earlier, you can see the word "Sample" in the menu displayed in the actual fonts themselves. Even better, Elements also gives you a quick way to preview what your actual text will look like in other fonts. First, select the text, and then click in the Font box in the Options bar. Use the up and down arrow keys to run down the font list. You'll see your words appear in each font as you go down the list.

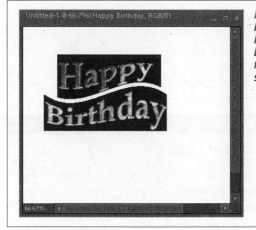

Figure 14-4:
If you change your mind about what you want to say, no problem. Here, the text is highlighted so that the words can be changed. The best part is that you can change the text to say anything, and all the formatting stays exactly the same. You can't do this after you simplify a type layer, though.

You can make all these changes as long as you don't *simplify* your type. Simplifying is the process of changing text from a vector shape that's easy to edit to a rasterized graphic (see the box on page 355). In this respect, text works just like the shapes you learned about in Chapter 12: Once you simplify text, Elements doesn't see it as text anymore, just as a bunch of regular pixels.

You can either choose to simplify text yourself (by selecting Layer → Simplify Layer), or wait for Elements to prompt you to simplify, which it will do when you try to do things like apply a filter or add an effect to your type.

NOTE   While the text effects included with Elements don't simplify your text, it's possible that effects you download may automatically simplify your text without asking first. So it's a good idea to make sure you've made all the edits you want to your text before using these effects.

Smoothing type: anti-aliasing

Anti-aliasing smoothes the edges of your type. It gets rid of the "jaggies" by blending the edge pixels on letters to make the outline look even, as shown in Figure 14-5. In Chapter 5 (page 135), you read about anti-aliasing for graphics; anti-aliasing has a similar effect on type.

Elements always starts you off with anti-aliasing turned on, and 99 percent of the time you'll want to keep it on. The main reason to turn it off is to avoid *fringing*—a line of unwanted pixels that make it look like the text was cut out from an image with a colored background.

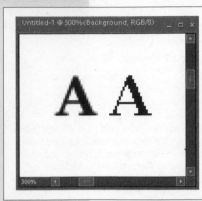

Figure 14-5:
An extremely close look at the same letter with and without anti-aliasing. The left letter A has anti-aliasing turned on, making the edges smooth (well, smoother). If you look at the letter A on the right, you can see how the edges are much more jagged and rough looking.

TROUBLESHOOTING MOMENT

How Resolution Affects Font Size

It's easy enough to pick the font size in the Text tool's Options bar. But you may find that what you thought would be big, bold, headline-size type is so tiny on your image that you can hardly see it. What gives?

In Elements, the actual size of text in your image is tied to the resolution of your image. So, if you thought that choosing 72-point type would give you a headline that's an inch high, it will, but only if the *resolution* of your file is also 72 pixels per inch (ppi). The more you increase the resolution, the smaller that same type is going to be. If you double the resolution to 144 ppi, your 72-point text prints half an inch high. If you triple it to 216 ppi, it's one-third of an inch high.

If you're working with high-resolution images, you have to increase the size of your fonts to allow for the extra pixel packing that comes from increased resolution.

It's not uncommon to have to choose sizes that are much higher than anything listed in the size menu in the Options bar. Don't be afraid of really big sizes if you need them—just keep entering larger numbers in the size box until the text looks right in proportion to your image.

Another thing that sometimes causes confusion is that Elements is creating the type based on the actual size of your image, not the view size. People often try to put very small type on a very big image and wonder why it looks so bad. If you aren't sure about the actual size of your document, try going to View → Print Size before typing. This view offers only an approximation, but it helps you get a better idea of what your text will look like.

You turn anti-aliasing on and off by clicking the Anti-aliasing button (the two As) in the Options bar. The button shows a dark outline when anti-aliasing is on. You can also turn anti-aliasing off and on by going to Layer → Type → Anti-Alias Off or Anti-Alias On. Once you simplify type, you can't change the anti-aliasing setting for the type.

> **TIP** If you're seeing really jagged type even with anti-aliasing turned on, check your resolution. Type often looks poor at low resolution settings—just as photos do. See page 89 for more about resolution.

Warping Type

With Elements, you can warp the shape of your type in all sorts of fun ways. You can make it wave like a flag, bulge out, twist like a fish, arc up or down, and lots more. These complex effects are really easy, too, and best of all, you can still edit the type once you've applied the effects. Figure 14-6 shows just a few examples of what you can do. If you add a Layer style (explained on page 382), warping is even more effective.

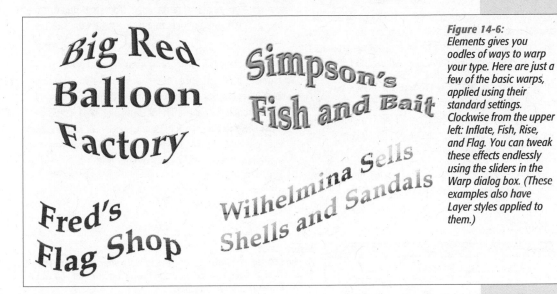

Figure 14-6:
Elements gives you oodles of ways to warp your type. Here are just a few of the basic warps, applied using their standard settings. Clockwise from the upper left: Inflate, Fish, Rise, and Flag. You can tweak these effects endlessly using the sliders in the Warp dialog box. (These examples also have Layer styles applied to them.)

To warp your type, follow these steps:

1. **Enter the text you want.**

   Use the Move tool (page 148) to reposition your text if necessary.

2. **Select the text you want to warp.**

   Make sure the Text layer is the active layer, or you won't be able to select what you typed. Click the Text layer in the Layers palette if it's not already highlighted there.

3. **Click the Create Warped Text button in the Options bar.**

   The Type tool must be active for the Warped Text button to appear. It's the T with a curved line under it. The Warp Text dialog box, shown in Figure 14-7, appears.

4. **Tell Elements how to warp your text.**

   Select a warp style from the pull-down list. Next, make any changes you want to the sliders or the horizontal/vertical orientation of the warp. Tweaking these settings can radically alter the effect. Push the sliders around to experiment.

Using Asian Text Options to Control Text Spacing

Getting letters spaced correctly when using the Vertical Type tool can be tough. Elements lets you set the *leading*, but with vertical type, your leading setting affects the spacing between *columns* of letters, not the spacing of the letters within a column. Also, sometimes you may want to adjust the spacing between letters written in horizontal text. Elements lets you make either of these fixes, but you need to employ a bit of a trick—the program's Asian Text Options—even if you're writing in English.

To get started, go to Edit → Preferences → Type and turn on the checkbox for Show Asian Text Options. Then, the next time you click in an image with the Type tool, you'll see an Asian character in the Options bar, just to the left of the Cancel button.

Click the symbol for a pop-out menu with three options: *Tate-Chuu-Yoko*, *Mojikumi*, and a pull-down menu with

percentages on it. You want the pull-down menu, which is for *Tsume*, which reduces the amount of space around the characters or letters you apply it to.

To apply Tsume, just highlight the characters you want to change and select a percentage from the pull-down menu. The higher the percentage, the tighter the spacing becomes.

You can select a single letter or a whole word when using Tsume. Since it reduces the space all the way around each letter you apply it to, you can use it for either vertical or horizontal text, although for horizontal type, you'd be most likely to use it to tidy up the spacing of just one or two letters. For vertical type, Tsume is a great way to tighten up the vertical spacing of your text.

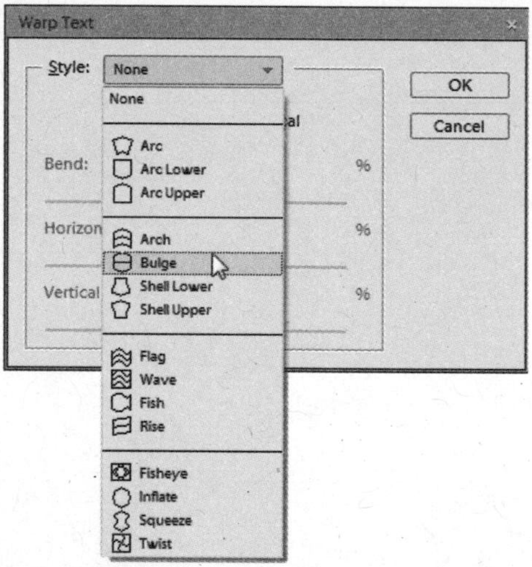

Figure 14-7:
As you can see, you have lots of ways to warp your text. Once you choose a warp style, you see sliders in the dialog box that you can use to further customize the effect.

You can preview the results right in your image. Your choices are described in more detail in the next section.

5. **When you come up with something you like, click OK.**

NOTE   You can't warp type that has the Faux Bold style applied to it. If you forget and try to do so, Elements politely reminds you. The program even offers to remove the style and continue with your warp.

Elements gives you lots of different warp styles to choose from, and you can customize the look of each style by using the settings in the Warp Text dialog box, described in the next section.

The Warp Text Dialog Box

The little dialog box that comes up when you click the Create Warped Text button is pretty straightforward. Your setting choices are:

• **Warp Style.** This is where you choose between warping patterns like Arc, Flag, and so on. To help you select, Elements gives you thumbnail icons demonstrating the general shape of each warp.

• **Horizontal/Vertical.** These radio buttons control the orientation of the warping. Most of the time, you'll want to leave the button the same as the text's orientation, but you can get interesting effects by warping the opposite way.

A vertical warp on horizontal text gives more of a perspective effect, like the text is moving towards you or away from you. You can get some very funky effects by putting a horizontal warp on vertical text.

• **Bend.** This is where you tell Elements how much of an arc you want. If you want to change the arc from Element's standard setting, type a percentage in the box or just move the slider until you get what you want. A higher positive percentage makes a bigger warp. A negative number makes your text warp in the opposite direction. For example, if you want an inverted arc, choose the Arc style and move the slider into the negative region.

• **Horizontal/Vertical Distortion.** These settings control how much your text warps in the horizontal or vertical plane. Moving the sliders gives you a very high degree of control over just how and where your text warps. They work pretty much the same way as the Bend setting—type a negative or positive percentage or move the sliders.

The best way to find the look you want is to experiment. It's lots of fun, especially if you apply a Layer style first (page 382) to give your type a 3-D look before warping it.

TIP   Many of the warps look best on two lines of type, so that the lines bend in opposite directions. However, you can also get very interesting effects by putting two lines of type on separate layers and applying a different warp to each.

To edit your warp after it's done, double-click the Warp thumbnail icon for the text layer in the Layers palette. Doing that automatically makes the text layer active and highlights the text. Then, click the Create Warped Text button in the Options bar. The Warp dialog box opens and shows your current settings. Make any changes you want or set the style to None to get rid of it.

Adding Special Effects

Besides warping your type, you can apply all kinds of Layer styles, filters, and special Text effects to give text a more elaborate appearance. You can change the color of your text, make the letters look 3-D, add brushstrokes for a painted effect, and so on. (There's more about Layer styles, filters, and effects in Chapter 13.)

Elements gives you lots of different ways to add special effects to your text. The following sections demonstrate three of the most interesting: applying the Text effects, using a gradient to make rainbow-colored type, and using the Liquify filter to warp text in truly odd ways.

Text Effects

The Content palette contains an entire category dedicated to special Text effects (Figure 14-8). You apply Text effects just the way you would apply any other effect—make the type layer active and double-click the effect you want.

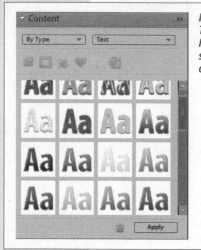

Figure 14-8:
The Content palette includes an entire section for Text effects. Most, like Animal Fur Zebra and Denim, are unique to this section. Others, like Bevel, are just shortcuts for effects you could also achieve using Layer styles, gradients, or other Elements tools.

If you already have Layer styles on your text, it's hard to predict how much the effects will respect the existing Layer styles. Some effects build onto the changes you've previously made with Layer styles; most undo anything you've done before. Experimenting is the best way to find out what happens when you combine Layer styles and effects.

Type Gradients

Gradient palette patterns fill your text with a spectrum of color. The simplest way to get these rainbow effects is to apply one of the Layer styles or Text effects that include a gradient. On the other hand, these features give you no control over the colors or direction of the gradient. If you have a specific look in mind, you may have to start from scratch and do it yourself. The easiest way is to start with a Type Mask, as explained on page 414. But if you already have some existing text, as long as it's not yet simplified, you can easily fill it with a gradient.

> **TIP** A heavier, chunky font shows off your rainbow better than a thin, spidery one. Fonts with names that end in Extended, Black, or Extra Bold are good, like Arial Black or Rockwell Extra Bold.

First, make sure you've got some text in your image, and then follow these steps:

1. **Create a new layer for your gradient. Make sure it's directly above your text layer in the Layers palette.**

   You're going to group the two layers, which is why they need to be next to each other. To create the new layer, press Ctrl+Shift+N or go to Layer → New → Layer. In the New Layer dialog box, turn on "Group with Previous Layer".

   Look at the Layers palette to be sure the new layer is the active layer. If it isn't, give it a click in the Layers palette to highlight it.

2. **Activate the Gradient tool.**

   Click the Gradient tool in the Toolbox and choose a gradient style in the Options bar. (See page 385 for more about how to select, modify, and apply gradients.)

3. **Drag across your new layer in the direction you want the gradient to run.**

   Because the layers are grouped, the gradient appears only in your type. If you don't like the effect, press Ctrl+Z and drag again until you like what you see. That's all you have to do, except of course, save your work if you want to keep it.

> **NOTE** You may have noticed that the new Smart Brush tool (page 189) includes Rainbow Map as one of the adjustments you can brush on to your image. Sounds like it might be just the ticket for avoiding all this layer creation and so on, doesn't it? Unfortunately, it applies a gradient *map* (see page 396), not a regular gradient, to your image. Your type is all the same tonal level, so you'll just get a one-color result on the letters with the Smart Brush Rainbow Map, not a rainbow at all.
>
> However, there are a number of gradients in the Text effects, so you might want to check out the Content Palette before trying the steps above. If you find an effect that's exactly what you want, you'll save yourself some effort.

Applying the Liquify Filter to Type

The Create Warped Text button in the Options bar (explained earlier on page 407) gives you lots of ways to reshape your type. But there's an even more powerful way to warp type: the Liquify filter (see Figure 14-9).

> **NOTE** You can actually use the Liquify filter to warp anything in an image—not just text. Use it to alter objects in photographs and drawings, for example. Fix someone's nose, make your brother look like E.T., give a scene a watery reflection, and so on.

Hot Deals

Hot Deals

Figure 14-9:
The Liquify filter can reshape text in many different ways, including adding a flame-like effect (shown here), making letters twirl around on themselves, or making text undulate like it's underwater.

Top: Text with a bevel Layer style applied.

Bottom: Use the Liquify filter's Warp tool to pull these little "flames" from the text.

To use the Liquify filter, you first need to simplify the layer your text is on (Layer → Simplify Layer, or just click OK when the Liquify filter asks if you want to simplify). (Remember, you can no longer edit your text once you simplify it.) Then, call up the Liquify filter dialog box by going to Filter → Distort → Liquify. You can also get to it by double-clicking the Liquify filter thumbnail in the Distort section of the filters in the Effects palette.

You see yet another large Elements dialog box. Like most of them, it's fairly straightforward once you learn your way around it. In the upper-left corner of the Liquify dialog box is a little toolbox with some very special tools in it (see Figure 14-10).

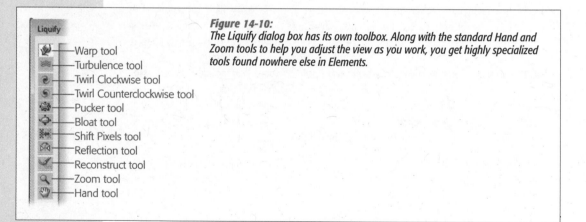

Liquify
— Warp tool
— Turbulence tool
— Twirl Clockwise tool
— Twirl Counterclockwise tool
— Pucker tool
— Bloat tool
— Shift Pixels tool
— Reflection tool
— Reconstruct tool
— Zoom tool
— Hand tool

Figure 14-10:
The Liquify dialog box has its own toolbox. Along with the standard Hand and Zoom tools to help you adjust the view as you work, you get highly specialized tools found nowhere else in Elements.

From top to bottom they are:

- **Warp tool.** This lets you push the pixels of your image in whichever direction you want, although it usually takes a fair amount of coaxing to create much of an effect.

- **Turbulence tool.** You can use the Turbulence tool to create clouds and waves. This tool is dependent on the Turbulent Jitter setting on the right side of the window (explained later). A higher number creates a smoother effect.

- **Twirl Clockwise tool**. Hold this tool down on your image, and the pixels under your cursor spin in a clockwise direction. The longer you apply this tool, the more extreme the spin effect.

- **Twirl Counterclockwise tool**. The opposite of the Twirl Clockwise tool, it makes the pixels under the cursor spin counterclockwise.

- **Pucker tool**. This tool makes the pixels under the cursor move toward the center of the brush.

- **Bloat tool**. The opposite of the Pucker tool, it makes pixels move *away* from the center of the brush.

- **Shift Pixels tool**. The pixels you drag this tool over move perpendicularly in relation to the direction of your stroke. For example, if you drag from the top of an image in a straight line down, the pixels you pass over will move to the right. Alt+drag to change the direction of the shift.

- **Reflection tool**. Drag to create a reflection of the area the tool passes over. Overlapping strokes create a watery effect.

- **Reconstruct tool**. Pass this wonderful tool over areas where you've gone too far, and you selectively return them to their original condition without wrecking the rest of your changes.

- **Zoom and Hand tools**. These are the same Zoom (page 87) and Hand (page 88) tools you find elsewhere in Elements.

Your image appears in the preview window in the center of the dialog box. You can adjust the view with the Zoom tool or by using the magnification menu in the lower-left corner of the image area.

> **TIP** It often helps to zoom in very close when using the Liquify filter. If you've added text to a large image, select the text with the Marquee tool (page 123) before activating the Liquify filter. Then you'll see only the selected area in the filter preview, which makes it easier to get a high zoom level.

At the right side of the dialog box are the Tool Options settings:

- **Brush Size**. You can enter a number as low as 1 pixel or as large as 600 in the space provided.

- **Brush Pressure**. This is how much the brush affects the pixels you drag over. The range is from 1 to 100. The higher the pressure, the stronger the effect of the brush. If you're using a graphics tablet, turn on Stylus Pressure so that the harder you press, the more effect you get.

- **Turbulent Jitter**. This controls how smooth your changes look. The higher the number, the smoother the effect you get from your changes.

- **Stylus Pressure**. Turn this on if you're using a graphics tablet (page 492) and you want the tool to be sensitive to how hard you press.

To use the filter, just pick your tool, modify your Tool Options (if you want), and then drag across your image. This is a very processor-intense filter, so there may be a fair amount of lag time before you see results, especially if your computer's slow. Give the filter time to work.

If you like what you see in the preview, click OK and wait a few seconds while Elements applies your transformations. Then you're done. But if you don't like what you see, you can always have another go at it. Use the Revert button, which returns your image to its original condition before you started using the Liquify filter. Another option is to Alt+click the Cancel button to turn it to a Reset button (which resets the tool settings as well as your image).

Type Masks: Setting an Image in Type

So far in this chapter, you've been reading about how to create regular type and how to glam it up by applying Layer styles and effects. But in Elements, you can also create type by filling letters with the contents of a photo, as shown in Figure 14-11. (You'll find *gourds.jpg*, the photo used as the basis for Figure 14-11 and Figure 14-13, on the Missing CD page at *www.missingmanuals.com*.)

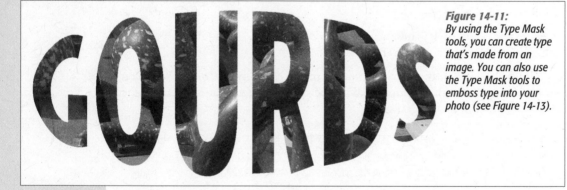

Figure 14-11:
By using the Type Mask tools, you can create type that's made from an image. You can also use the Type Mask tools to emboss type into your photo (see Figure 14-13).

The Type Mask tools work by making a selection in the shape of your letters. Essentially, you're creating a kind of stencil that you'll place on top of your image.

Once you've used the Type Mask to create your text-shaped selections, you can perform all sorts of neat modifications to your text: emboss type into your image (which makes it looks like it's been stamped into your image); apply a stroke to the outline of your text (useful if your font doesn't have a built-in outline option); or copy and move your text to another document entirely.

Using the Type Mask Tools

The following steps show how to create a Type Mask and lay it over an image so that the letters you create are filled with whatever's in your image:

1. **Open the image that you want to use as your source for creating the text.**

2. **Activate the Type Mask tool.**

   Click the Type tool in the Toolbox or press T. Select the Type Mask tool you want—horizontal or vertical. (Use the pop-out menu.) The Type Mask tools behave just like the regular Type tools—a horizontal mask goes across the page, a vertical mask goes up and down. The Type Mask tool has the same Options bar settings as the regular Type tool, except for Color and Style.

3. **Click your image and start typing.**

   When you click, a red film covers your entire image. The red indicates the area that *won't* be part of your letters. By typing, you're going to cut a visible selection through the red area (see Chapter 5 if you need a refresher on selections).

   When you type, instead of creating regular type, you're creating a type-shaped selection. You can see the shape of the selection as you go.

   It's important to choose a very blocky font for the type mask, since you can't see much of the image if you use thin or small type.

   It's hard to reposition your words once you've committed them, so take a good look at what you've got. While the mask is active, you can move the mask by dragging it, as explained in Figure 14-12.

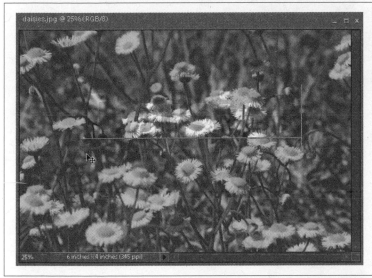

Figure 14-12:
Once you've activated the Type Mask tool and clicked on your image, you'll see a red mask appear over your picture. As you start typing, your text appears, as shown here. To move a selection made with the Type Mask tool, hold down Ctrl, and then you can easily drag your selection around in your image as long as you haven't committed it yet.

4. **Don't click the Commit button until you're satisfied with what you have.**

   Once you click the Commit button (the green checkmark on the right side of the Options bar), you can't alter your type as easily as you can with the regular Type tool. That's because the regular tools create their own layers, while the Type Mask tools just create selections. Once you commit, your type is just like any other selection—Elements doesn't see it as type anymore, so you can no longer change the size by highlighting the text and picking a different size, for example.

5. **When you're happy with your selection, finish by clicking the Commit button.**

   Once you click the Commit button, you see the outline of your type as an active selection. You can move the selection outline by nudging it with the arrow keys.

6. **Remove the non-text portion of your image.**

   Go to Select → Inverse and press Backspace to remove the rest of the image. Or you can copy and paste the selection into another document.

Figure 14-13 shows the effect of pressing Ctrl+J and placing a Type Mask selection on a duplicate layer of its own, and then adding Layer styles (page 382) to the new layer.

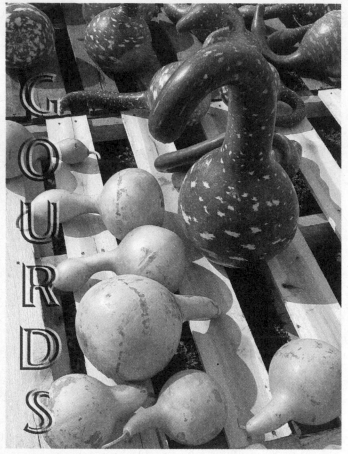

Figure 14-13:
By copying text to another layer, you can bevel or emboss it into your photo. Notice that this photo shows what you need to watch out for—the G is kind of hard to see because it blends right into the image. You may need to place your text a few times before you get it positioned correctly. Or you could also add a colored outline to make it stand out more, as described below.

Creating Outlined Type

If the font you're using doesn't come with a built-in outline style, there are three ways to create outlined type in Elements. The Text Effects in the Content palette (page 410) include an outlined type effect that you can apply with just a double click. If you don't like what you get with that, you can also use the Stroke Layer styles or the Type Mask tools to outline type. Both these methods are easy, but do require a bit more time than using the Content palette. The tradeoff is that you have more control over what you wind up with. Use the Layer styles if you want your text outline to be filled in, since the Type Mask gives you an empty outline.

Using the Stroke Layer style

To add an outline to type:

1. **Open your image or create a new one; then activate the Type tool.**

   Click it in the Toolbox or press T until you get either the Horizontal or Vertical Type tool (not the Type Mask tool).

2. **Choose your Options bar settings.**

   Select the font, size, style, and so on that you want.

3. **Enter the type and commit it.**

   Press Enter or the checkmark in the Options bar.

4. **Apply a Stroke Layer style.**

   Go to the Effects palette → Layer styles → Strokes and double click the one you want. If you don't like any of the Stroke styles, that's okay because you can edit the result in the next step.

5. **Edit the outline if you wish.**

   In the Layers palette, double click the Layer style icon for the text layer to bring up the Layer style editor. This is where you can change the width and color of the stroke (see page 385).

Using the Type Mask tool

To make a text outline like the one shown in Figure 14-14:

1. **Open your image or create a new one (if you just want the type by itself). Activate the Type Mask tool of your choice.**

   Click the Type tool or press T. Then select either of the Type Mask tools.

2. **Choose your font and size.**

   Use the settings in the Options bar. Outlined type works better with a fairly heavy font rather than a slender one. Bold fonts also work well here, rather than regular fonts.

3. **Enter your type.**

Type in your image where you want the text to go. If you want to warp your type, do it now, before you commit the type.

4. **Click the Commit button (the checkmark).**

Be sure you like what you've got before you do, because once you commit the text, it changes to a selection that's hard to edit. If you'd rather start over, click the Cancel button (the "no" symbol) instead.

5. **Add a stroke to your outline.**

Be sure the type selection is active, and then go to Edit → Stroke (Outline) Selection. Choose a line width in pixels and the color you want, and then click OK. (There's more about your choices in the dialog box on page 359.) Your selection is now a linear outline of the text you typed.

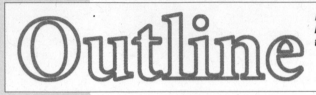

Figure 14-14:
By using the Type Mask tools, you can create outline type almost as quickly as ordinary type.

NOTE   You can also create a hollow outline using the Stroke Layer styles. Just simplify the layer (Layer → Simplify), then select the inside color of the text with the Magic Wand (page 133; be sure to turn off Contiguous). Then delete the selected color. The downside to this approach is that your text is no longer editable once you simplify it.

CHAPTER 15

Creating Projects

If you're into making scrapbooks, greeting cards, and other photo concoctions, Elements is perfect for you. You can dress up your pictures in all sorts of creative ways without using—or buying—any other software. Elements is crammed with add-on graphics, frames, and other special effects; you can even create multipage documents.

This chapter kicks off with an in-depth look at how to create a photo collage. Once you've got those steps under your belt, all the other projects (summarized starting on page 430) use the same basic method. You'll also learn how to create photo books and calendars using Kodak EasyShare, Adobe's online photo-printing partner.

> **NOTE** You can also create online albums (photo-filled Web pages) and slideshows in Elements. Learn all about those projects in Chapter 18.

Photo Collages

The Create tab (in both the Editor and the Organizer) helps you create fancy pages featuring your photos, which you can then share either in print or as digital files. Although Elements gives you lots of preset layouts to start from, you can customize every aspect to create projects that are totally your own.

A Photo Collage is a page displaying one or more of your photos, with or without a themed background. (Flip ahead to Figure 15-3 to get a glimpse of what Elements can help you do.) Elements' *wizards* (a series of guided questions that lead you from start to finish) all begin with one or more suggested photo placeholders, but you can add or remove photos at will. You can also change the background, frame styles, and other details.

TIP Photo Collages, like all the printable projects on the Create menu, start off at a resolution of 220 ppi. That's perfectly fine print quality for most people's taste. But if you want a higher resolution, your best bet is to cook up your own project from scratch, since increasing the resolution of a pre-built Elements project often throws the layout out of whack. (Photo Books are a little different. If you try to print a single, double-paged spread it prints at 72 ppi—in other words, you're likely to get poor results—unless you first save your book as a PDF.)

To create a Photo Collage:

1. **Open some photos in the Editor or select them in the Organizer.**

   This step is optional, but if you preselect photos, Elements can automatically place them into your layout for you, if you like.

2. **Go to Create → Projects → Photo Collage.**

   If you start from the Organizer, Elements bounces you over to the Editor to create your collage. The pane shown in Figure 15-1 appears.

3. **Choose your page size from the Page Size pull-down menu.**

   If you don't like the measurement units listed in the Page Size menu, you can change them. Go to Edit → Preferences → Units & Rulers → Photo Project Units, and change the Photo Project Units setting to inches, centimeters, or whichever system you prefer.

4. **From the "Choose a Theme" section, if you want, select a theme.**

   Themes give you coordinated backgrounds and frames for your photos. (You can always choose a different background later if you don't like the one that comes with the frame, or a new frame to replace the one that comes with the background.) Click once on a theme to select it, and a larger thumbnail appears, giving you a closer look at your choice.

   If you choose a theme and then decide you don't want any theme at all, click the upper-left thumbnail in the list of thumbnails to choose No Theme. If you go theme-less, you just get a blank background, but you can always add backgrounds from the Content palette later.

5. **Choose a Layout style.**

   Scroll through the thumbnails and click the one you like. You can rearrange your layout after you've chosen it: Add more photos, remove photos, rotate the images, and so on. The layouts are arranged from one picture per page at the start of the list, to many pictures at the bottom of the group.

6. **Choose from the Additional Options, if you like.**

   If you leave "Auto-Fill with Project Bin Photos" turned on, the pictures you chose in the Organizer automatically appear in your collage when Elements creates it. If you want to determine which photos go into which slots in the layout yourself, turn off the checkbox.

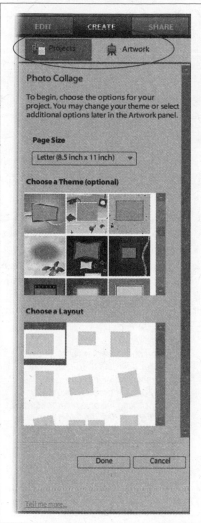

Figure 15-1:
Figure 15-1:
Once you're in the Create pane in the Editor, you have a choice of two tabs (circled). Select and start your project from the Projects tab. Here you see the Photo Collage pane, where you start your collage. Once you've completed your basic layout here, click the Artwork tab to see the Content palette—that's where you can choose frames, graphics and other doodads to add to your project.

There's also a checkbox for having captions you've added to your photos appear in the collage. (You can add text or edit the captions later, so you're not tied to what's in the Caption field.) This checkbox is grayed out if you haven't selected any photos with captions.

If you selected some photos before you started, the "Number of Pages" box tells you how many pages long your creation will be. This number updates to reflect your current Layout choice. So, for example, if you select three photos in the Organizer and choose a single photo per page, the number of pages is three. If you click a layout that uses three photos per page, the number of pages changes to one. (If you haven't selected any photos yet, you can specify how many pages you want by typing in a number.)

7. **When you've made all your choices, click Done.**

Elements gets to work creating your collage. If you preselected photos and left autofill turned on, Elements puts your photos right into the frames for you. Your document will have as many pages as needed to place all your photos in the layout you chose. If you didn't select any photos, you see "Click here to add photo or Drag photo here." That's fine, because you can add photos in the next step.

8. **Adjust your photos.**

If you haven't already picked photos for your project, click a frame and then choose a photo from the dialog box that appears, or drag a photo from the Project bin to a frame.

Regardless of how you get photos into the collage, you can make a number of adjustments to them once they're in. Click once to resize the frame, or double-click any photo and you see the controls shown in Figure 15-2, which let you make a number of different photo tweaks without changing the frame size. Click the green checkmark to apply your changes, or the red Cancel button to get rid of them.

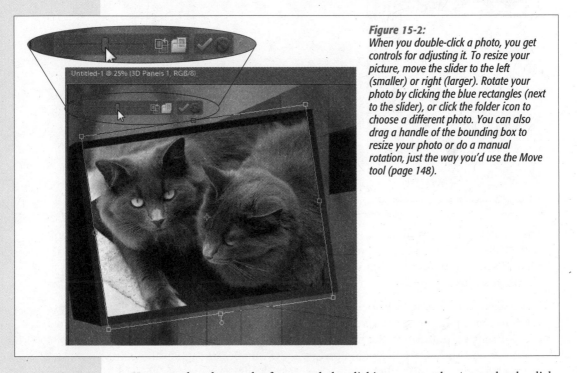

Figure 15-2:
When you double-click a photo, you get controls for adjusting it. To resize your picture, move the slider to the left (smaller) or right (larger). Rotate your photo by clicking the blue rectangles (next to the slider), or click the folder icon to choose a different photo. You can also drag a handle of the bounding box to resize your photo or do a manual rotation, just the way you'd use the Move tool (page 148).

You can also change the frame style by clicking over to the Artwork tab, clicking a photo in your collage, and then choosing a new style from the Content palette (page 427). To change to the new frame, double-click the new style, or drag it to the photo. You can also click it once and then click Apply.

9. **Customize your collage.**

Here's the fun part. Click a photo in your collage and drag it into a different position. Drag in art from the Content palette. These graphics are vector images (page 355), which means they'll look great no matter how big or small you resize them. You can also add text to your collage (find out how to do that in Chapter 14). You can change the background by selecting a new one in the Content palette (page 427). You can even flatten your image and use filters on the entire page. Figure 15-3 shows an example of what you can do with a Photo Collage.

If you click back to the Editor, you can use any tool or filter on your collage, but you may need to simplify a layer (page 355) or flatten your image first, so save that step till you're sure you like your collage. You can use the Move tool to rearrange your collage layers after you simplify them, but once you simplify layers, you can't make their contents larger than 100 percent without losing quality, just like any normal photo.

10. **Save your collage.**

When finished, press Ctrl+S to name your project and save it. You can save it in any standard file format if it's a one-page collage, but if you have more than one page you must save it as a PSE file, which is a special format just for multipage Elements documents.

There's almost no limit to what you can do in a Photo Collage. Anything you've read in the other chapters of this book works here, too. Plus, here are a few special things you can do with photos in a collage:

- **Remove a photo from your collage.** Right-click the photo and then choose Clear Photo. To remove the photo's placeholder and frame as well, choose Clear Frame.

- **Make your photo appear without a frame.** Right-click and then choose Clear Frame.

- **Resize a frame.** You can resize a frame, either before or after you put a photo into it. Click once on the frame to bring up handles, and then drag a corner of the frame to make it larger. You can also rotate a photo using the handles on the frame.

- **Resize the frame to fit the photo.** If you want to make the frame fit the photo, instead of the other way around, right-click the photo and then choose "Fit Frame to Photo".

TIP You can do all of the above in Full Edit, too, once your collage is complete, but you need to activate the Move tool first or you won't see correct options when you right-click.

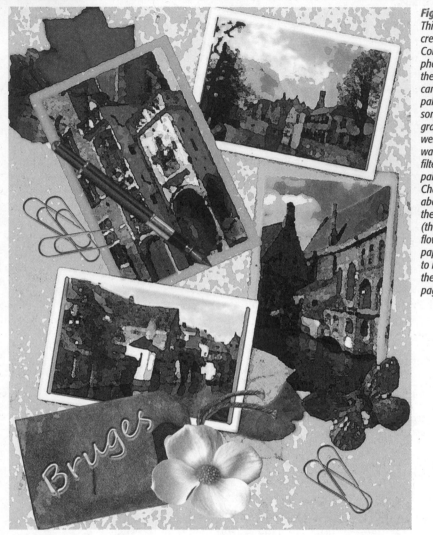

Figure 15-3:
This composition was created as a Photo Collage. Except for the photos themselves, all the additional artwork came from the Content palette. The photos and some of the background graphics (like the leaves) were added first, the file was flattened and several filters applied to give it a painted effect (see Chapter 13 for more about filters), and then the remaining graphics (the pen, the dogwood flower, and the paperclips) were added to make them look like they're lying on a painted page.

- **Add another photo.** Just drag a frame from the Content palette to a blank area in your collage. If you get too close to an existing frame, the new frame may just replace the one on an existing photo. If that happens, just press Ctrl+Z to undo it and drag again, more carefully, to another blank spot. You can also drag a photo into your collage from the Project bin.

- **Change your theme.** If you wish you'd gone with a different theme after you've already created your Photo Collage, go to Content → By Type → Themes for a list of all the Create themes. Double-click a thumbnail or drag the new theme to your photo, or click the thumbnail once and then click Apply. Presto—you've got your existing layout with new frames and background.

- **Edit the Layer style of a Frame.** Click the Edit tab to get back to Full Edit, and in the Layers palette, most of the frames have a Layer style icon. Double-click the icon to edit things like the size of the drop shadow on the frame. (See page 385 for more about editing Layer styles.)

What's more, you can add and delete pages from Photo Collages, as explained in the next section.

> **TIP**   You can apply artwork from the Content palette to any image, not just those in Photo Collages and other Create projects.

Creating Multipage Documents

Elements makes it easy to create a file that's more than one page long. A Photo Collage automatically starts with as many pages as needed to hold all your pre-selected photos, but you can add pages to any of the Create projects anytime—and remove them, too. (You can also add and remove pages from any Elements file, not just the Create projects.)

The size and resolution of your existing page determines the size and resolution of pages you add. In other words, if your current file is just a single 3"×5" photo and you add a page to it, you get a 3"×5" page. If you want to add a letter-size page to a small photo file, you must first add canvas to the photo (page 96) or resize it. (But check page 96 to see why resizing a small photo to letter size probably won't work well.)

POWER USERS' CLINIC

Smart Objects

Smart Objects are one of the ways Adobe makes Elements projects so fun and easy. Like their big-shot cousins in the full version of Photoshop, these objects seem to know where they are and what you're trying to do—and behave accordingly. Here are some of the things that make Smart Objects so smart:

- When you apply a new background from the Content palette, it immediately zooms down to the bottom of the layer stack to replace the existing background, without any assistance from you.

- Similarly, the frames in the Content palette automatically target your photos, but only as long as you're in the Create tab. (Add a frame from the Content palette in the Editor instead of the Artwork pane and you'll find that it's not so smart. It just sits there on top of your photo, if you have one open, waiting for you to help it out by placing a photo inside it, unless you're adding to an existing Create project.)

- You can resize, transform, or distort objects from the graphics section of the Content palette as much as you want without affecting the image quality. This behavior is something like how vector art works, but what's going on under the hood is quite a bit different. (The preview may appear pixelated if you hugely resize a graphic, but the actual object should be okay once you click the green checkmark.)

Anything you drag from the Project bin into your project while you're in the Create pane will behave like a Smart Object (you can resize it to any size, for instance).

By the way, if you've used Photoshop, you'll find that Smart Objects in Elements don't do nearly as many interesting things as they do in the full version of Photoshop. You can't create linked objects, for instance, where painting on one makes your painting appear on all of them. In fact, if you try to paint on a Smart Object in Elements, you just get the dialog box shown in Figure 15-4.

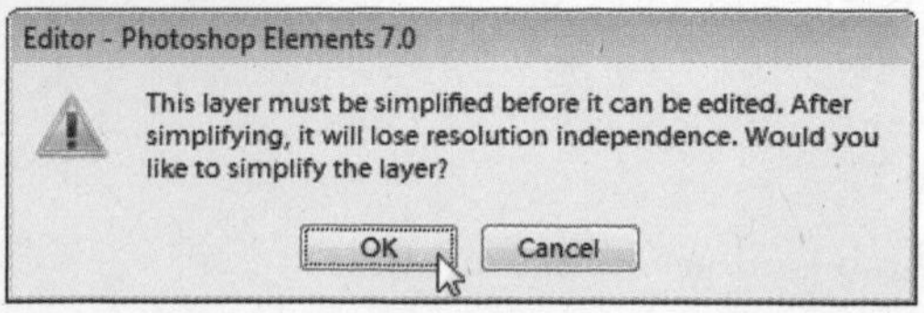

Figure 15-4:
You can enlarge, reduce, transform, and distort Smart Objects, but if you try to paint on them, or to apply filters or effects, you get this message. It's fine to click OK, but once you do, your formerly Smart Object will behave like any other object. (You can't increase its size to more than 100 percent, for instance, or it'll go all pixely on you.)

To add a new page to your document, go to the Editor's Edit menu and choose one of the following commands:

- **Add Blank Page (keyboard shortcut: Alt+Ctrl+G)**. This command creates a new, totally empty page with the same dimensions and resolution as your existing page.

- **Add Page Using Current Layout (shortcut: Alt+Shift+Ctrl+G)**. When you choose this option, Elements creates a page that's exactly like the current state of your existing page, including any changes you've made. Instead of photos, there are placeholders for you to fill in. So, for example, if you've changed frame styles and dragged a photo to another position, the new frame and positioning (without the photo) appears in your new page. Any graphics you've added from the Content palette show up as well. This option is a big help when you're making photo books or scrapbooks.

You can navigate through all the pages in your document using the Project bin, as shown in Figure 15-5. If you decide you've got too many pages, go to Edit → Delete Current Page, and the currently active page is history. You can also do any adding and deleting of pages right from the Project bin by right-clicking and choosing what you want to do from the pop-out menu, a big help when you're editing a multipage project.

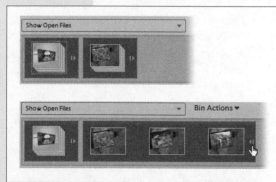

Figure 15-5:
You can expand and collapse the pages of your file so they don't hog all the visible space in the Project bin.

Top: A collapsed Photo Book and a multipage Photo Collage in the project bin. (Note how each type of project reflects the page shape for the project and even shows the project's chosen theme.) Collapsed multipage documents have a special outline in the bin to make them easy to recognize.

Bottom: Here's the expanded thumbnail for the collage, so you can select a single page to edit. Click the arrow again to collapse the thumbnail.

No matter what kind of file you start with—whether it's from the Create projects or just a regular JPEG—you must save your file as a PSE format file if you add pages to it. Elements reminds you with the dialog box in Figure 15-6. While it's very, very nice to be able to create multipage documents in Elements, the PSE format has some drawbacks, too, as explained in the box on page 427.

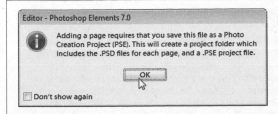

Figure 15-6:
You can't save a document with multiple pages in common file formats like TIFF or PSD. Your only option is PSE, as this dialog box reminds you every time you add a second page to any document. See the box that follows to learn why PSE is mixed blessing.

Working with the Content and Favorites Palettes

Adobe gives you a ton of artistic goodies to use for customizing your projects, and a special palette just to hold it all: the Content palette. You also get a Favorites palette, where you can keep the items you use most often from the Content palette (and from the Effects palette, too).

TROUBLESHOOTING MOMENT

About PSE Files

Anytime you create a multipage document in Elements, you get one file format choice when it's time to save—PSE. This special format has both advantages and disadvantages.

When you create a PSE file, you actually create a folder containing a separate .psd file for each page (for each double-page spread for a Photo Book) and the PSE project file, which contains all the information Elements needs to reassemble your document the next time you open it. That's very handy when you're working in Elements, but the drawback is that hardly any other program can read these files. PSE files work just fine if you

print at home or use Kodak EasyShare Gallery for online printing. You can send PSE files to EasyShare as easily as you send JPEGs.

The rub comes if you want to use a different printing service. If you make, say, a book that you want to print at Lulu.com or MyPublisher.com, there's no way they can work with your PSE file—at least not at this writing. Most printing services require PDF format files. Fortunately, Elements 7 can save your multiple-page PSE file as a multi-page PDF that you can upload to your printing service of choice. (Be aware, though, that Elements creates very large PDF files.)

The Content Palette

This palette holds backgrounds, frames, graphics, shapes, text effects, and themes to use in projects. The Content palette works something like the Effects palette, with menus and a row of little icons for each of its major categories (see Figure 15-7). Here's how it works:

1. **Make the Content palette visible.**

   Go to Create → Artwork. This palette is always visible in the Artwork pane, but you can make it visible in Full Edit, as well, by going to Window → Content. (It still appears in Artwork, even when you make it visible in the Editor. You can't remove it from the Artwork pane, even if you wanted to.)

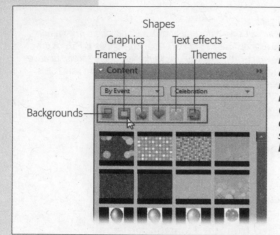

Shapes

Graphics — Text effects

Frames — Themes

Backgrounds —

Figure 15-7:
Once you've winnowed down your choices by selecting from the two pull-down menus shown here, use these little category icons (labelled) to further control which thumbnail patterns appear in the Content palette. Elements starts you off by including all the categories (a gray outline around a button means it's active and that category is included in your search). Click any of the buttons to turn them off and exclude that category from your search. So here you see the results of searching By Event → Celebration. And since the Frames button is turned off no frames appear in the thumbnail area.

2. **Choose how you want to search.**

   In the left-hand pull-down menu, choose to search by type (like backgrounds, frames, and so on), or choose Show All to see everything in the palette.

3. **Refine your search.**

   In the right-hand pull-down menu, choose specifically what you want. The contents of this menu change depending on your choice in the left-hand menu. So if you choose By Type on the left, you see Backgrounds, Frames, Graphics, and so on. If you choose By Mood, the right-hand menu offers you choices like Active, Adventurous, Fun, Romantic, or Thoughtful.

4. **If you like, filter your results.**

   Here's where those category buttons below the menus come into play. You may still get an awful lot of results from some of your menu choices, so you can use the buttons to filter out items you don't want. If you chose By Seasons and Winter in the menus but don't want to see frames, just turn off the Frames button (click it to get rid of the gray highlight around it) and frames are excluded from your results. (From left to right the buttons are Backgrounds, Frames, Graphics, Shapes, Text Effects, and Themes.) You can turn on and off as many buttons as you want, to include or exclude as many kinds of content as you like. To bring something you've excluded back into your search results, click its button again to turn it back on.

   Of course, if you're like a lot of people, most of the time you'll want to stick with By Type and choose the category you want. In that case the buttons are dimmed out.

5. **Add your choice to your image.**

   To use anything from the Content palette, double-click the thumbnail, or drag it to your image. (You can also click your selection once and then click Apply.)

To remove it, press Ctrl+Z if you just added it, or click the object with the Move tool and then press Backspace. If you use the Backspace key, Elements asks if you want to "Delete the Layer." You do.

WARNING   Don't use the trashcan icon in the Content palette to delete an object from your project. That seems like a logical thing to do—after all, that's how it works for the Layers palette. But with the Content palette, the trashcan deletes the graphic, frame, or whatever from the *palette*, not just from your image. Only use the trashcan for Content palette items you never want to use again. For example, if you've downloaded and installed a frame (as described on page 500) and know you don't want to use it again, then it's time to use the trashcan.

If that seems like a lot of navigation, check out the Favorites palette (described in the next section) for a faster way to reach Content palette items you use a lot.

NOTE   One advantage of signing up for a Photoshop.com account (page 18) is that the Content palette displays a lot of extra items that you can download. Free downloads display a blue banner across the corner of the palette thumbnail, while items only available for those with paid accounts have a gold banner.

The Favorites Palette

If you use the same effects, graphics, and styles over and over, you may find it tedious to keep navigating to them in the Content or Effects palettes. Make your life simpler by saving your Content and Effects standbys in the Favorites palette. Then you can get to these items with just a click or two.

To see the Favorites palette, go to Create → Artwork; you should see it at the bottom of the bin. To see the Favorites palette in the Editor, go to Window → Favorites to bring it up as a free-floating palette. (You can make sure it's always visible in the Palette bin, even when you're not in Artwork mode, by opening it as a floating palette, clicking the More button [the double arrows], and then choosing "Place in Palette bin when closed".)

To add an item to Favorites, right-click its thumbnail in the Content or Effects palette and then choose "Add to Favorites", or just drag its thumbnail to the palette.

To streamline the process of adding Content items to the Favorites palette, Elements lets you expand Create → Artwork into a full-screen view. Just click the arrows at the top of the Create pane, to the right of the Artwork tab; the Artwork pane expands to fill the Elements window. You can't add anything to an image from here, though. It's just to make it easier to see and drag things from the Content palette into the Favorites palette. When you're done, click the arrows again to collapse the Artwork pane back to its usual size.

To delete a favorite, right-click its thumbnail and then choose "Remove from Favorites". Or click it once to highlight it and then click the trashcan icon at the bottom of the palette (unlike the Content palette, trashing something here just removes it as a favorite, not from the program altogether). If you forget what a thumbnail is for, right-click it and choose Details, and Elements will tell you about it.

Photo Books

Elements lets you create 10.25"×9" pages for use in a bound book of photos—a very popular gift item. If you wish to order yours from Kodak's EasyShare Gallery (see page 430 to learn how to set up an account), you need at least 20 pages.

Creating a photo book is something like creating a collage; Elements walks you through the process with plenty of hand-holding:

1. **If you want, choose your photos.**

   If you want Elements to automatically layout your photos in the book, make sure you have them open in the Project bin and in the correct order before you start. Or if you prefer, you can wait and add each picture manually after you create the book layout.

2. **Start your book.**

   In either the Editor or the Organizer, go to Create → Photo Book. Elements switches over to the Editor, if you aren't there already, and presents your first set of choices for your book.

3. **Choose a title page photo.**

   Photo books usually have a cutout cover through which you can see one large image on the title page. This page has a different layout from the rest of the book. If you're using photos in the Project bin, drag the photo you want for the title page so that it's the first photo in the lineup. If you prefer, you can wait and choose your title page photo after you complete the book layout.

   Click Next to go to the next pane.

4. **Choose a layout and theme for your book.**

   You have two choices:

   • **Random Photo Layout.** Elements makes the decisions for you about how many photos will be on each page; every page may be different. It's best to avoid this option unless you have a *lot* of photos, since some of the layouts have as many as 20 tiny photos on a page—although, of course, you can edit things later.

   • **Choose Photo Layout.** Click this option and Elements presents you with a long list of possible page layout thumbnails. Click a thumbnail to select it. You need to pick left-and right-hand page layouts, which can be the same or different, as you prefer. Click Next to return to the main Photo Book pane.

   Now choose a theme. When you click a thumbnail in the theme list, Elements takes a few seconds, and then displays a little thumbnail showing the selected theme's style.

Your other choices are the same as for a Photo Collage. "Number of Pages" says 20 when you start your Photo Book; you need to have *between* 20 and 80 pages for a book. If you choose a number outside that range, you'll get a warning. (You don't have to enter a number here, incidentally, if you don't feel like counting. If you have more photos than will fit on 20 pages, the number of pages updates automatically.)

5. **Create your book.**

   Click Create, and Elements creates and opens a PSE file for you. You can edit anything in the file, exactly the same way you can change things in a Photo Collage. Once Elements creates the book, you see it, along with some special controls for navigating through the layout, as explained in Figure 15-8. The bright aqua lines towards the boundaries of the pages are the printing guides—they mark the actual page edges, so anything outside them will be cut off when your book is printed. Pay attention to them when moving or resizing your photos.

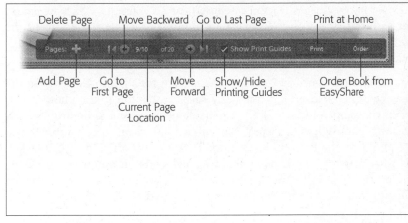

Figure 15-8:
When you click Create, Elements gives you a helpful double-page view of your book so that you can make any edits to the pictures or changes to the layout. The control strip shown here lets you move through your pages to see each double-page spread, or add or remove pages. You can reposition it anywhere in the work area that's convenient so it doesn't cover up your photos.

Don't forget to save the PSE file. When you're ready to print, you can upload the book to EasyShare for printing (page 437) right from the Editor by clicking the Order button in the control strip (see Figure 15-8). If you don't want to order from EasyShare, you can save your book as a PDF file to send to other photo book publishers.

NOTE   If you want to print your Photo Book pages somewhere other than Kodak's EasyShare Gallery, you'll need to use the workaround explained in the box on page 427.

You can also create a book of photos without using the Elements Photo Book feature at all. You can connect to EasyShare and upload your photos, as explained on page 437, and choose to have EasyShare print them in its own style of photo book. (You don't get any page decorations or layout choices when you use the EasyShare wizard, though.) One thing to keep in mind if you're getting a bound photo book:

Whether you order from EasyShare or another publisher, almost all books use only a single photo for the first page because that's what shows through the cover cutout.

Greeting Cards

Adobe calls them Greeting Cards, but they're more like what most people would call postcards. An Elements Greeting Card is a 4"×6" or 5"×7" single-sided page rather than a folded card. Go to Create → More Options → Greeting Card to get started. The layout and template choices are identical to those offered for Photo Collages, and the procedure is exactly the same, too. Just follow the steps for Photo Collages (page 419).

> **TIP**   You can also order greeting cards from Kodak EasyShare Gallery, as explained on page 433.

CD/DVD Jacket

In Elements, you can create CD jewel case inserts or DVD inserts, which appear on the front and back of the case. To make a CD insert, in either the Editor or the Organizer, just go to Create → More Options → CD Jacket; you get a variety of different templates, all the correct size for use in a CD case.

The steps for creating your CD Jacket are the same as for a Photo Collage, but the layout choices, of course, are different. Pay special attention to the photo placement when choosing your layout: The right side of the layout is the front cover. You can turn "Auto-Fill with Project Bin Photos" off or on to suit you. (If you have five photos in the Project bin, you don't want to get a five-page CD Jacket, which is what may happen. If there aren't enough slots on one page for all the open photos, Auto-Fill will just make extra pages to place the open images. So turn Auto-Fill off if you don't want all your open photos used.)

Unfortunately, only the "2 Centered" CD insert layout even approximately marks out the general spine area, where most CDs display their titles. If you decide to enter text that you want to appear on the spine, click the Horizontal Type tool (page 399), type away, and then go to Image → Rotate → Layer 90° Left. Then use the Move tool to place the text where you want it.

> **TIP**   If you use a theme (page 420) and want to add spine text, remember that home inkjet printers don't do a good job printing small white type on a dark background. You're better off going with dark type on a light background.

The DVD Jacket wizard (Create → More Options → DVD Jacket) is identical except for the layout choices.

CD/DVD Label

You can create stick-on labels for CDs and DVDs with Elements (Create → More Options → CD/DVD Label) and print them on blank label sheets from any office supply store. Elements gives you templates that create a single label layout. When you're done, you need to place your work into the template that goes with your brand of labels. (Most CD or DVD labels print two to a page.) The major brands, like Avery (*www.avery.com*) and Neato (*www.neato.com*), have free downloadable templates on their Web sites to help you position labels properly on the page.

> **NOTE** While labels make your discs look great, it's risky to put a stick-on label on any disc you'll use in a computer. If the label gets stuck in the disk drive, you may have to replace the drive. Consider using a marker to label discs for computer use, or buying printable discs if you have a printer that will take them.

Online Creations

Besides what you can do in Elements, you can create a handful of projects online at Kodak's EasyShare Gallery (page 437). You can order Kodak greeting cards (using their formats and templates instead of the Elements Greeting Card choices), for example. First, select your photos in the Organizer or open them in the Editor.

Then go to Create → More Options → Order Kodak Photo Greeting Cards. Elements automatically uploads your photos, and you see them in the EasyShare wizard, which walks you through creating and ordering cards. You need to set up an EasyShare account the first time you use the service. Setting up an account and using EasyShare are explained on page 437.

You can also create calendars with EasyShare. Before you start, you must select 12 photos in the Organizer. Then go to Create → Photo Calendar, and Elements whisks you off to EasyShare. You can access the Photo Calendar menu choice from either the Organizer or the Editor, but it's the photos you've selected in the Organizer that get uploaded. If you select fewer than 12 photos, the EasyShare wizard nags you to add more, and you don't have the option of using the same photo for each month. (Elements doesn't include templates for creating calendars to print at home or take to your local print shop.)

Another online ordering option (if you're in the United States) is PhotoStamps. This is real, legitimate postage that features the photo of your choice. If you've always wanted to be immortalized on a stamp, here's your opportunity. Select one or more photos if you like, and then go to Create → More Options → PhotoStamps. Elements automatically uploads your photos to Stamps.com. Create an account with Stamps.com, and then order away.

> **NOTE** While PhotoStamps are fun, they're definitely for people with lots of disposable income, or for very special occasions, like sending wedding announcements, for example. Before you spend a lot of time preparing photos, check the price list to see whether you really think the stamps will be worth the cost.

CHAPTER 16

Printing Your Photos

Now that you've gone to so much trouble making your photos look terrific, you probably want to share them with other people. This chapter and the next two look at the many different options Elements gives you for sharing your photos with the world at large.

This chapter covers the traditional method: printing your photos. You can print your photos at home on an inkjet printer, take them to a kiosk at a local store, or use an online service. Elements makes it especially simple to use Kodak's Easy-Share Gallery, Adobe's online printing partner. You also get an easy connection to several other popular online photo services (page 491). The best thing about using an online service nowadays is that you're not limited merely to ordinary prints: You can create hardcover books, calendars, embarrassing t-shirts—you name it.

> **NOTE** If you create online albums at Photoshop.com (page 467), you can let friends order prints directly from your Photoshop.com Web page, if you like. Those prints come from Shutterfly.

Getting Ready to Print

Whether printing at home or sending photos to a printing service, you need to make sure your image file is set up to give you good-looking prints.

The first thing to check is your photo's resolution, which controls the number of pixels per inch (ppi) in your image. If you don't have enough pixels in your photo, then your print will look grainy and pixelated. Most photo aficionados consider three hundred ppi ideal; at a minimum, a quality print needs a resolution of at least 150 ppi to avoid the grainy look you see in low-resolution photos. See page 93 for more on reviewing and setting your photo's resolution.

NOTE Be sure to set your resolution to a whole number—decimals may cause black lines on your prints with some printers. In other words, 247 ppi is fine, but you may have problems if the ppi is 247.32. Older printers are most likely to have problems with decimals.

When printing on photo paper or sending your photos out for printing, check to be sure that your images are cropped to fit a standard paper size. (Cropping is covered starting on page 79.) When printing at home, the paper and ink you use make a big difference in the color and quality of your output. It may seem like a marketing scam, but you really will get the best results by using your printer manufacturer's recommended paper and ink.

Ordering Prints

You don't even need to own a printer to print your photos. There's no shortage of companies hoping you'll choose them for that privilege. You can order prints online or use a print kiosk at a local store. Elements makes it very easy to prepare your photos for printing either way. Just save your photos in a compatible file format (see page 60 for more about picking different file formats). The JPEG format is usually your best bet, but always check with the service you plan to use to see if it has any special requirements.

If you plan to physically take your photos in for printing (as opposed to ordering them online), burn the photos to a CD, and then take that in. To do so, use the Organizer to export your photos to the desktop, as explained in Figure 16-1.

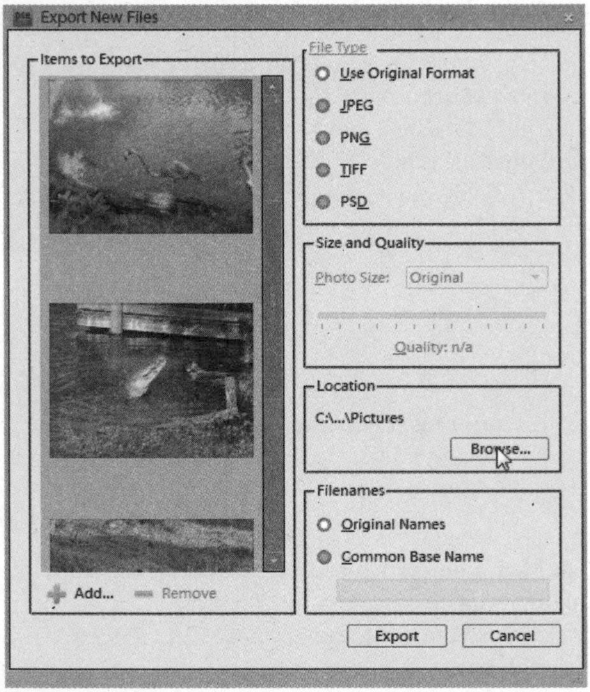

Figure 16-1:
Use the Export New Files dialog box to get your images ready for in-store printing (at a kiosk, for example). First, in the Photo Browser, select your photos. Then choose File → Export As New File(s) to send them to your desktop for easy burning to a CD. Click the Browse button to choose the desktop as your desired location, and then change the format of your files, if needed (if you have TIFFs and the store wants JPEGs, for example). For printing, always choose maximum quality (the quality slider becomes active only when you choose to export as JPEGs). File renaming is up to you.

NOTE   You can choose to burn a CD within Elements; that's fine as long as your photos are in the correct format and you don't include any photos from stacks or version sets. Stacks and version sets may cause problems for commercial printers and kiosks, which don't understand them.

Ordering Prints Online

Adobe has partnered with Kodak's online photo-printing service, EasyShare Gallery, to make it simple to upload photos directly from the Organizer. You can order prints, books, or any of the other photo-bearing items that Kodak would love to sell you. Of course, you're free to use any other online printing service (see page 491 for some suggestions), but the process for using them isn't integrated right into Elements the way it is with EasyShare.

NOTE   If you've ordered online from an early version of Elements but haven't done so in a while, EasyShare Gallery is the current name for what used to be Ofoto.com. If you have an Ofoto account, then you can still use it with EasyShare.

Once you've edited your photos and are ready to place your order, just follow these steps:

1. **In the Organizer, select the photos you want to print.**

   If the photos you want are scattered around, you may find it easier to make an album (see page 53) so you can easily see them all at once. Alternatively, just Ctrl+click to select a collection of individual pictures.

2. **Select a recipient in the Organize pane's QuickShare palette (Figure 16-2).**

   Drag the photos to the name of the person you want to receive the prints. If the person isn't already in your list, then drag the photos to where it says "Drag photos here to create an order". The New Order Prints Recipient window opens so you can enter that person's info. Or use your Contact Book (page 464) to create a new recipient, as explained in Figure 16-3. If you want to send photos to yourself, then just create your own Contact Book entry.

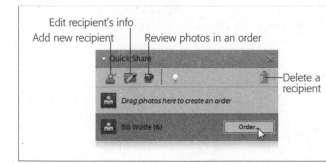

Figure 16-2:
The buttons marked here let you manage your contact information—your recipients' names and shipping details—when you're ready to order prints. You can add, edit, or delete a recipient. You can also check to see which prints you've chosen to send to your various friends—helpful when you can't remember which photos you've already chosen.

TIP   You need to create recipients for only those people with whom you regularly share photos. If you're going to send photos to someone just once, like guests from a wedding whom you rarely see, then skip the whole New Recipient thing by selecting your photos, and then going to File → Order Prints. That step takes you to EasyShare, and you can enter the recipients' information there instead.

3. **Confirm your order.**

If you want to review which photos you've chosen, then click the "View Photos in <Recipient's Name>" button to see them. It's the button just to the right of the Edit Recipient button (the pencil icon) at the top of the QuickShare pane.

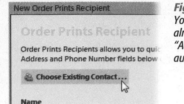

Figure 16-3:
You can add a new recipient to the QuickShare pane by copying information that's already stored in your Contact Book (page 464). To do so, click the button labeled "Add new recipient" in Figure 16-2, and then click Choose Existing Contact. Elements automatically creates a new Print Order recipient for the name you choose.

Add more photos by dragging them to the recipient's name in the QuickShare pane. You can also delete a photo from your order once you're in the Easy-Share window (Figure 16-4) by clicking Remove under the photo's EasyShare thumbnail.

The number of photos ordered for each person appears in parentheses in the recipient list, to the right of the person's name. When you're ready to order, click the Order button, and Elements whisks you off to the EasyShare site (although you're still actually in an Elements window, bearing the headline "Welcome to Adobe Photoshop Services").

NOTE   In Vista, you may have to give Elements permission to get through the Windows Firewall before you can connect to EasyShare. To do that, go to Start → Control Panel → Security → "Allow a program through Windows Firewall" → Continue → Add Program → Adobe Photoshop Elements 7.0.

4. **Order your prints.**

An easy-to-follow *wizard* (a series of guided question screens) appears to help set up your account. (If you already have an EasyShare account, then just sign in.) Select the size and number of prints for each photo, as shown in Figure 16-4. You'll receive an envelope of prints in the mail in a few days.

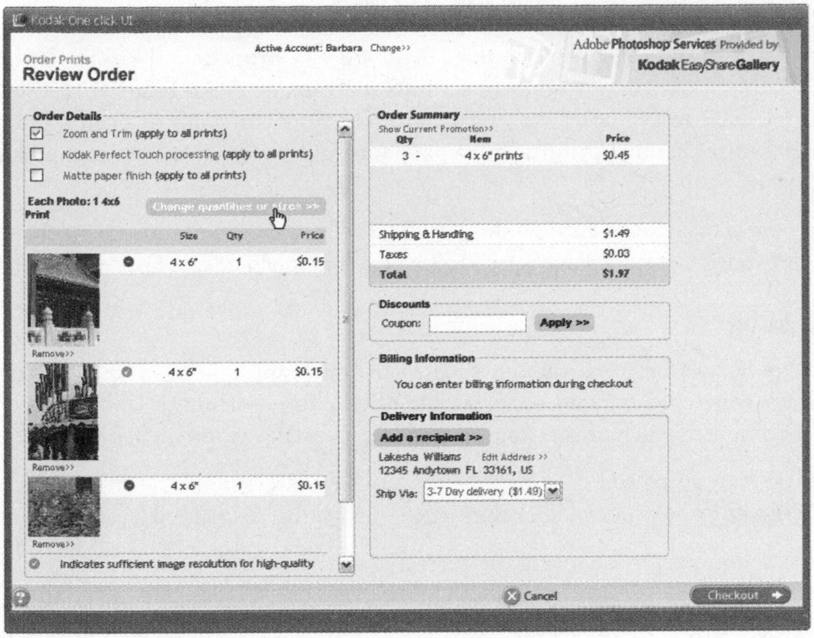

Figure 16-4:
You can add additional sizes or order more than one copy of a particular photo once you're in the EasyShare wizard. If your photo's resolution is too low for a good print, then you see a red circle next to it, as you can see in the top and bottom photos here. If you can, select an alternate photo with a higher resolution; if that's not an option, see page 96 for more on dealing with low-resolution images.

TIP   Elements automatically checks for updates to the EasyShare service, and does you the dubious favor of assuming you want to be notified of special promotions. You can turn off either by going to Organizer → Edit → Preferences → Adobe Partner Services. You can also tell Elements how to handle updates when it finds them by going to Organizer → Help → Updates → Preferences, where you can choose whether Elements should check for updates and install them automatically, or ask before it installs anything. In order to see the Updates Preferences, first you have to let the Updater run. Then the preferences appear as a choice in the window that's displayed when the Updater is finished.

Elements makes ordering prints from EasyShare very convenient. Of course, you can use EasyShare without the Organizer, and you can use other online print services like Shutterfly (*www.shutterfly.com*) or Snapfish (*www.snapfish.com*) if you like. The real advantage of ordering from Elements is the convenience of being able to work right from the Organizer.

If you're using Adobe's new Photoshop.com service (page 18), then you can connect to many popular online print services right from the personal Web page you get as part of Photoshop.com. And when you share an album online, you can let friends order prints of your photos right from your Web page. See page 470 for more details.

Printing at Home (from the Editor)

If you want to do your own printing, then you can print directly from the Elements Editor. You can print only one photo at a time from the Editor, but at least you don't have to switch to the Organizer every time you want to print a photo. (The Organizer handles printing multiple photos, like contact sheets, as explained later in this chapter.)

Before you actually print your photos, for the best results, you need to check the settings in two windows: the Page Setup dialog box, and the Elements Print window.

Page Setup

The Page Setup window is the same for all the programs you have on your computer. It's where you set your page size and orientation (portrait or landscape), and tell the computer which printer you want to use, if you have more than one printer.

Summon it by going to File → Page Setup. You can also press Ctrl+Shift+P or, on the Elements Print window, click the Page Setup button (explained later).

In Page Setup, start by choosing the correct printer by clicking the Printer button. Next, in the main Page Setup window, choose the paper size you want, and the orientation (portrait or landscape). When you've selected these settings, you're ready to go to the Elements Print window.

Print Window

Elements's Print window (Figure 16-5) is your control center for printing from Elements. It offers you lots of ways to tweak your prints, from simply positioning your photo correctly to making very sophisticated color adjustments.

Press Ctrl+P in the Editor to call up the Print window. For simple printing, make sure the photo is properly positioned on the page, and then click Print. If you're lucky, you'll get a perfect print. If you don't like the color, the next section on color management explains your options.

Don't be intimidated by the Print window. You probably won't need all the settings every time you print, but each setting comes in handy sooner or later. If you've used Elements before, this window may look more complicated, but it's really not. It's just that now you can see all the extra settings that were hidden in earlier versions. It still works pretty much the same as ever.

On the left side of the Print window, you see an image preview showing where your photo will print. So, for example, in Figure 16-5, the actual printed image would be surrounded by about an inch or so of white space on all four sides. Normally, Elements shows a *bounding box*, the black outline with handles on the corners indicating the edges of your photo. Don't worry, the bounding box itself doesn't print along with your photo. The box gives you a way to move and resize your image by dragging the handles. If seeing the bounding box bothers you, then get rid of it by turning off the Show Bounding Box checkbox near the bottom of the window.

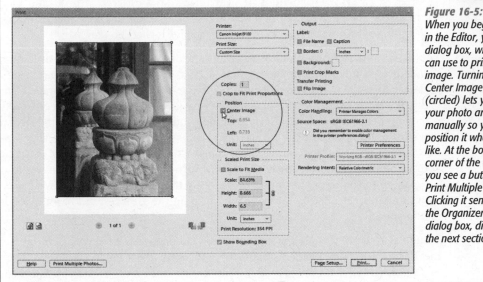

Figure 16-5:
When you begin printing in the Editor, you see this dialog box, which you can use to print a single image. Turning off the Center Image checkbox (circled) lets you drag your photo around manually so you can position it wherever you like. At the bottom-left corner of the window you see a button labeled Print Multiple Photos. Clicking it sends you to the Organizer's Print dialog box, discussed in the next section.

The familiar Elements Rotate symbols appear below the image windows' right corner. Use these symbols if you want to change the orientation of your photo. If you need to rotate the paper in order to fit your photo onto it, then use the small white buttons below the image preview area's lower-left corner.

You can resize your photo in the Print window in several ways:

- **Print Size menu.** This is where you can pick the size at which you want your photo to print. Choose any print size from the list or enter a Custom Size. Fit On Page changes the size of your image, if necessary, to fit the size of the paper you're using. If you choose a size with a different aspect ratio (length to width proportions) than your photo, Elements automatically crops your photo to fit. So that means if you want to control what gets chopped off, do the cropping yourself first. If Elements intends to crop your photo, it turns on "Crop to Fit Print Proportions" (explained below), and then shows you a preview of what it plans to do.

- **Scaled Print Size.** Use the settings in this section if you're feeling lazy and want to resize your photo right in the Print window, rather than using the Image Size dialog box (page 93). Resize your photo by entering either a percentage (in the Scale box) or new dimensions (in the Height and Width boxes). When you turn on "Scale to Fit Media", Elements automatically resizes your photo to fit on the page size you chose in Print Setup. You may wind up with a bit of white space along some of the edges if your photo isn't the same shape as the paper.

- **Bounding Box.** You can use the bounding box to change the size of your image. This option's good if you're looking to just tweak the size of your photo by a tiny bit (but as always, you get better results making your photo smaller rather than larger). Drag one of the handles (they look like tiny white boxes) on any of the bounding box's corners to make your image larger or smaller.

- **Crop to Fit Print Proportions**. If your image has a different aspect ratio than the paper you're printing on, and you're willing to let Elements decide which portions of your photo get cropped, then turn this checkbox on.

You need to be cautious about resizing in the Print window, though. If necessary, Elements re-samples your image (page 96) to make it fit the size you choose. Don't go larger than 100 percent, or the quality of your photo starts to deteriorate. Generally, it's better to do most resizing *before* you get to the Print window, especially when you're making a photo larger. Enlarging your photo in the Print window can make for grainy, poor-quality prints. If you can see pixelation in the preview window, then you know that something's amiss, and you should start by checking your resolution. (Early versions of Elements warned you if the resolution was low; now it's up to you to pay attention to the ppi setting in the Print window's Scaled Print Size area; see page 93 for more advice about the ideal resolution for a good-looking photo.)

To adjust your photo's placement on the printed page, use the settings grouped in the Position section. Elements starts you out with the Center Image checkbox turned on (it's circled in Figure 16-5). You need to turn it off before you can reposition your image. To change the location of your photo, either drag it in the left side of the dialog box or, in the boxes provided, type in the amount of space you want between the photo and the edges of the page, in the measurement unit of your choice. ("Top" controls how far your image is from the top of the page, and "Left" controls the distance from the left edge of the page.)

The right side of the Print window contains settings that were hidden in early versions of Elements. These settings are divided into two groups: Output and Color Management. Color Management is explained in the next section. The Output settings give you the following options:

- **Label**. You can print the file name and/or caption directly on your photo by turning on the relevant checkbox. The image preview area shows where your text gets printed. Caption text comes from what you entered in the Organizer, or you can go to File → Info in the Editor to add a caption in the relevant field.

- **Border**. When you want to add a border to your photo, turn on this checkbox, and then enter the size you want for your border (in inches, millimeters, or points). Elements shrinks your photo to accommodate the border, even if there's plenty of empty space around the picture, so you may need to enlarge the photo a bit before printing to get the size you originally chose. Then click the white square to bring up the Elements Color Picker (see page 209) so you can choose a border color.

- **Background**. If the page has empty space you want to fill with a background color, then turn on this checkbox. Then choose a color by clicking its color square to bring up the Elements Color Picker.

- **Print Crop Marks**. This setting lets you print guidelines in the margins of your photo to make it easier to trim it exactly. Crop marks are useful mainly for trimming bordered photos so that the borders are exactly even.

• **Flip Image.** Turn this checkbox on to horizontally reverse your image. Use it when printing transfers for projects like t-shirts.

> **NOTE** The Print window isn't *color managed*, which means that what you see in the window isn't meant to show you the exact colors you'll get when you print. Instead, you're looking only at the position of your photo.

Color management

Elements gives you several advanced color-related settings in the Print window. If you're content with the way your prints look without adjusting these settings, just be happy and ignore them. But if you don't like the color you're getting from Elements, then use these advanced controls to make adjustments.

> **TIP** Color management can be a dauntingly complicated subject to understand. The advice in the following pages should be enough to get you started, but if you're determined to learn more, a good place to start is Brad Hinkel's *Color Management in Digital Photography* (Rocky Nook, 2007). It covers Photoshop but many of its explanations are suitable for Elements users as well.

If you remember from Chapter 7, Elements is a *color-managed* program, which means it tries to coordinate the color settings used by various devices and programs: your photo (which may retain color settings applied by your camera), your monitor, your Elements settings, and your printer. Sometimes you need to step in and help Elements decide which settings are best, since different devices and programs can have different interpretations of what individual colors look like.

WORKAROUND WORKSHOP

Economical Print Experiments

If you've just gone out and bought top-quality photo paper, you may be suffering from a bit of sticker shock and perhaps are even thinking, "Oh yeah, great. Now I'm supposed to use this stuff up experimenting? At that price?"

The good news is, while you have to bite the bullet and sacrifice a sheet or two, you don't need to waste the whole box. Instead, try this: Make a small selection somewhere in a photo you want to print, press Ctrl+C, and go to File → New → "Image from Clipboard". You get a new file with only a small piece of your photo in it.

This is your test print. In the Editor's Print window, turn off the Center Image checkbox, and then drag your small photo to the page's upper-left corner. Try printing the page using Elements' standard settings. If your print looks good, then you're ready to print the whole photo.

On the other hand, if you don't like the result, then press Ctrl+P to bring up the Print window again. This time, move your test strip over to the right a little bit. Change your settings (keeping note of the changes you've made), and then print again on the same piece of paper. Your new test prints out beside the first strip. Keep moving the test area around on the page, and you can try out quite a few different combinations of settings, all on the same sheet of paper.

Your most important decision is whether you want Elements or your printer to manage your photo's color settings. (You can let both Elements *and* your printer have a say in color management, but that almost always mucks things up.) The good news is that Elements does its best to keep you from making that kind of mistake, and it tries to make managing the color in your prints as painless as possible.

You have four main choices to make in color management:

- **Color Handling**. You decide who's going to be in charge: Elements (Photoshop Elements Manages Colors), your printer (Printer Manages Colors), or nobody (No Color Management). The choice you make here determines your options in the rest of the settings. Elements also gives you some hints about your printer settings, as you can see in Figure 16-6.

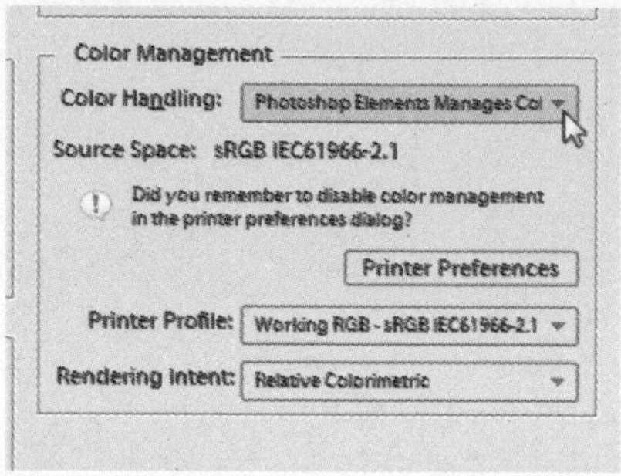

Figure 16-6:
Elements thoughtfully reminds you to turn color management off in your printer when you choose Photoshop Elements Manages Colors or No Color Management. Click the Printer Preferences button to get to the settings for your printer.

- **Source Space**. This setting shows you which, if any, color space your file is tagged with (for example, sRGB or Adobe RGB). You don't actually choose a setting here; instead, this line tells you the color space associated with your file. See page 196 for more about color spaces.

- **Printer Profile**. This setting is grayed out unless you chose Photoshop Elements Manages Color in the Color Handling menu. If Elements is managing the color, then you can choose the profile you want from a list of all the possible profiles that Elements can find on your computer.

- **Rendering Intent**. You can use this setting to tell Elements what to do if your photo contains colors that fall outside the color range of the print space you're using. Your choices are explained in the box on page 446. When you choose No Color Management for your Color Handling setting, this setting isn't available.

The easiest way to set up color management, and a good way to start, is to choose Printer Manages Color. This means that Elements hands your photo over to your printer, and lets your printer take care of the color management duties. Then all you need to do is select the proper paper profile and settings for your printer.

Selecting a paper profile sounds complicated, but it's usually as simple as choosing, say, Photo Paper Plus Glossy from the list of options in your *printer driver*, the utility program that lets you control your printer's settings. Just click the Printer

Preferences button below the Source Space area to get to these settings. The exact wording differs depending on what kind of printer you've got, but Figure 16-7 shows a typical printer's settings.

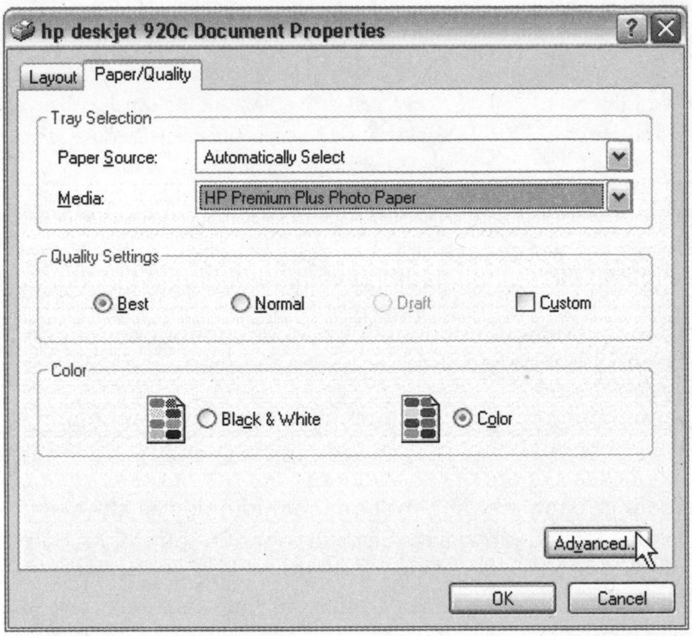

Figure 16-7:
Even a basic model like this older HP inkjet printer includes some options for color management, if you feel you need them. Clicking the Advanced button calls up another window that shows your color management options. Most of the time, selecting the right settings in Elements' Print window and choosing the correct paper type gives you good prints. Most modern printer drivers automatically choose the correct ink setting for the paper you've chosen. Don't override these settings unless you have a good reason.

TIP If your camera takes photos in sRGB, and you've been editing them in No Color Management or "Always Optimize Colors for Computer Screens", then don't alter your workflow by choosing Adobe RGB for the printer profile. Your colors may shift drastically. If for some reason you want to change the color space for the printer, first go to Image → Convert Color Profile, and then apply the Adobe RGB profile to your photo. If you aren't absolutely sure that your printer understands Adobe RGB (many inkjets don't), and you don't have a compelling reason for changing, then it's best to leave things alone.

You have limitless variations on how you can use the color settings in Elements, and you may need to experiment a bit to find what works best for you. See the box on page 443 for advice on how to cheaply test out a bunch of different print settings. If you go looking around for more information, then you'll find that this subject is very controversial. Everyone has a different approach that's the "right one." In fact, you have many options that can lead to good results.

Printing at Home (from the Organizer)

Elements also lets you print from the Organizer, which gives you many more output options than the Editor, including the ability to print several photos on one page. You can create contact sheets of thumbnails and picture packages (like you'd

---

What's Your Intent?

For most people, the Rendering Intent setting in Elements Print window is the most confusing of the color management options. Here are the basics you need to know to choose a setting. Sometimes your photo may contain colors that fall outside the color boundaries of the print space you're using. Intent just tells Elements what to do if that happens. You have four choices:

- **Perceptual** tells Elements to preserve the relationship between the colors in your image—even if that means Elements has to do some visible color shifting to make all the colors fit.

- **Saturation** makes colors very vivid but not necessarily very accurate. This setting is more for special effects than for regular photo printing.

- **Relative Colorimetric** tries to preserve the colors in both the source and the output space by shifting things to the closest matching color in the printer profile's space. Relative Colorimetric is Elements' standard setting, and it's usually what you want because it keeps your colors as close as possible to what you see on your screen.

- **Absolute Colorimetric** lets you simulate another printer and paper. This setting is for specialized proofing situations.

order from a professional photographer). You can also easily add all kinds of fancy borders to your photos in the Organizer. Elements 7 gives you improved print options from the Organizer. For example, in previous versions of Elements, everything printed from the Organizer at 220 ppi, but now you can choose any maximum resolution you like.

You probably want to select your photo(s) before starting, but you don't have to—you can do that in a moment, if you'd prefer. The Print Photos dialog box is the Organizer's print control center. Press Ctrl+P or go to File → Print Multiple Photos to bring it up (see Figure 16-8).

Print Photos has a strip down the left side of the window that displays the thumbnails of the photos you've selected for printing. You can add or remove photos here by using the buttons in the window's lower-left corner. Click Add to bring up a window where you can search for additional photos, or highlight a photo's thumbnail, and then click Remove to get rid of it.

The center of the dialog box has a preview window, and the right side gives you a few easy-to-understand options to choose from:

- **Select Printer.** Choose your printer (if you have more than one). The little icon to the right of the printer name is a shortcut to your printer preferences.

- **Select Type of Print.** Here's where you decide whether to make individual prints, a contact sheet, or a picture package of multiple photos. The next sections explain how to use the multiple print options.

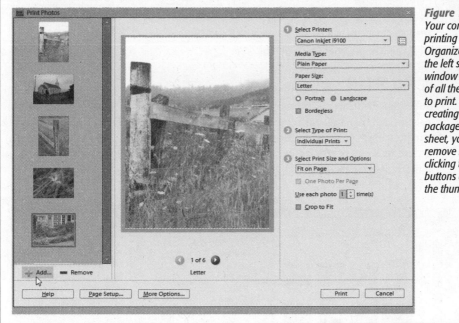

Figure 16-8:
Your control center for printing from the Organizer. The strip on the left side of the window holds thumbnails of all the photos you plan to print. When you're creating a picture package or a contact sheet, you can add or remove images by clicking the + or – buttons at the bottom of the thumbnail strip.

- **Select Print Size and Options.** This is where you select the size of your prints and how many times you want to use each photo, if you're printing multiple images. For example, you can choose to print one photo four times or four different photos once each. If you're printing picture packages, and you turn on the One Photo Per Page checkbox, then each image prints out on a separate page. "Crop to Fit" tells Elements to perform any cropping necessary. (If you want to decide where to crop your photos, then use the cropping tools you learned about on page 79.)

NOTE The size options you see are dependent on the page size you selected in Page Setup (page 440). So if you see only letter-size options and you want, say, A4, then check in Page Setup to be sure you've chosen A4 as your paper size.

At the bottom of the Print Photos window, click More Options, and you get the same options that you get in the Editor, along with some limited color management choices, and the ability to change the maximum resolution of your prints from the Organizer's standard setting of 220 ppi. When you're ready to print, enter your settings, and then click Print.

Printing Multiple Photos

The Organizer really shines when it comes to printing more than one photo at a time. You can print a contact sheet that shows small thumbnails of many images. You can also choose to create a picture package that features multiple pictures in multiple sizes.

TIP You can also get to the Organizer's Print Photos window by clicking Print Multiple Photos at the bottom of the Editor's Print window. You can also go to File → Print Multiple Photos or, if you have more than one photo open, then in the Project bin, go to Bin Actions → Print Bin Files. Both methods take you to the Print Photos window.

Contact Sheets

Contact sheets show thumbnail views of multiple images on a single page. They're great for creating a visual reference guide to the photos you've archived on a CD, for instance. Or you may want to print a contact sheet of all the photos on a memory card as soon as you download the photos to your computer, even before editing them (see Figure 16-9).

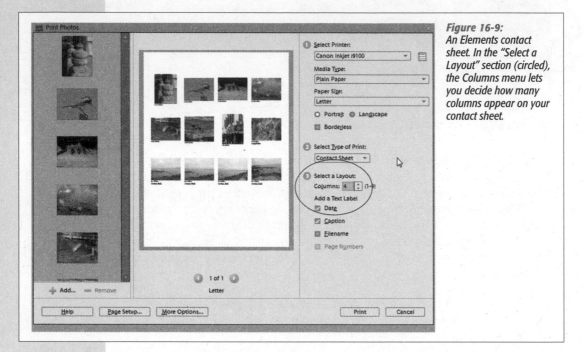

Figure 16-9:
An Elements contact sheet. In the "Select a Layout" section (circled), the Columns menu lets you decide how many columns appear on your contact sheet.

To print a contact sheet, in the Print Photos dialog box, go to "Select Type of Print", and then choose Contact Sheet. Your options immediately change to show "Select a Layout", and you can use the following settings to customize your contact sheet:

- **Columns.** Here's where you decide how many vertical rows of photos to have on a page. Choose up to nine columns per page. The more columns you have, the smaller your thumbnails. Even if you have only one image currently chosen, increasing the number of columns shrinks the thumbnail size.

- **Add a Text Label.** When you want a caption on each image, choose the Date, Caption (any text in the image's caption field), and/or Filename here. You can add page numbers if you're printing multiple pages. When all your photos fit on one page, Page Numbers is grayed out.

You can add and remove images as explained earlier. When you like your layout, click Print.

Picture Package

Elements' Picture Package tool lets you print several images on one sheet. You can print a package that's one photo printed repeatedly, or create a package that includes multiple photos.

To get started, press Ctrl+P, and the Print Photos dialog box appears. Go to "Select Type of Print" and choose Picture Package. Next, under "Select a Layout", choose which composition style you want (choices include four 3×5-inch photos, one 5×7-inch photo, and so on). Then choose a frame, if you'd like one, by picking from the "Select a Frame" menu. Add photos to your package by clicking the Add button in the lower-left corner of the dialog box. Figure 16-10 shows you how to change the layout of your photos once they're on the page. If you turn on "Fill Page with First Photo", then you get an entire page dedicated to each photo showing multiple sizes of the image, instead of a group of different photos on each page.

Elements crops your photos to fit their slots if you turn on "Crop to Fit", but you're probably better off doing that yourself in the Editor (page 79) before you start. When you've got your package arranged as you want it, click Print.

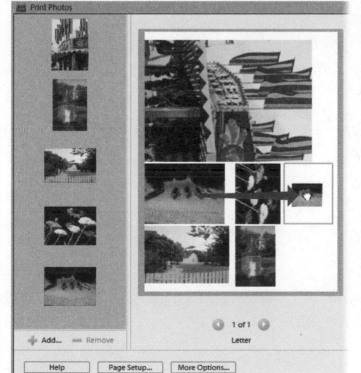

Figure 16-10:
Reorganizing your package is drag-and-drop easy. If you have empty space in your layout and want to fill it, then drag a thumbnail from a slot in the layout, or from a thumbnail on the left, into the slot where you want to use the photo again. Here you see a photo being dragged from one of the large slots into an empty part of the layout to create a smaller print of the same photo. You can easily change the size of a photo, too. Just drag it from the box it's currently in to a different-size box, and it automatically swaps places with the photo that was there originally. To remove a photo from the package, highlight it on the left side of the main window, and then click Remove (grayed out in this figure). To remove one of the photos you dragged from the package, right-click, and then choose "Revert to original".

WORKAROUND WORKSHOP

Creating Your Own Package

You may find that you want a layout for your picture package that's different from any of the choices that Elements offers. You can make your own picture package from scratch, and it's not hard to do:

1. Save all the photos you want to use at the same resolution.

2. In the Editor, create a new document (Ctrl+N or File → New). Make sure it's the size you want your complete package to be. Also make sure it has the same resolution as your photos. (See "Choosing Resolution" on page 93 for more about setting a file's resolution.) You can save time by choosing the Letter preset size from the New file menu. That size is already set to 300 ppi.

3. Drag each photo into your new document. Drag the photos from the Layers palette (page 179), and then position them as you wish. You can use the Move tool (page 148) or scale (page 324) to resize them.

When you have all your photos positioned and sized to suit you, save the combined file, and then print it. You can make the file smaller by flattening the layers first (Layer → Flatten Image). Flatten only if you don't think you'll want to tweak your layout later on.

You can also create new layouts for yourself in the Organizer. Go to *C:\Program files\Adobe\Photoshop Elements 7.0\Assets\locale\en_us (this will be different if you aren't in the US)\layouts*. Choose the layout that's closest to what you want. Open it in the text editor of your choice, save it with a new name, and then make the changes you want. When you're done, save your changes, and then put the new file into the same folder as the original. If you're not sure about what to change, the layouts folder has a helpful ReadMe file that explains what to do.

CHAPTER 17

Email and the Web

Printing your photos is great, but it costs money, takes time, and doesn't do much to instantly impress faraway friends. And to many people, printing is just so Twentieth Century. Fortunately, Elements comes packed with tools that make it easy to prep your photos for onscreen viewing, and email them in a variety of crowd-pleasing ways.

Image Formats and the Web

Back in the Web's early days, making your graphic files small was important, because most Internet connections were as slow as snails. Nowadays, file size isn't as crucial; your main obligation when creating graphics for the Web is ensuring they're compatible with the Web browsers people use to view your Web pages. That means you'll probably want to use either of the two most popular image formats, JPEG or GIF:

- **JPEG** (Joint Photographic Experts' Group) is the most popular choice for images with lots of detail, and where you need smooth color transitions. Photos are almost always posted on the Web as JPEGs.

   TIP   JPEGs can't have transparent areas, although there's a workaround for that: Fill the background around your image with the same color as the Web page you want to post it on. The background blends into the Web page, giving the impression that your object is surrounded by transparency. See Figure 17-4 for details on how this trick works.

- **GIFs** (Graphics Interchange Format) are great for images with limited numbers of colors, like corporate logos and headlines. Text looks much sharper in the GIF format than it does as a JPEG. GIFs also let you keep transparency as part of your image.

- **PNG** (Portable Network Graphic) is a Web graphics format that was created to overcome some of the disadvantages of JPEGs and GIFs. There's a lot to like about PNG files. They can include transparent areas, and the format reduces the file size of photographs without losing data, as happens with JPEG files (see page 64 for more about that). PNG files' big drawback is that only newer Web browsers deal with them very well. Older versions of Internet Explorer are notorious for not supporting the PNG format, so if you've got potential viewers with ancient computers, then you probably don't want to use PNG.

Elements makes it a breeze to save your images in any of these formats. You do so by using the Save For Web dialog box, covered in the next section.

Saving Images for the Web or Email

If you plan to email your photos or put them up on your Web site, Save For Web is a terrific tool that takes any open image and saves it in a Web friendly format; it also gives you lots of options to help achieve maximum image quality while keeping file size to a minimum. Save For Web aims to create as small a file as you can without compromising the image's onscreen quality.

Save For Web creates smaller JPEG files than you get by merely using Save As, because it strips out the EXIF data, the information about your camera's settings (see page 59). To get started with Save For Web, go to File → "Save for Web" or press Alt+Shift+Ctrl+S. The dialog box shown in Figure 17-1 appears.

The most important point to remember when saving images for the Web is that the resolution (measured in pixels per inch, or ppi) is completely irrelevant. You just care about the image's pixel dimensions, such as 400×600. When you have a photo that you've optimized for print, you almost certainly need to drastically downsize it. You can easily downsize in Save For Web.

Elements gives you a lot of useful tools in Save For Web, like the Hand (page 88) and Zoom (page 88) tools for adjusting your view. But the main attraction is the before-and-after image preview in the two main preview panes. On the left is the original and on the right is what the image will look like after resizing.

Below each image preview, you see the file size. Below the right preview, you see the estimated download time, which you can adjust by modifying your assumptions about your recipient's Internet connection speed, as explained in Figure 17-2. You can also adjust the zoom percentage (using the Zoom menu at the bottom of the window), but usually you want to stick to 100 percent because that's your image's size on the Web.

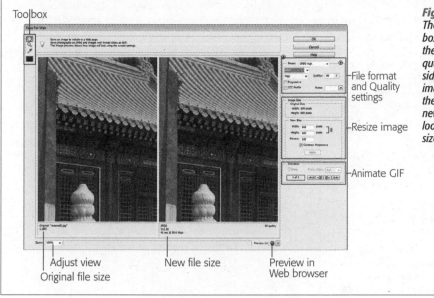

Figure 17-1:
*The Save For Web dialog
box makes it easy to get
the exact image size and
quality you want. The left
side shows your original
image. The preview on
the right shows what your
newly sized image will
look like at its new file
size.*

Toolbox

File format
and Quality
settings

Resize image

Animate GIF

Adjust view

Original file size

New file size

Preview in
Web browser

The upper-right corner of the window has your file format and quality choices.
What you see varies a bit depending on which format you've chosen. Below that
are your options for resizing your image. If you want to create animated GIFs
(those tiny moving images you see on Web pages), then set up the animation at the
bottom of the settings panel. How to create animated GIFs is explained later.

Using Save For Web

When you're ready to use Save For Web, follow these steps:

1. **Open the image you want to modify.**

2. **Launch the Save For Web dialog box.**

   Go to File → "Save for Web" or press Alt+Shift+Ctrl+S. The Save For Web dialog
   box appears.

3. **Choose the format and quality settings you want for your Web image.**

   Your choices are explained in the following section.

4. **If necessary, resize your image's dimensions.**

   If you want to make sure that anyone can see the whole image, no matter how
   small his monitor, enter 650 pixels or less for the longest side of your photo in
   the New Size area. (650 pixels is about the largest size that can fit on small monitors without scrolling, but if you're sending to someone with a really old monitor, you may want to stay below 500 pixels. If your friends all have big new
   monitors, you can go much larger.) As long as Constrain Proportions is turned
   on, you don't have to enter the dimension for the other side of your photo.

You can also resize your image by entering a percentage (for example, entering 90 shrinks your image by 10 percent). When you're finished entering the new dimensions, click Apply.

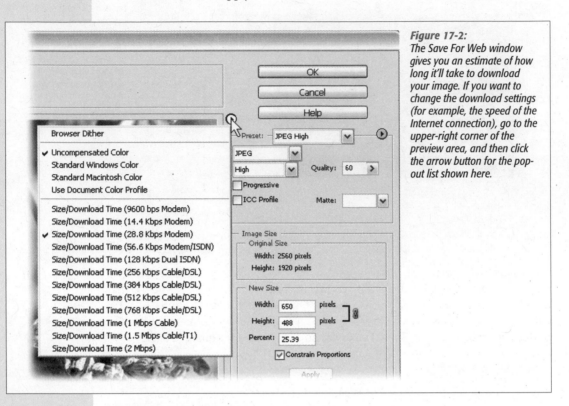

Figure 17-2:
The Save For Web window gives you an estimate of how long it'll take to download your image. If you want to change the download settings (for example, the speed of the Internet connection), go to the upper-right corner of the preview area, and then click the arrow button for the pop-out list shown here.

5. **Check your results.**

   Look at the file size again to see if it's small enough, and take a close look at the image quality in the preview area. Use Elements' file size optimization feature, if necessary, as explained in Figure 17-3. You can also preview your image in your actual Web browser (see the section "Previewing Images and Adjusting Color" on page 457).

6. **When everything looks good, click OK.**

   Name the new file, and then save it to the location of your choice. There's no Undo option in Save For Web, but you can Alt-click the Cancel button to change it to a Reset button. If you're processing several photos with the same settings, Alt-click the Help button to change it to say Remember. Then next time Save For Web opens, it'll have your current settings preselected.

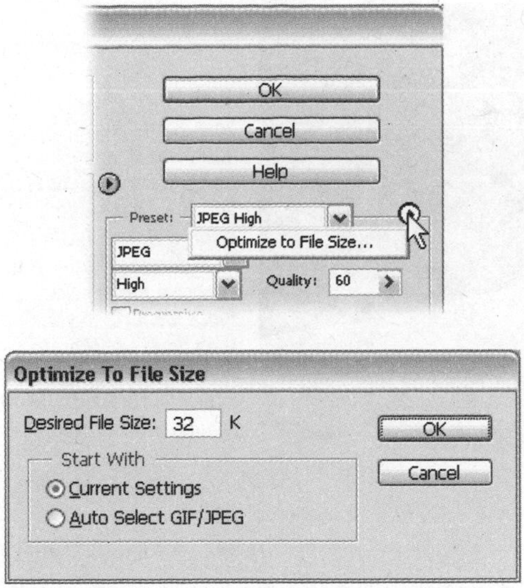

Figure 17-3:
Elements' Save For Web dialog box has a helpful file-size optimization feature for when you need to send a file someplace that puts limits on your total file size.

Top: When you click the triangle next to the Preset menu, and then choose "Optimize to File Size", Elements gives you a dialog box so you can enter your desired file size.

Bottom: Use K (kilobytes) as your unit of measurement in the Optimize To File Size dialog box. Picking Current Settings tells Elements to start with whatever settings you've entered in the main Save For Web window, like the format and quality. Autoselect GIF/JPEG means you want Elements to decide between GIF and JPEG for you. Once you've finished making your selections, click OK. Elements then reduces your image to the size you requested.

Save For Web file format options

You can reduce file size when you reduce the length and width, as explained in step 4. But you can also make your file smaller by adjusting the quality settings. Your quality options vary depending on which format you're using.

• **JPEG**. Elements offers you a variety of basic JPEG quality settings: Low, Medium, High, Very High, and Maximum. You can further adjust the quality by entering a number in the Quality box on the right. A higher number means higher quality. Generally, Medium is usually enough if you're saving for Web use. If you use Save For Web to make JPEG files for printing, then you want Maximum.

If you turn on the Progressive checkbox, then your JPEG loads from the top down. This option was popular for large files when everyone had slow dial-up connections, but it makes a slightly larger file, so it's not as popular today. Using the ICC profile checkbox, you can keep any color space profile embedded in your image. (See page 196 for more about color spaces.) With Matte, you can set the color of any area that's transparent in your original (see Figure 17-4). When you don't set a matte color, you get white. By choosing a matte color that matches the background of your Web page, you can make it look like your image is surrounded by transparency. In Elements, you have three ways to select your color: Click the arrow on the right side of the matte color box, and then choose from the menu; click the arrow, and then sample a color from your image with the eyedropper tool; or click the color square in the matte color box to call up the Color Picker. (See page 209 for more about using the Color Picker.)

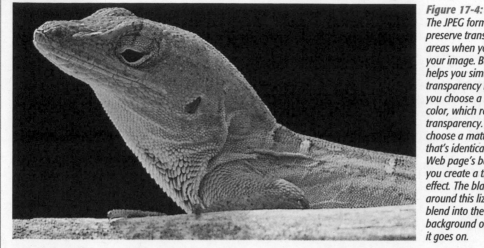

Figure 17-4:
The JPEG format doesn't preserve transparent areas when you save your image. But Elements helps you simulate transparency by letting you choose a matte color, which replaces the transparency. When you choose a matte color that's identical to your Web page's background, you create a transparent effect. The black matte around this lizard will blend into the black background of the page it goes on.

- **GIF.** The fewer colors a GIF contains, the smaller the file. In Elements, GIF format names tell you the number of colors in your GIF. For example, GIF-128 means there are 128 colors, and GIF-32 tells you there are 32 colors. You can also use the Colors box to set your own number of colors. Use the arrows on the left edge of the box to scroll to the number you want, or just type it into the box.

  If you turn on Interlacing, then your image downloads in multiple passes (sort of like an image that's slowly coming into focus). With today's computers, interlacing isn't as useful as it used to be on slower machines. If you want to keep transparent areas transparent, then leave Transparency turned on. If you don't want transparency, then choose a matte color the way you do for a JPEG, as described in the previous bullet point. When you create a GIF that you plan to animate, turn on Animate. (You have to have a layered file to make an animated GIF. See page 458 for more about animated GIFs.)

  Dithering is an important setting. The GIF format works by compressing and flattening large areas of colors. When you choose dithering, Elements blends existing colors to make it look like you have more colors than your GIF actually has. For instance, Elements may mix red and blue pixels in an area to create purple. You can choose how much dither you want. Sometimes you don't want any dithering—it depends on the image.

- **PNG-8.** The more basic of your PNG choices in Elements, PNG-8 gives you pretty much the same options as you get with GIF.

  With both PNG-8 and GIF, you get advanced options for how to display colors (generating the color lookup table if you're a Web-design maven). You can totally forget this option even exists, but if you're curious, here are your choices: Selective, the standard setting, favors broad areas of color and keeps to Web-safe colors; Perceptual favors colors to which the human eye is more sensitive;

Adaptive samples colors from the spectrum appearing most commonly in the image; and Restrictive keeps everything within the old 216-color Web palette.

- **PNG-24.** This is the more advanced level of PNG. Technically, both levels of PNG let you use transparency, but more Web browsers understand transparent areas in PNG-24 than in PNG-8. Your save options are the same as some of those for JPEG files.

NOTE   The Elements Color Picker lets you limit your choices to Web-safe colors, if you turn on Only Web Colors. But do you need to stick to this limited color palette for Web graphics? Not really. You need to be seriously concerned about keeping to Web-safe colors only if you know the majority of people looking at your image will be using very old Web browsers. All modern Web browsers have been able to cope with a normal color range for several years now.

Getting colors to display consistently in all browsers is another kettle of fish entirely. See the next section, "Previewing Images and Adjusting Color".

Previewing Images and Adjusting Color

Elements gives you a few different ways to preview how your image will look in a Web browser. You can start by looking at your image in any Web browser you have on your computer (see Figure 17-5).

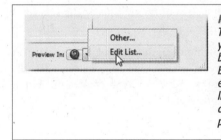

Figure 17-5:
To preview your image in a Web browser, click the Preview In icon to launch your computer's standard Web browser, or click the arrow and choose a browser from the list. The first time you click this icon, you may need to go to Edit List, as shown in the figure, and then click Find All. Elements sniffs out every browser on your computer, and automatically adds what it finds to the list of available browsers. The icon you see may vary, because Elements displays your chosen browser's icon (or the last browser you used for previewing in Elements).

To add a new browser, in the Save For Web dialog box, click the Preview In drop-down list, and then choose Edit List. Then, in the dialog box that appears, click Add Browser and navigate to the one you want. If you want to have all your browsers listed, then click Find All. From now on you can pick any browser from the list. When you do, Elements launches the browser with your image in it.

If you want to get a very rough idea of how your image will look on other people's monitors, click the arrow that's just above the upper-right corner of the right preview window. Above the modem specifications, you see a list of color options:

- **Uncompensated Color.** This option shows colors the way they normally appear on your monitor. This setting makes no adjustment to the color. It's what you usually see.

- **Standard Windows Color.** The Standard Windows Color option shows colors the way they should look on an average Windows monitor.

- **Standard Macintosh Color.** This option shows colors the way they should look on an average Mac monitor.

- **Use Document Color Profile.** If you kept the ICC profile (page 196), then this setting tries to match how your image will look as a result.

- **Browser Dither.** If an image contains more colors than a Web browser can display, the browser uses dithering (see page 456) to create the additional colors. Select this option to get an idea of how your image will look if a browser has to dither the colors.

These are all only rough approximations. You need only take a stroll down the monitor aisle at your local electronics chain to see what a wacky bunch of color variations are possible. You really can't control how other people are going to see your image unless you go to their homes and adjust their monitors for them.

> **NOTE** Changing any of these color options affects only the way the image displays on your monitor in Save For Web; it doesn't change anything in the image itself.

Creating Animated GIFs

With Elements, it's simple to create *animated GIFs*, those little animated illustrations that make Web pages look annoyingly jumbled or delightfully active, depending on your tastes. If you've ever seen a strip of movie film or the cels for a cartoon, Elements creates a similar series of frames with these specialized GIFs.

Animated GIFs are made in layers. (If you download an animated GIF, and open it up in Elements, then it appears as a multi-layered image.) When you create an animated GIF, you make a new layer for each frame. Save For Web creates the actual animation, which you can preview in a Web browser.

> **NOTE** It's a shame that you can't easily animate a JPEG the way you can a GIF. Most elaborate Web animations involving photographs are done with Flash, which is another program altogether. You can learn a little more about Flash on page 467. However, Elements offers another option if you want to make a standalone animation as opposed to an animated graphic for a Web page. Check out flipbooks on page 484. You can build cartoon-like Windows Media format animations using flipbooks.

Probably the best way to learn how to create an animated GIF is to make one. Here's a little tutorial on making twinkling stars:

Before you start, set your background color to black and your foreground color to some shade of yellow. (See page 209 if you need help setting your foreground and background colors.)

1. **Create a new document.**

   Press Ctrl+N. Set the size to 200 pixels × 200 pixels, choose RGB for the Color mode, and then choose Background Color for your Background Contents.

2. **Activate the Custom Shape Tool.**

From the Shapes palette (in the Options bar), click the arrow at the upper right of the palette, and then, from the menu, select Nature. Choose the Sun 2 shape, which is in the top row, second from the left.

3. **Draw some stars.**

Draw one yellow star, and then, in the Options bar, click the "add to shape area" square before drawing four or five more stars. (This step puts all the stars on the same layer, which is important, since then you won't have a bunch of layers to merge.)

4. **Merge the star layer and the background layer.**

Choose Layer → Merge Down. You now have one layer containing yellow stars on a black background, like the bottom layer shown in Figure 17-6.

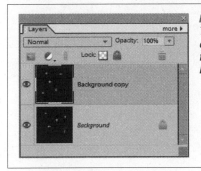

Figure 17-6:
This animated GIF has only two frames, which makes for a pretty crude animation. The more frames you have, the smoother the animation. But more frames make a bigger file, too. On a tiny image like this one, size doesn't matter, but with a larger image, your file can get huge pretty fast.

5. **Duplicate the layer.**

Choose Layer → Duplicate Layer. You now have two identical layers.

6. **Rotate the top layer 90 degrees.**

Click any other tool in the Toolbox, and then go to Image → Rotate → Layer 90° Left (if the Move Custom Shape tool is active, then the Rotate command doesn't work). You should now have two layers with stars in different places on each one, which is why you did the rotation.

7. **Animate your GIF.**

Go to File → Save For Web, and then turn on the Animate checkbox. (Select GIF as your Save format if Elements hasn't already done so; you don't see the Animate checkbox for other formats.) You can adjust the time between frames if you want. Leave Loop turned on. That step makes the animation repeat over and over. When you turn Loop off, your animation plays once and stops.

8. **Preview your animation.**

You can use the arrows in the animation controls to step through your animation one frame at a time, but for a more realistic preview, view the image in a Web browser (explained in the previous section). The stars should twinkle. Well, OK, they flash off and on—think of twinkle lights. Save your animation, if you like, by clicking OK.

ON THE WEB

Creating Web Buttons

Elements makes it a snap to create buttons to use on Web pages. Here's what you need to do:

1. Create a new blank file (File → New → Blank File) choosing one of the Web sizes, and then set the background to be transparent.

2. Set the Foreground color square to the color you want to use for your button, and use the Shape tool to draw the shape you want.

   (It helps to choose Actual Pixels for your view size when doing Web work, because that gives you the same size you'll see in a Web browser.)

3. Apply one or more Layer styles (page 382) to make your button look more three-dimensional.

   Bevels, some of the Complex Layer styles, or the Wow Layer styles are all popular choices.

4. Add any necessary text using the Type tool (page 399).

   You may want to apply a Layer style to the text, too.

5. Save as a GIF.

Emailing Your Photos

With Elements, emailing your photos is a piece of cake. With just a few clicks, Elements preps your image, fires up your email program, and attaches your image to an outgoing email. Of course, you can email images yourself (without Elements' help), and you may prefer that method since you get more freedom to specify settings like file size.

Emailing Images

The Organizer gives you an almost bewildering array of formatting choices for emailing your photos. You can send simple attachments, send prearranged groups of photos, frame your photos, change the background color, and so on. Here are your main choices:

- **E-mail Attachments.** This is the most traditional option, whereby you send each photo as a standard email attachment.

- **PhotoMail (HTML).** Elements lets you send emails formatted in HTML, the language used to create Web pages. This option gives you all kinds of fancy design choices, and your photo gets embedded in the body of the email—it's basically like emailing someone a custom-built Web page featuring your image.

The catch is that the recipient has to be using a mail program that understands HTML mail. Most newer email programs fit the bill, but if you're emailing someone who uses ancient software like AOL 4, then your email formatting doesn't appear correctly. An even larger problem, though, is if your recipient has her email program's HTML option turned off; your email doesn't appear with all its formatting intact. Page 463 gives you more information about Elements' HTML mail options.

- **PDF Slide Show.** This option creates a basic PDF-format slideshow of all your images. All you have to do is name your slideshow. Read more about slideshows on page 465.

You need to choose the kind of email you want to send before you start; you do that by clicking the one you want in the Create pane. The main procedure is pretty similar for all three types, and is explained in detail below.

> **NOTE** Remember that description a few paragraphs ago about Elements prepping your image and automatically launching your email program? That works only if you're using Vista's Windows Mail, Outlook Express, Outlook, or Adobe's own mail server. You can't use other email programs, like Yahoo Mail or Thunderbird, for instance. If you want to use a different email program, just use the Attach button in your email program instead. (You can export your image from the Organizer to the desktop to make it easier to find, if necessary.)

Sending from the Organizer has one big annoyance, though: You get an ad for Elements in every message you send from Elements.

> **TIP** Don't want to be in the advertising business? To get rid of the Adobe ad at the bottom of your messages, highlight it in the message, and then press Backspace. Or, if you want to eliminate it from all your Elements emails, go to *C:\Program Files\Adobe\Photoshop Elements 7.0\Assets\locale\en_us\email\signatures*. Open the files you find there using a text editor like Notepad and remove the advertising lines. Save the change, and from now on, your email will be ad free.

Individual attachments

To send your files as regular email attachments, just follow these steps:

> **TIP** If you want to email photos not already in the Organizer, open them in the Editor before you start, and then choose Share → E-Mail Attachments.

1. **In the Organizer, select your photos, and then go to Share → E-Mail Attachments.**

   You can preselect photos before you start, or add or change them once the email pane appears. Figure 17-7 explains how.

   In the email pane, below the image thumbnails, you see some information that can help you decide how many photos to send and how large to make them:

   - **Number of Items.** Indicates how many photos you've selected to mail.

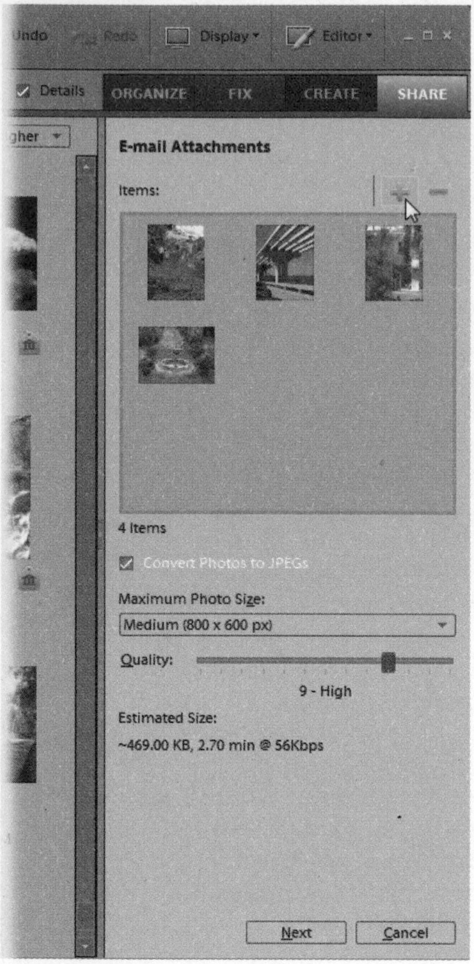

Figure 17-7:
The Organizer's email pane is pretty easy to use. You can start with one photo or a selected group, as shown here. To send more photos, just drag the photo thumbnails from the Photo Browser into the email pane. You can also highlight the photos in the Photo Browser, and then, at the top of the window, click the Add button (the green + sign). Remove photos you don't want by highlighting them, and then clicking Delete (the red – button, which is grayed out in this image). Drag your photos in the pane to change their order.

- **Convert Photos to JPEGs**. JPEG is the preferred format for emailing photos, so you can turn on this checkbox to make all your photos into JPEGs. If your photos are already JPEGs, then the option's grayed out. If you just want to convert some of your photos to JPEGs, select their thumbnails, and then turn on this checkbox.

- **Maximum Photo Size**. This sets how large you want your emailed photos to be. Remember that it can take a very long time to download a large image with a dial-up connection, and many email providers have a 10 MB limit per mailbox. If you need to change the size, then use the pull-down menu to choose a new size.

- **Quality**. If you're just emailing photos for viewing onscreen, then you can get away with a lower-quality setting than you can for photos that the recipient is going to print.

Finally, below these settings you can see Elements' calculations as to how large the attachment will be and how long it'll take to download with a dial-up connection (a useful warning if you're sending to people with slow Internet connections). When you're satisfied with your attachment, click Next. (The first time you use this feature, you also get asked to choose the email program you want Elements to use.)

2. **Enter your message (optional).**

    In this pane, you can change or remove the message that automatically comes up, which says, "Here are the photos that I want to share with you." To remove or change it permanently, follow the steps listed on page 461 for changing the signature. The message is in the same folder.

3. **Address your email (optional).**

    Decide whether you want to enter an email address now. You can:

    • **Do nothing**. Wait until Elements is through, and then type the address in the completed email before you send it.

    • **Select Recipients**. Elements keeps a Contact Book—a list of people to whom you regularly send emails. You can simply select names from the list. Read more about it in the box on page 464. If you haven't used the Elements email feature before, then start by clicking the Edit Contacts button (the little silhouette just above the Select Recipients window), and entering the contact information of your recipient.

    • **Edit Contacts**. If you want to enter a new recipient or change the information for someone in your list, then click the Edit Contacts button (the silhouette), and enter the information in the Contact Book.

    • **Save as Quick Share Flow**. If you want to make the recipient one of your regular options in the Order Prints pane, turn this on, and then choose a name you'll recognize. Then the next time you go to Order Prints, you see it in the list. You can just click to select it and save typing it over again.

4. **To finish, click Next.**

    Elements launches your email program, creates a new message, and attaches the files for you. You can make any changes to the message or recipient in your email program now, if you'd rather do it here. (If your files are large for emailing, then Elements warns you about it, and suggests burning a CD instead.)

PhotoMail options

Elements also gives you a ton of options for gussying up your photos if you choose PhotoMail, which is actually HTML mail. When you send HTML mail, your message gets formatted using a *template*, a stationery design in which your photo appears.

ORGANIZATION STATION

The Contact Book

The Organizer makes it easy to call up the addresses of people you regularly email by keeping a Contact Book. Any time you send email to a new recipient, you first have to add the address to the Contact Book by clicking the Edit Contacts button (the silhouette) in the E-mail window. You can also get to the Contact Book by choosing Edit → Contact Book in the Photo Browser or Date view.

Once you've got the Contact Book open, click the New Contact button to add an address. Then you can enter a name, email address, phone number, and other contact info. To edit or delete a contact, just highlight it in the list, and then click the relevant button.

You can also create groups of names in the Contact book, for times when you want to send the same photo to several people at once. To do this, click New Group, enter a name for the group, select an entry or entries in the Contact

Book, and then click Add. The name goes into the Members list. To remove a name from the group, highlight it in the Members list, and then click Remove.

You can easily coordinate the Contact Book with your existing address book. You can choose to import addresses from Vista's Windows Mail, Microsoft Outlook or Outlook Express, as well as any that you saved as V-cards (an industry standard for digitally storing business card information) in other programs. Just click Import and choose your source. You can also export your Contact Book addresses as V-cards for use in other programs.

In Elements 7, if you have a Photoshop.com account (see page 18), then your Contact Book is stored online, so Elements nags you to connect to Photoshop.com if you try to use it when you aren't connected. If you don't use Photoshop.com, then your Contact Book is stored on your computer and should always be available to you.

The procedure for sending PhotoMail is pretty much the same as for regular attachments, but in the first pane you can choose whether to display captions along with your photos.

When you click Next in Step 4, a wizard (a series of guided question screens) presents a long list of stationery theme categories with several choices in each. The preview window updates to show each one as you click it. You can add a caption to any photo in this window by highlighting the text below the photo and typing what you want. When you find a style you like, click Next Step to go to the next window.

When you're mailing more than one photo, you have a choice of several different page layouts. Below the layouts, you can choose a typeface (from a list of five common fonts). Click the box to the right of the font name to choose a color for the text. You can also customize the frame or border around your photos, as shown in Figure 17-8. Each time you make a change in the left pane of the window, Elements updates the preview so you can see just what you're getting.

When you've adjusted everything to your liking, click Next. (Click Cancel if you don't want to send the email after all, or Previous Step if you want to go back and choose a different theme.) Elements now creates your ready-to-send email. You can make any changes to the message and address just as you would to any other email. And you send it off like any other email, too.

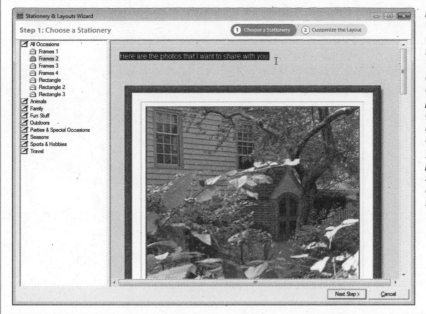

Figure 17-8:
You can choose from various frame styles in the Stationery & Layouts Wizard. If you've chosen a frame style that leaves empty space around the photo, then you can customize the background color of your email. For some styles, you can adjust the padding (the matte-like space between the photo and the frame) and the frame size.

PDF slideshows

You can also email a group of your photos as a slideshow. Elements uses the popular PDF format, which lets your recipients page through each slide using the ubiquitous Adobe Reader program. They just open the PDF and view the photos one by one. You can create a PDF slideshow from the Create menu's More Options choices (see page 472) if you don't want to deal with the Slide Show Editor (covered in more detail on page 473).

To do so, just select your photos as described earlier, and then go to Share → More Options → PDF Slide Show. You get offered a choice of sizes and quality, just as you do for regular email attachments. Name the slideshow, and then click Next. In the next pane, enter a message or recipients if you like, and then click Next. Elements generates a standard email message with the slideshow as a PDF attachment.

> **TIP**   You may have noticed that Elements lacks a feature that lets you send photos to Palm PDAs and smartphones. Here's Adobe's suggested workaround for sending photos to your Palm handheld with Elements: Create a slideshow using photos sized to fit the screen of the device you want to use as a viewer, and then save in the PDF format. Upload the PDF file using whatever software you normally use to send files to your Palm, and then use Adobe Reader for Palm OS to view the show. (You can download Reader for Palm OS at *www.adobe.com/products/acrobat/readerforpalm.html*.)

CHAPTER 18

Online Albums and Slideshows

Last chapter, you learned how to email your photos. But what if you've got legions of friends? Do you have to email your pictures to everyone? Not with Elements, which makes it incredibly simple to post photos online, thanks to Photoshop.com, a one-stop shop where you share your photos and back them up online. You can create fancy online albums complete with professional-looking effects, courtesy of Flash, the ubiquitous Adobe program that's responsible for zillions of nifty online animations.

Elements can also help you put together elaborate slideshows, complete with slick between-photo transitions like wipes and dissolves, clip art, and even audio. And for the perfect combination of high-tech wizardry and old-school charm, you can make digital *flipbooks*, simple slideshows that are easy to share with friends. Like the flipbooks of yore, these little shows can make a series of still photos appear to move, like an animated cartoon. Finally, Adobe has teamed up with Yahoo to give photo-taking map lovers a way to indulge both passions: customizable Yahoo maps sprinkled with photos detailing your latest road trip. In this chapter, you'll learn the ins and outs of all these ways of sharing your photos.

Online Albums

Adobe calls these "albums," but the online albums you create from Elements 7 aren't just boring grid-like rows of photos like you see on most photo Web sites. Instead they're elaborate Flash-based displays in which your photos do things like appear in an animation of old-fashioned slides dropped onto a table, and your friends sift through the pile and click the slides they want for a closeup view. Cool.

You can choose whether to share your album with the whole world or limit viewing to your family and friends. You won't believe how easily you can create and share these elaborate online creations:

1. **If your photos aren't already in an album, create one.**

   Flip back to page 53 for details.

2. **In the Organizer's Album pane, click the name of the album you want to use.**

   If you want to change the order in which the photos display, now's the time to do so. Just drag the photos to rearrange them.

3. **Click the Share button (see Figure 18-1, circled).**

   If you're already signed into Photoshop.com, you go straight to the Online Album wizard. If not, you get the sign-in screen first.

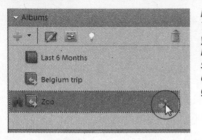

Figure 18-1:
The circled button takes you to Photoshop.com. If you aren't signed in, then you get a window to enter your password, or create an account if you don't have one yet (see page 18 for more about Photoshop.com). Once you're signed in, you get taken to the Online Album wizard, a series of guided question screens that walks you through the process of creating your online gallery.

4. **Choose a different template, if you wish.**

   Elements starts you off by displaying your photos in an automatically playing fancy little slideshow where the thumbnails glide along beneath the larger image area. If you want something different, click Change Template (next to the album thumbnail). In the pane that appears, choose a template category from the pull-down menu, and then click around on the various template thumbnails that appear. When you see one you like, click Apply. The left side of the window gives you a large preview of what your photos will look like in the selected template, and there's a text description of the template below the thumbnails area, too.

   NOTE In the template list, you see the same little blue and gold banners on some thumbnails that you see in the Content palette (page 429). They mean the same thing here: If a template has a blue banner, you can download it to your computer for free (if you have a Photoshop.com account). If the banner is gold, you need a Plus account (the paid version) to download it. Once you download a template you won't see the banner anymore.

   Some templates play as a slideshow automatically, others are interactive, as explained in Figure 18-2. (If you don't click Apply, then the last template style you clicked on gets applied when you move to the next step, but if that wasn't what you wanted, don't worry. You get another chance later to change the template.) Click Next to continue, or Cancel if you decide you don't want to share your album.

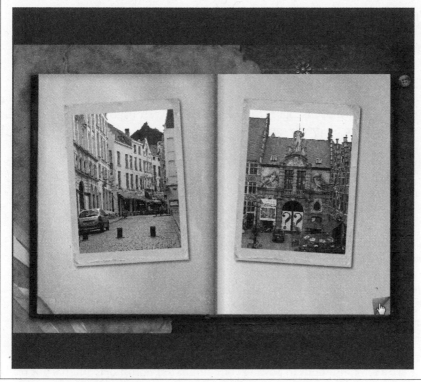

Figure 18-2:
Some of the album styles automatically start playing their slideshows, while others, like the Scrapbook template shown here, are interactive. Your friends "turn" the pages of the book to go backwards and forwards through your album.

5. **Give your Album a title.**

   If you don't add your own title, then the album is boringly titled "My Photos." Just highlight that text, and then type what you want. You can add a sub-title, too, if you like (just type what you want in the box provided), and choose whether or not to include captions you've added to your photos (turn on the checkbox). Click Refresh to see your title appear in the Preview area. Click Next when you're done with this step.

6. **Finally, share your new creation with your friends and family.**

   This last pane is where you decide who gets to see the album and what you want them to be able to do with it. If you want to show your work to the world, then choose "Share publicly with everyone". If you want to keep your album private, choose "E-mail my friends only (don't share publicly)".

   Then, in the box provided, type the message you want to send about the album, and then turn on the checkboxes next to the people you want to notify. This list is based on your Elements Contact Book (page 464). If you want to tell someone who's not currently in the list, then you can create new Contact Book entries by clicking the Edit Recipients icon (above the right corner of the recipient's list). Your chosen recipients receive an email with your message (plus a big Adobe ad) and a link to your album.

TIP   If you don't want to hassle with creating contacts every time you invite different people to view an album, just send the invitation to yourself, copy the link from the email you receive, and then paste that into a regular email to send to your recipients. You can also just copy the URL from the address bar of your Web browser, once the album is posted on Photoshop.com.

Lastly, you can turn on two checkboxes if you want to let people download your photos or order prints right from the album's Web page. Prints ordered this way come from *Shutterfly.com*.

NOTE   You can put your album into an existing album group if you have any setup. Just choose the group you want from the pull-down menu. (You can't create a new group in the wizard.) See page 55 for more about creating album groups. If you have so many albums it's hard to keep track of them, or you just like to be very organized, then groups can be useful.

7. **Click Share, and wait for the compliments on your photos and your Web design skills to pour in.**

NOTE   If you aren't in the US, then when you create an Online Album, you do so at Adobe's Photoshop Showcase Web site (page 3) rather than Photoshop.com. The procedure is exactly the same, and so are the templates available. However, your options for downloading and sharing the photos from the completed album may be different.

There are a few limitations to posting your album to Photoshop.com. It's not really private, for one thing—anyone who can figure out your Photoshop.com Web address can see your albums, whether you invite them or not. And maybe you have friends with dial-up Internet connections—the online albums take forever to appear for those with a slow connection. Fortunately, Adobe gives you two other ways to share the galleries you build using the wizard: you can post them to your own Web site, or burn them to a CD or DVD and mail them to friends. The next section explains how.

Other Ways to Share

You're not limited to creating these snazzy galleries at Photoshop.com. Even if you never sign up for a Photoshop.com account, you can still create the same galleries and impress friends with them, since you can also upload a gallery to your own Web site via FTP (File Transfer Protocol, the way you'd send any other files to your site), or just burn a CD or DVD.

To do either one, in the Organizer's Albums pane, just right click the album's name for a pop-out menu that gives you several options, including two for sharing:

- **Export to FTP.** Choose this and the right side of the Organizer presents you with a pane where you can choose a different template if you like, or rename your album. Then enter the FTP address of your Web server (get this from your site host if you don't know it), your username and password, and the name of the folder where you want Elements to place the gallery.

Then click Export. Elements builds your album and sends it to your server. If all goes well, you'll have the same album on your site that you could have built at Photoshop.com. (The only options missing are the ones for printing and downloading.)

> **TIP** If you want to check to be sure that Elements can "see" your server, click "Test Access to Server". Elements contacts your Web host and presents you with a window where you can watch the steps as it tries to log on and upload the file. As it completes each step a green checkmark appears. If you see the red "no" symbol, then there was a problem with that step and you have to figure out what went awry.

- **Export to CD/DVD.** Here you get the same options for renaming and changing the template as you do for an FTP export, but instead of entering server information, you choose the drive to use to burn the disc and enter a name for the CD or DVD. Click Export, and Elements asks you to insert a disc. Put one in, then click OK. Elements burns the disc, then asks if you want to verify it. You do. Finally, it reminds you to label the completed disc before it ejects it.

Discs made this way play in a computer, not in a DVD player. If your friends use Windows, the disc should play automatically when they put it into their computer. If that doesn't work (sometimes the Flash loading animation loops endlessly and the slideshow never runs), or if they're using Macs, tell them to open the disc, navigate to the Root folder, and then double-click the Index.html file inside that. The slideshow plays in their Web browser.

You can share albums this way even if you also uploaded them to Photoshop.com. It's a really handy way to make a very fancy slideshow.

> **NOTE** You can also choose one of these sharing methods when you first create an album in the Organizer's Album pane—just click Share rather than Done at the bottom of the new album panel. After your album has been created, Sharing takes you to straight to Photoshop.com if you have an account there. (In other words, you won't see the same options again.)

Slideshows

Online albums are about the easiest way you'll find to make a fancy slideshow, but maybe you want more control than they give you, or maybe you'd like to add features like music or panning and zooming over your photos, à la Ken Burns. Elements makes it easy to create very slick little slideshows—some even with music and transitions between the images—that you can play on your PC or send to your friends.

By using the Slide Show feature, you can make extremely elaborate slideshows. If you prefer the simple life, you can quickly create a plain vanilla PDF slideshow in about as much time as it takes to email a photo.

The simple PDF slideshow is really straightforward to create, and looks quite impressive, but you can't add audio to it or control how your slides transition. On the plus side, you can send a PDF slideshow to anyone, regardless of what operating system that person uses. As long as your recipients have Adobe Reader or another PDF-viewing program, they can watch your show.

The Slide Show Editor, on the other hand, lets you indulge your creativity big time. You can add all sorts of snazzy transitions, mix in sound in the form of background music or narration, add clip art, pan around your slides, and more. It's a bit more complex to work with the Slide Show Editor than to make a PDF, but the real drawback to the Slide Show Editor comes in your choices for the final output. The slideshow you create isn't as universally compatible as the PDF slideshow, as explained later in this chapter.

> **NOTE**   If you plan to create a simple PDF slideshow, then you need to do all your photo editing beforehand. The Slide Show Editor, on the other hand, lets you edit as much as you like before you finalize your slideshow.

PDF Slideshows

Elements gives you two ways to create a PDF slideshow. The first, the Simple PDF slideshow, is very basic, just a quick run-through of the photos you choose. If you make a PDF in the Slide Show Editor, then you can create something slightly more elaborate.

Simple PDF slideshow

The hardest thing about creating a PDF slideshow in Elements is figuring out where to start. Elements hides the Simple PDF slideshow option under Share → More Options → PDF Slideshow. Once you find it, it's as easy as sending an email. You can read more about it on page 465. This slideshow has no transitions, no clip art, and no custom type, but it's the most compatible kind of slideshow you can make in Elements. And you can easily create a reasonable-sized file so anybody can watch it, no matter how underpowered their computer.

Making a PDF in the Slide Show Editor

You have another way to create a PDF slideshow, although it's not as intuitive as the method just described. When you create a show in the Slide Show Editor, you can choose between saving your slide show as a Windows Media Video (WMV) file or a PDF. If you want to preserve your show's multimedia bells and whistles, then you need to choose WMV. But then there's that tantalizing PDF option. You may think this PDF slideshow sounds like the best of both worlds—a very compatible format and all the fancy effects you created with the Slide Show Editor.

Unfortunately, that's not quite how it works. When you create a PDF this way, you lose the pan and zoom feature (page 481), the audio, and the transitions that you set. You do keep any custom slides, text, and clip art that you added, though. On the whole, this feature's best used when you've created a full-scale slideshow, but one or two of the people you want to send it to can't view it in Windows Media format. The people who get the PDF can't see everything the WMV recipients do, but it's faster than trying to recreate a separate version for the WMV-challenged.

To create a PDF using the Slide Show Editor, just follow the instructions in the following section for creating a slideshow. When you're ready to create your PDF, click Output, and then choose "Save As a File" in the Slide Show Output window that opens. On the right side of the Slide Show Output window, click the PDF File button. This step brings up a series of settings just for your PDF:

- **Slide Size.** This setting starts out at Small. If you're going to burn a CD, then you can choose a larger size. If you want to email the final file, then choose Small or Very Small for your images. You also have a Custom choice for when you want to create a size that's different from one of the presets.

- **Loop.** Turn this on, and the slideshow repeats over and over until your viewer stops it by pressing the Escape key.

- **Manual Advance.** If you want recipients to be able to click their way through the slideshow instead of having each slide automatically advance to the next one, turn this on.

- **View Slide Show after Saving.** Turn this on, and as soon as Elements is through creating your slideshow, it launches Adobe Reader so you can watch the results of your work.

    TIP If you want to make a PDF from an existing slideshow, in the Photo Browser, right-click the slideshow's thumbnail, and then choose Edit. Once the Slide Show Editor opens, click Output → "Save As a File".

When you've got everything set the way you want it, click OK to bring up the Save As dialog box. Name your file, and then save it.

Using the Slide Show Editor

The Slide Show Editor lets you add audio, clip art, and nifty slide-to-slide transitions. You also get several different ways to share your completed slideshow, including making a Video CD (VCD) or—if you also have Premiere Elements—a DVD that your friends can watch in a regular DVD player. If your operating system is Vista (Home Premium or Ultimate) or Windows Media Center Edition, then you can even send your slideshow to your TV and watch it there (as long as you have your television hooked up to your computer, Xbox 360, or other device that can play WMV files).

To get started, from the Organizer, select the images you want to include. You may want to set up an album (page 53), which lets you control the order of your images. (You can change the order once you're in the Slide Show Editor, but for large shows, you save time if you have things arranged in pretty much the correct order when you start.) You can also start with a single photo and, once you're in the Slide Show Editor, click the Add Media button to add more photos. In any case, once you've got your initial photos selected, go to Create → Slide Show.

UP TO SPEED

Choosing a Slideshow

A couple of versions ago, people sometimes slammed Elements for not offering much in the way of slideshows. Now Elements gives you so many slideshow options you might get overwhelmed trying to decide which one to choose. Here are some suggestions to help you out:

- **Slideshows for the Web**. If you want to share your slideshow on the Internet, create an Online Album (page 467).

- **Slideshows with audio**. If you want a soundtrack for your slideshow, use the Slide Show Editor to create your show, and burn it to a disc to share with friends, who can watch the show on their computers, using Windows Media Player.

- **Slideshows to view on TV**. If you have Vista Home Premium or Ultimate or Windows Media Center Edition, use the Slide Show Editor, and choose "Send to TV" as your output choice. If you want to send a slideshow to someone else to watch on her TV, you can try a VCD. But frankly, you'd be better off using another program like Adobe's Premiere Elements or any other DVD-authoring software to create a true DVD, if your computer has a DVD burner.

- **Slideshows for people uncomfortable with technology**. You've got two options here, neither of which is guaranteed to prevent Uncle Joe from badgering you that he can't see pictures of his new grand-niece. You can create an Online Album (page 467) and send a disc or email a link, but of course recipients need a Web browser with Flash installed. The simple PDF slideshow (page 456) is also pretty straightforward. (However, your recipients still have to have Adobe Reader or another PDF viewer to watch the show. If you know they don't have Reader and won't know how to install it, try a Flipbook [page 484] at the slowest setting.) For the severely techno-challenged, consider a photo book, described on page 430.

Finally, if you still don't think Elements offers enough choices for you, ProShow Gold from Photodex (*www.photodex.com*) is probably the most popular slideshow program for Windows. And if you don't like the Elements Photo Galleries, JAlbum (*http://jalbum.net*) is a popular free alternative, although these days many people just use one of the photo sharing services mentioned on page 491 to create their slideshows online.

Slide Show Preferences

Once you choose to create a slideshow, Elements presents you with the Slide Show Preferences window before you get into the actual Slide Show Editor. You can click right past this window if you like, but it does give you some useful options for telling Elements how you want it to handle certain aspects of all your shows, like the duration of each slide and the color of the background. (You can also change these settings for a particular show in the Slide Show Editor itself.)

In the Slide Show Preferences, you can adjust:

- **Static Duration.** This determines how long each slide displays before it moves on to the next one.

- **Transition.** This setting tells Elements how to move from one slide to the next. You get many different transition styles to choose from, like a pinwheel effect or having the next slide move into view from the side. If you choose a different transition from the pop-out menu, then you can audition it in the little preview area at the right of the window, as explained in Figure 18-3.

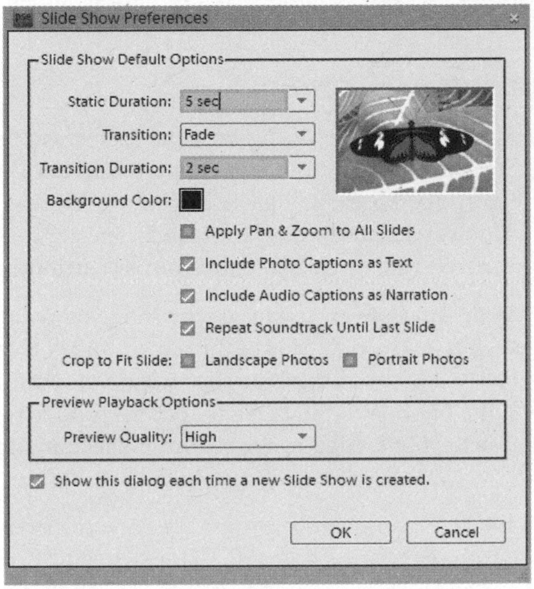

Figure 18-3:
You can set the slide duration and background color for all your slideshows in the Slide Show Preferences window. It's also a great place to audition different transitions. If you want to see how a particular transition looks, select it from the Transition drop-down menu. You see it play in the little preview area on the right. If you choose a transition here, then Elements automatically applies it to every slide. But you can override this setting for individual slides in the Slide Show Editor's Storyboard by clicking the transition you want to change, and choosing a different one.

- **Transition Duration.** Use this to set how fast you want the transitions to happen.

- **Background Color.** Click the color square for the Elements Color Picker (see page 209) if you want a different background color.

- **Apply Pan and Zoom to All Slides.** If you set up the Pan and Zoom feature (explained later in this chapter) for one slide, turn this on, and the camera swoops around every slide.

- **Include Photo Captions as Text.** If you want to display a photo's Caption field, turn on this checkbox. (This works in reverse, too—you can hide your captions by just turning off this checkbox.)

- **Include Audio Captions as Narration.** If you've recorded audio captions for your slides, leave this checkbox turned on if you want your audience to hear them.

- **Repeat Soundtrack Until Last Slide.** Leave this checkbox turned on, and if you run out of music on your soundtrack, then Elements fixes things for you by repeating your song as many times as necessary.

- **Crop to Fit Slide**. Turn on either of these checkboxes (for landscape- and portrait-oriented photos) and, if your image is too large for the slide, then Elements chops off the excess for you. However, it's best to do any cropping (page 79) yourself before starting your slideshow.

- **Preview Playback Options**. Choose the quality for previewing your show while you're working on it. The quality you pick for previewing doesn't affect the quality of the final slideshow.

Once you're through with these preferences, click OK. If you don't want to see the preferences every time you start a new show, then just turn off "Show this dialog each time a new Slide Show is created". You can still get back to the window at any time when you're in the Slide Show Editor by going to Edit → Slide Show Preferences.

Creating your slideshow using the Slide Show Editor

After you click OK in the Slide Show Preferences dialog box, the Elements Slide Show Editor launches. It's crammed with options, but everything is laid out very logically—in fact, it's pretty similar to the Elements Full Edit window. You get a menu bar across the top of the window, but most of the commands here are available elsewhere via a button or a keystroke (like Ctrl+Z to undo your last action).

On the left side of the window, in the preview area, you see the slide you're currently working on. There's a Palette bin on the right side of the screen, and you can collapse it just like the Full Edit Palette bin, by clicking its edge when you want to get it out of your way. Collapsing the bin makes the preview space expand across the window. Click the hidden Palette bin's edge again to bring the bin back onscreen.

At the bottom of the window, in the *Storyboard*, you see your slides and the transitions between them. (If you didn't preselect any photos, the Storyboard just says "Click Here to Add Photos to Your Slide Show".) Click a slide or transition here, and its properties (duration, background color, pan and zoom settings) appear in the Palette bin. If you don't want to see the Storyboard anymore, go to the Slide Show Editor's View menu, and then turn it off by removing the checkmark next to its name. You can turn it back on again there, too.

> **TIP** If you want to add photos to your slideshow, click the Add Media button at the top of the Slide Show Editor's preview window. The advantage to bringing photos in this way (as opposed to selecting them before you start creating your slideshow) is that you can choose to use photos, videos, and audio clips that *aren't* in the Organizer, by choosing either the "Photos and Video from Folder..." or the "Audio from Folder..." option and then navigating to the files you want. You can even edit your photos right in the Slide Show Editor. The disadvantage is that you have to choose each photo separately or you have no control over the order in which Elements brings them into the show.

You can finesse your show in lots of different ways in the Slide Show Editor. For instance, you can:

- **Edit your slide.** You can make any kind of editing changes to your photo right here in the Slide Show Editor. In the preview window, just double-click your image, and then, using the choices that appear in the Properties palette (Figure 18-4), you can rotate your slide, change its size, crop it, and apply the Auto Smart Fix (page 105) and the Auto Red Eye Fix (page 105). If you want to do more substantial editing, then just click the More Editing button, and Elements whisks your slide over to Full Edit.

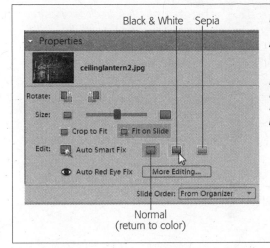

Figure 18-4:
The three little thumbnails to the right of the Slide Show Editor's Auto Smart Fix button let you change your photo to black and white or sepia and back to color again, if you change your mind. To change your slide to black and white or sepia, just click the button for the effect you want. To undo a color change you make here, click the Normal button. The changes you make with these buttons affect only the photo on your slide, not the original photo.

- **Duration.** You see a duration number (listed below each slide in the Storyboard and also in the Properties area) indicating how long a slide appears on the screen before it transitions to the next slide. Click the arrow to the right of the number (it's very hard to see, but it's there) for a pop-up menu that lets you change how long that particular slide appears onscreen. You don't need to assign the same amount of time to each slide. You can also use the pull-down menu next to the slide's thumbnail in the Properties palette, but only if you want to choose a duration between 3 and 7 seconds. Otherwise, in the Storyboard's pull-down menu, use the Custom choice. (Click the transition time beneath the slide to see this menu.)

- **Transition.** Elements gives you a lot of different ways to get from one slide to the next. These transitions appear in the Storyboard, and are represented by small thumbnail icons between the two slides they connect. (The transition icon changes to reflect the current transition style when you choose a new transition.)

On the right side of the Storyboard transition icon, you see a tiny arrow. Click it to see a pop-out menu listing all transitions, and then choose a different kind of transition, if you like.

Transitions have their own Properties palettes, which appear when you click a transition in the Storyboard. You can choose how long a transition is going to take and, for some transitions, the direction in which you want the transition to move.

If you like to make long slideshows, you'll appreciate the Quick Reorder feature, explained in Figure 18-5. When you switch over to the Quick Reorder window, you see all your slides in a view that looks like a contact sheet, making it easy to reposition slides that would be annoyingly far apart if you had to move them in the Storyboard. In Quick Reorder, you can easily drag them to another spot in the lineup without the hassle of scrolling.

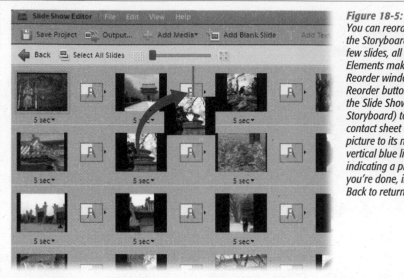

Figure 18-5:
You can reorder slides by dragging them in the Storyboard, but if you have more than a few slides, all that scrolling is a pain. Elements makes it easier with the Quick Reorder window. Just click the Quick Reorder button in the lower-left corner of the Slide Show Editor (just above the Storyboard) to bring up what looks like a contact sheet of your slides. Then drag any picture to its new location. You see a vertical blue line (the arrow points to one), indicating a photo's new position. When you're done, in the upper-left corner, click Back to return to the main editing window.

You can also change the order of all your slides by using the Slide Order drop-down menu above the right side of the Storyboard, although your choices there are limited. If you start a slideshow by first selecting your photos from the Organizer, then the Slide Order menu reads From Organizer, but you can choose Date (Oldest First), Date (Newest First), Random, Folder Location, Custom (this is what you see if you manually drag slides to new locations), and Reset (which puts your photos back in the order they were in when you first brought them into the Slide Show Editor).

Adding special effects

Elements gives you all kinds of ways to gussy up your slideshow, including adding clip art, text, and sound. If you want a slide that lists credits, for instance, start by creating a blank slide. (Click the slide immediately before the spot where you want the blank slide, and then, above the preview area, just click the Add Blank Slide button.) Elements produces a blank slide, to which you can then add whatever you like—your credits, for instance. Here's a rundown of what you can add to your blank slide (or to any of your slides, for that matter, as shown in Figure 18-6). Just click the relevant button (Graphics, Text, or Narration) in the Extras section at the top of the palette to see your options.

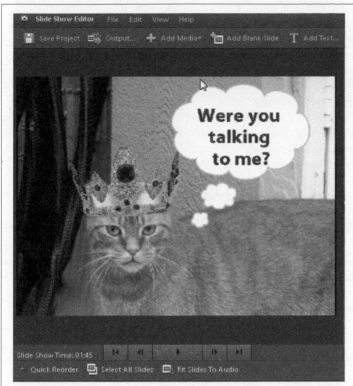

Figure 18-6:
You can add all sorts of clip art to your slides, as well as create slides that include only art or text. If you're wondering how to angle clip art, like the crown here, see the Tip on page 480.

- **Graphics.** Elements gives you a whole library's worth of clip art you can add to your slides. The art is divided into these categories: animals, backgrounds, costumes, flowers, food, frames, holidays and special occasions, home items, miscellaneous, ornaments, scrapbooks, sports and hobbies, and thought and speech bubbles.

Use the backgrounds on a blank slide, because they cover a whole slide, but the rest of the clip art can be added to slides that already have something on them. To add a piece of clip art to a slide, just double-click the clip art object's thumbnail in the palette. It appears on your slide surrounded by a frame. You can grab the corners of the frame and drag them to resize the clip art object to the size you want, or use the slider in the Properties palette. You can also reposition clip art by dragging it. To remove it, right-click it, and then choose Delete.

TIP If you play around with the costumes (hats, outfits, and glasses that you can paste onto your friends' pictures), you may notice that you can't rotate the clip art on the slide. If you want to adjust the angle for any of the clip art, here's a workaround. All the art lives in *C:\ProgramData\ Adobe\Photoshop Elements\7.0\Slideshow Graphics* if you have Vista. In Windows XP it's *C::\ DocumentsandSettings\All Users\Application Data\Adobe\Photoshop Elements\7.0\Slideshow-Graphics*. (Program Data and Application Data are hidden folders, so you need to turn on hidden folder viewing to see them.) Open your slide in Full Edit, and then add the clip art there (by importing it from the Graphics folder listed in the previous sentence). Then, use the Move tool (page 148) to place the clip art just so, and the transform commands (page 321) to adjust the shape, if necessary. When you're done, you can re-import your image into the Organizer as a version (page 59) and use the new version in your slideshow. You can also open the clip art images themselves, change them, and then save them as PNG files under a new name in the same folder as the originals, and they appear right in the clip art section along with the originals.

- **Text.** You can add text to your slides, and also apply a number of fancy styles to your text. Click the Text button at the top of the palette, and then double-click the text style you like. The Edit Text window pops up. Type in the words you want to add to your slide. When you're finished, click OK. The text appears in your slide, surrounded by a bounding box (dotted lines), which you can use to place the text where you want it.

  NOTE When the Edit Text window is active, you can't click OK by pressing the Enter key. You just create a line break in your text. You need to click the actual OK button.

  At the same time, the Text Properties palette appears at the lower right of the Slide Show Editor. You can change the font, size, color, and style in the palette. You can even choose a different color here for the drop shadow if you're using shadowed text. If you want to edit text later on, just click the letters on the slide to bring back the text bounding box and the Text Properties.

  NOTE You can remove text by right-clicking and choosing Delete, but you may need to do it more than once, since the first Delete may just remove a drop shadow, for instance, if one exists.

- **Narration.** You can record a narration for your slideshow if you wish. Just click the slide you want to add your voice to, and then, in the palette, click the Narration button. You see the recording window shown in Figure 18-7. (Of course, you need to have some kind of microphone hooked up to your PC to record your voice.)

- **Music.** You can add a full-scale soundtrack to your slideshow. To do that, click the bottom of the Slide Show Editor where it says, "Click Here to add Audio to Your Slide Show". In the window that opens, navigate to the audio you want, and then click Open. You can choose from any MP3, WAV, AC3, or WMA files you have on your PC.

  NOTE If you use iTunes, then you need to convert your iTunes AAC files to one of these formats before Elements acknowledges their existence. To do so, right-click any song name and choose, from the pop-up menu, "Convert Selection to MP3".

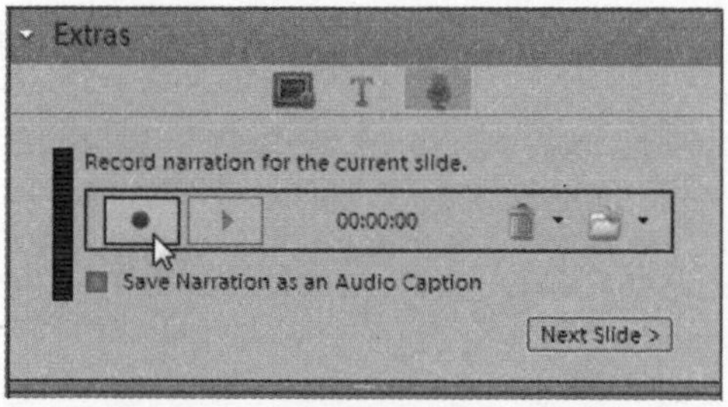

Figure 18-7:
Adding a narration to your slides is pretty simple. Just click the red Record button and start talking, and then click again when you're done. Click the Play button to preview what you've got. If you don't like how things turned out, click the Trash can icon, and then choose Delete This Narration. If you want to permanently save your narration as an audio caption for the original photo, then turn on "Save Narration as an Audio Caption". You can also click the folder icon to the right of the recording controls to import an existing audio caption to use with this slide.

You can make your slideshow fit the duration of the music, if you like. At the top of the Storyboard, click "Fit Slides to Audio", and Elements spins out your slideshow to last the entire length of your song. Or, if you'd rather repeat a short audio clip over and over, go to Edit → Slide Show Preferences, and then turn on "Repeat Soundtrack Until Last Slide". If you don't choose either one, then Elements doesn't make any attempt to synchronize the length of the soundtrack and the length of the slideshow.

TIP If you have problems getting the Organizer to play one of your MP3 files, then you may find you have better luck if you use an audio program to re-encode your MP3 as a variable bit-rate MP3 file. Check the audio program's options or help files for instructions on how to do this.

• **Pan and Zoom.** Filmmaker Ken Burns popularized this technique, where the camera moves around a still photo, giving the impression of motion. To create this effect in Elements, just click the slide you want to pan over. In the Properties palette, turn on the "Enable Pan and Zoom" checkbox.

TIP If you've lost the Pan and Zoom properties because you double-clicked over to the slide's Edit properties, then you can get back to Pan and Zoom by clicking once in the preview area outside the slide itself.

The Properties palette has two little thumbnails, Start and End. Click the Start thumbnail to choose where to begin panning over your photo. The pan frame appears in your photo, marking the spot where Elements will begin panning over your slide. Drag the frame to another place on the slide to change the starting point for your pan, or drag a corner to resize the frame.

Then, click the End thumbnail in the Properties palette and repeat the process to set the end point for panning and zooming. If you decide you want to edit the effect, then you can always click either thumbnail again to bring back the pan frame. You can also click the buttons between the thumbnails to swap where you start and end.

You can control the zoom level by how large you make your start and end frames. A small frame means the camera has to zoom in to fill the slide; an end frame that's larger than the start frame makes the camera zoom out.

NOTE   Panning and zooming usually looks pretty jerky when you preview your slideshow, but it should be smooth in the final slideshow.

You can pan more than once on a slide, too. To do that, click "Add Another Pan and Zoom to This Slide". If you want all your slides (or selected slides) to show the same pan and zoom you just set up, go to the Edit menu, and then, from the pop-out menu, choose what you want to do: "Apply Pan and Zoom to Selected Slide(s)" or "Apply Pan and Zoom to All Slides".

TIP   While Elements doesn't give you a way to create scrolling credits, you can fake them by creating a slide with a list of people you want to credit, and then applying the pan and zoom effect to the slide multiple times.

Saving and sharing your slideshow

After all the work you've done creating your slideshow, needless to say, you want to save it. (If you forget, then Elements reminds you to do so when you exit the Slide Show Editor.)

TIP   You can watch a full-screen preview of your slideshow by clicking the button of the same name above the Palette bin, or by pressing F11. Press Escape (Esc) to get back to the Slide Show Editor window.

Before saving, you need to decide what you want to do with your slideshow (burn it to a CD, email it as a file, and so on). It's important to remember that no matter what you choose (except for saving as a PDF), you're going to end up with a Windows Media Video (WMV) file.

That doesn't matter as long as everyone you want to share your slideshow with is using a computer or DVD player that uses a recent version of Windows Media Player. (It's part of the Windows operating system [if you've disabled Windows updates you can download the latest version from Microsoft]; for Macs, you find a free plug-in at *www.flip4mac.com*.) But unfortunately, that's not always the case. If you need to send a slideshow to someone who doesn't have Windows Media Player, your options are to create a PDF file as explained on page 472, upload your slideshow to YouTube (*www.youtube.com*) and send a link to your friends, or use other software to change the format to something your recipients have, like Quick-Time, for example.

To see your Output options, click the Output button above the Slide Show Editor's preview window. You get a new window (Figure 18-8) where you can choose from several ways to save and share your slideshow.

- **Save As a File**. Choose this option to save your slideshow to your hard drive as a PDF or Windows Media Video (WMV) file. The PDF options are explained on page 473. If you choose WMV, you get several choices for size and quality. Choose the one that best suits how you plan to share your slideshow. (If you're curious about the various choices, choose the one you want to know more about, and then click the Details button. You get a pop-up window giving more information about that size and its suggested uses.)

- **Burn to Disc.** You can create a Video CD (VCD) using Elements. This is a disc that plays in a DVD player, just like a regular DVD, but you don't need a DVD recorder to create one (because you're just using a plain old CD). The downside is that VCD is a very tricky format—the quality is low, and you can expect to have some problems getting the discs to play in some DVD players. If you want to send VCDs, you may want to make a short test slideshow for your friends to be sure they can watch one before you invest a lot of time in creating a large project.

TIP If you'd like to check which players can handle VCDs, or if you just want to know more about the format, head over to *www.videohelp.com/vcd*, where you'll find links to lists of compatible players and a lot more information.

You can also choose to include other slideshows on the same disc if you turn on the "Include additional slide shows I've made on this disc" checkbox in the Output window. Then click OK to bring up the "Create a VCD with Menu" window where you can choose the slideshows you want to include.

In the "Create a VCD with Menu" window, you must choose between the NTSC or PAL formats for your disc. Choose PAL if you're sending your slideshow to Europe or China; choose NTSC for most other areas, including the United States. Then click Burn to begin burning your disc.

NOTE If you also have Adobe's Premiere Elements software (and a drive that can create DVDs), then you can send your slideshow to Premiere Elements to make a true DVD. (If you have a DVD recorder, but no Premiere Elements, you can save your slideshow, and then use any other DVD-authoring software you've got loaded on your PC.)

- **Send to TV.** If you have Vista Home Premium or Ultimate, or Windows Media Center Edition running on your PC, and your television is connected to your computer, or if you have a device like an Xbox360 that can play WMV files, you can send your slideshow straight to your TV for large-screen viewing. In the Output window, click "Send to TV", and then type a name for your slideshow in the Name box. Next, choose the option in the Settings pull-down menu that correctly describes your TV, and then click OK. (If you aren't sure what to choose in the Settings menu, click the Details button to learn more about the currently selected choice.)

NOTE As long as you save your slideshow as a Slide Show (by clicking Save Project), you can always go back and edit it whenever you like. To edit an existing slideshow, in the Organizer, just right-click its thumbnail, and then from the pop-up menu, choose Edit. Elements opens your show in the Slide Show Editor so that you can make your changes. If you want to work on your slideshow again, then you need to save the actual Slide Show file, too, in addition to your PDF or WMV file, if you created one. You can't edit PDFs or WMVs in the Slide Show Editor.

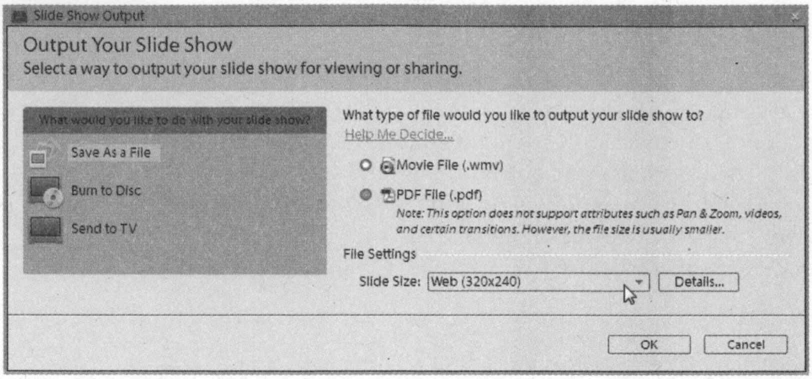

Figure 18-8:
To pick a format for your slideshow, in the Slide Show Editor, click the Output button above the preview area. This action brings up the window you see here. Choose what you want to do from the list on the left. Your options on the right change to reflect your choice. If you're creating a WMV file, then you get a number of different slide size options. For items that offer PAL and NTSC variations, PAL is the format you should choose if you plan on viewing the slideshow in Europe or China; choose NTSC for most other areas of the world, including the United States.

Flipbooks

In some ways, a *flipbook* is like a very simple slideshow without any transitions, audio, or fancy panning and zooming. After slogging through the last section, you may be thinking you've had enough slideshow options in Elements, thank you very much. But all that's different about a flipbook is the speed at which the images appear. A flipbook's *frame rate* (how fast one image appears and disappears) is very fast. When you put a stack of photos you took with your camera in burst mode into a flipbook, you can create an animation where the images change so fast it appears that your subject is moving.

> **TIP** Flipbooks are great for creating a time-lapse effect. For instance, if you take a photo of the building progress of your new house each day from the exact same spot, you can combine all the photos and watch your house go from an empty lot to finished in just a few seconds.

The flipbook effect is similar to an animated GIF (page 458), but you can use JPEGs in your flipbook, so the image quality is much higher than with a GIF. The downside is that you can't easily include a flipbook on a Web page. Your completed flipbook is a Windows Media file, so all you or your friends can do is watch it like a movie or regular slideshow. That said, Elements does give you several different output sizes, so you can pick one that's suitable for watching on a regular television (although you need Adobe's Premiere Elements or some other video creation program to make a version your television understands).

You may also want to create a flipbook to use as a plain old slideshow, since they're quick to produce and easy to email. Regardless of how you plan to use your flipbook, here's how to get started:

1. **In the Organizer, select the photos you want to include.**

   You must choose at least two photos, or you'll get a warning (instead of the Flipbook wizard) when you try to continue. You can't add or delete photos once you're in the wizard, so be sure you have all the photos you want before you start. You may want to make an album (page 53) to help you keep track.

   The flipbook displays your photos in order based on their file names or numbering. For example, files with names like *img_0617.jpg*, *img_0618.jpg*, and so on, appear in numerical order. The only control the Flipbook wizard gives you is that you can reverse the order of the entire group of images. See page 247 for advice on renaming a batch of photos using a sequential number scheme.

2. **Go to Create → More Options → Flipbook.**

   The Flipbook wizard shows you the window in Figure 18-9. You can preview your flipbook by pressing the Play button below the image area.

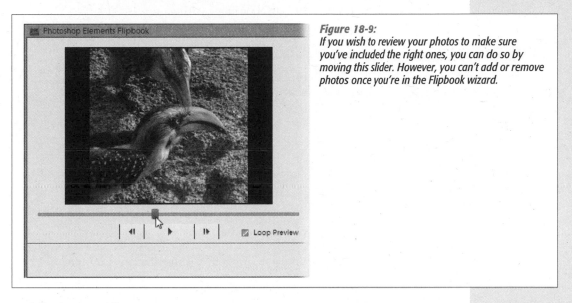

Figure 18-9:
If you wish to review your photos to make sure you've included the right ones, you can do so by moving this slider. However, you can't add or remove photos once you're in the Flipbook wizard.

3. **Adjust your settings.**

   You have only a limited number of choices in the flipbook window. Because the images move so fast, flipbooks don't let you use any kind of transitions between slides. All you can do is choose:

   - **Playback Speed.** Here's where you control the number of frames per second (each photo is one frame). One frame per second is the slowest option, and even that's pretty zippy for a regular slideshow. The more frames per second you choose, the faster and smoother the animation effect, and the shorter the total playback time for the flipbook.

- **Reverse Order.** If you want to see your slides from last to first, instead of first to last, then turn on this checkbox.

- **Output Settings.** These settings determine the final size of your flipbook. You get a variety of file formats to choose from. *Computer Monitor* is a good medium size that gives you a convenient balance between file size and image size. *Web* is a good size for use on a Web page (assuming your viewers have broadband Internet connections). *E-mail* creates a very tiny show that you can send to people with dial-up connections. You can also choose to create your flipbook as *VCD-NTSC* or *VCD-PAL*, or *DVD-NTSC* or *DVD-PAL*. NTSC is for video players in the United States and most other areas, and PAL is used in Europe and China. (If you choose any of these settings, then you need a program like Premiere Elements to create your final DVD for television viewing. Although you can create a flipbook in a format for use on a DVD, Elements can't create the menus and extra files your DVD player needs in order to play the file.) Unfortunately, the VCD choices are subject to the same quality limitations discussed on page 483. Figure 18-10 gives you more advice if you need help choosing a setting.

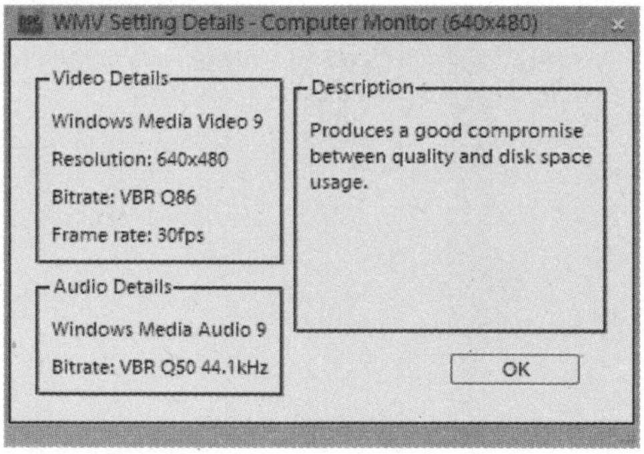

Figure 18-10:
If you're unsure which output format to use for your flipbook, click the Details button in the Photoshop Elements Flipbook window. As shown here, you get a window with more information about the size that's currently selected.

- **Loop Preview.** Turn this box on, and your preview plays endlessly once you click the Play button, until you stop it by clicking the Pause button.

4. **Create your flipbook.**

   When you're happy with how your flipbook performs, click Output. If you want to make large changes, like adding or removing photos, or if you decide you don't want to make a flipbook after all, then click Cancel. (You need to start from the beginning if you wish to change your photo selection.)

   When you click Output, a new window opens where you must name and save your video, which automatically gets added to the Organizer. Then you're all done.

Sharing Photos with Yahoo Maps

Elements gives you another fun way to share your photos online: placing them as virtual pins stuck in a Yahoo map. Your first reaction may be a yawn and, "So what? I know where I've been." But this is actually a very cool feature.

It's so great because you can choose to use a satellite view of the map, and in many places, you can zoom in to the level where you can see individual buildings. This means you can place your photos *exactly* where you took them. Want to sell your house? Find it on the map and attach your photos. Click the mountain lodge where you spent your vacation, and then attach your photos. Trace out the route of your trip to Europe, and then place the photos of each site you visited.

Once you've created your photo-speckled map, you aren't limited to admiring your work on your own computer. You can create an Online Album to post it on the Internet, where your friends can click the pins on the map to view a slideshow of your photos for that spot, or send it straight to Flickr (*www.flickr.com*)—the enormously popular photo sharing site. Adobe has made this very easy by building the map feature right into the Organizer. You even find a map view in the Organizer, as explained in Figure 18-11.

> **NOTE** If your camera has built-in GPS (a Global Positioning System that always knows where the camera is), then Elements automatically reads your GPS data, and places your photos on the map. The camera writes the GPS coordinates into your EXIF data (see page 59). You don't have to do a thing except enjoy the view. At least, that's how it's supposed to work. Unfortunately, some cameras write this information in places that Elements doesn't expect to find it, so you may have to go back and add it manually.

To create a map with your photos, just follow these steps:

1. **Place your photos on the Map.**

   You have several choices for getting photos onto the Map:

   - Right-click a photo thumbnail, and then choose "Place on Map". You get a dialog box where you can enter the general location (London, for example, or North Carolina) or even the specific address where your photos should go.

   - Drag and drop photos where you want them when the Map pane is open. You may need to use the Map Move tool (more on how to use that in a moment) to reposition the photos exactly where you want them.

   - Assign a Place tag (page 50) to a group of photos, and then place the tag on the map using either of the two previous methods. All photos with this Place tag get positioned on your map.

> **TIP** The map is pretty grabby. When you're dragging in a photo to a location close to a spot where you already have photos, it may get sucked into the existing group, even though that's not where you want it. Sometimes it's easier to drop a photo some distance from where you want it, and then use the Move tool to bring it to a location close to existing pins.

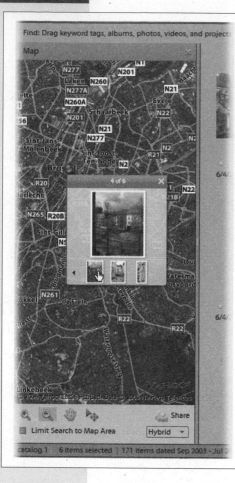

Figure 18-11:
To see the Yahoo map pane, go to Display → Show Map at the Organizer's upper right. Or right-click a photo or tag (label) and choose "Place on Map", and then enter the location where you want to attach the photo. Once you're in Map View, you can click a pin to see the photos attached to that spot. Click the large thumbnail on the little pop-out window for a full-screen slideshow of the pin's photos with options like music and captions. Press the Esc key to get back to the map.

Use the Map tools to adjust the view to your liking, and then use the Map Move tool (see Figure 18-12) to reposition your photos, if necessary. The more you zoom the view, the more accurate your placement.

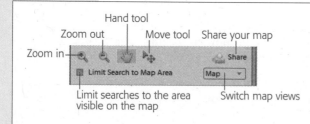

Figure 18-12:
The Map pane has its own little toolbox, used only to adjust your view of the map and to rearrange your photos, if necessary. Click one of the Zoom tools, and then click the map to zoom in or out. The area you click becomes the center of the map. The Hand tool works just like the regular Hand tool (page 88), but it only moves the Map around. The Map Move tool lets you reposition your photos on the map.

2. **View your photos on the map.**

   Click any visible pin to display the little pop-up window you can see in Figure 18-13. To see a particular photo, click it in the little thumbnail strip along the bottom of the pop-up window.

   The pin icon is always one pin for each location, no matter how many photos you have attached there. It would be nice if the number of pins corresponded to the number of photos, but whether you have 2 photos or 20 attached to a particular spot on the map, the icon shows one pin for any group of photos. If you have more than one pin in an area and you're zoomed out too far to show each location, then the map shows a group of three pins, no matter how many pins actually are in the area.

3. **When you've got all your photos positioned as you want them, share your map.**

   Click the Share button, and then choose how you want to share your map. Your choices are explained below. If you aren't ready to share it yet, your pins stay on the map even if you don't use the Share button—you don't need to do anything special to save them for later.

The map pane gives you three ways to view the map. If you click the Map pull-down menu, you can see:

- **Map.** This is like a standard street map: a drawing with street names and numbers on it.

- **Hybrid.** Hybrid combines the satellite view and the map view, so you see a satellite photo with the street names marked on it.

- **Satellite.** This is an aerial photo of the map area, taken by satellite, but the detail level is pretty amazing if you zoom it all the way in. (Not all areas have the same zoom level available. The map tells you if it can't zoom to the maximum level.)

The Map pane also includes a little tool set below the map to help you get things arranged to your liking. You can see it in Figure 18-12.

The Zoom and Hand tools work like the regular Elements Zoom (page 87) and Hand tools (page 88), but they work only on the map (not on the photos). The Map Move tool is very handy for repositioning photos. It's tough to position your photos precisely on the first try. Click the Map Move tool, and then grab a pin and drag it where you want it. If you have multiple photos on a pin and you want to move only one photo, the easiest way is to right-click it, choose "Remove from Map", and then add it in again.

> **TIP** The map can be a little cranky about scrolling long distances. If you find it's hard to maneuver the map to the spot where you want to put your photos, try right-clicking a photo, choosing "Place on Map", and then entering your area in the search box. You can always remove the photo (right-click, and then select "Remove from Map") once the map shows the region you want.

If you've already placed a photo on a map, you can go right to that location by right-clicking the photo in the Photo Browser, and then choosing "Show on Map". The Map pane opens, showing your photo's current location. When you want to get rid of a photo, right-click it, and then choose "Remove from Map". (You can do this in the Photo Browser or from its pin in the map.)

Once you've arranged all your photos to your satisfaction, you can share your map. Click the Share button and agree to the Yahoo Map terms of use (in that window, click Share), and you can choose whether to share to Photoshop.com (Photoshop Showcase if you're not in the US) or Flickr. If you choose Photohop.com (Photoshop Showcase), then Elements sends your map to the Album wizard (see page 467). Just name your album, and then choose whether to share to Photoshop.com, export to a CD or DVD, or export your album to send to your own Web site. Online Albums are covered in detail starting on page 467. You can change from the Map template to another style of Online Album while you're creating the album, if you like. Just click Change Template when you get to the Album Details pane of the wizard. Figure 18-13 shows a completed Yahoo Map Online Album.

NOTE When you share a map, the Photo page that Elements generates automatically opens with the plain Map view showing, so you need to explain to friends how to change to one of the other views by clicking on the word Hybrid or Satellite, as they prefer, for a more realistic look.

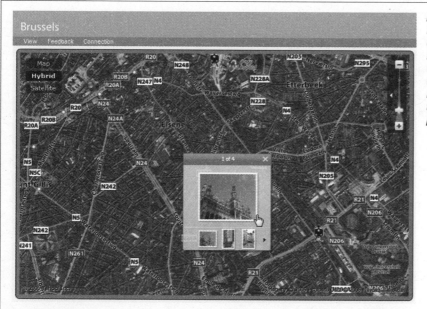

Figure 18-13:
Here's an example of a completed Yahoo Map Photo Gallery. It's a great way to share your photos with friends. They just need to click a pin to see the photos "pinned" to a particular location.

If you choose Flickr, then a wizard appears and walks you through authorizing and uploading your photos. They'll be displayed on Flickr's map feature. The first time you send photos, you have to create a Flickr account if you don't have one.

ON THE WEB

Sharing Photos Online

In addition to Photoshop.com, Elements makes it simple to post your photos to several other popular online services, so that your friends can view your photos online. You can quickly send photos to Kodak Easy-Share Gallery, SmugMug, and others, right from within Elements. (The list changes depending on Adobe's current partnerships.) Once your photos are posted, you and your friends can order not only prints, but also T-shirts, mugs, bags, and other items with your photos on them. (Merchandise options vary, depending on which service you're using.) Here's a quick rundown of what you can do with each service, and what it'll cost you:

- **Kodak EasyShare**. Besides ordering prints from EasyShare (page 437), you can upload your photos for your friends to view online. Once your friends set up free accounts, they can order prints directly from Kodak. EasyShare also offers a wide variety of gift items with your photos on them, like mugs, bags, shirts, and more. EasyShare's free, except for the cost of what you order.

- **SmugMug**. SmugMug is another online gallery service with a lot of different gift items you and your friends can order. It has a 7-day free trial, and your friends can order prints and merchandise without a paid account. If you want to maintain a gallery there, however, it's $39.95 a year for a basic account after the trial period expires.

- **Flickr**. A very popular photo sharing site, where you can create galleries and slideshows, or order many different kinds of merchandise featuring your photos. Basic accounts are free.

- **Send to a CEIVA brand Frame**. It's not exactly online sharing but if you have a CEIVA Digital Photo Frame, Elements makes it very simple to send your photos to it. (The CEIVA Frame is an electronic gadget that looks like a regular picture frame, but displays photos you send to it digitally over a phone line.) Just choose Share → More Options → "Send to CEIVA Digital Photo Frame" to connect and upload your photos. A basic CEIVA account that lets you send photos to someone's frame is free, but you have to sign up for it; the frames themselves are pretty expensive. Connect to the service from the Share menu or go to *www. ceiva.com* to learn more.

To upload a photo to any of these services, just select it in the Organizer, click the Share tab → More Options, and then choose the service you want. (You can also select and upload more than one photo at a time.)

You're asked to sign in if you already have an account, or to create one if you don't. Each site has a simple-to-use wizard that walks you through the sign-up process, and they also have tours so that you can take a look around before you decide to join.

If you aren't sure which one(s) to try, ask your friends which one they like. Each service has pros and cons. You may want to try them all out before you decide.

CHAPTER 19

Beyond the Basics

So far, everything in this book has been about what you can do with Elements right out of the box. But as with many things digital, there's a thriving cottage industry devoted to souping up Elements. Of course, signing up for a Photoshop.com account (page 18), gives you access to a lot of extra goodies from Adobe, but there's a ton of other stuff available, too. You can add new brush shapes, Layer styles, actions, and fancy filters. Best of all, a lot of what's out there is free. And many of the tools are especially designed to make Elements behave more like Photoshop. This chapter looks at some of these extras, how to manage the stuff you collect, and how to know when you really do need the full version of Photoshop instead. You'll also learn about the many resources available for expanding your knowledge of Elements beyond this book.

Graphics Tablets

Probably the most popular Elements accessory is a *graphics tablet*, which lets you draw and paint with a pen-like stylus instead of a mouse. A tablet is like a souped-up substitute for a mouse: you control your onscreen cursor by drawing directly on the tablet's surface—an action that many artists find offers them greater control. If trying to use the Lasso tool with a mouse makes you feel like you're trying to write on a mirror with a bar of soap, then a graphics tablet is for you.

> **NOTE** Some deluxe-model graphics tablets act as monitors and let you work directly on your image. But you need to budget close to a thousand dollars for that kind of convenience.

Most tablets work like the one shown in Figure 19-1. You use the special pen on the tablet just as you would a mouse on a mousepad; any changes you make appear right on your monitor.

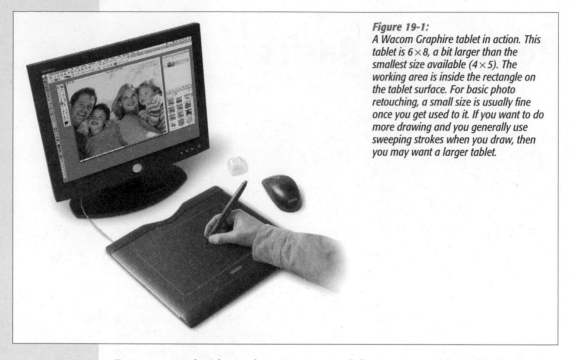

Figure 19-1:
A Wacom Graphire tablet in action. This tablet is 6×8, a bit larger than the smallest size available (4×5). The working area is inside the rectangle on the tablet surface. For basic photo retouching, a small size is usually fine once you get used to it. If you want to do more drawing and you generally use sweeping strokes when you draw, then you may want a larger tablet.

For most people, it's much easier to control fine motions with a tablet's pen than with a mouse. Moreover, when you use a tablet, many of the brushes and tools in Elements become *pressure sensitive*—the harder you press, the darker and wider the line becomes. The tablet pen lets you create much more realistic paint strokes, as shown in Figure 19-2.

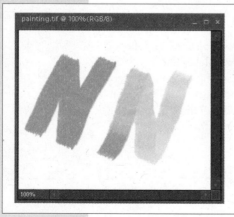

Figure 19-2:
Two almost identical paint strokes, starting with fairly hard pressure and then easing up. Both were made using the identical brush and color in Elements. The only difference is that the stroke on the left was drawn with a mouse, and the one on the right came from a tablet. You can see what a difference the pressure sensitivity makes.

When using the Brush tool, you'll see Tablet Options (it's a tiny black triangle) just to the right of the Airbrush setting in the Options bar. Many brushes and tools are automatically pressure sensitive when you hook up a tablet. You can choose whether to let the pressure control the size, opacity, roundness, hue jitter, and scatter for your brushes. (See page 328 for more about Brush settings.)

With a tablet, you can also create hand-drawn line art—even if you don't have an artistic bone in your body—by placing a picture of what you want to draw on the surface of the tablet and tracing the outline. Also, if you find constant mousing troublesome, you may have fewer hand problems when using a tablet's pen. Most tablets come with a wireless mouse, which works only on the surface of the tablet. Or you can use your regular mouse on a mousepad or your desk the way you always do, if you like to switch back and forth between the stylus and a mouse.

Tablet prices now start at less than a hundred dollars, a big drop from what they used to cost. There are lots of different models, and their features vary widely. Sophisticated tablets offer more levels of sensitivity and respond when you change the angle at which you hold the stylus.

Wacom, one of the big tablet manufacturers, has some pretty nifty tablet demos on its Web site (*www.wacom.com*), if you click on the various product tours. You can't actually simulate what it's like to use a tablet, but the animations give you a good idea of what your life would be like if you went the tablet route.

Free Stuff from the Internet

You have to spend some money if you want a graphics tablet, but there's a ton of free stuff—tutorials, brushes, textures, and Layer styles, for example—available online that you can add to Elements. Most of these add-ons say they work with Photoshop, but since Elements is based on Photoshop, you can use most of them in Elements, too.

Here are some popular places to go treasure hunting:

- **Adobe Exchange** (*www.adobe.com/cfusion/exchange/*). On Adobe's own Web site, you can find hundreds and hundreds of downloads, including more Layer styles than you could ever use, brushes, textures, and custom shapes (to use with the Shape tool). They're all free, once you register. This site is one of the best resources anywhere for extra stuff. About 99 percent of the items listed are made specifically for Photoshop, but Photoshop's brushes, swatches, textures, shapes, and Layer styles work with Elements, too. See the box on page 500 for help with installing your finds in Elements.

- **Creative Mac** (*www.creativemac.com*). Don't let the name put you off. Almost everything on this site works in Windows, too. It's not what it once was, but it's still a wonderful source for specialty brushes, especially for tricky things like hair and skin.

- **MyJanee** (*www.myjanee.com*). You'll find lots of tutorials and free downloads on this site.

- **Sue Chastain** (*http://graphicssoft.about.com*). This is another Web site with lots of downloads and many tutorials.

- **Panosfx** (*www.panosfx.com*). Panos Efstathiadis produces some wonderful actions (see the section "When You Really Need Photoshop" later in this chapter) for Photoshop, and now he's adapted many of them for Elements as well. Most are free; some cost a few dollars.

- **Optik Verve Labs** (*www.optikvervelabs.com*). This is the home of Virtual Photographer, one of the most amazing plug-ins (add-on utilities) for Elements. Best of all, it's free.

- **Hidden Elements** (*www.hiddenelements.com*). Richard Lynch has been creating wonderful add-on tools for Elements practically as long as the program has existed. Some are free, many are not, but all are worth the investment.

- **Grant's Tools** (*www.cavesofice.org/~grant/Challenge/Tools/index.html*). Here's another source of popular free tools for Elements, though it often takes a while for Grant to update it for new versions. But it's well worth checking to find out.

If you're willing to pay a little bit, you've got even more choices. You can find everything from more elaborate ways to sharpen photos to really cool collections of special edges and visual effects. Prices range from donationware (pay if you like it) to some quite expensive and sophisticated plug-ins that cost hundreds of dollars. You can also buy books like the *Wow!* series (Peachpit Press), which have loads of illustrations showing the styles available on the included CD.

> **NOTE** Elements 7 is based on Photoshop CS3, so CS3 downloads are compatible. Plug-ins and other goodies designed for older versions of Photoshop or Elements usually work with newer versions, but not the other way around. For example, a brush made for Photoshop CS3 works in Elements 7 but not Elements 3.
>
> Mac plug-ins don't work in Windows, and vice versa, but many plug-ins offer two versions, one for each platform. When buying a plug-in, check with the developer to be sure it works with Photoshop Elements, and if you're using Windows Vista, check on Vista compatibility, as well.

With so many goodies available, it's easy to find yourself overwhelmed trying to keep track of everything you've added to Elements. Your best bet is to make backup copies of anything you download so you'll have it if you ever need to reinstall Elements.

Elements also includes a Preset Manager (Figure 19-3) that can help manage certain kinds of downloads. Go to Edit → Preset Manager to launch it.

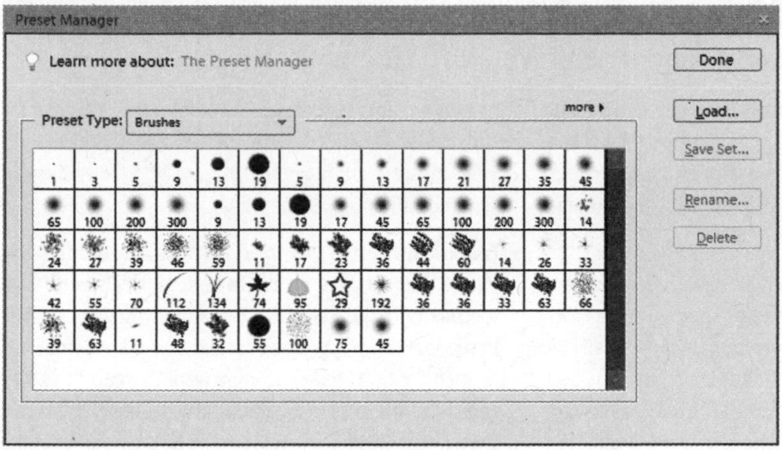

Figure 19-3:
The Elements Preset Manager offers a place to see all your brushes, swatches, gradients, and patterns in one place. You can use it to switch which groups are loaded, to add or remove items, and so on—the same way you do in the main brush window.

When You Really Need Photoshop

You can do an enormous amount with Elements, but some people do need the full version of Photoshop. For example, if you want the ability to write your own *actions* (little scripts, like macros, that automate certain things in Photoshop) or if you have to work extensively in CMYK mode, then you need Photoshop.

CMYK is the color mode used for commercial printing—it stands for Cyan, Magenta, Yellow, and blacK, which are the colors professional printers use. When you send a file to a print shop, the printer usually tells you it needs to be a CMYK file. You can't convert files to CMYK in Elements. If you need CMYK files on a regular basis, it's worth the extra price of Photoshop to avoid the aggravation. If you only occasionally need CMYK, you might just ask your printer about converting the file for you for an additional charge.

> **NOTE** Richard Lynch (*www.hiddenelements.com*) created a workaround for CMYK conversion for earlier versions of Elements. You may want to check his Web site to see what workarounds and other goodies he's come up with for Elements 7.

In Photoshop you get more of everything: more choices, more tools, more settings, more types of adjustment layers, and so on.

Beyond This Book

You can do thousands of interesting things with Elements that are beyond the scope of this book. If you install the Photoshop Inspiration Browser, you have access to dozens of interesting tutorials right from Elements. Also, bookstores have loads of titles on Elements and Photoshop, and a lot of procedures are common to both programs. All kinds of specialized books on everything from color management to making selections to scrapbooking are available.

Making Elements Behave More Like Photoshop

While each version of Elements is more talented than its predecessor, there's one thing about Elements 7 that you may not like if you're a longtime member of the Elements community: Some of the tools and actions you find online won't work in Elements 7.

Ever since Elements first came out, there's been quite a cottage industry devoted to figuring out ways to get Elements to behave more like Photoshop. If you've used Elements 3 or earlier versions, the odds are pretty good that you're familiar with the extra tools and action players created by Richard Lynch, Paul Shipley, Grant Dixon, and Ling Nero. Unfortunately, Adobe decided to write Elements 4 in a way that disabled the traditional route used

by add-on tools to access some of the underlying Photoshop code needed for these additional features to work. That meant that many of the existing add-on tools stopped working in Elements 4.

For now, it's best to stick to actions that state they're written for Elements 4, 5, 6, or 7, to be sure they'll work. (See the box on page 500 for more about installing action-based tools.) If you've been using extra tools or actions in Elements 2 or 3, then you may want to keep the older version of the program around just for them. (You can have as many different versions of Elements as you like installed on your computer, but Adobe recommends that you run only one version at a time.)

NOTE If you're looking to learn some photo-shooting and -editing techniques from a pro who's been at it since the birth of digital cameras, check out *Stephen Johnson on Digital Photography* (O'Reilly).

In addition, you'll find hundreds of tutorial sites on the Web. Besides those mentioned earlier in the chapter, other popular sites include:

- **Adobe** (*www.adobe.com*). You'll find plenty of free online training for Elements here.

- **Jay Arraich** (*www.arraich.com/elements/psE_intro.htm*). This longtime Photoshop guru provides lots of Elements information, both basic and advanced.

- **Radiant Vista** (*www.radiantvista.com/workbench*). This site's Photoshop Workbench section features many video tutorials. They're for full Photoshop, but many are applicable to Elements, too.

- **Photoshop Support** (*www.photoshopsupport.com/elements/tutorials.html*). Despite the name, this site isn't run by Adobe, but it does have a whole section of Elements tutorials.

- **YouTube** (*www.youtube.com*). Yep, that's right: You can find videos about almost anything on YouTube, including lots of Elements tutorials.

- **Photoshop Elements User** (*www.photoshopelementsuser.com*). This is the Web site for a subscriber-only print newsletter, but it also includes some free online video tutorials, a forum, and a good collection of links. This is the only publication especially for Elements. Their forums are hosted at *www.elementsvillage.com*.

If you search Google, you're sure to find a tutorial for any project you have in mind, although many of them are written for full Photoshop. In most cases, you can adapt them for Elements. If you get stuck or need help with any other aspect of Elements, there's a very active online community that's sure to have an answer for you. Besides the sites already mentioned, try:

- **Adobe Support forum** (*www.adobe.com/support/forums/index.html*). Scroll down the page to the Photoshop forums and, in that group, you'll find the Elements User-to-User forum, where you'll find lots of helpful and friendly people. It's your best bet for getting answers without calling Adobe support.

- **Digital Photography Review** (*www.dpreview.com*). You'll find many camera-specific forums on this site. You can also get a lot of Elements answers in the Retouching forum if you specify in your question that you've got Elements rather than Photoshop.

- **Retouch Pro** (*www.retouchpro.com*). The forums here cover all kinds of retouching and artistic uses of Elements and Photoshop.

Many sites are devoted to scrapbooking using Elements. A good place to start is Scrapper's Guide (*www.scrappersguide.com*), a commercial site run by Linda Sattgast.

No matter what you're looking for—add-ons, tutorials, communities—try a Google search, and you're sure to find a site that has what you want.

There's no question about it: Once you get familiar with Elements, it's addictive. Lots of other folks have found out how much fun this program is, and you shouldn't have any trouble finding the answer to any question you have.

The only limit to what you can do with Elements is your imagination. Enjoy!

Adding Layer Styles, Shapes, and Actions to Elements

Adding your online finds to Elements 7 is a good news/bad news situation. The good news is that it's quite easy to add Layer styles, shapes, and actions (see the box on page 498 for more about using actions in Elements). The bad news is that if you want to categorize them or have them show up in your Content palette searches, you're in for a trip through some pretty techie territory.

To add your extras, just put them into the folders described below; the next time you launch Elements, they'll show up in the Show All section of the relevant palette. Here's how to add them:

- **Layer styles**. Just put them into *C:\Program files\ Adobe\ Photoshop Elements\7.0\Presets\Styles*.

- **Actions**. In Elements 7, the easiest installation route for most actions is via the Guided Edit's Action Player, explained on page 380. The drawback is that if you install an action that requires you to use the Layers palette during a step (to choose the target layer for the action's next step, for instance), you can't do that in Guided Edit. And since many add-on tools for Elements are really actions, you want to be able to use them in Full Edit. You can't do that with actions installed in the Action Player.

    If you do want to use actions in Full Edit, you can, but it's a bit more complicated. First, you need two files: one for the action itself (the .atn file) and one to use as a thumbnail so that you can find the action to launch it. The thumbnail needs to be a 64-pixel square PNG image with *exactly* the same name as the action (except for the file extension), including spacing, capitalization, and so on. Put both the thumbnail and the .atn file (individually, not in a folder) into *C:\Documents and Settings\All Users\ Application Data\Adobe\Photoshop Elements\7.0\ Photo Creations\Photo Effects* if you use Windows XP, or *C:\ProgramData\Adobe\Photoshop Elements\7.0\ Photo Creations\Photo Effects*, if you use Vista. (In both Windows XP and Vista, you'll need to enable viewing hidden files to see these folders. To do that, go to Control Panel → Classic View → Folder Options → View → "Show Hidden Files and Folders".)

- **Shapes**. After all that, you'll be relieved to know that adding more shapes to the Shape tool is much simpler. Just put your downloaded shapes (which need to have the .csh file extension) into: *C:\Program Files\Adobe\Photoshop Elements\ 7.0\ Presets\Custom Shapes or, for Vista, C:\Program-Data\Adobe\Photoshop Elements\ 7.0\Presets\ Custom Shapes* and they'll appear in the Shape tool.

Once you've put everything in the right place, your Layer style or shape will show up in Show All in the Content Palette. Actions installed by the directions here appear in the Effects palette → Photo Effects → Show All. For mere mortals, that's all there is to it, but if you're a techie who understands XML, read on.

You can make your content appear in its own category if you also create an XML file (a little snippet of code that gives Elements directions for how to categorize the file and search for it). The easiest way to do this is to find an XML file for an existing Layer style, photo effect, or whatever you have, duplicate it, and then edit its contents. You can find these XML files in *C:\Documents and Settings\All Users\Application Data\Adobe\Photoshop Elements\ 7.0\Locale\en_US\Photo Creations Metadata* in Windows XP, and *C:\ProgramData\Adobe\Photoshop Elements\7.0\en_US\Photo Creations Metadata* in Vista.

Regardless of whether you completed the XML steps or not, to remove new content that you've added, just right-click it in the palette and choose Delete Content from the shortcut menu, or click the icon once and then click the trashcan icon at the bottom of the palette. If you created a metadata (XML) file, go dig that out and remove it as well.

XML is pretty intimidating, but you can also simplify the whole process by using something like Graffi's Add-O-Matic, which installs add-on content for you. You'll find it at *www.graficalicus.com*, along with a bunch of add-ons for Elements. At the time of this writing it's for Elements 5 and 6, but it seems quite likely he'll update it for Elements 7. It costs ten dollars, but if you're addicted to Elements add-ons, it may be worth the money for the convenience.

The Organizer, Menu by Menu

This appendix gives you a quick tour of the main menus in the Organizer—the ones listed at the top of the screen. The Organizer has two main windows: Photo Browser and Date View. Both offer the same menu choices—everything listed here is available in either window. There are keyboard shortcuts and buttons in the Organizer windows that give you access to many of these menu items. When there's more than one method, both are mentioned in the text.

In addition to the main menus discussed here, the Organizer is chock-full of shortcut (also called contextual) menus. That means you can right-click almost anywhere in the Organizer, and you'll get a menu with several options specific to the object you clicked. Right-click a tag (page 50), for instance, and you get a menu that includes choices for editing the tag or changing it to a category.

> **NOTE** If you also have Premiere Elements or Photoshop installed, you'll see a few additional menu choices not listed here.

System Menu

The Photoshop Elements icon (a blue square with "PSE" on it) at the far left of the menu bar is actually a button. Click it for the System menu, where you can minimize, maximize, move, resize, or close the Organizer. (You also have the standard Windows window buttons on the right side of the Organizer.)

Welcome Menu

Click the little blue and white house to the right of the System menu to bring up the Elements Welcome window that you see when the program first launches. This is where you connect to Photoshop.com (page 18).

File Menu

This menu is where you import photos, start new projects, manage catalogs, and export photos. It's also where you quit the Organizer when you're done.

Get Photos and Videos

Here's where you import photos into the Organizer. You can tell Elements to find and import photos and videos:

- **From a camera or card reader** (or press Ctrl+G).

- **From a scanner** (or press Ctrl+U).

- **From Files and folders** (or press Ctrl+Shift+G).

- **By Searching** tells Elements to search your computer for photos. You can choose to search all your hard drives (if you have more than one attached to your PC), your C drive only, your My Documents folder, or you can browse to a particular folder or drive to search only its contents.

New

You can choose to create a new blank file that will appear in the Editor. (The Organizer itself doesn't create blank files.) Your other options here are:

- **Image from Clipboard.** You can copy a photo in the Organizer (Ctrl+C) and then start a new Editor file by copying your photo from the Clipboard (the invisible file that stores what you copy until you paste it somewhere).

- **Photomerge Group Shot.** Group Shot lets you move people from one group photo to another, similar photo (page 313). You can use it to replace someone who's looking away from the camera or blinking, for example.

- **Photomerge Faces.** This one lets you combine parts of different faces, just for fun (page 310).

- **Photomerge Scene Cleaner.** This new feature lets you remove unwanted people or other details from a photo by copying over bits of other photos (page 313).

- **Photomerge Panorama.** Create a panorama from files you've selected in the Organizer. (Choosing this feature takes you to the Editor for the actual merge. See page 304 for more about panoramas.)

Open Recently Edited File in Editor

Choose a file from the list, and the Organizer opens it in the Editor so you can work on it there.

Catalog

This is where you manage your catalogs (page 48). A window opens where you can choose a catalog to open, repair, or optimize from a list of your existing catalogs. You can also create a new catalog, and rename, move, or delete a catalog here. Keyboard shortcut: Ctrl+Shift+C.

Make a CD/DVD

Use this menu option to quickly burn a project or a group of photos to a CD or DVD. Choose this for sharing photos, and use "Copy/Move to Removable Disk" (described next) when making alterations in your storage location. Ctrl+Alt+C also brings up the same window.

Copy/Move to Removable Disk

If you want to move a photo or a group of photos to a CD or DVD, choose this command. Page 67 has more information about backing up your files. Keyboard shortcut: Ctrl+Shift+O.

Backup Catalog to CD, DVD, or Hard Drive

It's wise to keep a backup of your catalog, and this command makes it easy to do so. You can choose to back up your entire catalog or just a few photos. See page 67 for detailed directions on using Backup. Keyboard shortcut: Ctrl+B.

Restore Catalog from CD, DVD, or Hard Drive

Choose this option when you want to replace your catalog with an archived version, or if you accidentally delete photos or otherwise run into trouble with the current version.

Duplicate

Highlight a photo or a Create project and choose this menu item (or press Ctrl+Shift+D) to make a duplicate.

Reconnect

Sometimes your Organizer catalog (page 48) can't find a file when you ask for it. Usually this happens when you move or rename a file using a method outside of Elements (like Windows Explorer). This command tells the Organizer to find the file again. You can choose to reconnect:

- **Missing File.** Choose this to reconnect one file.

- **All Missing Files.** The Organizer searches for all the files it can't find.

Watch Folders

Use this command if you regularly import photos into certain folders. Elements monitors the folders you choose and checks for new graphics stored inside them. You can tell Elements to automatically place any photos it finds into your catalog. If you prefer, Elements can just notify you that it found new files and let you decide what to do with them.

Rename

If you want the Organizer to keep track of your photos, you need to move and rename them from within Elements (rather than using, say, Windows Explorer). So if you want to change the name of a photo, choose this menu item or press Ctrl+Shift+N.

Write Tag and Properties Info to Photo(s)

Normally your Organizer tags exist only in your catalog's database. If you want to make the tag information part of the photo file itself, first select it in the Photo Browser, then choose this menu item. Elements writes your tags into the file's IPTC metadata (page 59). You can select multiple photos and use this command on the whole group at once.

Move

If you want the Organizer to keep track of your photos, you must move them within Elements once they're in your catalog. To move a photo, choose this menu item and then select a destination in the window that appears. You can also move files by dragging them if you go to Display → Folder Location or press Ctrl+Alt+3. You'll see a new pane on the left of the Photo Browser with a schematic view of the folder structure of your hard drive (just like you see elsewhere in Windows). You can drag your photos into the folders you want. Keyboard shortcut for Folder View: Ctrl+Shift+V.

Export As New File(s)

If you want to export a group of photos for use by another program, this is one way to do it. Choose Export As New File(s) from the menu, and you get a dialog box where you can choose the destination of your files and rename them if you like. You can also choose to convert the exported files to a different format. Your choices are JPEG, PSD, TIFF, and PNG. This menu option is a useful feature if you need to create JPEGs for printing at a store kiosk, for example.

Page Setup

This menu item calls up your system's regular Page Setup window, where you choose the page size, the orientation of your document, and the printer you plan to use. Page 445 has more about printing from the Organizer. Keyboard shortcut: Ctrl+Shift+P.

Print

Choose this command, and you get the Organizer's Print Photos window, which is discussed in detail inChapter 16. Keyboard shortcut: Ctrl+P.

Order Prints

This is one way to connect to the online Kodak EasyShare Gallery to order prints or photo books. See page 437 for details on how to order prints online from the Organizer.

Exit

You can close the Organizer here or by pressing Ctrl+Q. The Editor doesn't quit along with the Organizer. If the Editor is also running, you must exit it separately.

Edit Menu

This menu contains choices that let you make changes to your files. It's also where you can access your Elements preferences to change their settings.

Undo

You can undo your last action in the Organizer by selecting Undo or by pressing Ctrl+Z.

Redo

If you undo something and then change your mind, select Redo or press Ctrl+Y.

Copy

To copy something to the Clipboard, highlight it and select this menu item or press Ctrl+C.

Select All

To select all the photos in any window in the Organizer, choose this menu item or press Ctrl+A.

Deselect

To clear all selections, choose this menu item or press Ctrl+Shift+A.

Delete from Catalog

Select the photo you want to get rid of and choose this option to remove it from the catalog database. You can press Delete to do the same thing. If you want to remove the photo from your hard drive as well, the dialog box that appears gives you the option to do so.

Rotate 90° Left

To rotate a photo 90 degrees counterclockwise, select it, and then choose this menu item or just press Ctrl+left arrow key.

Rotate 90° Right

To rotate a photo 90 degrees clockwise, select it, and then choose this menu item or just press Ctrl+right arrow key.

Auto Smart Fix

To instantly apply the Auto Smart Fix command to your photo, choose this item or press Ctrl+Alt+M. See Chapter 4 for more about Auto Smart Fix.

Auto Red Eye Fix

Choose this option or press Ctrl+R to automatically find and correct red eye problems in all the selected photos. See page 104 for more about how this feature works.

Edit 3GPP Movie

This is where you can edit movies to send to wireless devices, like cellphones, that have the ability to play video. Your movie must be in the 3GPP or MPEG-4 format. Select this menu item for a window with your editing controls.

Adjust Date and Time

If you want to adjust a file's date and time settings, select this item or press Ctrl+J. You get three choices:

- **Change to a specified date and time.** This lets you adjust the date and time manually.

- **Change to match the file's date and time.** This changes the time and date to reflect the last time you modified the file.

- **Shift by a set number of hours (time zone adjust).** This lets you change the date and time of a selected group of photos. Any changes you make get made to all the photos you've selected. For example, if you elect to move the time back three hours (via the Time Zone Adjust dialog box), all your selected photos have their times moved back three hours.

Add Caption

To add a caption to a selected image, choose this menu item or press Ctrl+Shift+T.

Update Thumbnail

If a thumbnail stops displaying correctly or doesn't show the correct image, select the thumbnail by clicking it, and then choose this menu item or press Ctrl+Shift+U.

Set as Desktop Wallpaper

To use one or more of your photos as wallpaper for your desktop, just click its thumbnail in the Photo Browser, and then choose this menu item or press Ctrl+Shift+W. If you select multiple photos, Elements arranges them like tiles so that they all appear as a sort of collage.

Ratings

Choose this menu item and you can assign your selected image(s) a rating of zero to five stars, so you can quickly find your favorites or sort out the duds.

Visibility

Using the pop-out menu here you can mark photos as Hidden or Visible, or make all your Hidden photos visible. See page 52.

Place on Map

To stick photos onto a Yahoo map, choose this menu item and you get a dialog box where you can enter the location where each photo should appear. (Learn more about maps on page 487.)

Remove from Map

If your photo already has a place on a Yahoo map and you want to take it off, choose this menu item.

Show on Map

If you've assigned a photo to a spot on a Yahoo map, choose this menu item to see the map showing the photo's location.

Stack

This is where you create and manage *photo stacks*. Stacks are groups of photos that you want to store together. Only the top photo shows in the Photo Browser until you expand the stack. Stacks can be made from unrelated photos, unlike version sets (see the next section).

Your stacking options are:

- **Automatically Suggest Photo Stacks**. If you've taken photos using your camera's burst (rapid advance) mode or bracket mode, this menu item sorts related photos into their own stacks. (Elements isn't smart enough to look through a folder and find all the photos you took of Yellowstone National Park, though. The photos must be similar in subject and taken very close together in time—using your camera's burst mode, say—for this command to work.) Keyboard shortcut: Ctrl+Alt+K.

- **Stack Selected Photos.** Highlight your photos, and then choose this menu item or press Ctrl+Alt+S to put the images into a stack.

- **Unstack Photos.** This modifies a selected photo stack so that the photos it includes are no longer joined together.

- **Expand Photos in Stack.** Choose this option or press Ctrl+Alt+R to see all the photos in a stack.

- **Collapse Photos in Stack.** To compress an expanded stack again, choose this command or press Ctrl+Alt+Shift+R.

- **Flatten Stack.** This reduces your stack so you see only the top photo, and not the ones below it.

- **Remove Selected Photos from Stack.** Use this to remove one or more photos from a stack. This item and the next one appear only for expanded stacks.

- **Set as Top Photo.** Highlight a photo and choose this to send that photo to the top of the stack. From now on, it becomes the visible photo.

Version Set

This is where you manage your *version sets*. When you make changes to a photo in the Editor, you have the option of creating a *version set*, as long as your photo is stored in the Organizer. In a version set, each time you save your photo, Elements saves it as a copy with a new name, that is, a different version. In this way, you can save many files containing your changes and go back to any one at any time. Your options here are:

- **Expand Items in Version Set.** Choose this item, or press Ctrl+Alt+E, to see all your versions at once.

- **Collapse Items in Version Set.** To return an expanded version set to single image view, choose this command, or press Ctrl+Alt+Shift+E.

- **Flatten Version Set.** Use this to reduce a version set to one photo—the top one.

- **Convert Version Set to Individual Items.** If you want to be able to work with the files in a version set as though they were separate photos, choose this item and, instead of a version set, you get multiple individual photos.

- **Revert to Original.** This deletes later versions, leaving only your original photo as it was in when you first brought it into the Organizer.

- **Remove Item(s) from Version Set.** If you find you've saved more versions than you need, highlight the ones you want to get rid of and choose this menu item. You have to expand your version set to see this choice.

- **Set as Top Item.** Highlight a photo and choose this option to send that photo to the top of the set. From now on, it becomes the visible photo. You only see this for expanded version sets.

Color Settings

This is where you can set your color space (page 196). You can also press Ctrl+Alt+G to bring up Elements color settings.

Contact Book

If you want to see or edit your Contact Book of email addresses (to use when sending your photos from Elements), you can get to it here. See page 464 for more about the Contact Book.

Preferences

This is where you can make changes to your Organizer settings for getting and saving photos; connecting to cameras or scanners; emailing; editing; and creating tags, albums, and calendars. If you're using the online sync feature at Photoshop.com (page 66), this is where you control album syncing. You can also adjust the settings for what you want to see in Folder view, and for using the online Kodak Easy-Share Gallery here. In addition, it's where you tell Adobe whether or not you want to see ads for special offers. You can also get to the Editor's preferences from this menu.

Find Menu

This menu is really the heart of the Organizer. From it, you can search for your photos in many different ways.

Set Date Range

Choose this menu item, and a dialog box appears that lets you specify start and end dates. The Organizer shows all the photos that fall in the date range you specify. Keyboard shortcut: Ctrl+Alt+F.

Clear Date Range

After you've searched for a date range, choose this menu item to return to your complete catalog in the Photo Browser, or press Ctrl+Shift+F.

By Caption or Note

When you choose this item, you get a dialog box that lets you search for any text in your captions or notes. It doesn't have to be the entire caption. The Organizer finds all the photos with those words in either field. Keyboard shortcut: Ctrl+Shift+J.

By Filename

Enter part of a filename and the Organizer finds the file for you. Keyboard shortcut: Ctrl+Shift+K.

All Version Sets

Choose this, and Elements shows you all the version sets in your catalog. Keyboard shortcut: Ctrl+Alt+V.

All Stacks

This menu item makes Elements show you all the photo stacks you've made. Keyboard shortcut: Ctrl+Alt+Shift+S.

By History

Choose to find your file based on any of the following factors:

- **Imported On.** This is the date you brought your file into the Organizer.

- **E-mailed to.** You can search by the names of people you've emailed your photos to, but only if you sent the messages from the Organizer.

- **Printed On.** Search for the photos you printed on a certain date.

- **Exported On.** Search for all the photos you exported from the Organizer on a particular date.

- **Ordered Online.** Search for the photos you've ordered from Kodak EasyShare Gallery (page 436).

- **Shared Online.** Search for the photos you've shared on Kodak EasyShare Gallery or Photoshop.com (page 491).

- **Used in Projects.** Search for all the photos you've used in your Create projects.

By Media Type

The Organizer doesn't organize only still photos. You can also use it to keep track of movies and audio files. Here, you can search for all the files of a particular type:

- **Photos.** Find all your still photos (press Alt+1).

- **Video.** Find all your video clips (press Alt+2).

- **Audio.** Find all your audio files (press Alt+3).

- **Projects.** Find all your Create projects (press Alt+4).

- **PDF.** You can import and tag PDF files in the Organizer. If you want to see all your PDFs, choose this option or press Alt+5.

- **Items with Audio Captions.** If you've recorded captions for any of your photos (see page 480), you can search for them by choosing this menu item or pressing Alt+6.

By Details (Metadata)

If you want to search your photos according to what's stored in their metadata, like the EXIF information (page 59) from your camera, this is where you start. See page 57 for more about how to perform these searches.

Items with Unknown Date and Time

Choose this menu item if you want to find any photos that haven't been properly tagged with the date and time. Keyboard shortcut: Ctrl+Shift+X.

By Visual Similarity with Selected Photo(s)

This is a very cool feature. If you want to find photos that have colors and tones that are similar to a particular photo (or group of photos), select the photo(s) you want to match, and then choose this item. Elements ranks all your photos by color. The closest matches appear at the top of the list.

Untagged Items

To find photos that you haven't tagged yet, choose this menu item or press Ctrl+Shift+Q.

Items Not in Any Album

Choose this menu item to find all the photos you haven't used in albums yet.

Find Faces for Tagging

Choose this, and Elements searches your photos for pictures with people's faces in them. You can't choose to search for a particular person, only for all faces. The idea behind this feature is that once you have all your family's and friends' faces gathered together in one window, you can quickly tag them with the appropriate tags. Once you've used Find Faces, you can choose to find only untagged photos on future searches, speeding up the process considerably. You can also click the Faces button in the Organize pane to do the same thing.

View Menu

This menu lets you control how your photos are presented in the Organizer. It also includes two very cool ways to look through a group of photos or compare photos.

Refresh

If you need to make the Organizer redraw its screen, choose this menu item or press F5.

Media Types

Choose this item to bring up a window where you can decide what kinds of media the Organizer displays, or you can use the keyboard shortcuts. Your choices are photos (Ctrl+1), video (Ctrl+2), audio (Ctrl+3), Projects (Ctrl+4), and PDF files (Ctrl+5). Just turn on the ones you want and turn off the ones you don't.

Hidden Files

Use this option to see or hide all your files with the Hidden tag (page 52).

Details

When Details is turned on (it usually is unless you've turned it off), you see the information about your photos in the Photo Browser window, like the date and the tag icons. Toggle Details off to see just the thumbnails with no other information. Keyboard shortcut: Ctrl+D.

Show File Names

Turn this on to see your photos' names displayed below their thumbnails.

Show Grid Lines

Turn this on to see the dividing lines between each thumbnail.

Show Borders Around Thumbnails

Although you may not really be able to see it, Elements displays a very fine border around each thumbnail, unless you turn this off.

Expand All Stacks

To see every photo in every stack, choose this menu item.

Collapse All Stacks

To return all your stacks to single photo view so you see only the top photo, choose this menu item.

Window Menu

This menu is where you choose which parts of the Organizer are visible. Most of the items are grouped in pairs, because you must choose one or the other. For instance, you can choose to show the Timeline (page 56), or to hide the Task Pane here.

Hide Task Pane

If you want to have the entire Organizer window for viewing thumbnails, you can turn off the Task pane here, or just click its edge. (If the Task pane is hidden, this menu item reads "Show Task Pane" instead.)

Timeline

If you turn on the Timeline, you see each group of photos as a bar on a graph across the top of the Photo Browser area. The height of the bar shows how many photos are in each group. The groups are arranged according to your choice in the Date pull-down menu at the top of the thumbnails area. Ctrl+L is the keyboard shortcut to toggle the Timeline on and off.

Quick Share

The Quick Share pane (page 437) makes it easy to order prints for friends and family. If you don't want to see the Quick Share pane (if you never order prints via Elements, for instance) you can turn it off here.

Properties

To see the Properties window for a photo, highlight the photo and then choose this menu item or press Alt+Enter.

Upload Progress Window

When you send photos to Kodak EasyShare Gallery for printing or sharing, or to Photoshop.com, the Upload Progress Window lets you track how close your upload is to being completed. Turn the window off or on here.

Help Menu

This menu is where you find the Elements Help files, as well as information about the program itself.

Photoshop Elements Help

When you call up the Elements Help files here or press F1, Elements launches your Web browser to display the Help Files.

About Photoshop Elements

Choose this to see a window with information about the version of Elements you've got. You'll also see a very long list of patents and credits—an impressive testimony to the complexity of the engineering that went into Elements.

Patent and Legal Notices

If you want the Organizer's patent numbers, you can view and copy them here.

Glossary of Terms

The Elements Help files include a glossary of terms relating to digital imaging. If you're wondering what a particular term means, choose this menu item and it'll take you to the glossary so you can look it up.

System Info

Choose this item for a window showing information about Elements itself and also about your Windows operating system. If you can't remember which service pack you have, for instance, you can check here. There's also information about some important plug-ins. If you're not sure whether you have QuickTime, for example, that information is here, too.

Registration

If you didn't register Elements with Adobe the first time you used the program, you can choose this menu item to bring up the registration window again.

Updates

Select this menu item and Elements searches for updates. You can also change the update preferences by clicking the Preferences button in the window that opens when it's done updating or searching for updates or trying to connect to the server.

Online Support

Choose this option, and Elements launches your Web browser and opens Adobe's support Web site. If it fails because you're not connected to the Internet, Elements launches an Internet connection window.

Online Learning Resources

This menu item takes you to the main product page for Photoshop Elements on Adobe's Web site. As with the online support link, Elements launches your browser and offers to connect to the Internet if you're not already online.

Welcome Button

When you're signed on to your Photoshop.com account (page 18), you'll see text that says "Welcome, <your name>." Click it to go directly to your Photoshop.com account online. If you're not signed on, you see "Sign In" instead.

Undo

Click this button or press Ctrl+Z to undo your last action.

Redo

Click here or press Ctrl+Y to redo your last action.

Display Menu

This menu lets you choose how you'd like to arrange your photos for viewing.

Thumbnail View

For the basic Photo Browser view, where you see thumbnails of your photos, choose this menu item or press Ctrl+Alt+1.

Import Batch

Select this menu item to see your photos grouped according to when you imported them. Each batch is separated by a header giving the import date and time. Ctrl+Alt+2 is the keyboard shortcut.

Folder Location

Choose this option for a view of your photos grouped by the folders that contain them, You also get a folder tree view of your computer and networked drives on the left of the window. The header for each group of thumbnails in the middle of the window gives you a button you can click to assign the name of the enclosing folder as an Instant Keyword Tag. Keyboard shortcut: Ctrl+Alt+3.

Date View

Date View displays your photos on a calendar. You can switch to Date View by selecting this menu item, or by pressing Ctrl+Alt+D. (If you're in Date View this menu item reads Photo Browser, so you can get back to the usual state of the Organizer.)

Show Map

Choose this option to bring the Yahoo map into view. There's more about using Yahoo maps on page 487.

View Photos in Full Screen

Choose this menu item or press F11 to get a full-screen slideshow of your photos. Elements presents you with a floating control strip to help you navigate through the photos, but it appears only when you pass your mouse over it. It's a great way to check through a group of newly imported photos, and you can even choose music to listen to while you watch your slideshow. The Escape key takes you out of Full Screen view.

Compare Photos Side by Side

This option is similar to "View Photos in Full Screen" in that you get a full-screen view. But in "Compare Photos Side by Side", you get to see any two photos of your choice side by side. It's great for choosing which photos you want to keep or print. You can also get to "Compare Photos Side by Side" by pressing F12. To bring in a new photo for comparison, click the photo that you want to get rid of. Press Escape to exit this view.

Editor Menu

Use this menu to go to any of the editing modes.

Quick Fix

Choose this item to go to the Editor's Quick Fix window (see Chapter 4).

Full Edit

Choose this item to go to the main Edit window. Keyboard shortcut: Ctrl+I.

Guided Edit

This option takes you to Guided Edit mode where Elements walks you through some basic editing tasks (page 28).

The Editor, Menu by Menu

The Editor's menus are far more complex than the menus in the Organizer. All three editing modes—Full Edit. Quick Fix, and Guided Edit—have the same menus, although some choices are grayed out when you're in Quick Fix or Guided Edit mode. When you need a menu item that's unavailable in Quick Fix or Guided Edit, just switch back to Full Edit to use it.

Several of the menus in Elements are dynamic: They change quite a bit to reflect the choices currently applicable to your image. That means the choices you see in this appendix represent only what you *may* see depending on the situation. The Layer menu, for instance, offers you very different options depending on the current state of your image and which layer is active.

> **NOTE** If you have Adobe Premiere Elements installed, then you'll see some extra menu options not included in this basic list.

System Menu

This is actually a button—a blue square with "PSE" on it—at the upper left of the Elements window. Click it to get a pop-out menu for opening, closing, moving, maximizing, and minimizing the Editor, as well as restoring it to its original size.

Welcome Screen

To the right of the System Menu button is button that looks like a little house. Click it when you want to see the Welcome screen (page 13), and to connect to Photoshop.com.

File Menu

The commands listed here let you create, import, open, save, and print files.

New

Choose this menu item if you want to start a new file in Elements. Your options are:

- **Blank file** (or press Ctrl+N).

- **Image from Clipboard**. This automatically pastes anything you've copied into a new file.

- **Photomerge Group Shot**. This lets you move a person from one photo of a group into another photo of the same group (page 313).

- **Photomerge Faces**. Use this one to combine parts of different faces for caricatures and other fun effects (page 310).

- **Photomerge Scene Cleaner**. This new feature lets you remove unwanted people or other details from a photo by copying over bits of other photos (page 313).

- **Photomerge Panorama**. Use this option to combine your photos into panoramas (page 304).

Open

Choose this menu item or press Ctrl+O to open an existing file.

Open As

This menu option (or Alt+Ctrl+O) lets you choose the format for a file as you open it. Select it when you want to use the Raw Converter on non-Raw formats like JPEG or TIFF (page 239).

Open Recently Edited File

Here's you'll find a pop-out list of the most recent files you've had open in Elements.

Duplicate

When you need to make a copy of your photo, choose this option.

Close

To close the active image window, choose this menu item or press Ctrl+W.

Close All

To close all your open image windows, choose this option or press Alt+Ctrl+W.

Save

To save your work, select this option or press Ctrl+S.

Save As

To save your image under another file name or in a different format, choose this command or press Shift+Ctrl+S.

Save For Web

To save an image so that it's optimized for posting on a Web page or sending by email, choose this menu item or press Alt+Shift+Ctrl+S. For more on the Save For Web window, see page 452.

File Info

Choose this menu item to bring up the File Info window, which displays general information (file creation date, file format, and so on) about your image.

Place

Use this command to place a PDF, Adobe Illustrator, or EPS file into an image as a new layer. When the artwork's larger than the image you place it in, Elements automatically makes it small enough to fit.

Organize Open Files

Choose this menu option to add the files you have open in the Editor to the Organizer.

Process Multiple Files

This is where you batch process your files to rename them, change their format, add copyright information, and so on (see page 245 for everything that Elements lets you do to groups of files).

Import

This is where you bring certain file formats into Elements. It's also where you can connect to external devices like scanners. (They'll show up in this menu if you install their drivers.) Your basic choices before you connect or install anything are:

- **Frame from Video** (page 43)
- **WIA Support** (the built-in support for scanners that's part of the Windows operating system)

Export

This command is always grayed out. That's normal. Adobe left it in for the benefit of any third-party plug-ins that may need it to be there—but you don't need it in Elements to use the program's standard tools and commands. (The Organizer contains an active Export command.)

Automation Tools

Like Export, this command is only here for a few third-party plug-ins that may need it. Normally, it's grayed out.

Page Setup

This menu option calls up your system's regular Page Setup window, where you choose the page size and the orientation of your document and select the printer you plan to use. Read more about printing from the Editor on page 440. Keyboard shortcut: Shift+Ctrl+P.

Print

Choose this command and you get the Print window, which is discussed in detail in Chapter 16. Keyboard shortcut: Ctrl+P.

Print Multiple Photos

With this command, you get the Organizer's Print Photos window, which is discussed in detail on page 445. Keyboard shortcut: Alt+Ctrl+P.

Order Prints

This is your portal to connecting to Kodak EasyShare Gallery to order prints, calendars, or photo books. See page 437 for how to order prints online.

Exit

You can close the Editor here or by pressing Ctrl+Q. The Organizer doesn't quit along with the Editor. If the Organizer is also running, you must exit it separately.

Edit Menu

The menu choices listed here let you make changes to your files. This is also where you can access your Elements preferences to change their settings.

Undo

You can back out of your last action by selecting Undo or by pressing Ctrl+Z. You can keep applying this command to undo as many steps as you've set in the Undo History palette preferences (Edit → Preferences → Performance → History States).

Redo

If you undo something and then change your mind again, redo it here or press Ctrl+Y.

Revert

Choose this command to return your image to the state it was in the last time you saved it.

Cut

To remove something from your image and store it on the Clipboard (so that you can paste it into another file), choose this menu item or press Ctrl+X.

Copy

To copy something to the Clipboard, highlight it and select this menu item or press Ctrl+C. The Copy command copies only the top layer in a file with layers. To copy all the layers in your selected area, use Copy Merged instead.

Copy Merged

To copy all the layers in the selected area to the Clipboard, choose this menu option or press Shift+Ctrl+C. To copy just the top layer to the Clipboard, use Copy instead.

Paste

Use this command or press Ctrl+V to add whatever you have cut or copied into an image.

Paste Into Selection

Use this special command for pasting something within the confines of an existing selection. See page 125 for more on how this command works. Keyboard shortcut: Shift+Ctrl+V.

Delete

This command removes what you've selected without copying it to the Clipboard—it's just gone. You can press Backspace to do the same thing.

Fill, Fill Layer, Fill Selection

Choose this menu item to fill your active layer with a color or pattern (page 176). When you make a selection in your image, this menu item changes to Fill Selection. You can also choose a blend mode and opacity for your fill.

Stroke (Outline) Selection

This command lets you place a colored border around the edges of a selection.

Define Brush, Define Brush from Selection

If you want to create a custom brush from your photo or from an area of your photo, choose this command. The process is explained in detail on page 336.

Define Pattern, Define Pattern from Selection

This command creates a pattern from your image or selection. See page 264 for more about applying patterns.

Clear

Use this command to permanently remove information from the Undo History, Clipboard Contents, or All (both of them). If you have a corrupt image in the Clipboard (or one that's too large), it may cause Elements to slow way down or quit on you. Once in a while, the Clipboard may get stuck, too—you try to copy and paste an item but still get whatever you copied previously. Clear fixes all these problems.

Add Blank Page

This command lets you add a new, blank page to your current project. Find out more about working with multipage files on page 425. Keyboard shortcut: Alt+Ctrl+G.

Add Page Using Current Layout

If you're working with a Photo Collage (page 419) and you want to use that page as a template for new pages, choose this command instead of Add Blank Page. Keyboard shortcut: Alt+Shift+Ctrl+G.

Delete Current Page

If you're working with a multipage document and you decide you want to get rid of your current page, choose this command.

Color Settings

Here's where you choose your color space for Elements (page 196). Keyboard shortcut: Shift+Ctrl+K.

Preset Manager

This is where you access the window that helps you manage your brushes, swatches, gradients, and patterns. See page 496 for more on how the Preset Manager works.

Preferences

This menu item gives you access to the many Elements settings you can customize. You'll find the following preference windows available from this menu:

- **General** (or press Ctrl+K)

- **Saving Files**

- **Performance** (where you set the number of history states and assign scratch disks)

- **Display & Cursors**

- **Transparency**

- Units & Rulers

- Grid

- Plug-Ins

- Type

- **Organize & Share** (brings up the Organizer's preferences)

Image Menu

This menu lets you make changes to your image. Here you can rotate a picture, change its shape, crop or resize it, or change the color mode.

Rotate

Use these commands to change the orientation of your image (page 74). The first group of options applies to your whole image:

- **90° Left**

- **90° Right**

- **180°**

- **Custom**

- **Flip Horizontal**

- **Flip Vertical**

The next group does the same thing but on a layer or selection. The menu choices change depending on whether you have an active selection in your image. If you have a selection, you'll see the word "Selection" instead of "Layer."

- **Free Rotate Layer**

- **Layer 90° Left**

- **Layer 90° Right**

- **Layer 180°**

- **Flip Layer Horizontal**

- **Flip Layer Vertical**

Finally you can choose to:

- **Straighten and Crop Image**

- **Straighten Image**

These last two commands are mostly for use with scanned images when you need to straighten the position of the entire image. To straighten the *contents* of an image, use the Straighten tool (page 76).

Transform

These commands let you change the shape of your image by pulling it in different directions. They're explained in detail on page 321. Your choices are:

- **Free Transform** (Ctrl+T) incorporates the other three commands.

- **Skew** slants an image.

- **Distort** stretches your photo in the direction you pull it.

- **Perspective** stretches your photo to make it look like parts are nearer or farther away.

> **TIP** You might prefer to use the Correct Camera Distortion filter for transforming your images to correct perspective. See page 316.

Crop

Choose this menu item to crop your image to the area you've selected (page 83).

Divide Scanned Photos

You can create a group scan by placing several photos on your scanner glass at once and then choosing this command. Elements then cuts your photos apart and straightens and crops each individual photo. See page 71 for more about how this works.

Resize

Here's where you change the actual size of your image (as opposed to changing the size of the view on your screen). Resizing is explained in Chapter 3. Your choices are:

- **Image Size** (page 89). Keyboard shortcut is Alt+Ctrl+I.

- **Canvas Size** (page 96).

- **Reveal All**. If you drag a layer from another image into your photo and part of the layer falls outside the perimeter of the target image, then use the Reveal All command to see the entire dragged layer. It basically resizes the canvas to fit all of the image(s). Also, some versions of Photoshop hide the area outside a selection when you use the Crop tool. When someone sends you one of these images, use this command to see the area that was hidden by the crop.

- **Scale** (page 324).

Mode

This is where you can change the color mode for your image (page 45). Your choices are:

- **Bitmap**

- Grayscale

- Indexed Color

- RGB Color

You'll find two other commands in this menu:

- **8-bits/Channel** reduces images from 16-bit color to 8-bit (see page 238).

- **Color Table** shows you the color table (the colors of your image as swatches) for an Indexed Color image.

Convert Color Profile

If you need to change the ICC (International Color Consortium) profile of an image, you can do it from this menu, which lets you apply an sRGB or Adobe RGB profile, or you can remove the profile from an image. For more on color profiles, go to page 196.

Magic Extractor

Use this command or press Alt+Shift+Ctrl+V to call up the Magic Extractor window, which automates the process of selecting an object in your photo and removing it from the background. See page 139 for details.

Enhance Menu

This menu contains the commands you use to adjust the color and lighting of your images. The first six options apply changes automatically, and the remainder let you adjust your changes.

Auto Smart Fix

Choose this option or press Alt+Ctrl+M to adjust lighting, color, and contrast at the same time (page 105).

Auto Levels

Use this command or press Shift+Ctrl+L to adjust the individual color channels of your image (page 108).

Auto Contrast

Choose this command or press Alt+Shift+Ctrl+L to adjust the brightness and darkness of your image without changing the colors (page 109).

Auto Color Correction

Use this option or press Shift+Ctrl+B to adjust your color in much the same way that Levels does. Auto Color Correction looks at different information in your photo to make its decisions, though (page 110).

Auto Sharpen

This command applies the same one-click sharpening you get when you use the Auto Sharpen button in Quick Fix (page 112).

Auto Red Eye Fix

Use this command or press Ctrl+R to apply the same auto red-eye correction found in the Organizer (page 104).

Adjust Smart Fix

This command is the same as Auto Smart Fix, except you get a slider to adjust the degree of change Elements makes to your photo. Keyboard shortcut: Ctrl+Shift+M.

Adjust Lighting

Your choices for adjusting the light and dark values in your photos are:

- **Shadows/Highlights** (page 187).
- **Brightness/Contrast** (page 185).
- **Levels.** You can also press Ctrl+L to bring up the Levels dialog box (page 198).

Adjust Color

With these settings you can change a color, replace a color, remove a color cast, remove all the color from your image, or add color to a black-and-white photo. Choose from:

- **Remove Color Cast** (page 206).
- **Adjust Hue/Saturation** (page 271). Keyboard shortcut: Ctrl+U.
- **Remove Color** (page 283). Keyboard shortcut: Shift+Ctrl+U.
- **Replace Color** (page 276).
- **Adjust Color Curves** (page 267). The Color Curves tool lets you adjust the brightness and contrast of specific tonal ranges (like highlights or midtones) in your photo.
- **Adjust Color for Skin Tone** (page 117). This setting adjusts the colors in your image based on the skin tones of someone whom you select in the photo.
- **Defringe Layer** (page 143). This setting gets rid of the rim of contrasting pixels you may get when you remove an object from its background.
- **Color Variations** (page 207).

Convert to Black and White

Use this menu item or press Atl+Ctrl+B to convert a color photo to a black-and-white image (page 283).

Unsharp Mask

This is the most popular traditional method for sharpening your photos (page 214).

Adjust Sharpness

Choose this menu item to use Adobe's newest sharpening tool (page 216).

Layer Menu

Here's where you'll find the commands for creating and managing Layers. (Chapter 6 is all about Layers.) This is the most dynamic menu in Elements—what you see at the bottom of the menu changes depending on the layers in the image that's open and on the characteristics of the active layer. This is a basic rundown of the main menu options you'll usually see if your open image has only a Background layer. (Sometimes you'll see choices visible but grayed out.) The choices for merging and combining layers change the most as your layers change.

New

This is where you create new, regular (as opposed to Adjustment) layers. Your options are:

- **Layer** (or press Shift+Ctrl+N).
- **Layer from Background.**
- **Layer via Copy** (or press Ctrl+J).
- **Layer via Cut** (or press Shift+Ctrl+J).

If your image doesn't currently have a Background layer, you see "Background from Layer" instead of "Layer from Background".

Duplicate Layer

Use this command to make a duplicate of the active layer. As long as you don't have a selection, you can also use Ctrl+J to do the same thing.

Delete Layer

If you want to eliminate a layer, click it in the Layers palette to make it the active layer and choose the Delete Layer command.

Rename Layer

Choose this option to—you guessed it—rename a layer. You can also double-click the layer's name in the Layers palette to rename it.

Layer Style

If a layer has a Layer style applied to it (page 382), you can adjust it here.

- **Style Settings** brings up the dialog box where you can adjust some of the settings of a Layer style. Double-clicking the Layer style icon in the Layers palette brings up the same dialog box.

- **Copy Layer Style** lets you copy any styles applied to a layer to the Clipboard so you can apply them to another image or layer.

- **Paste Layer Style** applies your copied style to a new layer, even in a new image.

- **Clear Layer Style** removes all the styles applied to a layer.

- **Hide All Effects** hides all the styles applied to a layer so that you can see what your image looks like without them. If you hide all the styles, this menu item reads "Show All Effects" instead.

- **Scale Effects** lets you adjust the size of certain aspects of Layer styles.

New Fill Layer

Choose this option to create a layer that's filled with a color, gradient, or pattern. You can also do this from the Layers palette by clicking the Create Adjustment Layer icon. Your options are:

- **Solid Color** (page 176)

- **Gradient** (page 390)

- **Pattern** (page 176)

New Adjustment Layer

This command creates a new Adjustment layer (page 176). The types of layers you can create are:

- **Levels** (page 198)

- **Brightness/Contrast** (page 185)

- **Hue/Saturation** (page 275)

- **Gradient Map** (page 396)

- **Photo Filter** (page 242)

- **Invert** (page 281)

- **Threshold** (page 282)

- **Posterize** (page 281)

Change Layer Content

For Adjustment and Fill layers, you can change the type of layer you've got, as long as you haven't flattened your layers. For example, you could change a Levels layer into a Hue/Saturation layer. You can also change an Adjustment layer to a Fill layer, and vice versa. The choices include all the layers listed in the two previous sections.

Layer Content Options

Use this option to bring up the dialog box for an Adjustment or Fill layer. You can also double-click the left icon for the layer in the Layers palette.

Type

This command gives you ways to modify a Type layer, as long as it hasn't been simplified (page 355). You can choose:

- **Horizontal**. Change vertical type to horizontal type.

- **Vertical**. Change horizontal type to vertical type.

- **Anti-alias Off**. Anti-aliasing is explained on page 405.

- **Anti-alias On**.

- **Warp Text**. See page 407.

- **Update All Text Layers**.

- **Replace All Missing Fonts**. When your image is missing fonts, this command replaces them, but you can't choose the replacement. It's usually just as easy to replace fonts by highlighting the text and selecting a new font in the Options bar.

Simplify Layer

The Simplify Layer command rasterizes your layer, turning the layer content from a vector or smart object to one that's built pixel by pixel. See page 355 for more about the difference between vectors and pixels.

Group with Previous

This command links two layers together in such a way that the bottom layer determines the opacity of the upper layer (page 172). Keyboard shortcut: Ctrl+G.

Ungroup

This command separates grouped layers so that they're now two unrelated layers. Keyboard shortcut: Shift+Ctrl+G.

Arrange

Use these commands to change the order of layers in the layers stack, or just drag them in the Layers palette. See page 167 for details on rearranging layers. (Front is the top of the stack, and back is directly above the Background layer.)

- **Bring to Front** (or press Shift+Ctrl+]).

- **Bring Forward** (or press Ctrl+]).

- **Send Backward** (or press Ctrl+[).

- **Send to Back** (or press Shift+Ctrl+[).

- **Reverse.** Select two or more layers, and this command reverses the order in which they appear in the layer stack.

Merge Layers

Choose this command or press Ctrl+E to combine multiple layers into one layer. You may also see Merge Down, which merges a layer with the layer immediately beneath it, or Merge Clipping Mask, which merges grouped layers.

Merge Visible

Use this option or press Shift+Ctrl+E to merge all the visible layers into one layer.

Flatten Image

This command merges all the layers into one Background layer.

Select Menu

Here's where you make, modify, and save selections in your image. See Chapter 5 for more about selections.

All

Choose this command or press Ctrl+A to select your entire image.

Deselect

Use this command or press Ctrl+D to remove all selections from your image.

Reselect

If you apply the Deselect command, but then want your selection back again, choose this menu item or press Shift+Ctrl+D.

Inverse

This command switches the selected and unselected areas of your image. The area that wasn't previously selected is now selected, and the previously selected area is now unselected. Keyboard shortcut: Shift+Ctrl+I.

All Layers

Use this command to select all the layers in your image, including hidden layers.

Deselect Layers

Choose this option to unselect all the layers in your image.

Similar Layers

Use this command to select all the layers of your image that are the same type, such as all Adjustment layers or all regular layers.

Feather

Choose this option or press Alt+Ctrl+D to feather (blur) the edges of a selection (page 135).

Refine Edge

This command lets you groom the edges of a selection (page 128).

Modify

These commands let you change the size or edges of your selection. They're all explained in Chapter 5.

- **Border** selects the edge of your selection (page 147).

- **Smooth** rounds the corners of selections (page 147).

- **Expand** moves the edge of your selection outward (page 146).

- **Contract** moves the edge of your selection inward (page 146).

Grow

This command expands your selection to include more contiguous areas of similar color (page 146).

Similar

This option expands your selection to include more areas of similar color, but—unlike the Grow command—it doesn't restrict the growth to contiguous areas (page 146).

Load Selection

If you have saved a selection, choose this command to use it again.

Save Selection

If you wish to save a selection so that you can use it another time without recreating it, use this command (page 149).

Delete Selection

Use this command to permanently remove a saved selection.

Filter Menu

Filters let you change the appearance of your image in all sorts of ways. Elements comes with some filters that are mostly for correcting and improving your photos, while others create artistic effects. The filters are grouped into categories to make it easier to find one that does exactly what you want. You can also apply filters from the Effects palette. Learn more about using filters in Chapter 13. Every image responds to filters differently, so the descriptions here are a very rough guide.

Last Filter

The top item in the Filter menu always features the last filter you've applied. Choose it or press Ctrl+F to reapply that filter with the exact same settings you previously used. If you want to change the settings, then you need to choose the filter from its regular place in the list of filters or press Ctrl+Alt+F.

Filter Gallery

This option lets you try the effects of different filters, rearrange them, and preview what they'll look like in your photo (page 367).

Correct Camera Distortion

Use this filter to correct various kinds of lens distortion problems (page 316).

Adjustments

This group of filters is used primarily (but not exclusively) for correcting and enhancing photos. The filters are discussed on page 280, unless otherwise noted.

- Equalize
- Gradient Map (page 396)
- Invert (or press Ctrl+I)
- Posterize
- Threshold
- Photo Filter (page 242)

Artistic

Use these filters to apply a variety of artistic effects to your image, ranging from a pencil-sketch look to a watercolor effect.

- **Colored Pencil** makes your photo look like it was sketched with a colored pencil on a solid colored background.

- **Cutout** makes your image look like it was cut from pieces of paper.

- **Dry Brush** makes your photo look like it was painted using dry brush technique.

- **Film Grain** adds grain to make your photo look like old film.

- **Fresco** makes your photo look like it was painted quickly in a dabbing style.

- **Neon Glow** adds vivid color to your image while softening the details.

- **Paint Daubs** gives your photo a painted look.

- **Palette Knife** makes your photo look like you painted it with a palette knife. While you may think of a palette knife as a tool for blending heavy paint daubs, Adobe describes the effect of this filter as looking like a thin layer of paint that reveals the canvas beneath it.

- **Plastic Wrap** makes your image look like it's covered in plastic.

- **Poster Edges** gives your image accented, dark edges while reducing the number of colors in the rest of the photo.

- **Rough Pastels** makes your image look like it was quickly sketched with pastels.

- **Smudge Stick** uses short diagonal strokes that soften the image by smearing the detail.

- **Sponge** paints with highly textured areas of contrasting color like you'd get by sponging on color.

- **Underpainting** makes your image look like it's painted on a textured background.

- **Watercolor** simplifies the details in your image the way they would be if you were creating a watercolor painting.

Blur

Soften and blur your images with these filters.

- **Average Blur** (page 376)

- **Blur**

- **Blur More**

- **Gaussian Blur** (page 374)

- **Motion Blur.** You apply this pretty much the same way as the Radial blur, described on page 374, but it creates a one-way blur, like you'd see behind Road-Runner when he's scooting away from Wile E. Coyote.

- **Radial Blur** (page 374)

- **Smart Blur.** This filter reduces grain and noise without affecting the edge sharpness of your photo. It's also used for special artistic effects.

- **Surface Blur.** This new filter blurs without reducing edge contrast (page 377).

Brush Strokes

These filters give your image a hand-painted look.

- **Accented Edges** emphasizes the edges of objects as though they were drawn in black ink or white chalk.

- **Angled Strokes** creates diagonal brush strokes that all run in the same direction.

- **Crosshatch** creates diagonal brush strokes that crisscross.

- **Dark Strokes** paints dark areas of your image with short, tight, dark strokes, and light areas with long, white strokes.

- **Ink Outlines** makes your image look like it was drawn with fine ink lines.

- **Spatter** gives the effect you'd get from a spatter airbrush.

- **Sprayed Strokes** paints your image with diagonal, sprayed strokes in its dominant colors.

- **Sumi-e** gives the effect of drawing with a wet brush full of black ink, in a Japanese influenced style.

Distort

These filters warp your image in a variety of ways.

- **Diffuse Glow** makes your image look as though you're viewing it through a soft diffusion filter.

- **Displace** lets you create a map to tell Elements how to distort your image.

- **Glass** makes your image look like you're viewing it through various kinds of glass, depending on the settings you choose.

- **Liquify** (page 411).

- **Ocean Ripple** gives an underwater effect by adding ripples to your image.

- **Pinch** pulls the edges of your photo inward toward the center.

- **Polar Coordinates** lets you create what's called a cylinder anamorphosis. With this kind of distortion, the image looks normal when you see it in a mirrored cylinder.

- **Ripple** creates a pattern like ripples on the surface of water.

- **Shear** distorts your image along a curve.

- **Spherize** makes your image expand out like a balloon.

- **Twirl** spins your photo, rotating a selection more in the center than at the edge, producing a twirled pattern.

- **Wave** creates a rippled pattern but with more control than the Ripple filter gives you.

- **ZigZag** creates a bent, zigzagging effect that's stronger in the center of the area you apply the filter to.

Noise

Use these filters to add *noise* (graininess) to your photos or remove noise from them. (Unless otherwise specified, these filters are explained on page 258.)

- **Add Noise** (page 372)

- **Despeckle**

- **Dust & Scratches**

- **Median**

- **Reduce Noise** (page 371)

Pixelate

These filters break up the appearance of your photo into spots or blocks of various kinds.

- **Color Halftone** adds the kind of dotted pattern you see in commercially printed color.

- **Crystallize** breaks your image into polygonal blocks of color.

- **Facet** reduces your image to blocks of solid color.

- **Fragment** makes your image look blurry and offset.

- **Mezzotint** creates an effect something like that of a mezzotint engraving.

- **Mosaic** breaks your image down to square blocks of color.

- **Pointillize** creates a pointillist effect by making your photo look like it's made of many dots of color.

Render

This is a diverse but powerful group of filters that transform your photo in many ways.

- **3D Transform** makes your image look like it's on a cube, cylinder, or sphere.

- **Clouds** covers your image with clouds using the foreground/background colors.

- **Difference Clouds** also creates clouds, but blends them in your image in Difference mode.

- **Fibers** creates an effect like spun and woven fibers.

- **Lens Flare** creates starry bright spots like you'd get from a camera lens flare.

- **Lighting Effects** is a powerful and complex filter for changing the light in your photo. For an in-depth tutorial on how to use this filter, see the Missing CD page at *www.missingmanuals.com*.

- **Texture Fill** lets you use a grayscale image as a texture for your photo.

Sketch

Here's another group of artistic filters. Most of them make your image look like it was drawn with a pencil or graphics pen.

- **Bas Relief** gives your photo a slightly raised appearance, as though it's carved in low relief.

- **Chalk & Charcoal** makes your photo look like it was sketched with a combination of chalk and charcoal.

- **Charcoal** gives a smudgy effect to your image, like a charcoal drawing.

- **Chrome** is supposed to make your image look like polished chrome, but you might prefer the Wow chrome Layer styles in the Effects palette.

- **Conté Crayon** makes your image look like it was drawn with conté crayons (a drawing medium originally made of graphite and wax, now made from chalks, that is used for making bold strokes) using the foreground/background colors.

- **Graphic Pen** makes the details in your image look like they were drawn with a fine pen using the foreground color, with the background color for the paper color.

- **Halftone Pattern** gives the dotted effect of a halftone screen, like you see in printed illustrations. The effect only *looks* like a halftone—this filter doesn't create a true halftone that your print shop might request.

- **Note Paper** makes your image look like it's on handmade paper. The background color shows through in spots in dark areas.

- **Photocopy** makes your photo look like a Xerox copy.

- **Plaster** makes your image look like it was molded in wet plaster.

- **Reticulation** creates an effect you might get from film emulsion—dark areas clump and brighter areas appear more lightly grained.

- **Stamp** makes your image look like an impression from a rubber stamp.

- **Torn Edges** makes your photo look it's made from torn pieces of paper.

- **Water Paper** makes your photo look like it was painted on wet paper, making the colors run together.

Stylize

These filters create special effects by displacing the pixels in your image or increasing contrast.

- **Diffuse** makes your photo less focused by shuffling the pixels according to the settings you choose.

- **Emboss** makes objects in your image appear stamped or raised.

- **Extrude** gives a 3-D effect by pushing some of the pixels in your image up, something like toothpaste squeezed from a tube.

- **Find Edges** emphasizes the edges of your image against a white background.

- **Glowing Edges** adds a neon-like glow to the edges in your photo.

- **Solarize** produces an effect like what you'd get by briefly exposing a photo print to light while you're developing it. It combines a negative and a positive image.

- **Tiles** breaks your image up into individual tiles. You can choose how much to offset them.

- **Trace Contour** outlines areas where there are major transitions in brightness. The result is supposed to be something like a contour map.

- **Wind** makes your image appear windblown.

Texture

These filters change the surface of your photo to look like it was made from another material.

- **Craquelure** produces a surface effect like cracked plaster.

- **Grain** adds different kinds of graininess to your photo.

- **Mosaic Tiles** is supposed to make your photo look like it's made of mosaic tiles with grout in between them.

- **Patchwork** reduces your image to squares filled with the image's predominant colors.

- **Stained Glass** is supposed to make your photo look like it's made of stained glass. The effect's usually more like a mosaic.

- **Texturizer** makes your photo look like it's on canvas or brick. You can select a file to use as a texture.

Video

These filters are for use with video images.

- **De-Interlace** smoothes images captured from video by removing the odd or even interlaced lines.

- **NTSC Colors** restricts your colors to those suitable for television reproduction.

Other

This is a group of fairly technical filters.

- **Custom** lets you create your own filter.

- **High Pass** is discussed on page 219.

- **Maximum** replaces pixel brightness values with the highest and lowest values of surrounding pixels. It spreads out white areas and shrinks dark areas.

- **Minimum** does the opposite of the Maximum filter. It spreads out dark areas and shrinks white ones.

- **Offset** moves your selection by the number of pixels you specify.

Digimarc

Use this filter to check for Digimarc watermarks in photos. Digimarc is a commercial system that lets subscribers enter their information in a database so that anyone who gets one of their photos can find out who the copyright holder is by searching the Digimarc database.

View Menu

This menu features different ways to adjust how you see your image on your screen. For more details on adjusting your view, see page 86.

New Window for...

This command lets you create a duplicate window for your image so that you can see it at two different magnification levels at once. The new window goes away when you close your image—it doesn't create a copy of your photo.

Zoom In

To increase the view size, you can choose this menu item or press Ctrl+=. You can also use the Zoom tool (page 87).

Zoom Out

To reduce the view size, choose this menu item or press Ctrl+−. You can also use the Zoom tool (page 87).

Fit on Screen

Use this command or press Ctrl+0 to make your photo as large as it can be without your having to scroll to see part of it.

Actual Pixels

Choose this option or press Alt+Ctrl+0 to see your image the exact size it would appear on the Web or in other programs that can't adjust view size (as Elements can).

Print Size

Elements makes its best guess as to how large your image would print at its current resolution (page 93).

Selection

When this menu item is turned on, the outlines of your selections are visible. You can toggle the setting off and on here, or by pressing Ctrl+H.

Rulers

If you want to see rulers around the edges of your image window, toggle them on and off here, or by pressing Shift+Ctrl+R. You can adjust the unit of measurement in Edit → Preferences → Units & Rulers.

Grid

If you want to see a measurement and alignment grid on your photos, use this setting to toggle it on and off. You can adjust the grid size in Edit → Preferences → Grid.

Guide Presets

The preset document sizes for new files include a couple of video sizes with guidelines to help you know the workable areas of the document. The Guide Presets menu item becomes active when you're working with a DV (digital video) file, or if someone sends you a Photoshop file with guides. It's normally grayed out.

Annotations

This command is available only for files that contain voice annotations. Toggle the annotation on and off here. You may get a file with a voice annotation from someone working with Photoshop, which lets you record sound annotations that you can add to your files.

Snap to

If you want to control the Elements autogrid (a hidden system that determines how precisely you can place things when you move them in your images), use these commands.

- **Guides.** When you're working with one of the video document sizes that includes guidelines, or if someone sends you a Photoshop file that includes them, this setting is where you toggle on and off whether you want objects you add to snap to the guidelines.

- **Grid.** When this setting is turned on, Elements automatically jumps to the nearest gridline. If the way your tools and selections keep jumping away from you bothers you, then turn off the Grid here. Then everything stays exactly where you place it. You have to make the Grid visible (View → Grid) before you can change its settings.

Window Menu

This menu controls which palettes and bins you see, as well as letting you adjust how your image windows display. Windows that are currently visible have a checkmark next to their names. A dash next to a name means the window is visible in another pane, but not in the current pane.

Images

Use these commands to control how your images display. The choices are explained in detail on page 86.

- **Maximize Mode.** Each image takes up the entire available space.

- **Tile.** Your images appear edge to edge so that all windows are equally visible.

- **Cascade.** Your image windows appear in overlapping stacks. (Cascade is the usual view when you start Elements for the first time.)

- **Match Zoom.** Choose Match Zoom to get the same magnification level in all open windows as in the active image window.

- **Match Location.** When you have only part of a photo visible in a window, choose Match Location to make all open windows display the same part of their images, too, like the upper-left corner, for example.

Tools

The Tools setting hides and shows the Toolbox.

Color Swatches

Use Color Swatches to show and hide the Color Swatches palette (page 212).

Content

The Content palette holds frames, backgrounds, graphics, shapes, themes, and text effects to use in projects. It's always visible in Create → Artwork, but if you want to see it in Edit mode as well, this is where you make it visible. See page 427 for more about how to use this palette.

Effects

Effects shows and hides the Effects palette, from which you apply filters, Photo Effects, and Layer styles. See page 366.

Favorites

You can put your favorite items from the Content and Effects palettes into the Favorites palette for easier access (page 429). Like the Content palette, it's always visible in Create → Artwork, but you can use the setting here to make it visible in Full Edit or hide it again once it's visible.

Histogram

Use the Histogram to show or hide the Histogram in its own palette (page 199).

Info

Use this setting to bring up a palette with information about your photos, like the file size and color value numbers.

Layers

Make the Layers palette visible or hidden by toggling this setting. See page 153.

Navigator

Turn the Navigator off and on here. The Navigator lets you adjust which portion of a large image is visible on your screen and also adjust the zoom. See page 89.

Undo History

The Undo History setting makes the Undo History palette visible or hides it. The Undo History palette shows a record of all the changes to your image up to the number of states you set in Edit → Preferences → Performance → History States. See page 32 for more about the Undo History palette.

Palette Bin

This setting minimizes (hides) and maximizes (reopens) the Palette bin (page 26). You can also just click the edge of the bin to hide or expand it.

Reset Palette Locations

Use this command to return all palettes to their original locations.

Welcome

Choose this menu item to see the Welcome window that appears when Elements starts up. This is where you connect to Photoshop.com (page 18).

Project Bin

This setting minimizes (hides) the Project bin. Select it again to maximize (reopen) the bin.

Image Windows

At the bottom of the Window menu you see a list of all the files you have open in Elements. Choose one to bring it to the front as the active window.

Help Menu

The Help menu is where you find the Elements Help files, as well as information about the program itself.

Photoshop Elements Help

When you call up the Elements Help files here, or press F1, your Web browser launches to show you the Help files.

About Photoshop Elements

Choose this to see a scrolling window with information about the version of Elements you've got. You'll also see a very long list of patents and credits—an impressive testimony to the complexity of the engineering that went into Elements.

About Plug-In

Select this option for a long pop-out menu displaying all the plug-ins in your copy of Elements. Choose a plug-in from the list to see its version and date information.

Patent and Legal Notices

This menu item displays a long list of the various patents for Elements, as well as trademark information for some of the components used in the program.

Glossary of Terms

The Elements Help files include a glossary of terms relating to digital imaging. If you're wondering what a particular term means, choose this menu item and it'll take you to the glossary index so you can look it up.

System Info

Choose this item for a window showing information about Elements itself and also about your Windows operating system. If you can't remember which service pack you have, for instance, then you can check here. You'll also find information about some important plug-ins. If you're not sure whether you have QuickTime, for example, that information's here, too.

Registration

If you didn't register Elements with Adobe the first time you used the program, you can choose this menu item to bring up the registration window again.

Updates

This is where you check for updates to Elements components. Go to Adobe Updater window → Preferences and you can set your preferences for how you want Elements to handle updates.

Online Support

Choose this option and Elements launches your Web browser and attempts to go to Adobe's support Web site. If you're not connected to the Internet when you select Online Support, then Elements launches an Internet connection window.

Online Learning Resources

This menu item takes you to the main product page for Photoshop Elements on Adobe's Web site. As it does with the online support link, Elements launches your browser and offers to connect to the Internet if you're not already online.

Welcome Button

When you're signed on to your Photoshop.com account (page 18), you'll see text that says "Welcome, <your name>." Click it to go directly to your Photoshop.com account online. If you're not signed on, you see "Sign In" instead.

Undo

Click this button or press Ctrl+Z to undo your last action.

Redo

Click here or press Ctrl+Y to redo your last action.

Organizer

Click here to go to the Elements Organizer.

Installation and Troubleshooting

Elements is quite easy to install and is pretty trouble free once it's up and running. This appendix explains a couple of things you can do to ensure that your installation goes smoothly, and it also provides cures for most of the little glitches that can crop up once you're using the program.

Installing Elements

Before you install Elements, it helps to make sure your PC is ready to receive its newest arrival. First of all, if your computer's on a network, take it off the network temporarily. (You can go back on as soon as you've installed Elements.) Also, it's important to disable any antivirus software, as well as *any* products from Symantec (whose programs tend to quarrel with Adobe software during installation). You can turn any of these programs back on as soon as you've finished the installation.

Also, you need to install Elements when logged into an administrative account on your computer. (If you've never done anything to change your account and you have only one account on your machine, it's almost certainly an administrative account.)

> **NOTE**   If you already have a previous version of Elements, then there's no need to remove it before installing Elements 7. All versions of Elements run as separate programs, and you can keep the older version, too, if you want.

Make sure you have your Elements serial number handy. You won't be able to install the program without it. If you have a retail version of Elements, the serial number is on the label on the install disc's case. If you got it bundled (when you bought a scanner, for example), you'll usually find the serial number on the paper sleeve the disc's in. (It's not a bad idea to write your serial number right on the disc so that you'll always have it around if you need to reinstall.)

It's a good idea to make a complete backup of any existing Organizer catalogs before you start, just in case (see page 67 for information on backing up).

Installing Elements

1. **Put the install disc in your computer's drive.**

   The disc window should open automatically. If for some reason it doesn't, then double-click the disc's icon or right-click it and choose Open, then double click Setup.exe to start the installer.

2. **Choose a language and accept the software agreement.**

3. **Click Install Adobe Photoshop Elements.**

   The installation *wizard* (a series of guided question-and-response screens) launches.

4. **Decide whether to remove any older versions of Elements.**

   If you already have one or more versions of Elements on your computer, the installer reminds you about them, asking if you want to add the new version or get rid of the previous version(s). It's up to you whether or not to remove them. If you want to remove your older versions, click No to cancel the installation and then remove the older versions yourself before starting the Elements 7 installer again. (In Vista, do this by going to Start → Control Panel → "Uninstall a Program": in Windows XP, Start → Control Panel → "Add or Remove Programs".) You can choose which versions to leave or to remove—it's not an all or nothing decision. You need to uninstall each version individually, if you decide to remove the old ones.

5. **Accept the license agreement.**

   Yes, you already accepted a software agreement. That was for all the stuff on the disc, and this one's specifically for Elements.

6. **Enter the Serial Number.**

   This is new in Elements 7: You can't install without your serial number.

7. **Choose where you want Elements to install itself.**

   Unless you have a specific reason to do so (if you install all your programs on a separate drive, for example), just agree to the location the installer suggests.

8. Click Install to begin the installation.

Elements installs. When the installer is done, click Finish to exit the installer, and restart your computer.

The installer creates a desktop shortcut to Elements. To launch Elements, double-click the shortcut or right-click it and choose Open.

Registration

When you first launch Elements, it asks you to register the program. You can run Elements without registering it, but you get a couple of advantages if you register. For one thing, Adobe hangs onto a record of your serial number, so if you ever misplace the number, you can get it from Adobe. Also, when Adobe releases new versions of Elements, there's usually a rebate for registered owners of previous versions. And if you agree to let Adobe send you email, they often offer discounts on other programs, like a big discount on the full version of Photoshop, if you want to move on later.

> **TIP**   In the Registration pull-down menu, you can choose to have Elements remind you to register a week from now, or you can choose not to register. If you choose the latter option and change your mind later on, go to Help → Registration (in either the Editor or the Organizer) to bring up the Registration window.

Scratch Disks

Elements uses a *scratch disk*—reserve space on a hard drive to supplement your PC's memory—when it's busy making your photos gorgeous. The calculations Elements makes behind the scenes are very complex, and Elements needs someplace to write stuff down while it's figuring out how to make changes to your image. It does so by using a scratch disk if the task at hand is too heavy-duty for your system's main memory alone to cope with.

You probably have just one hard drive in your computer, and Elements automatically uses that drive as the scratch disk. That's fine, and Elements can run very happily without a dedicated scratch disk.

> **TIP**   You can make Elements *really* happy by keeping your hard drive defragmented and making sure there's plenty of free space available for Elements to use. To defragment in Vista, go to Control Panel → "System and Maintenance" → Administrative Tools → "Defragment your hard drive". In Windows XP, it's Control Panel → "Performance and Maintenance" → "Rearrange items on your hard disk to make programs run faster".

If you're fortunate enough to have a computer with more than one internal drive, you can designate a separate disk as your scratch disk to improve Elements performance. Your scratch disk needs to be as fast as the drive Elements is installed on or there's no point in setting up a special scratch disk. (If you have a USB external drive, for instance, forget it [USB isn't fast enough, even USB 2.0] and just leave your main drive as your scratch disk.)

To assign a scratch disk, go to the Editor → Edit → Preferences → Performance and choose your preferred disk. You can choose up to four disks to use as scratch disks.

Troubleshooting

If Elements behaves badly from the moment you install it, something probably went funky during your installation. That's easy to fix. Uninstall Elements and reinstall it.

To remove Elements, in Vista go to Control Panel → "Uninstall a Program" (in Windows XP, Control Panel → "Add or Remove Programs") and then remove Elements. Then reinstall the program.

> **NOTE** You can't perform a Repair Install for Elements—you just get an error message that keeps asking for "Disk 1". (Repair installs are used for some programs to fix problems without having to do a full reinstall.)

Fortunately, Adobe makes very good software that looks after itself very well. There is, however, one simple procedure you can perform if things start acting funny in Elements: delete your Elements *preferences file*, which is where Elements keeps track of your preferred settings for the program. Deleting it fixes the overwhelming majority of problems you may develop. In Elements, you'll most likely to need to delete the preferences file when dealing with Editor-related problems.

> **NOTE** There is one downside to throwing out your preferences file: Once Elements supplies you with a replacement (which it generates automatically), you'll have to re-enter any changes you made to things like window behavior (page 86) and the Editor's preferences. Your palettes also go back to their original locations; you'll need to rearrange them if you pulled any of them out of the bin. (However, deleting the preferences doesn't affect your image files at all.)

The following steps explain what you need to do.

1. **Quit the Elements Editor if it's currently running and then relaunch the Editor.**

   Press Ctrl+Alt+Shift before you start the program, and keep holding those keys down as you start the Editor.

2. **Delete your preferences.**

   A window appears asking if you want to delete the Elements settings. Click Yes. If you don't see the window, quit the Editor and try again.

It's much less common to need to reset the Organizer's preferences, but if you do want to reset the Organizer, that's easy, too. When you're in the Organizer, go to Edit → Preferences → General and click the Restore Default Settings button at the bottom of the window.

Elements is usually pretty zippy, but if you find that it's really slowing things down on your computer, follow the instructions in the box on page 48 for disabling the Adobe Active File Monitor in your Windows services. (You'll also lose the ability to use Watched Folders and to see added content like Layer styles and actions if you do this.)

> **NOTE** Elements stores your catalog (page 48) separately from the actual program files. You can install and uninstall Elements as many times as you like without damaging or losing your existing catalog (if you have one from a previous version of Elements). However, as mentioned above, it's a good idea to back up any existing catalogs from older versions before installing Elements 7.
>
> When you first install Elements 7, if the Organizer doesn't find your existing Elements catalog, go to File → Catalog → Open. Then navigate to your catalog (usually called something like *My Catalog*) and open it. Elements automatically makes a backup copy of your catalog and adds the number -1 to its name (for example, *My Catalog-1*). Elements 7 then uses your existing catalog (the one *without* the -1 in its name). Just remember that any changes you make in Elements 7 won't appear in the old version of the catalog (the one *with* the -1 in its name).

Index